# THE CAMBRIDGE HISTORY

## OF

# ENGLISH LITERATURE

VOLUME X

## THE AGE OF JOHNSON

# The Cambridge History
of
# English Literature

Edited by

## Sir A. W. Ward, Litt.D., F.B.A.

Master of Peterhouse

and

## A. R. Waller, M.A.

Peterhouse

Volume X

## The Age of Johnson

New York: G. P. Putnam's Sons
Cambridge, England: University Press

COPYRIGHT, 1913

BY

G. P. PUTNAM'S SONS

Made in the United States of America

The Knickerbocker Press, New York

# PREFATORY NOTE

THE late Mr. D. C. Tovey's chapter on *Gray*, as well as the accompanying bibliography, reached us a very short time before his lamented death; and the proofs were not seen by him. Mr. Tovey's contribution to this *History* represents his last labour upon a subject which he had gradually made his own, and with which his name will always be associated in the minds of all lovers of English literature, and especially of members of his own and Gray's university.

We have to thank Mr. A. T. Bartholomew, of Peterhouse and the University Library, for contributing to this volume the bibliographies to which his initials are appended, and for other assistance chiefly of a bibliographical nature.

A. W. W.
A. R. W.

*July*, 1913.

# CONTENTS

## CHAPTER I

### RICHARDSON

By L. CAZAMIAN, Maître de Conférences at the
Sorbonne, Paris

PAGE

Antecedents of the change introduced by Richardson into the history of the English Novel. Richardson's life before 1741. *Pamela:* its qualities and extraordinary success. Continuation, Stage adaptation and Parody. Fielding and Richardson. *Clarissa:* its unique place among its author's works; its Sentimentalism. *Sir Charles Grandison:* its shortcomings and its psychological value. Richardson's later years and death. Decline of his popularity. Limitations of his art. His momentous influence upon English and European Literature. His literary descendants. His influence upon French Literature and national sentiment: Prévost, Voltaire, Diderot. Richardson and Rousseau. His influence in Germany: Gellert, Wieland, Klopstock and Goethe. Dutch and Italian reproductions.

## CHAPTER II

### FIELDING AND SMOLLETT

By HAROLD CHILD, sometime Scholar of Brasenose College, Oxford

Fielding and Smollett compared. Fielding's descent and earlier life. His first and subsequent Plays. His Farces and cognate Dramatic Pieces. His marriage. *Pasquin* and *The Historical Register.* Journalistic work: *The Champion. Joseph Andrews* and *Pamela.* The character of Parson Adams. Fielding and Cervantes. *Miscellanies. Jonathan Wild.* Political Journalism: *The True Patriot* and *The Jacobite's Journal.* Magisterial work and humane efforts. *Tom Jones.* The morality and the realism of the book: the author's openness of soul. Further pamphlets on social reform. *Amelia:* its distinctive charm. *The Covent Garden Journal.* Fielding seriously ill. His journey to Lisbon, and his posthumous account of it. His death. Smollett's parentage and early training as a surgeon. His arrival in London, with *The Regicide* in his pocket. His stay in the West Indies. Satirical and other verse. *Roderick Random* and the *Picaresque* Novel. *Ferdinand Count Fathom. The Critical Review;* Historical and Miscellaneous work. *Sir Launcelot Greaves. Travels through France and Italy. Humphrey Clinker.* Smollett's last journey and death. Final comparison between the literary achievements and influence of Fielding and Smollett

# Contents

## CHAPTER III

### STERNE, AND THE NOVEL OF HIS TIMES

By C. E. VAUGHAN, M.A., Balliol College, Oxford, Professor of English Literature in the University of Leeds

## CHAPTER IV

### THE DRAMA AND THE STAGE

By GEORGE HENRY NETTLETON, Ph.D., Assistant Professor of English in Yale University

## CHAPTER V

### THOMSON AND NATURAL DESCRIPTION IN POETRY

By A. HAMILTON THOMPSON, M.A., F.S.A., St. John's College

## CHAPTER VI

### GRAY

By the late Rev. DUNCAN C. TOVEY, M.A., Trinity College

## CHAPTER VII

### YOUNG, COLLINS AND LESSER POETS OF THE AGE OF JOHNSON

By GEORGE SAINTSBURY, M.A., LL.D., D.Litt., F.B.A., Professor of Rhetoric and English Literature in the University of Edinburgh

# Contents

# Contents

## CHAPTER X

### THE LITERARY INFLUENCE OF THE MIDDLE AGES

By W. P. KER, M.A., F.B.A., Fellow of All Souls College, Oxford, Professor of English Literature, University College, London

## CHAPTER XI

### LETTER-WRITERS

#### I

By HENRY B. WHEATLEY, F.S.A.

#### II. THE WARWICKSHIRE COTERIE

By the Ven. W. H. HUTTON, B.D., Archdeacon of Northampton, Canon of Peterborough and Fellow of St. John's College, Oxford

# Contents

## CHAPTER XII

### HISTORIANS

#### I. Hume and Modern Historians

By the Rev. WILLIAM HUNT, D.Litt., Trinity College, Oxford

PAGE

## CHAPTER XIII

### HISTORIANS

#### II. Gibbon

By Sir A. W. WARD, Litt.D., F.B.A., Master of Peterhouse

# CHAPTER XIV

## PHILOSOPHERS

By W. R. SORLEY, Litt. D., F.B.A., Fellow of King's College,
Knightbridge Professor of Moral Philosophy

### I. DAVID HUME

### II. ADAM SMITH

### III. OTHER PHILOSOPHICAL WRITERS

# CHAPTER XV

## DIVINES

By the Ven. Archdeacon W. H. HUTTON, B.D.

# Contents

# CHAPTER I

# Richardson

AFTER a protracted period of tentative effort, the English novel in the eighteenth century sprang into complete being from a soil not upturned by any violent social upheaval, but in which a deep movement of vitality had been secretly at work. The moral revolution sometimes called the renascence of sentiment cannot be said to have preceded the birth of Richardson's masterpieces; but their success, to some extent, was favoured by it, while they contributed to give it weight. The literary growth into which the sap that had permeated the Elizabethan drama was again to flow could thus be sustained by a radical energy equal in depth, if not in breadth, to that by means of which Shakespeare's plays had flourished. From the age of Milton to that of Wesley, puritanism, to all appearance, had been struck out of art, as it had out of the brilliant, superficial life of the world. Yet, Bunyan had dreamt his dream, and visualised for ever his imaginings; Addison had reconciled literature with the earnest purposes of human life; Defoe had grasped the concrete substance of things and breathed truth into fiction. From the beginning of the Georgian era, the rise of the trading class had been slowly infusing into public opinion a new spirit of probity and fervour. About 1740, the methodist movement was in full activity, and the sentimental reaction was gathering an impetus destined to contribute to no less a result than the romantic revival. A contemporary as he was of Wesley and of Young, Richardson signalises the advent of a momentous change, the full extent of which was never to become perceptible to himself. But the new birth of puritanism, together with the resurrection of emotion as a native energy, bore along his naturally narrow genius with something of the amplitude and force of a tidal wave. He was the poet, as he was one of the prophets, of middle-class religious faith, and united in himself much of the literary significance of Bunyan, Addison and Defoe. Like Bunyan, he owed a vivid strength of imagination to spiritual intensity; like Addison, he turned to account for dramatic purposes a wealth of psychological observation and insight into human character; like Defoe, he established the greatness of the English novel on its unique faculty of graphic realism. With him, the moral purpose of art reigned supreme, and, from it, he derived alike his wonderful power and his most obvious limitations. The score of edifying volumes in which he conveyed instruction through emotion make up a triple allegory, a thrice-told *Pilgrim's Progress*, illustrating the road to salvation by both positive and negative examples. Pamela's trials, Clarissa's sufferings, Sir Charles Grandison's difficulties, all open the way to final happiness; and the inner drift and purpose of the three novels is no other than the traditional impulse which had driven Bunyan's naïve fancy, together with the pilgrim soul, from the slough of despond to the eternal city. But Richardson's faith and hope fall short of Bunyan's rapt singlemindedness. In *Clarissa* only, the higher regions and finer air of religious enthusiasm are approached; in the other books, a more grossly utilitarian atmosphere prevails, and it is in this world that Sir Charles's, like Pamela's, conscious expectations meet with their reward.

Of Samuel Richardson's life, not much is interesting, and little need be said here. Though his family resided in London before, and soon after, his birth, he was born in Derbyshire, as the son of a well-to-do joiner. It is characteristic of leanings which were natural to him that, of his early history, he left what he could in the dark, while what he mentioned he tried to idealise. He seems to have received but a slight education, and certainly was without any university training. Recent investigation has not materially added to the scant knowledge of his boyhood and youth derived from eighteenth century sources. His father's wish was, first, to make him a clergyman; but, owing to money losses, young Richardson remained unprovided with the usual accomplishments; and, eventually, he chose to be apprenticed to a printer. Due emphasis is com-

monly laid on the early symptoms of his later literary temperament, as revealed in the boy's love of letter-writing and
propensity to preaching, as well as on the experience which the
moralist was enabled to gather from his employment by girl
friends as penman and inditer in their love affairs. He set up
a printing business in 1719, and, in 1721, married the daughter
of his old master; she bore him six children, five of whom died
in infancy. A year after her death, in 1731, Richardson
married a second time; and, again, he had to undergo sad
family bereavements. The tenor of his blameless but humdrum
existence was broken only by a few unimportant incidents,
while his steady rise in the world can be gauged from his
employment as printer to the House of Commons, and from
his taking on lease a country residence at Hammersmith, in
1739.

By this time, Richardson was fifty years of age; he had
long shown signs of declining health, was much troubled with
nervousness and adopted the diet of a valetudinarian. He had
not produced anything of consequence in the way of literature,
when, in the same year, he was asked by two friends, printers
like himself, to prepare for them "a little volume of letters,
in a common style, on such subjects as might be of use to those
country readers who were unable to indite for themselves."
These letters came out in January, 1741, and, as was intimated
on the title-page, furnished not only a pattern in style and form,
but, also, directions "how to think and act justly and prudently
in the common Concerns of Human Life." One of the subjects
emphasised in this collection was the danger surrounding the
position of a young woman—especially when goodlooking—as
a family servant. How Richardson's first novel grew out of
the treatment of this theme is pretty generally known. That
the book should have been written in the form of letters was
thus due to the accident of its origin; but, underlying all mere
chance and circumstances were a deep-seated habit and the
irresistible bent of genius. *Pamela; or, Virtue Rewarded*, was
published in two volumes (November, 1740), and immediately
met with an eager reception; two further volumes, describing
Pamela's life after her marriage, were given to the public in
December, 1741.

*Pamela's* supposed indebtedness to Marivaux's *Marianne*

has been discussed, and definitively negatived, by Austin
Dobson, in his study of Richardson.  It seems safer to consider
the first notable English novel of sentimental analysis, in the
light in which its author looked upon it, as an entirely spontaneous production, the rough outline of which had been suggested
to him by facts.  From this point of view, it is impossible not
to agree with the verdict generally passed upon the book, as,
in truth, a crude first attempt, redeemed by unmistakable
genius.  The originality and power of Richardson are recognisable throughout; but, both matter and manner are spoiled
by his characteristic faults, which are here at their worst.  The
novel, as a whole, lacks unity of conception and construction;
one readily perceives that the plan was not decided upon from
the first, but that it grew on the author as he became more
conscious of his faculties and aim.  The two volumes added as
an afterthought are a mere tag and make a very heavy demand
upon the reader's patience; whatever interest we may take in
Pamela's fate, her triumph and happiness bring all our anxieties to an end, and we should like to be spared her married
experiences, together with all the new ensamples furnished by
her unfailing virtues.  If she no longer appeals to us, so soon
as her persecutor has been reformed into her husband, it is
because she is the least sympathetic of Richardson's heroines;
and this, again, is closely connected with the fact that his
moral teaching, in this work, is at its lowest.  The deeplying
energy of the puritan spirit makes itself felt in its most uncritical and narrowest form; it relies entirely on our acceptance
of religious utilitarianism as an all-sufficient principle and
motive.  That Pamela's honour should be threatened is held
out as an irresistible demand on our sympathy; that her
resistance should be rewarded, as an edifying conclusion and a
most improving lesson.  That Pamela's innocence should be
self-conscious and designing is an unavoidable corollary of a
moral ideal of this nature; and the indelicacy implied in the
plot and in the treatment of many scenes is only a natural
consequence of the hard, materialistic, calculating and almost
cynical view of virtue and vice stamped on the whole book.

But the student of literature cannot forget that the publication of *Pamela* produced an extraordinary effect; it swept
the country with a wave of collective emotion; indeed, few

readers, even in our days, are likely to give the story a fair
trial without feeling its grip. The most interesting feature of
Richardson's works, in general, and more particularly of his
first novel, is that he should have found a substitute and an
equivalent for conscious art in the creative power of moral
earnestness and imaginative intensity. The instrument which
the new writer had unwittingly chosen for himself was shapeless and unwieldy; the difficulties and conventions implied
in the development of a narrative by means of letters make
themselves felt more and more, as the action proceeds; a
moment soon comes when Pamela's epistles are exchanged for
her journal, and, though the patience and fertility of correspondents in Richardson's circle may have equalled the stupendous performances of his heroine, yet, it is difficult to reconcile
an impression of truth or likelihood with the literal record of
lengthy conversations. Nevertheless, the reality of the story
grows upon us from the very first. It is due, partly, to the
vividness of presentment which the epistolary form makes
possible; partly, to that realistic grasp of minute facts which
Richardson shared with Defoe, though, perhaps, not in the
same measure. This faculty may be traced back to the positive
bent of his middle-class instincts, as well as to the mysterious
affinity of the traditional puritan genius with the concrete.
Throughout the story, the reader remains aware that the un-
speakable importance of each trifling event in the moral order
of things, according as it makes for eternal life or perdition,
is the source of the unfailing attention which it exacts from him,
as well as the incentive to the imagination which forces the series
of events upon his notice. Only the grim pathos of the life-
drama of all religious souls can account for the strange and
cruel power with which Richardson wrings the very heart of his
heroine—and the hearts of his readers.

Last, the energy of the puritan scrutiny of motives and
searching of conscience develops into a wonderful intuition of
character. Richardson's experience had made him acquainted
with the nature of women; and his tremulous, sensitive temperament was spontaneously attuned to theirs; so, by far the
most remarkable of his creations are feminine. Mr. B. is
almost a woman's man; of the secondary figures, only those
of Lady Davers and Mrs. Jewkes are carefully particularised,

and testify to Richardson's power of bitter realism; but Pamela herself stands out in strong relief. Our predominant impression of her is not, as might have been expected, that of a tame and rose-pink, or dull and priggish, character, marked with conventional idealism or moral pedantry. Though there is a good deal of both in her, she is far more real than the heroines of works against which Richardson's common sense and puritan strictness rose in protest. The artist in him, unknown to himself, got the better of the moralist; and Pamela's personality seems to grow, as it were, independently of his purpose, according to the inner law of her being. Her little tricks and ways, her conscious or semi-conscious coquetry, her more than innocent weakness, counterbalance the almost miraculous correctness of her conduct, as judged by the author's ethical standard. The growth of her affection for her master and persecutor, the subtle traits which reveal it to us and the fine gradation of her confession of it to herself, belong to an order of artistic achievement and psychological truth to which English literature had hardly risen since the decay of the Elizabethan drama.

The success of *Pamela*, whether it was due to a dim recognition of this merit, or, more simply, as we have reason for thinking, to the sentimental interest taken in a moving tale, is a landmark in the history of the novel. Directly through the imitations, or indirectly through the satires or parodies which it called forth, the book stands at the very fountain-head of the teeming period in which the ascendency of modern fiction asserted itself. (A fourth edition came out within six months of the first.) We know from contemporary evidence that it was the fashion to have read *Pamela;* and that, while fine ladies made a point of holding a copy of it in their hands, it stirred the emotions of middle-class or lower-class readers; and, in at least one instance, it was recommended from the pulpit. In September, 1741, was published an anonymous sequel, *Pamela's Conduct in High Life*, which thus preceded the author's own continuation of his novel. The story was adapted for the stage so early as 1741. According to Richardson, "the publication of the History of Pamela gave birth to no less than 16 pieces, as remarks, imitations, etc." Among the less famous skits directed against it, mention should be made of *An*

*Apology for the Life of Mrs. Shamela Andrews* (April, 1741),
the authorship of which is still under discussion; it was followed
by Fielding's *History of the Adventures of Joseph Andrews, and
his friend Mr. Abraham Adams* (February, 1742). It must
be left to a subsequent chapter[1] to show how Richardson's
sentimentalism and overstrained morality provoked into expression the broader naturalism of his great rival, and how
the English novel thus started, at the same time, on the two
main lines of its modern advance.

Though *Pamela* was published without its author's name,
and Richardson was not, at once, generally associated with it,
its unexpected reception gradually raised him to literary fame.
No material change, however, seems to have taken place in his
regular, precise and laborious way of living; and he did not give
up his business as a printer. But the circle of his friends and
correspondents was much enlarged; and he was brought into
contact with not a few of the distinguished men of the time.
The group of admirers, principally ladies, of which he was the
centre, and the ways of the quiet country household in which
he was wont to read out his morning's work to appreciative
listeners, are of moment to us here only because they throw
light upon the far more deliberate method and clearer knowledge of his own powers which distinguish his second novel from
the first. How far he was indebted to the suggestions and
criticism of his daily audience cannot, of course, be estimated;
but we know that he expanded in an atmosphere of warm,
responsive sympathy, and that, to his sensitive nature, encouragement and praise were as the bread of life.

The conception of *Clarissa* was prompted by something
besides his natural desire to turn his newly revealed faculties
to fuller use. Indeed, the design of the book was not only to
convey a moral; it was to improve on the teaching of *Pamela*,
and to correct any rash or unfair inference that might have been
drawn from it. Well might Richardson be alarmed lest the
teaching of his first novel should be misconstrued: would
not romantic serving-maids and confident damsels dream of
conquering their masters' or lovers' unruly passions, and was
not Mr. B. too apt a confirmation of that dangerous axiom that
"a reformed rake makes the best husband"? While the author

[1] See Chap. II, *post*.

of *Pamela* had been optimistic, because it was his main purpose
to point out a positive example, the author of *Clarissa* thought
it his duty, rather, to offer a warning, and to lay stress on the
exceptional nature of conversions. *Clarissa, or, the History
of a young Lady*, was, thus, doomed to end in gloom, and to be
a demonstration of the perfidy of man. As the title-page declared, the book was designed to show "the Distresses that may
attend the Misconduct both of Parents and Children in relation
to Marriage." The first edition consisted of seven volumes,
two of which were issued in November, 1747, two more in
April, 1748, and the last three in December of the same year.

The higher merit and the unique place of *Clarissa* among
Richardson's works are due to a deepened consciousness of
his purpose and to a nobler energy of conscience. Puritan
ardour and intensity is better able here to take the place of the
suggestions of art, inasmuch as it is itself exalted into its most
refined essence. That Clarissa's heroic virtues should be
sustained by her trust in a heavenly reward is, no doubt, a
lesson unpleasantly thrust upon us during the latter part of the
story; indeed, the piety of the poor sorely-tried soul partakes
of the strictest and sternest spirit of an austere Christianity,
and, in the rapture of her penitence and expectation, she re-
fuses to see her friends, because "God will have no rivals."
Again, the gusto with which the author deals out fit endings
and terrible deaths to the wicked, and his claim that every
personage in the novel finally receives his or her due, belong,
rather, to the sphere of edification than to that of realistic
observation or artistic effect. But, leaving out the last episodes,
and the constantly implied or expressed hope of a Providential
remedy for human wrongs, the tragedy of suffering and sorrow
which Richardson's genius has spun out of itself reaches a
greater breadth and height on the familiar stage of this world;
it is free from the trammels of religious utilitarianism as well
as of moral convention. The literary formula he had invented
and made his own is thus afforded a wider scope. Whatever
intrinsic artificiality it may contain is, of course, not less apparent here than elsewhere; the reader's goodwill and com-
plaisance are required on many points; a painful ingenuity
has to be expended by the author in order to squeeze the writing,
and, frequently, even the copying, of the epistles, into the bare

limits of time allowed by the story; the network of the letters retains many items of trifling interest and, necessarily, implies a good many repetitions, while not a few incidents of the plot which could hardly be transmuted into the self-consciousness of the personages of the novel or into their knowledge of one another have to be allowed to slip through. The deliberate style of almost all the correspondents drags along into unparalleled lengthiness; and Lovelace's self-revelation in his cynical confessions to his friends is, at times, irreconcilable with psychological truth. Still, when all is said, the clumsy framework of this epistolary drama is so constantly hidden under the creative wealth of a wonderfully minute imagination, and the enormous body of the narrative, as a whole, is borne along by so irresistible a flow of emotion, that Richardson's masterpiece remains one of the great novels of the world's literature.

Its appeal is to the heart. No doubt, the psychological interest of the book is broader and more varied than that of *Pamela*. Though Clarissa is proposed as an example to all young ladies, she accomplishes the all but impossible feat of remaining an attractive pattern of virtue. Not that she is faultless—a fact of which Richardson was well aware, though, perhaps, less so than he would have allowed. But there is a true nobleness, a natural dignity in Clarissa, a power of stedfast suffering, a true delicacy, an ardour of affection; while, together with her serious bent of mind, she has the supreme touch of a winning naturalness, fresh, unexpected and even provokingly spontaneous, which makes her a match for her friend, the sprightly Miss Howe. Nothing is finer or truer than the evolution of her feeling for her unworthy lover; nowhere else did Richardson's knowledge of the feminine heart stand him in better stead. Lovelace, undoubtedly, is the forerunner of a long series of romantic heroes; the drawing of this character reveals a strangely penetrating insight, on the part of the author, into motives and moods, together with an almost naïve exaggeration. His is a divided soul, a study in the subtle degradation wrought by desire; he is, at the same time, more than a mere human personage—a power of darkness, the prince of lies; and the weird letter in which he murders his own conscience and himself tells the tale of the bloody deed is a triumph of imaginative art though a sin against realistic truth. The

Harlowe family, and several of the less important figures, are depicted with a remarkable wealth and vigour of characterisation. In the history of the English novel, no such group of boldly and strongly sketched personalities had, hitherto, served as a background for so individualised a pair of lovers. And yet, the mere aesthetic appreciation of a profound study of the working of the human mind is, as we read, lost in our sympathy with a heart-rending story of undeserved woe. The family tragedy of the first volumes seizes upon our emotions like the slow, oppressive, inevitable approach of a storm; the circle of fate grows narrower and narrower as it closes round the unprotected Clarissa; and the chain of circumstance and event is woven with an extraordinary strength of dramatic cohesion. No sooner has Clarissa fallen into Lovelace's power, than the crushing of her will and pride in a hopeless struggle is impressed upon us with the relentless, terrible determination of religious enthusiasm; only Dante or Bunyan could have painted such scenes with the same inflexible rigour. When her heart is broken, and she has nothing left to her but to die, the pathos of her long agony is overdone. Such cheap means of emotion as the coming of death, with all its attending circumstances, had not yet been exploited to satiety by domestic dramatists and sentimental novelists; Richardson avails himself of them only too fully, and our overwrought nerves are offended by his want of artistic taste. But, as is well known, his contemporaries were not so fastidious. During the months of breathless suspense when Clarissa's fate hung in the balance, many letters reached the author deprecating a catastrophe; and, when the heroine, having settled all her affairs and written her eleven posthumous letters, actually departed this world, England burst into a wail of lament; nor was it long before the contagion of sorrow spread to the continent.

As *Clarissa* had grown out of *Pamela*, so *Sir Charles Grandison* grew out of *Clarissa*. Richardson's female friends would not rest satisfied with his portrait of a good woman; he must now give them a good man. Moreover, had not Fielding's *Tom Jones* (1749) insolently, and, as Richardson thought, most unfairly, encroached upon his own province of holding up examples and depicting heroes, and, immediately, found many readers for itself? The easy morals and "low" tone of his rival's book were all the more odious to Richardson's sense of propriety, because his vanity, ever a weak point with him, was sorely tried. Before the end of 1749, he had, though reluctantly, undertaken the difficult task which his admirers and his conscience were, alike, pressing upon him. The slow progress of the novel bears witness to the particularly arduous nature of the task; it came out, in seven volumes, between November, 1753, and March, 1754. *The History of Sir Charles Grandison; in a Series of Letters published from the Originals* professed to be "by the Editor of *Pamela* and *Clarissa*"; but, in the preface, Richardson practically admitted his authorship.

None of his three novels has set modern criticism so much at variance as *Grandison*. The student of literature must, primarily, bear in mind that the success of the last effort was not unequal to that of its predecessors. At the same time, the aim and conception of the book show a marked falling off from the higher artistic level of *Clarissa*. The didactic purpose is as glaring as it is in the previous novels, without being, in the present instance, relieved by the wealth of human pathos which made the story of Clarissa, in itself, a moving tragedy. Sir Charles's trials are but slight, as befits the good fortune of a man not less beloved by Providence than by a consensus of mere mortals; and the embarrassing predicament in which he finds himself between half-a-dozen women admirers—even the annoying prospect of being obliged, on principle, to marry Clementina, while, at heart, preferring Miss Byron—cannot ruffle the well-founded composure of his mind. Richardson, of course, took care that the Italian signorina should be very attractive indeed, though we feel sure that where Sir Charles's duty lies his affections will soon enough follow. Those readers—and they are not few—who find Harriet Byron lacking in genuine delicacy and unaffected charm, are, of course, not privileged to take an interest in her doubts and anxieties. The disappointed ladies—Clementina and Emily—certainly appeal more strongly to our sympathies; though Clementina's madness is not so successfully devised that the touch of cheap romanticism in it can be passed over. Thus, our emotions, on the whole, are little stirred. Apart from the first incidents, which concern Miss Byron's abduction and her rescue by Sir Charles, the development of the story is not very exciting to blunted tastes; while the Italian episodes, and the lengthy negotiations with the della Porretta family, are wholly tedious.

The despairing reader falls back upon the psychological value of the book.  Here, indeed, lies its greatness—if great it can, indeed, be said to be.  The characters are more numerous than in either *Pamela* or *Clarissa;* they are more varied, and more of them are interesting.  Sir Hargrave and the wicked personages in general are merely awkward performers who play at being naughty while remaining very conscious of the difference between good and evil;  so that their conversion, in due time, by Sir Charles's triumphant example, seems to us merely a matter of course.  But there is a vein of fresh observation in such comic figures as that of Sir Rowland Meredith, and an almost delicate intuition of girlish feeling in Miss Jervois;  as for Charlotte Grandison, she is not less true to life than she is perversely and abnormally provoking.  It seems as if the artist in Richardson had availed himself of this character to wreak some obscure unavowed revenge on the constraint which the moralist was imposing upon him in the rigid self-consistency of Sir Charles.  Of the hero and overwhelmingly predominant personage of the book, it is difficult to speak in cold blood—so irritating to our noblest (and to some of our worst) instincts is his self-possessed, ready-made, infallible sense of virtue.  The most we can say in his favour is that, considering the difficulties of the task, Richardson has managed to create a remarkably acceptable "*beau idéal*" of a gentleman, more genuine in his ways, and freer from the most objectionable features of puritanic priggishness, than might reasonably have been expected.

All through the composition of his last novel, Richardson had been aware of declining powers and failing health.  He still kept up his epistolary intercourse with his admirers and friends;  and his letters, most of which, duly prepared by himself for the use of posterity, have been preserved and handed down to us, are a mine of information for the student of the period.  Our knowledge of his life is, to this day, mainly based on the selection of his correspondence, published, in 1804, by Mrs. Barbauld.  Besides a pamphlet (1753) aimed against certain piratical Irish booksellers who had forestalled the authorised issue of the last volumes of *Grandison*, and a letter to *The Rambler* on the change in the manners of women (no. 97, for

19 February, 1751), perhaps his most characteristic, though not his most interesting, literary productions still remain to be mentioned. One of these is *A Collection of the Moral and Instructive Sentiments, Maxims, Cautions, and Reflexions, contained in the Histories of Pamela, Clarissa, and Sir Charles Grandison* (1755). As every reader of the novels knows only too well, they are rich with the ore of wisdom ready coined; and on such subjects as duelling, education, marriage and family relations, Richardson has even provided us with elaborate treatises. The other is *Meditations collected from the Sacred Books, and adapted to the different Stages of a Deep Distress; gloriously surmounted by Patience, Piety and Resignation. Being those mentioned in the History of Clarissa as drawn up for her own Use* (1750). These meditations are thirty-six in number, only four of which are inserted in the novel.

In 1754, Richardson removed from North end to Parson's green, Fulham; and, in the following year, his printing-house in Salisbury square had to be rebuilt on an adjoining site. This expenditure points to a prosperous condition of affairs; in fact, Richardson's means and social position were so far improved that he had become master of the Stationers' company. Though he never was in touch with the most brilliant society of the time, he numbered among his acquaintances men of a standing far superior to his own, and certainly did something to promote the gradual recognition of literary genius as a distinction equal to any other. His eldest daughter, Mary, made a good match in 1757; and, on the occasion of her marriage, he wrote his will, which Austin Dobson describes as "very lengthy, and having four codicils." His last years were afflicted with increasing nervous disorders, and insomnia. He died, from a paralytic stroke, on 4 July, 1761.

At the present day, the interest taken in Richardson's works is very largely historical. Their popularity, which did not show any symptoms of decline down to the beginning of the nineteenth century, is now, mainly, a thing of the past. Several causes may help to account for the neglect of them, even by cultivated readers, in our liberal-minded age. The length of the novels is, obviously, the first stumbling-block, as is testified by the many abridgments which have, more or less in vain, sought to adapt the cumbrous volumes to the exigencies of a more hurried life. Their epistolary form, probably, is another drawback. If, as has been said above, it permits a fresh and particular presentment of everyday facts to us, yet it is apt to seem hopelessly slow and antiquated; it savours of a time when letters were a work of leisure and love, and people liked to piece together the different threads of a story. More subtle elements in Richardson's writings, certainly, contribute to envelop them in an atmosphere of faint appreciation and widespread indifference. Together with the limitations of his art, those of his psychology and of his morals have grown more and more apparent, while their real strength is easily forgotten. His essential power was hardly personal; it was that of puritanism. His genius reached as deep as the consciousness of sin and the source of tears; but, in the depth of his emotions and in matters of conscience, he did not pass beyond the bounds of his time and of his class; and his intuitions possessed but little creative originality. With the passing of the sentimental age, and with the toning down of the puritan spirit, he ceased to be a prophet and sank into the part of a representative thinker and writer. The light thrown by him into the obscure undergrowths of the soul does not break from heaven like the flashes of a Shakespeare; it is a humble ray of poring, searching intensity. In these latter days, new shades have been added to our notions of conduct; morality has been revived in new forms and touched with an unwonted delicacy, a more anxious self-diffidence; and Richardson's hard, plain idea of duty cannot but appear blunt and harsh to us, as his analysis of the soul seems poor when compared with the luxuriant growth of modern psychology. Thus, the wonderful penetration of his genius has not maintained its supremacy, and time has pitilessly revealed its narrowness.

But his novels deserve more than the disinterested curiosity of students; their significance is other than relative. Taken by themselves, they constitute a literary achievement of enduring worth. The moral passion with which they are instinct may not appeal to us unreservedly; yet the forceful grasp of the stories holds us fast so soon as we have become reconciled to the atmosphere; and those regions of the human heart in which nature and grace, selfishness and love are always at war slowly and pitilessly open themselves to us, while we read, together with some part, at least, of the free, individual, spontaneous life of the shallow self. Richardson's realism is great in its handling of minute details, its imaginative power, its concatenation of events. Though the picturesque aspects of the world are hardly ever called up by him, the material circumstances of the drama in which his characters are engaged stand depicted with diligent fulness, and the inner incidents of the sentient, struggling soul have never been more graphically or abundantly narrated. His style is a self-created instrument of small intrinsic merit but of excellent utility; it shows variety enough to adjust itself to the personalities of different correspondents; it moves on with a certain elaborate ease, but knows how to rise, at times, to a straightforward, telling energy. It is not free from artistic, or even from grammatical, flaws, but, considering Richardson's personal lack of culture, it bears witness to a remarkable natural gift. Its tone is most often slightly self-conscious, with a preference for Latin, genteel words and phrases; but it not unfrequently displays the strength of racy idioms and the charm of native English simplicity.

Richardson's influence upon the course of English and European literature cannot be overestimated. To understand the extent and meaning of the effect exercised by him at home, the state of the English novel before and after him should be borne in mind. The assertion, frequently made, that he put an end to the romance of fancy, after the pattern of *The Grand Cyrus*, should not be repeated without qualification; the vogue of the D'Urfé and Scudéry school had long been on the wane, and the tendency to realism had already come to the front, principally through Defoe and Swift. But it is certain that *Pamela*, besides being the first notable English novel of sentimental analysis, heralded the advent of everyday manners and common people to artistic acceptance. The claims of Richardson to the favour of contemporary readers were, thus, manifold; he stirred their emotions, and gave definite satisfaction to their latent thirst for sentiment; he presented them with living, actual, flesh-and-bone heroes and heroines, and responded to their longing for reality and substance in fiction; he imparted a moral lesson, and, thus, found himself at one with the rising reaction against the sceptical levity of the preceding age. One more point should be emphasised: at the very moment when the social power of the middle classes was growing apace, Richardson, himself one of them, exactly expressed their grievances and prejudices. His novels are filled with a spirit of *bourgeois*—it might almost be said, popular—criticism of the privileges and the corruption of the great; and, at the same time, they are flavoured with the essence of snobbishness. It is easy to exaggerate the fondness with which Richardson dwells on the manners of servants or "low" people; the class with which he deals, that forming, so to say, the social plane of his novels, is the gentry. To him, the right of birth is an all but impassable barrier, and Pamela is no exception; she remains an inferior in her own eyes, if not exactly in those of her husband. No doubt, the higher circles of society in which Sir Charles Grandison moves were not known to Richardson from personal experience, and it is unnecessary to dwell on the mistakes with which he has been charged in his description of aristocratic life; still, he took a secret delight in holding intercourse, though it were of a more or less imaginary sort, with the nobility, and his conception of a gentleman was certainly not in advance of his time. Both the impatient self-assertion of the middle class, and its quiet settling down into conservative grooves of feeling, are thus foreshadowed. The story of Pamela is an illustration of the Christian equality of souls, quite in keeping with the widespread modern tendency to exalt a sentimental, theoretical democracy; it breathes, on the other hand, an involuntary subservience to the intrinsic dignity of rank and riches. In both ways, the social tone of Richardson's novels was that of a class, which, thenceforth, contributed its own elements to the formation of the literary atmosphere.

This general, diffused effect is of more importance than the direct and particular influence of Richardson on his imitators or disciples in England. The course of the English novel was not shaped by him alone, since Fielding rose to eminence almost simultaneously with him; but who can gauge the exact indebtedness of *Tom Jones* to *Pamela* and *Clarissa?* Is not a negative impulse an efficient motive power in its way; and, besides, was not the example of the older writer of positive value to the younger? Among the novelists who came after them, Sterne, in a large measure, may be included among the descendants of Richardson. So may Henry Brooke, whose *Fool of Quality* (1766–70)[1] bears some resemblance in matter to *Sir Charles Grandison*, Oliver Goldsmith, the kind-hearted moralist of *The Vicar of Wakefield* (1766),[2] and Henry Mackenzie, author of *The Man of Feeling* (1771).[3] Special mention should, also, be made of Fanny Burney, who wrote her first novel *Evelina* (1778) in the epistolary style,[4] and of Jane Austen, who used the same method in the first form of *Sense and Sensibility* (1811).[5] With both these writers, Richardson's influence, engrafted on a passionate admiration, was supreme; yet it need hardly be added that they both and, preeminently, Jane Austen, achieved distinct originality. It is a characteristic fact that, within the fifty years which followed Richardson's death, it should be impossible to single out any novelist on whom his individual spirit may be said to have descended, while there is hardly one who might not be said to have inherited something from him. With the new century and its new literature, his action did not cease to be felt; but it sank into subterranean channels, and dissolved into the general tendency in fiction to realism, accepted morality and mental analysis. These sources of inspiration are still fresh and running in the English novel of the present day; and, through them, the impulse given by Richardson is as notable as ever.

Whatever estimate may be formed of the relative merits of Richardson and Fielding individually, the significance of the former is seen to be immeasurably superior to that of his great rival, so soon as the wider field of European literature is taken into account. From the author of *Clarissa* is derived one of those pervading lines of influence out of which was woven the web of international life and thought in the latter half of the eighteenth century. By falling in with the revival of feeling on the continent, Richardson helped the wave of sentimentalism to break loose, and, thus, had a large share in the rise of the cosmopolitan age. In France, his works may be said to have played as great a part as any indigenous production. The admirable disquisition of Joseph Texte has thrown full light on this episode, which is one of paramount importance in the history of French letters. Public taste was then in a state of

[1] Cf. *ante*, Vol. IX, Chap. XII.　　　　[2] Cf. Chap. IX, *post*.
[3] Cf. Chap. III, *post*.　　　[4] Cf. Chap. III, *post*.　　　[5] Cf. Vol. XI, *post*.

transition. The latent possibilities of French genius were stirred as by the coming of a new springtime; fresh powers of imagination and emotion were seeking to assert themselves in the dry atmosphere of philosophical rationalism. The decay of classical ideals left room for new subjects and a new treatment; not only the manners of man in the abstract, but the complexity of the individual, not only the dignity of tragic or epic heroes, but the charm of real, everyday scenes and characters, were dimly felt to lie still unexplored—a field of boundless promise for a resolutely modern and original literature. Akin to the craving for sentiment and to the desire for reality in fiction was the moralising propensity; the spirit of the time indulged easily in free enquiries into problems of conduct, since the power of the old beliefs was in all spheres shaken by criticism. Richardson's novels answered to all those aspirations. The *Anglomanie* had fairly set in before he became the idol of the French public; but no English writer was more widely read in France during the eighteenth century. He was fortunate in being translated by abbé Prévost, himself a distinguished novelist and a warm admirer of English manners. *Pamela* was gallicised as early as 1742; *Clarissa* in 1751; *Grandison* from 1755 to 1758, with that freedom of adaptation and suppression which is characteristic of the time.

It would be out of place here to attempt more than a summary notice of the fortune with which Richardson's novels met in France. They were eagerly welcomed and only a very few dissentient voices made themselves heard in the chorus of praise; their author was worshipped by the swelling crowd of the votaries of sensibility. A series of imitations and sequels of the novels, and of plays founded upon them, bore witness to the lasting favour of the public. The reception of *Clarissa* was still more enthusiastic than that of *Pamela;* and even the somewhat stiff self-consciousness of *Grandison* could not blunt the appetites of French readers, forgetful, for once, of their keen susceptibility to the ridiculous. The versatile genius of Voltaire himself was carried away by the fashion of the day, and his *Nanine* (1749) was a strangely dissimilar dramatisation of *Pamela;* later, the irrepressible antipathy of his temperament broke out in angry condemnations of the novels.[1] Worthy of special

[1] For other French dramatic adaptations of *Pamela* see bibliography.

notice is Diderot's *Éloge de Richardson* (1761), a somewhat indiscriminate, but, on the whole, penetrating, criticism, laying eloquent stress on some of the main aspects of the English writer's real greatness, and turning them to account as a confirmation of Diderot's own dramatic theory. Still more momentous in the history of French and European literature is the admiration of Jean-Jacques Rousseau for Richardson. That his *Nouvelle Héloïse* (begun 1756, completed 1760) was suggested by *Clarissa* has, from the first, been a commonplace of literary criticism. The similitude in the theme and in its treatment, indeed, is extremely striking. Rousseau's heroine conquers her passion for Saint-Preux when virtue claims her under the more pressing form of duty to a husband, as Clarissa subdues her love for Lovelace when he has proved unworthy of her. In both stories, the death of the heroine crowns a pathetic tale with a supreme consummation. The French Claire and the English Miss Howe play pretty much the same part as *confidantes*. That both novels are written in the form of letters furnishes tangible proof of an influence which Rousseau never attempted to deny. The inner analogies are of still greater importance. A didactic spirit breathes through *La Nouvelle Héloïse*, a spirit of sober and earnest morality; the book aims at vindicating the sanctity of marriage, and at illustrating the artistic interest of domestic manners; it stands opposed to the artificial, aristocratic tone of older French fiction, as well as to the cynical mockery of Lesage. Needless to say, Rousseau's genius touched the book with its own originality; a more impassioned fervour of emotion, a poetical worship of nature, a self-indulgent enjoyment of melancholy moods, set upon it the distinct stamp of romanticism, while Richardson's sensibility kept within the bounds of the inner life, and was checked by his puritanism when half-way to romantic morbidity. It was his fate, nevertheless, to become one of the most active among the literary forces from which was to spring, together with the revival of letters, a state of moral unrest which would have caused his conscience many an anxious qualm. Not only most French novelists after 1760, but the leaders of the new school, from 1790 to 1830, either directly or through Rousseau, felt the inspiring and guiding influence of Richardson.

Hardly less deep-reaching or extensive was his influence in
Germany. "Richardson," says Erich Schmidt, in his still
indispensable study, "belongs as well to the history of the
German, as to that of the English, novel." The chords which
the author of *Clarissa* struck in the hearts of his earnest, religious and sentimental German readers were no other than
those which he had stirred in his light and sceptical French
admirers—so true it is that one great tide of emotional enthusiasm swept, at that time, over the bounds of nationality and
race. But the individual genius of each nation was, of course,
recognisable in the chorus of praise by a tone of its own. The
state of German romance before Gellert, says the critic just
quoted, was much the same as that of English fiction before
Richardson—with this difference only, that Germany had no
Defoe. Gellert, who translated *Pamela* and *Grandison*, was,
indeed, a writer after Richardson's heart; and his novel, *Das
Leben der schwedischen Gräfin von G.* (1746), though it falls far
short of his model, still affords ample proof of the most
praiseworthy intentions. Meanwhile, the German literary
market, just like the French, was flooded with imitations and
sequels; "histories" of an individual or of a family, in epistolary form, became the fashion. Among novelists who followed
Gellert's example may be mentioned Hermes (*Geschichte der
Miss Fanny Wilkes*, 1766) and Sophie La Roche (*Geschichte
des Fräuleins von Sternheim*, 1771). Wieland's admiration
found vent in a drama on the unfortunate *Clementina della
Poretta* (1760), after he had planned a series of letters from
Sir Charles Grandison to Miss Jervois (1759). In their im-
pulsive eagerness, many admirers would visit the scenes which
Richardson had described or make a pilgrimage to those in
which he had lived. Characteristic, in this respect, is Klopstock's longing to be personally acquainted with the author of
*Clarissa*, and the touching episode of his young wife's correspondence with a man upon whom, in her naïve enthusiasm,
she looked as little less than a saintly painter of angelic figures.
As years went by, the rationalists and disciples of the *Auf-
klärung* grew rather bitter against the sentimental influence
wielded by the English writer; Wieland himself somewhat
recanted his undiscerning praise; and the parody of Musäus
(*Grandison der Zweite*, written in 1759, recast in 1781) pointed,

at least, to some irreverence in the minds of a few. But the popularity of Richardson was rooted in the love of all tender hearts, and, as is well known, tender hearts were then, and remained long afterwards, the majority in Germany. Moreover, to the direct action of Richardson must be added that which he exercised through Rousseau and *La Nouvelle Héloïse;* and, thus, the puritanic, insular English genius is brought into close association with the world-wide, supremely liberal intellect of the author of *Werther's Leiden*. This summary would be too manifestly incomplete if a brief mention were not made of the Dutch translation of *Clarissa*, by John Stinstra; and of the sensation which *Pamela* created in Italy, where Goldoni adapted it for the stage.

# CHAPTER II

# Fielding and Smollett

THE two novelists with whom this chapter is to deal were very different in character, aims and achievement. Fielding was humane, genial, sweet-tempered; Smollett rancorous and impatient. Fielding, a philosopher and moralist, tried to show by a wide and deep representation of life the beauty of certain qualities of virtue; Smollett, to whom, in his old age at any rate, life seemed "a sort of debtors' prison, where we are all playthings of fortune," was more concerned with the superficial absurdities of men and circumstance. Fielding established the form of the novel in England; Smollett left a myriad of brilliant episodes. But, as men and as authors, they have, also, their resemblances. Both lived lives of hardship and labour with courage; both indulged the irony born of shrewd and independent minds. And both, by developing the study of the actual life around them as a subject for fiction, which had been begun by Bunyan and carried on by Defoe, Addison and Swift, conquered new kingdoms, and left the novel supreme in English imaginative literature.

Henry Fielding was born at Sharpham park, near Glastonbury, Somerset, on 22 April, 1707. In 1713, his father, Edmund Fielding (who was directly descended from the first earl of Desmond), moved, with his wife and family, to East Stour, a few miles to the west of Shaftesbury, in the northern corner of Dorset, where Henry's sister Sarah, the author of *David Simple* (1744–52), was born. His tutor here was a clergyman, named Oliver, of whom parson Trulliber, in *Joseph Andrews*, is said by Murphy to be a portrait. At the end of 1719 or beginning of 1720, he was sent to school at Eton, where he made friends with George (afterwards "the good" lord) Lyttelton, author of

*Dialogues of the Dead* (1740), his firm friend in later years, to whom he dedicated *Tom Jones*. Here, too, he acquired a knowledge of the classics to which his works bear witness. At Lyme Regis, when eighteen years old, he fell violently in love with a daughter of a deceased local merchant named Andrew, and appears to have planned an abduction. The girl was removed to Devonshire, and Fielding worked off his emotion in an English version of Juvenal's sixth satire, which he published, some years afterwards, revised, in his *Miscellanies*.

The next news of him is the production of his first play at Drury lane, in February, 1728. A month later, his name appears as *Litt. Stud.* in the books of the university of Leyden. He was still at Leyden in February, 1729; but within a year his name disappeared from the roll. In January, 1730, his second play was produced at Goodman's fields theatre. His schooling being over, and the paternal remittances few or none, he had now come to London to make a living. A big, strong young man, well-educated and well-connected, with a great appetite for life, and small experience of it, he began his activity as author and dramatist.

Unlike Smollett, Fielding never wrote a tragedy; but his work for the stage comprises every other then known kind of drama-comedy, farce, ballad farce, burlesque and adaptation from the French. The first play produced by him was *Love in Several Masques*, a comedy accepted by Cibber, Wilks and Booth for Drury lane, and acted in February, 1728, by Mrs. Oldfield and others, with great success. His second, brought on the stage of the Goodman's fields theatre, in January, 1730, was the comedy *The Temple Beau*. In the following March, at the Haymarket theatre, he gave an example of a vein which was to suit him better than experiments in imitation of Congreve, of which his comedy mainly consists. *The Author's Farce, and The Pleasures of the Town*, by "Scriblerus Secundus," as Fielding now for the first time called himself, satirises the prevalent taste for opera and pantomime. For the character of Luckless, the young, gay and impecunious author of the "puppet-show" *The Pleasures of the Town*, Fielding has evidently drawn upon himself; and the first two acts, which serve as introduction to the puppet-show, abound in that vivacious, satirical observation of the life about him in which

Fielding excelled. He pokes fun at wellknown people, among them Henley the preacher, Cibber and Wilks; while the relations between booksellers and their hack-writers are amusingly exhibited. In the same year, 1730, appeared not only *The Coffee-House Politician*, a comedy in which justice Squeezum anticipates justice Thrasher in *Amelia*, while the principal character is obsessed with politics much like Mrs. Western in *Tom Jones*, but, also, Fielding's longest-lived and most enjoyable dramatic work, the burlesque *Tom Thumb*. In the following year, this play, enlarged from two acts to three, was revived under the title *The Tragedy of Tragedies; or, The Life and Death of Tom Thumb the Great.*[1] In 1731, Fielding produced three comparatively unimportant plays; in 1732, besides writing *The Covent Garden Tragedy*, a burlesque of Ambrose Philips's *The Distrest Mother*, and two other plays, he adapted Molière's *Le Médecin Malgré Lui* under the title *The Mock Doctor*. The work is well done, and the version keeps fairly close to the original, though Fielding did not scruple to touch it up here and there, or, with his eye for the life about him, to introduce some personalities about Misaubin, a quack of the day, to whom he dedicated the printed play. In the next year, he adapted *L'Avare*, under the title *The Miser;* after which he remained almost silent till the beginning of 1734, when Kitty Clive, for whom he had a warm admiration and friendship, appeared in his comedy, *The Intriguing Chambermaid*, partly adapted from Regnard's *Le Retour Imprévu*. Together with this, an enlarged and altered version of *The Author's Farce* was produced. *Don Quixote in England*, another play (1734) (begun, as the preface tells us, at Leyden, in 1728), is chiefly remarkable for the character of squire Badger, who is very like squire Western, for the famous hunting song beginning "The dusky Night rides down the Sky," and for parliamentary election scenes which, possibly, were in the mind of Fielding's friend Hogarth when he designed his election prints. With the year 1735, in which were brought out a successful farce and an unsuccessful comedy, we come to a break in Fielding's activity as a playwright. As a writer of comedy, Fielding suffered under three disabilities—inexperience

---

[1] See, as to Fielding's dramatic burlesques and satires, and their significance in the history of the English drama and stage, Chap. IV, *post*.

of the human heart; the haste of a young man about town in urgent need of money to relieve him of duns or provide him with pleasures; and the prevalence of the decaying form of comedy inherited from Congreve. He is at his best when exhibiting the external features of the life of his time; his characterisation is neither deep nor interesting. In farce and burlesque, he was far happier. Here, his high spirits, his gift for amusing extravagance, had free play.

On 28 November, 1734, at St. Mary Charlcombe, near Bath, Fielding was married to Charlotte Cradock, of Salisbury, whom he appears to have been courting, by poems (afterwards published) and in other ways, since 1730 or an earlier date. In February, 1735, Charlotte Fielding's mother died, leaving one shilling to her daughter Catherine (we think of Amelia and her sister, and their mother's will) and the residue of her estate to Charlotte. It was probably this legacy that enabled Fielding to take his wife away from the ups and downs of an author's life in London, to the house at East Stour, where he had spent his boyhood. Here, he seems to have lived a jolly, and rather extravagant life; it is not improbable that Booth's experiences on his farm in *Amelia* are taken partly from Fielding's own, and partly, perhaps, from those of his father. In something less than a year, he was back in London and again hard at work.

Early in 1736, he took the Little theatre in the Haymarket, formed a company of actors, and in this and the following year produced *Pasquin* and *The Historical Register for the year* 1736. Of these celebrated dramatic satires something will be said elsewhere,[1] as well as of the share which the second of them had in bringing about the Licensing act of 1737. For Fielding, the passing of this act meant, practically, the end of his career as a dramatist. Two or three plays, written by him in whole or in part, were, indeed, produced in 1737; but, in the same year, he dismissed his company and turned to other fields of work. Of himself, he said, later, that he "left off writing for the stage when he ought to have begun."[2] He resumed his legal studies, and, in the month of November, became a student of the

---

[1] See Chap. IV, *post*.
[2] He afterwards produced *The Wedding Day* (in 1743). *The Good-Natured Man* appeared posthumously.

Middle Temple.   There is evidence that he worked hard—without, apparently, ceasing to live hard—and he was called to the bar in June, 1740.   Meanwhile, he had not given up authorship altogether.   An "Essay on Conversation," published in the *Miscellanies* of 1743, was probably written in 1737.   In November, 1739, appeared the first number of *The Champion*, a newspaper published thrice a week, and written mainly by Fielding (whose contributions, signed C. or L., are the most numerous[1]) and his friend James Ralph.   He adopted the not uncommon plan of inventing a family or group as supposed authors or occasions of the various essays—in this case, the Vinegar family, of whom captain Hercules, with his famous club, is the most prominent.   Among the best papers are the four called "An Apology for the Clergy."   Fielding had attacked the clergy in *Pasquin;* in "An Apology," his ironical method exposes even more clearly the vices of place-hunting and want of charity then prevalent among them, while he reveals the deep admiration and reverence for the qualities which were afterwards to glow in his portrait of parson Adams. In an essay on Charity, again, the Fielding of the future is evident in the warm-hearted common sense with which the subject of imprisonment for debt is treated.   The personal interest in these papers is strong.   One of them has high praise for the humour and moral force of Hogarth's "Rake's Progress" and "Harlot's Progress."   Another furnishes a glimpse of Fielding's own personal appearance, familiar from Hogarth's drawing.   Yet others continue the persistent attacks on Colley Cibber which Fielding had begun in his plays.   Cibber, when, in his *Apology* (1740), noticing the Licensing act, retorted by an opprobrious reference to Fielding.   Thereupon, Fielding vented all his humour, all his weight and all his knowledge of the law and of the world in slashing replies, in which Colley and his son Theophilus are successfully held up to ridicule.   The last paper in the essays collected from *The Champion* is dated Thursday, 12 June, 1740,[2] just before Fielding was called to the bar.   He went the western circuit.

Perhaps, in spite of himself, writing must have been still

---

[1] Some of Fielding's papers in *The Champion* were collected in book-form in 1741.

[2] He seems, however, to have continued to write for the paper till June, 1741.

necessary to him as a means of subsistence. In any case, accident had something to do with his finding his true field. In November, 1740, Samuel Richardson had published *Pamela*. Fielding had had some experience in parody: and he set to work to parody *Pamela*. But, just as *Pamela* had grown under its author's hands into something much larger than the original conception, so the parody grew beyond Fielding's first intention till it became his first published novel, *The History of the Adventures of Joseph Andrews, and of his Friend Mr. Abraham Adams*. As Pamela was tempted by her master, squire Booby (the full name given by Fielding is concealed by Richardson under the initial B.), so her brother, Joseph Andrews, is tempted by his mistress Lady Booby, another member of the family. Clearly, the fun of the inverted situation would soon be exhausted; and Fielding would speedily tire of a milksop. Thus, before he had composed his title-page and his preface, his whole design had changed. Of Lady Booby, we hear practically nothing after the tenth chapter. Andrews himself, though transformed into a hearty and vigorous youngster, has slipped into the second place, and the chief character in the story is the poor clergyman, parson Adams. Twice in the book, Fielding defends himself against the charge of drawing his characters from living originals; but, among others, Richardson (who was much hurt at the "lewd and ungenerous" treatment of his *Pamela*, and, henceforth, never lost an opportunity of carping at Fielding) declared that parson Adams was drawn direct from William Young, a clergyman of Gillingham, in Dorset, who (curiously enough) witnessed Fielding's signature to the assignment of the copyright in *Joseph Andrews* for £183.11s. 0d., and who, also, later, intended to join him in a translation of Aristophanes, which was never completed. If so, William Young must have been a fascinating character; but it is more important to notice that, with all the contradictions in his nature, parson Adams does not show any of those lapses from verisimilitude which are usually the result of a slavish imitation of life. He is, in truth, one of the immortal characters in fiction. Something of him appears in the vicar of Wakefield, something in my uncle Toby; and, wherever in fiction simplicity, self-forgetfulness, charity and hard riding of a hobby are combined in one person, there will be found traces of parson

Adams. He is often ridiculous; the absurdest accidents happen to him, for Fielding, though he was nearly thirty-five when the book was published, had not yet lost his love of farce. But, just as Cervantes preserved the dignity of Don Quixote, so this novel ("written in imitation of the manner of Cervantes," as the title-page tells us), by preserving the spirit of comedy through all the episodes of farce, preserves the dignity of one of the most loveable of men. In the preface, Fielding explains that the only source of the ridiculous is affectation, springing either from vanity or from hypocrisy. Vanity and hypocrisy were the objects of Fielding's life-long enmity; but it is unsafe to trust too much to his own explanation of his motives. For parson Adams is, certainly, free from affectation; and it is this very freedom which gives rise to all his misfortunes. In this novel, we find, for the first time, the distinguishing character- istic of Fielding's attitude towards life—his large-hearted sympathy. Hypocrisy he hated, together with all cruelty and unkindness; but, when he comes to exhibit a hypocrite, a scold, or a rogue of any kind, he betrays a keen interest, sometimes almost an affection, rather than hatred or scorn. Mrs. Slip- slop, that wonderful picture of a sensual, bullying, cringing lady's-maid; Peter Pounce, the swindling skinflint; Mrs. Towwouse, the scolding virago, parson Trulliber, the boor and brute—all are satirised genially, not savagely. Perhaps the one character invented by him for whom he shows hatred pure and simple, the one character at whom we are never allowed to laugh, is Blifil in *Tom Jones*.

By stating on his title-page that *Joseph Andrews* was "written in imitation of the manner of Cervantes," Fielding meant more than that parson Adams was a Quixotic character. He meant that he was writing something new in English litera- ture, though familiar to it from translations of Cervantes's work. Scott traced in *Joseph Andrews* a debt to Scarron's *Roman Comique;* Furetière's *Roman Bourgeois*, Marivaux's *Paysan Parvenu* and *Histoire de Marianne* have, also, been mentioned as possible origins of the novel. Fielding himself, in the pre- face, explains that he has written "a comic epic poem in prose," with a "light and ridiculous" fable instead of a "grave and solemn" one, ludicrous sentiments instead of sublime and characters of inferior instead of superior rank. It is necessary

to disentangle his motives (which may have been afterthoughts) from the facts of his novel's descent.  The author
of *Tom Thumb* began *Joseph Andrews* as a burlesque; and burlesque—not of *Pamela* but of older works—he allowed it to
remain, so far as some parts of the diction are concerned.
But the origin of *Joseph Andrews*, as we have it, is not to
be found in Scarron, or Cervantes, or any parody or burlesque.   In spirit, it springs from the earlier attempts, made
by Bunyan, by Defoe, by Addison and Steele in *The Spectator*, to reproduce the common life of ordinary people.  Until
*Joseph Andrews* came out, that life had never been exhibited
in Engla ld with so much sense of character, so clear an insight
into motives, so keen an interest.  What the book owes to Cervantes is its form, in which the loosely-knit plot follows the
travels and adventures of Adams, Andrews and Fanny, and
is summarily wound up when the author pleases.  Fielding's
achievement in the construction was not yet equal to his
achievement in the spirit of fiction; nor could he yet be
called "the father of the English novel."

Seven years were to pass before the novel which justly
earned him that title was published.  Meanwhile, Fielding, who
appears to have been still attempting to gain a practice at the
bar, had not relinquished writing.  In or about April, 1743, a
little more than a year after the publication of *Joseph Andrews*,
he issued by subscription three volumes of *Miscellanies*.  The
first volume contains a preface, largely autobiographical,
followed by some poems.  Fielding's poetry is almost negligible in view of his other work, though the songs in his plays
have plenty of spirit.  The poems included in the *Miscellanies*
are mainly early compositions, "productions of the heart
rather than of the head," as he calls them.  They include love
poems and light verse, addressed to Charlotte Cradock and
others, and episties, together with some prose essays.  The
second volume contains more interesting matter: the long
Lucianic fragment, *A Journey from this World to the Next*,[1]
which begins with some of Fielding's happiest satire in the
coach-driver of the spirits from earth.  The judgment of
Minos affords more excellent fun; and the talk of Homer (with

---

[1] A paper in *The Champion* (Saturday, 24 May, 1740) contains the germ of
the idea fitfully elaborated in this fragment.

Mme. Dacier in his lap), Addison, Shakespeare, Dryden and others is good. Then come sixteen less interesting chapters on the migrations of the soul of the emperor Julian, the tale of which remains incomplete; and, in a final chapter, Anne Boleyn relates her life.

In the third volume of the *Miscellanies*, Fielding printed the most brilliant piece of work that he had yet achieved, *The Life of Mr. Jonathan Wild the Great*. Hitherto, his irony had but flashed. In *Jonathan Wild*, it burns through the book with a steady light. The point of view is a familiar one with Fielding, who was a sworn foe of pretentious appearances. The confusion of greatness with goodness is common. "Bombast greatness," therefore, is to be exposed by dealing with its qualities as if, indeed, they were the qualities of goodness; and, since "all these ingredients glossed over with wealth and a title have been treated with the highest respect and veneration" in "the splendid palaces of the great," while, in Newgate, "one or two of them have been condemned to the gallows," this kind of greatness shall be taken as it is seen in Newgate, glossed over with no wealth or title, and written of as if it were the greatness of Alexander, Cæsar or—as we of a later time might add—Napoleon. So we have Jonathan Wild, thief, "fence" and gallows-bird, steadily held up before us throughout fifty-six chapters as a hero, a great man; while Heartfree, the simple, affectionate, open nature—the good man—is treated as "silly," "low" and "pitiful." The book has distressed many, including Scott, whose recollection of it was not very exact; but not even Swift has produced so remarkable a piece of sustained irony, so full of movement, so various, so finely worked in its minutest particulars, or so vivid in its pictures of "low" life. Its humour is often broad—especially in the passages relating to Miss Laetitia Snap, afterwards Mrs. Jonathan Wild; but its merciless exposure of hypocrisy, meanness and cruelty, even more than the difference between the rewards ultimately meted out to greatness and to goodness, makes it a work of excellent morality. The way to true honour, the book claims, lies open and plain, the way of the transgressor is hard.

About this time, Fielding's own way became hard; and, if the gout which was taking an ever firmer hold on him was partly due to his own transgressions in youth, fate had in store for him a blow which he had not done anything to bring upon himself. After the publication of the *Miscellanies*, he devoted himself to the law as closely as his gout would permit. Literature, he forswore: partly, perhaps, by reason of the precarious nature of its rewards, partly because, as we learn from his preface to his sister Sarah's novel, *David Simple* (1744), he was disgusted at being "reputed and reported the author of half the scurrility, bawdry, treason, and blasphemy, which these few last years have produced"—especially "that infamous, paltry libel," *The Causidicade*. Six months later, in November, 1744, his wife died at Bath, after a long illness. Fielding had loved her passionately. Sophia Western is one portrait of her; Amelia is another—even to the broken, or scarred, nose. The passage describing Allworthy's feelings about his dead wife[1] has, no doubt with justice, been described as autobiographical. No disproof of his affection for his Charlotte is to be found in the fact that, in November, 1747, he married her maid, Mary Daniel, a good soul, who made him a good wife. Their son, William, was born in February, 1748.

Fielding's efforts to break away from writing were spasmodic and never successful for long. In November, 1745, the expedition of the young pretender sent him to journalism again. He started a paper, *The True Patriot*, in which he tried to rouse the nation out of the sluggish indifference and the acquiescence in bad government, that were a greater danger than the advance of the Highlanders on Derby. It was for this purpose, probably, that he let his robust humour and his hatred of what he considered the affectations of the Jacobite party find free play in a series of violently overdrawn pictures of what would happen if the rebels took London. Almost the sole interest of the journal for modern readers lies in the reappearance of parson Adams, who is made to trounce, with effect, a young English fribble, more fond of French wine than adverse to French government. Fielding, though less insular than Smollett, was a thorough John Bull. In December, 1747, he engaged once more in political journalism, with *The Jacobite's Journal*, a paper conducted on the same lines as *The True Patriot*, in one number of which he generously praises the first two volumes of his detractor Richardson's *Clarissa*. The writing of these

[1] *Tom Jones*, bk. I, chap. II.

journals brought on Fielding the reproach of being a "pensioned scribbler," and may have helped to obtain his commission as justice of the peace for Westminster. The last number of *The Jacobite's Journal* is dated 5 November, 1748. A commission as justice of the peace for Westminster had been granted him on the previous 25 October; and a similar commission for Middlesex was, apparently, granted to him soon afterwards. The duke of Bedford had become secretary of state early in the year. From the terms in which he is mentioned in the preface to *Tom Jones* and from Fielding's letter to him of 13 December, 1748,[1] it seems clear that his "princely benefactions" included something besides the present of leases enabling Fielding to qualify for the office in Middlesex by holding landed estate of £100 a year.

When Fielding took the magistrate's post, it was one of small honour, and of only such profit as could be made out of one or both parties to the cases brought before him. Squeezum and Thrasher were probably only too faithful portraits of the trading justices, as they were called. Fielding, however, took his work very seriously; considerably reduced its emoluments by his honesty; and endeavoured to remedy at the root the appalling evils due to ignorance, poverty, drink and the lack of an efficient police force. His *Proposals for erecting a county work-house* may, to modern ideas, seem repellently brutal; to his own age, they seemed sentimentally humane.

Within four months of his Westminster appointment, that is, in February, 1749, there appeared in six duodecimo volumes *The History of Tom Jones, A Foundling*. When Fielding began to write his masterpiece, there is no evidence to show. The years preceding his appointment as magistrate seem to have been years of pecuniary, as well as of other troubles, relieved by the generosity of Lyttelton, and of Ralph Allen of Prior park, Bath. In the letter dedicating *Tom Jones* to Lyttelton, Fielding acknowledges his debt to both these friends, and says that the character of Allworthy is taken from them. The book, then, was probably written slowly (it took, Fielding says, "some thousands of hours") in the intervals of other occupations, during sickness and trouble; and the circumstances only make the achievement more surprising.

[1] Godden, p. 196.

Fielding had called *Joseph Andrews* a comic epic poem in prose; the title is better deserved by *Tom Jones.* His debt to the great epics is patent in such passages as the fight in the churchyard, where he indulges in open burlesque. A greater debt becomes evident when a perusal of the whole book shows the coherence of its structure. The course of the main theme is steadily followed throughout; and to it all the by-plots, all the incidents in the vast and motley world which the story embraces, are carefully related. ˙ It is true that the art is lower at some points than at others. Into *Joseph Andrews,* Fielding introduced two independent stories, those of Leonora and of Mr. Wilson, which are excusable only on the ground of the variety obtained by the insertion of scenes from high life. *Tom Jones* contains its independent story, that of the Man of the Hill; and, though this story forms part of the book's theme, its introduction violates the laws of structure more forcibly than could be the case with the earlier and more loosely built novel. The episode of the widow, again, which occurs in the eleventh chapter of the fifteenth book, is so grave a fault in construction that even the need of proving that Tom could say no to a woman scarcely reconciles us to believing it Fielding's work. But, in spite of these and other blemishes of form, *Tom Jones* remains the first English novel conceived and carried out on a structural plan that secured an artistic unity for the whole. It set up for prose fiction a standard which nearly all its great writers have followed, and which is to be found practically unchanged in Thackeray.

The question of the "morality" of *Tom Jones* is so closely bound up with the realism which is another of its main characteristics, that it is almost impossible to treat them apart. In *Jonathan Wild*, Fielding had a double object—to carry on his lifelong war against humbug, and to show how poorly vice rewarded its votaries. Both these aims underlie *Tom Jones;* but both are subdued to a wider aim—to show life as it is. "The provision which we have here made is Human Nature." The implication is that, if we can see the whole of human nature, we shall find that some of it is, in itself, ugly, and some, in itself, beautiful. That which is ugly makes people unhappy; that which is beautiful makes them happy. Fielding was content to leave to Richardson the conventions of society, of "good form," as it is called—the code of Sir Charles Grandison. Its place is taken in *Tom Jones*, if at all, by that "prudence" which Allworthy preached to Jones, and which is no more than the moderation that keeps a man out of reach of what is ugly in human nature, and of those who practise it. The gist of the book's moral purpose is to show human nature, ugly and beautiful alike, raised to a high power of activity, so that the contrast between what is itself beautiful and what is itself ugly shall be clearly perceived. Incidentally, meanness, cruelty, hypocrisy, lasciviousness will be found to bring unhappiness in their train; but it is a worse punishment to be a Blifil than to suffer as Blifil ultimately suffered.

Since no man can see life whole, the question of the moral value of *Tom Jones*—which has been considered a great moral work and a great immoral work—resolves itself into the question of how much of human life Fielding could see. To much of it he was blind. He could have understood a saint as little as he could have understood an anarchist. The finer shades—such as were clear to Richardson—were lost to him. Of love as a spiritual passion, he shows himself almost entirely ignorant. He was wholly in sympathy with the average morality of his time; and he takes, quite comfortably, what would nowadays be considered a low view of human nature. He had never known a perfect character; therefore, he will not put one in his book; and even Allworthy, who stands nearest to his ideal of a good man, comes out, against Fielding's intention no doubt, a little cold and stiff. But, of human nature that was not perfect, not exalted by any intellectual or moral or religious passion, he knew more than any writer, except, possibly, Shakespeare. In *Tom Jones*,

we shall represent human nature at first to the keen appetite of our reader, in that more plain and simple manner in which it is found in the country, and shall hereafter hash and ragoo it with all the high French and Italian seasoning of affectation and vice which courts and cities afford.

True to his promise, he shows us the whole of life as he saw it, in its extremes of poverty and luxury—from Molly Seagrim to Lady Bellaston; its extremes of folly and wisdom—from Partridge to Allworthy; its extremes of meanness and generosity—

from Blifil to Tom Jones. And every character in the book has been thought out, not merely adumbrated. Fielding had used to the full his opportunities of exercising his enormous interest in men and women; his experience had brought him into contact with nearly all kinds in nearly all circumstances; and the distinguishing feature of *Tom Jones* is the solidity of thought and judgment with which the numberless types included in it have been built together into a coherent whole.

The question then arises: what use did the author of *Tom Jones* make of his knowledge? Reference has been made to his realism; and, if by a realist is meant an artist conscientiously determined to express life exactly as he sees it, then Fielding was one. But, if a realist is one to whom all the facts of life and character, all aims and emotions are of equal value, Fielding cannot be called by that name. He is without the golden dream of what life should be which shines through the work of nearly every other great artist; but, in the place of that dream, his passionate sympathy with certain human qualities supplies so much of direct moral as may be found in his book, and, through it as a medium, he sees which of these qualities are ugly, and which of them beautiful. Chastity, to him, is not a thing of much account; but, in considering the much-discussed licence of *Tom Jones*, it must be remembered, first, that, in the episode of Nightingale, a line is shown over which even Tom will not step; next, that all Tom's lapses—even the affair, painful as it is to modern feeling, of Lady Bellaston —leave unimpaired the brightness of his prominent quality; and, last, that, in Fielding's eyes, those very lapses were caused by the untrained excess of that very quality—his generous openness of soul. If you have that quality, in Fielding's opinion, you cannot go very far wrong; if you are mean, envious, cruel, you can never go right. There is a strong spice of fatalism in the doctrine, if pressed home— a reliance on instinct which the villains have as much right to plead in excuse as have the generous-minded. But a candid, steady view of so much of life as we can take in shows generosity to be beautiful and meanness to be ugly. Tom Jones is no hero; Fielding was concerned to draw, not heroes, which, to him, were impossible abstractions or inventions, but men as he knew them. Finally, a word should be added on

Fielding's utter absence of pretence. His own sturdy wisdom (often, to us of later times, commonplace) is always at hand —and not only in those introductory chapters to each book which tell us, in his manliest, most humorous, prose, what he is thinking and what he is trying to do. In every incident throughout the crowded story, and in every character throughout the wonderful array of personages high and low, the force of his own knowledge and conviction may be felt.

The years 1749 and 1750 found Fielding assiduous in his duties as magistrate. In May of the former year, he was chairman of quarter sessions; and, in the following month, he delivered a famous charge to the Westminster grand jury. His published works for the two years consisted only of pamphlets: one, in defence of his action in sentencing one Bosavern Penlez to death for rioting and theft; the other, the weighty *Enquiry into the Causes of the late Increase of Robbers*, which shows how earnestly he studied and desired to remove the causes of crime. Hogarth's "Gin Lane" is supposed to have been inspired by this pamphlet.

Fielding was at work, meanwhile, upon his last novel, *Amelia*, which was published in December, 1751, and dedicated to his benefactor, Ralph Allen. Fielding was now nearly forty-five; he was a very busy man, and his health was breaking up. It is not surprising that *Amelia* lacks some of the ebullience, the strength and the solidity of the novel into which Fielding had packed all his youth and prime of life. In form, the story is distinctly inferior to *Tom Jones*. The writer had given further attention and thought to the social evils with which his official position brought him into daily touch. He had more to say about the evils of the sponging-houses, about the injustice of the laws of debt, the insolence and cruelty of the servants of justice, the blind cruelty of punishments and similar topics. Instead of putting these thoughts into such incidental essays as had enriched *Tom Jones*, he attempted to incorporate them with the story, and thereby at once dislocated his tale and roused the reader's impatience. The course of the narrative, again, harks backward and forward more often than that of *Tom Jones*. Miss Matthews, Booth, Mrs. Bennet must each have a separate narrative, and nearly a chapter must be devoted to the previous history of Trent. There are signs, also, of interruption, or of carelessness, in the work.[1]

In spite of these blemishes, *Amelia* has merits which Fielding's other novels lack. In place of the huge and turbulent world of *Tom Jones*, we have a much smaller canvas, and a more intimate revelation of shadows and depths in character. In losing some of his ebullience, Fielding has gained insight into things unknown to him before. The character of Amelia, Fielding's "favourite child," has been so fervently admired that, perhaps, it is rash to miss in her the courage and the strength of the ever dear Sophia. Booth who lacked the excuse of Tom Jones's youth and vitality, seems a weakling and a fool rather than a man of generous impulse; and, while the reader is touched—as no sensitive reader can fail to be touched—by the pathos of which Fielding here, for the first time, shows himself a master, the doubt may arise whether Sophia would have endured so much from her husband without a hearty trouncing. There is, in fact, just a dash in Amelia Booth of that other Amelia who married George Osborne; and such women help to bring their troubles on themselves. For all that, there is no resisting the beauty of Amelia's character, which is drawn with a depth of understanding far in advance of Fielding's time. There are novelty and daring, too, in the study of Miss Matthews; and colonel Bath, with his notions of honour, is an admirable piece of comedy. The story, as a whole, is the work of a mellower, soberer Fielding than the author of *Tom Jones*— a Fielding touched with tears, yet as much in love as ever with nobility and generosity of character, and equally full of interest in men and women. The novel rouses a wonder as to what he would have gone on to achieve, had time and health been granted him.

"I will trouble the World no more with any Children of mine by the same Muse." So he wrote in an early number of *The Covent-Garden Journal*, a Tuesday and Saturday paper which he started, under the pseudonym Sir Alexander Drawcansir, in January, 1752, a month after the appearance of his last novel. *The Covent-Garden Journal* contains the best of

[1] One of these, as is well known, is the inconsistency of the statements as to Amelia's nose—which Fielding himself practically admitted in *The Covent-Garden Journal*.

Fielding's occasional writing. He takes a rather gloomy view of letters, manners and morals; he has forsworn Aristophanes and Rabelais; but his irony is still awake, and his earnestness unabated. Incidentally, the *Journal* is interesting, inasmuch as it involved him in several literary quarrels, among others with Smollett. Smollett had attacked Fielding and Lyttelton in *Peregrine Pickle;* Fielding, in return, had a fling at that novel and at *Roderick Random;* and Smollett retorted with the savage pamphlet about "Habbakuk Hilding, Justice and Chapman" which will be mentioned again later. *The Covent-Garden Journal* came to an end in November, 1752. In April of that year, Fielding issued his *Examples of the Interposition of Providence, in the Detection and Punishment of Murder.* In January, 1753 appeared his *Proposal for Making an Effectual Provision, for the Poor*, which included *Proposals for Erecting a County Work-house* previously referred to. In March, 1753, he published a pamphlet in which he espoused (wrongly, as it appears) the cause of one Elizabeth Canning, whose accusation of kidnapping had nearly brought an old gipsy-woman to the gallows and a procuress to punishment.

By the middle of 1753, Fielding was very ill. He was just setting out for Bath, when he was commissioned by the duke of Newcastle to frame a plan for checking the prevalence of robbery and murder. This he prepared, in the midst of his heavy work as magistrate. He stayed in London, and succeeded in breaking up a gang of ruffians. His illness, now, had become a combination of dropsy, jaundice and asthma, and he was unfit to take the journey to Bath. The winter of 1753–4 was long and severe. In May, he betook himself to his house, Fordhook, at Ealing, where he found some relief in drinking bishop Berkeley's tar-water, though his dropsy grew worse. He was ordered to Lisbon; and, on 26 June, 1754, he left Fordhook, never to return.

Of his voyage to Lisbon, in the company of his wife and daughter, on *The Queen of Portugal*, he has left an account which has more in it of the quality of charm than anything else that he wrote. It shows his courage and his zest for life undiminished by the sufferings that had wasted his great frame, and mellowed by a manly patience; his courtesy and consideration for others; his sound sense and sincerity. Neither his eye for character nor his power of ironical expression had deserted him; and the portraits of captain Veale, and others, are as shrewd and complete as any in his novels. The book was published in February, 1755, in a version which omitted portions of the manuscript; the whole text being issued in December of that year. But, before the earlier issue appeared, the author had passed away. Fielding died at Lisbon on 8 October, 1754, and lies buried in the English cemetery there. He had lived hard. A self-indulgent youth had been succeeded, after his first marriage, by a manhood crammed with arduous work in literature and in the law. As justice of the peace, he had seen further than his contemporaries into the causes of crime, and into the remedies for it; as writer, he had poured ridicule and contempt on meanness, on pretence and on vanity, and had fixed the form of a new branch of literature. Poverty, sorrow, ill-health and detraction could not quench his delight in life; and he used his energies, his good-sense and his knowledge of the world consistently in the service of what he saw to be the right.

In speaking of Smollett, we have to deal with a man of very different character from Fielding, though of scarcely less ability. Born in the spring of 1721 at Dalquhurn, Cardross, in the vale of Leven, Dumbartonshire, Tobias George Smollett was the grandson of Sir James Smollett of Bonhill, judge and member of the Scottish and the united parliaments. Tobias's father, Sir James's youngest son, died in the future novelist's childhood. The account of Roderick Random's childhood and youth, Smollett afterwards said, was not autobiographical; but the main outlines were the same. He was educated at the school at Dumbarton, and, in 1736, went to Glasgow university. In the same year, he was apprenticed to a surgeon and apothecary in Glasgow, by name Gordon, whom, though he ridiculed him as Potion in *Roderick Random*, he honoured in *Humphrey Clinker*. He came to London at the age of eighteen; obtained a commission as surgeon in the navy, and, in 1740, sailed on *The Cumberland*, to join the fleet in the West Indies under admiral Vernon, whose previous expedition against Porto Bello had been celebrated in a poem by Fielding. Smollett's object in coming to London was not, it seems, to obtain an appointment in connection with his profession. Like Johnson, a year or two before, he had in his pocket a tragedy—*The Regicide*. He was not, however, a dramatist; and no manager was found to put *The Regicide* on the stage. This disappointment Smollett never forgot or forgave. In boyhood, he had shown a disposition for savage sarcasm; and the rejection of *The Regicide* was to lead to fierce attacks on Garrick, Lyttelton and others. After Vernon's disastrous expedition to Cartagena, Smollett sailed with the fleet to Jamaica. There, he left the service in disgust, and in Jamaica he stayed till 1744, when he returned to London, betrothed to Anne Lascelles, a Jamaican lady of some fortune, whom he married in or about 1747. On his return to London, he set up as a surgeon in Downing street, and seems to have had no thought of literature as a profession, for he wrote but little. The suppression of the rising in 1745 drew from him a poem, *The Tears of Scotland*. In 1746, he published *Advice*, a satire; in 1747, *Reproof*, another satire; both in the heroic couplet, both characteristic in spirit and diction. In the same year, the fate of *The Regicide* still rankling, he made a brutal attack on Lyttelton in *A Burlesque Ode on the Loss of a Grandmother*, a parody of Lyttelton's monody on the death of his wife. None of these works is of any importance to literature; but, in 1748, they were succeeded by a work of very high importance, *The Adventures of Roderick Random*.

Smollett admitted that he modelled his story on the plan of Le Sage's *Gil Blas*. In the country of Defoe, the *picaresque* novel—the realistic novel of travel and adventure—was not absolutely new; nor was the device of stringing the episodes of the story together along the thread of a single character. What Smollett achieved in *Roderick Random* and, later, in *Peregrine Pickle*, was to show how much could still be done with this form, to introduce new life and new types, and to present them with unequalled brilliance and energy. The new type for which he is most famous is not the hungry and adventurous Scot, like Roderick Random himself or Strap, his faithful attendant, but the British sailor. The expedition to Cartagena had given great opportunities for knowledge of the navy to a man who had great skill in expressing that knowledge. So vivid a picture of a certain kind of life peopled with such clcar-cut types as Morgan, the Welsh surgeon, Bowling, Oakum, Mackshane, Jack Rattlin, had never been presented before and has not been surpassed since. The British tar was all but new to English literature, and, in this direction alone, Smollett's influence has been as important as his achievement. Though he sees men and women chiefly from the outside, he sees them with extraordinary clarity, and has a way of hitting them off in the first few words which keeps the attention arrested all through the rambling, ill-constructed book. Smollett was not a moralist; he was even without a view of life and conduct such as might have lent unity to his several works. Dickens, in boyhood, found Roderick "a modest and engaging hero"; to the adult reader, he is one of the most shameless young scoundrels in fiction. In his preface to the work, Smollett writes of Roderick's "modest merit," and he may have been sincere. The truth is that he did not care. He aimed almost exclusively at what he abundantly secured— movement and variety; and his taste for farce, horseplay and violence was inexhaustible. It should be added that Smollett's study of medicine had doubtless inured him to the contemplation of certain physical facts, and that he revels in contemplating them.

The publication of *Roderick Random* brought Smollett immediately into fame. The first advantage he took of it was to publish his unfortunate tragedy *The Regicide*, with a preface full of railing at the blindness, the jealousy and so forth, of those who would not see its merits. He made—or revised and corrected—an English translation of *Gil Blas*, which was published in 1749. Yet, just as Fielding tried to live by the 'aw, Smollett seems to have gone on hoping to make a living by medicine. In 1750, he took the degree of doctor of medicine in Marischal college, Aberdeen. In the autumn of that year, however, he set out for Paris with Dr. John Moore, the author of *Zeluco*, in order to collect material for another novel. The result of the tour was *The Adventures of Peregrine Pickle*, published in 1751. In some respects, this is the most remarkable of Smollett's novels; it is, also, the longest, and it maintains its vivacity and vigour throughout. In morality, the treatment of the main theme (if such a book can be said to have a main theme) shows scarcely any advance on *Roderick*

*Random.* Peregrine is a scoundrel with a very moderate sense of shame; he is also, in his elegant and rather witty way, a bully of the most refined cruelty, who is not content to feast on others' folly, but likes to pay for the feast with all kinds of insult and annoyance. It would be easier to insist on the fact that morality and good taste have nothing to do with the effect that Smollett wished to produce, were it not that the same novel contains the finest character he ever drew. In a work of this kind, coherence is of little moment; and, that Smollett clearly changed his mind as he went on, not only about Pickle's mother, and his aunt Grizzle, but about his aunt Grizzle's husband, commodore Trunnion, does not lessen the beauty of the commodore's character in its final form. A modern reader, by reason of a satiety that must have been almost unknown in Smollett's day, wishes that Trunnion could open his lips just once or twice without using a nautical metaphor; but metaphor was never more finely used than in the famous death-scene of that simple, wise, lovable old sea-dog. This character alone (supposing that there had been no Matthew Bramble or Lismahago to follow) would prove that Smollett had it in him to be a humourist of a high order, if his savageness and brutality had not stifled the humourist's qualities. In *Peregrine Pickle*, much of the characterisation is on the highest level ever reached by Smollett. The household at "The Garrison," where Hawser Trunnion lived, included that "great joker," lieutenant Hatchway, and Tom Pipes, the silent and faithful, who is more attractive, if not better fun, than Strap. Though Mrs. Pickle is an impossible person, her husband Gamaliel lives from the first line of the story; and the adventures of the painter and the doctor, the banquet in the manner of the ancients and the "escape" from the Bastille, offer a concurrent development of farcical incident and oddity of character hardly to be paralleled for vivacity and inventiveness. In *Roderick Random*, many of the characters were taken from life; so it was with *Peregrine Pickle;* and, in the first edition, Smollett attacked several of those whom he considered his enemies—Lyttelton (under the name Sir Gosling Scrag), Garrick, Rich and Cibber, his rancour against whom, on account of the rejection of *The Regicide*, was continuous, besides Akenside and Fielding. At this date, he cannot have had any cause of complaint against Fielding, unless it were the belief that Partridge in *Tom Jones* was imitated from Strap in *Roderick Random;* and, in the main, the secret of his dislikes seems to have been jealousy. Fielding's retorts, in two numbers of *The Covent-Garden Journal*, drew from Smollett one of his most savage and indecent performances: *A Faithful Narrative of the Base and Inhuman Acts that were lately practised upon the Brain of Habbakuk Hilding, Justice, Dealer and Chapman* . . . (1752). In the second edition of *Peregrine Pickle*, however, which was issued before the end of 1751, the attacks on Fielding were withdrawn. It remains to add that the form of the book is still the picaresque novel; but even this loose construction is disturbed by the interpolation of the immoral but vivacious *Memoirs of a Lady of Quality.*

Smollett had not yet given up all idea of practising as a doctor. He took up his abode in Bath; but, failing to meet with success, he wrote a pamphlet to prove that Bath water was but little more efficacious than any other water, and, returning to London, definitely took up literature as his profession. He settled in Chelsea, at Monmouth house, where he was visited by Johnson, Garrick, Goldsmith, Sterne and others; and here he held those Sunday dinners which he was to describe later in *Humphrey Clinker*, for the benefit of the hacks who worked in the "literary factory" established by him. His next novel, published in 1752, was *The Adventures of Ferdinand Count Fathom*. If Partridge owed something to Strap, Fathom undoubtedly owed something to Jonathan Wild; but Smollett's book lacks the unity to which Fielding attained by his consistent irony and by the intellectual conception of the relations of goodness and greatness. And Smollett betrays his half-heartedness by leaving Fathom converted and repentant, in which not very convincing or edifying condition he is found again in *Humphrey Clinker*. Yet, if the book, as a whole, be unsatisfactory, it is, like all Smollett's fiction, vivacious and brilliant, and its influence may be traced in *Pelham*, in *Dennis Duval* and in other works.

After *Ferdinand Count Fathom*, Smollett did not write any more novels for some years. He was constantly in need of money, for he was always overspending his income, considerable as it was. Of his wife's fortune, only a small part ever reached him; but Smollett was practically the first man to conduct a "literary factory" with success; and, at one time, his profits came to about £600 a year. After the publication of *Ferdinand Count Fathom*, the factory and the trade of book-making absorbed him. In 1755, he published a translation of *Don Quixote*, which critics have declared to be only a *réchauffé* of Jervas's translation (published, posthumously, in 1742), Smollett not having Spanish enough to be capable of making an entirely new version. In 1756, Archibald Hamilton, formerly an Edinburgh printer, put Smollett at the head of the contributors to his new monthly paper, *The Critical Review*, started in opposition to Ralph Griffiths's *Monthly Review*. Smollett, as we have seen, was trenchant in attack; and his writings in *The Critical Review* involved him in quarrels with Grainger, Joseph Reed, Churchill, Shebbeare and several others. To digress for a moment from the chronological order of his doings, in January, 1757, Garrick brought on the stage at Drury lane Smollett's farce of life at sea, *The Reprisal, or the Tars of Old England*, a rollicking play, full of the oddities of national character and sure of popularity because of its attacks on the French. Garrick having gone out of his way to see that Smollett was well remunerated, Smollett has praise for him in *The Critical Review*, and, later, more of it in "a work of truth," his *History of England*. In 1759, Smollett was fined £100 and suffered three months' not uncomfortable imprisonment in the king's bench prison (which he was afterwards to describe in *Sir Launcelot Greaves*) for impugning, in *The Critical Review*, the courage of admiral Sir Charles Knowles.

Meanwhile, at the close of 1757, he published the first four volumes of his *History of England*, bringing it down to the treaty of Aix-la-Chapelle in 1748. The work seems to have been a mere bookseller's venture. Hume had already published two volumes on the Stewart period, and was known to be at work on the Tudors.[1] In order to take the wind out of his sails by bringing out a complete history before him, Smollett worked very hard, reading, he said, 300 volumes; and, in twenty months, completed a work written, though in haste, with his usual clearness and force. What he really thought of public affairs was not to become evident till the publication of

[1] Cf. Chap. xii, *post*.

*The History of an Atom*, some years later. Between 1761 and 1765, he added five more volumes to his *History of England*, bringing the story down to the moment of publication, and taking opportunities, by the way, of praising Fielding, Hume and others whom he had attacked in earlier days.

The work of these strenuous years included, also, the preparation of Dodsley's *Compendium of Voyages* in seven volumes, among which appeared Smollett's own account of the expedition against Cartagena; the compiling of a *Universal History*, in which he composed the histories of France, Germany and Italy, besides painfully revising the contributions of his hacks; eight volumes entitled *The Present State of the Nations;* a translation,with Thomas Francklin,of the works of Voltaire; and two further excursions into journalism—one of them as editor of *The Briton*, a tory paper started in May, 1762, in support of Lord Bute.[1] While Smollett was in the king's bench prison, in 1759, Newbery, the bookseller, secured his services for his new monthly paper, *The British Magazine*. Its first number, published in January, 1760, contained the first instalment of Smollett's fourth, and feeblest, novel, *The Adventures of Sir Launcelot Greaves*. Sir Launcelot is an eighteenth century gentleman who rides about the country in armour, attended by his comic squire, Timothy Crabshaw, redressing grievances. When one remembers their originals, Don Quixote and Sancho Panza, it is impossible to feel much interest in this pair; and the fun of the story, almost entirely, is horseplay. Some of the lesser characters, however, are well done, including the sour and crafty rogue, Ferret, said to be a caricature of Shebbeare. Though the talk of captain Crowe, the naval man, whose adventures as knight-errant are a burlesque of the hero's, in the main resembles that of commodore Trunnion, it is very suggestive, at times, of Alfred Jingle; and to Mrs. Gobble, the justice's wife, Bob Sawyer's landlady unquestionably owed her indignation at being addressed as "woman." Another feature of note in the book is that it begins straight away with an admirable piece of description, in the manner of Scott, leaving out the exordium which had till then been usual.

By 1763, Smollett's health was broken by incessant overwork, disappointment in his hopes of aid from Bute, and the ex-

[1] Cf. Chap. XVII, *post.*

cesses of his own *systema nervosum maxime irritabile*. And, in
April of that year, the violent, affectionate man suffered the
heaviest of blows in the loss of his only child, Elizabeth, at the
age of fifteen. For the sake of his own health and his wife's
spirits, he left England in the month of June, and travelled
across France to Nice. In the autumn of 1764, he visited
Genoa, Rome, Florence and other towns of Italy; for the winter,
he returned to Nice, and, by June, 1765, he was back in London.
In the following year, he published an account of his *Travels
through France and Italy*, one of the most entertaining books of
travel extant, and a mine of information, on the whole remarkably accurate, concerning the natural phenomena, history, social
life, economics, diet and morals of the places described. Smollett had a lively and pertinacious curiosity, and, as his novels
prove, a very quick eye. He foresaw the merits of Cannes,
then a small village, as a health-resort, and the possibilities of
the Corniche road. The chief interest of the book, however,
for the general reader, lies in its unsparing revelation of the
author's character. In place of the bravery, serenity and
sweetness of the dying Fielding, we have here little but spleen,
acerbity and quarrelsomeness. Smollett's fierce engagements
with innkeepers, postillions and fellow-travellers; his profound contempt for foreigners, now fortified by first-hand
observation; his scorn of the Roman catholic faith and cere-
monies, of duelling, of such domestic arrangements as the
*cicisbeo*, of petty and proud nobility, of a hundred other French
institutions and ways; and the shrewd sense and the keen eye
(keener than Carlyle's) for shams which fortify all his violent
prejudices, combine to make the book a masterpiece in description and ironic criticism of men and manners. Not that
he was wilfully blind to merit or beauty; he has good words,
now and then, even for a foreign doctor. But he was determined to see everything with his own eyes; and, being a sick
man and splenetic, he saw everything, from politics to statues
and pictures, with an eye more or less jaundiced. Sterne, who
met Smollett in Italy, hit off the truth, with his usual pun-
gency, in the portrait of Smelfungus in *A Sentimental Journey*.

Smollett was better, but far from well, when he returned
home. In 1766, he travelled in Scotland, revisited the scenes
of his childhood, and was made much of by learned Edinburgh.

Here, and in Bath, whither he now went as a patient, he gathered material, and possibly laid plans, for his last novel. Before *Humphrey Clinker* appeared, however, Smollett was to show himself in his most rancorous and pseudo-Rabelaisian mood in *The History and Adventures of an Atom* (1769). In this work, the Atom relates, to one Nathaniel Peacock, his experiences while in the body of a Japanese. Since Japan stands for England, and the names in the story (many of them formed on the principle afterwards adopted by Samuel Butler in *Erewhon*) each represented a wellknown figure in British public life, the work is merely a brutal satire on British public affairs from the year 1754 to the date of publication—and the *Travels* of Lemuel Gulliver are fragrant beside it.

In the last month of 1769, Smollett's health compelled him, once more, to leave England. He went to Italy, and, in the spring of 1770, settled in a villa near Leghorn. Here, he wrote his last and most agreeable novel, *The Expedition of Humphrey Clinker*. In its way, this is another picaresque story, insomuch as, during its progress, the characters (who relate everything in letters to their friends) pursue their travels in England and Scotland. But its tone and temper (owing, possibly, to the influence of Sterne, possibly, to the pacific mood which often blesses the closing days of even the angriest men) are very different from those of *Roderick Random* and of *Peregrine Pickle*. Smollett the humourist, of whom we have had but brief glimpses in his earlier works, is more evident here than anywhere else. Matthew Bramble, the outwardly savage and inwardly very tender old bachelor, his sister Mrs. Tabitha Bramble, smart Jery Melford, their nephew, and his sister Miss Lydia, Mrs. Winifred Jenkins, the maid, and Humphrey Clinker himself, the "methodist" manservant whom they pick up on their travels—all these are characters more deeply and kindly seen than any of their predecessors except Hawser Trunnion. The best among them all is Lismahago, the Scottish soldier, needy, argumentative, proud, eccentric—a figure of genuine comedy, among whose many descendants must be reckoned one of great eminence, Dugald Dalgetty. The novel is planned with a skill unusual in Smollett's fiction. In Richardson, the device of telling the story in letters leads to wearisome repetitions and involutions. Smollett contrives to avoid much repetition; and the story, though loosely built, as picaresque novels must be, goes steadily and clearly forward to reach a more or less inevitable ending. This was his last work. He died at his villa in September, 1771, and is buried in the English cemetery at Leghorn. After his death, his *Ode to Independence*—not a great poem, but a vigorous expression of his sturdy temperament—was published; and, in 1795, there appeared under his name a curious pamphlet, foretelling the revolt of America and the French revolution. Whether he wrote this pamphlet or not, he had shown a prevision hardly less remarkable in certain political forecasts to be found in his *Travels*.

One of the marks of Hazlitt's "common-place critic" was that he preferred Smollett to Fielding. To dilate on preferences is less profitable than to enquire, first, what the two greatest of English eighteenth century novelists achieved between them. Both tried their hands in youth at the drama; and both failed almost precisely in so far as they followed the prevalent fashion of the drama. Fielding's comedies and Smollett's tragedy are attempts at expression through outworn media. The long-enduring somnolence which overtook the English drama early in the eighteenth century had already begun. In turning from the stage to the new field of prose fiction, Fielding and Smollett together raised the novel to the chief place among contemporary forms of literary expression, and showed how much it could contain of philosophy, of incident, of humour and of fun. Of the pair, Smollett was the more learned, and, perhaps, the more inventive in finding value for the purposes of his art in modes of life hitherto untouched. Fielding's mind went deeper.

"I should be at a loss," wrote Hazlitt, "where to find in any authentic documents of the same period so satisfactory an account of the general state of society, and of moral, political, and religious feeling in the reign of George II as we meet with in The Adventures of Joseph Andrews and his friend Mr. Abraham Adams."[1]

In other words, the novel had already taken "the whole of life" for its province. It remained for Scott to sweep into its

---

[1] *Lectures on the Comic Writers*, vol. VI. Waller and Glover's Hazlitt, vol. VIII., p. 106.

compass all the past, with its romance and its ideals, and the novel had conquered the empire in the possession of which it has not yet been disturbed.

The direct influence of Fielding is harder to estimate than that of Smollett. Episodes and characters have been borrowed from him, freely enough. *The Vicar of Wakefield, Tristram Shandy, Quentin Durward, Pendennis, Barry Lyndon*—each of these, among a hundred others, shows clear traces of the study of Fielding. But the very completeness and individuality of Fielding's work prevented his founding a school. The singleness of intellectual standpoint which governs all his novels makes him difficult of imitation; and he is no less different from those who have taken him as model than he is from Cervantes, whom he professed to follow. But this it is safe to say: that Fielding, a master of the philosophical study of character, founded the novel of character and raised it to a degree of merit which is not likely to be surpassed. What his successors have done is to take advantage of changes in social life since his day, and to study, from their own point of view, character as affected by those changes. His greatest disciple is Thackeray, who had much of his genius, much of his power of seeing human nature beneath the robes of a peer or the rags of a beggar, much of his satirical power; but who lacked the large-hearted geniality of his master. The novel of character must always go to Fielding as its great exemplar.

Smollett's novels have about them more of the quarry and less of the statue. He is richer in types than Fielding; and it needs only a mention of his naval scenes and characters to raise memories of a whole literature, which, receiving an impetus from the naval battles won a few years after Smollett's death, has persisted even after the disappearance of wooden ships. The picaresque novel in general, which burst into activity soon after the publication of *Roderick Random*, was under heavy obligations to Smollett, and nowhere more so than in its first modern example, *Pickwick*. Dickens, indeed, who was a great reader of Smollett, was his most eminent disciple. In both, we find the observation of superficial oddities of speech and manner carried to the finest point; in both, we find these oddities and the episodes which display them more interesting than the main plot; in both, we find that, beneath those oddities, there is often a lack of real character. Dickens's fun is purer than Smollett's; but it is not less rich and various. Although, at the present moment, the picaresque novel has fallen a little out of fashion, Smollett will continue to be read by those who are not too squeamish or too stay-at-home to find in him complete recreation.

## CHAPTER III

# Sterne, and the Novel of His Times

THE subject of this chapter is, virtually, the history of the English novel from 1760 to 1780, a crucial period in the earlier stages of its growth. And the chief questions to be asked are: what are the new elements which these years added to the novel? how far has each of them proved of lasting value? and what is the specific genius of the two or three writers who stand out above the rest?

The answer to the first of these questions may be given, in summary form, at once. In the hands of Sterne and a group of writers who, though it may be without sufficient reason, are commonly treated as disciples of Sterne, sentiment began to count for more than had hitherto been held allowable. As a natural consequence, the individuality of these writers impressed itself more and more unreservedly upon a theme which, in the days of Defoe and even Richardson, had been treated mainly from without. Sterne, it need hardly be said, is undisputed master in this way of writing; and here, so far, at least, as his own century is concerned, he stands absolutely alone. Others, such as Brooke and Mackenzie, may use the novel as a pulpit for preaching their own creed or advancing their own schemes of reform. But their relation to Sterne, on this head, is, manifestly, of the slightest, and the effect produced is utterly different. A little more of personality, a great deal more of emotion and sentiment, may come into their work than any novelist before Sterne would have thought possible. But that is all. That is the one link which binds them to him, the one tangible mark which he left upon the novel of his generation.

Sterne is the sole novelist of first-rate importance in the period under review; for even Fanny Burney, inventive and sparkling though she is, can hardly lay claim to that description. And, thanks to his very originality, he stands aloof from the main stream of contemporary fiction. Apart from him, the writers of the time fall, roughly, into three groups: the novelists of "sentiment and reflection," who, though far enough from Sterne, are yet nearer to him than any of the others; the novelists of home life, who, in the main, and with marked innovations of their own, follow the chief lines laid down by Richardson in the preceding generation; and, finally, the novelists of a more distinctly romantic bent, Horace Walpole and Clara Reeve, who drew their theme from the medieval past, and supported the interest by an appeal to the sense of mystery and terror—Horace Walpole, no doubt, the more defiantly of the two and, perhaps, with less seriousness than has sometimes been imputed to him. It should be added that the romantic writers are of far less importance for their own sake than for that of the writers who followed during the next fifty years, and of whom, in some measure, they may be regarded as precursors.

The main facts of Laurence Sterne's life (1713–1768) are sufficiently well known. After a struggling boyhood, he went to Cambridge, where he made the friendship of Hall-Stevenson, the Eugenius of his great novel. In 1738 he became vicar of Sutton, the first of his Yorkshire livings, and a few years later prebendary of York, of which his great-grandfather had been archbishop. In 1741 he married Eliza Lumley, for whom he soon ceased to feel any affection and from whom he was formally separated shortly before his death. By her he had one daughter, Lydia, subsequently Mme. Medalle, whom he seems to have genuinely loved. The greater part of his life was passed in a succession of love affairs, mainly of the sentimental kind, with various women of whom Mrs. Draper is the best known. The publication of *Tristram Shandy* was begun in 1760 (vols. I and II), and continued at intervals until the year before his death. In 1762 his health, which had always been frail, broke down and he started on travels in France and Italy which lasted, with an interval, till 1766 and of which the literary result was *A Sentimental Journey* (1768). He died, of pleurisy, in March, 1768.

Few writers have thrown down so many challenges as

Sterne; and, if to win disciples be the test of success, few have
paid so heavily for their hardihood. He revolutionised the
whole scope and purpose of the novel; but, in his own country,
at any rate, years passed before advantage was taken of the
liberty he asserted. He opened new and fruitful fields of
humour; and one of the greatest of his successors has denied
him the name of humourist. He created a style more subtle
and flexible than any had found before him; and all that Goldsmith could see in it was a tissue of tricks and affectations.
But, if the men of letters hesitated, the public had no doubt.
The success of *Tristram Shandy* swept everything before it.
And here, as is often the case, the popular verdict has worn
better than the craftsman's or the critic's.

Sterne was nothing if not an innovator. And in no innovation was he more daring than in that which widened the
scope and loosened the structure of the novel. This was the
first of his services to his brethren of the craft. It is, perhaps,
the only one which has left a deep mark upon the subsequent
history of a form which, when he wrote, was still in the early
stages of its growth.

When *Tristram Shandy* began to appear (1760), there was
real danger that the English novel would remain little more
than a mirror of contemporary life: a reproduction, often pho-
tographically accurate, of the social conditions of the time.
Defoe, Fielding, Smollett, each in his own way and according
to the measure of his genius, had yielded to the impulse;
Richardson alone, by striking into tragedy, had partially escaped. Sterne defiantly throws himself athwart the tradition
of the elders. He delivers one blow after another at the fashion they had set. Tale of manners, picaresque adventure,
types of contemporary humanity, plot itself, all go by the
board. His very title is a resounding challenge to all accepted
notions of what the novelist should attempt. And even the
title falls very far short of what the novel actually provides.
The *Life and Opinions* of the hero is the subject we are bidden to
expect. The opinions, the character, the caprices of his father,
his uncle, his uncle's servant—above all, of the author himself—
is what we actually find. In other words, the novel has ceased
to be a mirror of life and manners. It has ceased to be what
Johnson, himself a heretic against his own theory, thought it

must naturally be, "a smooth tale, mostly of love." It has become a channel for the outpouring of the author's own personality and idiosyncrasy; a stage from which, under the thinnest of disguises or with no disguise at all, he lays bare the workings of his heart, his intellect, his most fleeting imaginations, before any audience he can gather round him. If we compare *Tristram* with *Tom Jones*, with *Roderick Random*, with *Moll Flanders* —if we compare it even with *Pamela* or *Clarissa*—we shall see that the wheel has come full circle. Every known landmark has been torn up. And, in asserting his own liberty, Sterne, little as he may have cared about it, has won unbounded liberty for all novelists who might follow. Whatever innovations the future might have in store, it was hardly possible that they should go beyond the freedom triumphantly vindicated by Sterne. For whatever purposes future writers might wish to use the novel, it was hardly conceivable that they would not be covered by the principle which he had victoriously, though, it may be, unconsciously, laid down. The purpose for which Sterne used the novel was to give free utterance to his own way of looking at life, his own moral and intellectual individuality. So much granted, it was impossible to quarrel with those who used it for a more limited purpose; for embodying in a narrative form the passions stirred by any burning problem of the day; for giving utterance to their own views on any specific question, political, social or religious. The perils of such a task might be great. They could hardly, however, be greater, they would almost certainly be less great, than those which Sterne had already faced and conquered. And, with the success of *Tristram* before him, no critic could maintain that, given sufficient genius, the venture was impossible. The challenge of Sterne was wide enough to include all the other challenges that have followed. *The Fool of Quality*, *Nature and Art*, *Oliver Twist*, *Wilhelm Meister*, *Les Misérables*—all are covered by the unformulated formula of *Tristram*.

Not, of course, that the whole credit of the widening process should be given to Sterne. *Rasselas* in England, if *Rasselas* is, indeed, to be counted as a novel, much more *Candide* in France, had already pointed the way in the same direction. Both appeared in the year 1759, before the publication of the first volume of *Tristram*. Neither of them, however, attempts more than a fragment of the task which Sterne attempted and performed. In neither case does the author stake his whole personality upon the throw; he lets his mind work, or play, round a single question, or group of questions, and that is all. It was an easier venture, a smaller venture and one far less rich in promise, than that which, a few weeks later, launched the Shandy family upon their voyage round the world.

It is, then, as liberator that Sterne comes before us in the first instance. And it is as liberator that he has left his chief, perhaps his only enduring, mark upon the subsequent history of the novel. His other great qualities are almost purely personal to himself. His very originality has caused him to count for less, as a moulding influence, than many a writer not to be compared with him in genius.

And, first, his humour. The elements which go to make up this are strangely various and, for the most part, as strangely baffling and elusive. His handling of character is humorous to the very core. It is so with the figures that merely flit across the stage: Susannah and the scullion, Obadiah and Dr. Slop, Eugenius and Yorick. It is so a hundred times more with those constantly before the footlights: above all, the undying trio, Walter Shandy, my uncle Toby and corporal Trim.

The last three are humorous in a whole sheaf of senses, each of which fades insensibly into the others. In the first place, to employ a term sanctioned by long usage, they are themselves humourists of the first water. Each of them is fast astride on his own hobby-horse, galloping as hard as may be in pursuit of his own fad. In this sense, though in no other, they are akin to Puntarvolo and Fastidious Brisk, to Morose and Volpone. They are akin, also, to Tom Bowling and commodore Trunnion. Sterne, however, had far too subtle a spirit to content himself with the mere oddities in which Smollett and, in his own masterful way, Jonson also, had delighted. His characters may be born humourists, in the Jonsonian sense. But they have been born anew, and have taken on an entirely new nature, in the soul of a writer who was a humourist in another, and a far higher, sense: the sense in which we apply the term to Fielding and Walter Scott, to Cervantes and Shakespeare. And the second birth counts for infinitely more than the first. All that in the original draft of the character may have been overcharged, distorted and ungenial is now inter-woven with so many softer strands, crossed by so many subtler strokes, touched to so many finer issues that the primitive harshness has altogether vanished, and the caricature become a living creature, of like nature with ourselves. The "humour," in the sense of Jonson and Smollett, is still the groundwork of the character. But it is so transformed and humanised by the subsequent touches as to have passed without effort into a nobler plane of being. It is soon recognised as something scarcely differing from that leaven of idealisation which is the indispensable condition of the highest creative work and which, much as we may desire to fix it, is, in this, as in many other instances, lost in the general effect of the whole. Compare "my Uncle Toby," the supreme instance of this subtle trans-formation, with Tom Bowling or commodore Trunnion, and the difference proclaims itself at once.

The name of Cervantes has been mentioned. And Sterne himself does not make any attempt to conceal that Cervantes was his model. Others—Rabelais, Montaigne, Burton, the last especially—may have provided hints and suggested methods. That, however, is only for the more discursive and abstract parts of the story. In the humorous handling of character, Sterne's master was Cervantes and none other. My uncle Toby and corporal Trim are variations, but variations of genius, upon Don Quixote and Sancho Panza. Yet, on taking over the suggestion, Sterne has made it entirely his own. And the differences are even more strongly marked than the resem-blance. Neither master nor servant, in Sterne's creation, has the universal significance which makes itself felt even to the most casual reader of *Don Quixote*. And this is true of the relation between the two men no less than of each as taken by himself. There is nothing in Sterne of the contrast between sense and spirit, between the ideal and the material, which gives a depth of unfathomable meaning to the twofold creation of Cervantes. Trim is in no wise the foil of his master. Still less is he his critic. The very thought would have filled him with dismay. He is uncle Toby's devoted follower, the ardent sharer of his dreams, the zealous agent of their fulfilment, hardly less warm-hearted, hardly less overflowing with kindness, a point or two shrewder and less unworldly, by many points less simple and more studious of effect, moulded of slightly coarser clay but on the same general pattern; altogether, far more his counterpart than his opposite. The relation between the two is full of beauty, as well as of humour. And, just because it is so, it is wholly different from that which Cervantes has cunningly woven between Sancho and Don Quixote.

But yet further differences are to be noted. Both Don Quixote and uncle Toby are possessed with a dream. So, for that matter, is Walter Shandy. But the dream of the knight, though absurd in appearance, is, in essentials, noble and heroic. Those of the Shandy brothers—no ingenuity can conceal the fact—are futile and childish. To follow them is to watch "Nestor play at push-pin with the boys." Don Quixote may tilt at windmills; but all his thoughts are for the weak and the oppressed. As for uncle Toby, "our armies in Flanders" may be upon his lips; but all he cares about is toy cannons and tin soldiers. The one point of vital resemblance is the fervour with which each rushes in pursuit of his delusion. The heavens might fall; but Don Quixote would still worship Dulcinea as a princess. The world might come to an end; but Toby would still be rearing midget demilunes, his brother still be spinning paradoxes and striking impressive attitudes.

Thus, when all is said and done, the contrast goes even deeper than the resemblance. And this accounts for a difference of method which could hardly otherwise be explained. Cervantes is so sure of his hero's nobility that he is not afraid to cover him with every outward mark of ridicule. Sterne puts forth all his art to make us forget the futility of the craze which he has imagined for the central figure of his story. There are moments, it must be confessed, when the ridiculous in Don Quixote is pushed further than we are willing to endure. In such moments, it is clear that the satirist has got the better of the creative artist; and it is not on the hero, but on the author, that our resentment is, instinctively, apt to fall. Our admiration is proof against all that Cervantes himself can do to undermine it. Could the intrinsic nobility of his conception be more decisively driven home? Put either Toby or Walter Shandy to the same test, and who shall say that either of them would come through it? The delicate raillery of Sterne is not

too much for them to bear.  Before the relentless satire of
Cervantes, they would shrivel into nothing.

It is just here, however, that Goethe found not only the
most characteristic, but, also, the most helpful, quality of
Sterne's genius—that from which there is most to be learned
for the practical conduct of our lives.  The very detachment
from all that is commonly reckoned to belong to the serious
interests of life, the readiness to escape from that for which
other men are striving and fighting, to withdraw into the cit-
adel of our bare, naked self and let the world go its way, to count
all for nought, so long as our own ideal is kept intact, had, for
him, a moral worth, a "liberating" value, which it was hard to
overrate.  That it was the whole truth, Goethe was the last
man to suppose.  *Wilhelm Meister* is there to protest against so
impossible a charge.  But, as a half-truth, and one which the
world seems forever bent on denying, he held, and he was right
in holding that it was beyond price.  He recognised and he was
right in recognising, that, of all men who ever wrote, Sterne was
the most firmly possessed of it himself, and the most able, by the
magic of his art, to awaken the sense of it in others.  "Shandy-
ism," he says, in the words of Sterne himself, "is the incapacity
for fixing the mind on a serious object for two minutes together."
And Sterne himself he defines as "a free spirit," "a model in
nothing, in everything an awakener and suggester."[1]

So much as to Sterne's humour in the creation of character.
This, however, is anything but the only channel through which
his humour finds an outlet.   He is rich in the humour of situation; rich, also, in that which gathers round certain instincts
of man's nature.  On the former, there is no need to enlarge:
the less so, as it is often inseparably interwoven with the humour of character, which has already been sufficiently discussed.  If we consider such scenes as that of Trim's kitchen
discourse on mortality, or the collapse of Mr. Shandy the elder
upon his bed, or, above all, the curse of Ernulphus and all that
leads up to it, we shall see at once the infinite art with which
Sterne arranges his limelights and the astounding effects which
he makes them produce.  To say, as Goldsmith came near to
saying, that Sterne's humour depends upon a judicious use
of dashes and stars, upon the insertion of marbled sheets and

---

[1] Goethe, *Sprüche in Prosa.  Werke*, vol. XLII, ii, pp. 200–205 (Weimar ed.).

other mechanical or pert devices, is not even a parody of the truth. As a criticism, it is incredibly beside the mark; only less so than Thackeray's—"The man is not a great humourist; he is a great jester."[1]

On the other head, Sterne is more open to attack. It is useless to deny that the instincts round which he best loves to let his humour play are just those which lend themselves most readily to abuse, and that, in his handling of them, there is a pruriency which justly gives offence. There is none of the frankness which takes the sting out of the obscenity of Aristophanes or the riotous coarseness of Rabelais. On the contrary, there is a prying suggestiveness which is nothing but an aggravation of the misdeed. Yet, so much being granted, it is right to guard ourselves against two possible misconstructions. It is an injustice if we read what we know of the author's life and conduct into his writings. It is an injustice if we fail to take into account what may fairly be said in mitigation of the charge, on this score, against the writings themselves.

With Sterne, as a man, it is hard to have much patience. He was unkind to his wife, and he philandered persistently with other women. His pruriency, moreover, is a blot upon his character; and, in a man of his cloth, it is doubly distasteful. The two former defects, however, have nothing to do with his genius as a writer. And the last, as a trait of character, would concern us much more than it does if he made any attempt to conceal it in his writings. Exactly the contrary is the case. The charge, and the just charge, against him is that he parades it at every turn. There is no need to go to the records of his life for the knowledge of it. It is proclaimed upon the housetops in his books. If a man makes great professions of nobility of soul in his writings, it is, no doubt, a disenchantment to discover that they are contradicted by his life. The very suspicion of hypocrisy may and does interfere with the pleasure we take in a work even of imaginative creation. But hypocrisy, at least in this connection, is the very last thing that can be charged upon the work of Sterne. His sins go before him to the judgment; and it is by his writings that they are made known.

Again, offensive as his pruriency is, the specific, and very

---

[1] Goldsmith, *Citizen of the World*, pp. 50, 52; Thackeray, *Lectures on English Humourists* (Sterne).

peculiar, appeal it makes to the intellect and imagination, may be urged as a mitigating plea. The two things are closely connected; the former, in fact, is a consequence of the latter. The indecency of Sterne is of a peculiarly intellectual kind. He holds it jealously aloof from all that can touch the passions or emotions. It works, as it were, in a void which he has created specially for the purpose and of which he alone, of all writers, holds the secret. In this dry handling of the matter, the affections of the reader are left unenlisted and unmoved. He is too much engrossed in following the intellectual ingenuity of the writer, the rapid quips and turns of his fancy, to have much attention left for the gross insinuations which too often form the primitive groundwork of the arabesque cunningly stencilled on the surface. Certainly, he is not carried off his feet, as he might easily be by warmer, if far more innocent, descriptions.

The sentimentalism of Sterne goes much deeper and, in its more extreme forms, is, perhaps, less capable of defence. Here, again, no doubt, we are mainly, though, in this case, not solely, concerned with the actual effect stamped by the artist's hand upon our imagination. We have little—and, in that little, we have nothing *directly*—to do with the havoc which sentiment, as he nursed it, may have wrought with his personal conduct and his practical outlook on life. The truth is that sentiment so highly wrought—still more, sentiment so deliberately cultivated and laid out with such a manifest eye to effect—can hardly fail to rouse the suspicion of the reader. When the limelights are manipulated with design so palpable as in the death of Le Fevre or the story of the dead ass, the author goes far to defeat his own purpose. The spontaneity which is the first charm of sentiment is immediately seen to be wanting, and the effect of the whole effort is largely destroyed. More than that. We instinctively feel that, with the author himself, as a man, all can hardly be well. We are driven to cast doubts on his sincerity; and, when we look to his life, we more than half expect our doubts to be confirmed. Such suspicions inevitably react upon the imaginative pleasure which the picture itself would otherwise have given. There is an air of unreality, if not of imposture, about the whole business which, with the best will in the world, it is impossible wholly to put by.

Yet, the same command of effect, which, in matters of

sentiment, is apt to prove perilous, is, elsewhere, brought into play with the happiest results. Give him a situation, a thought which appeals strongly either to his imagination or to his humanitarian instincts—for Sterne also, in his own curious way, is among the prophets—and no man knows so well how to lead up to it; how to make the most of it; how, by cunning arrangement of light and shade and drapery, to show it off to the best possible advantage. As stage-manager, as master of effective setting, he is without equal, we may almost say without rival, among novelists. And there are moments when such mastery is pure gain. Take the curse of Ernulphus, take Trim's reading of the sermon on conscience, take his oration upon death; and this will hardly be denied. There are, no doubt, other moments —those of sentimentality or indecency—when, from the nature of the theme, approval is not likely to be so unreserved. Yet, even here, we cannot but admire the cunning of the craftsman, deliberate yet light-handed, deeply calculated yet full of sparkle, nimbleness and humour.

From Sterne to his alleged disciples the descent is abrupt. Two only of these call for notice in this sketch: Mackenzie and Brooke.

Henry Mackenzie (1745–1831) passed a long and peaceful life at Edinburgh, where he held the post of attorney for the Crown, and subsequently of comptroller of the taxes, for Scotland. After the publication of *The Man of Feeling* (1771, the year of Scott's birth) he was recognised as the literary leader of Edinburgh society, and he may be said to have held that post by courtesy until his death, a year before that of Scott. In addition to his three novels, he wrote a successful play (*The Prince of Tunis*, 1773) and edited two successive periodicals, *The Mirror* (1779–80) and *The Lounger* (1785–7). He was also chairman of the committee which reported on Macpherson's *Ossian* (1805).

He is, of course, best known by his earliest work, *The Man of Feeling* (1771). At the time, this won for him a name which still survives as a tradition, but which is hardly justified by the intrinsic merits of the book, either in conception or in execution. It is, in fact, mainly remarkable as a record of the influences which, at this period, were battling for the mastery of the novel.

The form of it, which, at first sight, might be taken for picaresque, is, in reality, a reversion to a yet more primitive type of structure: that familiar to us from the Coverly papers. And it may be noted that *The Life of John Buncle, Esq.*, by Thomas Amory,[1] the first part of which appeared some fifteen years earlier (1756), shows, with much better justification for itself, something of the same peculiarity. Mackenzie, however, does not, like Amory, write what professes to be an autobiography. He has not, therefore, the excuse of recording what give themselves out for "actual facts." On the contrary, he sets about to write a novel with a full-fledged hero to its credit. The hero and the beggar, the hero on a visit to Bedlam, the hero in a stage-coach, the hero in the park and at the gambling-table—such are the disjointed fragments tacked together by way of apology for a story. We are back again at Sir Roger in the Abbey, Sir Roger at the play, Sir Roger and the gipsy-woman; which gives a significant meaning to the title of "the northern Addison," given to Mackenzie, on quite different grounds, by Scott. The author, indeed, is nothing if not apologetic. He is at pains to account for the lack of connection by the lame expedient of a middleman—a curate with a turn for sport and literature—who gives or withholds material as suits the humour of the moment, suppressing ten chapters at the beginning and some thirty more as the story slowly creeps towards an end. It is manifest that the episodes are chosen, not in the least for the sake of the excitement they may offer, but solely to make call upon the virtuous, if ill-regulated, "feelings," and, still more, upon the tears, of the hero. And, neither in the spirit of the story, nor in its incidents, is there the smallest trace of humour. These things alone are enough to show that *The Man of Feeling* owes little or nothing to Fielding or Smollett; but that in form, if in nothing else, it casts back to Addison and the essayists. Some of the elements which, in the interval, the picaresque writers had employed for their own ends, may, doubtless, be fairly recognised as present. But they are bent to uses alien, indeed hostile, to those for which they were originally devised. They are no longer there for their own sake, or for the humour which they offer. The sole purpose they serve is to furnish the stage

[1] As to Amory, see Vol. XI, Chap. XII.

on which the "sentimental education" of the hero—and, through him, of the reader—is carried out.

It is in working the mine of sentiment that Mackenzie comes as near as he ever comes to Sterne. His methods and aims are utterly different. With him, as with the great humourist, the raw material is sentiment. But how raw the material remains in Mackenzie's hands! What a wide difference between his clumsy insistence and the light, airy touch of Sterne! Define Mackenzie as sentimentalist or sentimental moralist, and you have told almost the whole truth about him. Describe Sterne by the same terms, and almost everything remains unsaid. A slenderer thread of affiliation could not easily be conceived.

The debt of Mackenzie to Rousseau is, undeniably, more substantial. It is, however, a debt purely of sentiment, of the humanitarian feelings which Rousseau did more than any man to spread abroad through Europe. From the nature of the case, these feelings could not fail to make their way, sooner or later, into the novel. They had done so already in Sterne, and, by anticipation, even in Richardson; nor can it have been an accident that, in the preface to *The Man of Feeling*, Mackenzie should have placed himself behind the shield of Richardson and Rousseau; though he certainly goes far to destroy the force of the appeal by tacking on the name of Marmontel. For, in spite of their title, the *Contes Moraux* of that writer belong to a wholly different order.

In his next book, *The Man of the World* (1773), Mackenzie returned to the same theme, but from the other side. This time, he has taken the precaution to provide himself with a villain, the nominal hero of the story; and the villain, in a long career of intrigue and seduction, brings a plot in his train. The plot may not be specially good; but, after the disconnected episodes of *The Man of Feeling*, it is an untold relief to have any plot at all. This is the one new element of importance. In all else, *The Man of the World* moves in the same circle as *The Man of Feeling*. The influence of Rousseau may, perhaps, be still more strongly marked, and beyond doubt is so in one passage, which exalts the virtues of the Cherokee over the corruptions of Europe with a fervour clearly inspired by the second *Discourse* and the *Letter to Philopolis*. But, even this outbreak might be met by an attack on our east Indian conquests, which is to be found in the earlier novel, and which reveals the same train of thought and feeling.

Mackenzie's last and best book, *Julia de Roubigné* (1777), strikes a wholly different vein and places him in the straight line of descent from Richardson. The work is planned on a much smaller scale; the intrigue is far simpler, and less elaborately prepared. But it is, none the less, the direct offspring of *Clarissa*, and one of the very few tragedies to be found in the early stages of the English novel. In scale and general treatment, *Julia* may, perhaps, have owed something to certain French models: to *La Princesse de Clèves*, and, still more, to *Manon Lescaut*. But, when all allowance has been made for this, the star of Richardson—and that, in the letter form as well as in the tragic substance—still remains in the ascendant. Still, whatever Mackenzie might write, he was still for the men of his own day the man of feeling and nothing else. And it was as the man of feeling that he was known to the younger generation, Scott and others, who looked up to him as a venerable oracle of the past. Such are the curious freaks of literary reputation.

With Brooke, we return once more, in however loose a sense, to what may be called the sphere of influence of Sterne; and, like Mackenzie, he, too, has sat at the feet of Rousseau. To many readers, perhaps to most, the spirit of Brooke will seem much healthier, as his outlook is undoubtedly much wider, than that of Mackenzie. He writes in a far breezier spirit; and, as the picaresque model is more unreservedly adopted, there is far more variety in his incidents and his settings. The extreme looseness of structure which inevitably results from this is, no doubt, something of a drawback; but it is amply redeemed by the vivacity of the characters, and by the vividness of the ever-changing scenes through which they are led. It is redeemed, also, by the unfailing zest with which the author throws himself into the varying fortunes of his hero—whose pugnacity is hardly less conspicuous than his overflowing benevolence—and of the motley crew among whom his lot is cast. Moreover, full of "feeling" as the book is, it is of the kind which leads as often to laughter as to tears. After a course of Mackenzie, we cannot but be grateful for this relief.

Henry Brooke (1703?–83) was born in Ireland and educated

at Trinity college, Dublin; he lived in Dublin for the greater part of his life. In addition to his work in the novel, drama and poetry, he took some part in the political controversies of his time; issuing a warning against the Jacobite tendencies of the Irish catholics in the panic of 1745 (*The Farmer's Letters*), and subsequently pleading for a mitigation of the penal laws (1761). He was deeply affected by the religious movements of his day, that of the methodists as well as that of the mystics; a fact which did much to popularise his most important work, *The Fool of Quality*.

For our purposes, two things in particular deserve notice in the work of Brooke. In the first place, *The Fool of Quality* (1766) is more deeply stamped with the seal of Rousseau—the Rousseau of the second *Discourse* and of *Émile*—than is any other book of the period. The contempt which Rousseau felt for the conventions of society, his "inextinguishable hatred of oppression" in high places, his faith in the virtues of the poor and simple, his burning desire to see human life ordered upon a more natural basis—all this is vividly reflected upon every page of *The Fool of Quality*. It is reflected in the various discourses, whether between the personages of the story or between the author and an imaginary friend (of the candid sort), which are quaintly scattered throughout the book: discourses on education, heroism, debtors' prisons, woman's rights, matter and spirit, the legislation of Lycurgus, the social contract, the constitution of England—on everything that happened to captivate the quick wit of the author. Clearly, Brooke had grasped far more of what Rousseau came to teach the world, and had felt it far more intensely, than Mackenzie. Before we can find anything approaching to this keenness of feeling, this revolt against the wrongs of the social system, we have to go forward to the years immediately succeeding the outbreak of the French revolution; in particular to the years from 1790 to 1797—the years of Paine and Godwin, of Coleridge's "penny trumpet of sedition"; or, in the field of the novel, the years of *Caleb Williams*, of *Nature and Art*, of *Hermsprong, or Man as he is not*. There, no doubt, the cry of revolt was raised more defiantly. For, there, speculation was reinforced by practical example; and the ideas of Rousseau were flashed back, magnified a hundredfold by the deeds of the national assembly, the convention and the reign of terror.   And this contrast between the first and the second harvest of Rousseau's influence is not the least interesting thing in the story of the eighteenth century novel.

The second point which calls for remark is connected with the mystical side of Brooke's character, of which notice has been taken in an earlier chapter.[1]   Through the mystics, it will be remembered, Brooke was brought into touch with John Wesley and the methodists.   It is, in fact, the methodistical, rather than the mystical strain which comes to the surface in *The Fool of Quality* —though, in the discourse on matter and spirit, mentioned above, the author boldly declares,"I know not that there is any such thing in nature as matter."[2]   Such defiances, however, are rare, and, in general, the appeal of Brooke is of a less esoteric kind.   He dwells much on conversion; and, as revised by Wesley, the book was long a favourite with methodists.   The importance of this is to remind us of the bond which unites the literary with the religious revival of the eighteenth century.   It is, of course, only in a small number of writers— Collins, Smart, Cowper, for instance—that the two strands are visibly interwoven.   But it is probable that the emotional appeal of the religious revival was an awakening force to many writers, whether poets or novelists, who, in the outward ordering of their lives, were indifferent, or even hostile, to the "enthusiasm" either of the methodist or of the evangelical. And it is certain that, from the general change of temper of which the religious revival was at once the cause and the symptom, both poet and novelist found the hearts of men more ready to receive their creations than would have been possible at any earlier period of the century.   The same thing holds good as to the corresponding movement in the literature of Germany and, to a less degree, as to that in the literature of France.   If the pietists had not prepared the ground, Goethe, who himself owed not a little to intercourse with the "beautiful soul"—the Moravian sister—would have found it much harder to win a hearing for his youthful poems and for *Werther*.   If, in his earlier writings, Rousseau had not roughly challenged the speculative creed of "the enlightenment," *La Nouvelle Héloïse* and the *Rêveries* would probably have been written in a very

[1] Cf. Vol. IX, Chap. XII.    [2] Vol. I, p. 81, ed. 1766.

different spirit; conceivably they might never have been written at all.

On the other novel of Brooke—*Juliet Grenville or the History of the Human Heart* (1774), it is not worth while to linger. His plays and poems may be passed by here.[1]  He lives, indeed, by *The Fool of Quality*, and by that alone.

From the novel of sentiment to that of terror, or of the far past, is a startling transition.  And the harvest in this field is so poor that our account of it may be brief.

The fountainhead of both streams of romance is to be found in *The Castle of Otranto*, which was struck off at feverheat by Walpole in the summer of 1764 and published at the end of the year, or the beginning of the next.  The execution is weak in the extreme.  The "history" is one vast anachronism, and the portents are absurd.  Yet, in spite of these glaring defects, of which it is hard to suppose that the author was not in some degree aware, an entirely new turn is here given to the novel, and elements are brought into it which, at a later time and in hands more skilful, were to change it out of all knowledge. The book, as Walpole himself tells us, was written in conscious reaction against the domesticities and the sentiment of Richardson.  It was a deliberate attempt to divert fiction from the channel along which it had hitherto flowed; to transport it from the sphere of close observation to that of free invention; to substitute for the interest of the present that of the past, for the world of experience that of the mysterious and the supernatural. The performance is bungling; but the design is in a high degree original and fruitful.  It was, in fact, so original that, as sometimes happens in such cases, Walpole himself took fright at his own boldness.  He is at the pains to explain that, all appearances to the contrary, his heart is still half with the novel of every-day life.  "It was not so much my intention to recall the glories of ancient romance as to blend the wonderful of old stories with the natural of modern novels."[2]  And he appeals, in proof of his sincerity, to Matilda's avowal of her passion for Theodore.  We are not bound to take him at his word.  He may, with more kindness, be regarded as a whole-hearted

[1] As to his contributions to the drama, see Vol. XI.
[2] Letter to Élie de Beaumont, 18 March, 1765.

rebel, who led the forlorn hope in a cause which, years after, had its day of triumph. It is that which makes *The Castle of Otranto* a marked book—even more marked perhaps for its ultimate bearing on foreign literature than on our own.

Clara Reeve, to whom we now pass, led an entirely uneventful life (1729–1807), marked only by the publication of various tales, of which *The Old English Baron* has alone survived, and by her friendship with Mrs. Brigden, Richardson's daughter, who revised that work in its earlier shape, *The Champion of Virtue*.

If there is some doubt about the intentions of Walpole, about those of Clara Reeve, his successor and disciple, there is none whatever. *The Old English Baron* (1777)—it had been published earlier in the same year as *The Champion of Virtue, a Gothic Tale*—is undeniably what *The Castle of Otranto* professes to be, "an attempt to unite the merits and graces of the ancient Romance and of the modern Novel." There is "a sufficient degree of the marvellous," in the shape of a ghost, "to excite attention; enough of the manners of real life," or what passes for such, "to give an air of probability; and enough of the pathetic"—in the form of a love-story, with an interesting peasant, who turns out to be son and heir of the ghost (a murdered baron), for hero—"to engage the heart in its behalf." It is quite true that the ingredients of *Otranto*, including the irresistible young peasant, were much the same. But they were differently mixed. In Walpole's book, the chief appeal was to "terror" and to the romantic past. In *The Old English Baron*, these have sunk into little more than trimmings. The main stress on the part of the author lies upon a tale of righteous vengeance and of love. About the use of the marvellous, she is manifestly nervous. She reduces it, therefore, to the presence of an ordinary ghost, who contents himself with groaning beneath the floor, by way of instituting proceedings against his murderer. Even the medieval is a source of some alarm. And, considering what she makes of it, we can hardly be surprised. Walpole, absurd as novelist of the crusades—his scene is laid with delightful vagueness during the century and a half which covered them—at least contrives to give some faint flavour of the later middle ages to his characters and their setting. Clara Reeve can boast of no such success. A trial by combat, her

supreme effort in this direction, is conducted with all the
flourishes of forensic etiquette. The manners of the eighteenth century are transplanted straight into the fifteenth.
The scene may be labelled "A Feudal Castle"; in reality, it is
the cedar parlour of Miss Byron and Sir Charles. The Gothic
element and the element of terror being thus disposed of, nothing is left but that which "engages the heart on its behalf":
the eternal theme of "virtue rewarded," of injured innocence
triumphant over treachery and crime. In the compromise
which the authoress strove to effect, the "modern Novel"
carries off all the honours; the "ancient Romance" is represented by little beyond garnish and appurtenance.

How far can it be said that the works comprised in the
above group did anything to prepare the way for the historical and romantic novel, as it was subsequently shaped by
Scott? The answer is: only in the vaguest and most rudi-
mentary sense. The novel of terror—if by that we understand
the terror which springs from the marvellous and super-
natural—has never taken kindly to English soil. And it is
manifest that Scott fought shy of the marvellous as an element
of prose fiction. In appealing to terror, accordingly, neither
Walpole nor Clara Reeve did much more than enter a claim
that the borders of the novel might without treason be enlarged; that the novel was not bound down by the charter of its
being to the presentation of current life in its most obvious
respects—of buying and selling, of marrying and giving in
marriage. That, if judged by the permanent results, was all;
but it was enough. The appeal to history told in the same
direction; but it was far more fruitful of results. Walpole, it is
true, did not make much of it; Clara Reeve still less. But
they pointed the way which, with a thousand modifications suggested by his genius, Scott was triumphantly to follow. And
the very defects of *The Old English Baron* may have aided him
in the discovery, so often missed by his successors, that, in the
historical novel, the history is of far less importance than the
human interest and the romance. The earlier and greater
*Waverleys*, in fact, can be called historical only by a stretch.
It was not until Scott had worked for years upon the near past
—a past which still made itself felt as a living force upon
the present—that he plunged into the middle ages. More-

over, in spite of its stirring adventure, *Ivanhoe* has always counted for less with the English reader than with those of Germany and France.

Frances Burney (1752–1840), the last novelist of note belonging to our period, was daughter of Dr. Burney, the historian of music. During her youth, and until some years after the publication of her second novel, *Cecilia* (1782), she lived in the most brilliant literary society of her day, including that of Johnson, Mrs. Thrale and Burke. In 1786 she was appointed second keeper of the robes to queen Charlotte, a post which she held for four years, to her own great discomfort, but to the delight of those who read her fascinating *Diary*. After her release, she married (1793) a French officer of the name of d'Arblay, one of the emigrants who gathered at Juniper hall and of whom her *Diary* contains many striking and amusing notices. From 1802 to 1812 she lived in France, returning only to publish her last novel, *The Wanderer* (1814). The later years of her life (1815–40) were passed peacefully in England.

With the novels of Fanny Burney we pass into another world. They stand far nearer to the novel as we know it than anything which had yet appeared. The picaresque scaffolding, the obtrusive moral, the deliberate sentiment—much more the marvellous and the medievalism—of the writers who had immediately gone before her are thrown to the winds. She sets herself to tell a plain story—enlivened, doubtless, with strange adventures, with characters still stranger—and that is all.

Yet in this very simplicity is contained a new and, as time has proved, a very fruitful conception of what the novel might achieve. Starting from the general plan laid down by Richardson, she limits, she adds, she modifies, until the result is something entirely different. The tragic element is the first to go. This, with other modifications, leaves her with a story of home life for the groundwork of her picture. And the introduction of a whole gallery of oddities, dogging the steps of the heroine at every turn, gives variety, zest and sparkle to what otherwise would have been a humdrum, and, perhaps, a slightly sentimental, tale. The novel of home life, it is not too much to say, is the creation of Fanny Burney. There is a great deal else, and a great deal more brilliant, in her creations. But it is this that makes them a landmark in the history of fiction.

Her method is simplicity itself. *Evelina* is the "History of a young lady's entrance into the world." And the same description would apply to every one of the stories which followed. Her unvarying plan is to take a young girl "with a virtuous mind, a cultivated understanding and a feeling heart," but wholly "ignorant of the forms and inexperienced in the manners of the world"; to provide her with a guardian instead of parents and so throw her on her own resources; to place her in circumstances unusual but not, except in *The Wanderer*, unnatural; and, with an inexhaustible fertility of invention, to devise incidents and situations such as will draw out her character and keep the interest of the reader on the stretch. In *Cecilia*, no doubt, she added to this something of the tragic purpose, the solemn moral, of Richardson; and very few are likely to regard the addition as an improvement. But, with this partial exception, her aim was always what has been said; and she had two gifts which enabled her triumphantly to attain it.

The first is a talent, not easily to be matched among English novelists, for telling a story; an unaffected delight in telling it, which wakens a like pleasure in the reader. The second is an amazing power—a power in which she is surpassed by Dickens only—of giving flesh and blood to caricature. "My little character-monger" was Johnson's pet name for her;[1] and, in the sense just hinted at, she earned it ten times over. With infectious zest, she adds touch after touch of absurdity to her portrait, until the reader is fairly swept off his feet by the drollery of the figure she has conjured up. This particular talent is, no doubt, most conspicuous in her earliest two works, *Evelina* (1778) and *Cecilia* (1782). But it flashes out often enough in *Camilla* (1796), and, on occasion, even in *The Wanderer* (1814). In all this gallery of "humourists" the most laughable is Mr. Briggs, the ill-bred but not unkindly skinflint of *Cecilia*. But he is hard run by the Branghtons, still harder perhaps by Mr. Smith, the "gentleman *manqué*," as Mrs. Thrale called him, of *Evelina;* while Sir Hugh Tyrold and Dr. Orkborne, the

---

[1] The story is told in the dedication to *The Wanderer*. There was a party at Lady Galloway's, shortly after the appearance of *Cecilia*. "Johnson endeavouring to detain me when I rose to depart, by calling out 'Don't go yet, little character-monger,' Burke followed, gaily but impressively exclaiming, 'Miss Burney, die to-night!'"

Admiral, Sir Jasper Herrington and Mr. Tedman keep up the succession not quite unworthily, in the two later novels. But even to mention instances is to do injustice. For, after all, the most surprising thing is their unlimited abundance; the way in which they start up from every corner, from each rung of the social ladder, at the bidding of the author. For vulgarity, in particular, she has the eye of a lynx. Right and left, high or low, she unmasks it with unflagging delight, tearing off the countless disguises under which it lurks and holding it up, naked but not ashamed, to the laughter, and, sometimes, though not often, to the contempt of the reader. By the side of these lively beings, the figures of Smollett seem little better than stuffed birds in a museum.

Spontaneity is among the best gifts of the novelist. And few novelists are more spontaneous than Fanny Burney. We should have guessed this from the novels themselves. The *Diary*,[1] in some ways a yet greater masterpiece, puts it beyond doubt. It is evident that all she saw and all she heard presented itself to her instinctively in dramatic form; that all the incidents through which she passed naturally wove themselves into a story—one might almost say, into a novel—before her eyes. In the *Diary*, as in the novels, the two gifts are intertwined beyond possibility of separation. The observation which enabled her to take in the passing scene, to seize the distinctive features of every man and woman she met, may have put the material in her hands. But the material would have lost half its effect, it would have lost more than half its charm, if the genius of the born story-teller had not been there to weave it into a coherent whole, to give it life and movement. The *Diary* is a better test of this even than the novels. The incidents recorded in it are, for the most part, what might happen to any of us. The men and women it brings before us are, with some marked exceptions, such as might be met at any party. Who but themselves would have cared a straw for Miss Streatfield or M. de Guiffardière, for colonel Blakeney or even the "sweet Queen"? Yet, through the magic glass of the *Diary*, each of them takes distinct form and feature; all have gestures, mannerisms, gesticulations of their own; and each, without the smallest effort, fits into a

[1] Cf. Chap. XI, *post*.

drama as lively as any that could be put upon the stage. It is of course, perfectly true, and it is as it should be, that, when she has an incident of intrinsic interest to record, the portrait of a really marked figure to paint, she surpasses herself. Her portraits of Johnson and Mrs. Thrale, of George III and the French *émigrés*, are among the best ever drawn. Her account of the king's madness, of the escape of the duc de Liancourt, is as good as anything in Saint-Simon or Carlyle. These, however, were the chances of a lifetime. And it is in her more level work that her peculiar talent is most readily to be traced. There we can almost see the portrait growing, the incidents moving each into its own place, under the hand of the diarist. And we know that the same process must lie behind the triumphs of the novelist.

It is an injustice that her last two books, *Camilla* in particular, should have been allowed utterly to drop out. The old brilliance is, doubtless, largely gone. But the more solid qualities remain almost untouched. There is the old keenness of observation, the old narrative genius, the old power of contriving ingenious and, in the main, natural situations. The secondary figures are certainly less laughable, but that, as Macaulay hints, is largely because they are less freakish and more human; because their humour is often next door to pathos and the laughter they call out, to tears. This is true even of *The Wanderer*, when we can once forget the grotesque opening —the writer can think of no better machinery for introducing her heroine, a beautiful English girl, than the make-up of a negress—and the woeful touches of grandiloquence—the heroine is described as "a female Robinson Crusoe"—which the authoress of *Evelina* would have been the first to laugh out of court. Such lapses, however, give no fair impression of the book; and, with the best will in the world, Macaulay has made them bulk for more than they are worth. Strike out a few paragraphs, and *The Wanderer* is not written in "jargon"—any more than, with the exception of a few pages, the language of *Cecilia* is Johnsonese.

To the end Miss Burney remains what she was at the begining: a keen observer, a great "character-monger," a supreme story-teller, the first writer to see that the ordinary embarrassments of a girl's life would bear to be taken for the main theme of a novel. "To her we owe not only *Evelina*, *Cecilia* and *Camilla*, but also *Mansfield Park* and *The Absentee*." When Macaulay ended his estimate of Miss Burney with these words, he said better than he knew. He was thinking of her as the first of a long line of woman novelists. He forgot that the innovation applied not only to her sex, but to her theme.

## CHAPTER IV

# The Drama and the Stage

THE term "eighteenth century English drama" suggests a somewhat arbitrary chronology. Yet it has, perhaps, other justification than that of convenient reference. The year 1700 marks the death of Dryden, the dominant figure in restoration drama, and the retirement of Congreve, its most brilliant comic dramatist. Etherege, Wycherley, Lee, Otway and many other contemporaries of Dryden had already passed from the ranks of active dramatists. The growing protest against the immorality of the drama, vigorously expressed in Jeremy Collier's invective, *A Short View of the Immorality and Profaneness of the English Stage* (1698), shows that the old order has changed and is soon to yield place to new.[1]

The reign of queen Anne (1702–14) may be regarded, therefore, as a period of transition in English drama. Though the current of restoration comedy still runs strong in the first decade of the eighteenth century, in Vanbrugh's later works and in Farquhar's plays, the tide of drama turns with the moralised comedies of Colley Cibber[2] and the sentimental dramas of Richard Steele.[3] Cibber strove deliberately to moralise the drama. He ascribed the success of his first comedy to the "moral Delight receiv'd from its Fable," and, in reviewing his own dramatic career, claimed to "have had the Interest and Honour of Virtue always in view."[4] Imperfect as his ethical standards often appear to modern critics, there is little reason to question the sincerity of his intention to reform comedy. To the moral aim of Cibber, Steele united sentiment. Without the epigrammatic

[1] Cf. *ante*, Vol. VIII, Chap. VI, pp. 185 ff.
[2] Cf. *ibid.*, pp. 200–201.  [3] Cf. *ante*, Vol. IX, pp. 32–34, 71.
[4] *An Apology for the Life of Mr. Colley Cibber*, edited by Lowe, R. W., vol. I, pp. 220, 266.

brilliancy of Congreve or the fertile invention of Farquhar, he sought to sustain comedy by a different method. If comedy was moralised by Cibber, it was sentimentalised by Steele.

Meanwhile, tragedy, also, was showing signs of transition. The heroic drama of the restoration had torn passion to tatters; but the queen Anne age inclined more toward classical constraint than toward romantic licence. Even Nicholas Rowe, who, in *The Fair Penitent* (1703), followed an Elizabethan model and wrote *Jane Shore* (1714) "in imitation of Shakespear's style," shows classical tendencies in limitation of the number of characters, in restriction of dramatic action and in rejection of comic relief. His chief dramas—to use his own phrase, "she-tragedies"—have an almost feminine refinement of tone.[1] In the moralised sentiment with which they enforce their pathetic appeals there is a close kinship between the tragedy of Rowe and the comedy of Steele. In sentimental drama, pity is akin to love.

The conventional critical distinction between tragedy and comedy should not, then, be unduly pressed. Doubtless, it is unnecessary to find fault with the term "sentimental comedy," which is sanctioned by contemporary usage and actually adopted by Goldsmith in his attack upon sentimental drama. But it is important to recognise that the wave of sentiment swept over a wider field than that of English comedy, or even of English drama. It invaded the continent. Destouches, whose residence in England brought him, like Voltaire, into direct contact with English influences, admitted into several of his later comedies (1727–53) a serious undertone. Marivaux touched comedy with pathos and sentiment. Nivelle de la Chaussée, who followed Steele's dictum that "laughter's a distorted passion" more closely than did its author, developed sentimental comedy into *comédie larmoyante*. Voltaire, though by no means ready to permit comedy to forget her function of mirth, found "melting pity" admissible. Diderot drew inspiration from Lillo's moralised *bourgeois* tragedy. The very term *drame* suggests the obliteration of the rigid line between comedy and tragedy.[2] In England and on the continent alike,

---

[1] Cf. *ante*, Vol. VIII, Chap VII, pp. 221–223.

[2] Saurin, *Épître Dédicatoire* to his *drame*, *Béverlei* (1768), declares that he does not know whether Sedaine's *Philosophe sans le Savoir* (1765) is tragedy or comedy, but that it is *un drame très beau et très original*.

sentiment tended to break down the barriers of dramatic convention.

Notwithstanding the far-reaching influence of sentimental drama, the record of its rise and progress is but part of the English dramatic history of the eighteenth century. The queen Anne period was, essentially, a critical age, which fixed its standards largely on classical authority. To a very considerable degree, its playwrights reflect the influence of French classical drama and dramatic theory. Racine and Corneille were adapted for the English stage in a whole series of versions.[1] Addison, whose critical influence was cast in favour of dramatic rule and regularity, put classical theory so effectively into practice in *Cato* (1713) that Voltaire hailed it as the first *tragédie raisonnable* in English.[2] Stimulated by the successes of Ambrose Philips[3] and Addison, other English playwrights turned to classical models and translated, though often with considerable freedom, such dramas as *Le Cid*, *Cinna* and *Iphigénie*.

Though the influence of French classical drama and dramatic standards upon eighteenth century English drama demands ample recognition, it should not be overestimated. Not even under queen Anne was the Elizabethan tradition forgotten. Shakespeare's tragedies, Jonson's comedies and Beaumont and Fletcher's romantic plays continued to hold the stage. Rowe turned freely to Elizabethan models and sought to imitate Shakespeare's style. Even Addison, a confirmed classicist, in at least one memorable passage,[4] treated Shakespeare's genius as above artificial restraints. English translators of French tragedy sometimes abated the rigid classical conventions in their adaptations for the freer English stage. In reality, English drama, even during the Augustan period, was often an unconscious compromise between the restraint of French theory and the inherited freedom of English dramatic practice. Furthermore, the English element in queen Anne drama is not confined to the survival of Elizabethan influences. The note of sentiment struck in contemporary comedy by Steele is per-

[1] Cf. *ante*, Vol. VIII, Chap. VII, pp. 204–205.

[2] Cf. *ante*, Vol. IX, Chap. II, pp. 70–71.

[3] *The Distrest Mother* (adapted from Racine's *Andromaque*) was produced in 1712.

[4] *The Spectator*, no. 592.

ceptible, not merely in the tragedy of Rowe, but, perhaps, even in classical English drama itself. The triumphs of Philips and Addison were founded on the distresses of the heroine and the moralised sentiments of the hero. Despite, then, the dominance of classical standards, queen Anne drama is not a merely Gallicised product. It is the resultant of English and continental forces.

If critical survey of the period be broadened so as to include the history of the stage as well as of the drama, the dramatic currents will appear still more complex. Dorset gardens theatre had catered more and more to the popular demand for spectacle. Foreign singers and dancers invaded the boards of the patent theatres. The successful advent of Italian opera made the judicious Cibber grieve and Steele demand that Britons should "from foreign insult save this English stage."[1] But even Colley Cibber, sworn advocate of regular drama, compromised his convictions and, as a manager, "had not Virtue enough to starve by opposing a Multitude that would have been too hard for me."[2] Meanwhile, the attacks of Collier and his followers were continued, through almost a generation, until, in 1726, William Law published his treatise, *The Absolute Unlawfulness of the Stage Entertainment fully demonstrated*. Thus, beset by foes without and by rivals within the theatre, regular drama had fallen on evil days.

To the adverse factors which threatened the ascendancy of formal tragedy and comedy must be added two theatrical developments of great significance. The second decade of the eighteenth century marks the introduction of English pantomime; the third, that of ballad-opera. The elements of pantomime had long been present on the English stage before John Rich fused them into an extraordinarily popular type of theatrical entertainment. "Dumb-shows," introduced as early as *Gorboduc*, scenic and mechanical elements in masque and the spectacular accessories of restoration opera anticipate salient features of Rich's productions. Yet, even if Cibber's suggestion[3] be accepted that the "original hint" for pantomime is to be found in Weaver's Drury lane production of *The Loves of Mars and Venus* (1717), John Rich was the dominant factor

[1] Epilogue to *The Tender Husband* (1705).
[2] *Apology*, vol. ii, p. 182.    [3] *Apology*, vol. ii, pp. 180 ff.

in establishing the popular type. He had none of Cibber's scruples about catering to "the vulgar taste." A remarkable mimic, but without the gift of stage speech, Rich cleverly turned his limitation to advantage. The speaking harlequin, familiar on the Italian stage and already introduced on the English, now became dumb; but Rich made actions speak louder than words. To a theme usually drawn from fabulous history or classical myth, the pantomime added the comic courtship of harlequin and columbine, heightening the effect with spectacular transformations, elaborate scenery and music. The patent theatres vied with each other in producing pantomimes; for the receipts from them doubled those from regular drama. Henceforth, pantomime had to be numbered as one of the stock attractions of the eighteenth century stage.

Hardly had pantomime firmly established itself in popular favour, when Rich produced another formidable rival to regular drama in John Gay's *Beggar's Opera* (1728).[1] This work marked the triumph of ballad-opera. "The vast Success of that new Species of Dramatick Poetry" was, to Colley Cibber,[2] further proof of the "vulgar taste" which had already welcomed pantomime. But the influence of Gay's opera is not confined to its introduction of popular lyrics. In satirising not merely the absurdities of Italian opera but the conscious moralisings of sentimental drama, and in providing happy issues out of all the afflictions of its "charmingly pathetic" prison scenes, Gay points towards the dramatic burlesques of Fielding and Carey. Palpable hits at Sir Robert Walpole and other politicians of the day open the vein of social and political satire, worked to the full in Fielding's farces. *The Beggar's Opera*, accordingly, holds an important place in English dramatic annals. Like pantomime, ballad-opera, henceforth, must be regarded as a stock attraction of the theatre. During the Garrick era, its popularity was maintained by many operas like those of Isaac Bickerstaff, and the initial run of Sheridan's *Duenna* surpassed that of *The Beggar's Opera*.

Even this general survey of those earlier aspects of eighteenth century drama, which form a necessary background to any account of its later history, must make it clear that English drama is the resultant of many forces. So complex, indeed, is

---

[1] Cf. *ante*, Vol. IX, Chap. VI, pp. 182–183.  [2] *Apology*, vol. I, pp. 243, 245.

the interaction of these various forces that it is idle to seek to resolve actual dramatic products exactly into their precise component parts. Still more futile are attempts to warp the actual facts of dramatic history into conformity with a rigid preconceived theory of dramatic evolution. The convenient distinction between tragedy and comedy, if converted into an arbitrary critical formula, becomes a stumbling-block to the critic of sentimental drama. To attempt to explain English classical drama simply from the standpoint of French classical, or pseudo-classical, theory is to ignore English influences which directly affected the dramatic practice, and even the theories, of Voltaire himself. To regard the transition from the immorality of restoration comedy to the sentimentalised morality of the eighteenth century as a complete moral regeneration is to forget the frank licence of Mrs. Centlivre and the imperfect ethical standards of even professed moralists like Cibber.

Broadly viewed, eighteenth century drama shows decided reaction from the immorality that provoked the attacks of Sir Richard Blackmore and Jeremy Collier. Yet, despite many evidences of an awakening sense of moral responsibility in the attitude of the court, of society and of administrators of the law, the conversion of drama was neither sudden nor complete. Farquhar, whose dramatic work is subsequent to Collier's attack, maintains, essentially, the spirit of restoration comedy. Even *The Careless Husband*, despite Cibber's good intentions, presents the stock characters of restoration comedy purged of their gross excesses, doubtless, but yet not wholly chastened in spirit. The tendencies of earlier comedy are maintained in the dramatic work of Mrs. Centlivre. The sins of various dramatists of her sex seem to have been visited chiefly upon Mrs. Aphra Behn;[1] but, though Mrs. Centlivre has largely escaped the notoriety of the "chaste Aphra," the character of her drama is without fear rather than without reproach. A certain concession to Collier's charge that "the Stage-Poets make their Principal Personages Vicious, and reward them at the End of the Play," may, perhaps, be detected in the fifth-act repentance which she allows to sinners whose consciences have lain comfortably dormant through the earlier acts. Yet, for the most part, she can be acquitted of any intention "to moral-

---

[1] Cf., as to Aphra Behn, *ante*, Vol. VIII, Chap. v, pp. 159–161.

ise the stage." With considerable skill in dramatic structure and facility in securing comic effect, she was content to achieve theatrical effectiveness with little hesitation as to methods. An early attempt at blank-verse tragedy, *The Perjur'd Husband, or The Adventures of Venice* (1700), proves that her dramatic aptitude did not extend either to verse or to tragedy. Her *forte* lay in cleverness of comic intrigue and fluency of prose dialogue. Her characters often have the salient traits which are within the ready grasp of the actor, while the best of them are more vital comic creations. Marplot, in *The Busy-Body* (1709) and its sequel (1710), *Marplot in Lisbon,*[1] is much more than a copy from Molière's *L'Étourdi;* and Don Felix, in *The Wonder! A Woman Keeps a Secret* (1714), became one of Garrick's most popular parts. From Molière and from Spanish sources, Mrs. Centlivre drew materials freely for various plays; but she deserves credit for ability in adaptation and for the addition of effective original touches. Of her later plays, *A Bold Stroke for a Wife* (1718) was a successful comedy, and *The Artifice* (1722) reflects in some measure the influence of sentimental drama. Mrs. Centlivre serves as a convenient illustration of the fact that comedy had not wholly responded to the movement for its moral improvement; but it is fair to recall, at the same time, that the epilogues appended to some of Young's dramas maintain the restoration practice of enlivening tragedy with coarsely comic epilogues.

Like the current of moral reform, the current of classical influence, which was very strong in queen Anne drama, encountered various obstacles in its course. Some of the early Georgian tragedies of Edward Young (1683–1765)[2] have much of the violent action of Elizabethan drama and the unrestraint, though not the poetic imagination, of Lee's dramatic utterance. It needed but little exaggeration for Fielding to turn the heroics of *Busiris* (1719) to mockery in his burlesque tragedy, *Tom Thumb*. *The Revenge* (1721), in striving to depict "the tumults of a Godlike mind," recalls the heroic drama of the restoration, though Zanga, the Moor, is reminiscent of Othello. Thus, these tragedies of Young seem, in reality, to follow English, rather than strict continental, models. In *The Siege of Da-*

---

[1] The title by which the sequel was later known.
[2] Cf. Chap. VII, *post*.

*mascus* (1720), a tragedy far superior to the mediocre work of Young, John Hughes had turned to an English source in borrowing from D'Avenant's play, *The Siege*.[1] While the ponderous tragedies of James Thompson, to which reference is made elsewhere,[2] lent weight rather than dignity to the cause of classical drama, the rather uneventful course of English tragedy during the second quarter of the eighteenth century was broken by one radical innovation.

In *The London Merchant, or The History of George Barnwell* (1731), George Lillo introduced prose domestic tragedy. Brought up to his father's trade of jeweller in the city of London, Lillo became the dramatist of domestic life. His first theatrical venture was an insignificant ballad-opera, *Silvia, or The Country Burial* (1730). The production at Drury lane theatre, on 22 June, 1731, of *The London Merchant, or The History of George Barnwell*, is, however, an important landmark in English dramatic history. Domestic tragedy, in a sense, was no novelty on the English stage. Elizabethan dramas such as *Arden of Feversham*, *A Yorkshire Tragedy* and *A Woman Killed with Kindness*, forego the usual noble preferences of tragedy. Otway, Southerne and Rowe found that pathos was not dependent upon rank and title. The prologue to Rowe's *Fair Penitent*, indeed, deliberately announces the creed which Lillo followed.[3] Yet the father of the fair Calista is a Genoese nobleman and her lover is a young lord. *Jane Shore* tells the ruin of a woman of lower class; but it is a great noble who compasses her downfall. Otway's *Orphan*, like most of the domestic tragedies that precede Lillo's, seems rather to neglect the aristocratic tone of tragedy than to magnify its democratic character.

With Lillo, domestic tragedy becomes positively and insistently familiar. He deliberately dramatises ordinary commercial life, and teaches the importance of the commonplace. The prologue to *George Barnwell* dwells on the fact that the tragic muse, after moving in the very highest social spheres, has "upon our stage" been sometimes seen, nor without applause,

---

[1] Cf. *ante*, Vol. VIII, p. 220.  [2] Cf. Chap. v, *post*.
[3] See the lines beginning:

> Long has the fate of kings and empires been
> The common bus'ness of the tragick scene.

in a humbler dress—
Great only in distress.   When she complains
In Southern's, Rowe's, or Otway's moving strains,
The brilliant drops that fall from each bright eye
The absent pomp with brighter jems supply.
Forgive us then, if we attempt to show,
In artless strains, a tale of private woe,
A London 'Prentice ruin'd is our theme.


Lillo puts Rowe's earlier creed into aggressive practice.  The atmosphere of *George Barnwell* is that of the trading class, and its ideal the virtue of the merchant's calling.   Thorowgood, the honest merchant, gratifies the "laudable curiosity" of his faithful apprentice, Trueman, as to the political situation,

because from thence you may learn how honest merchants, as such, may sometimes contribute to the safety of their country, as they do at all times to its happiness;  that if hereafter you should be tempted to any action that has the appearance of vice or meanness in it, upon reflecting on the dignity of our profession, you may with honest scorn reject whatever is unworthy of it. . . .  As the name of merchant never degrades the gentleman, so by no means does it exclude him.

Even the rapid downward course of Lillo's erring prentice-hero is interrupted, at the opening of the third act, to allow Thorowgood to continue his instructions to Trueman on the ethics of business and the moral mission of commerce.   Trueman is bidden to observe how trade

has promoted humanity, as it has opened and yet keeps up an intercourse between nations, far remote from one another in situation, customs, and religion;  promoting arts, industry, peace and plenty; by mutual benefits diffusing mutual love from pole to pole.

The merchant's vocation is thus defined:   "It is the industrious merchant's business to collect the various blessings of each soil and climate, and, with the product of the whole, to enrich his native country."   Even when, with something of a sigh, he descends to the routine of the day's work, he delivers such business maxims as, "Method in business is the surest guide."

In conscious moral aim, Lillo is akin to the sentimental dramatists. He seeks deliberately

> thoughtless youth to warn, and shame the age
> From vice destructive.

Thorowgood is "a man of sentiment," and, unlike Joseph Surface, "acts up to the sentiments he professes." From his store of commonplaces, he draws apposite maxims for moral as well as business emergencies—"When innocence is banish'd, modesty soon follows"; "When vice becomes habitual, the very power of leaving it is lost." Maria inherits her father's gift for sentiment. Even when Barnwell yields precipitately to Millwood's seductions, he ejaculates such unavailing precepts as these: "To ease our present anguish, by plunging into guilt, is to buy a moment's pleasure with an age of pain"; "The law of Heaven will not be revers'd; and that requires us to govern our passions." Sentiment attends him even to the gallows. He parts from his mistress with this cold consolation:

From our example may all be taught to fly the first approach of vice; but, if o'ertaken

> By strong temptation, weakness, or surprize,
> Lament their guilt and by repentance rise!
> Th' impenitent alone die unforgiven;
> To sin's like man, and to forgive like Heaven.

In the moralised drama of the eighteenth century, didactic sentiment is not merely the reward of virtue but a very present help in trouble.

The plot of *George Barnwell*, as Lillo says, is "Drawn from the fam'd old song that bears his name." Ballad and play tell alike the story of the ruin of an apprentice by a courtesan. The theme suggests Hogarth's plates[1]—Trueman is the industrious, and Barnwell the idle, apprentice. Lillo ekes out the somewhat meagre materials of the ballad by introducing Maria, Trueman and Millwood's servants, and by expanding the shadowy figure of the merchant into Thorowgood. He presents his hero in a more sympathetic light by shifting to Millwood the responsibility for the suggestion of his uncle's murder,

---

[1] Hogarth's first work of importance, *A Harlot's Progress*, appeared the year after *George Barnwell*.

and by emphasising his "fear and sting of conscience," of which the ballad makes but passing mention.

In portrayal of character, Lillo is often crude and sometimes inconsistent. At the outset, Barnwell, "young, innocent, and bashful," is an unsuspecting innocent, whose response to Millwood's leading question as to his thoughts of love would, in a less sentimental age, stamp him as either a prig or a hypocrite:

If you mean the love of women, I have not thought of it all. My youth and circumstances make such thoughts improper in me yet. But if you mean the general love we owe to mankind, I think no one has more of it in his temper than my self. I don't know that person in the world whose happiness I don't wish, and wou'dn't promote, were it in my power. In an especial manner I love my Uncle, and my Master, but, above all, my friend.

Yet he yields to temptation, almost without resistance; nor can he be defended on the score of innocent ignorance, since the moral aphorisms with which he meets Millwood's advances clearly betray his consciousness of guilt. His morality is but a thin veneer, penetrated at the first touch. Yet, assuredly, this is not the conception of character which Lillo sought to impart. Millwood is a more consistent study in passion and depravity, and became the prototype of more than one powerful dramatic figure.[1]

To Lillo's influence on the subjects of English tragedy must be added his no less marked influence upon its language. He deliberately adopted prose as the vehicle of expression for domestic tragedy. He accepts, indeed, the convention of rime-tags at the end of every act and at the conclusion of some scenes during the act; but his main intent is to give domestic drama the vocabulary and phrase that suit his theme. Judged by modern standards, his attempt to abandon the sublime frequently achieves the ridiculous. So firmly fastened was the habit of verse tragedy that Lillo's dialogue often preserves the inverted phrases and general rhythmic movement, and, at times, the actual scansion, of blank verse.

The martyr cheaply purchases his heaven. Small are his sufferings, great is his reward; not so the wretch who combats love with duty. . . . What is an hour, a day, a year of pain, to a whole life of tortures such as these?

[1] Notably of Marwood in Lessing's *Miss Sara Sampson.*

The habit of ornate description also persists even with the honest merchant: "The populous East, luxuriant abounds with glittering gems, bright pearls, aromatick spices, and health-restoring drugs. The late found Western World glows with unnumber'd veins of gold and silver ore." Most grotesque is the dialogue of the scenes of the uncle's murder. His prophetic soul forebodes evil and his "imagination is fill'd with gashly forms of dreary graves, and bodies chang'd by death." His apostrophe to "Death, thou strange mysterious power—seen every day, yet never understood but by the incommunicative dead"—unnerves the murderer for the moment, and hardly has the deed been perpetrated when Barnwell throws himself on the body of the "expiring saint," his "martyr'd uncle," with an outbreak of inflated rhetoric which expires in moralised heroic couplets. Judged by the modern standards of prose drama that has felt the influence of Ibsen, Lillo's prose is sheer travesty. Yet his was an age accustomed to the artificial rhetoric of sentimental drama, as it was to the "grand manner" in acting. Even so classical a critic as Pope deemed that, if Lillo "had erred through the whole play, it was only in a few places, where he had unawares led himself into a poetical luxuriancy, affecting to be too elevated or the simplicity of the subject."[1] In Lillo's hands, the old shackles of verse tragedy are broken; but cruel marks of the fetters remain visible. Beyond doubt, he sinned greatly; yet much may be forgiven to one who showed, however imperfectly, that serious drama might find expression in prose.

In *The Christian Hero* (1735), Lillo relapses into more conventional tragedy. Prose gives way to blank verse, the London prentice to "a pious hero, and a patriot king," and London to Albania. In *Fatal Curiosity: A True Tragedy of Three Acts*[2] (1736), Lillo retains blank verse, but reverts to domestic tragedy. "From lower life we draw our scene's distress."[3] The elder Colman, in his prologue written for the revival of the play in 1782, proclaimed Lillo's kinship with Shakespeare in disregard of dramatic rules and boldly suggested that

---

[1] *The Lives of the Poets of Great-Britain and Ireland.* By Mr. (Theophilus) Cibber, and other Hands. (1753), vol. v, p. 339.

[2] The original title was *Guilt Its Own Punishment, or Fatal Curiosity.*

[3] Fielding's prologue.

Lillo's plantations were of forest growth,
Shakespear's the same, great Nature's hand in both!

The strong verbal reminiscences of *Macbeth* and *Hamlet* would
seem rather to indicate that Shakespeare's hand was in Lillo's.
The plot itself, based on an old story of a Cornish murder, shows
how old Wilmot, urged by his wife to relieve their poverty, kills
the stranger that is within their gates, only to find that he has
murdered his son, whom "fatal curiosity" has led to conceal his
identity.    In Lillo's play, fatality, not poverty, is the real
motive force.    With something of the Greek conception,
destiny dominates the tragedy.    Old Wilmot, to be sure, expires with the confession that "We brought this dreadful ruin
on ourselves."    But Randal, whose couplets point the conventional moral,

The ripe in virtue never die too soon,

protests against any censure of

Heaven's mysterious ways.

In Lillo's tragedy of destiny, we are not "to take upon 's the
mystery of things, as if we were God's spies."
Lillo's other dramatic works may be dismissed with brief
mention.    *Marina* (1738), a three-act drama, based on *Pericles,
Prince of Tyre*, is additional evidence of Lillo's indebtedness to
Shakespeare.    The brothel-scenes, which tend to abandon
decency as well as blank verse, can hardly be justified by a
conclusion that shows "Virtue preserv'd from fell destruction's
blast."    *Britannia and Batavia*, a rather belated instance of
masque, *Elmerick, or Justice Triumphant*, a regular blank-
verse tragedy which won Fielding's praise, and *Arden of
Feversham*, which gives further evidence of Lillo's interest in
domestic tragedy and of his indebtedness to Elizabethan drama,
were published posthumously.
In the history of English drama, Lillo holds a position wholly
disproportionate to his actual dramatic achievement.    Like
D'Avenant, his importance is chiefly that of a pioneer.    The
modern reader sympathises more readily with Charles Lamb's
familiar strictures upon Lillo than with Fielding's praise.    But,
artificial as his work appears to-day, Lillo set in motion powerful

forces that pointed toward natural tragedy.    He deliberately put aside the dignity of rank and title and the ceremony of verse.    He animated domestic drama, and paved the way for prose melodrama and tragedy.

The influence of Lillo is not to be measured simply in the records of English drama.    On the continent, especially in France and Germany, the effect of his domestic tragedy was striking.    In French drama, this influence may best be observed in Diderot.    From the previous discussion of the rise of sentimental drama and its development on the continent as well as in England, it is evident that French drama had already responded to the influences of sentimental drama before the success of *George Barnwell* moralised *bourgeois* tragedy.    Destouches had admitted a serious undertone in his *Philosophe marié* (1727), and Marivaux, in his *Jeu de l'Amour et du Hasard* (1730), had delicately touched sentiment with pathos.    In the score of years between the English production of *George Barnwell* and the French translation which probably directly influenced Diderot, *drame sérieux* was developing toward *comédie larmoyante*.    Nivelle de la Chaussée bathed virtue in tears, and, in dramatising *Pamela*, had brought the influence of Richardson's novel of sentiment to swell the tide of sentimental drama.    Even Voltaire borrowed from *Pamela* and found praise for *George Barnwell*.

Though the general tendencies of the time should thus be remembered, there is no need to belittle Lillo's direct and powerful influence on Diderot.    Like Voltaire, Diderot's influence on drama was twofold—in actual dramatic production and in dramatic theory.    But Diderot set himself in direct opposition to the classical standards which, despite some inconsistencies, Voltaire maintained.    In *Le Fils Naturel* (printed 1757), and in *Le Père de Famille* (printed 1758), with the critical discourses that accompany them, Diderot set forth the type of drama which he sought to introduce into France.    His very term, *tragédie domestique et bourgeoise*, suggests the nature of Lillo's influence upon him.    Diderot carried his enthusiasm for *George Barnwell* to the point of comparing the prison scene between Barnwell and Maria with the *Philoctetes* of Sophocles.    He followed his English master in the choice of characters drawn from ordinary life, in the moralisation of tragedy and in the use of prose. Diderot, in fact, carried his belief in prose into more consistent practice than did Lillo. In his treatise *De la Poésie Dramatique*, he expresses the conviction that domestic tragedy should not be written in verse, though, doubtless, it is French verse that he has in mind rather than the English blank verse to which Lillo himself reverted in *Fatal Curiosity*. The length of time before Diderot's plays were put on the stage, and their rather indifferent reception by the public,[1] suggest that his own dramatic accomplishment was less significant than his influence upon dramatists like Sedaine and Lessing.

Largely through Diderot, Lillo's influence was extended to German drama. Lessing's translations of Diderot's plays and his critical interpretations of his dramatic theories fell on favourable soil in Germany. Lessing's own domestic tragedy, *Miss Sara Sampson* (1755), which dissolved its audience in tears, has the general tone of Lillo's drama. To the influence of *George Barnwell* upon German domestic tragedy (*bürgerliches Trauerspiel*) should be added that of *Fatal Curiosity* upon the German tragedy of destiny (*Schicksalstragödie*). During the last two decades of the eighteenth century, versions of *Fatal Curiosity* appeared in German, its actual theme was taken for a brief play by Werner (1812), and other examples of the "tragedy of destiny" were borne along on the passing wave of popularity.[2]

Though the effect of Lillo's dramas was far-reaching and persistent, it must not be supposed that his *bourgeois* tragedy thereafter dominated the English stage. Occasional plays, like Charles Johnson's *Caelia, or The Perjured Lover* (1732), reflect Lillo's influence. But, year after year, the English stage continued to produce a remarkable variety of theatrical productions, from classical tragedy to nondescript farce. Not until the days of Edward Moore did Lillo find a conspicuous follower. Moore, like Lillo and Gay, was an apprentice turned playwright. The mob of gentlemen who wrote with ease, in days when playwriting was more in fashion, had noticeably, like the old drama itself, given way to a less high-born school. Moore's early comedy, *The Foundling* (1748), has some suggestion of Steele's

---

[1] *Le Fils Naturel*, publicly produced in 1771, failed. *Le Père de Famille* had found moderate favour on the Parisian stage in 1761.

[2] For further details, see the study of Lillo's work and its influence in Ward's, A. W., edition of *The London Merchant* and *Fatal Curiosity* (Belles Lettres Series).

last sentimental comedy, while *Gil Blas* (1751) darkens the comic action with a tragic underplot.   But Moore's tragic and moral bent unite most clearly and forcibly in *The Gamester* (1753).

In *The Gamester*, prose domestic tragedy again prevails. Moore dramatises a new commandment—"Thou shalt not gamble."   To the playful hits of Pope and the more vigorous attacks of Addison upon gambling, Moore gave tragic intensity. The very singleness of his purpose gives unity to his drama. Without remarkable dramatic skill, he conceived his framework on large lines, and, in many ways, executed it impressively. He stoops, at times, to melodrama, in the use of surprise; but, like Lillo, he shows dramatic restraint in not permitting Mrs. Beverley to expire on her husband's corpse.   His failure to introduce his hero in the actual setting of the gaming-house seems, however, a needless sacrifice of a situation that would have strengthened at least the acting possibilities of the drama. Moore's prose, despite obvious evidences of unnaturalness, marks an advance over Lillo's.   Yet the later writer's own confession,[1] that in scenes of elevated passion, it was harder to refrain from verse than to produce it, helps to explain Lillo's inflated diction.   Diderot coupled *The Gamester* and *The Merchant of London* as instances of English tragedies in prose, and Saurin's vein in *Béverlei* (1768) is further evidence of Moore's influence on the continental drama.

While Lillo and Moore were thus enlarging the field of tragedy by extending it to the concerns of ordinary life and developing, however crudely, a new medium of prose expression, the influence of Voltaire was being exerted in behalf of classical standards.   In 1726, he began a residence of almost three years in England which brought him into contact with English drama. *Cato* he regarded as a masterpiece of classical tragedy.   Yet, like Addison, he confessed, once, at least, that creative energy such as Shakespeare's "leaves far behind it everything which can boast only of reason and correctness."[2] The greater freedom and vigour of action of the English stage clearly affect both Voltaire's classical dramatic standards and his own dramatic practice.   In a letter of 1735, he declares that French drama "is ordinarily devoid of

---

[1] See *Introduction* to *The Gamester*.

[2] Quoted by Lounsbury, T. R., *Shakespeare and Voltaire*, p. 52.

action and of great interests," and, in another of 1750, full of
his usual strictures on the barbarities of English tragedy, he
concedes that "'t is true we have too much of words, if you
have too much of action, and perhaps the perfection of the art
should consist in a due mixture of the French taste and the
English energy."[1]  His own dramas borrow from Shakespeare
with a freedom that impressed even those who translated and
adapted Voltaire's plays for the English stage.   In the prologue to Aaron Hill's *Zara* (1736), a version of Voltaire's *Zaire*,
Colley Cibber says plainly:

> From English plays, *Zara's* French author fired,
> Confessed his muse, beyond himself, inspired;
> From rack'd Othello's rage he raised his style,
> And snatched the brand that lights his tragic pile.

The prologue to James Miller's version of *Mahomet* (1744) is
equally frank:

> Britons, these numbers to yourselves you owe;
> Voltaire hath strength to shoot in Shakespeare's bow.

The monstrosities which Voltaire took pains to point out in
Shakespeare's tragedies did not prevent him from borrowing
from such dramas as *Othello*, *Julius Caesar*, *Hamlet*, *Macbeth*
and *King Lear* far more than he troubled himself to acknowledge.   Nor did his borrowings from Shakespeare measure his
indebtedness to English drama.   William Duncombe's adaptation of *Brutus* (1734), which begins the long list of English
stage versions of Voltaire, brought upon the French dramatist
the charge of plagiarism from Lee's restoration tragedy, *Brutus*.
Voltaire's influence upon English drama is, accordingly,
not that of an uncompromising continental classicist.   In the
main, he supported the cause of classical drama; but it is wholly
misleading to ignore the strength of the counter influences of
English drama upon him.   Criticism, likewise, has frequently
exaggerated the influence of Voltaire's dramas on the English
stage.   Of the various versions of Voltaire that appeared during
the second quarter of the eighteenth century, which include,
besides those already mentioned, Hill's *Alzira* (1736) and
*Merope* (1749), the most successful was the same writer's *Zara*.

[1] Quoted by Lounsbury, T. R., *Shakespeare and Voltaire*, pp. 71, 138.

Yet its continuous run of fourteen nights was an exceptional success. The early recognition of Voltaire's large indebtedness to Shakespeare helps to explain why he failed to supplant the native genius from whom he borrowed. Performances of Shakespearean drama far outnumbered those of English versions of Voltaire's plays. The succession of critical editions of Shakespeare, beginning with that of Rowe (1709),[1] increased Shakespeare's influence with readers. David Garrick powerfully advanced his popularity with playgoers. The tide of patriotic feeling rose in increasing resentment against Voltaire's strictures on English drama. Even Aaron Hill, the zealous adapter of Voltaire, in the preface to *Merope*, asserts that

so much over-active sensibility to his own country's claims, with so unfeeling a stupidity in judging the pretensions of his neighbors might absolve all indignation short of gross indecency towards one who has not scrupled . . . to represent the English as incapable of tragedy; nay, even of painting or of music.

The plain speech of Voltaire's English sympathisers became violent invective, when Foote, in 1747, denounced him as "that insolent French panegyrist who first denies Shakespeare almost every dramatic excellence, and then, in his next play, pilfers from him almost every capital scene," and pictured him in his dual *rôle* of critic and dramatist as "the carping, superficial critic and the low, paltry thief."[2] Such bursts represent the extreme of patriotic ire rather than the mean of ordinary criticism; yet there is abundant evidence that the mid-eighteenth century stage which acclaimed Garrick's Shakespearean productions was in little danger of blind allegiance to a continental authority.

Even before the deference at first accorded to Voltaire had perceptibly abated, classical drama did not hold the English stage unchallenged. Lillo's bold innovations threatened its prestige, and pantomime its popularity. The vein of dramatic burlesque struck by Gay in *What-d'ye-Call-it* and *The Beggar's Opera* was developed by Fielding and Carey. In *Tom Thumb; A Tragedy* (1730), afterwards called *The Tragedy of Tragedies; or, The Life and Death of Tom Thumb the Great* (1731), Fielding

---

[1] Cf. *ante*, Vol. V, pp. 298 ff.      [2] Cf. Lounsbury, *u.s.*, pp. 148-9.

(of whose comedies something has been said in an earlier chapter)[1] ridiculed the absurdities of contemporary drama, and,
in his later mock critical and explanatory notes, satirised the
theories of Corneille and such tragedies as *Cato*, *Busiris* and
Fenton's popular *Mariamne* (1723). The coarser burlesque
of Fielding's *Covent Garden Tragedy* (1733) is directed, in part,
against Philips's *Distrest Mother*. The spirit of *Tom Thumb*
is maintained in Henry Carey's *Chrononhotonthologos, the Most
Tragical Tragedy that ever was Tragediz'd by any Company
of Tragedians* (1737), and, less effectively, in his burlesque
opera, *The Dragon of Wantley* (1734), which displays, in the
words of its dedication, "the beauty of nonsense, so prevailing
in Italian opera."[2] While Fielding and Carey thus out-Heroded
Herod, they, too, were on the side of sanity in English drama.
*Tom Thumb* is the ironic expression of that revolt against conventional English tragedy which Fielding phrased seriously
in his prologue to Lillo's *Fatal Curiosity*:

> No fustian Hero rages here to-night;
> No armies fall, to fix a tyrant's right.

To the negative effect of burlesque, Fielding added a positive influence against the accepted dramatic conventions by
devoting a large share of his energies to the composition of
short dramatic pieces. Though some of his plays accept the
five-act formula, most of them do not exceed three acts. The
production of brief dramatic pieces by Samuel Foote and other
followers of Fielding is intimately connected with the eighteenth
century fashion of appending to regular drama an after-piece,
usually farce or pantomime. The ultimate effects of this
practice may be illustrated by the fact that Sheridan's *Critic*
was produced, originally, as an after-piece to *Hamlet*.

In still another way, Fielding shook the conventions of
formal drama. Improving on Gay's "local hits" at politicians
of the day, Fielding carried personal allusion and innuendo to
daring extremes. *Pasquin* (1736) is "a dramatick Satire on
the Times," and *The Historical Register for* 1736 (acted 1737)
overruns with political, theatrical and social satire. Fielding's
bold political references were largely responsible for the licens-

---

[1] Cf. *ante*, Chap. II, pp. 23–25.     [2] Cf. *ante*, Vol. IX, Chap. VI, p. 212.

ing act of 1737, which limited the metropolitan theatres to two, and brought plays, prologues and epilogues under direct legal supervision.  Though Sir John Barnard, in March, 1735, had interested himself, in the House of Commons, in the question of restricting the theatres, and, though the immediate stimulus to the licensing act is usually held to have been an abusive piece, called *The Golden Rump*, there is little reason to doubt that Walpole recognised in Fielding his most dangerous foe. The licensing act restricted Fielding's lawless freedom; already, however, he had set in motion forces which the censorship of the stage might in part check, but could not wholly control.  Essentially the playwright of his own day, Fielding influenced drama in the direction of themes of contemporary life.  Even Lillo, who set his face against a social restriction of the sphere of tragedy, passively conceded the historic background in giving, nominally, at least, an Elizabethan setting to *George Barnwell*, in assigning *Fatal Curiosity* to the reign of James I and in choosing *Arden of Feversham* as the theme of "an historical tragedy." Fielding's actual dramatic works resembled cartoons rather than finished works of comic art.  Yet, his burlesque of conventional drama, his development of short dramatic pieces that challenged the authority of the five-act formula and his attention to the subjects and personages of contemporary life, powerfully combined towards enlarging the freedom and advancing the naturalness of dramatic expression.

The transfer of Fielding's literary activity from drama to novel suggests another potent factor in the decline of the drama. To the forces of Italian opera, pantomime, burlesque, balladopera, farce and spectacle, whose constant inroads had grievously thinned the ranks of regular drama, was now added a more dangerous, if more subtle, rival off the boards.  *Robinson Crusoe* (1719–20) and *Gulliver's Travels* (1726–7) had already fired the fancy of English readers.  With Richardson's *Pamela* (1740), the English novel began its great period of literary dominance.[1]  It is not an accidental coincidence that the middle of the eighteenth century is marked by poverty in dramatic composition as well as by the strenuous advance of the novel. Nevertheless, two powerful forces helped to sustain the vitality of the theatre.  Provided with a strong repertory of stock

[1] Cf. *ante*, Chap. I

plays, the genius of actors was able to triumph even over the mediocrity of contemporary drama. It was the age of the player, not of the playwright. The period of which we speak is the era of Garrick.

The record of David Garrick belongs, primarily, to theatrical annals. Yet his own dramatic work, his Shakespearean revivals and the influence of his natural method of acting, which indirectly affected the artificiality of the drama itself, while directly opposing the old school of acting, entitle him to a place in English dramatic history. His mythological skit *Lethe* (1740) gained a place on the boards in the year before its author's histrionic triumph as Richard III. Reynolds's picture showing Garrick torn between the rival muses of tragedy and comedy suggests his range and versatility both as actor and as manager. He produced on the stage more than a score of Shakespeare's dramas, and himself appeared in the great majority of them. He was the dominant factor in confirming Shakespeare's popularity with audiences in the middle of the eighteenth century. Yet his service consisted rather in accelerating the popular current than in setting it in motion. Rich's noteworthy Shakespearean revivals, in 1738, which included many long unacted plays, Macklin's famous triumph as Shylock and the Drury lane productions of Shakespearean comedies, in 1740–1, are but instances of increasing interest in Shakespearean performances before Garrick's advent. Furthermore, though Garrick's influence, in the main, was salutary, his versions of Shakespeare were, at times, unfaithful both to the original text and to its spirit. Early in 1756, he produced, within a month, alterations of three Shakespearean dramas, excising most of the first three acts of *The Winter's Tale*, despite the protestation of the prologue,

> 'T is my chief Wish, my Joy, my only Plan,
> To lose no Drop of that immortal Man!

Theophilus Cibber indignantly demanded, "Were Shakespeare's ghost to rise, would he not frown indignation on this pilfering pedlar in poetry—who thus shamefully mangles, mutilates, and emasculates his plays?"[1] Though sweeping generalisations as to Garrick's fidelity to his original are thus disproved by

[1] Genest, *Some Account of the English Stage*, vol. IV, p. 452.

actual facts, his services to Shakespearean drama must not be rated beneath their real value. It was in his hand to set the fashion, and he set it beyond dispute. His own masterly acting of Shakespearean characters far outweighs the infelicities, and occasional outrages, of his acting texts.

The popularity of Shakespeare during the Garrick era did not, however, lead to general adoption of Elizabethan models by playwrights of the period. Adaptations like Garrick's *Gamesters* (1757), altered from Shirley's *Gamester*, seem somewhat accidental. Otway, Southerne and Rowe were greater favourites on the stage than any Elizabethan writer of tragedy save Shakespeare. In *The Earl of Essex* (1753), Henry Jones worked over again the theme of one of John Banks's quasi-heroic English dramas; but tragedies such as Johnson's *Irene* (1749) follow stricter classical models. The classical cause, indeed, may be said to have received a new impetus of some importance in William Whitehead's successful version of *Horace* in *The Roman Father* (1750). The wave of influence from Philips's *Distrest Mother*, which had led to more than a dozen translations of plays by Thomas and Pierre Corneille and Racine within a dozen years, seems to have subsided with William Hatchett's *Rival Father* (1730). Whitehead's success revived the interest that had lain dormant for a score of years. *The Roman Father* remained a stock play throughout the rest of the century, and, doubtless, was the chief stimulus to some eight or ten other translations from French classical drama during that period. In *Creusa, Queen of Athens* (1754), Whitehead continued to work the vein of classical tragedy; but *The School for Lovers* (1762) is an excursion into the realm of comedy. The latter is not without some comic energy, but Sir John Dorilant, "a Man of nice Honour," and Caelia, who justifies the complaint that she talks at times "like a sentimental lady in a comedy," have a "nicety of sentiments" which brings them dangerously close to the pitfalls of sentimental drama.

Despite vigorous attacks upon his critical authority, Voltaire maintained, during the third quarter of the eighteenth century, some hold on the English stage. Of English versions of his plays the most successful was Arthur Murphy's *Orphan of China* (1759). *Orestes* (1768), *Almida* and *Zobeide* (1771) and *Semiramis* (1776) adapt other tragedies of Voltaire, while some of his comedies had an English rendering, as in Murphy's *No One's Enemy but his Own* (1764) and Colman's *English Merchant* (1767).[1]  *Merope* was, occasionally, revived at Drury lane and seems to have inspired Hoole's *Cyrus* (1768). Yet, even the most successful of these pieces could not outrun several tragedies by English playwrights of the period or rival in popularity Shakespearean plays.   Voltaire's influence still counted strongly in maintaining the belief that Shakespeare was not a great dramatic artist; but it could not successfully challenge his actual triumph on the boards.

In contrast to many conventional dramas of the period, Home's *Douglas* (first acted at Edinburgh in 1756, and in London in 1757) strikes a distinct romantic note.   In the desert of Scottish drama, *Douglas* was an oasis, and, to some patriotic enthusiasts, its author seemed a Scottish Shakespeare.   The philosopher Hume ascribed to his friend Home "the true theatric genius of Shakespeare and Otway, refined from the unhappy barbarism of the one and licentiousness of the other." Even Gray, in August, 1757, wrote to Walpole: "The author seems to me to have retrieved the true language of the stage, which has been lost for these 100 years."   Age has withered *Douglas*, and custom staled the declamation of Young Norval. Yet the plot of Home's drama, based on an old Scots ballad, its native background, and its atmosphere of brooding melancholy, invest it with something of the romantic atmosphere of his friend Collins.   A succession of later tragedies showed that Home was unable to repeat his first theatrical success; but Sheridan's palpable hits in *The Critic* are incidental proof of the continued stage popularity of *Douglas*.

The general poverty of original English drama in the middle of the eighteenth century is apparent in comedy as well as in tragedy.   Benjamin[2] Hoadly's popular comedy *The Suspicious Husband* (1747), which gave to Garrick a most successful part in Ranger, has something of the comic power of earlier drama. But, for the most part, sentimental drama had so constrained formal comedy, that laughter sought free outlet in the larger licence of farce, burlesque and spectacle.   Among multifarious theatrical entertainments, attention must be directed to the efforts of Samuel Foote.   Early appearances as an actor showed

[1] Founded, respectively, on *L'Indiscret* and *L'Écossaise*.
[2] His brother John is supposed to have assisted him.

that his *forte* lay in comic mimicry.   In April, 1747, he established himself at the Little theatre in the Haymarket, evading the licensing act by announcing "a Concert of Musick," or "an Auction of Pictures," or inviting his friends to drink a "dish of Chocolate" or a "dish of Tea" with him.   Thus, for two seasons, Foote found pretexts for mimicry and caricature of Garrick, Mrs. Woffington and other familiar figures of the day. Though he found little trouble in evading the law, he was fortified with a patent in 1766.   The grant, though covering only performances during the summer season and limited to his own lifetime, in reality created a third patent theatre.

Foote's career as playwright coincides almost exactly with Garrick's managership at Drury lane (1747–76).   He was a direct descendant of Fielding, fully developing personal satire through the medium of brief dramatic sketches.   Of about a score of printed dramatic pieces, none exceeds three acts.   With Foote, as with Fielding, most of the zest of his "local hits" is now lost.   Taylor the quack oculist, the extortioner Mrs. Grieve, chaplain Jackson and many other once familiar personages whom he boldly caricatured are now shadowy or forgotten figures.[1]   Foote's characters often have animation and theatrical effectiveness; but they are not developed in action. Though his pieces are usually printed as comedies, they mainly belong to the realm of farce.   Like his own art as an actor, they tend to substitute mimicry for original delineation of character.

The zest of Foote's farces, without their personal bitterness, is seen in various contemporary after-pieces.   Garrick produced a number of lively farces, such as *The Lying Valet* (1741), *Miss in her Teens* (1747), *The Irish Widow* (1772) and *Bon Ton* (1775). James Townley's *High Life below Stairs* (1759) proved a welcome variety to those who, like George Selwyn, were tired of "*low* life above stairs," and it long maintained its popularity.

Of the playwrights of the Garrick era, Arthur Murphy may serve as a type of prolific industry.   His dramatic efforts include farces, like *The Upholsterer* (1758), in the general vein of Fielding's political satire; adaptations from Voltaire; comedies,

---

[1] The satire against Whitefield and his methodist followers in *The Minor* (1760) and that against the suitors of Elizabeth Linley before her romantic marriage to Richard Brinsley Sheridan in *The Maid of Bath* (1771), have a personal interest.

often, like *All in the Wrong* (1761) and *The School for Guardians*, based on Molière; and tragedies such as *Zenobia* (1768) and *The Grecian Daughter* (1772). Without enough originality to channel out his own way, he drifted easily with the tide, appropriating whatever came within easy reach. His comedy has the usual didactic note, schooling wives in the way to keep their husbands,[1] and husbands in the lesson that constancy should not be shamefaced. His tragedy preserves the conventional cast, and *The Grecian Daughter* owes its place in theatrical traditions largely to Mrs. Siddons. Yet, Murphy had the cleverness required for fashioning successful acting plays, and to some ingenuity added much industry.

Another popular Irish playwright of the day was Isaac Bickerstaff. His facile pen turned most successfully to opera *libretti*. With much of Murphy's ability in adaptation and sense of theatrical effectiveness, he blended materials from such divergent sources as Charles Johnson, Wycherley and Marivaux into his successful comic opera, *Love in a Village* (1762), and found in Richardson's *Pamela* the basis for his popular *Maid of the Mill* (1765). In 1768, he scored two popular hits at Drury lane by his "musical entertainment," *Padlock*, and by his version of Cibber's *Non-Juror*, and produced successfully at Covent garden (1768) *Lionel and Clarissa* (published anonymously in 1768).[2] To many of his operatic works, Charles Dibdin, later a prolific playwright, supplied much of the music.

A more important dramatist than either Murphy or Bickerstaff was George Colman the elder, who, amidst prevalent sentimentality, maintained something of the earlier and more genuine comic spirit. *Polly Honeycombe* (1760), his first dramatic venture, produced anonymously in deference to his uncle's dislike of his dramatic aspirations, became a popular after-piece. In its satirical thrusts at the sentimental school, it anticipates Sheridan's *Rivals*. The opening scene between Polly and her nurse suggests Lydia Languish's discussion with Lucy of the sentimental novels of the circulating library, and enforces the satirical hits of Colman's prologue at the sentimental novel. Polly and Lydia Languish are alike familiar

[1] *The Way to keep him* (1760).
[2] It was reprinted, in 1773, with the title *A School for Fathers*.

with "ladders of ropes" and other accessories of sentimental elopements. A decade and a half before Sheridan, Colman turned the laugh against "The goddess of the woful countenance—The Sentimental Muse."

It is not surprising that Colman, who made the sentimental novel a target for satire, turned to Fielding's *Tom Jones* for the ground-work of a genuine comedy. *The Jealous Wife* (1761) is conspicuous as an early example of successful dramatisation of a popular novel. Tom Jones, Sophia, Lady Bellaston, Lord Fellmar, squire Western and Blifil become respectively Charles Oakly, Harriot, Lady Freelove, Lord Trinket, Russet and Beagle. Yet, Colman is more than a copyist. He introduces new characters in Mr. and Mrs. Oakly, and effectively transfers to Beagle squire Western's sporting instincts. Furthermore, in welding his material into effective drama, he "took some hints from *The Spectator*, a suggestion from The Adelphi of Terrence"[1] and advice from Garrick. The dramatic structure shows skill in developing action through effective stage-situations, while Harriot's flight to Oakly's house, which arouses the suspicions of the jealous wife, firmly links the two plots. The solution is kept somewhat in suspense; but, finally, with a belated touch of Petruchio's manner in taming his shrew, Oakly breaks his wife's spirit.

Though the tide of sentimental drama was yet to reach its height in Hugh Kelly and Cumberland, *The Jealous Wife* has some foreshadowings of Sheridan's comic masterpieces. It inherits something of the spirit, without the gross immorality, of restoration comedy. The restoration contempt for the country and the exaltation of good manners at the expense of good morals reappear in Lady Freelove and Lord Trinket, as they do in Lady Teazle and her scandal school. Lord Trinket's French phrases have the familiar Gallic affectation; Lady Freelove, in action as in name, recalls a stock restoration character; and Sir Harry Beagle's rough-and-ready love-making somewhat resembles that of sailor Ben in Congreve's *Love for Love*, with the lingo of the stable replacing that of the sea.[2] Charles Oakly, with his easy morals, is an earlier instance of

---

[1] Advertisement to *The Jealous Wife*.

[2] Compare *The Jealous Wife*, act IV, scene 2, with *Love for Love*, act III, scene 3.

a type more familiar in Charles Surface. Captain O'Cutter, with his readiness for a duel without inquiry as to its cause, suggests the Irish ancestry of Sir Lucius O'Trigger. Though without Sheridan's brilliant wit and masterly dramatic skill, Colman fashioned the rough materials of drama into really popular comedy.

During the next two years, he produced successfully two after-pieces, *The Musical Lady* and *The Deuce is in Him*, and a revision of *Philaster*. With the collaboration of Garrick, he rose again to genuine comedy in *The Clandestine Marriage* (1766). Taking a hint from one of Hogarth's plates in his *Marriage-à-la-Mode*, and animating, at least, some characters said to have been drawn from Townley's *False Concord*, Colman and Garrick produced a highly effective comedy. Lord Ogleby, a late connection of the Fopling Flutters and Foppingtons of restoration comedy, is a distinct character creation. In the illiterate Mrs. Heidelberg, some have sought the original of Mrs. Malaprop, but there is a decided difference between her blunders in pronunciation and Mrs. Malaprop's "select words so ingeniously mis*applied*, without being mis*pronounced*."

After *The Clandestine Marriage*, Colman's theatrical record continues for more than a score of years, but without any notable contribution to original drama. During the seven years of his management of Covent garden theatre (1767–74), he produced various minor pieces of his own composition, ranging from comedy to operetta. The credit attaching to his Shakespearean revivals is lessened by his retention of a happy ending for *King Lear*, and the honour of having produced *The Good-Natur'd Man* and *She Stoops to Conquer* is clouded by the obstacles which he allowed to obstruct Goldsmith's path.[1] Yet, as a member of the Literary club, as a successful dramatist and manager, translator of Terence's comedies, editor of the dramatic works of Beaumont and Fletcher and writer of prologues and epilogues—among them the epilogue to *The School for Scandal*—the elder Colman was a noteworthy figure in the theatrical and literary world of the latter half of the century.

The success of occasional comedies like *The Jealous Wife* and *The Clandestine Marriage* did not, for the time being, seri-

[1] Cf. Chap. IX, *post*.

ously check the popularity of sentimental drama. Six days
before Goldsmith's *Good-Natur'd Man* finally achieved its belated production at Covent garden, Garrick triumphantly produced at Drury lane Hugh Kelly's *False Delicacy* (1768). It
was the clash between sentimental comedy and an upstart rival,
and for the moment victory rested with the established favourite. In contrast with the moderate favour accorded to Goldsmith's piece, *False Delicacy* won a theatrical triumph. Three
thousand copies of it sold in a day, it was translated into several
languages and was acted with applause at Lisbon and Paris.
*False Delicacy* is full of the wise saws and "modern instances"
of sentimental comedy. One of its phrases, indeed, may be
taken, not merely as Kelly's own motto, but as the creed of
sentimental drama—"The stage should be a school of morality." Two characters, Mrs. Harley and Cecil, afford some comic
relief to the usual didactic banalities of the dialogue. Yet the
"elevated minds" of the chief personages continue to deal in
"delicate absurdities" and to emit moral platitudes until the
final fall of the curtain.

Kelly's next comedy, *A Word to the Wise* (1770), despite its
sentimental appeal, was refused a fair hearing by his political
opponents and was driven off the stage. *Clementina* (1771),
a dull tragedy, was followed by a happier return to comedy,
*A School for Wives* (1773), which achieved five editions within
two years, and had various stage revivals during the next forty
years. The failure of a later comedy, *The Man of Reason*,
marked the close of Kelly's theatrical efforts. With Kelly,
as with Richard Cumberland, dramatic probability is sacrificed
on the altar of sentiment.

The development of English drama during the period
reviewed in the present chapter is too varied and complex to
admit of being summarised in a narrow formula. Yet, despite
the diversity of counter currents, the stream of sentimental
drama runs strong from Steele to Hugh Kelly and Richard
Cumberland. Pantomime, ballad-opera, burlesque and farce
often oppose its progress. The current of tragedy frequently
flows from classical or Elizabethan sources. The breadth of
the restoration spirit still, at times, ripples the placid waters of
formal comedy. Yet, moralised tragedy and moralised comedy
contribute alike to the stream of sentimental drama. Even

Lillo and Moore, who sturdily stemmed the tide of conventional tragedy, were submerged in the waves of sentiment, and *The Jealous Wife* and *The Clandestine Marriage* did not prevent the course of sentimental comedy from running smooth in Kelly's *False Delicacy* and Cumberland's *West Indian*. Nevertheless, the undercurrent of reaction was gathering strength. To the satirical attacks of burlesque upon sentimental drama, Fielding had added his description in *Tom Jones*[1] of that "very grave and solemn entertainment, without any low wit, or humour, or jests," in which there was not "anything which could provoke a laugh." Goldsmith, who dared to challenge[2] the authority of the epithet "low" with which critics were wont to stigmatise comedy which was not "genteel," and who learned the power of that "single monosyllable" from the excision of his own bailiffs' scene in *The Good Natur'd Man*, was not to be daunted in his attack upon "this species of bastard tragedy" called sentimental drama. In his *Essay on the Theatre; or, A Comparison between Laughing and Sentimental Comedy*,[3] he put the pertinent query: "Which deserves the preference,—the weeping sentimental comedy so much in fashion at present, or the laughing, and even low comedy, which seems to have been last exhibited by Vanbrugh and Cibber?" The answer was given in the comedies of Goldsmith and of Sheridan.

[1] Description of the puppet-show, *The Provoked Husband*, bk. XII, chap. V.
[2] *The Present State of Polite Learning*, ed. 1759, p. 154.
[3] *The Westminster Magazine*, December, 1772.

## CHAPTER V

# Thomson and Natural Description in Poetry

IN a general estimate of the poetry of the earlier half of the eighteenth century, Thomson's work, from the exceptional character of its subject, may, perhaps, be apt to receive undue prominence.  It called attention to a field of verse which his contemporaries, absorbed in the study of man, in ethical reflection and moral satire, had ceased to cultivate; it looked back with admiration to models which were almost forgotten, and, through its influence on the poetry of Collins and Gray, it lent impulse to the progress which was to culminate in the romantic movement.  On the other hand, Thomson was not the champion of an opposition or the apostle of a new order, contending against prejudices and destroying barriers.  In essential qualities of thought, he was at one with the taste of his day; and, if his talent was most happily exercised in the observation and delineation of nature, his point of view was the very antithesis of that emotional treatment of the subject which marked the ultimate revolt against the limitations of eighteenth century convention.

James Thomson was born at Ednam in Roxburghshire, where his father was parish minister, in September, 1700.  In the following year, his father obtained the cure of Southdean, at the head of the Jed valley, and here Thomson spent his boyhood.  For some time, he went to school in the abbey church of Jedburgh, and, in 1715, he entered Edinburgh university, intending, as it seems, to become a presbyterian minister.  His early surroundings could hardly fail to disclose to him the natural charms of a district which, seventy years later, kindled the romantic imagination of Scott; and they duly received Thomson's tribute when he wrote

> The *Tweed* (pure *Parent-stream*,
> Whose pastoral banks first heard my *Doric* reed,
> With, silvan *Jed*, thy tributary brook).[1]

In these early experiments, which show little promise, he was encouraged by a neighbour, Robert Riccaltoun, the author of a poem called *Winter*. At Edinburgh, Thomson's talents developed, and, after coming to London in 1725, he had his own *Winter* ready for publication in March, 1726. About this time, he gave up all intention of a clerical career, and devoted himself to poetry, earning a stipend as tutor in various noble families. His friend David Mallet was tutor in the household of the duke of Montrose; and it was, probably, through him that Thomson obtained introductions which brought him into the society of possible patrons of his verse. He spared no pains to make himself agreeable to the kindly disposed Aaron Hill; and the prose dedications of the first three *Seasons*, which were fortunately cancelled in later editions in favour of lines inserted in the poem, are remarkable examples of the effusiveness of bad taste. *Winter* soon reached a second edition. Sir Spencer Compton, to whom it was inscribed, showed a tardy gratitude for the compliment; but George Bubb Dodington, the patron of *Summer* (1727), proved a more useful friend. Thomson visited Dodington's seat, Eastbury park, near Blandford; and the acquaintance thus formed probably led to his friendship with George Lyttelton and to his adhesion to the political party which supported the prince of Wales. *Britannia* (1729) eulogised the prince and condemned Walpole's policy. In the printed copies, this monologue is said to have been written in 1727. In that year, Thomson dedicted his *Poem sacred to the Memory of Sir Isaac Newton* to Walpole himself. The sincerity of the patriotism which was laboriously expressed in *Liberty* cannot be doubted; but the patronage of Walpole, had it rewarded Thomson's advances, might have curbed his enthusiasm for an aggressive policy.

Meanwhile, *Spring*, inscribed to Frances countess of Hertford, appeared in 1728. *Autumn*, dedicated to Arthur Onslow,

---

[1] *The Seasons, Autumn,* ll. 913-15.

speaker of the House of Commons, completed the collected edition, under the title of *The Seasons*, in 1730. Thomson began his career as a dramatist with *Sophonisba* (1729). Of his plays, more will be said later: they have a special historical interest, in that, for the most part, their choice of subject and outspoken treatment were directed against the court party on behalf of the prince. In 1730, he went abroad as travelling tutor to a son of Sir Charles Talbot, solicitor-general and, afterwards, lord chancellor. He complained that the muse did not cross the channel with him, and his ambitious poem *Liberty* (1734–6), in which there are some touches due to his foreign tour, confirms the accuracy of his judgment. Thrown out of employment by the death of his pupil in 1733, he received from Talbot the sinecure secretaryship of briefs in chancery. He could afford, on the failure of *Liberty*, to cancel generously his bargain with the publisher, and, in 1736, to retire to a small house at Richmond, where he was able to enjoy the society of Pope and other friends. In these circumstances, he made a thorough revision of *The Seasons*, the fruits of which are seen in the transformed text of 1744. A copy of the 1738 edition in the British museum proves that he sought and took the advice of a friend whose poetical skill was considerable; but whether this helper, as has been assumed, was Pope or another, is a question upon which experts in handwriting differ. The new text, while omitting a certain amount which may be regretted, bears testimony to a judicious pruning of florid diction; and passages hitherto enervated by excess of colour gained in vigour what they lost in diffuseness. The poem, however, was lengthened by the insertion of new matter, much of which increased its general value. One personal feature of these additions is the introduction of references to Amanda, the subject, also, of the graceful lyric "Unless with my Amanda blest." Too much may be made of attachments expressed in verse; but there is no doubt of Thomson's genuine affection for Elizabeth Young, a sister-in-law of his friend Robertson, and this fact may be set against one side of the charge of sensuality imputed to him by Johnson, probably on the untrustworthy information of Savage. *The Castle of Indolence*, published in May, 1748, after a long period of elaborate revision, may stand as the personal confession of a poet whose industry was not proof against his love of ease and luxury.    Thomson's later days were not without reverses of fortune.    The story of his arrest for debt and delivery from the spunging-house by Quin the actor may be a legend; but he lost his sinecure after Talbot's death in 1737, through negligence (so it is said) in applying for its renewal.    Through the instrumentality of Lyttelton, who was one of the lords of the treasury, he obtained the surveyorship-general of the Leeward islands, a sinecure well suited to a poet who had often surveyed the phenomena of nature from the pole to the tropics in his easy chair.    A pension from the prince of Wales, who had received the dedication of *Liberty* and about 1737 heard from Thomson that his affairs were "in a more poetical posture than formerly," was stopped when Lyttelton fell into disgrace with the prince.    This was not long before Thomson's death.    One evening in the summer of 1748, after a journey by boat from Hammersmith to Richmond, he was attacked by a chill.    A short recovery was followed by a relapse, and he died on 27 August.    His tragedy *Coriolanus* was produced during the next year: the story of the emotion shown by Quin in the delivery of the prologue is a testimony to the affection which Thomson inspired in his friends.

The body of Thomson's poetry, excluding the dramas, is not large, and, historically, *The Seasons* is his most important poem.    Its form of *The Seasons* was suggested by the example of Vergil's *Georgics:* Thomson expressly reminds his readers of the similarity of his themes to those of Vergil,[1] of whom he imitated more than one famous passage.[2]    In this respect, he had a conspicuous forerunner in John Philips, author of *Cyder*, and it is impossible to overlook the debt which Thomson owed to the older writer.    Philips was an imitator of Milton's poetic manner, and it may have been through Philips's poetry that Thomson first felt that Miltonic influence which moulded his style and the characteristic shape of his phrases.    Johnson, it is true, denied the influence of Milton upon Thomson:

As a writer, he is entitled to one praise of the highest kind: his mode of thinking, and of expressing his thoughts, is original.    His blank verse is no more the blank verse of Milton, or of any other

[1] *Spring*, ll. 55–8: cf. ll. 446, 447.        [2] *E. g. Summer*, ll. 1151 *seq.*

poet, than the rhymes of Prior are the rhymes of Cowley.  His numbers, his pauses, his diction, are of his own growth, without transcription, without imitation.[1]

This criticism can be justified only to a limited extent.  Thomson's characteristic modes of thought were too much those of his age to bear a very close resemblance to those of Milton. His choice of blank verse, while sanctioned by Milton's authority, was, on the other hand, natural to a poet whose language was too voluble and ornate to be easily confined within the couplet.  Its regular flow and even beat imply a strictly limited command of those musical resources of which Milton was master.  Thomson's prosody is adequate to the contents of his verse; but it would be difficult to cite a passage of *The Seasons* in which the sound becomes a direct echo of the sense. Yet, if we allow these differences and admit a limitation of thought and a florid expansiveness of language which afford a strong contrast to Milton's pregnancy of thought and phrase, there cannot be any question as to the attraction which Milton exercised upon the method of natural description and upon the diction of *The Seasons*.

In the second of these relations, the likeness is at once evident.  Such passages as the contrast in *Winter* between the studious retirement of the scholar and the diversions of the village and the town are reminiscent in phrase, as in subject, of *L'Allegro* and *Il Penseroso*.[2]  The love of inversion which provoked Thomson's boldest experiments in style, the constant and frequently adverbial use of epithets derived from Latin sources, are Miltonic characteristics.  That rich literary imagery in which Milton excelled quickened Thomson to bring into contrast with the more homely scenes of his poem the unfamiliar scenery of the tropics, and to enrich his verse with the ornament of carefully chosen proper names.  Lines such as these,

> All that from the tract
> Of woody mountains stretch'd thro' gorgeous *Ind*
> Fall on *Cormandel's* coast, or *Malabar;*
> From *Menam's* orient stream, that nightly shines
> With insect-lamps, to where *Aurora* sheds
> On *Indus'* smiling banks the rosy shower,

[1] Johnson, *Life of Thomson*.            [2] *Winter*, ll. 424 *seq.*

are one instance out of many in which Thomson echoed harmonies which Milton had awakened.  To reproduce the full charm, the magic melody of the original, was impossible for a poet who had no great reserve of imagination on which to draw; but the imitation is obvious and its effect is, to some extent, a success.

The poetry of Thomson's day had ceased to hold direct communion with nature.  Occasional contact, however, could not be avoided.  Dyer's *Grongar Hill* (1727) showed a spontaneous attitude to nature which was too exceptional to capture the public taste at once: the age preferred the conventional and generalised descriptions in which poets not preoccupied with nature were accustomed to indulge—descriptions on which the example of Milton, who regarded nature through the medium of literary reminiscence, had a far-reaching effect.  It is Thomson's peculiarity that the description of natural phenomena, in an age which overlooked their artistic value, was his chief concern.  His observation was keen and intelligent.  His eye, in the phrase of Wordsworth, was "steadily fixed upon his object"; his feelings "urged him to work upon it in the spirit of genuine imagination."[1]  The spectacles of books enlarged his range of vision; but his commerce with the more familiar aspects of nature was direct and unimpeded.  This process marks a point of departure from the fashion set by the commanding genius of Milton, and a return to earlier methods.  But, for the expression of his genuine, though limited, imagination, he was bound by the necessities of a diction which had become formal and stereotyped.  What he saw with his own eyes, he conventionalised in terms which were the common property of his age.  No one, however, since Milton had given so much attention to the varied aspects of nature, and, consequently, Thomson's description of the stock elements of conventional scenery, of

> hill and dale, and wood and lawn,
> And verdant field, and darkening heath between,
> And villages embosom'd soft in trees,
> And spiry towns by surging columns mark'd
> Of houshold smoak,[2]

[1] Wordsworth, *Essay, supplementary to the preface to* Lyrical Ballads.
[2] *Spring*, ll. 947–51.

was governed by an accuracy of observation and depth of enjoyment which, while perpetuating the Miltonic tradition in poetry, distinguished Thomson from poets who, without observation and feeling for nature, had passively accepted the superficial qualities of that tradition.

At the same time, Thomson's obedience to the conventional diction of poetry was in no sense reluctant. The broad view of the general aspects of nature which such a diction reveals was essential to his habit of mind. His observation, if accurate, shared the tendency inherent in the art of the later seventeenth century to group details in broad masses of colour and striking contrasts of light and shadow. The pictorial medium through which he approached scenery is indicated by a stanza in *The Castle of Indolence:*

> Sometimes the pencil, in cool airy halls,
> Bade the gay bloom of vernal landskips rise,
> Or autumn's varied shades embrown the walls:
> Now the black tempest strikes the astonish'd eyes;
> Now down the steep the flashing torrent flies;
> The trembling sun now plays o'er ocean blue,
> And now rude mountains frown amid the skies;
> Whate'er *Lorrain* light-touch'd with softening hue,
> Or savage *Rosa* dash'd, or learned *Poussin* drew.[1]

Of such pictures, Thomson was the receptive recorder. His intelligence was not of that vigorous and active type which searches in nature for a life instinct with emotions akin and responsive to his own. Nature, to him, is a succession of phenomena of varied form and colour which compose a series of landscapes, as they affect the senses with their charm. Beneath the changes of the sky, he notes with delight the changes of colour of the earth. Over the country-side in spring,

> One boundless blush, one white-empurpled shower
> Of mingled blossoms,[2]

rise the clouds, big with rain, "a dusky wreath . . . scarce staining ether," gathering quickly until the massed vapour "sits on th' horizon round a settled gloom."[3] At evening, the

---

[1] *The Castle of Indolence*, canto I, st. 38.    [2] *Spring*, ll. 110, 111.
[3] *Ibid* ll. 147–51.

clouds lift; the sunset casts its light on mountains and rivers, and tinges the mist which rises from the soaked plain with yellow, while every blade of grass sparkles with raindrops, and the rainbow is refracted from the eastern sky.[1] In summer, when night gathers over the hot day, the glow-worm twinkles in the hedges, and the evening star rises in the calm sky, as black vesper's pageants dissolve.[2] In autumn, truthful observation notes the gathering mists through which the sun "sheds, weak and blunt, his wide-refracted ray,"[3] the shower of meteors in the night-time,[4] the heavy dews of morning,[5] and the "peculiar blue" of the midday sky.[6] If, in winter, the rich colours, congenial to Thomson's fancy, of "Autumn beaming o'er the yellow woods,"[7] give place to more livid hues, yet there remain the red sunset which precedes the frosty night, the "blue film" breathed by the icy wind over pool and stream, the "crystal pavement" of the arrested water-course, the glitter of the stars, the pallor of the dawn which reveals the "dumb cascade" of icicles hanging from the eaves and the arabesque of frostwork woven over window-pane and frozen soil, the cold gleam of the icebound brook and the "plumy wave" of white snow on the forest trees.[8]

Nor is sight the only sense which is alive to the charm of the progress of the year in earth and sky. In the spring garden, the violet, polyanthus, hyacinth and tulip, "the yellow wall-flower, stain'd with iron brown," combine their bright colour with the scent of the stock and jonquil, while sight and touch alike combine in the note of

> auriculas, enrich'd
> With shining meal o'er all their velvet leaves.[9]

Sensitive to perfume, Thomson invites Amanda to walk

> Where the breeze blows from yon extended field
> Of blossom'd beans,[10]

or wanders in the spring morning from the fragrant garden into country lanes, among sweet-briar hedges, or "tastes the smell of dairy" as he walks past a farm.[11] The fisherman, when the

[1] *Spring*, ll. 186 *seq.*     [2] *Summer*, ll. 1683 *seq.*     [3] *Autumn*, ll. 623 *seq.*
[4] *Ibid.* ll. 1019 *seq.*     [5] *Ibid.* ll. 1081 *seq.*     [6] *Ibid.* l. 1130.
[7] *Ibid.* l. 969.     [8] *Winter*, ll. 714 *seq.*     [9] *Spring*, ll. 516 *seq.*
[10] *Ibid.* ll. 499, 500.     [11] *Ibid.* ll. 101 *seq.*

noonday sun scatters the light clouds borne across the sky before the west wind, may retire with a book to the shady bank where sight is attracted by the purple violet, and the air is scented by the "balmy essence" of the lily of the valley, or beneath the shade of a mountain ash where "the sounding culver" builds its nest in the cliff.[1] Few of Thomson's pictures are without their accompaniment of sound. The silence of the winter morning is broken by the foot-fall of the shepherd on the hard crust of frozen snow.[2] The song of birds in spring, which forms the subject of one of the most attractive passages in *The Seasons*,[3] intensifies, as it ceases, the stillness of autumn, when the only sound is that of the distant gun or of the wood-man's axe in the "sadden'd grove."[4] Such sounds are used chiefly to give emphasis to quiet and solitude. His happiest effects in this direction are summed up in a stanza of *The Castle of Indolence* beginning

> Join'd to the prattle of the purling rills,
> Were heard the lowing herds along the vale.[5]

In all the scenes to which this stanza makes reference, the part of man is incidental. The poet roams with "eye excursive" for the sake of the varied pleasure to be derived from his wanderings. He has his own stock of readily awakened sentiment, susceptible to the gloom and terror of storm, or to the coming of the "Power of Philosophic Melancholy" in autumn;[6] but there is no subjective sense of revolt in his own breast to make his spirit at one with the warring elements, no natural melancholy which colours Nature with its own hue and translates her death into personal terms. Similarly, man is introduced only so far as he forms a telling feature in the landscape, just as the human element in Salvator Rosa's pictures is subordinated to a position which gives scale to nodding rocks and adds terror to frowning forests. The village haymaking and sheepwashing in *Summer* are mild attempts at *genre* pictures; the "rural smell" of the harvest, the "dusky wave" of mown hay on the meadow, the "russet hay-cock" of the one, the "pebbled shore" and "flashing wave" of the washing-pool in the other, meant more

---

[1] *Spring*, ll. 443 *seq.*    [2] *Winter*, ll. 755–9.    [3] *Spring*, ll. 582 *seq.*
[4] *Autumn*, ll. 886 *seq.*    [5] *The Castle of Indolence*, canto I, st. 4.
[6] *Autumn*, ll. 920 *seq.*

to Thomson than the perfunctory rustics who form part of the
scene.[1]   His one elaborate picture of the pursuits of his fellow-
men is the description of the feast after a day's hunting;[2] and
this, conceived in a spirit of heavy playfulness, was transferred
by his executor Lyttelton, as unworthy of *The Seasons*, to a
place by itself in his collected works, where it appears as *The
Return from the Fox-Chace, a Burlesque Poem, in the Manner of
Mr. Philips*.   More characteristic is his introduction of the
horseman, vainly awaited by his wife and children, and perish-
ing in the swamp, to heighten the terrors of the marsh, lit by
treacherous wildfire, on an autumn night.[3]   A parallel tragedy
adds effect to the description of the snowdrift.[4]   The famous
picture in *Summer* of the caravan swallowed in the sandstorm
ends with lines which, in pointing a contrast to the scene
described, are invested with an unusual element of human interest—an element which, in the scene itself, is entirely subject
to the irresistible power of nature.

In this objective attitude to nature, which, while recognising
her power, dissociates her from an active participation in the
interests and emotions of man, Thomson stands midway
between two periods.   Milton, a lover of nature less for her
own sake than for the echoes of poetry and music which she
aroused in him, felt in her being the breath of an animating
and sustaining creative power.   Twenty-one years after Thomson's death, Gray, travelling in north-west Yorkshire, as he
looked on Ingleborough wrapped in clouds and stood "not
without shuddering" in the gloomy ravine of Gordale scar, felt
the presence of a sentient life in nature responding to his own
thought and quickening his emotions.[5]   The chief characteristic of this point of view is the local colour which it lends to
description, its attempt to register every shade of subjective
emotion by a definition of the spirit of place which gives it its
special hue.   Thomson's descriptions of individual scenes are
guiltless of local colour.   Most of them were introduced into
later editions of *The Seasons*, and, in these, the thought of the
patron or friend whose "hospitable genius" presides over the
landscape inspires the passage, while the details of the landscape itself are characterised in the most general terms.   The

[1] *Summer*, ll. 352 *seq.*     [2] *Autumn*, ll. 488 *seq.*     [3] *Autumn*, ll. 1061 *seq.*
[4] *Winter*, ll. 276 *seq.*                                    [5] Gray, *Journal in the Lakes*.

prospect from Richmond hill is described with affection and with a keen sense of its natural beauty.[1] From the hill above Hagley park, the Welsh mountains are noted in the western distance,[2] and, at Stowe, the poet's eye is quick to mark the autumnal colour of the woods.[3] But it is precisely in such places, with their memories of friendship and social pleasure, that Thomson is most in harmony with the poetic taste of his day. The landscape is merely the setting to a compliment or a tribute of personal regard. An enumeration of the general features of the landscape, a ready perception of points of colour, the occasional introduction of a place-name, are indicative of the poet's personal enjoyment, but do not by themselves evoke the special qualities of the prospect. And, if these passages have a certain prominence in *The Seasons*, it must be owned that, as pictures of nature, they are inferior to passages, such as that which describes the eagle rearing its young "on utmost *Kilda's* shore,"[4] where Thomson's imagination, although untouched by personal experience, is unfettered by the claims of man upon its object.

It is true that the poetry of nature, even where deeply imbued with the spirit of place, frequently shows a tendency to vagueness of description. Wordsworth's *Lines composed a few miles above Tintern Abbey*, or the sonnet *Composed after a journey across the Hambleton hills*, are records not of the peculiar beauties of particular spots, but of the emotions which they kindle in an individual mind. With Thomson, the external aspect of nature was never made sublime by intensity of spiritual feeling. We, who have never known Lyttelton or held converse with Pitt, or had the privilege of directing the downcast eyes of Amanda to the dwelling of Pope or the shades where "the worthy Queensb'ry yet laments his Gay," may admire the pictures of Hagley or Stowe or the Thames near Richmond as skilful arrangements of colour, but cannot regard them as expressions of the permanent element in nature. They are interesting landmarks in the history of poetic taste; but their emotional quality, such as it is, is slight, and typical of a state of mind which had not yet recognised in nature the presence of a being independent of period and place. Nevertheless,

[1] *Summer*, ll. 1402 *seq.*  [2] *Spring*, ll. 899 *seq.*
[3] *Autumn*, ll. 953 *seq.*  [4] *Spring*, ll. 750 *seq.*

in common with his generation, Thomson had his conventional philosophy of nature. Just as Milton's habit of generalised description had tinged the verse of his successors with a pale reflection, so his devout conception of a controlling Deity manifesting Himself in nature had left its impression upon his imitators. Thomson, with a reminiscence of Vergil, pays repeated tribute to the Divine force which

> pervades,
> Adjusts, sustains, and agitates the whole,[1]

and writes of it with a reverence which indicates the effect upon his thought of the Miltonic idea of the Creator, limited by a general agreement with the deism of his own day. The "Source of Being" has touched "the great whole into perfection."[2] Supreme Perfection attracts "life rising still on life, in higher tone"[3] into Its own Being. As we gaze on nature, "we feel the present Deity,"[4] and know it to be full of a "mighty Breath,"[5] an "inhaling spirit."[6] The seasons in their course embody this pervading energy, and "are but the *varied* God."[7] The paragraphs of *The Seasons* which contain such sentiments, or the hymn which is their most eloquent expression at the end of the poem, leave us in doubt as to Thomson's actual adherence to any connected system of religion or philosophy. Deism alternates with a vague pantheism according to the feeling of the moment; and, in one place, at any rate, there are signs of a leaning towards Pythagorean doctrines.[8] Thomson himself might have found it hard to define the religious emotion which nature excited in him. His sincere gratitude to the Creator is at times prompted by a sense of duty, when its terms unconsciously resemble those in which he recognised the disposing hand of Lord Cobham at Stowe or saw the "pure *Dorsetian* downs" at Eastbury decorated by the union of human graces in Bubb Dodington. The greater patron and the wider area of power called for the more elaborate compliment.

Such temperate rhapsodies are, in fact, among the digressions of *The Seasons*. Thomson felt the necessity of giving some

---

[1] *Spring*, ll. 849, 850.
[2] *Spring*, l. 560.
[3] *The Castle of Indolence*, canto II, st. 48.
[4] *Spring*, l. 897.
[5] *Ibid*. l. 846.　　　[6] *Summer*, l. 108.
[7] *A Hymn*, l. 2.
[8] *Spring*, ll. 335 *seq*.

relief to description, and, in the successive revisions to which *The Seasons* was subjected, the poem gained in arrangement and in variety of surface. The most striking digressions are, undoubtedly, those surveys of foreign scenery which provide necessary contrast to the limited area of Thomson's own experience. The longest and best of these, in *Summer*,[1] was remodelled and transformed in the later editions, when Thomson removed from it the eloquent and highly coloured picture of the African city buried in the sand[2]—an alteration which probably involved some self-sacrifice. We have already noticed Lyttelton's treatment of the hunting episode in *Autumn*, a digression which arises naturally out of the subject. The most popular passages of *The Seasons*, which were long the admiration of English readers and did much to gain the poem its vogue on the continent, were those episodes which take the form of sentimental anecdotes appropriate to the season under discussion. Of these, three in number, two are in *Summer*. A description of a thunderstorm suggests the story of Celadon and Amelia, the lovers separated by a fatal thunderbolt.[3] This is quickly succeeded by a passage on summer bathing, illustrated by the tale of Damon and Musidora, which, in its present form, is entirely altered, and altered for the worse, from the form which it assumed in the earliest draft of the poem.[4] The episode of Palemon and Lavinia in *Autumn* is a tale of harvest, modelled upon the history of Boaz and Ruth.[5] At their best, these stories are merely elegant decorations of Thomson's verse. Their popularity in their own day was due to an artificial taste which sought in such poetry the distractions of an unreal world, and tolerated the questionable morality and spurious sentiment of the story of Damon and Musidora, for the sake of its superficial prettiness.

Moral reflections, such as those upon love and jealousy suggested by the song of the birds in spring[6] are among the incidental passages of *The Seasons*. No subject, however, was more congenial to Thomson than the glory of his country, and the patriotic enthusiasm excited by the prospect seen from

---

[1] *Summer*, ll. 629 *seq.*
[2] Printed in the appendices to Tovey's edition of Thomson.
[3] *Summer*, ll. 1170 *seq.*  [4] *Ibid.* ll. 1270 *seq.*
[5] *Autumn*, ll. 182 *seq.*  [6] *Spring*, ll. 959 *seq.*

Richmond hill in *Summer* was more than a conventional sentiment exacted by duty to the political sympathies of his friends
and patrons.   His convictions, on this head, found their earliest
expression in the monologue *Britannia*, and were developed at
tedious length in *Liberty*.   In this poem, his art failed him, and
the careful arrangement of topics which gave much variety to
*The Seasons* was abandoned for the prolix discussion of a single
theme.   Stirred to his subject by the sight of the ruins of Rome,
he indulged in a historical survey, related by Liberty herself, of
her progress from Greece to Italy, her temporary eclipse in
"Gothic darkness," and her revival at the renascence to find
in Britain a field for her untrammelled sway.   In her autobiography, Liberty displays a remarkable lack of modesty,
and the width of her claims is the only original feature of
Thomson's political philosophy.   The poet himself plays the
part of an admiring listener to her oration, making, from time to
time, respectful interruptions which serve to let loose new floods
of verbiage.   He evidently grew weary of his task.   The prophecy contained in the fifth book, awaited by a steadily decreas-
ing number of subscribers, begins with an uninspired adaptation
to Britain of Vergil's famous tribute to Italy in the second
*Georgic*, and "goes dispiritedly, glad to finish" to an abrupt
and hurried end.   After Thomson's death, Lyttelton, following, as he said, the author's own design, condensed the five
books of *Liberty* into three.   His rearrangement, when compared with the earlier text, is a symptom of the loose construction
and redundancy of the original, which made such drastic treatment possible.   Thomson's friend Murdoch appears to have
set his face against the application of a similar process to *The
Seasons;* but it must be owned that, even after all the revision
which it underwent from the author himself, *The Seasons* is not
without a considerable amount of repetition, which testifies to
the limitations of Thomson's material.

Although *Liberty* was a failure, Thomson evidently intended
to try his fortune once more with a patriotic poem.   The
ominous promise, recorded in *The Castle of Indolence*,[1] was
not fulfilled, for a reason which must be found in *The Castle
of Indolence* itself.   The elaboration of this short poem occupied
many years, and, even in its final condition, bears signs of incom-

[1] *The Castle of Indolence*, canto I, st. 32.

pleteness.   Each of the two cantos ends abruptly with a homely realistic simile which forms an inappropriate conclusion to a romantic allegory.   The poem might, indeed, have been extended to an indefinite length: its merit lies, not in the story which it contains, but in the polish of its style and the success with which Thomson, following a fixed model, contrived to display in it his own best qualities.

This poem (says the advertisement prefixed to it) being writ in the manner of *Spenser*, the obsolete words, and a simplicity of diction in some of the lines, which borders on the ludicrous, were necessary to make the imitation more perfect.   And the stile of that admirable poet, as well as the measure in which he wrote, are, as it were, appropriated by Custom to all allegorical Poems writ in our language; just as in *French* the stile of *Marot*, who lived under *Francis i*, has been used in tales, and familiar epistles, by the politest writers of the age of *Louis xiv*.

Already, in 1742, Shenstone had attempted, in *The School-Mistress*, to imitate Spenser's

language, his simplicity, his manner of description, and a peculiar tenderness of sentiment remarkable throughout his works.

Thomson's poem, however, had been conceived at an earlier date than Shenstone's.   It shows, not merely an admiration of the external qualities of Spenser's verse, but some intimacy with his methods of description and personification.   At the same time, the use of the Spenserian stanza, of obsolete words and of a studied simplicity of diction, could not repress the characteristic tastes of the poet of *The Seasons*.   In the habit of poetical inversion Milton stood between Spenser and Thomson; and Thomson had assimilated this habit so thoroughly that *The Castle of Indolence* could hardly fail to be leavened with it. With Spenser, the employment of obsolete words, if, primarily, an affectation, became an essential feature of his poetry. With Thomson, it was purely a quaint imitation of Spenser: his old-fashioned words were dragged in as a necessity, and the poem would lose none of its attractiveness without them.

The point at which Thomson most closely approaches Spenser is in the deliberate movement and varied melody of his stanza. Otherwise, it may fairly be claimed that his resemblance to his model is of the most general kind. The landscape with which the poem opens is his highest achievement in that type of description, combining soft colour with suggestions of perfume and sound, with which *The Seasons* has made us familiar. There is little emphasis on small details: effects of colour, of light and shadow, are conveyed in such general and inclusive phrases as

> gay castles in the clouds that pass,
> For ever flushing round a summer-sky.[1]

If, in such passages, the luxurious beauty of Spenser's descriptions is reflected, it is rather in their form than in their contents. Here, once more, the influence of Milton in poetry, of "savage *Rosa*" and "learned *Poussin*" in painting, are too strong to make insistence on detail possible. In his personifications, Thomson comes nearer to Spenser. The incidental persons, the "comely full-spread porter"[2] and his "little roguish page,"[3] the diseases of body and mind in the dungeon of the castle,[4] "the fiery-footed boy, benempt *Dispatch*,"[5] who is page to the Knight of Arts and Industry, are portraits which have Spenser's power of giving individual being to abstract qualities. On the other hand, the chief portraits of *The Castle of Indolence*, the sketches of the friends of the poet as inhabitants or visitors of the castle,[6] suggested though they may have been by Spenser's habit of interweaving traits of his contemporaries with his personified abstractions, were drawn with a personal feeling which owed little to imitation. Written by one who has himself fallen under the dominion of the enchanter, the poem has a note of confession and complaint which gives its contents a special interest, apart from questions of derived form and style.

The slightness of *The Castle of Indolence* and its allegory do not bear comparison with the sustained complication of the fable which Spenser made the vehicle of his high philosophy. Thomson's imagination was unrefined by exalted philosophical thought, and his poem is certainly not improved by excursions into conventional moralising. The eleven stanzas of perverted morality, which are sung with an energy foreign to his character

---

[1] *The Castle of Indolence*, canto I, st. 6.   [2] *Ibid.* st. 24.   [3] *Ibid.* st. 25.
[4] *Ibid.* st. 73 *seq.*   [5] *Ibid.* canto II, st. 32.   [6] *Ibid.* canto I, st. 57 *seq.*

by Indolence as he sits at the gate of his castle,[1] do not add anything to the allegory, but simply mark a breathing-space between the opening description and the admirable remainder of the first canto.   With the appearance, in the second canto, of the "generous imp of fame"[2] whose vigorous accomplishments are to be fatal to the wizard's abode, Thomson was easily betrayed into paths which his muse had trodden bare.   After a life passed in varied climes, the Knight of Arts and Industry has at length found his proper home in Britain, encircled by the protection of Britannia's thunder on the main, and aided in his efforts by Liberty, "th' Eternal Patron,"[3] who handsomely atones for her overpowering egoism in an earlier poem by allowing him to encroach upon her extensive functions.   The mechanic arts, the learning, the constitution of Britain, meet with due compliment.   Threatened by the minions of Indolence, they are protected by the knight, who sets out to overthrow the castle.   The song of the bard Philomelus, tuned to the British harp, stands in contrast to the song of Indolence, and proceeds through its fifteen stanzas with equal smoothness and fluency.[4]   Supreme Perfection is invoked from the point of view which, in the concluding hymn of *The Seasons,* sees "life rising still on life, in higher tone" to absorption with deity. The examples of Greece and Rome and of the great poets are cited to encourage the energy which is the antithesis to slothful repose.   A contrast is drawn between health and disease, and a final exhortation to the use of godlike reason has the desired effect of stirring the knight's followers to the attack.   While these sentiments are polished with the care which distinguishes the whole poem, they are drawn from a stock-in-trade which Thomson and his contemporaries had well-nigh exhausted, and their commonplace nobility is at the very opposite pole to the grave philosophy of Spenser or to Milton's lofty morality.

Thomson's dramatic work consists of five tragedies and the masque of *Alfred,* written in conjunction with Mallet.   He had no special talent for the stage, and, at a period when rhetoric was the chief ambition of the dramatist, Thomson's rhetoric was no distinguishing excellence.   His dramas are devoid of characterisation; his characters are vehicles of lofty sentiment, the

[1] *The Castle of Indolence,* canto I, st. 9 *seq.*       [2] *Ibid.* canto II, st. 4.
[3] *Ibid.* st. 23.                                         [4] *Ibid.* st. 47 *seq.*

prevailing tone of which is the belligerent patriotism of the party to which Thomson was sincerely devoted. *Sophonisba*, however, the earliest of the tragedies, is without noticeable political bias. It is simply a classical drama of the conventional type. Its subject, to be sure, is patriotic, and its choice of a queen who died for her country may have been intended to spur the queen, to whom it was dedicated, to free herself from an influence to which Thomson's associates were bitterly opposed. There can be no question as to the meaning of the later plays. Between *Sophonisba* and the production of *Agamemnon*, there was an interval of nine years. It is easy to read into the characters of Clytemnestra and Egisthus the queen and the minister whom the prince's coterie was bent on deposing. The Orestes of *Agamemnon* was flattered more openly in *Alfred*, which was played before the prince and princess at Cliveden in 1740; while the application of *Edward and Eleonora* was so obvious that it was rejected for the stage. *Agamemnon* and *Edward* were published with dedications to the princess of Wales; the last of the political plays, *Tancred and Sigismunda*, was inscribed to the prince himself. *Coriolanus*, posthumously produced, is a return to pure tragedy without party bias. It may fairly be said that not one of these plays has the least dramatic interest. Their blank verse, however, is, as might be expected, easy and fluent. Thomson, possibly in imitation of the constant habit of the later Jacobean and Caroline dramatists, permitted himself a free use of weak endings to his lines, a practice which may promote ease in delivery, but becomes monotonous to the reader. His rhetoric is respectable; but the nobility of sentiment which it clothes is not above the ordinary level of the conventional sentiment of the classical drama of his day, and provokes no striking bursts of eloquence. His subjects do not afford scope for his gift of natural description, and there is only an occasional touch to remind us that his true genius lay in his appreciation of natural atmosphere and colour. His philosophy, on the other hand, is frequently introduced, but without any material addition to the contents of the passages in which its vague principles had been embodied in *The Seasons*. On the whole, the main interest of the plays is the debt which they owe directly to Greek tragedy, and not merely to the antique drama through the medium of the French stage. This virtue may, to some extent, be claimed for *Agamemnon;* it cannot be denied to *Edward and Eleonora*, where the self-sacrifice of Eleanor of Castile is imitated at first hand from the devotion of Alcestis, and the famous description of the Cretan queen's farewell to life is almost translated in the narrative given by Daraxa to the earl of Gloster. Otherwise, the dramas fail to offer any special feature that raises them above the ordinary competence of their time; they are deficient in action, and their division into five acts is a theatrical convention which only emphasises the poverty of their construction. The masque of *Alfred*, the greater part of which, in its first form, seems to have been supplied by Mallet, was afterwards rewritten by Thomson, and the music, "excepting two or three things which being particularly Favourites at Cliefdon, are retained by Desire," was "new-composed" by Arne.[1] Among the lyrics to which Arne provided new music for the edition of 1753 was *Rule, Britannia*, the sentiments of which embody Thomson's enthusiasm for his country and liberty in its most compact form.

The influence of Thomson was strongly felt by the younger generation of poets: by Collins, who dedicated a beautiful *Ode* to his memory, and by Gray, in whose work reminiscences of the elder poet are frequent. The vogue of *The Seasons* was followed by a period in which blank verse, such as Thomson had employed, was used with some fluency and skill for the treatment of rural subjects. Milton was the original model on which this type of verse was founded, and the example of John Philips, "*Pomona's* bard," was felt in the choice both of metre and of subject. Somerville, in his preface to *The Chace*, defends his blank verse against "the gentlemen, who are fond of a gingle at the close of every verse."

For my own part (he adds), I shall not be ashamed to follow the example of Milton, Philips, Thomson, and all our best tragic writers.

William Somerville, born in 1675, was a year older than Philips and twenty-five years older than Thomson; but it was not until 1735 that he published *The Chace*, by virtue of which

[1] Title-page of the 1753 edition of *Alfred*.

his name survives. He was educated at Winchester and New college, Oxford, and was elected fellow of New college. On succeeding to the family estate of Edstone, near Henley-in-Arden, he settled down to a life in which the ordinary occupations of a country gentleman were varied by the study and composition of poetry. Much of his verse is poor doggerel in the form of fables and tales, dull and coarse after the usual manner of such productions. But Somerville was a scholar and something of a critic. His *Occasional Poems* (1727) contain appreciative verses addressed to Addison and Pope; he enjoyed the friendship of Allan Ramsay, and criticised the "rude notes" of the youthful Jago. In a set of couplets, he welcomed the first edition of *The Seasons* in a tone of patronage which, if justified by his age, was hardly warranted by his own poetry. Prophesying a great future for the young poet, he regretted that his muse should "want the reforming toilet's daily care," and urged him to abandon novelties of diction which, dangerous in southern poets, became all the more so "when minted on the other side of Tweed."

> Read Philips much, consider Milton more;
> But from their dross extract the purer ore.[1]

Somerville himself had nothing to teach Thomson; and his *Chace*, when it appeared, shows the influence of the verse of *The Seasons*, or, at any rate, a strong inclination to come into line with it. The poet's "hoarse-sounding horn" invited the prince of Wales, the friend of Lyttelton and the patron of Thomson,

> to the Chace, the sport of kings;
> Image of war, without its guilt.[2]

After a short sketch of the history of hunting from the rude but thorough methods of Nimrod to the days of William the conqueror, and a compliment to Britain, the "fair land of liberty," as the true home of horse and hound, the country gentlemen of Britain are summoned to hear the poet's instructions upon his favourite sport. He discusses at length and with much practical knowledge and good sense, the position and

[1] *Epistle to Mr. Thomson, on the first edition of his Seasons.*
[2] *The Chace*, bk I, ll. 13-15.

proper design of the kennels, with the advice, not inapplicable
to a day when Palladian symmetry was being pursued to excess
by the architects of country houses and their out-buildings,
"Let no Corinthian pillars prop the dome."[1]　The habits of
hounds, the best breeds—a subject which gives Somerville
the true hunter's opportunity to express his contempt for
coursing[2]—and the mysteries of scent conclude the first book.
Hare-hunting is the main subject of the second and fox-hunting
of the third; but Somerville was not a mere sportsman, and his
literary digressions and allusions to the great Mogul's battue of
wild beasts "taken from Monsieur Bernier, and the history of
Gengiscan the Great,"[3] and to the story of the tribute of wolves,
heads imposed by Edgar, show that he followed his own advice
and spent days on which sport was impossible in improving
converse with his books.　From one of these digressions upon
oriental methods of hunting, his "devious muse" is recalled,
with an appropriate reference to Denham's *Cooper's Hill* and a
flattering eulogy of the royal family, to Windsor and the king's
buckhounds; and the third book ends with an example of
royal clemency to the stag and a compliment to the throne.
The concluding book contains instructions upon breeding and
the art of training puppies, from which a transition is made to
the diseases of hounds and the fatal effect of bites.　Otter-
hunting concludes the series of descriptions, and is followed by
a final congratulation, in the spirit of Vergil's *O fortunatos
nimium*, on the felicities of the hunter in his unambitious
country life.

*The Chace* was followed a few years later by the short poem
entitled *Rural Sports*, also dedicated to the prince of Wales.
*Hobbinol*, a burlesque narrative in blank verse, dedicated to
Hogarth, was inspired by Philips's *Splendid Shilling*, and is a
lively account of the quarrelsome May games of some rustics
in the vale of Evesham.　In his preface, as in that to *The Chace*,
Somerville indulged in a short critical explanation of his chosen
form of verse, and defined his burlesque as "a satire against the
luxury, the pride, the wantonness, and quarrelsome temper, of
the middling sort of people," which he condemned as respon-

---

[1] *The Chace*, bk 1, l. 143.　　　　　　　　　　　　　　　　[2] *Ibid.* ll. 227–30.
[3] Argument to *The Chace*, bk II.　The *Voyage* of François Bernier (1625–88),
who had been for a time physician to Aurungzebe the great, was published in 1699.

sible for the decline in trade and the depressed condition of the
rural districts. These poems do not add anything to the qualities displayed in *The Chace*, and the mock heroics of *Hobbinol*
are unduly prolonged into three cantos. Somerville, however,
was always lively in description; he knew his subject, whether
he wrote of sport, or of the amusements of the Gloucestershire
rustic "from Kiftsgate to remotest Henbury,"[1] and he had a
genuine feeling for classical poetry. Philips appears to have
been his favourite English author, appealing to his rural tastes
and to his particular vein of somewhat coarse humour. Natural
description is purely incidental to his verse; but the scene and
atmosphere of the various forms of sport which he described
are suggested in adequate general terms.[2] Where he approaches detail, as in his description of unfavourable weather
for hunting, the resemblance of his methods to those of Thomson is noticeable. Like Thomson, he was fond, as has been
noticed, of oriental and of patriotic digressions. His tendency
to moralising is slight when compared with Thomson's and from
quasi-religious rhapsody he was as entirely free as he was from
Thomson's sympathy with the victims of the chase. His
poems are in no sense dull reading; but his blank verse, suave
and regular, is somewhat monotonous, and is seldom broken
by any variation of accent, such as that frequent employment
of a trochee in the first foot of a line which gives variety of
movement to the verse of *The Seasons*.

In the *Edge-Hill* of Richard Jago, a strong taste for moralising was combined with appreciation of "Britannia's rural
charms, and tranquil scenes."[3] Warwickshire, a fertile nurse
of poets, was his native county and provided him with his
subject. His father, a member of a Cornish family, was rector
of Beaudesert near Henley-in-Arden, where Jago was born in
1715. Somerville, whose estate Edstone lay some three miles
distant, was a friend of his boyhood.[4] At Solihull, where he
went to school, he made the friendship of Shenstone, a year

---

[1] *Hobbinol*, canto 1, l. 246.

[2] It may be mentioned that *The Chace* was a favourite of Mr. Jorrocks in the
sporting novel *Handley Cross*, where several quotations from it occur which have
become familiar to readers who know nothing about Somerville's poem.

[3] *Edge-Hill*, bk 1, l.1.                    [4] *Ibid.* ll. 365–70.

his senior, which he continued to share at Oxford and long afterwards.[1] He entered University college as servitor, and, about 1739, took holy orders and became curate of Snitterfield near Stratford-on-Avon. In 1746, he was presented to the vicarage of Harbury, with which he held the perpetual curacy of the neighbouring church of Chesterton. To these, he added, in 1754, the vicarage of Snitterfield; and, in 1771, resigning Harbury vicarage, he was presented to the rectory of Kimcote near Lutterworth. He retained his three livings until his death in 1781. He was buried at Snitterfield.

His poems consist of a few miscellaneous pieces, an oratorio called *Adam*—a cento from *Paradise Lost* intended to combine the passages of that poem most suitable for music—and *Edge-Hill*. The design of the last poem is very simple. In four books, he describes the prospect of Warwickshire as seen at various times in the day from the famous ridge which separates the vale of the Cherwell from the plain through which the Avon flows to meet the Severn. At morning, he looks westward over the vale of Red Horse to Stratford and Alcester. At noon, afternoon and evening, from different standpoints on the hill, his eye, to some extent aided by imagination, roams over other portions of the county and dwells upon its principal towns and gentlemen's seats. These comprehensive panoramas are broken up by a large amount of digressive morality; and a large portion of the third book is a scientific discourse on the theory of sight, addressed to Lord Clarendon, and pointed by an extremely long, if appropriate, anecdote of a blind youth restored to sight by the help of a gentle friend named Lydia. When the fourth book has run a third of its course, and the survey of Warwickshire has been completed by the compliments to the owners of Arbury and Packington, Jago turns the sober evening hour to account by reviewing the scene "with moral eye," and descants upon the instability of human affairs. This is well illustrated by the death of the seventh earl of Northampton, the master of Compton Wynyates—an allusion which shows that this part of the poem, at any rate, was written in 1763; and the local calamity introduces the

[1] See *Edge-Hill*, bk III, ll. 355 *seq.*, and the stanzas *To William Shenstone, esq. on receiving a gilt pocket-book*, 1751, and *The Goldfinches, an elegy. To William Shenstone, esq.*

chief memory of the place, the battle of Edge-Hill and the lessons and warnings to be derived from it. Jago's moralising has a distinctly religious end. His master was Milton, whose phraseology he copies closely and even borrows, although, in such lines as

Nature herself bids us be serious,[1]

his ear can hardly be said to have caught the charm of Milton's verse. His topography is conscientious: he mentions every country seat of any importance in the county, and adds footnotes with the owners' names. In such passages, he may have felt the influence of Thomson; but his catalogues have little picturesqueness or colour; while his verse, although it is not without the accent of local association, is typical, as a whole, of the decadence of the Miltonic method of natural description in the eighteenth century. Every group of trees is a grove, every country house a dome, and every hill a precipice. The classicism of the renascence has degenerated into a fixed and stilted phraseology.

As he looks from Edge-Hill to the distant Cotswolds, Jago refers to the *Monody* written by George Lyttelton in 1747 to the memory of his wife, Lucy Fortescue, whose home was at Ebrington near Chipping Campden. Lyttelton, the son of Sir Thomas Lyttelton of Hagley, Worcestershire, was the friend of Pope, Thomson and Shenstone, and his house at Hagley was a favourite resort of men of letters. His life was largely political. Born in 1709, and educated at Eton and Christ Church, Oxford, he made the usual grand tour, and entered parliament as member for Okehampton in 1735. He was a prominent supporter of the "patriotic" party against Walpole, and, after Walpole's fall, became a lord of the treasury. In 1751, he succeeded to his father's baronetcy, and, in 1756, after his retirement from a short tenure of the chancellorship of the exchequer, was created baron Lyttelton of Frankley. He died in 1773. His later years saw the publication of *Dialogues of the Dead* and of his *History of the Life of Henry II*. But at no season of his life was literature entirely neglected. He wrote poetry at Eton and Oxford; on his foreign tour,

[1] *Edge-Hill*, bk IV, l. 254.

he addressed epistles in couplets to his friends at home; and, soon after his return, he appears to have composed the four eclogues called *The Progress of Love*. His poems include some songs and stanzas, of which the best are those addressed to his wife. His affection for her is a pleasing trait in a character which excited genuine devotion in his friends; and his *Monody*, composed in irregular stanzas, with a motto taken from Vergil's description of the lament of Orpheus for Eurydice,[1] is written with some depth of feeling, although its reminiscences of *Lycidas* invite a comparison which it cannot sustain. The influence of French literature presides over his imaginative prose works: the very titles of the satiric *Persian Letters*, written in his youth, and the more mature but less sprightly *Dialogues of the Dead*, are copied from Montesquieu and Fénelon, their contents suffering from the usual inferiority of imitations. The graver tone of his later work, as distinguished from his licence of thought and expression in the letters of the Persian Selim from England to Mirza and Ibrahim Mollac at Ispahan, is due to his change of opinion from deism to Christianity. He flattered himself that his *Observations on the Conversion and Apostleship of St. Paul*, which took the form of a letter to Gilbert West, translator of Pindar, brought about the conversion of Thomson on his death-bed. However this may have been, the mutual attachment between himself and Thomson calls for some mention of him in this place. He is said to have supplied the stanza which characterises the poet in *The Castle of Indolence*;[2] he wrote the prologue, recited by Quin, to the posthumous *Coriolanus*, and, as we have seen, he put a liberal interpretation upon his duties as Thomson's executor. In this connection, it is interesting to remember the criticism of Thomson which Lyttelton introduced in the most valuable of the *Dialogues of the Dead*. In answer to a question by Boileau, Pope says:

Your description points out Thomson. He painted nature exactly, and with great strength of pencil. His imagination was rich, extensive, and sublime: his diction bold and glowing, but sometimes *obscure* and *affected*. Nor did he always know when to

---

[1] *Ipse, cava solans*, etc. (*Georgic* IV, 464-6).
[2] *The Castle of Indolence*, canto I, st. 68. The first line, "A bard here dwelt, more fat than bard beseems," is Thomson's own.

*stop*, or what to *reject*. . . . Not only in his plays, but all his other works, there is the purest *morality*, animated by *piety*, and rendered more touching by the fine and delicate sentiments of a most *tender* and *benevolent* heart.[1]

Lyttelton's early poems show him to have followed in the footsteps of Pope, and the letters written to his father from France and Italy are mainly concerned with foreign politics; the only prolonged passage of description in them is a formal account in French of his journey across Mont-Cenis. In 1756, he wrote two letters to the historian Archibald Bower, describing a journey in north Wales. The master of Hagley, by this time, had developed a strong taste for scenery. His descriptions are excellent and accurate, and he visited the castles of Wales with the enthusiasm of a historian, although he fell into the error of imagining that the ruins of Rhuddlan were those of a castle built by Henry II. The beauty of the valleys charmed him; the situation of Powis castle, the vales of Festiniog and Clwyd, the wooded shores of the Menai straits and the view of the Dee valley from Wynnstay, excited him to enthusiasm. Bala seemed to him an oasis in the desert of Merionethshire, "a solitude fit for Despair to inhabit." Snowdon filled him with "religious awe" rather than admiration, and its rocks excited "the idea of Burnet, of their being the fragment of a demolished world." It is characteristic of the taste of his day that the magnificent prospect of the Carnarvonshire mountains from Baron hill above Beaumaris, on which Suckling had looked more than a century before, seemed to Lyttelton inferior to the view of Plymouth sound and Dartmoor from mount Edgcumbe. The love of nature in her wilder moods was not yet part of English literature. "Nature," said Lyttelton of the Berwyn mountains, "is in all her majesty there; but it is the majesty of a tyrant, frowning over the ruins and desolation of a country."

[1] *Dialogues of the Dead*, XIV.

# CHAPTER VI

# Gray

THOMAS GRAY, a poet whose influence upon subsequent literature was largely in excess of the volume of his published works, was born in Cornhill, 26 December, 1716. His father, Philip Gray, was an exchange broker, but seems to have combined with this other and more hazardous pursuits. He was a selfish, despotic, ill-tempered man, passionate even to the verge of lunacy. He owned the house in which the poet was born, and, about the year 1706, let it, and the shop connected with it, to two sisters, Mary and Dorothy Antrobus, milliners. At the same date, approximately, he married Dorothy and came to live with her and Mary. Thomas Gray was the fifth and only surviving child of this marriage; the rest, to the number of seven, died in infancy; and his own life was saved by the prompt courage of his mother, who opened one of his veins with her own hand.

Dorothy Gray had two brothers, Robert and William Antrobus. Robert was a fellow of Peterhouse, and had a considerable reputation at Cambridge. He was Gray's first teacher, not only in classical knowledge, but, also, in the study of natural history, especially botany, and imbued his nephew with a life-long passion for scientific observation of the minutest kind in almost every department of vegetable and animal life. Robert Antrobus was sometime assistant master at Eton, but had probably resigned before Gray entered the school in 1727. The poet's tutor there was William, Robert's younger brother.

During the earlier part of his stay at Eton, Gray, probably, was housed with his uncle Robert, then residing in retirement either in the town or in the college precincts. As an oppidan, the delicate boy had not to endure the hardships of the colleger,

and the horrors of Long Chamber.  His chief friend there, in
the first instance, was Horace, son of Sir Robert Walpole, the
prime minister, of whose wife his cousin Dorothy was a humble
intimate.  Another of his Eton contemporaries was Richard
West, son of the lord chancellor of Ireland, and grandson of
bishop Burnet.  At Eton, West was accounted the most brilliant of the little coterie formed by the three and Ashton,
afterwards fellow of King's and of Eton, and called the quadruple alliance.  A scholar, with a thin vein of poetry, West was
absent-minded, with a tendency to melancholy, to some extent
resembling Gray's own, and he died prematurely in 1742.

The year 1734 brought a dislocation of the alliance.  Gray
went for a time to Pembroke college, Cambridge,[1] pending
his admission to Peterhouse in July.  In March, 1735, West
went to Christ Church, Oxford, whence he wrote to Gray,
14 November, 1735:

Consider me very seriously here in a strange country inhabited
by things that call themselves doctors and masters of arts; a country
flowing with syllogisms and ale, where Horace and Virgil are equally
unknown.

But, as a matter of fact, all these young Etonians exhibit a
petulance for which youth is the only excuse; and Gray himself
writes, "It is very possible that two and two make four, but
I would not give four farthings to demonstrate this ever so
clearly." Then follows the splenetic outburst:

Surely it was of this place, now Cambridge, but formerly known
as Babylon, that the prophet spoke when he said "the wild beasts
of the desert shall dwell there, and their houses shall be full of
doleful creatures, and owls shall build there, and satyrs shall dance
there; their forts and towers shall be a den for ever, a joy of wild
asses; there shall the great owl make her nest, and lay and hatch
and gather under her shadow; it shall be a court of dragons; the
screech owl also shall nest there, and find for herself a place of rest."

But he was saved from the temptation to dilettantism, which
beset his friends, by the scientific bias which his uncle Robert
had given him, and which would have found quick recognition

[1] From this brief sojourn we may probably date the beginning of his friendship
with Thomas Wharton ("*dear, dear*" Wharton).

and encouragement in the Cambridge of another day. Late in life, he regretted his early neglect of mathematics, and dreamt even then of pursuing it, while he lamented that it was generally laid aside at Cambridge so soon as it had served to get men a degree.

His vacations were chiefly spent at Burnham, where, at Cant's hall, he stayed with his uncle Rogers, his mother's brother-in-law, a solicitor fond of sport, or of the habits of sport. Gray, however, had some little literary companionship:

We have old Mr. Southern, at a gentleman's house a little way off, who often comes to see us; he is now seventy-seven years old, and has almost wholly lost his memory; but is as agreeable as an old man can be, at least I persuade myself so when I look at him, and think of *Isabella* and *Oroonoko*.

This interesting letter serves also to explain to us the lines towards the conclusion of the *Elegy*. He writes:

My comfort amidst all this is that I have at the distance of half-a-mile, through a green lane, a forest (the vulgar call it a common) all my own, at least as good as so, for I spy no human thing in it but myself. It is a little chaos of mountains and precipices; mountains, it is true, that do not ascend much above the clouds, nor are the declivities quite so amazing as Dover cliff; but just such hills as people who love their necks as well as I do may venture to climb, and craggs that give the eye as much pleasure as if they were dangerous: Both vale and hill are covered with the most venerable beeches, and other very reverend vegetables, that like most other ancient people, are always dreaming out their old stories to the winds,

> And as they bow their hoary tops relate,
> In murmuring sounds, the dark decrees of fate;
> While visions, as poetic eyes avow,
> Cling to each leaf, and swarm on every bow.[1]

At the foot of one of these squats Me I (il penseroso) and there grow to the trunk for a whole morning.

It seems that Gray's first destination, so far as it was definite, was the law (as was also West's); for, so early as December,

---

[1] If Gray's own, these are the earliest of his original English verses which we possess. The last two lines are frequently quoted by Hazlitt.

1736, he writes to his friend: "You must know that I do not take degrees."[1] He lingered at Cambridge, somewhat aimlessly. However, this inertia was dispelled by a journey abroad which he undertook in company with Walpole. His first extant letter from Amiens is written to his mother and tells how, on 29 March, N. S., 1739, the friends left Dover. At Paris, Walpole goes out to supper with his cousin Lord Conway; but Gray, though invited too, stops at home and writes to West. He was, however, delighted to dine "at my Lord Holdernesse's" with the abbé Prévost, whom he knows as the author of *L'Histoire de M. Cleveland, fils naturel de Cromwel*, while omitting to mention *Manon Lescaut*. He saw in tragedy Mlle. Gaussin who had been Voltaire's *Zaïre*; saw, also, with Walpole, Racine's *Britannicus*, and, in 1747, reminded him of the grand simplicity of diction and the undercurrent of design which they had admired in the work. His own fragmentary *Agrippina* (1747 c.) is, structurally, borrowed from this tragedy.[2]

From Paris, the travellers went to Rheims. Gray's grand tour is illustrated by him in a double set of notes, sometimes "bones exceeding dry" of quotations from Caesar in France, or Livy on the Alps; he draws less frequently than Addison from Latin poets, but still frequently enough; and records his impressions of architecture, and especially of painting; and we note among other evidences of his independence of judgment that he finds Andrea del Sarto anything but "the *faultless painter*." In this adverse judgment, he is seconded by Walpole, who comes nearer to Gray in artistic than in any other tastes.

On their way into Piedmont, Gray received, from his first view of mountain scenery, impressions which, on his return to England, remained for a while dormant, but had been

---

[1] In June, 1738, he begins a sapphic ode to West (Favonius)

> Barbaras aedes aditure mecum,
> Quas Eris semper fovet inquieta,
> Lis ubi latè sonat, et togatum
>     Aestuat agmen.

[2] Compare, with the union of Junia and Britannicus (Racine), that of Otho and Poppaea (Gray), Nero's passion being the obstacle in both cases. Nero overhears a conversation in both Racine and Gray; the place of Burrhus is taken by Seneca; the false Narcissus reappears in Anicetus, Agrippina's confidante Albina in Aceronia

wakened again when he wrote in *The Progress of Poesy* of scenes

> Where each old poetic mountain
> Inspiration breath'd around.

On 24 April, 1741, the pair set out from Florence, intending to go together to Venice, there to see the doge wed the Adriatic on ascension day. At Reggio, they quarrelled. It would seem that the discrepancy in their tastes became more and more a trial to both; and they were alike open in their comments on one another to their common friend Ashton, who disclosed Gray's to Walpole. Ashton did not display any particular displeasure with Gray at the time, but was put up by Walpole, in the interview at which a reconciliation was at last brought about, to affect that Gray's letter had roused his anger. Walpole was left at Reggio, and would have died there of quinsy but for the kind aid of Spence, the friend of Pope. Gray went with two new friends, made at Florence, to Venice, and thence took his homeward way. He paid a second visit to the Grande Chartreuse, and it was probably on this occasion that he left in the album of the fathers the beautiful alcaic ode *O tu severi Religio loci*, of which a fine English version has been composed by R. E. E. Warburton.[1]

On 7 September, 1741, we find Gray in London, causing a sensation among the street boys "by the depth of his Ruffles, the immensity of his Bagg, and the length of his sword." He was still in town in April, 1742, maintaining a correspondence with West, then ruralising in quest of health at Pope's house near Hatfield in Hertfordshire, on Tacitus and on the fourth *Dunciad,* which had just appeared. The yawn of Dulness at the end Gray describes as among the finest things Pope has written; and this young unknown critic here sounds the first note of discriminating praise, which has since been repeated by all good judges, from Johnson to Thackeray. In the same

---

[1] The later story of Gray's alcaics is curious. Mitford sought the original in vain at the monastery. He says that collectors who followed in the wake of the French revolutionary armies made away with it. But we find that a certain Mrs. Bigg, when resident in France, was arrested in the reign of terror, and a copy of Gray was found in her possession. The opening line, *O tu severi Religio loci*, suggested to the Jacobin investigators the comment: *Apparemment ce livre est quelque chose de fanatique.*

letter, he enclosed the first example of English verse which we
certainly know to be his, a fragment of *Agrippina*, a tragedy
never completed, of which Mason discovered the general
design among Gray's papers.   As has been already seen, it is
manifest that, in *Agrippina*, Racine's *Britannicus* was to have
been copied with almost Chinese exactness, just as Gray's details, like Racine's are often Tacitus versified.   The dignity of
style to be discovered in these *disjecta membra* still impresses
us.   But, more important than any question of their merits,
is the friendly criticism which they occasioned.   Few known
passages in critical literature furnish more instructive details
as to English poetic diction than these unpretending sentences
in a letter to West of April, 1742:

As to matter of stile, I have this to say:   *The language of the age
is never the language of poetry* except among the French, whose
verse, where the thought or image does not support it, differs in
nothing from prose.   Our poetry, on the contrary, has a language
peculiar to itself; to which almost every one, that has written, has
added something by enriching it with foreign idioms and deriva-
tives: nay sometimes words of their own composition or invention.
Shakespear and Milton have been great creators in this way: and
*no one more licentious than Pope or Dryden*, who perpetually borrow
expressions from the former.   Let me give you some instances
from Dryden, whom every body reckons a great master of our
poetic tongue.—Full of *museful mopeings*—unlike the *trim* of love—
a pleasant *beverage*—a *roundelay* of love—stood silent in his *mood*
—with knots and *knares* deformed—his *ireful mood*—in proud *array*
—his *boon* was granted—and *disarray* and shameful rout—*wayward*
but wise—*furbished* for the field—the *foiled doddered* oaks—*dis-
herited*—*smouldering* flames—*retchless*[1] of laws—*crones* old and
ugly—the *beldam* at his side—the *grandam-hag*—*villanize* his
Father's fame.

Gray goes on to admit that expressions in his play—"*silken*
son of *dalliance*," "*drowsier* pretensions," wrinkled *beldam*,"
"*arched* the hearer's brow and *riveted* his eyes in *fearful extasie*"
—may be faulty; though why they should be thought so, in
view of his own theory, must remain a mystery.   To take but
two examples, he has compounded "*silken* son of *dalliance*"
from that "New Dunciad" which he has just been reading, and

[1] *Palamon and Arcite.*   The form traces back to *Piers Plowman.*

from Shakespeare's *Henry V;*[1] and he gets his "arched brow" from Pope.[2]  More generally, it is a testimony to the great transformation of literary tastes which Gray ultimately helped to bring about, that words so familiar even in our everyday speech as "mood," "smouldering," "beverage," "array," "boon" and "wayward" were, in 1742, thought by some to be too fantastic even for poetry.  While this correspondence, sometimes little more than a pretty dilettantism and strenuous idleness, was passing between them, Gray was lulled into a false security about his friend West.  In April, he writes: "I trust to the country, and that easy indolence you say you enjoy there, to restore your health and spirits."  On the 8th, he has received a poem on the tardy spring and "rejoices to see you (West) putting up your prayers to the May: she cannot choose but come at such a call."  Pretty verses enough;[3] but chiefly interesting because they are the last poetic effort of the young and sorrow-stricken spirit to whom Gray sent the *Ode on the Spring*, which he first called "Noon-tide, an ode," and has left transcribed in his commonplace-book with the note "at Stoke, the beginning of June, 1742, sent to Fav[-onius, West]: not knowing he was then Dead."  In fact, West died on the first of June.  It was strange that the same theme of the opening year should have been respectively the first and the last efforts of the devoted friends, and that the month which silenced one young voice for ever should have wakened the survivor into an unwonted luxuriance of song.

A very brief period of efflorescence in verse preceded Gray's return to Cambridge.  From Stoke, to which, after the death of his father in 1741, his mother and his aunt Mary Antrobus had gone to live with their widowed sister Mrs. Rogers, he had sent (early in June, 1742) the *Ode on the Spring;* he wrote there

---

[1]      "And silken dalliance in the wardrobe lies."

*Henry V*, ii, chor. 1, 2.
"To where the Seine, obsequious as she runs
Pours at great Bourbon's feet her silken sons."

*Dunciad* iv.
[2]      "Whom have I hurt? has poet yet, or peer
Lost the arch'd eyebrow, or Parnassian sneer?"

*Ep. to Arbuthnot,* 1735.
[3]  They may be read in the volume *Gray and his Friends* (Cambridge, 1890), in which all West's remains are collected.

in August his *Sonnet on the Death of Richard West*, his cento
the *Hymn to Adversity*, his *Ode on a Distant Prospect of Eton
College* and a very splenetic *Hymn to Ignorance* (which, happily,
remains a fragment), on his projected return to Cambridge.
But we must refer to the same date the most touching of all
his tributes to the memory of West, in which the sad thoughts
of his English poems on the same theme are combined and concealed in a Latin dress.  His ambitious fragment *De Principiis
Cogitandi*, begun at Florence in 1740, and dubbed by him
"Tommy Lucretius" is, after all, so far as it goes, only a
*résumé* of Locke; but, in June, so soon as he heard of his loss,
he added, apparently without effort, a lament prompted by
the keen stimulus of grief, which seems to be more spontaneous
than his sonnet or the Eton *Ode*, and is, in fact, the first source
of these familiar verses.  It will bear comparison with Milton's
*Epitaphium Damonis*—Charles Diodati, the friendship between
whom and Milton, in many ways, is an exact counterpart to
that between West and Gray.  Nor can it be denied that Gray's
effort is without a certain artificiality, which, *pace* Masson,
renders Milton's poem more passionless, and more self-centred
and discursive.[1]

From his letters, we see that, for the first two years after
his return to Cambridge, now as a fellow-commoner of his
college, Gray was idle, so far as he could be for one still *in
statu pupillari*. He must have had arrears of lectures and
disputations to make up, in order to qualify for the degree of
LL.B., an easy task for him, though he writes ironically to
Wharton,

by my own indefatigable Application for these ten years past and
by the Care and Vigilance of that worthy magistrate The Man-in-
Blew,[2] (who I 'll assure you has not spared his Labour, nor could
have done more for his own Son) I am got half-way to the Top of
Jurisprudence.

But he had previously spoken of his allegiance to "our sovereign
Lady and Mistress the President of Presidents, and Head of
Heads (if I may be permitted to pronounce her name, that

---

[1] For the rest, a close comparison between Milton's Latin poems and Gray's
would show how much Gray owed to Milton in this department alone.

[2] The vice-chancellor's servant.

ineffable Octogrammaton) the power of *Laziness.*" Nevertheless, though the poetic impulse of 1742 had spent its force, his
interest in current literature is as keen as ever.  He criticises
Akenside's *Pleasures of Imagination* and at once put his finger
on that young poet's chief blemish; it is infected, he says, with
the jargon of Hutcheson, the disciple of Shaftesbury.  It is
the fault which he noted later in certain verses of Mason; there
was a craze for Shaftesbury among the young men of his time,
and beauty and morality were as identical for them as truth
and beauty were to Keats at a later date.

In 1745, Gray and Walpole were reconciled.  Of this consummation, Gray wrote a satirical account to Wharton, in
which his contempt for Ashton was clearly enough expressed.
After this strange pronouncement, the irony of fate brought it
about that Gray's next poetic effort was his *Ode on the Death
of a Favourite Cat,* which has been discussed with a solemnity
worthy of an epic.  Walpole had two favourite cats; and has
not told Gray which of these was drowned.  One of them was
a tortoiseshell, the other a tabby.

During the whole of the next four years, Gray seems to
have relapsed into his normal state of facile and amusing
gossip and criticism.  He is "a chiel taking notes," but with
no intention of printing them: yet we also discover that he is
a real power in the society that he pretends to despise, using
his influence to get fellowships for his friends, including Mason;
interesting himself in the wild and reckless Christopher Smart,
then a fellow of Pembroke, and deploring the loss of the veteran
Middleton, with whose views he was in sympathy, and whose
house was the only one in which he felt at his ease.  At the
same time, his studies were remarkably various, and his curiosity about foreign, and especially French, literature, intense,
as is particularly illustrated by his welcome of Montesquieu's
*Esprit des Lois,* which forestalled some of the best thoughts in
the fragmentary *Alliance of Education and Government* (1748).
At length, 12 June, 1750, he sends from Stoke to Walpole "a
thing with an end to it"—a merit that most of his writings have
wanted—and one whose beginning Walpole has seen long ago.[1]

---

[1] Probably in 1745 or 1746.  See *Gray's Poems* (Cambridge, 1898), p. 130.
Mason's statement that the *Elegy* was begun in 1742 is possibly true of the epitaph
at the end.

This is the famous *Elegy*, and Walpole appears to have circulated it somewhat freely in manuscript, with the result that the magazines got hold of it; and Gray, to protect himself, makes Walpole send it to Dodsley for immediate printing. Between *The Magazine of Magazines* and Dodsley, the *Elegy*, on its first publication, fared but badly: "Nurse Dodsley," Gray says, "has given it a pinch or two in its cradle that I doubt it will bear the marks of as long as it lives"; and, together, these publishers, licensed and unlicensed, achieved some curious readings. The moping owl complained of those who wandered near her "sacred bow'r": the young man went "frowning," not "smiling" as in scorn: the rustic's "harrow" oft the stubborn glebe had broke; and his frail memorial was decked with uncouth rhymes and shapeless "culture." And the mangled poet writes, "I humbly propose for the benefit of Mr. Dodsley and his matrons, that take *awake* for a verb, that they should read *asleep*, and all will be right."[1]

In contrast with this *incuria*, so far as the public is concerned, was the pains which he took, as evidenced by the MS preserved at the lodge at Pembroke college, to set down what he *did* write beyond the possibility of mistake.

The quatrain of ten syllables in which the *Elegy* was written had been used before, but never, perhaps, with conspicuous success, except in Dryden's *Annus Mirabilis*. In Gray's hands, it acquired a new beauty, and a music of its own. It does not appear that either the form or the diction of the poem struck the general reader as novel. The prevalent taste was for a sort of gentle melancholy and the mild and tranquil surroundings which minister to the reflective spirit. There is a little truth under the gross exaggeration with which the poet declared that he would have been just as successful if he had written in the prose of Hervey's *Meditations among the tombs*. Certain it is that Young's *Night Thoughts*, completed five years before the *Elegy*, was, for the time being, almost as popular. In Young's work, the sentiment is everything; hence, perhaps, its vogue on the continent, where discriminating judgments on our literature were few and far between.

---

[1]
    "the voice of Nature cries
   Awake, and faithful to her wonted fires."
(As if "awake" were an imperative.)

The *Elegy* seems to us simple in expression, and by no means abstruse, and we have said that there was in it nothing that struck even Gray's contemporaries as revolutionary. Perhaps it was Johnson who first scented the battle from afar. He parodied, in a version of a chorus of *Medea*, the style, as he conceived it, of the *Elegy*, in which adjectives follow their substantives, old words are revived, epithets are doubled and hyphenated, while subject and object are inverted. Contrasted with this was Johnson's own serious rendering of the same passage, in which the language was the current language of the day, with scarcely a word in it that was distinctly poetical.[1] The eccentricities which he noted still remain pitfalls. In the line "And all the air a solemn stillness holds," stillness, in spite of commentators, is the nominative, and we almost invariably quote, with so careful a reader as Conington,

> Await alike the inevitable hour,

although Gray wrote "Awaits," and "hour" is subject not object. (The thought is that of Horace, "One night awaits us all"; we should be less absorbed in our ambitions if we kept death in mind.) Again, Gray wrote "The lowing herd wind slowly o'er the lea," where not only is the plural suggestive of a line of cattle, but some of these are pictured as returning from the pasture and others from the plough. Once more, he wrote

> The paths of glory lead but to the grave

meaning that whatever the path chosen, the terminus is the same.[2]

The *Elegy* may be looked upon as the climax of a whole series of poems, dating from 1745, which had evening for their theme. In his 17th year, Thomas Warton, in his *Pleasures of Melancholy*, had all the accessories of the scene which Gray describes; there is a "sacred silence," as in a rejected but very beautiful stanza of the *Elegy* there was a "sacred calm"; there is the "owl," and the "ivy" that "with mantle green Invests some wasted tower." But the young poet, in his character of devotee of melancholy, takes us too far, when, with that

---

[1] Cf. Gray to West, April, 1742, quoted *supra*.

[2] The true readings were all recognised and translated by the late H. A. J. Munro, who, in his striking Latin version of the poem, is often its best interpreter.

gruesome enjoyment of horrors which is the prerogative of youth, he leads us at midnight to the "hollow charnel" to "watch the flame of taper dim shedding a livid glare." We are at once conscious of the artificial and ambitious character of the effort, precocious as an essay in literature, but without genuine feeling, without the correspondence between man and nature, which alone can create a mood. And it was the power to create a mood which was the distinctive merit of the best poems of this class and at this date.

Joseph Warton, with the same environment, and, still more, Collins, in his magical *Ode to Evening*,[1] achieved this success. Contrast these with the conventional beings of *The Seasons*, and we become aware that we are nearing an epoch where description is subordinated to the real emotions of humanity, and the country bumpkin no longer chases the rainbow, or "unfolds," with Akenside, "the form of beauty smiling at his heart."

The *Elegy* in its MS forms brings another noteworthy fact into prominence. These show how pitilessly the poet excised every stanza which did not minister to the congruity of his masterpiece. We feel for instance that Wordsworth, apt to believe that his most trivial fancies were inspirations, would never have parted, for any considerations of structure, with such lines as

> Hark how the sacred Calm, that broods around
> Bids ev'ry fierce tumultuous Passion cease,
> In still small accents whisp'ring from the Ground
> A grateful Earnest of eternal Peace.

Gray himself seems in one instance to have repented of his infanticide, and writes in the Pembroke MS the marginal note "insert" over the stanza (evidently adapted but compressed from Collins's *Dirge in Cymbeline*) about the violets scattered on the tomb and the little footsteps of the redbreast which lightly print the ground there. Memory and affection have something to do with the epitaph, which sounds the personal note of which Gray was fond, but is, unquestionably, the weak-

---

[1] Friendship and compassion did not reconcile Johnson to the poetry of Collins, who is nearest to Gray in the diction which their critic loathed. See Johnson's *Life of Collins, ad fin.*

est part of the poem, and was, perhaps, written about 1742, and inserted in the *Elegy* by afterthought.   In general, no poet better understood, or more strictly followed, the Popian maxim "survey the whole," that golden rule which a later generation seldom remembers or practises.

The *Elegy* had a curious sequel in *A Long Story*.   After her husband's death, in 1749, Lady Cobham must have left the famous Stowe for the mansion house at Stoke Pogis; she had seen the *Elegy* when Walpole was circulating it in MS, and learnt that the author was in her neighbourhood.   Accordingly, she caused her niece, Miss Speed, and Lady Schaub, the wife of Sir Luke Schaub, to visit him, at the house of Mrs. Rogers, ostensibly to tell him that a Lady Brown, one of his friends, who kept open house in town for travellers young and old, was quite well.   Gray was not at home, and this visit of fine ladies may have caused, as Gray pretends, some perturbation to his quiet aunt and mother.   A graceful intimacy (nothing more) grew up between the poet and Miss Speed, though gossip declared they were to be married.[1]

*A Long Story*, written with facile pen, goes far to bear out Walpole's statement that Gray never wrote anything easily except things of humour.   His serious efforts are always the fruit of long delay and much labour.   Next followed (1752) what remains a fragment, only because Mason found a corner of the sole MS copy torn, supplying, *more suo*, words of his own to complete it.   It was entitled *Stanzas to Richard Bentley*, who made *Designs for six Poems by Mr. T. Gray*.   We cannot feel sure that Mason has given us the unmutilated part of the poem correctly.   Gray knew Pope and Dryden too well to write

> The energy of Pope they might efface
> And Dryden's harmony submit to mine.

It may be suspected that Mason has clumsily transposed these epithets.   As evidence how Gray nursed his thoughts we may note that the line

> And dazzle with a luxury of light

is a reminiscence of a version which he made in 1737 from Tasso's *Jerusalem Delivered*, bk. 14.

[1] The lady died as comtesse de Viry in 1783.

One other line in this brief poem lives in the memory—that in which he attributes to Shakespeare and Milton in contrast to "this benighted age," a diviner inspiration,

> The pomp and prodigality of heaven.

He is, later, in February, 1753, in a great fret about the title of the six poems, and, in his desire to seem unaffected, displays a great deal of affectation.  It was quite absurd to imagine that the poems, including the *Elegy*, could be regarded as secondary to the designs.  It was his foible to pose; but he indulged it with scanty success.  In March, 1753 died Gray's "careful tender mother," as he calls her in the inscription for the vault in which she was laid by the side of her sister Mary Antrobus. In July of the same year, he went to see his friend Wharton, who was living in Durham.  Here, the author of the *Elegy* was made much of; but the visit was important in another way. It coincides with a change in Gray's poetic tendencies, and helped to encourage them.  He now reverted to that love of the bold and majestic which appears in the alcaics on the Grande Chartreuse.  In the neighbourhood of Durham, he found a faint image of those more august scenes.

I have (he writes) one of the most beautiful vales here in England to walk in, with prospects that change every ten steps, and open something new wherever I turn me, *all rude and romantic;* in short the sweetest spot *to break your neck or drown yourself in* that ever was beheld.

On 26 December, 1754, was completed the ode entitled *The Progress of Poesy;* it had been nearly finished two years before. It was not published until 1759, when Walpole secured it for the Strawberry hill press, together with *The Bard;* the motto φωνᾶντα συνετοῖσι from Pindar belongs to them both.[1]

Gray did not attach any great value to the rule of strophe and antistrophe, but he strongly objected to the merely irregular stanzas which Cowley introduced.  It was probably Congreve who first wrote a real pindaric ode; and, whatever the value of his *Ode to the Queen*, it did something, as Mason points out, to obviate Gray's objection to this form.  It was written

---

[1] Subsequently the words that follow in Pindar, ἐς δὲ τὸ πᾶν ἑρμηνεύων, were added, when Gray found explanatory notes were needed.

in short stanzas, and the recurrence of the same metre was more recognisable to the ear than when it was separated by a long interval from its counterpart.

In Gray's time, the muse was always making the grand tour. If the title of Collins's *Ode to Simplicity* were not misleading, we should find in it an embryo *Progress of Poesy*, in which inspiration passes, as with Gray, from Greece to Italy and from Italy to England. The clue to the mystery of the title is found when we discover that, to Collins, "simplicity" is "nature," as Pope understood the word—nature identified with Homer, and with all her great poetic interpreters, who idealise but do not distort her. These pilgrimages of the muse were started by Thomson, who, in his *Liberty*, chose her as his travelling companion, and brought her home intolerably dull, and, not long before Gray's death, by Goldsmith in his *Traveller*.

The most easy way of criticising *The Progress of Poesy* and *The Bard* is to start by criticising their critics, beginning with Francklin, regius professor of Greek at Cambridge, who mistook the "Aeolian lyre" invoked in the first line of *The Progress* for the instrument invented by Oswald, and objected that "such an instrument as the Aeolian harp, which is altogether uncertain and irregular must be very ill adapted to the dance which is one continued regular movement." Garrick, who spoke from professional knowledge, grasped the truth better, and said that Gray was the only poet who understood dancing. His original in the place which he has in mind is a line of Homer (*Odyss.*, bk. VIII, l. 265); but he borrows without acknowledgment the word "many-twinkling" from Thomson (*Spring*, l. 158) who uses it of the leaves of the aspen. The poem begins appropriately with an imitation of Horace's description of Pindar,

> In profound, unmeasurable song
> The deep-mouth'd Pindar, foaming, pours along.

This beautiful poem is marred by a personal reference at the end, as in the case, to which we have already referred, of the *Elegy*.

Between *The Progress of Poesy* and *The Bard* comes the Fragment of an Ode found in the MS at Pembroke. It is without a title: that which it now bears, *On the pleasure arising from Vicissitude*, is probably due to Mason, who attempted to complete the poem and excelled himself in infelicity, filling up the last stanza as we have it, thus:

> To these, if Hebe's self should bring
> The purest cup from Pleasure's spring
> Say, can they taste the flavour high
> Of sober, simple, genuine Joy?[1]

In *Vicissitude*, some critics have discovered an anticipation of Wordsworth, but we ought to distinguish. When Gray says that "the meanest flouret of the vale" is "opening paradise" to the convalescent, he describes the human being under limited and exceptional circumstances. But when Wordsworth, in robust health, derives from the meanest flower, thoughts that "often lie too deep for tears," and reproaches his Peter Bell for finding the primrose a yellow primrose and nothing more, he expects from humanity in general more than experience warrants.[2]

Though this fragment probably comes chronologically between *The Progress of Poesy* and *The Bard*, we are not justified in interposing it between them. They are dissociable from it, not only on account of their being printed and published in juxtaposition, as Ode I and Ode II, and of the motto which clearly applies to both, but because together they herald a generic change. *Vicissitude*, with every promise of a beautiful poem, carries on the meditative spirit in which all Gray's serious work had been executed hitherto. But the two odes are conceived in an atmosphere rather intellectual than sentimental. They are a literary experiment. They idealise great facts, historic or legendary, out of which reflection may be generated —but mediately, not directly from the poet's mind. While they have this in common, there remains a point of contrast between them. *The Bard*, more clearly than the other ode, bears traces of those studies from the Norse which Gray had already made and which found expression in *The Fatal Sisters* and *The Descent of Odin*.

[1] For another stanza he is indebted to a suggestion in Gray's pocket-book, but has made a poor use of it.

[2] Gray almost directly imitates here Gresset, a favourite poet with him (*Sur ma convalescence*).

It inaugurates the last stage of the poet's literary history. The design has been marred by many editors through heedlessness in printing. They have not observed that the bard sings his song at first as a solo, until, in the distance, he sees the ghosts of his slain brethren, and invites them to join the chant, while together they weave the winding sheet of Edward's race. That done, they vanish from the bard's sight, and he finishes his prophecy alone. The fault, perhaps inevitable, of the poem, lies in the conclusion, which smells too much of the lamp. The salient characteristics of the great poets of the Elizabethan era are described with much skill, though with a certain vagueness proper to prophecy; and yet we cannot help asking, how he can know so much about these his very late successors, while he shows himself rather a discerning critic, than a mighty prophet who has just been foretelling tragic horrors and retribution. They ill suit the majestic form graphically described before his prophecy begins.

A curious evidence of the influence of Gray's *Bard* upon the συνετοί is to be found in the history of the Ossianic imposture. In Cath-Loda Duan I of this so-called collection of reliques, we have the expression "Thou kindlest thy hair into meteors," and in the "Songs of Selma" Ossian sings:

I behold my departed friends. Their gathering is on Iona, as in the days of other years. Fingall comes like a watery column of mist! his heroes are around: and see the bards of song, grey-haired Ullin; stately Ryno! Alpin with the tuneful voice! *the soft complaint* of Minona! How are ye changed, my friends, etc.

Gray, who had at first welcomed the frauds of Macpherson, because he discerned in them the romantic spirit, became more reticent as time went on, and as his common sense, against which he feebly struggled, gained the mastery. He either did not or would not observe that in them he was imitated or parodied. On the other hand, he repudiated for himself the suggestion that the opening of *The Bard* was modelled upon the prophecy of Nereus in Horace (*Carm.* I. 15). We cannot accept the repudiation, for the resemblance is unmistakable, although it makes but little against the real originality of his poem, and is on the same plane with his acknowledgment that the image of the bard was modelled on the picture by Raphael of the

Supreme Being in the vision of Ezekiel, or that of Moses breaking the tables of the law by Parmegiano. *The Bard* still remains the best evidence we possess that Gray, imitative as he is, was, also, an inventive genius.

It might, after all, have come down to us as a colossal fragment, lacking the third antistrophe and epode, but for a stimulus of which Gray gives an account. He heard at Cambridge Parry, the blind Welsh harper, and his sensitive ear was so fascinated that "Odikle" was put in motion again. So completely did he associate his verse with music, that he gave elaborate directions for its setting, and it is a very high compliment to Gray's taste that Villiers Stanford, though he knew nothing of these instructions, carried them out to the letter.

Before this, in 1756, occurred an event which Gray describes only vaguely "as a sort of aera in a life so barren of events as" his. The affair has been treated with so much difference of opinion that we can only summarise the conclusion at which we have arrived. Gray had been much tormented by some young men, of whom two were certainly fellow-commoners residing on his staircase, and he had a nervous dread of fire, upon which they probably played. He accordingly got Wharton to bespeak him a rope-ladder, a strong temptation to the young men to make him put it to the proof. It is possible that, before the outrage, they had begun kindling fires of shavings on his staircase. At last, an early hunting party caused the huntsmen to shout "fire" under his window, some of them, perhaps, before joining the party, having made the usual blaze on the stairs. The poet put his night-capped head out of the window and, discovering the hoax, drew it in again. This was all that was known to Sharp, fellow of Corpus, who wrote only six days after Gray's migration to Pembroke. The exaggerated form in which the story is still current was shaped in 1767 by a certain Archibald Campbell, a scribbler in a production called *The Sale of Authors*, who expressly confesses that he vouches for no details in what he describes as a harmless pleasantry. Suffice it to say that the master, Dr. Law, to whom Gray complained, made light of this "boyish frolic," as he called it, and Gray, in consequence, changed his college.

The year 1759 was mainly spent in London, near the British

museum, which was opened to the public in January. Gray revelled in MS treasures there, and made copious extracts from them; the most interesting, perhaps, to the general reader are letters from Richard III, and the defence of Sir Thomas Wyatt, the poet; both of which transcripts he made for Walpole, who used them in his *Miscellaneous Antiquities* and *Historic Doubts*. At this time, also, he probably composed the treatise called *Metrum*, and *Observations on the poems of Lydgate*, probably in view of a design for the history of English poetry which was never executed.

In 1762, Gray made a tour in Yorkshire and Derby, and saw Kirkstall abbey, the Peak, of which he thought but little, and Chatsworth. On his return to Cambridge, he found the professorship of modern history vacant, and caused his claim to be represented to Lord Bute. But the professorship was given to Lawrence Brockett, who had been tutor to Sir James Lowther, son-in-law of the favourite Bute. In 1764, possibly with Wharton as his companion, he made his first visit to Scotland, and, in 1765, he repeated this visit as the guest of Lord Strathmore, formerly a fellow-commoner of Pembroke. On this second visit, he met Robertson and other *literati*. It is a proof of the remarkable catholicity of Gray's love of scenery that, in the earlier of these years, possessed though he was with the sublime grandeur of the mountains, he could also enjoy and describe graphically the charms of a gentler landscape, in a part of England (Winchester, Southampton, Netley abbey, etc.) dear to Collins.

In the following year, he once more visited Scotland and became acquainted with Beattie, author of *The Minstrel*, to the last an unfinished poem, the earliest part of which he helped to correct. His criticism is just but with two notable exceptions. He truly remarks that too much is given to descriptions and reflections; Beattie does not know what to do with his minstrel when he has made him. Yet Gray's remarks are in two particulars disappointing. In direct contrast to his doctrine as stated to West in April, 1742, he says "I think we should wholly adopt the language of Spenser's time or wholly renounce it. You say, you have done the latter; but, in effect, you retain *fared, forth, mead, wight, ween, gaude, shene, in sooth, aye, eschew,* etc." And he objects to Beattie's use of alliteration: if he had confined himself to censuring one line in the part of the poem which was sent him

> The long-robed minstrels wake the warbling lyre

it would have been well.   As it is, Beattie had an easy retort upon him with

> Nor cast one longing, lingering look behind

in the *Elegy*.

In 1768, Gray's poems were republished by Dodsley, and for *A Long Story* were substituted the two Norse odes, *The Fatal Sisters*, and *The Descent of Odin*.   A similar edition came, at the same time, from the press of Foulis (the Glasgow Elzevir). When Gray wrote *The Bard*, he had already made some study of Scandinavian poetry.   He had *The Fatal Sisters* in mind when he wrote

> Weave the warp and weave the woof
> The Winding sheet of Edward's race.

Perhaps, *The Descent of Odin*, in one passage of which[1] it is impossible not to recognise an anticipation of Scott, is, in this respect, still more suggestive.

In 1768, Brockett, Cambridge professor of modern history, met with a fatal accident on returning from Hinchingbrooke. Stonehewer, who had been one of Gray's closest friends at Peterhouse and who acted as the duke of Grafton's secretary, pleaded Gray's claims to the professorship of history, and with success.   The office was a sinecure; he had some intention of delivering lectures, but the form of his projected inaugural lecture is in Latin, and whatever his design was it fell through. In his new capacity, it was his task to write the installation ode when Grafton was made chancellor of the University.   The work proved the one exception to the fact that he never wrote

[1]
> " Right against the eastern gate
> By the moss-grown pile he sate
> Where long of yore to sleep was laid
> The dust of the prophetic Maid,
> Facing to the northern clime
> Thrice he traced the runic rhyme ;
> Thrice pronounc'd, in accents dread,
> The thrilling verse that wakes the dead."

well unless spontaneously. He lingered long before he began. At last, he startled Nicholls by throwing open his door to his visitor and shouting, "Hence, avaunt! 't is holy ground," and the new ode was completed. A sort of heraldic splendour characterises this, his last great effort; in places, it seems to step out of a page of Froissart, and, notwithstanding the bile of Junius, the pomp and circumstance of the closing personal panegyric do not convey any impression of inappropriateness.

This business over, Gray went with Wharton towards the English Lakes, but his companion fell ill at Brough, and Gray pursued his journey alone. The fruit of it was a journal which he sent from time to time to Wharton, and of which, with a Porsonian delight in his own beautiful handwriting, there is reason to believe that he made more than one copy. The journal was never published until after his death, and the public did not know till then how exactly he had surveyed the scenery. Wordsworth, if he knew, ignored the fact that a poet whom he habitually depreciated was, as a minute admirer of the views of nature, not less enthusiastic than his censor. The credit of discovering the Lakes belongs really to neither of these. It belongs to poor crazy Brown, the author of *The Estimate*, who wrote of a night scene near Keswick:

> Nor voice, nor sound broke on the deep serene;
> But the soft murmur of soft-gushing rills
> (Unheard till now, and now scarce heard), etc.

The whole of Gray's journal is precious, abounding in description, facts of natural history, historical detail, antique records, experiences gained with a persistent effort, very creditable to one generally very nervous and timid, but careless of fatigue and risk in his fascinating quest.[1]

At the beginning of 1770, Gray, through Nicholls, found a strange young friend, to beguile for a short time his solitary days, and give his waning life a sort of Martin's summer. Young Charles-Victor de Bonstetten came to him to fascinate, but, also, to perplex, him. The undergraduates puzzled the foreigner; he could not understand the young seigneurs traves-

---

[1] He travelled, of course, much on foot, but it is not probable that he always did so. It was not his way to record on all occasions how he travelled. The distances which he walked have been absurdly exaggerated.

tied as monks in the university glorified by Newton. He knew
so little of the real life of these neophytes as never to suspect
that their conduct and character were far from ascetic. It was
a secret Gray prudently withheld from him, jealously keeping
his disciple for himself. Bonstetten spent most of his time in
Gray's room, having, however, a young sizar to wake him in the
morning and read Milton to him. He studied from morning
to night and spent his evenings with Gray. His own experience
was, in truth, already much wider than that of his now ageing
friend. He had seen Rousseau, he had talked with Voltaire;
he had even tried suicide, anticipating Werther under the spell
of that *Weltschmerz* which the Briton imperfectly understood.
All this, Gray never knew, or thought it best not to notice.
He wrote to the young man, who relapsed for a time into melancholy on his return to Switzerland, as Fénelon's Mentor might
talk to Telemachus; and epitomises for his benefit the sixth
book of Plato's *Republic*. In the end, Bonstetten became an
excellent magistrate, and served Switzerland well, until the
revolution drove him into exile. He never forgot Gray, the
old poet whose last days he had brightened, and who had
parted from him with pathetic regret.[1]

The scene had begun to close in when, in the company of
Nicholls, he went through five of the western counties, descended the Wye forty miles in a boat, saw Tintern and, at
Malvern, on receiving a copy of *The Deserted Village*, exclaimed
emphatically "this man is a poet." But there was not, for
the first part of 1771, much sign of any serious ailment; apart
from some indications of failing vitality in his frame, his mind
was as active as ever, till, in June, he became conscious of a
new complaint, and, on 24 July, was taken suddenly ill in hall.
On the 30th, he was dead.

A survey of Gray's work would include MSS. of incredibly
larger volume than the few poems published in his lifetime.
Yet no small part of his reputation rests, for us, upon copious
MSS., carefully preserved by him, but never intended to be
seen, except by an esoteric circle. To begin with, his invaluable
letters are an index to his whole character, and to the humorous
spirit that is often, as in the case of Hood, twin sister to melan-

[1] See the story told more at length in the second volume of Gray's *Letters*
(1904).

choly. In his letters, his life lies spread out before us; they
are the only absolutely trustworthy records for his biographers.
Their interest lies in their infinite variety. Walpole was a better
historian of social life; but his claims to erudition were slight,
his obligations to Gray, acknowledged and unacknowledged,
were great,[1] and his scientific knowledge was *nil;* while, whatever the interest of his letters for political and social history,
they contain nothing comparable to the depth and pathos of
Gray's more limited memories and friendships.[2] On the other
hand, Gray's letters are an excellent guide as a survey of continental literature; the best French writers he literally devoured;
his liking for inferior fiction he shared with the fashionable
world, partly because it *was* fashionable, but such writers as
Montesquieu, Buffon and the encyclopaedists he read with
enthusiasm. With Rousseau, except his *Émile,* and with
Voltaire, he is utterly out of sympathy. He plunges deep into
the pages of Froissart, "the Herodotus of a barbarous age,"
of Sully's *Mémoires,* of Madame de Maintenon's letters, and
the memoirs of that French Fanny Burney, Madame de Staal
Delaunay. He knows, beside Froissart, all the old French
chroniclers, and gives advice as to the order and method of their
study. While, at times, like a market-gardener, he exchanges
with Wharton notes as to the dates of the returns of the seasons
and the state of the crops, he is also a man of science. He is
in touch with Linnaeus, through his disciple at Upsala, and
with the English naturalist Stillingfleet. Classical literature
has, for him, no dry bones. He rises to enthusiasm on such
subjects and expects Wharton to share his delight in the description of the retreat from Syracuse, which his friend has just
reached in the seventh book of Thucydides.

In December, 1757, he was offered the laureateship, but
contemptuously declined it; the offer, nevertheless, was a
tribute to him, as the first poet of his generation. And,
indeed, in 1748, before he had written very much, he sat in
scornful judgment upon his contemporaries. In Dodsley's
collection of that year, the only living poets whom he can praise
unreservedly are Shenstone for *The Schoolmistress,* Johnson

---

[1] See his *Anecdotes of Painting* and Gray's comments; also, Gray's criticisms
on *Historic Doubts* (read between the lines).

[2] As to Walpole's letters, see Chap. XI, *post.*

for *London* and *Verses* on the opening of Garrick's theatre,
Dyer for *Grongar Hill*, and, of course, Walpole. But, he adds

What shall I say to Mr. Lowth, Mr. Ridley, Mr. Rolle, the Rev.
Mr. Brown ("Estimate Brown"), Seward, etc. etc. If I say Mes-
sieurs! this is not the thing; write prose, write sermons, write
nothing at all: they will disdain me and my advice.

Of Gray's most persistent friend and correspondent, Mason,
it is difficult to speak with justice or moderation. Gray has
described him with kindliness and sincerity, and it is, perhaps,
the one redeeming trait in Mason's edition of the correspondence
that he has preserved this description with almost Boswellian
self-sacrifice. According to Gray, he is a creature of childlike
simplicity, but writes too much, and hopes to make money by
it, reads very little, and is insatiable in the matter of preferment; the simplicity we may question, and it seems incompatible with the rest of the description. He garbled Gray's
letters ruthlessly; in their unmutilated form, they would have
disposed for ever of his claims to be his friend's *compère*. He
may be excused for not wishing to figure before the public as
"dear Skroddler"; but, when he pleads the boyish levity of
some of the letters as an excuse for his expurgations, he knows
better, and is simply posing, often substituting his own bombast for Gray's plain speaking. Gray recognised merit in
Mason's *Musaeus, a Monody on the death of Pope*, spite of
shells and coral floors; he liked, moderately, *Elfrida* and,
immoderately, *Caractacus*, from which, in *The Bard*, he quotes
an example of the sublime. His elegies and other verses it
would be profitless to enumerate. They have no place in the
history of our literature. He wrote political pasquinades of
no great merit; but it may be reckoned to his credit that he
was a consistent Whig, so that, on the accession of George III,
he lost all chance of further preferment. He showed very little
magnanimity in attacking, in his *Isis*, the university of Oxford,
then (1746 sq.) out of favour with the court, the bulk of whose
patronage went to Cambridge. He was answered in *The Triumph of Isis* by Thomas Warton, then a youth of twenty-one,
with spirit and good temper; yet, such was his vanity that
he believed he had inflicted a mortal wound, and, years after,
congratulated himself on entering Oxford at night, without

fear of a crowd of "booing undergraduates." His superficial resemblance to the manner of Gray did the greater poet some harm. Their contemporaries, and certain critics of a later generation, did not see any difference between Mason's frosty glare and constant falsetto and the balanced eloquence of Gray.

If the project of a joint work with Mason on the history of English poetry had not fallen through, Gray must have found his associate a terrible incubus. No greater contrast existed at that date than Mason's slipshod, as compared with Gray's scholarly accuracy. Even the work of Warton was an inadequate substitute for that which Gray might have given us; the probability is that its only fault would have been too much, even as Warton has too little, method.

There was one of Gray's preferences that contributed greatly to the appreciation which, as the historian of our poetry, he would have shown of its earlier stages. In strong contrast to the elaborate and stately diction of his own verse, he loved best the poets who were almost models of simplicity: Matthew Green, and the French Gresset, and Dyer of *Grongar Hill*, and whatever Shenstone and even Tickell had written in the same vein. His mind was early ripe for the ballads of Percy's *Reliques*. He finds, accordingly, in *Gil Morrice*, all the rules of Aristotle observed by some unknown ballad-writer who had never read Aristotle. He derives from Macpherson's fragments and his Fingall evidence that "without any respect of climates poetry reigns in all nascent societies of men." The theory itself is intrinsically better than the support on which he chose to rest it. He was struggling in that portentous Ossianic mist which spread from Britain to the continent, a mist through which people of genius, the greatest as well as the least, wandered for a time, bewildered by their own shadows. The last efforts of his muse, dating from *The Bard*, are, in the history of our literature, incomparably the most important. From his Latin verse, which, if we except his jocular or satiric efforts, was alone fluent and spontaneous, and is still significant as marking the first stage in his poetic development, we pass to a meditative mood sufficiently conventional in form except in its extreme classicism, and transcendent only because impressed by genuine feeling, and thence to the scanty product by virtue of which we regard him as a pioneer, who seems, like Hesperus, to lead a starry host, but really moves with the rest in obedience to the same mysterious impulse.   His fame, in this character, has obscured without effort that of many lesser bards whose course was in the same direction, until the magic was transmitted to Coleridge, and then to Scott, who used it with more persistent energy and more conspicuous effect.

# CHAPTER VII

## Young, Collins and Lesser Poets of the Age of Johnson

THE posthumous experience, if it may be so described, of most of the poets to be treated in the present chapter, like that of their predecessors, noticed in an earlier section of this *History*,[1] illustrates certain doctrines, both of the less, and of the more, vulgar philosophy of life. For more than a century and a half, through the successive collections of Dodsley, Pearch, Johnson, Anderson and Chalmers, they have had opportunities of being generally known which can hardly be said to have been shared by the verse writers of any other period of English literary history. But, for the last century at any rate, this familiarity with their productions has, also, brought about its proverbial consequence. Collins, indeed, if not *nemine contradicente*, yet, by a strong body of the best critical judgment, has (putting range of kind and bulk of production out of the question) been allowed poetical quality of almost the rarest and purest sort. Young, despite the great volume of now imperfectly interesting matter comprehended in his poetical works, and the extreme inequality of his treatment of it, despite, too, the defects of his temper and other drawbacks, enjoyed, for a long time, great and almost European popularity; he possesses, for the literary historian, the attraction of having actually anticipated Pope in one of the most characteristic directions of Pope's satiric energy; and he can never be explored by any patient and unbiassed investigator without the recognition of flame under the ashes, flowers in the wilderness and fragments of no contemptible moulding among the ruins. Shen-

[1] See *ante*, Vol. IX, Chap. VI, sec. II.

stone, Dyer, Green ("Spleen"-Green), Blair, Armstrong, Akenside, Beattie, Smart—there are associations with each of these names which ought not to be forgotten; and, even from the *numerus* which may be grouped with them, there remains something to be gathered as to the general state and fortunes of literature and of poetry which ought not to be missing in such a work as the present.

An extensive notice of biographical data, not generally included in the plan of this *History*, would be altogether out of place in a collective chapter; but some references of the kind will be found to be occasionally indispensable. Young's long life, from the time when he entered Winchester in 1695, was exactly divided between residence at school and in three colleges at Oxford (New college, where he missed securing a place on the foundation, Corpus Christi, and, lastly, All Souls, of which he became a lay fellow in 1708) and tenure of the college living of Welwyn, to which, having given up plans of professional and parliamentary life and taken orders, he was presented in 1730. Throughout each of these long periods, he appears (except at the moment of his election at All Souls) as a disappointed man, baffled as to regular promotion at school; wandering from college to college; not, indeed, ever in apparent danger of the jail, but incessantly and fruitlessly courting the patron; an unsuccessful, or but once successful, dramatist; a beaten candidate for parliament; and, in his second stage, perpetually desiderating, but never, in the very slightest measure, receiving, that ecclesiastical promotion which, in some not quite comprehensible way, almost every eighteenth century divine seems to have thought his plain and incontestable right. In both parts of his career, moreover, there can be little doubt that Young suffered from that curious recoil or rebuff for which, perhaps, not enough allowance has been made in meting out praise or blame among the successive literary generations of the eighteenth century. Addison's administrative, and Prior's diplomatic, honours were not unmixed blessings to their possessors; but there cannot be any doubt that they made Grub street, or even places much more agreeable and less "fabulous" than Grub street, all the more intolerable to the younger generation.

Before applying the light of this (of course not novel) consideration to Young's work, let us see what that work (most of it now utterly forgotten) actually was. He began with addresses and odes of various kinds (one on the queen's death) in the last two years of Anne, and produced the play *Busiris*, a paraphrase of *Job* and his *Letters to Tickell*, in 1719. In 1721 appeared his one famous play *The Revenge*, and, a little later, in parts (1725–8), the most important work of his younger, but not very young, years, *The Universal Passion*. During the years 1728 to 1730 were published the amazing pieces called *Ocean* and *Imperium Pelagi*, with others. *The Complaint, or Night Thoughts on Life, Death and Immortality*, began to appear in 1744, when the author was nearly sixty-two. A third play, *The Brothers*, followed in 1753: and his last work of importance, *Resignation*, in 1762.

The immense and long enduring popularity of *Night Thoughts* hardly requires much comment, even now that it has utterly vanished and is never likely to return. This popularity was not, as it has been in some other cases, due to lack of insight on the part of the public that bestowed it; but, as perhaps nearly always happens, it was due to the fact that the merits of the work, in part, at least, were exactly such as that public could best appreciate, and the faults such as it was most disposed to pass over. *Night Thoughts* is hard reading, nowadays, even for the most catholic lover of poetry; and the rest of Young, even *The Universal Passion*, is harder. But he must be a very exceptional critic who can do Young justice, either without a complete reading of his poems, or at a first reading only. Two keys, perhaps, are wanted to unlock the cabinet. The first is an easy and wellknown key—the effect of personal disappointment. To this feeling, in various forms, poets are proverbially liable; but it is difficult to remember any poet who shows it so constantly and in such various forms as Young. It is not always very noisy in him: but it shows itself everywhere—in his satire as well as in his preachings and moralisings, in the innumerable passages, whether longer or shorter, of a form of flattery which sometimes carries with it a despairing sense that nothing, or nothing adequate, will, after all, come from the flattered; in the elegies over apparent triumphs such as Addison's, and apparent failures like that of Swift's "little Harrison," who was Young's intimate friend; last of all, but

not least of all, and, perhaps, most pathetically, in the title
and the substance alike of his swan-song *Resignation*. That
his disappointment, on the whole, was rather unreasonable is
a feeble, as well as a "philistine," way of dismissing the matter:
unreasonable disappointments are apt to be the most, not the
least, keenly felt.

But there was something else wrong with Young. Johnson,
in one of that great majority of his judgments on which one
cannot do better than fall back, pronounced that "with all his
defects he was a man of genius and a poet." He was this; but,
of almost all men of genius and almost all poets, he was the
most singularly lacking in art; and he seems, to some extent,
to have been aware of it, if we may judge from the frequency
with which he dismissed his own work as not worth republica-
tion. It is quite astonishing how bad an artist Young is; for,
whatever its deficiencies in other respects and whatever its
limits in the domain of art, the eighteenth century did not
usually, according to its lights, make default in questions concerning art. In gross and in detail, Young's art, even his mere
craftsmanship, is absolutely untrustworthy. His rimes are
the worst that we have from any English poet, except Mrs.
Browning. He constantly ventures, in narrative blank verse,
upon the dramatic redundant syllable, which is always a
blemish, and sometimes fatal, out of drama. The almost
incredible absurdities of *Ocean*, *Imperium Pelagi* and other
odes come partly from want of taste in selection of stanza,
partly from infelicities of phrase which few schoolboys would
commit.

In the greater matter (as some hold it) of construction, he
is equally weak. He really did precede Pope in certain turns,
as well as in a general atmosphere, of satire, which, it may be
suspected, is the reason why some not illiterate persons are in
the habit of attributing lines and passages in Young to his
greater successor. But, in the earlier poet, the inequality,
the awkwardness, the verbiage, are still constantly present.

It ought to be set down to the credit of public taste, which
seldom receives, and does not often deserve, praise, that these
defects (except the verbiage) are somewhat less perceptible in
what was long held to be a masterpiece, and is Young's masterpiece still. Even the annoying and defacing redundant syllable

may be excused, to some extent, on the plea that *The Complaint*,
to all intents and purposes, is an enormous soliloquy—a lamentation in argumentative and reflective monologue, addressed
by an actor of superhuman lung-power to an audience of still
more superhuman endurance. It has, throughout, the character of the *epideictic*—the rhetorical exercise deliberately
calculated and consciously accepted as a matter of display—
which is frequent in more serious eighteenth century verse.
What Shakespeare, in a few lines of *Hamlet* and of *Macbeth*, compressed and sublimed into immortal poetry, Young watered
down or hammered out into rhetoric, with endless comments
and "uses" and applications. But, in passages which are
still unforgotten, he allows himself a little concentration and
something that is strangely like, if it is not actually, sincerity;
and, then, he does become, in his day and in his place, "a man
of genius and a poet." Indeed, if he were judged by single
lines, both of the satiric and of the reflective kind, these titles
could still less be refused him. And it is only fair to say that
such lines and passages occur not merely in *Night Thoughts*,
not merely in *The Universal Passion*, but almost everywhere
(except in the odes), from the early *Last Day* and *Job* to
the final *Resignation*.

As we turn to William Collins, we come, perhaps, to the
only name the inclusion of which in this chapter may raise a
cavil. "If Collins is to be classed with lesser poets," it may
be said, "then who, in Collins's time, or in his century, is a
greater?" There is no space here for detailed controversy on
such points; yet, without some answer to the question, the
literary history of the age would be obscured or left imperfect.
In the opinion of the present writer, Collins, in part, and the
chief part, of his work, was, undoubtedly, a "greater poet,"
and that not merely of his own time. There is no time—
Elizabethan, Georgian or Victorian—at which the best things
in the *Odes* would not have entitled their author to the verdict
"poetry *sans phrase*." But there is another part of his work,
small as it may be in bulk—the whole of it is but small, and,
in the unhappy circumstances of his life, could hardly have been
larger—which is not greater poetry, which, indeed, is very distinctly lesser; and this "minority" occurs also, we must almost

say constantly, in the *Odes* themselves.    Further, this minority
or inferiority is of a peculiar kind, hardly exampled elsewhere.
Many poets are unequal: it would scarcely be an exaggeration
to say that, in varying measure, every poet is unequal.  The
string, be it of bow or of lyre, cannot always be at full tension.
Some—we have but just quoted an example in Young—are
unequal with an inequality which cannot take any benefit
from the old metaphor.    But, at certain times, hardly any
poet, and few poets at any time, exhibit the peculiar inequality
which Collins displays; and, for historical and critical purposes,
the analysis of the special character of this difference is, perhaps, of almost as much importance as that of the discovery
and recognition of his poetic idiosyncrasy and merit when he is
at his best; perhaps, it is of even greater importance than this.

For, here, the cross-valuation of man and time, easily
abused down to mere glib futility, yet very significant when
used rightly, becomes of the very first moment; in fact, it
would not be an exaggeration to say that there is hardly
another case where it counts for so much, and where it explains
so much.   Almost everything that is good in Collins belongs
to the man; almost everything that is not good belongs to the
time.   And, consequently, there is, again, hardly a poet of
whom it may be said, with less of this futility, that even supposing his unhappy mental affliction to have remained the same
(which, in the different circumstances, it very conceivably
might not), his production, as a contemporary of Shakespeare
or of Milton, of Coleridge or of Tennyson, would have been
entirely different in all the features that are not its best.
The Collins of the *Odes*, at his best, is the poet of all time in
general and no time in particular; the Collins of the *Eclogues*
is everywhere the poetaster of the eighteenth century.   Nor is
the distinction to be confined to this easy and sweeping separation; for, in the *Odes* themselves, it constantly, and, to the
critical reader, not at all tiresomely, presents and represents
itself.   In two succeeding poems of the collection, in two stanzas
of the same poem, in two successive lines, nay, in the very same
line of the same stanza, two writers—the Collins of eternity
and the Collins of his day—are continually manifesting themselves.   The latter talks about a " British shell " when he means
" English poetry "; intrudes the otiose and, in fact, ludicrous

detail of "its southern site," a sort of auctioneer's item, in his description of the temple of Pity; indulges in constant abuse of such words as "scene." And he sometimes intrudes upon, though he cannot quite spoil, the loftiest inspiration of the Collins who writes "How sleep the brave" and the *Ode to Evening*.

When this is thoroughly understood, it not merely brings the usual reward—the fact of this understanding—but a distinct increase of enjoyment. On the full perception of the difference between the two Collinses, there follows, not merely pardon, as in the proverb, but a possibility of neglecting what would otherwise annoy. The "British shell" no longer suggests artillery or oysters; the "turtles" have no savour of the tureen; and nothing interferes with our appreciation of the dewy eyes of Pity and the golden hair of Peace, when the sense of incongruity is, as Coleridge says of the sense of disbelief, "suspended."

In regard, indeed, to the *Eclogues*, the critical is almost the only satisfaction. They occupy but little room—less than a score of pages, containing scarcely more than three hundred lines, form not a very severe tax upon the reader. But, in them, we certainly find the Collins of the hour almost unrelieved by a single exhibition of individual poetic quality. Eastern apologues in prose or verse had been patented for the whole eighteenth century by the authority of Addison; and Collins was merely following one of the various fashions beyond which it was reckoned improper, if not positively unlawful, to stray. The consecrated couplet furnishes the metre; the *gradus* epithet—"radiant morn," "wanton gales," "tender passion" —lends its accustomed aid to swell and balance the line; and, though we sometimes come on a verse that shows forth the poet, such as

> Cold is her breast like flowers that drink the dew,

unreasonable expectations of more instances of the same sort are promptly checked by such flatnesses as the statement that "the virtues *came along*," or such otiosities as

> In *distant* view along the *level* green.

Had these attempts to compose something that might represent the poetry of Saadi and Hafiz and Omar Khayyam stood alone, Collins might certainly have justified the strictures[1] of *The Gentleman's Magazine* on his fellow-contributors to *Dodsley*. Fortunately, they do not stand alone, but are accompanied and effaced by the *Odes*. Besides the two pieces to which reference has already been made—the *Ode to Evening*, with its almost, if not quite, successful extension of the "blank" principle to lyric, and the exquisite softness and restraint of "How sleep the brave"—at least three others, in different degrees, have secured general admiration. These are the slightly "time-marked," but, surely, charming for all time, *Dirge in Cymbeline*, the splendid outburst of the *Liberty* ode and the posthumous *Superstitions of the Highlands*, of which the text may, perhaps, admit of dispute, but certainly not the spirit and the poetic quality. Hardly one of these, unless it be "How sleep the brave," is, as a whole poem, faultless; but Longinus would have made no mistake about the "slips" and "faults" of Collins, as compared with his sublimity—and why should we?

The other poets to be mentioned in the present chapter are inferior to these two; but, with rare exception, each has something that would make it improper to batch or group him with others, as was done on a former occasion; while hardly one is so distinctly eminent that, in his case, chronological order need be disregarded as it has been in that of Collins. We shall, therefore, observe it, with the very slight further liberty (possibly no liberty at all) of mentioning John Dyer, who was certainly not born within the eighteenth century, but whose exact birth-year is unknown, before Green and Blair, who can be positively claimed for the seventeenth.

For Dyer, though his real claims rest upon one short piece only, and that not belonging to the very highest style of poetry, must be recognised as a poet, and as a very remarkable poet, from curiously different points of view. *The Fleece* and *The Ruins of Rome* are merely examples of the extraordinary mistakes as to subjects proper for poetry, and the ordinary infelicity in dealing with them, which have condemned eighteenth century verse as a whole to a lower place than it deserves.

[1] Cf. *ante*, Vol. IX, Chap. VI, sec. II, p. 214.

*The Country Walk*, not disagreeable in itself, is either a vastly
inferior first draft, or a still more surprisingly unsuccessful
replica, of *Grongar Hill*.   But *Grongar Hill* itself is one of those
poems which occupy a place of their own, humble though it
may be, as compared with the great epics and tragedies, simple
and of little variety, as compared with the garlands or paradises
of the essentially lyrical poets, but secure, distinguished and,
practically, unique.   That even Johnson, though he thought
it "not very accurately written," allowed it to be "pleasing,"
and felt sure that "when once read it would be read again," is
a striking testimony in its favour.   For it deals almost wholly
with "prospects," to which Johnson was contemptuously indifferent; and its "inaccuracy" (which, in truth, is the highest
accuracy) was to prove a very crowbar for loosening the
foundations of the prosody that he thought accurate.

The poem is really a little wonder in subject and form alike.
The devotees of "the subject" cannot fail, if they know the
facts, to recognise in it the first definite return to that fixing of
the eye on the object in nature which, though not so absent
from Dryden as Wordsworth thought, had been growing rarer
and rarer (save in such obscure work as Lady Winchilsea's) for
generation after generation, and which was to be the most
powerful process in the revived poetry of the future.   The
student of form cannot fail to perceive in that inaccuracy
which Johnson (for him) gently blamed something neither
more nor less than a return to the peculiar form of the octo-
syllabic couplet which, after being developed by Shakespeare
and Fletcher and the pastoral poets of the early seventeenth
century, had been exquisitely employed by Milton in the twin
masterpieces of his youth.   The poem appeared, in 1726, in the
*Miscellany* of that remarkable person Lewis.[1]   Even the first
of *The Seasons* had but just been published; and, if there is a
certain identity of spirit between this poem and Dyer's, the
expression is wholly different.   Even those who are free from
any half-partisan, half-ignorant contempt for the age of Pope
and the age of Johnson, must own how strange and sweet, amid
the ordinary concert of those ages, is the sound of

> Who in the purple evening lie
> On the mountain's lonely van . . .

[1] Cf. *ante*, Vol. IX, p. 210.

or

> A little rule, a little sway,
> A sunbeam on a winter's day . . .

or

> Sometimes swift, sometimes slow,
> Wave succeeding wave, they go
> A various journey to the deep,
> Like human life, to endless sleep.

That Dyer was a painter as well as a poet goes, no doubt, for something; that, at least, he liked to think he had married a collateral descendant of, in his own phrase, "everybody's Shakespere," may go for a great deal.

In Dyer—or, at least, in *Grongar Hill*—we see some of the first, and almost best, fruits of the romantic spirit and style. In Matthew Green, both style and spirit are of the other kind, but hardly less agreeable in their own way. He, also, so far as good verse goes, is a "single-speech" poet; but he derives some advantage from the fact that he hardly tried to speak on any other occasion, though a few minor pieces usually accompany *The Spleen*, and a few more might, it seems, be added to them. Green was a quaker-freethinker (a curious evolution) and a clerk in the custom-house, where he amiably prevented a reform which would have disestablished, or, at least, dismilked, the cats. He seems, on the whole, to have been more like a French man of letters of the time than like an Englishman possessing a temperament which may, at once, have qualified and disqualified him for treating "the English disease." It must be admitted that his treatment is somewhat superficial, and more than a little desultory; but it certainly exhibits a condition completely opposite to that of the ailment, and even, for the time of reading, provides an antidote. The octosyllables, "accurate," as Johnson would say, without stiffness or limpness, and slipping lightly along without any Hudibrastic acrobatism, frame a succession of thoughts that, if never very profound, are always expressed with a liveliness of which the well-known

> Fling but a stone, the giant dies

is by no means too favourable a specimen. Sometimes, we have satiric glances at individuals, as that, near the beginning, at Gildon; sometimes, lively "thumbnails" of contemporary manners; once or twice, more elaborate drawings, as of the often quoted

> Farm some twenty miles from town.

The epicurean attitude of the lighter, but not the coarser, kind has seldom been better illustrated in verse.

Chronology could hardly have been more complacent in contrast-planning than by putting the author of *The Grave* next in order. Here, also, we have a poet of one poem; but the subject of that poem has at once greater possibilities and greater dangers. A poet who writes unpoetically on death at once proves himself to be no poet; and Blair has not failed to pass the test. But he has passed it with the qualification of his time; and, perhaps, so universal a subject ought to receive rather more universality of treatment. Even the fine *coda* (which did not form part of the original edition of the poem) dates itself a little too definitely; and the suicide passage, to name no other, is somewhat rhetorical, if not even melodramatic. But there is no doubt that it had a powerful influence. The very fact that contemporary critics thought the language lacking in "dignity" offers the best testimony to its freedom, at least sometimes, from the always irksome, and sometimes intolerable, buckram which mars Young and Thomson, Armstrong and Akenside, and which is by no means absent from Collins or from Gray. The blank verse, like nearly all dating from this period, though not so badly as some of it, abuses the abrupt full-stopped middle pause, and is too much given to dramatic redundancy. But it has a certain almost rugged massiveness, and occasionally flings itself down with real *momentum*. The line

> The great *negotiators* of the earth

possesses sarcastic force of meaning as well as prosodic force of structure. It would be hard to find two poets of more different schools than Blair and Blake. Yet it was not a mere association of contradictories when Blake illustrated Blair.[1]

---

[1] The close coincidence of *The Grave*, which was certainly written by 1742, though not published till the following year, and *Night Thoughts*, the first part of

The peculiar "tumid and gorgeous" style of the eighteenth century in blank verse, in which Johnson professed to find the only excuse—and that inadequate—for the metre he detested, not unfrequently gives the wary critic a certain pause before he absolutely excludes the notion of conscious or half-conscious burlesque on the part of its practitioners. There had been no doubt about this burlesque in the case of *The Splendid Shilling,*[1] which, undoubtedly, had led not a few of them to Milton. Even in Thomson, a later and much stronger influence —in fact, one which directly mastered most blank-verse writers after 1726—it is not certain whether the temper which avowedly exists in *The Castle of Indolence* may not sometimes lie concealed in *The Seasons.* And John Armstrong, Thomson's intimate friend and more than countryman—for their birthplaces, just inside the Border, were within a few miles of each other—one of the garrison invalids of the castle itself, was, by common consent of tradition, a remarkable specimen of that compound of saturnine, and even churlish, humour with real kindliness, which Scotsmen have not been indisposed to acknowledge as a national characteristic. He seems to have pleaded actual burlesque intent for his *péché de jeunesse* (as it would be called in French literary history), *The Economy of Love.* But it is difficult to discern much difference of style between this and the more respectable *Art of Preserving Health.* The preposterous latinising, which has made his "gelid cistern" for "cold bath" a stock quotation, and the buckram stiffness of style which usually goes with it, appear in both. His well-known contribution to *The Castle of Indolence* itself is avowed burlesque, and not unhappy; while, though his imitations of Shakespeare are about as much like Shakespeare as they are like Walt Whitman, his *Epistle to Wilkes*, from the army in Germany to which he was attached, is not without good touches. He seems to have possessed literary, if not exactly poetical, power, but to have been the victim of personal bad taste, exaggerating a particular bad taste of the time.

Richard Glover, like Armstrong, belongs to the "tumid and

---

which appeared in the earlier year, has given occasion to the usual idle disputes about priority. The conception of each of these poems was, probably, quite independent.

[1] See *ante*, Vol. IX, Chap. x, p. 286.

gorgeous" blank-verse division; but, unlike him, he offers not the slightest provocation to direct or indirect amusement, and, unlike him also, he has nothing of real vigour. His celebrated ballad, *Admiral Hosier's Ghost*, is a curious success; but it is not certain how much of its reproduction of the half-pathetic, half-bathetic style of the broadside is art and how much nature. Of his "great" performances, *Leonidas* and *The Athenaid* (rash as literary prophecy is), it may, with little fear, be said that no age will ever resuscitate their popularity—a popularity which, even at the time, was not lasting and, perhaps, to some extent, had been politically engineered; while, almost certainly, the main cause of it was the already mentioned fancy for the newly resuscitated blank verse. Glover, perhaps, is not so absurd as is Blackmore; but he is equally dull in substance; and, in form, he pushes one mannerism to an almost maddening length. The effect which Milton produces by occasional strong full-stops of sense coinciding with the metrical middle pause is well known and unquestionable. But Milton uses it carefully, and in combination with the utmost and most artful variety of other pauses, and of stopped or overrun lines. His imitators, from the first, were tempted to employ and overdo this obvious device; and Thomson himself is by no means impeccable in respect of it. Glover uses it on every possible occasion, not unfrequently in several successive lines, and not unfrequently, also, stopping where no stops should be, in order to achieve it. It is difficult to imagine, and would be hardly possible to find, even in the long list of mistaken "long poem" writers of the past two centuries, more tedious stuff than his.

The immediate cause which places William Shenstone here next to Glover is merely chronological; but the sequence could hardly be better arranged for a reader of the two. As a relief from the probably vain attempt to read the London merchant, nothing could be better than the poems of the Worcestershire gentleman-farmer. Shenstone is not a great poet; but, perhaps, there has been a tendency, at all times, to treat him too lightly. Especially if his prose work on poetry be taken together with his poems, it may, not as a mere fancy, be found that very few of his contemporaries, perhaps none but Collins and Gray, had in them more of the root of the matter, though time and circumstance and a dawdling sentimental temperament intercepted and stunted fruit and flower. With his prose,[1] we are here not directly concerned; but it is certainly surprising how, in a few aphoristic touches, he lays a finger on some of the chief faults of the poetry of his day. He did not quite practise what he preached: and there is no doubt that posterity has not been wholly unjust in associating the *rococo* decorations and the trivial artifices of the Leasowes with the poems which partly show direct connection with that estate. But artificial-pastoral was only a stage on the return to real nature; and the positive achievements of Shenstone's poetry have much less of the toyshop and the marionette theatre about them than it has been customary to think or say. It is almost a pity that he was of Pembroke, Oxford; for, had he not been there, Johnson's belittling would hardly have been accompanied by a sort of patronising endeavour to make the best of it—the most damaging form of disparagement.

In fact, it is very easily possible to assign him far less than his real value in the return to nature itself. When Fanny Burney, many years after his death, saw Knowle for the first time, she ranked it next to Hagley as the finest park she had seen, acknowledging, however, with frankness the culpable or regrettable absence of improvement by temples and grottoes, obelisks and view-seats. We should, of course exactly reverse the estimate. Yet Hagley and the (as some will have it) Naboth's vineyard which patterned Hagley's beautification were only schoolmasters to bring public attention, at any rate, from town to country—if to a country "townishly" bedizened and interfered with. The proper study of mankind ceased to be man only, when he busied himself with nature at all; even though for a time he might officiously intrude his own works upon her. One may smile at

> But oh! the transport most ally'd to song
>     In some fair *villa's* peaceful bound
> To catch soft *hints* from Nature's tongue
>     And *bid* Arcadia bloom around—

but it is only fair to remember that the earlier part of the same

[1] See, as to his letters, Chap. XI, sec. II, *post*.

poem had almost expressly condemned meddling with nature as contained in the lines

> 'T is Nature only gives exclusive right
> To relish her supreme delight,

and, as if with half-surprise at its own boldness, allowed "pregnancy of [such] delight" to "thriftless furze" and "rough barren rock."

It may indeed be admitted that, both in his grounds and in his poems, Shenstone allowed the charms of the villa to overpower those of furze and rock.

One of the censor's ironical anecdotes is that "nothing roused Shenstone's indignation more than to ask if there were any fishes in his water." The obvious innuendo has a certain justice; but it may, to some extent, be retorted that he did try to "stock" some part of his poetical water—very profitably. His *Moral Pieces*, had they stood alone, would either have excluded him from notice here altogether, or have left him with a line of condemnation. *The Judgment of Hercules* has the smoothness, but also the insignificance, of the average eighteenth century couplet; *Economy, The Ruined Abbey*, and *Love and Honour*, the frigid bombast and the occasional sheer "measured prose" of its worst blank-verse. If *The Progress of Taste* deserves a less harsh judgment, it is because Shenstone, there, is writing autobiographically, and, consequently, with his heart in the matter; while, as to form, he takes refuge in the easy "Hudibrastics" which the age generally wrote well, and sometimes excellently. But, elsewhere, if the sense of *impar congressus* is too frequently with us, there are, also, frequent alleviations; while that other and consoling sense of reading one who, at least, is a seeker after true poetry is seldom absent. *The Schoolmistress* (which, we know, was undertaken irreverently and converted the author in the writing) has generally been admitted to be one of the happiest things of its kind, so far as its author intended (and he has defined his intention very strictly) to reach. Even the tea-garden "inscriptions" are saved by the best-known of them, " Here in cool grot," which, by the exclusion of some of the unlucky poetic lingo of the time, and the substitution for it of better phrase, could be made a really charming thing. Whether there are enough good things in *Levities* to save the others is a nicer question: but, some things are certainly good. And the same is the case with *Elegies*, which occupies the other wing of his array. But it has practically long been decided that Shenstone must be judged by *The Schoolmistress* and the *Miscellaneous Poems* conscientiously subtitled " Odes, Songs, Ballads *etc.*" Of *The Schoolmistress* we have spoken; of the others we may now speak.

To any one who has read much poetry, and has thought a little about it with due mixture of criticism and affection, some —relatively many—of these pieces have a strange attraction. The true and even profound notions as to poetical substance and form which are scattered about Shenstone's prose seem to have exercised some prompting, but no restraining, influence on his verse. A seldom quoted, and not in the least hackneyed, piece, *The Song of Valentine's Day*, illustrates this, perhaps, in a more striking fashion than any other. He appears, at first, to have caught that inestimable soar and sweep of the common measure which had seemed to be lost with the latest Carolines; and the charm of it, as it were, is in the distance throughout. But he never fully masters it. Some lines, beginning with the second—

> 'T is said that under distant skies,
> *Nor you the fact deny—*

are hopelessly prosaic. The fatal jargon of the time, " swain" and " grove" and the rest, pervades and mars the whole. The spell is never consummated; but the possibility is always there. Of the *Ode to Memory*, something the same may be said, and of others. His best known things, *The Dying Kid*, the *Jemmy Dawson* ballad and the four-parted *Pastoral*, are unequal, but only because they condescend nearer to the fashion. The three-footed anapaestics of the last are jingling enough, no doubt; and it is wonderful that Shenstone should not have anticipated the variations and ennoblings of the metre which, even then, though chiefly in light matter, had been sometimes hit upon, and which were perfected by Byron, Praed and Swinburne. But there is a favour and a prettiness about them that still appeal to all but very superior persons; and not merely they, but many of their companions, show that Shenstone was certainly a " called," if he could not quite rise to be a " chosen," poet.

It may be desirable, and should certainly be permissible, to use once more the often misused comparison, and observe that, while Shenstone would probably have been a better poet, and would certainly have written better poetry, in the seventeenth or the nineteenth century, there is little probability that Mark Akenside would at any time have done better than he actually did, and small likelihood that he would ever have done so well. His only genuine appeal is to the intellect and to strictly conventionalised emotions; his method is by way of versified rhetoric; and his inspirations are political, ethical, social, or almost what you will, provided the purely poetical be excluded. It is, perhaps, not unconnected with this restricted appeal to the understanding, that hardly any poet known to us was so curiously addicted to remaking his poems. Poets of all degrees and kinds, poets as different from each other as Thomson and Tennyson, have revised their work largely; but the revision has always, or almost always, been confined to omissions, insertions and alterations for better or worse of isolated phrase, line or passage. Akenside entirely rewrote his one long and famous poem, *The Pleasures of Imagination*,[1] and did something similar with several of his not very numerous smaller pieces.

Since his actual intellectual endowment was not small, and his studies (though he was an active practising physician) were sufficient, he often showed fairly adequate stuff or substance of writing. But this stuff or substance is hardly ever of itself poetical; and the poetical or quasi-poetical ornament is invariably added, decorative and merely the clothes, not the body —to borrow the Coleridgean image—of such spirit as there is.

He, therefore, shows better in poems, different as they are from each other, like the *Hymn to the Naiads* and *An Epistle to Curio*, than in his diploma piece. *The Pleasures of Imagination* might, by a bold misnomer or liberty, be used as the title of a completed *Kubla Khan*, and so might designate a magnificent poem. But, applied strictly, and in the fashion congenial to Akenside and his century, it almost inevitably means a frigid

[1] The title of the second edition (1757) runs: *The Pleasures of the Imagination.*

catalogue, with the items decked out in rhetorical figures and developments. The earlier form is the better; but neither is really poetry. On the other hand, the *Hymn to the Naiads*, in blank verse, does, perhaps, deserve that praise of being "the best example of the eighteenth century kind" which has been sometimes strangely given to *The Pleasures* themselves. More than one of the *Odes* and *Inscriptions*, in their formal decorative way, have a good deal of what has been called "frozen grace." But only once, perhaps, does Akenside really rise to poetic bloodheat: and that is in *An Epistle to Curio*. It may deserve, from the point of view of the practical man, the ridicule that Macaulay has applied to it. But, as an example of the nobler satiric couplet, fashioned in a manner between that of Dryden and that of Pope, animated by undoubtedly genuine feeling, and launched at its object with the pulse and quiver of a well-balanced and well-flung javelin, it really has notable merit.

Such a thing as this, and such other things as semi-classical bas-reliefs in description or sentiment, Akenside could accomplish; but, except in the political kind, he has no passion, and in no kind whatever has he magnificence, or the charm of life.

If Shenstone and Akenside present an interesting parallel contrast in one way, that presented to both of them by Christopher Smart is even more interesting; while, in another way, he approximates to Collins. Akenside, with all his learning, acuteness and vigour, never found the true spirit of poetry and, perhaps, did not even look for it, or know where it was to be found. Shenstone, conscious of its existence, and always in a half-hearted way seeking it, sometimes came near it or, at least, saw it afar off. Smart found it once for all, and once only; but that once was when he was mad. Since *A Song to David* at last gained its true place (and sometimes, perhaps, a place rather higher than that), it has been the fashion rather to undervalue the positive worth of those other poems from which, by certainly one of the oddest tricks in literary history, fortune separated the *Song* in the original edition of Smart's work, leaving it for Chalmers to find in a review fragment only, and for the nineteenth century at last to recover completely. Smart's Latin poems, original and translated, are now quite out of fashion;

and they are not, as a rule, strikingly good. He had not,
when sane, the power of serious poetry; but his lighter verse
in a Hudibrastic or Swiftian vein is, sometimes, really capital;
and neither in those great originals, nor in Barham, nor even in
Thackeray, can be found a better piece of *burla* rhyme than

> Tell me, thou son of great Cadwallader,
> Hast thou that hare? or hast thou swallowed her?

But, in *A Song to David*, as it has been said, *furor vere poeticus*
has seized and inspired his victim. It has been so much praised
in the last half-century as to be, perhaps, to some extent, in
the danger of Aristides; and it is anything rather than faultless.
The ideas, and, indeed, much of the language, are taken at
second-hand from the Bible; there is, as, in the circumstances,
there almost must have been, divagation, repetition, verbiage, inequality, with other things not good in themselves.
But, the tide of poetry carries the poem right through, and the
reader with it; the old romance-six or *rime couée*—a favourite
measure with the eighteenth century, but often too suggestive
of *Sir Thopas*—once more acquires soar and rush, and the
blood and breath of life, so that the whole crowd of emotional
thought and picturesque image sweeps through the page
with irresistible force.

There is little for us that is irresistible in James Beattie or
in William Falconer. But men not yet decrepit, who in their
youth were fond of haunting bookstalls, may remember that
few poems were commoner in "elegant pocket editions," as their
own times would have said, than *The Minstrel* and *The Shipwreck*. We know that Byron was strongly influenced by
Beattie in point of form; and it has been credibly asserted that
his influence, at least in Scotland, on young readers of poetry,
is not, or was not very recently, exhausted. It is difficult to
think that this can have been the case with Falconer. The
"exquisite harmony of numbers" which Chalmers could
discover has now completely vanished from such things as

> With joyful eyes th' attentive master sees
> Th' auspicious omens of an eastern breeze;

and scarcely will any breeze, of east or west, extract that

harmony again from such a lyre. The technicalities are not only unlikely to interest, but, to a great extent, are, unluckily, obsolete. The few personal touches are of the faintest; and even Falconer's Greece is a Greece which, if it was ever living, has ceased to live now. His smaller poems are few and insignificant.

Beattie, on the other hand, retains at least a historic interest as a pioneer of romanticism, and as the most serious and extensive handler, up to his own time, of the Spenserian stanza. He was hampered in general effect inasmuch as, if he was possessed of any strictly poetic faculty, it was of a singularly small and weak one; and he hampered himself in a special way by failing to observe that, to make a Spenserian stanza, you need a Spenserian line and Spenserian line-groupings. As it was (and he taught the fault to Byron), the great merit of the form—its complex and yet absolutely fluent harmony—is broken up by suggestions, now of the couplet, now of the old dramatic blank-verse line, now, again, of the Miltonic or pseudo-Miltonic paragraph arrangement. Nor, though the matter might more than compensate contemporaries and immediate posterity for a defect in manner which they would hardly notice, is it such as can give much enjoyment either now, or ever again. That it is not only plotless and characterless but, also, unfinished, need not be fatal. It has hills and vales and other properties of romanticism à la Rousseau; suggestions of knights and witches and so forth in the manner of romanticism à la Percy. But the drawing is all in wateredout sepia; the melody is a hurdy-gurdy strum.

His minor poems are more numerous than Falconer's, and intended much more greatly: but they have little more significance. He tries Gray's ode manner, and he tries his elegy manner: and he fails in both. A tolerable opening, such as that of *Retirement:*

> When in the crimson cloud of even,
> The lingering light decays,
> And Hesper on the front of Heaven
> His glistering gem displays

is followed by some twenty times the number of lines mostly rubbish. The *Pastorals*, if less silly, are not much better than pastorals usually are; and the most that can be said for *The Judgment of Paris*, wherein Beattie employs the elegiac quatrain, is that it is rather less bad than one would expect—a fact which may account for its unpopularity at the time as well as for its omission from his collected poems.[1]

The poets—for, in a few cases, they most certainly deserve that name—and the verse-writers—an indefeasible title—who have been mentioned in this and in an earlier chapter[2] do not require any peroration with much circumstance.   But it would not only be uncivil to give them none; it would amount to a sort of petty treason in failing to make good their claims to the place they have here received.   This place is, perhaps, justified in one case only—that of Collins—by the possession of intrinsic genius of the strictly poetical kind, in quality if not in quantity, sufficient to have made its way in any age; though, undoubtedly, in some ages, it would have been more fertile than in this.   Yet Collins acquires not only interest but intelligibility when he is considered in company with those who have been associated with him here.   "Why was he not as they?"   "What was it that weighed on him as on them?"   These are questions which those who disdain the historic estimate—who wish to "like grossly," as Dryden put it—may disdain likewise.   They add to the delight as much, at least, as they satisfy the intelligence of better exercised tastes.   So, again, in various ways, Garth and Watts, Young and Dyer and Green, Shenstone and Akenside and Smart, have special attractions—sometimes, if not always, strictly poetical; always, perhaps, strictly literary—in one way or another, sufficient to satisfy fit readers, if they cannot abide the same test as Collins.   And so, in their turn, have even the *numerus*, the crowd of what some harshly call poetasters, whom we have also included.   They, also, in their day and way, obeyed the irresistible seduction which urges a man to desert prose and to follow the call of poetry.   They did not go far or do much; but they went as far and did as much as they could.

[1] As to Beattie's once celebrated *Essay on the Nature and Immutability of Truth*, cf. Chap. xiv, *post*.

[2] *Ante*, Vol. ix, Chap. vi, sec. ii.

# CHAPTER VIII

# Johnson and Boswell

IT was a supreme fortune that gave Johnson the friendship of Reynolds and Boswell. His great personality is still an active and familiar force. We know him as well as if he had lived among us. But the first of Reynolds's portraits was painted when Johnson had completed *The Rambler* and was already "the great moralist," and Boswell did not meet him till after he had obtained his pension. The Johnson that we know is the Johnson "who loves to fold his legs and have his talk out." The years in which he fought poverty and gained his place in the world of letters are obscure to us, in comparison with those in which he enjoyed his hard-won leisure. He never cared, in later life, to speak about his early struggles; he never spoke much about himself at any time. Even when he wrote the lives of authors whom he had known and might have told his own experiences without disturbing the unity of his picture, he offered little more than the reflection of his feelings. Sir John Hawkins did not make full use of his great opportunity. He alone, of all Johnson's biographers, had known him almost from the start of their work in London, but he drew on his recollections fitfully and lazily. He has given enough to show how much more he might have given. Boswell, with all his pertinacious curiosity, found that he had to rely mainly on his own researches. There were in these early years subjects "too delicate to question Johnson upon." Much remained, and still remains, for others to discover.

New letters, anecdotes or facts will not disturb our idea of Johnson.[1] They will, at most, fill gaps and settle doubts. The

[1] A large amount of new material on Johnson's family and early life has recently been made accessible in *The Reades of Blackwood Hill and Dr. Johnson's*

man himself is known. Yet the very greatness of his personality has tended to interfere with the recognition of his greatness as a man of letters. No other author whose profession was literature seems to owe so little of his fame to his books. Many writers, Dryden and Scott among others, give the impression that they were greater than anything that they have written. It has been the unique fate of Johnson to be dissociated from his works. He would have welcomed the knowledge that he was to be remembered as a man, for he had no delusions about authorship. But he is to be found in his works as he wished to be known, and as he was. If the greatest of biographies catches him at moments which he would not have recorded, it is also true that his writings give us his more intimate thoughts, and take us into regions which were denied to his conversation.

He was born at Lichfield on 18 September, 1709, in the year in which his father, one of the chief booksellers of the midlands, was sheriff of the city. As a schoolboy, he seems to have been already distinguished by his ease in learning, his tenacity of memory, his lack of application, and delays adjusted to his power of rapid work. But the best part of his instruction he acquired for himself in his father's shop. There, he prowled about at leisure, and read as his fancy directed. He was never a laborious reader. The progress which the understanding makes through a book, he said, has more pain than pleasure in it. "Sir; do you read books through?" he once asked. There may have been few books that he read through himself. His defective eyesight had probably some bearing on what came to be an intellectual habit. But he had in a supreme degree the gift of discovering the matter and quality of a book, almost on opening its pages. The extent of his knowledge was the wonder of all his friends: Adam Smith declared that Johnson knew more books than any man alive. He had begun this knowledge by sampling his father's store. And in these days, before he had left school, he was already a good enough Latinist to be diverted from a search for apples by the discovery of a folio of Petrarch.

---

*Ancestry* (1906) by Reade, A. L., and in his *Johnsonian Gleanings* (1909 etc.). New material on his later life is given in Broadely and Seccombe's *Doctor Johnson and Mrs. Thrale* (1910).

He was intended to follow his father's business. Hawkins and Mrs. Piozzi both say that he could bind a book. But, after two years at home, he contrived to proceed to Oxford. He entered Pembroke college as a commoner on 31 October, 1728, and remained there continuously, with, at most, one week's break in the long vacation, till December, 1729. Thereafter, his residence was irregular, and he left the university without taking a degree.[1] The outstanding fact of his college career was the translation of Pope's *Messiah* into Latin verse, as a Christmas exercise. This was the first of his works that was printed, being included in *A Miscellany of Poems by Several Hands* (1731), collected by J. Husbands, fellow of Pembroke college. Latin was already almost as familiar a language to him as his own. Late in life, during his tour in France, he was "resolute in speaking Latin," though he had a command of French idiom that enabled him to supply the first paragraph to Baretti's translation of *Rasselas*.[2] "Though he is a great critic in French," said Baretti, "and knows almost as much Italian as I do, he cannot speak either language, but he talks Latin with all Cicero's fury."[4] His knowledge of the renascence poets was unusually wide. He regretted that they were not generally known, and that Pope's attempt to rescue them from neglect by his *Selecta Poemata Italorum* had been fruitless. The first book which he himself designed was an edition of Politian, with a history of Latin poetry in the fourteenth and fifteenth centuries. Proposals for printing it by subscription were issued in August, 1734; but nothing came of the scheme, and the Latin poems of Politian still await an editor.

Of his five and a half years in the midlands after his residence in Oxford, the records are fragmentary. His earliest extant letter (30 October, 1731) has reference to an unsuccessful application for the post of usher in the grammar school of Stourbridge. He acted in this capacity for some time, in 1732, at Market Bosworth, in Leicestershire. Later in the

---

[1] Boswell says he left "in autumn, 1731." There is much support for this date in Hawkins. But Croker argued that he never returned after December, 1729, though his name remained on the books till October, 1731; and this view has been commonly adopted. The arguments for residence till 1731 remain the stronger.

[2] See Prior's *Life of Malone* (1860), p. 161.

[3] See *Giuseppe Baretti*, Collison-Morley, L. (1909), p. 85.

same year, he paid a visit to his lifelong friend Edmund Hector, then settled as a surgeon in Birmingham; and it would appear that Birmingham was his home for the next three years.[1] What is certain is that his hopes had now turned to writing. He contributed to *The Birmingham Journal* a number of essays, all of which are lost; he planned his edition of Politian; he offered to write for *The Gentleman's Magazine;* and he completed his first book, *A Voyage to Abyssinia, by Father Jerome Lobo. With a Continuation of the History of Abyssinia, and Fifteen Dissertations, by Mr. Le Grand. From the French.* The volume was printed in Birmingham and published in London, anonymously, in January, 1735.

In this translation, there is much more of Le Grand than of Lobo. In parts, Johnson condensed freely; where he allowed himself least liberty was in the sixteen (not fifteen) dissertations, which occupy more than half the volume and deal with such subjects as the Nile, Prester John, the queen of Sheba and the religious customs of the Abyssinians. He was always an eager reader of books of travel; and it was fitting that the passion for whatever afforded views of human nature, which led him to describe his own experiences of another country and to urge others to describe theirs, should be shown in his first work. But the main interest of the volume now lies in the short preface. In the translation, he is content to convey the meaning of the original, and, while he follows in haste another's thought and language, we fail to find the qualities of his own style. But they are unmistakable in such a passage as this:

The Reader will here find no Regions cursed with irremediable Barrenness, or bless'd with Spontaneous Fecundity, no perpetual Gloom or unceasing Sunshine; nor are the Nations here described either devoid of all Sense of Humanity, or consummate in all private and social Virtues, here are no Hottentots without Religion, Polity, or Articulate Language, no Chinese perfectly Polite, and

---

[1] The issue of the Politian proposals at Lichfield in August, 1734, appears to be the only evidence for the common statement that he then returned to Lichfield. It was to be expected that the subscriptions should be received by his brother Nathanael, who, with his mother, had carried on the family business from the death of his father in 1731. *A Voyage to Abyssinia* was all written at Birmingham. If it was completed before August, 1734, there must have been a delay of six months in publication. The letter to *The Gentleman's Magazine* was written from Birmingham on 25 November, 1734.

complcatly skill'd in all Sciences: He will discover, what will always be discover'd by a diligent and impartial Enquirer, that wherever Human Nature is to be found, there is a mixture of Vice and Virtue, a contest of Passion and Reason, and that the Creator doth not appear Partial in his Distributions, but has balanced in most Countries their particular Inconveniences by particular Favours.

He who writes much, Johnson said, will not easily escape a manner. But here is Johnson's manner in his first book. And here, too, is a forecast of the philosophy of *The Rambler* and *The Vanity of Human Wishes*. There are no distinct periods in Johnson's literary development, no sudden access of power, no change in his outlook, no novelties in his methods. He continued as he had begun. He grew in confidence and facility; he perfected his command of expression; but there was not any change in the spirit of his expression or in what he wished to express.

His experience of letters at Birmingham had not promised success, and, on his marriage in July, 1735, with Mrs. Elizabeth Porter, the widow of one of his Birmingham friends, he set up a school at Edial, near Lichfield. His first reference to the new enterprise is found in a letter of 25 June, 1735, recently published for the first time.[1]

"I am going," he writes, "to furnish a House in the Country and keep a private Boarding-house for Young Gentlemen whom I shall endeavour to instruct in a method somewhat more rational than those commonly practised."

His "scheme for the classes of a grammar school," as given by Hawkins and Boswell, illustrates what he was to say about teaching in his *Life of Milton*. The school failed, and, on 2 March, 1737, he set out for London with one of his pupils, David Garrick. Henceforward, London was to be his home. Having no profession, he became by necessity an author.

He had no promise of work, but he looked to find employment on *The Gentleman's Magazine*, and he had hopes in the drama. He had written at Edial three acts of his tragedy *Irene*.[2] He worked at it during his first months in London,

---

[1] *Bi-Centenary of the Birth of Johnson. Commemoration Festival Reports*, edited by Raby, J. T. (1909), pp. 26–7.

[2] It was founded on a story in Knolles's *History of the Turks*, previously treated

and finished it on his visit to Lichfield to settle his affairs, in the summer of 1737. But there remained for him "the labour of introducing it on the stage, an undertaking which to an ingenuous mind was in a very high degree vexatious and disgusting"—as he wrote of another's experience while his own tragedy was still unacted. The goodwill of Garrick, whom he placed under a heavy debt by the great prologue which heralded his managership of Drury lane in 1774, at last brought it on the stage in February, 1749[1], and protracted its run to nine nights, so that there might be three third-night benefits. With all his knowledge of human nature, Johnson was unable to exhibit dramatically the shades which distinguish one character from another. *Irene* is only a moral poem in a succession of dialogues on the theme that "Peace from innocence must flow" and "none are happy but the wise and virtuous." And the thought struggles with the metre. He could not divest his blank verse of the qualities of the couplet. The same faults are to be found in his translation, made many years later, of a short passage of Metastasio. We expect the rime at the end of the line; and, when we come on it in the couplets with which each act closes, instead of feeling that they are tags, as we do in our great tragedies, we find the verse bound forward with unwonted ease. Johnson had too massive and too logical an intellect to adapt himself readily to the drama. He came to perceive this, but not till long after he had described the qualifications of a dramatist in his *Life of Savage*, and had proceeded with a second play, *Charles of Sweden*, of which the only record is an ambiguous allusion in a letter (10 June, 1742). The labour he spent on *Irene* led him to think well of it for a time; but, late in life, when he returned to it afresh, he agreed with the common verdict. He "thought it had been better." He could speak from his own experience when, in the passage on tediousness in his *Life of Prior*, he said that "unhappily this pernicious failure is that which an author is least able to discover."

---

in *The Tragedy of The Unhappy Fair Irene*, by Gilbert Swinhoe, 1658; *Irena, a Tragedy*, of unknown authorship, 1664; and *Irene, or the Fair Greek*, by Charles Goring, 1708. Before Knolles, the same subject had been treated in Peele's lost play *The Turkish Mahamet and Hyrin the fair Greek* (see Peele, ed. Bullen, A. H., vol. I, p. xxxvii, and vol. II, p. 394).

[1] The title on the play-bills was *Mahomet and Irene*. See *An Essay on Tragedy*, 1749, p. 12 note, and Genest, *English Stage*, 1832, vol. IV, pp. 265–6.

It was *The Gentleman's Magazine* that gave Johnson his real start as a man of letters. Founded by Edward Cave, under the name Sylvanus Urban, in January, 1731, it had been growing steadily from small beginnings. Its original purpose was to reprint, from month to month, a selection of the more interesting matter that had appeared in the journals; and the name "magazine" was, in this its first application to a periodical, intended as a modest title for a collection which made small claim to originality. The idea was not altogether new. *The Grub-street Journal* contains a section of "domestic news" extracted from other papers, and sometimes so treated as to suggest to the modern reader the more urbane comments in the pages of *Punch*. But, as the editors of *The Grub-street Journal* complained in the preface to *Memoirs of the Society of Grub-street* (1737), their rival of *The Gentleman's Magazine* took anything he fancied—news, letters, essays or verses—and printed as much or as little of them as he pleased. The success of the *Magazine* was never in doubt. The first number went into a fifth edition; and with success came ambition. In the number for January, 1739, a correspondent, who evidently was Johnson, observes that the extracts from the weekly journalists have "shrunk at length into a very few columns and made way for original letters and dissertations." The *Magazine* now included parliamentary reports, poetical essays, serial stories, mathematical papers, maps, songs with music, and a register of publications. Most of the devices of modern journalism were anticipated in these early numbers. Cave had the luck and the skill to hit on what the public wanted. If we may trust the preface to the collected numbers for 1738, there were immediately "almost twenty imitations." Yet *The Gentleman's Magazine* had many features in common with *The Gentleman's Journal; or the Monthly Miscellany*, which Peter Motteux had started in January, 1692, and carried on with flagging zeal to 1694. The earlier periodical had begun on a much higher literary level and remains a work of very great interest; but its fortunes were not watched over by a man of business. It had been modelled partly on *Le Mercure Galant*. *The Gentleman's Magazine* was, in its origin, independent of both its French and its English forerunners.

In the letter which Johnson sent to Cave from Birmingham

in 1734, besides offering to contribute, he suggested several improvements. For "the low jests, awkward buffoonery, or the dull scurrilities of either party," which were to procure for it or its imitators a place in *The Dunciad*, might be substituted, he thought, "short literary dissertations in Latin or English, critical remarks on authors ancient or modern, or loose pieces worth preserving." Nothing came of the letter; but the suggestion that the *Magazine* should take itself more seriously accorded with Cave's business instincts, and the changes gradually introduced were in accordance with Johnson's wishes. His first contribution, the Latin alcaics beginning *Urbane, nullis fesse laboribus*, did not appear till March, 1738. From that time, he was regularly employed; and he at once asserted some sort of literary control. There cannot be any doubt that the subsequent steady rise in the character of the *Magazine* was largely due to him. He also helped to guide its fortunes through a grave crisis. Reports of the proceedings and debates in parliament had been given in the *Magazine* since 1732; but, on 13 April, 1738, the House of Commons declared such reports to be "a notorious breach of the Privilege of this House." The *Magazine* could not easily omit a section on which much of its popularity depended, and, in June, 1738, there appeared "debates in the Senate of Magna Lilliputia." If, as Hawkins says, the device was Cave's, it had Johnson's approval; and his hand is unmistakable in the passage in which the device is explained. He began by editing the reports, which continued to be written by William Guthrie, the first of his many Scottish friends. He was their sole author only for the thirty-six numbers and supplements from July, 1741 to March, 1744, and author rather than reporter. According to Hawkins, he had never entered either House; according to Murphy, he had once found his way into the House of Commons. He expanded in Cave's printing-office, long after the actual debates, the scanty notes supplied to him, and invested them with his own argumentative skill and eloquence. Some of the speeches are said to represent what was said by more than one speaker; others he described as the mere coinage of his imagination. His reports are, in fact, original work, and a very great work. To us who know the secret of their authorship, it is surprising that they should not have been recognised as the work of a man of letters. They are on a high level of literary excellence, and there is an obvious uniformity in the style. Even when they succeed in suggesting the idiosyncrasies of the different speakers, they show one cast of mind and texture of language. They are Johnson's own debates on the political questions of the day, based—and based only—on the debates in parliament. He said, within a few days of his death, that he wrote them "with more velocity" than any other work—often three columns of the *Magazine* within the hour, and, once, ten pages between noon and early evening. The wonder is, not so much that debates thus written could have been so good, as that debates so good could have been accepted as giving the words of the speakers. Johnson had not expected this; and, when he recognised it, he determined not to be any longer "accessory to the propagation of falsehood." This is the explanation given for his sudden abandonment of them in 1744. But the secret was long kept, and they continued to be regarded as genuine. There is more of Johnson than of Pitt in the famous speech about "the atrocious crime of being a young man." And two speeches entirely written by him appeared, to his amusement, in the collected works of Chesterfield.

The extent of his other contributions cannot easily be determined. We have often only the evidence of style to guide us, and his editorial privileges make it difficult to apply. It is very doubtful, for instance, if the short notice, in November, 1739, of the poems of Joseph Warton and Collins printed in the previous number is, as Wooll states in his *Memoirs of Warton*, the work of Johnson. Our best authority is Boswell, but his list is only tentative. We know that he wrote the biographies of Sarpi, Boerhaave, Blake, Drake, Barretier, Lewis Morin, Burmann and Sydenham; and there are other articles about which there can be no reasonable doubt. The amount of his writing varies greatly from month to month. In the number for December, 1740, which contains his *Essay on Epitaphs*, most of the original contributions are his; in other numbers, we cannot safely ascribe to him more than the debates. The question of authorship has never been examined thoroughly; but, even with the help of Cave's office books, there would be obstacles to a conclusive finding. In addition to his work for Cave, he had brought out, with other publishers, *Marmor*

*Norfolciense* (April, 1739), an ironical discussion, with a political bearing, on the supposed discovery of a prophecy in "monkish rhyme," and *A Compleat Vindication of the Licensers of the Stage* (May, 1739), an ironical attack on the rejection of Brooke's *Gustavus Vasa*. Continued irony is rarely successful. Johnson did not try it again.

The early series of biographies was followed by the elaborate life of a poet whom Johnson had known intimately, and whose character required protection from the insults and calumnies which it invited. Richard Savage died in the prison of Bristol at the beginning of August, 1743; and, in the number of *The Gentleman's Magazine* for the same month, Johnson announced, in an unsigned letter, that a biography of him was in preparation. He wrote it with his usual speed—once he wrote as much as forty-eight printed pages at a sitting—and had it published in February, 1744. It is a work of remarkable and varied interest, and throws light on a period of Johnson's career of which we know too little. They had suffered poverty together and forgotten it in their companionship; they had spent whole nights in the streets when their combined resources could not find them a shelter; and the description of Savage's fortunes reflects what Johnson had himself endured, and might have still to endure. He was attracted to Savage by the story of his life, on which research had not yet cast any doubt, by his shrewd knowledge of human nature, by his social skill and experience and by his talent as a writer. Savage was eleven years older than Johnson, and in his varied life had much to tell. But the chief attraction was Savage's own character. His great capacities could not save him from his undoing. He was self-indulgent, petulant, aggressive and ungrateful; there was excuse for the indifference or resentment of those who had once been benefactors. All this Johnson brings out clearly in a narrative which, when it leans from impartiality, leans to the side of friendship. He related everything as he knew it, with no suggestion of censure, but with generous sympathy. *The Life of Savage* is one of those rare biographies which, by their perfect sincerity, tell us as much of the character of the author as of the man described. He included it, later, with only slight alterations, in *The Lives of the Poets*. It had been an adequate expression of his feelings when it was written, and he wisely decided to let well enough alone. But it is a different *Life* from the other *Lives*, and differs from them in more than scale and method. It is the study of a personality rather than of a poet, though at no time would Johnson have tried to make such a distinction. The criticism of Savage's works is the least part of it, and has not yet all the writer's easy mastery. The style, too, which, at its best, is as good as it ever was to be, sometimes lacks its later certainty and precision. And the frequent repetition of the same ideas, though always in different language, shows a desire to give in full the content of a full mind rather than to represent it by selection. The new setting of *The Life of Savage* invites a comparison which proves that Johnson's abilities were strengthening and maturing to his seventieth year. Yet he never revealed himself more fully than in this early tribute to the memory of a difficult friend.

Johnson's contributions to *The Gentleman's Magazine* had become less frequent in 1743, and they ceased in the following year. He was meditating larger schemes. And he had latterly been doing much other work. Since the end of 1742, he had been engaged with William Oldys in cataloguing the printed books in the library of the earl of Oxford, then newly purchased by Thomas Osborne, the bookseller. The *Proposals* for printing the catalogue by subscription were written by Johnson and issued in December, 1742, and the *Account of the Harleian Library*, which they contained, was afterwards made to serve as preface to the first of the four volumes of the catalogue—*Catalogus Bibliothecae Harleianae*, 1743-4. While the catalogue was in progress, the bookseller, who had remarkable luck in having secured the services of one of the greatest of English literary antiquaries and one of the most scholarly of English critics, was persuaded to publish a collection of the more scarce and valuable tracts or pamphlets in his possession, under the title *The Harleian Miscellany*. The bulk of the selective and editorial work fell to Oldys; but it was Johnson who, again, wrote the *Proposals*, and contributed the introduction (1744), which, when reprinted separately, he entitled *An Essay on the Origin and Importance of Small Tracts and Fugitive Pieces*. In this, his first attempt at literary history, he gives a short sketch of English pamphlets from the reformation to the reign of Charles II, and follows in the tracks of such works as *The*

*Phenix* (1707) and *The Phoenix Britannicus* (1731), *The Critical History of Pamphlets* (1716) of Myles Davies, and the *Dissertation on Pamphlets* (1731) of his collaborator Oldys. There is no evidence of Johnson's hand in the Harleian *Collection of Voyages and Travels* (1745).

On the completion of this congenial experience in bibliography Johnson proposed to edit Shakespeare. The work was not to be undertaken for many years yet; but it was the first of the larger schemes planned by him. *Miscellaneous Observations on the Tragedy of Macbeth*[1] (April, 1745) was intended to prepare the way. There was still room for a new edition, as Hanmer had given most thought to regularised metre and sumptuous printing, and Warburton seemed to have abandoned what he had announced as early as 1740. But, after the death of Pope and the completion of Hanmer's edition in 1744, Warburton set to work in earnest, and the prospect of early publication compelled Johnson to lay aside his scheme, which could not have had an equal chance of success, inasmuch as, like most of his work up to this time, it was anonymous. When Warburton's edition appeared, in 1747, Johnson had the meagre satisfaction of finding his *Miscellaneous Observations* singled out for praise in the vituperative preface. It was now that he turned to the *Dictionary*. He had "long thought of it," he said; "it had grown up in his mind insensibly." The *Plan of a Dictionary of the English Language* was issued in 1747, and, at the desire of Dodsley, was addressed to the earl of Chesterfield. This year—which is, also, the year of the Drury lane prologue —marks the turn in Johnson's fortunes, though the fitful struggle with poverty was not yet over. But what was Johnson doing in 1745 and 1746? Here again the records are deficient. Of more than a thousand letters of his that are known, there is not one to throw light on either of these years.

Johnson did not confine himself to the labours of the *Dictionary*. During the eight years of its preparation he wrote his greatest poem, and gave new life to the periodical essay.

His school verses, which were preserved by the pride of a

---

[1] The title continues:—*To which is affix'd, Proposals for a New Edition of Shakespear, with a Specimen.* The *Proposals* are commonly wanting. They were printed on a folio sheet and folded in at the end of the volume. The Bodleian library possesses the rare folio sheet, MS. Bodl. Add. C. 244 (387).

teacher and the admiration of a friend, and printed by Boswell, are of little interest except in relation to his later work. They show the study of *The Rape of the Lock* and the translation of Homer, and they occasionally indulge in the liberties of Dryden's triple rime and alexandrine—liberties from which Johnson afterwards refrained, though he came to say that the art of concluding the sense in couplets "has perhaps been with rather too much constancy pursued."[1] The piece entitled "The Young Authour" is a first study for the great passage in *The Vanity of Human Wishes* on the scholar's life, and, in the the music of the metre, and in the turn and balance of the expression, already discovers the quality of his mature verse. He acquired a reputation for ease in writing and for readiness to help a friend in need. His verses *Written at the request of a gentleman to whom a lady had given a sprig of myrtle* were remembered as having been made in five minutes, and those *To Miss Hickman, playing on the Spinnet*, or others like them, led the girl's father to opine that their author could write about anything. What he called "the endearing elegance of female friendship" had been, long before he met Mrs. Thrale, an effective spur to his facility. Some of the pieces written while he was still in search of occupation in the midlands afterwards found their way into *The Gentleman's Magazine* and Mrs. Williams's *Miscellanies in Prose and Verse* (1766). None of them is more characteristic than *Friendship, An Ode*. On the other hand, the collected editions include several pieces clearly not his. He could not have written *To Lyce, an elderly Lady*. It is no less certain that, though he did write some verses *To Stella*, the chance that a piece is addressed to Stella is not, as his editors seem to have believed, an argument of his authorship. His early poems have still to be discriminated;[2] but their chief interest will always be that they were written by the author of *London* and *The Vanity of Human Wishes*.

*London: a poem, in imitation of the Third Satire of Juvenal* was published in May, 1738, on the same day as Pope's *One Thousand Seven Hundred and Thirty-Eight, a Dialogue some-*

---

[1] *Life of Denham.*

[2] Boswell promised an edition of the poems, in which he would "with the utmost care ascertain their authenticity, and illustrate them with notes and various readings." Such an edition has not yet appeared.

*thing like Horace*, and thus, accidentally, invited a comparison which appears to have gone in Johnson's favour. Here was a new author who concealed his name, rivalling Pope in the very kind of verse which, after an indisputed career, he had found best suited to his genius. The poem went into a second edition within a week; and Pope himself, who was always generous in his recognition of excellence, and had said of Johnson's youthful translation of his *Messiah* that posterity would have to decide which form of the poem was the original, declared that the unknown author of *London* could not be long concealed. The method of "imitation" adopted in this poem was described by Johnson in his *Life of Pope* as "a kind of middle composition between translation and original design, which pleases when the thoughts are unexpectedly applicable and the parallels lucky." Brought into *vogue* by Boileau, it had been practised in English by Rochester, Oldham and Dryden (in his revision of Soames's translation of Boileau's *Art Poétique*), and many others; and it had recently been perfected by Pope, who had so written that a knowledge of the original might enhance the appreciation, but should not be indispensable to it. Juvenal's *Third Satire* lent itself to imitation and had already been copied by Boileau and Oldham. The chief criticism to be urged against Johnson's poem is that it does not show Pope's art in escaping from its model. He was still timid enough to wish to show himself scholar as well as poet. When he wrote that "falling houses thunder on your head," or that the midnight murderer "leaves unseen a dagger in your breast," he thought more of Juvenal than of modern fact. The need of a parallel forces him to say, "I cannot bear a French metropolis"; but this was not the London described in Voltaire's *Lettres Anglaises*. He himself admitted (in a manuscript note) that the description of Orgilio was "no picture of modern manners, though it might be true at Rome." His own opinion on the advantages of country life we shall find, not here, but in the passage on scenes of flowery felicity and the melody of the nightingale in *The Life of Savage*. His political views are more truly represented: the references to excise and pensions, as well as to patrons, anticipate the definitions in the *Dictionary*. But it is when Juvenal leads him to speak of poverty that he expresses his own feelings in his own person.

None of these objections can be urged against *The Vanity of Human Wishes*, written in imitation of Juvenal's *Tenth Satire* and published, with Johnson's name, in January, 1749. There is nothing in this poem to suggest to those unacquainted with the model that it is an imitation; it is, indeed, not so much an imitation as a companion study by one who, amid different circumstances, took a very similar view of life. Instead of the Roman illustrations, we have modern instances of hopes that lay in power, and learning, and war, and long life and beauty. The pictures of Wolsey and Charles of Sweden, and the description of the lot of the scholar, are distinct studies of human ambition, each complete in itself and easily taken from its setting, but all viewed in the same light, and united by the one lesson of inevitable disappointment. The poem is completely satisfying as a statement of its theme. It is not less valuable as a personal document. There is nothing in it but what Johnson consistently thought and felt. He was wont to say that there is more to be endured than enjoyed in the general condition of human life; and he had found that human happiness, if it ever comes, must come by our own effort. The concluding lines which he supplied many years later to Goldsmith's *Traveller* state his invariable experience. In *The Life of Savage* he had said that happiness is to be placed only in virtue, which is always to be obtained; and he had said much the same in *Irene*. But there were times when he doubted even this. "Where then shall hope and fear their objects find?" In his simple piety, he gave himself to the earnest exercise of religion. His *Prayers*, which were made public after his death, will win the admiration alike of idle curiosity and of doubting reason. And so, with his habitual sincerity, he gave to *The Vanity of Human Wishes* a religious conclusion which reflected his own practice. He was no pessimist. The sense of vanity may keep us from thinking that things are better than they are, but it need not make us think that they are worse. He would maintain in talk that the world was not half so wicked as it was represented to be, that there was very little gross wickedness in it, and very little extraordinary virtue. This we are told explicitly by Mrs. Piozzi, and we may learn it for ourselves from his writings.

Shortly before he wrote *The Vanity of Human Wishes*, he

had aided Dodsley in planning *The Preceptor* (April, 1748), a substantial work containing "a general course of education," and had contributed to it the preface and *The Vision of Theodore, the Hermit of Teneriffe.* He told Percy that he thought this fable the best thing he ever wrote. It states the part which he assigned to religion in the conduct of life, and should be read as a supplement to *The Vanity of Human Wishes.* It may, also, be regarded as a prelude to *The Rambler.*

This paper began on Tuesday, 20 March, 1750, and ended, with its 208th number, on Saturday, 14 March, 1752, three days before the death of Johnson's wife.

He that condemns himself to compose on a stated day, will often bring to his task, an attention dissipated, a memory overwhelmed, an imagination embarrassed, a mind distracted with anxieties, and a body languishing with disease.

So he wrote in the last number, reviewing his experiences.

But the paper appeared regularly every Tuesday and Saturday, though the printer might complain of the late hour of receiving the copy. The very title was chosen in haste. Johnson meant it to announce that he would pass in each essay from subject to subject. But it was not suited to his majestic deliberations. There is nothing of the rambler in any single essay. Each pursues its way in a steady, unswerving march.[1]

The conditions amid which Johnson revived the periodical essay differed widely from those amid which it originally flourished. In the interval of forty years, there had been a development of journalistic enterprise which was not paralleled in any other country. More than 150 periodicals, of one kind or another, had been meeting the needs of the reading public, and contributing to its steady growth in size and power. Some of these were on the model of *The Spectator*, while others, written with a different purpose, or planned to include a greater variety of matter, showed its influence. The periodical essay

[1] Such slight assistance as he received is scrupulously acknowledged in the last number. Four papers were written by others: no. 30 by Mrs. Catharine Talbot, nos. 44 and 100 by Mrs. Elizabeth Carter, and no. 97 by Samuel Richardson; and six letters were contributed, the four in no. 10 by Hester Mulso, afterwards Mrs. Chapone; the second in no. 15 and the second in no. 107, both of unknown authorship.

no longer offered any of the attractions of novelty. In its strict form, it was a type of journalism that was being crushed out of favour by politics and news. By 1750, *The Gentleman's Magazine* enjoyed a secure popularity, and had its rivals; and, in the previous year, *The Monthly Review* had been established. The time was not auspicious for beginning a paper devoted exclusively to meditations on matters of no immediate interest, without the assistance of any item of news, or of a single advertisement. But, in *The Rambler*, the periodical essay reasserted itself, and entered on the second of its two great decades, that of *The Rambler*, *The Adventurer*, *The World*, *The Connoisseur*, *The Idler* and *The Citizen of the World*.

The effect of *The Rambler* was the more remarkable, in that Johnson was deficient in the qualifications of a periodical writer. The maxim that "the drama's laws the drama's patrons give" is equally true of the essay. It was not in Johnson's nature to bow to the public, however much he believed in its ultimate verdict. He spoke in his first number as if success depended on the choice of subject. But, in the treatment of his choice, he lacked the art of going to meet his readers; and they never came in great numbers. The circulation of *The Rambler* was only about 500 copies. But it raised the literary level of the periodical essay and set a standard of excellence to such papers as *The World*, whose sale was numbered in thousands.

It found a larger public on being reprinted in volume form, and came to be the only periodical of the century to vie with *The Spectator* in popularity. Johnson revised it for the collected edition with unusual care.[1] It had been his most ambitious work; and he knew that it was best suited to a leisurely perusal. Yet there is little in *The Rambler* that is

---

[1] According to Alexander Chalmers, "the alterations made by Dr. Johnson in the second and third editions of *The Rambler* far exceed six thousand." Cf. Drake, Nathan, *Essays illustrative of the Rambler*, 1809, vol. I, pp. 273–280. Johnson created an impression that his care for his works ceased at their publication; but, to adopt his phrase about Pope, his parental fondness did not immediately abandon them. Boswell says that, in 1781, Johnson had not looked at *Rasselas* since it was first published; but a comparison of the two editions of 1759 shows a large number of alterations affecting the style. The poems were revised: James Boswell the younger transcribed into his copy of the edition of 1789 the "notes and various readings" in "Johnson's own handwriting on a copy of the fifth edition" of *London*.

now well known. Much of its literary criticism was superseded by the preface to his *Shakespeare* and by his *Lives of the Poets*. The allegories and stories have not the reputation of their models in *The Spectator*. Nor are Johnson's characters familiar as Addison's are. The explanation lies mainly in his inability to visualise. He did not number the streaks of the tulip because, in effect, he did not see them; but he remarked general properties and large appearances because he had the gift, which he assiduously developed, of viewing things in their moral aspects and human relationships. The real interest of the famous passage in *Rasselas* on the aims of the poet—a passage which, it must be remembered, leads to the humorous conclusion that "no human being can ever be a poet"—lies in its personal basis. The best poets of his century, and the poets of all time whom he most admired, numbered the streaks when they wished. But he did not number them, because they did not enter into his experience. We do not give a face or figure to any of his characters in *The Rambler*, because he did not see either clearly himself. Polyphilus, the quick wit without purpose; Suspirius, the fault-finder; Quisquilius, the virtuoso; Venustulus, the effeminate beau—are, each of them, bundles of habits, or a predominant habit. Even Prospero, who might have been drawn from Garrick, represents only the social failings of the rich man who has risen in life. Johnson reverted to the methods of the character-studies of the seventeenth century. Addison had set out by continuing them, but he was at war with them at heart, and he adapted them to his purpose. The superiority of Addison in this respect will never be denied. But Johnson shows a deeper knowledge of human nature "in all its gradations," and, while he lacks the familiar elegance which alone can play with foibles and frivolities, he offers a richer harvest of deep observation.

And Johnson had not the desire, even had he possessed the ability, to disguise his purpose. Addison, too, had been frankly didactic; he had said that he meant to bring philosophy to dwell on tea-tables and in coffee-houses. But he kept his readers from suspecting that they were being taught or reformed. Johnson's lessons are obvious. His aim was "only the propagation of truth"; it was always his "principal design to inculcate wisdom or piety." The great moralist lavishes the best instruction he can offer, the instruction of a man of the world who knows what the world cannot give; but he does not offer it in a way to attract unwilling attention. He recognised this himself and admitted that "the severity of dictatorial instruction has been too seldom relieved." His deep humour is present throughout, and is occasionally given scope, as in the essay on the advantages of living in a garret; but it is always controlled by the serious purpose.

In concluding *The Rambler*, he stated that he had laboured "to refine our language to grammatical purity, and to clear it from colloquial barbarisms, licentious idioms, and irregular combinations." At this time he was in the midst of a similar and greater task in his *Dictionary of the English Language*. Most of the earlier English dictionaries, to the beginning of the eighteenth century, had been dictionaries of "hard words." Then, Nathan Bailey, in his *Universal Etymological English Dictionary* (1721), had aimed at a record of all English words, irrespective of their *vogue* or repute. Johnson purposely omitted "many terms appropriated to particular occupations," and thought not so much of the reader as of the writer and the purity of the language. His *Plan* clearly states his objects, and it is cleverly supplemented in Chesterfield's two papers in *The World*.[1] He set out to perform, singlehanded, for the English language what the French Academy, a century before, had undertaken for French.[2] It was to be "a dictionary by which the pronunciation of our language may be fixed, and its attainment facilitated; by which its purity may be preserved, its use ascertained, and its duration lengthened." So Johnson hoped; and Chesterfield was ready to acknowledge him as a dictator who would free the language from its anarchy. But, when he came to write the preface, he had found that "no dictionary of a living tongue can ever be perfect, since, while it is hastening to publication, some words are budding,

---

[1] Nos. 100, 101.

[2] f Garrick's verses in *The Gentleman's Magazine* for April, 1755, ending
    And Johnson, well arm'd, like a hero of yore,
    Has beat forty French, and will beat forty more.
Cf., also, the review in Maty's *Journal Britannique*, 1775, XVII, p. 219: *Mr. Johnson peut se glorifier. . .d'être en quelque sorte une Académie pour son isle.* Adam Smith reviewed the *Dictionary* in the first number of *The Edinburgh Review* of 1755–6.

and some falling away." None the less, the mistaken hope gave the *Dictionary* its peculiar value. By aiming at fixing the language, he succeeded in giving the standard of reputable use.

Though there are many words in Bailey's dictionary which Johnson omitted, a hasty comparison will show that he added a large number. He held that the golden age of our language began with the reign of Elizabeth, and that the writers in the century before the restoration were "the pure sources of genuine diction." As his earliest authorities, he chose Sidney and Spenser. When he avowedly included obsolete words, they were to be found in wellknown authors, or appeared to deserve revival. "Cant words," as he called them, were occasionally admitted, because of their *vogue;* others were described as "low." But the most interesting departure from the rigid exclusiveness of an academic dictionary is his treatment of dialect. There is a much larger infusion of provincialisms than might have been expected. The great majority of these are Scottish, no doubt because five of his six amanuenses, as Boswell has proudly recorded, were "natives of North Britain"; but he was also affectionately disposed to words with which he had been familiar in his native county. With all his care for current reputable use, he had too great respect for the native stock to ignore its humbler members, and his selection and description of these have a clear historical value. His main fear for the language was that it would be corrupted by French. It seemed to him to have been, since the restoration, "deviating towards a Gallick structure and phraseology," and to be threatening to "reduce us to babble a dialect of France." So he set himself to denounce "the folly of naturalising useless foreigners to the injury of the natives." It was no vain boast that the book was devoted to the honour of his country. "We have long preserved our constitution, let us make some struggles for our language."

It appears from Spence's *Anecdotes* that Pope had discussed the plan of a dictionary, and had drawn up a list of authors, beginning with Hooker and Spenser, from whom words should be collected. The list is referred to in Johnson's *Plan;* and in terms which suggest a closer relationship than is now known to have existed. But there is nothing to show that Pope had favoured the inclusion of quotations. This was Johnson's most notable innovation in English lexicography. He had hoped that every quotation would serve a further purpose than that of illustrating the use of a word; but he found, as he proceeded, that he had to abandon the idea of combining a dictionary with an anthology. The quotations were frequently from memory and are seldom accompanied with exact references; but, considering the slightness of the assistance which he received, they supply a remarkable proof of the range of his knowledge, and they have a different kind of interest from those in other dictionaries, which, based on more scientific principles, record the use of a word with no attention to the quality of the writer. But the chief worth of the *Dictionary* lies where it should. Johnson had a supreme talent for definition. When it is remembered that the definitions are his own, that he was the first to attempt a thorough distinction of the different meanings (such words as *come* and *go* being each subdivided into more than fifty sections), and that the highest praises he has received have been paid by his successors, the extent of his services to the survey of the language will readily be estimated. The few explanations in which he gave play to his prejudice or indulged his humour were only a remission of the continued exercise of his keen and muscular intellect. Occasionally, he obscured a simple meaning; and no better statement is to be found than in his preface, of the difficulties of defining the obvious. He had, like every one in his century, little etymological knowledge to help him. But his common sense often kept him right in giving the original meaning of a word and distinguishing its later uses, where his successors, previously to the much later advance in philological science, by aiming at refinement introduced confusion and error.[1]

The publication of the *Dictionary* in eight years was a remarkable achievement of industry, and the more remarkable in that he had been doing much other work. Apart from his duties to his own *Rambler*, he held himself ready to assist his

---

[1] There were four editions of the *Dictionary* in folio during Johnson's lifetime. The last of them, "revised by the author," appeared in 1773. But Bailey's continued to hold the market. It was the popular English dictionary of the eighteenth century.

friends. He contributed a paper about once a fortnight, from March, 1753, to Hawkesworth's *Adventurer*. He helped Lauder, unsuspectingly, with a preface and postscript to his Miltonic hoax, and dictated his confession (1750–1); and he wrote the dedication for Mrs. Lennox's *Female Quixote* (1752) and *Shakespear Illustrated* (1753). He contributed the life of Cheynel to *The Student* (1751), and the life of Cave to *The Gentleman's Magazine* (1754). He composed Zachariah Williams's *Account of an Attempt to ascertain the Longitude at Sea*, (1755). And he furnished the *Dictionary* with a "History of the English Language" and a "Grammar of the English Tongue," including a section on prosody, as well as with its noble preface. And all this had been accomplished "amidst inconvenience and distraction, in sickness and in sorrow." He had so great a capacity for work, and when he had once started moved with so much ease, that he did not recognise his rapidity to be uncommon. The extreme concentration compelled periods of relaxation which he allowed to weigh on his conscience. He, too, was subject to the common delusion that his best was his normal. As he was, in all matters, a man of the most sensitive morality, it became a habit with him to be distressed at his idleness; and it has become a habit with us to speak of his constitutional indolence. He certainly had to make an effort to begin. But to the activity of the eight years from his thirty-eighth to his forty-sixth, it is not easy to find a parallel.[1]

The *Dictionary* has the accidental interest of having occasioned the letter to the earl of Chesterfield, which is sometimes said to have given the death-blow to literary patronage. Though always an object of curiosity, the letter was first made public by Boswell in 1790. In refusing to dedicate the *Dictionary*, Johnson adhered to his regular practice, from which only motives of business had suggested a departure. The *Plan* was a letter "addressed" to Chesterfield. Only once had he dedicated a work of his own—*The Voyage to Abyssinia*, and that was dedicated in the person of the Birmingham bookseller. But, though he made a rule for himself, he did not condemn the custom. He accepted dedications, and he continued to supply other writers with theirs. He told Boswell

---

[1] The second volume, L—Z, was begun on 3 April, 1753, and finished by March 1755. The introductory matter to vol. I also belongs to these two years.

that he "believed he had dedicated to all the Royal family round." He excelled in dedications.

His next scheme was a journal that should record the progress of European studies, and he planned it while the zest that came from completing the *Dictionary* concealed how far he had drawn on his energies. Such periodicals as *The Present State of the Republic of Letters* (1728–36) and *The History of the Works of the Learned* (1737–43) had now long ceased after having shown, at most, the possibility of success; and, since 1749, their place had been taken by *The Monthly Review*, of which, in its early years, Johnson had no reason to think highly. He now intended an English periodical that would rival those of Le Clerc and Bayle. But this scheme for "the Annals of Literature, foreign as well as domestic," was to yield to an older project. In June, 1756, he issued new *Proposals* for an edition of Shakespeare, and he hoped to have the work completed by the end of the following year. The long strain, however, had begun to tell. He had difficulty in facing any continuous work, and he suffered gravely from the mental depression to which he was always liable. He has described his unhappy condition in his Latin verses entitled *Γνῶθι σεαυτὸν post Lexicon Anglicanum auctum et emendatum*, which give a more intimate account of his feelings than he ever allowed himself in the publicity of English; and stronger evidence is to be found in his prayers, and in the reports of his friends. It was now that he confirmed himself in the habit of seeking relief in company, and, by encouraging the calls of anyone who wished for his help, established his personal authority in literature. Only the need of money made him write, and none of his work at this time required long effort. He brought out an abridgment of his *Dictionary* (January, 1756), but he probably had assistance in this mechanical labour. Having abandoned the idea of a critical periodical of his own, he contributed to the early numbers of Kit Smart's *Universal Visiter* (1756), and then undertook the control of *The Literary Magazine* (May, 1756–7). Here, he made his famous defence of tea; and, here, he exposed the shallow optimism of Soame Jenyns's *Free Enquiry into the Nature and Origin of Evil*, in an essay which, written with the convincing ease that had come from the experience of much painful thought, is an unsurpassed example of his method and power in argument. Another piece of journalistic work, at this time, was the introductory column of Dodsley's evening paper, *The London Chronicle* (1 January, 1757), which was to be distinguished from all other journals, probably on his advice, by its "account of the labours and productions of the learned." He also helped his friends with their books. He wrote a life of Sir Thomas Browne, with a criticism of Browne's style, for his own edition of *Christian Morals* (1756). With it may be grouped the later life of Ascham in the edition of Ascham's works nominally prepared by James Bennet (1761). The variety of his writings for some years after the completion of his *Dictionary* helps to explain how he found his memory unequal to producing a perfect catalogue of his works.[1]

His assistance was, once again, sought to give weight and dignity to a new periodical, and the starting of *The Universal Chronicle, or Weekly Gazette* was the occasion of his second series of essays, *The Idler*. They began 15 April, 1758, and appeared every Saturday till 5 April, 1760. The fact that *The Idler* was not an independent publication, but merely a section of a journal, will account for most of the differences between it and the *Rambler*. The papers are much shorter and do not show the same sense of sole responsibility. In one respect, however, they have a clear superiority. Their lighter touch is better suited to portraiture. Dick Minim the critic, Johnson's only character that may still be said to live, is a perfect example of his art at its best; nor can there be any difference of opinion about the shorter sketches of Jack Whirler and Tom Restless, or of Mr. Sober, in which the author represented himself. That the characters should no longer bear Latin names indicates a wider change. The critical papers also show the growth of ease and confidence. There is an obvious interest in those on "Hard Words," "Easy Writing" and "The Sufficiency of the English Language."

While *The Idler* was in progress, Johnson's mother died, and her death was the occasion both of his paper on the loss of a friend[2] and of his solemn novel on the choice of life, *Rasselas, Prince of Abyssinia* (April, 1759).[3] No work of his has been

---

[1] *Memoirs of the Life and Writings of Johnson* (1785), p. 38.　　　[2] No. 41.
[3] In all the editions published during Johnson's lifetime the title was simply

more frequently translated or is better known by name; but none has met with more contradictory judgments, or is a stricter test of the reader's capacity to appreciate the peculiar qualities of Johnson's thought and manner. There is little or no story, no crisis, no conclusion; there is little more than a succession of discussions and disquisitions on the limitations of life. *Rasselas* may be called the prose *Vanity of Human Wishes;* and it is the fullest, gravest and most intimate statement of his common theme.

It has been said that Addison would have written a novel, could he have cast the Coverly papers in a different form. Johnson proposed to write a novel, and produced an expanded essay. There are five "oriental tales" in *The Rambler*, and three were yet to appear in *The Idler*. They suited his purpose in their vagueness of background and their free scope for didactic fancies. *Rasselas* is another of these tales, elaborated to enforce his lesson by a greater range of observation. The first requirement of the story was a happy valley. Older writers would have placed it in Arcadia; Johnson takes us to the same undiscovered country, but calls it Abyssinia. He had not forgotten his early translation. The name "Rasselas" was suggested by it, and other instances of recollection are equally certain. There were "impassable forests and inaccessible cliffs" in the real Abyssinia,[1] and why not a happy valley behind them? But one of the attractions of Lobo's narrative had been that the reader found in it no regions blessed with spontaneous fecundity or unceasing sunshine. Johnson knew, quite as well as the critics who stumble at local and ethnographical discrepancies, that there is no happy valley; but he asked its existence to be granted as a setting for a tale which would show that "human life is every where a state in which much is to be endured, and little to be enjoyed." The gloom is heavy, but, to those who can appreciate Johnson, it is never depressing. He had cleared his mind of cant, and he wrote to give his readers the strength that comes from the honesty of looking straight at things as they are. He pur-

---

*The Prince of Abissinia, a Tale.* He had thought of calling it *The Choice of Life* (see his letter of 20 January, 1759).

[1] *Voyage to Abyssinia* (1735), p. 105. For other recollections in the first chapter of *Rasselas* cf. *ibid.*, pp. 97, 102, 204 and 259.

sues his way relentlessly through the different conditions that seem to offer happiness openhanded, and works to a climax in the story of the astronomer; "Few can attain this man's knowledge, and few practise his virtues, but all may suffer his calamity. Of the uncertainties of our present state, the most dreadful and alarming is the uncertain continuance of reason." This is one of the many passages which emphasise his perfect sincerity. The book ends in resignation to the futility of searching for happiness, and in resolution to pursue life as it is found. Stated in these words, the lesson may appear a commonplace. But so are the real things of human experience. And never was the lesson stated with more sympathetic knowledge, and enlivened with a greater wealth of aphoristic wisdom.

Meanwhile, the edition of Shakespeare was at a stand. Some of the plays—evidently, those in the first volume—had been printed by March, 1758; but, during the next four years, there was no sign of progress. In addition to *The Idler* and *Rasselas* Johnson had been writing dedications, prefaces, introductions and reviews, engaging in unsuccessful controversy on the structure of the new bridge at Blackfriars, and helping to lay the Cock lane ghost. The discontent of his subscribers, roughly expressed in Churchill's *Ghost* (1762), at last roused him to complete his work; and the financial ease that had come with his pension of £300 (1762) gave him what time he needed. The edition was published, in eight volumes, in October, 1765.[1]

There was nothing new in Johnson's methods as an editor. He aimed only at doing better what had been done already, and produced an edition of the old fashion at a time when the science of Shakespearean editing was about to make a distinct advance.[2] But he had qualifications sometimes wanting in editors with more painful habits or more ostentatious equipment—a good knowledge of Elizabethan English, and imperturbable common sense. Like almost every text of Shakespeare that had yet appeared, or was to appear till our own day, it was based on the text of the most recent edition. What he

[1] New facts about Johnson's receipts for his edition of Shakespeare are given in *The Athenaeum*, 11. IX. 1909, and in the *Bi-Centenary Festival Reports*, pp. 29–32. From the original agreement with Tonson, it would appear that Johnson received a much larger sum than was stated by Nichols, *Literary Anecdotes*, vol. v. p. 597.

[2] Cf. *ante*, Vol. V. pp. 305 ff.

sent to the printer was Warburton's text revised. But he
worked on the "settled principle that the reading of the ancient
books is probably true," and learned to distrust conjecture.
His collation was never methodical; his weak eyesight was a
serious hindrance to an exacting task. But he restored many
of the readings of the first folio, and, carrying on the system of
combination that had been started by Pope, was the first to
detect and admit many of the readings of the quartos. He
produced a text which, with all its shortcomings, was nearer
the originals than any that had yet appeared. Some of his
emendations, which are always modest and occasionally minute, find an unsuspected place in our modern editions. Though
his text has long been superseded, the advance of scholarship
will never impair the value of his notes. It was a proud boast
that not a single passage in the whole work had appeared to
him corrupt which he had not endeavoured to restore, or
obscure which he had not endeavoured to illustrate; and it
did not go beyond the truth. No edition, within its limits, is
a safer guide to Shakespeare's meaning. The student who
searches the commentators for help in difficulties, soon learns
to go straight to Johnson's note as the firm land of common
sense in a sea of ingenious fancies. The same robust honesty
gives the preface a place by itself among critical pronounce-
ments on Shakespeare. He did not hesitate to state what
he believed to be Shakespeare's faults. Yet Shakespeare remained to him the greatest of English authors, and the only
author worthy to be ranked with Homer. He, also, vindicated the liberties of the English stage. After conforming to
the "unities" in his own *Irene*, and then suggesting his doubts
of them in *The Rambler*, he now proved that they are "not
essential to a just drama." The guiding rule in his criticism
was that "there is always an appeal open from criticism to
nature." A generation later, the French "romantics" found
their case stated in his preface, and they did not better what
they borrowed.[1]

Hereafter, Johnson did not, on his own initiative, undertake any other large work. "Composition is, for the most

[1] Johnson's examination of the "unities" is translated word for word in Beyle,
Henri, *Racine et Shakespeare* (1822). See *Johnson on Shakespeare* by Raleigh,
Sir Walter (1908), and *Stendhal et l'Angleterre*, by Gunnell, Doris (1909).

part," he said, "an effort of slow diligence and steady perseverance, to which the mind is dragged by necessity or resolution."
His pension had removed the necessity, and, for the next
twelve years, his best work lay in talk. In 1763, he met Boswell; in 1764, he founded with Reynolds "The Club"—not
known till long after as "The Literary Club"; in 1765, he gained
the friendship of the Thrales. Companionship and elegant
comforts provided the relief that was still needed to his re-
curring depressions. He wrote little, but he engaged in personal kindnesses, and talked his best, and exerted an influence
which spread far beyond the circle of his conversation. He
was still, as at all times, ready to contribute to the publications
of his friends, and even dictated the arguments in some of
Boswell's law cases; but he did not undertake any writing that
required resolution or has added to his fame. His four political tracts—*The False Alarm* (1770), *Falkland's Islands* (1771),
*The Patriot* (1774) and *Taxation no Tyranny* (1775)—are known,
so far as they are known, because he was their author. Since
his early work on the debates in *The Gentleman's Magazine*,
he had always taken a keen interest in politics. Most of his
essays in *The Literary Magazine* had been on political topics.
Towards the end of 1765, he had undertaken to supply "single-
speech" Hamilton with his views on questions that were being
discussed in parliament and had written for him, in November,
1766, *Considerations on the Corn Laws*.[1] But now, he wrote
as a pamphleteer. The most judicious of the four tracts is
*Falkland's Islands*, which makes a just defence of the policy
towards Spain and is notable for its picture of the horrors of
war and for its reference to Junius. The best thing in *The
False Alarm*, his thoughts on the present discontents, is the
satirical picture of the progress of a petition. In *Taxation no
Tyranny*, his "answer to the Resolutions and Address of the
American Congress," he asks "how is it that we hear the loudest
yelps for liberty among the drivers of negroes?"

The prejudice in *A Journey to the Western Islands of Scot-*

---

[1] This was first published by Malone as an appendix to his edition of Hamilton's *Parliamentary Logick* (1808). Malone points out Boswell's error in deducing
from the prayer entitled "Engaging in Politicks with H—n" that Johnson was
"seized with a temporary fit of ambition" and thought of "becoming a politician."
See, also, *Boswell*, ed. Hill, G. B., vol. I, pp. 518–20.

*land* is of a different kind, and never displeasing. It is only the natural prejudice of John Bull as a tourist. He makes many acute observations which even the most perfervid Scot must have recognised to be just; but his impartiality is occasionally impeded by a want of knowledge which he himself was the first to admit. He had been conducted round Scotland by Boswell from August to November, 1773, and the book—which was published in January, 1775—is not so much a record of the ninety-four days of "vigorous exertion" as a series of thoughts on a different civilisation. It had a different purpose from that of Pennant's *Tour in Scotland* (1771), which Johnson praised highly. He had taken the opportunity of enquiring into the authenticity of the poems of Ossian, and convinced himself that "they never existed in any other form than that which we have seen." This is the best known section of his book; but the reader may find more interest in the remarks on the superstitions of the Highlands, on American emigration and on the Scottish universities. In July and August, 1774, he made a tour in north Wales with his friends the Thrales, and kept a diary which might have served as the groundwork of a companion volume to his Scottish *Journey;* but he did not make any use of it, and it remained in MS. till 1816. The beauty of the Welsh scenery had greatly impressed him, and this diary must not be neglected in any estimate of his feeling for wild landscape. The fragmentary records of his tour in France with the Thrales in 1775 were left to be printed by Boswell. Johnson was content to pass the rest of his days in leisure, working only as the mood prompted, when, on Easter Eve, 1777, a deputation of booksellers asked him to undertake, at the age of sixty-seven, what was to prove his masterpiece.

*The Lives of the Poets* arose out of a business venture. The London booksellers were anxious to drive out of the market an Edinburgh reprint of the English poets and to protect their own copyright; and, besides producing an edition superior in accuracy and elegance, they determined to add biographical prefaces by some writer of authority. The scheme took some time to mature, and Percival Stockdale[1] had hopes of the editorship. But Johnson was given the first offer and at once accepted. Writing to Boswell, on 3 May, 1777, he says he is

[1] *Memoirs* (1809), vol. II, pp. 193-7.

engaged "to write little Lives and little Prefaces, to a little edition of the English Poets." The work proved so congenial that he wrote at greater length than he had intended; and, when the edition was completed, the prefaces were issued without the texts under the title *The Lives of the Poets* (1781). Their independent publication, and the title by which they are now known, were alike afterthoughts; in origin, *The Lives of the Poets* is only editorial matter. It is even more important to remember that this great body of critical opinion—perhaps the greatest in the English language—was written on invitation and in conformity with conditions controlled by others. When he found the complete series labelled "Johnson's Poets," he was moved to write on a scrap of paper which has happily been preserved: "It is great impudence to put Johnson's Poets on the back of books which Johnson neither recommended nor revised." Of the fifty-two poets, five, at most, were included on his suggestion. In the life of Watts, he says that the readers of the collection are to impute to him whatever pleasure or weariness they may find in the perusal of Blackmore, Watts, Pomfret and Yalden; but it would also appear from the letter to Boswell cited above that he "persuaded the booksellers to insert something of Thomson." There is no evidence that he advised any omission. For only one of the fifty-two lives was he indebted to another hand—the life of Young by Sir Herbert Croft. He included his early life of Savage, with insignificant changes, and worked up his article on Roscommon in *The Gentleman's Magazine* for May, 1748. The other lives he now wrote specially for the booksellers, availing himself here and there of what he had written already, such as the "Dissertation on Pope's Epitaphs" in *The Universal Visiter* (1756), and the character of Collins in Fawkes and Woty's *Poetical Calendar* (1763).

The original plan had evidently been to include "all the English poets of reputation from Chaucer to the present day." It is no matter for regret that this scheme was curtailed. The poets of the seventeenth and eighteenth centuries, besides affording him ample scope for expounding his views on poetry, possessed for him the personal interest which was always a stimulus to his criticism. But, even could he be shown to have recommended Cowley as the starting point, it would be an error to infer that this was the limit to his knowledge and appreciation. Such an inference would neglect his preface to Shakespeare, his work on the Elizabethans for the *Dictionary* and his statement in *The Idler*[1] that "we consider the whole succession from Spenser to Pope as superior to any names which the Continent can boast." Of the earlier writers, he had not the knowledge possessed by Thomas Warton and other of his friends. But he wrote on Ascham, and corresponded on the manuscripts of Sir Thomas More, and devoted to him a considerable section of the introductory matter of his *Dictionary;* and he was always alert to any investigation, whether in modern English, or Old English, or northern antiquities. His comprehensive knowledge of English literature may be described as beginning with the reign of Henry VIII. In an interview with George III, he was enjoined to add Spenser to *The Lives of the Poets;* and he would readily have complied, could he have obtained new material.[2]

In the earlier interview which Boswell has recorded, many years before *The Lives of the Poets* was thought of, George III proposed that Johnson should undertake the literary biography of his country. It was a happy courtesy, for, though there had been good lives of individual poets since Sprat's *Life of Cowley*, the collections that had yet appeared had shown that much remained to be accomplished, and Johnson was specially fitted to write the lives of authors. Even had he not said so, we should have suspected that the biographical part of literature was what he loved most. The best of these collections had been *The Lives of the Poets of Great Britain and Ireland* (1753), nominally by "Mr. Cibber" (Theophilus), but really by Robert Shiels,[3] *The Royal and Noble Authors* (1758), of Horace Walpole, which is a "catalogue," and the literary articles in the very unequal *Biographia Britannica*.[4] It was

---

[1] No. 91.

[2] This interview appears to have been unknown to Boswell. The authority for it is a sentence in the *Memoirs* of Hannah More (1834, vol. I, p. 174), and an obvious allusion in the conversation with John Nichols given towards the end of Boswell's *Life*.

[3] The evidence on the authorship is given in Sir Walter Raleigh's *Six Essays on Johnson* (1910), pp. 120–5, note.

[4] Johnson was asked to undertake the second edition of this work and regretted his refusal. See *Boswell*, ed. Hill, G. B., vol. III, p. 174.

left to Johnson to impart a sustained excellence to this kind of writing, and, by engaging in what had not yet occupied an author of his authority, to raise it to a new level as an English literary form.

The most obvious features of *The Lives of the Poets* is the equipoise of biography and criticism. Johnson states the facts simply, but connects them with his impression of the writer, and, when he passes to the examination of poems, he is still thinking of their relation to the writer's personality. He finds the man behind the work. The truth is that he was much more interested in the man than in that part of him which is the author. Of "mere poets," he thought little; and, though he championed the dignity of authorship, he claimed for it no exclusive privileges, nor held that the poet was a man apart to be measured by standards inapplicable to other men. If the enduring freshness of *The Lives of the Poets* is due to any one quality more than to another, it is to Johnson's inexhaustible interest in the varieties of human nature. As detailed biographies, they have been superseded, though they remain our only authority for many facts and anecdotes, and include much that had been inaccessible. He made researches; but they were limited to his immediate needs. It is often easy to trace the sources of his information. He criticised Congreve's plays without having read them for many years, and he refused for a time to hear Lord Marchmont's recollections of Pope. Though, in general, he welcomed new details, his aim was to know enough to describe the man and to bring out his individuality in the estimate of his work.

The common result of this method in criticism is that the critic is at his best when he is in sympathy with the writer. Johnson meant to be scrupulously judicial; but he showed personal feelings. He disliked the acrimonious politics of Milton, the querulous sensitiveness of Swift and the timid foppery of Gray. This personal antipathy underlies his criticisms, though it is qualified, at times, even generously. Had Gray written often as in the *Elegy*, he says "it had been vain to blame and useless to praise him"; and *Paradise Lost* "is not the greatest of heroic poems only because it is not the first." Of Dryden and Pope he wrote in friendship, and there exists no finer criticism of them. But no critic has been severer on Dryden's negligences, or spoken more ruthlessly of the *Essay on Man*.

The passage on *Lycidas* is generally regarded as an error of judgment which marks Johnson's limitations as a critic. With his usual courage, he stated a deliberate opinion. He gave his reasons—the artificiality of the pastoral convention, the confusion of the allegory with actual fact and sacred truth, and the absence of the feeling of real sorrow. But there is the further explanation that he was opposed to some recent tendencies in English poetry. That he had more than *Lycidas* in his mind is shown by the emphasis of his statement. The same ideas reappear in his criticism of Collins and Gray. He objected to the habit of inverting the common order of words, and, on one occasion, cited Thomas Warton's "evening gray"; he might also have cited "mantle blue." It was Warton who occasioned his extempore verses beginning—

> Whereso'er I turn my view,
> All is strange, yet nothing new;

and Warton imitated, as well as edited, the early poems of Milton. Warton was one of many in whom he found faults which he traced to Milton as their original. In criticising *Lycidas*, he had in mind his own contemporaries. When the new tendencies had prevailed, he was said to have judged by a rigorous code of criticism. This code would have been difficult to reconcile with the preface to his edition of Shakespeare; with the praise given by him to Homer's heroes, that they are not described but develop themselves;[1] with his statement that "real criticism" shows "the beauty of thought as formed on the workings of the human heart";[2] and with his condemnation of "the cant of those who judge by principles rather than perception."[3]

His views on the matter of poetry are shown in his criticism of Gray's *Bard:* "To select a singular event, and swell it to a giant's bulk by fabulous appendages of spectres and predictions, has little difficulty, for he that forsakes the probable may always find the marvellous." The common growth of mother earth sufficed for him as for Wordsworth. The distinction

[1] *Boswell*, ed. Hill, G. B., vol. v, p. 79.
[2] *Ibid.*, vol. ii, p. 88.       [3] *Life of Pope*.

which he draws between the *Elegy* and *The Bard* was that which ultimately divided Wordsworth and Coleridge. There was enough for him in life as he knew it. And there was a personal reason why, more than the other writers of his century, he should tend to limit nature to human experience. The tumult in his mind was allowed no direct expression in his writings; but it made him look upon the world as the battle ground of thought, and passion, and will.

With the revision of *The Lives of the Poets*, Johnson's career as an author closed. In the three years of failing health which were left to him, he lived his accustomed life, honoured for the authority of his opinion, generous in his help to younger writers, and active in domestic benevolence. He revised Crabbe's *Village*, and dictated much to Boswell. Death removed some who had played a great part in his later life—Thrale, whose house at Streatham had been a second home, and two of the pensioners in his own house at Bolt-court, Levett and Mrs. Williams. The tribute to Levett, noble in its restrained emotion, is the most tender of his poems. The sadness of loss was embittered by Mrs. Thrale's marriage to Piozzi and the irreparable break in the long and happy friendship. He had so far recovered from a paralytic seizure as to be able, at the close of 1783, to found the Essex-Head club. By its ease of access, the old man sought to supply the need of new company. He dined at The Club, for the last time, in June, 1784. Next month, he set out for his native city, and returned by Birmingham and Oxford, the cities of his youth. His health had not found any relief, and, when he reached London in November, was rapidly declining. He died 13 December, and, on the 20th, was buried in Westminster abbey. Shortly before his death, he had destroyed his papers.

His long career had been uniform in its aim and methods, and the distinctions between his earlier and later writings are those which come from experience and confidence. The author of the preface to *A Voyage to Abyssinia* is unmistakably the author of *The Rambler* and *The Lives of the Poets*, with the same tastes and habits of thought, but younger, with a shorter reach and less precision in his skill. There had been no discipleship, and no time of searching where his strength lay; and no new influences had modified his purpose. The changes to be found in his work of forty-five years are those of a natural and undisturbed development, so steady that its stages cannot be minutely marked by us, and were probably imperceptible to himself. As he grew older, he related all art more and more to life. Though careful to give his thoughts their best expression, and severe on improprieties in others, he became impatient of mere proficiency in technique; and, though a scholar, he recognised the insufficiency of scholarship and the barrenness of academic pursuits. He had the "purposes of life" ever and increasingly before him, and his criticisms of the English poets are the richest of his works in worldly wisdom.

At the same time, his style became more easy. The Latin element is at its greatest in *The Rambler*. He was then engaged on his *Dictionary*. But he always tended to use long words most when he wrote in haste; and his revision was towards simplicity.[1] He used them in conversation, where alone he allowed himself the liberty of a daring coinage. They were in no sense an embroidery, but part of the very texture of his thought. "Difference of thoughts," he said, "will produce difference of language. He that thinks with more extent than another will want words of larger meaning; he that thinks with subtlety will seek for terms of more nice discrimination."[2] As we read him and accustom our minds to move with his, we cease to notice the diction. The strength of his thought carries the weight of his words. His meaning is never mistaken, though it may not be fully grasped at a glance; for he puts much in small compass, and the precision of his language requires careful reading for its just appreciation. "Familiar but not coarse, and elegant but not ostentatious"; "vanity produced a grotto where necessity enforced a passage"—could the thought be put more pointedly, or adequately, or shortly? When Latin diction cannot be changed without loss, or without affecting the tenor of the thought, it has made good its right. His humour and irony found an aid in the dignified phraseology. But he also used simple words. Wit is "that which he that never found it wonders how he missed"; "what he does best he soon ceases to do"; "a rage for saying something when

---

[1] See, in addition to the alterations in *The Rambler*, the corrections in *The Lives of the Poets* as given in Boswell's lists.

[2] *Idler*, No. 70.

there is nothing to be said"—these, also, are typical of his style. The letter to Chesterfield reaches its climax in the homeliest of English: "till I am known, and do not want it."

His parodists have been peculiarly unsuccessful. We lose their meaning in a jumble of pedantries; and we do not lose Johnson's. They inflate their phraseology; but Johnson is not tumid. And they forget that his balance is a balance of thought. His own explanation still holds good: "the imitators of my style have not hit it. Miss Aikin has done it the best; for she has imitated the sentiment as well as the diction." This was said in 1777. But better than Miss Aikin's essay "On Romances"[1] in the style of *The Rambler*, and the best of all the parodies, is *A Criticism on the Elegy written in a Country Church-yard* (1783), composed by John Young, the versatile professor of Greek at Glasgow, and designed as a continuation of *The Life of Gray*. The long list of his serious imitators begins with Hawkesworth and extends to Jeffrey,[2] who started by training himself in the school of the periodical essayists. Others, who did not take him as a model, profited by the example of a style in which nothing is negligent and nothing superfluous. He was the dominating influence in English prose throughout the second half of the eighteenth century. The lesson of discipline required to be taught, and it was learned from him by many whose best work shows no traces of his manner.

His death, says Murphy, "kept the public mind in agitation beyond all former example. No literary character ever excited so much attention." Collections of stories about him had begun to appear in his lifetime, and now his friends competed in serious biography. When Mrs. Piozzi wrote her account, she had heard of nine others already written or in preparation. Her *Anecdotes of the late Samuel Johnson* (1786) has a place by itself. It preserves much that would have been lost; but its importance lies chiefly in its picture of Johnson's character, and in its illustration of the qualities by which he was attracted. She writes with amiable pride in the ties that bound him to the hospitality of Streatham, and with an honest

[1] *Miscellaneous Pieces, in Prose*, by J. Aikin and A. L. Aikin (Mrs. Barbauld), 1773.

[2] See Cockburn, *Life of Jeffrey*, vol. I, pp. 31 etc.

effort to rise above their quarrel.   If her detractors can find
evidence of artfulness, no one can deny the clearness of her
vision; and, if, at times, her little vanities prevented her from
seeing the true bearing of Johnson's remarks, she must, at
least, be admitted to have been happy in the selection of what
she has recorded.   There is no work of the same size as her
*Anecdotes* that gives a better portrait of Johnson.   In strong
contrast is the *Life* (1787) by Sir John Hawkins.   It is the
solid book of an "unclubbable" magistrate and antiquary, who
has much knowledge and little intuition.   He had known
Johnson for over forty years and, on many points, is our chief
authority.   Much of the value of his book lies in the lengthy
digressions on contemporary literature.   His lack of sympathy made him unsuited for biography; but we are under
a debt to him for the facts which he threw together.

The merits of Mrs. Piozzi and Hawkins were united and
augmented by Boswell.   He had been collecting material
since his first interview in 1763.   He had told Johnson his
purpose by 1772, and he had spoken definitely of his *Life* in a
letter of 1775.   After Johnson's death, he set to work in earnest
and spared himself no trouble.

"You cannot imagine," he wrote in 1789, "what labour, what
perplexity, what vexation I have endured in arranging a prodigious
multiplicity of materials, in supplying omissions, in searching
for papers buried in different masses, and all this besides the exertion of composing and polishing: many a time have I thought of
giving it up."

But he was confident in the result.   It was to be not merely
the best biography of Johnson, but the best biography ever
written.

"I am absolutely certain," he said, "that my mode of biography,
which gives not only a *History* of Johnson's *visible* progress through
the world, and of his publications, but a *view* of his mind in his
letters and conversations, is the most perfect that can be conceived,
and will be more of a Life than any work that has ever yet appeared."

When the book at last came out, in May, 1791, the same confidence was expressed in the opening paragraphs.   There, he

admits that the idea of interspersing letters had been taken from Mason's life of Gray. He had made a careful study of the art of biography; and the *Anecdotes* of Mrs. Piozzi, which had shown the necessity of a careful handling of intimate material, and the facts of Hawkins, which had proved the inadequacy of simple narrative, had reassured him that he was engaged on the real life of his friend.

Johnson owes much to Boswell; but it was Johnson who gave us Boswell. His life is the story of failure turned to success by an irresistible devotion. He had always been attracted by whatever won the public attention, partly from scientific curiosity, as when he visited Mrs. Rudd, and partly with a view to his own advancement. In the first of his letters, he says that Hume " is a very proper person for a young man to cultivate an acquaintance with." He comes to know Wilkes, but doubts "if it would be proper to keep a correspondence with a gentleman in his present capacity." The chief pleasure that he foresaw in his continental tour was his meeting with Voltaire and Rousseau. Then, he proceeded to Corsica and became the friend and enthusiastic champion of Paoli. Having received a communication on Corsican affairs from the earl of Chatham, he asks: " Could your lordship find time to honour me now and then with a letter?" Again, he is found thinking of a life of lord Kames and satisfying himself that "he has eminence enough to merit this." There was cause for the sturdy laird of Auchinleck to complain, according to Sir Walter Scott's anecdote, that his irresponsible son was always pinning himself to the tail of somebody or other. But, of all his heroes, Johnson alone brought out the best qualities in his volatile character, and steadied him to the worthy use of his rare gifts. When Johnson is absent, his writings possess no remarkable merit, though they have always the interest of being the pellucid expression of his singular personality. The *Life* is the devoted and flawless recognition of an influence which he knew that his nature had required.

Born at Edinburgh in 1740, the son of a Scottish advocate who took his title as a judge from his ancient estate of Auchinleck in Ayrshire, Boswell reluctantly adopted the family profession of law, and, after studying at Edinburgh, Glasgow and Utrecht, was called to the Scottish bar in 1766. His heart was never in a legal career, and, to the last, he had a fond belief in sudden and splendid success in literature or politics. His earliest work appeared in *The Scots Magazine*, but has not been identified. He wrote much verse and published *An Elegy on the death of an amiable young lady* (1761), *An Ode to Tragedy*, dedicated to himself (1761), and *The Cub at Newmarket*, a humorous description of his experiences as the guest of the Jockey club (1762). Several of his earliest pieces are printed in *A Collection of Original Poems, by the Rev. Mr. Blacklock and other Scotch Gentlemen* (1760–2), the second volume of which he edited.[1] He frequented the literary society of Edinburgh, founded the jovial "Soaping Club" and engaged in regular correspondence with his friends. The *Letters between the Hon. Andrew Erskine and James Boswell Esq.*, in which, also, there is much verse, he published in 1763. "They have made ourselves laugh," says the advertisement; "we hope they will have the same effect upon other people." They were hardly worth publishing, though we should be sorry now not to have them. In the description of a long series of daydreams, given with the characteristic vanity which is always saved by its frankness, he says:

I am thinking of the perfect knowledge which I shall acquire of men and manners, of the intimacies which I shall have the honour to form with the learned and ingenious in every science, and of the many amusing literary anecdotes which I shall pick up.

This was published, from Flexney's shop in Holborn, in the very month that he met Johnson in Davies's parlour. Shortly before this, he had brought out, with Erskine and George Dempster, his two associates in much of his early work, the rare *Critical Strictures* on Mallet's *Elvira*. He returned to Edinburgh from his continental travels in 1766, and, being admitted to the bar in the midst of the excitement about the Douglas cause, found in it material for *Dorando* (June, 1767), which recounts the points at issue under a Spanish disguise, and

[1] The manuscripts of many of Boswell's poems written between 1760 and 1768, several of them unprinted, are in the Bodleian library—MS. Douce 193. The collection includes a "Plan of a Volume of Poems to be published for me by Becket and Dehorde."

appeared immediately before the thirteen Scottish judges, by a majority of one, arrived at a decision contrary to his wishes. The little story went into three editions within a fortnight, but it now disappoints the hopes excited by its rarity. As the case was sent up to the House of Lords, where the decision was ultimately reversed, Boswell continued to write about it and brought out the more serious *Essence of the Douglas Cause* (November, 1767). He took an energetic part in the riotous controversy concerning the Edinburgh stage and supplied the prologue for the opening of the first licensed theatre in Scotland.[1] At the same time, he was engaged on his Corsican experiences. *An Account of Corsica* had been read by Lord Hailes in manuscript in June, 1767, and was issued in March, 1768. It is Boswell's first considerable book, and, indeed, his only book, apart from those concerned with Johnson, that had a chance of being remembered on its merits. It won what he calls "amazing celebrity"; he could boast that he was "really the great man now." His head was full of Corsica and was not to be emptied of it, even on Johnson's advice. He made a collection of twenty letters by himself and others, and published them under the title *British Essays in favour of the Brave Corsicans* (January, 1769); and, in the following September, he appeared at the Shakespeare festival at Stratford in the dress of an armed Corsican chief and recited a poem that "preserved the true Corsican character." A description of the proceedings, an account of himself, and the poem were immediately contributed by him to *The London Magazine*. Two months later, he married, and then tried to settle to his legal practice. From this time, the influence of Johnson, already evident in *An Account of Corsica*, grew steadily stronger. He was not satisfied with Edinburgh after the splendour of London. "The unpleasing tone, the rude familiarity, the barren conversation," he complains, "really hurt my feelings." But he had to content himself with lengthy visits to London in vacation, which were the more indispensable when Johnson had procured his election to The Club, and he had become a

[1] The prologue was printed in *The Scots Magazine* for November, 1767; see, also, *The European Magazine* for May, 1791, and Dibdin, J. C., *Annals of the Edinburgh Stage* (1888), pp. 143–8, and 493. The *Songs in the Justiciary Opera*, privately printed for Alexander Boswell in 1816, belong to this time.

proprietor of *The London Magazine*. He contributed to it, monthly, a series of seventy periodical essays called *The Hypochondriack* (1777–83), for which he found much material in himself. There is also much in them that was inspired by the dominating friendship. They take *The Rambler* as their model, and are the most Johnsonian of his writings. After the death of his father and his own succession to Auchinleck, in 1782, he turned to politics, and carried out his ambition of becoming a member of the English bar, but to no purpose. He stood for parliament, and published two letters "to the people of Scotland"; one, *On the Present State of the Nation* (1783), and the other, *On the Alarming Attempt to infringe the Articles of the Union* (1785). All he obtained was the recordership of Carlisle, which he soon resigned. In his last years, which were saddened by the loss of his wife and troubled with financial difficulties, he is still found hoping that practice may come at any time and expecting "a capital prize." He confesses that he no longer lives with a view to have surprising incidents, though he is still desirous that his life "should *tell*." But he begins to waken from the long delusion and, in a melancholy moment, admits: "I certainly am constitutionally unfit for any employment." He was then on the point of achievement. His life was to tell better than he knew, and in another way than he had hoped. His friendship for Johnson was helping him in these years to do what he was unable to do for himself. Without Johnson, he relapses to the level of his early verse in *No Abolition of Slavery; or the Universal Empire of Love* (April, 1791).[1] And, when the effort of producing the great work is over, there remains only the record of steady decline, varied by new schemes of matrimony, and cheered by large sales and the preparation of new editions. He died in London, 19 May, 1795. From 1758 to within a few weeks of his death, he had corresponded regularly with William Johnson Temple, a fellow student in the Greek class at Edinburgh who became vicar of St. Gluvias in Cornwall; and these letters, which had been sold by a hawker at Boulogne and were rescued to be published in 1857, give us

[1] A copy of this rare piece is now in the Bodleian library. It was for long doubtful if it had been published, but a review with copious extracts had been given in *The Gentleman's Magazine* for April, 1791.

his real autobiography.[1] They tell us much more than the many descriptions of himself, from his *Ode to Tragedy* to the "Memoirs" in the *European Magazine* of 1791.[2] If they show why his descendants decided on a holocaust of his papers, they also explain the attraction which he exerted on those who took the trouble to try to understand him.

But, if Boswell without Johnson would have been forgotten, it was his own talent that gave the *Life* its surpassing excellence. Whenever he writes of Johnson, he succeeds in giving the impression that he saw things as they were, and not through the spectacles of his own personality. He never tried to conceal the part that he played; and yet, despite his vanities, and they were many, he knew how to make his readers think that they are looking at the facts for themselves. The very freedom from self-consciousness which was no help to his career was a great part of the secret of his skill in description. It also provided him with material denied to less sympathetic natures. "No man," he said, "has been more successful in making acquaintance easily than I have been. I even bring people quickly on to a degree of cordiality." Johnson, too, tells us that "Mr. Boswell's frankness and gaiety made every body communicative." He never tired of arranging new situations, in order to see what they would bring forth; and his interpretations of what he found are strong testimony to his insight into character and to his judgment. Minute as his observations are, he never offers a meaningless detail. It is easy to understand why Johnson made him postpone the *Journal of a Tour to the Hebrides*, which was intended as a supplement to his own *Journey*. He had given "notions rather than facts"; but Boswell had contrived to make the facts give Johnson. The

---

[1] Boswell thought of an autobiography. "My journal," he says, "will afford materials for a very curious narrative" (letter to Temple, 22 May, 1789). The first record of a journal is in his letter to Temple of 16 December, 1758. The journal was destroyed; but a portfolio of papers, each inscribed "Boswelliana," escaped. They are now in the possession of the marquess of Crewe, and were edited by Charles Rogers for the Grampian club in 1874. Boswell thought also of editions of Johnson's poems, Walton's *Lives*, and the autobiography of Sir Robert Sibbald; a work maintaining the merit of Addison's poetry; histories of Sweden, James IV, and the '45; a life of Thomas Ruddiman; and an account of the Isle of Man. These, and others, are mentioned in the *Life of Johnson;* and yet other projects are mentioned elsewhere.

[2] If he did not write these "Memoirs," he certainly supplied their material.

reproduction of his sayings and experiences was too minute to be published during his lifetime, and was more decently delayed till the year after his death.[1] The *Life* does not surpass the *Journal* in the sense of actuality; but it is a greater achievement. He had met Johnson only on some two hundred and seventy days, scattered over twenty-one years, and his material had to be gathered from many sources. He selects and arranges; he places his facts in the light and perspective that will create the situation; and Johnson lives in his pages. And he had the gift of the perfect style for his kind of biography— a style of no marked individuality, but easy, clear and flexible, which does its duty without attracting attention, and requires to be examined to have its excellence recognised.

[1] The *Journal* was revised by Malone while it was going through the press. Malone also revised the *Life*, and, on Boswell's death, completed the preparation of the third and final edition.

# CHAPTER IX

# Oliver Goldsmith

"NO man," wrote that authoritative but autocratic biographer, John Forster, "ever put so much of himself
into his books as Goldsmith, from the beginning to the
very end of his career." To many authors, this saying is only
partly applicable; but it is entirely applicable to the author
of *The Vicar of Wakefield*. His life and his works are intimately
connected. They accompany and interpret each other in such
a way as to make them practically inseparable; and it is, therefore, appropriate, as well as convenient, to treat them, so to speak,
in the piece, rather than to attempt any distribution of the
subject into divisions and sub-divisions of history and criticism.

Concerning Goldsmith's early years, there is much that is
obscure, or that, in any case, cannot be accepted without
rigorous investigation. He left his native island when he
was three-and-twenty, and never returned to it. Those who,
like Glover and Cooke, wrote accounts of him shortly after his
death, were the humbler associates of his later and more famous
years, while the professedly authentic "Memoir" drawn up
under the nominal superintendence of bishop Percy, and the
much quoted letter of Annesley Strean in Mangin's *Essay on
Light Reading*, did not see the light until the first decade of the
nineteenth century, when Goldsmith had long been dead. It
follows that much of the information thus collected after date
must have been imperfect and contradictory, often extracted
from persons more familiar with his obscure beginnings than
with his later eminence, and, possibly, in answer to those
unsatisfactory leading questions which usually elicit not so
much the truth as what the querist wishes to establish.

Goldsmith was born on 10 November, 1728; and it is usually held that the place of his nativity was Pallas, or Pallasmore, a village near Ballymahon, in the county of Longford, Ireland. But it has also been plausibly contended, though actual proof is not forthcoming, that his true birthplace was Smith-Hill house, Elphin, Roscommon, the residence of his mother's father, Oliver Jones, a clergyman and master of the Elphin diocesan school. His own father, Charles Goldsmith, was, likewise, a clergyman of the established church. When Oliver came into the world, Charles Goldsmith was acting as assistant to an uncle whose name was Green, the rector of Kilkenny West, and eking out a scanty subsistence by farming a few fields. In 1730, Green died; and Charles Goldsmith, succeeding to the vacant rectorate, transferred his residence to the hamlet of Lissoy, in Westmeath, a little to the right of the road from Ballymahon to Athlone. At this time, he had five children, two sons and three daughters, Oliver being the fifth child and second son. As already stated, the accounts of his earliest years are contradictory. By some, he was regarded as thick-witted and sullen; to others, he seemed alert and intelligent. That he was an adept at all boyish sports is admitted; and it is also recorded that he scribbled verses early. His first notable instructor was the village schoolmaster, Thomas, or "Paddy," Byrne, who had been a quartermaster in queen Anne's wars. Byrne was also a local rimer, and had even composed an Irish version of the *Georgics*. His endless stories of his continental adventures, and his inexhaustible legends of ghosts and banshees, held his pupils spellbound; and, by Goldsmith's family, were, later, made responsible for much of "that wandering and unsettled turn which so much appeared in his future life." When Goldsmith was seven or eight, he was attacked by confluent smallpox, which scarred him terribly and probably added not a little to the "exquisite sensibility of contempt" with which he seems to have been born. With this, at all events, is connected one of the two most-repeated anecdotes of his childhood. A ne'er-do-well relation asked him heartlessly when he meant to grow handsome, to which, after an awkward silence, he replied, "I mean to get better, sir, when you do." The other story also illustrates an unexpected gift of repartee. At a party in his uncle's house, during the pause

between two country-dances, little Oliver capered out, and
executed an extempore hornpipe.  His deeply-pitted face and
ungainly figure caused much amusement; and the fiddler, a
lad named Cumming, called out "Æsop."  To which the dancer
promptly answered:

> Heralds, proclaim aloud! all saying,
> See *Æsop* dancing, and his *Monkey* playing,

at once transferring the laugh to his side.  Whether improvised
or remembered, the retort certainly shows intellectual alacrity.

From Byrne, Goldsmith passed to the school at Elphin,
of which his grandfather had been master; thence to Athlone,
and, finally, to Edgeworthstown, where his preceptor, Patrick
Hughes, seems to have understood him better than his previous
instructors.  Hughes penetrated his superficial obtuseness,
recognised his exceptionally sensitive temperament, and contrived, at any rate, to think better of him than some of his
playmates who only succeeded in growing up blockheads.
There were traditions at Edgeworthstown of his studies—his
fondness for Ovid and Horace, his hatred of Cicero and his
delight in Livy and Tacitus; of his prowess in boyish sports and
the occasional robbing of orchards.  It is to the close of his
Edgeworthstown experiences that belongs one of the most popular of the incidents which exemplify the connection between
his life and his work.  Returning to school at the end of his
last holiday, full of the youthful pride begotten of a borrowed
mount and a guinea in his pocket, he lingered on his road, with
the intention of putting up, like a gentleman, at some roadside
inn.  Night fell, and he found himself at Ardagh, where, with
much importance, he enquired of a passer-by for "the best
house" (hostelry) in the neighbourhood.  The person thus
appealed to, a local wag named Cornelius Kelly, formerly
fencing master to the marquis of Granby, amused by his boyish
swagger, gravely directed him to the residence of the squire of
the place, Mr. Featherston.  Hither Goldsmith straightway
repaired, ordered supper, invited his host, according to custom,
to drink with him, and, being by that humourist fooled to
the top of his bent, retired to rest, after giving particular
directions as to the preparation of a hot cake for his breakfast.

Not until his departure next morning was it disclosed that he had been entertained in a private house. The story is too good to question; and accepted, as it has always been, supplies a conclusive answer to those after-critics of *She Stoops to Conquer* who regarded the central idea of that comedy—the mistaking of a gentleman's residence for an inn—as unjustifiably farfetched. Here, in Goldsmith's own life, was the proof of its probability.

At this date, he must have been between fourteen and fifteen; and, whatever his ability, it seems to have been decided that he should follow his elder brother Henry to Trinity college, Dublin, though not with the same advantages. Henry Goldsmith, who was five or six years his brother's senior, had gone as a pensioner and obtained a scholarship. For Oliver, this was impracticable. His father, a poor man, had, from family pride, further crippled himself by undertaking to portion his second daughter, Catherine, who had clandestinely married the son of a rich neighbour. In these circumstances, nothing was open to Goldsmith but to obtain his university education as a poor scholar, a semi-menial condition which, to one already morbidly sensitive, could not fail to be distasteful. For a long time, he fought doggedly against his fate; but, at length, yielding to the persuasions of a friendly uncle Contarine, who had himself gone through the same ordeal, he was admitted to Trinity college as a sizar on 11 June, 1744, taking up his abode in one of the garrets of what was then the eastern side of Parliament square.

The academic career thus inauspiciously begun was not worshipful. From the outset, he was dispirited and disappointed, and, consequently, without energy or enthusiasm. Moreover, he was unfortunate in his tutor, a clergyman named Theaker Wilder, who, though his bad qualities may have been exaggerated, was certainly harsh and unsympathetic. His *forte*, too, was mathematics, which Goldsmith, like Swift, like Gray, like Johnson, detested as cordially as he detested the arid logic of "Dutch Burgersdyck" and Polish Smiglesius. According to Stubbs's *History of the University of Dublin*,

Oliver Goldsmith is recorded on one or two occasions as being remarkably diligent at Morning Lecture; again, as cautioned for bad answering at Morning and Greek Lectures; and finally, as put down into the next class for neglect of his studies.

To this, he added other enormities. He was noted, as was
Johnson at Oxford, for much "lounging about the college gate";
and for his skill on that solace to melancholy and *laborum dulce
lenimen*, the German flute, of which, as readily as his own
"Man in Black," he had apparently mastered the "Ambusheer."
He became involved in various scrapes, notably a college riot,
including that ducking of a bailiff afterwards referred to in the
first version of *The Double Transformation*, on which occasion
he was publicly admonished *quod seditioni favisset et tumultu-
antibus opem tulisset*. Recovering a little from the stigma
of this disgrace by gaining a small (Smythe) exhibition, he was
imprudent enough to celebrate his success by a mixed entertainment, in what only by courtesy could be called his "apartments."
On these festivities, the exasperated Wilder made irruption,
knocking down the unfortunate host, who, after forthwith selling his books, ran away, vaguely bound, as on subsequent
occasions, for America. But a reconciliation with his tutor
was patched up by Oliver's brother Henry; and he returned to
his college to enjoy the half-peace of the half-pardoned. His
father was now dead; and he was miserably poor. He managed, however, to take his B.A. degree on 27 Feburary, 1749, and
quitted the university without regret, leaving behind him a
scratched signature on a window pane (still preserved), an old
lexicon scored with "promises to pay" and a reputation for
supplementing his scanty means by the ballads (unluckily *not*
preserved) which he was accustomed to write and afterwards
sell for five shillings a head at the Reindeer in Mountrath court,
stealing out at nightfall—so runs the tradition—to "snatch the
fearful joy" of hearing them sung. It must have been the
memory of these things which, years after, at Sir William
Chambers's, made him fling down his cards, and rush hurriedly
into the street to succour a poor ballad-woman, who had
apparently, like Rubini, *les larmes dans la voix*.

What was to happen next? For a Goldsmith of the Gold-
smiths, there was no career but the church; and he was too
young to be ordained. Thereupon ensued an easy, irresponsible time, which the new B.A. spent very much to his own
satisfaction. He was supposed to be qualifying for orders;
but he had never any great leaning that way. "To be obliged to
wear a long wig, when he liked a short one, or a black coat, when

he generally dressed in brown," observes one of his characters in *The Citizen of the World*, was "a restraint upon his liberty." Hence, as his biographer Prior sagaciously says, "there is reason to believe that at this time he followed no systematic plan of study," On the contrary, he passed his time wandering, like Addison's Will Wimble, from one relative to another, fishing and otter-hunting in the isleted river Inny, playing the flute to his cousin Jane Contarine's harpsichord, or presiding at the "free and easys" held periodically at George Conway's inn at Ballymahon, where, for the benefit of posterity, he doubtless made acquaintance with Jack Slang the horse-doctor, Dick Muggins the exciseman and that other genteel and punctilious humourist who never "danced his bear" except to Arne's "Water parted" or the favourite minuet in *Ariadne*. But these "violent delights" could have only one sequel. When, in 1751, he presented himself to Dr. Synge, bishop of Elphin, for ordination, he was rejected. Whether his college reputation had preceded him; whether, as on a later occasion, he was found "not qualified," or whether (as legend has it) he pushed his aversion from clerical costume so far as to appear in flaming scarlet smallclothes—these questions are still debated. That another calling must be chosen was the only certain outcome of this mishap. He first turned to the next refuge of lettered unemployment, tuition. Having, in this way, accumulated some thirty pounds, he bought a horse, and once more started for America. Before six weeks were over, he had returned penniless, on an animal only fit for the knacker's yard, and seemed naïvely surprised that his friends were not rejoiced to see him. Law was next thought of; and, to this end, his uncle Contarine equipped him with fifty pounds. But he was cozened by a sharper on his way to London, and once more came back—in bitter self-abasement. In 1752, his long suffering uncle for the last time fitted him out, this time to study physic at Edinburgh, which place, wonderful to relate, he safely reached. But he never saw Ireland, or his kind relative, again.

After two years' stay in the Scottish capital, where more memories survive of his social success than of his studies, he took his departure for Leyden, nominally to substitute the lectures of Albinus for the lectures of Monro. At Leyden, he arrived in 1754, not without some picturesque and, possibly, romanced adventures related in a letter to Contarine. The names of Gaubius and other Batavian professors figure glibly and sonorously in his future pages; but that he had much experimental knowledge of their instruction is doubtful. His name is not enrolled as a "Stud. Litt." in the Album Academicum of Leyden university, nor is it known where he received that "commission to slay" which justified him in signing himself "M.B." It was certainly not at Padua;[1] and enquiries at Leyden and Louvain were made by Prior without success. But the Louvain records were destroyed in the revolutionary wars. That, however, his stay at Leyden was neither prosperous nor prolonged is plain. He fell again among thieves; and, finally, like Holberg, or that earlier "Peregrine of Odcombe," Thomas Coryat of the *Crudities*, set out to make the grand tour on foot. "*Haud inexpertus loquor*," he wrote, later, in praising this mode of locomotion; though, on second thoughts, he suppressed the quotation as an undignified admission. He went, first, to Flanders; then passed to France, Germany, Switzerland and Italy, supporting himself, much as George Primrose does in *The Vicar of Wakefield*, by playing the flute, and by occasional disputations at convents or universities. "Sir," said Boswell to Johnson (who seems to have sustained the pun without blenching), "he *disputed* his passage through Europe." At some period of his wanderings he must have sketched a part of *The Traveller*, specimens of which he sent from Switzerland to his brother Henry. After a year's wandering, he landed at Dover on 1 February, 1756, "his whole stock of cash," says an early biographer, "amounting to no more than a few half-pence." By this time, he was seven-and-twenty.

His vocation was still as visionary as were his means of subsistence. He is supposed to have tried strolling, and was certainly anxious to play "Scrub" in later years. For a season, he was an apothecary's assistant on Fish street hill. Hence, with some assistance from an Edinburgh friend, Dr. Sleigh, he "proceeded" a poor physician in the Bankside, Southwark— the region afterwards remembered in *An Elegy on Mrs. Mary Blaize*. He is next found as corrector of the press to Richardson, at Salisbury court. Then, drifting insensibly towards literature, to which he seems never to have intentionally shaped

[1] *The Athenaeum*, 21 July, 1894.

his course, he is (again like his own George Primrose) an usher at the "classical Academy" of Dr. Milner of Peckham. He had already submitted a manuscript tragedy to the author of *Clarissa;* and, at Milner's table, he encountered the bookseller Ralph Griffiths, proprietor of *The Monthly Review.* Struck by some remark on the part of Milner's latest assistant, and seeking for new blood to aid him in his campaign against Hamilton's *Critical Review*, Griffiths asked Goldsmith whether he could furnish some "specimens of criticism." An arrangement followed under which, released from the drudgery of Peckham, Goldsmith was to receive, with bed and board, a salary which Percy calls "handsome," Prior "adequate" and Forster "small." For this, he was to labour daily from nine till two (or later) on copy-of-all-work for his master's magazine.

This, in effect, was Goldsmith's turning-point; and he had reached it by accident rather than design. Divinity, law, physic—he had tried them all; but, at letters, he had never aimed. With his duties "at the Sign of the Dunciad," in Paternoster row, began his definite bondage to the "*antiqua Mater* of Grub Street"; and we may pause for a moment to examine his qualifications for his difficult career. They were more considerable than one would imagine from his vagrant, aimless past. He was a fair classical scholar, more advanced than might be supposed from his own modest admission to Malone, that he could "turn an ode of Horace into English better than any of them"; and, as that sound critic and Goldsmithian, the late Sidney Irwin, remarked, it is not necessary to make him responsible for the graceless Greek of Mr. Ephraim Jenkinson. In English poetry, he was far seen, especially in Dryden, Swift, Prior, Johnson, Pope and Gay. He had a good knowledge of Shakespeare; and was familiar with the comic dramatists, particularly his compatriot Farquhar. French he had acquired before he left Ireland, and he had closely studied Molière, La Fontaine and the different collections of *ana.* For Voltaire, he had a sincere admiration; and, whether he actually met him abroad or not, it is probable his own native style, clear and perspicuous as it was from the first, had been developed and perfected by the example of the wonderful writer by whom the adjective was regarded as the enemy of the noun. Finally, he had enjoyed considerable experience of humanity, though mostly in the rough; and, albeit his standpoint as a pedestrian had, of necessity, limited his horizon, he had "observed the face" of the countries through which he had travelled, making his own deductions. On what he had seen, he had reflected, and, when he sat down to the "desk's dead wood" in Paternoster row, his initial equipment as a critic, apart from his individual genius, must have been superior, in variety and extent, at all events, to that of most of the literary gentlemen, not exclusively hacks, who did Griffiths's notices in *The Monthly Review*.

Even in his first paper, on *The Mythology of the Celtes*, by Mallet, the translator of the *Edda*, he opened with a statement which must have been out of the jog-trot of the *Dunciad* traditions.

"The learned on this side the Alps," he said, "have long laboured in the Antiquities of Greece and Rome, but almost totally neglected their own; like Conquerors who, while they have made inroads into the territories of their neighbours, have left their own natural dominions to desolation."

It would be too much to trace the *Reliques of English Poetry* to this utterance; but (as Forster says) "it is wonderful what a word in season from a man of genius may do, even when the genius is hireling and obscure and only labouring for the bread it eats." Meanwhile, the specimen review "from the gentleman who signs, D," although printed with certain omissions, secured Goldsmith's entry to Griffiths's periodical, and he criticised some notable books—Home's *Douglas*, Burke *On the Sublime*, Gray's *Odes*, the *Connoisseur*, Smollett's *History*—titles which at least prove that, utility man as he was, his competence was recognised from the first. The review of Gray, whose remoteness and "obscurity" he regretted, and whom he advised to take counsel of Isocrates and "study the people," was, nevertheless, the last of his contributions to *The Monthly Review*. Whether the fault lay in his own restless nature, or whether he resented the vexatious editing of his work by the bookseller and his wife, the fact remains that, with September, 1757, Goldsmith's permanent connection with Griffiths came to a close; and, for the next few months, he subsisted by contributing to *The Literary Magazine* and by other miscellaneous practice of the pen.

At this point, however, emerges his first prolonged literary effort, the remarkable rendering of the *Memoirs* of Jean Marteilhe of Bergerac, "a Protestant condemned to the Galleys of France for his Religion," which was published in February, 1758. This translation, perhaps because it has been sometimes confused with that issued by the Religious Tract Society, has never received the attention it deserves. It is an exceedingly free and racy version of one of the most authentic records of the miseries ensuing on the revocation of the edict of Nantes; and Goldsmith, drudge as he was supposed to be, has treated his theme sympathetically. He may, indeed, have actually seen Marteilhe in Holland; but it is more reasonable to suppose that he was attracted to the subject by the advertisement, in *The Monthly Review* for May, 1757, of the French original. The book is full of interest; and, as the fight of *The Nightingale* with the galleys, and the episode of Goujon, the young cadet of the Aubusson regiment, prove, by no means deficient in moving and romantic incident. Why, on this occasion, Goldsmith borrowed as his pseudonym the name of an old college-fellow, James Willington, it is idle to enquire. In his signed receipt, still extant, to Edward Dilly, for a third share in the volumes, they are expressly described as "my translation," and it is useful to note that the mode of sale, as will hereafter be seen, is exactly that subsequently adopted for the sale of *The Vicar of Wakefield*.

Anonymous or pseudonymous, Marteilhe's *Memoirs* had little effect on Goldsmith's fortunes; and the twenty pounds he received for the MS. in January, 1758, must have been quickly spent, for he was shortly at Peckham again, vaguely hoping that his old master would procure him a medical appointment on a foreign station. It was, no doubt, to obtain funds for his outfit that he began to plan his next book, *An Enquiry into the Present State of Polite Learning in Europe*, for we find him in this year soliciting subscriptions from his friends in Ireland. When, at last, the nomination arrived, it was merely that of physician to a Coromandel factory. What was worse, for some obscure reason, it came to nothing; and his next move was to present himself at Surgeons' hall—like Smollett's

Roderick Random—as a ship's hospital mate, with the result that, in December, he was rejected as "not qualified." To put the seal on his embarrassments, this new effort involved him in fresh difficulties with his former employer, Griffiths, who had helped him to appear in decent guise before the examiners—difficulties from which he only extricated himself with much humiliation by engaging to write a life of Voltaire.

We next find him domiciled at 12 Green Arbour court, Little Old Bailey,[1] where, in March, 1759, Percy, who had recently made his acquaintance through Grainger of *The Sugar Cane*, one of the staff of *The Monthly Review*, paid him a visit. He discovered him in a miserable room, correcting the proofs of his *Enquiry*, which appeared in the following month. For a small duodecimo of two hundred pages, it is, beyond doubt, ambitiously labelled. The field was too wide for so brief a survey; and, although the author professed that his sketch was mostly "taken upon the spot," it was obvious that he was imperfectly equipped for his task. What he had himself seen he described freshly and forcibly; and what he knew of the conditions of letters in England he depicted with feeling. He might talk largely of the learning of "Luitprandus" and the "philological performances" of Constantinus Afer; but what touched him more nearly was the mercantile avidity and sordid standards of the London bookseller, the hungry rancour of the venal writers in his pay, the poverty of the poets, the slow rewards of genius. Perhaps the most interesting features of the *Enquiry* are, primarily, that it is Goldsmith's earliest original work; and, next, that it is wholly free from that empty orotundity, that " didactic stiffness of wisdom, " which his French models had led him to regard as the crying sin of his English contemporaries. To be "dull and dronish," he held, was "an encroachment on the prerogative of a folio. " " The most diminutive son of fame, or of famine, has his *we* and his *us*, his *firstlys* and his *secondlys* as methodical as if bound in cowhide, and closed with clasps of brass." On the whole, the little book was well received, notwithstanding its censure of the two leading *Reviews*, and the fact that the chapter "Of the

---

[1] These premises were subsequently occupied by Smith, Elder & Co. as *The Cornhill Magazine* printing office, to which Thackeray sent his proofs. (Cf. *Roundabout Paper*, '*De Finibus*,' August, 1862, at end.)

Stage," enforcing, as it did, Ralph's earlier *Case of Authors by Profession* gave Garrick lasting offence—a circumstance to which may be traced not only some of Goldsmith's later dramatic difficulties, but that popular " poor Poll " couplet of which the portable directness rather than the truth has done much wrong to Goldsmith's reputation. To be as easily remembered as a limerick is no small help to a malicious epigram.

At this date, beyond a few lines dated " Edinburgh, 1753," the instalment of *The Traveller* sent to Henry Goldsmith from Switzerland, and the *Description of an Author's Bedchamber* included in another letter to the same address, little had been heard of Goldsmith's verse, although he had written vaguely of himself as a " poet." In the *Enquiry*, however, he published his first metrical effort, a translation of a Latin prologue in that recondite Macrobius with a quotation from whom, after an uncommunicative silence, Johnson electrified the company on his first arrival at Oxford. In the little periodical called *The Bee*, with which Goldsmith followed up the *Enquiry*, he included several rimed contributions. Of these, only one, some "topical" stanzas, *On the Death of Wolfe*, is absolutely original. But the rest anticipate some of his later excellences —and personal opinions. In the *Elegy on Mrs. Mary Blaize*, he laughs at the fashion, set by Gray, of funereal verse, and, in the bright little quatrains entitled *The Gift*, successfully reproduces the levity of Prior. But, what is more, he begins to exhibit his powers as a critic and essayist, to write character sketches in the vein of Addison and Steele, to reveal his abilities as a stage critic and censor of manners. One of the papers, *A City Night-Piece*, still remains a most touching comment on the shame of cities; another, the Lucianic reverie known as *The Fame Machine* (that is, " coach"), in which Johnson, rejected by Jehu as a passenger for his *Dictionary*, is accepted on the strength of his *Rambler*, may have served to introduce him to the great man who, ever after, loved him with a growling but genuine affection. *The Bee*, though brief-lived, with similar things in *The Busy Body* and *The Lady's Magazine*, also brought him to the notice of some others, who, pecuniarily, were more important than Johnson. Smollett enlisted him for the new venture, *The British Magazine*, and bustling John Newbery of St. Paul's churchyard, for a new paper, *The Public Ledger*.

For Smollett, besides a number of minor efforts, Gold-smith wrote two of his best essays, *A Reverie in the Boars' Head Tavern at Eastcheap*, and the semi-autobiographic *Adventures of a Strolling Player;* for Newbery, the *Chinese Letters*, afterwards collected as *The Citizen of the World*. This production was his first permanent success. With its assumed orientalism, as with what it borrows from Montesquieu or his imitators, we can dispense, although it may be noted that a summary of the vices of the contemporary novel, long supposed to be Goldsmith's own, is a literal transcript of Du Halde. What is most enduring in the correspondence of Lien Chi Altangi is the fuller revelation, already begun in *The Bee*, of Goldsmith as a critic, a humourist and a social historiographer. It is Goldsmith on quacks and connoisseurs, on travellers' tales and funeral pomp, on mad dogs, on letters and the theatre, on such graver themes as the penal laws and public morality, to whom we turn most eagerly now. And of even greater interest than their good sense and good humour, their graphic touches and kindly shrewdness, is the evidence which these passages afford of the coming creator of Dr. Primrose and Tony Lumpkin. In the admirable portrait of "the Man in Black," with his reluctant benevolence and his Goldsmith family traits, there is a foretaste of some of the attractive peculiarities of the vicar of Wakefield, while, in the picture of the pinched and tarnished little beau, with his parrot chatter about the countess of All-Night and the duke of Piccadilly, set to the forlorn burden of "Lend me Half-a-Crown," he adds a character sketch, however lightly touched, to that imperishable and, happily, inalienable gallery which contains the finished full-lengths of Parson Adams and Squire Western, of Matthew Bramble and "My Uncle Toby."

The last Chinese letter appeared on 14 August, 1761, and, in May of the following year, the collection was issued in two volumes as *The Citizen of the World*, a phrase first used in Letter xx, and, perhaps, suggested by Bacon's *Essays* (no. xiii). At this date, Goldsmith had moved from the Little Old Bailey to 6 Wine Office court, Fleet street, where, on 31 May, he had been visited by Johnson. He had been editing *The Lady's Magazine*, in which appeared the *Memoirs of Voltaire* composed by him for Griffiths. He wrote a pamphlet on the popular imposture, the Cock lane ghost, and he compiled or revised *A History of Mecklenburgh*, the native country of king George III's consort. He published an anecdotical *Life of Richard Nash*, the fantastic old king of Bath, and seven volumes of *Plutarch's Lives*. More important than these activities, however, was the preparation of *The Vicar of Wakefield*, on which, according to Miss Gaussen,[1] he was engaged as early as June, 1761. Internal evidence shows that the book must have been written in 1761–2; and it is certain that a third share of it was purchased in October, 1762 by Benjamin Collins of Salisbury, who afterwards printed it for Newbery.[2] It is to this date that must probably be referred the sale of the MS. familiar to Boswell's readers, which, in that case, took place at Wine Office court, where the author would be close to Johnson's chambers in Inner Temple lane, on the opposite side of Fleet street. But, for obscure reasons, *The Vicar* was not issued until four years later, at which date it will be convenient to return to it.

Meanwhile, alternating incessant labour with fitful escapes to " Bath or Tunbridge to careen," and occasional residence at Islington, Goldsmith continued in bondage to "book-building." In 1764, he became one of the original members of the famous (and still existing) "Club," afterwards known as "The Literary Club," a proof of the eminence to which he had attained with the *literati*. This brought him at once into relations with Burke, Reynolds, Beauclerk, Langton and others of the Johnson circle. His next important work, *The History of England in a Series of Letters from a Nobleman to his Son*, published in June, was, as had no doubt been intended, long attributed to Chesterfield and other patrician pens. Later, too, in the same year, Christopher Smart's *Hannah* moved him to the composition of *The Captivity*, an oratorio never set to music. Then, after the slow growth of months, was issued, on 19 December, 1764, another of the efforts for his own hand with which he had diversified his hackwork—the poem entitled *The Traveller; or, a Prospect of Society*.

In a spirit of independence which distinguishes this performance from its author's workaday output, *The Traveller* was

[1] *Percy: Prelate and Poet*, 1908, p. 144.
[2] This matter it discussed more fully in the bibliography.

dedicated to his brother, Henry Goldsmith, to whom the first sketch had been forwarded from abroad, and who, in Goldsmith's words, "despising Fame and Fortune, had retired early to Happiness and Obscurity, with an income of forty pounds a year"—the actual value of the curacy of Kilkenny West. The dedication further accentuates that distaste for blank verse which Goldsmith had already manifested in *An Enquiry*, as well as his antipathy, also revealed in *The Citizen of the World*, to the hectoring satires of Churchill; while the general purpose of the poem, anticipated by a passage in the forty-third letter of Lien Chi Altangi, is stated in the final words:

I have endeavoured to show, that there may be equal happiness in states, that are differently governed from our own, that every state has a particular principle of happiness, and that this principle in each may be carried to a mischievous excess.

Whether these postulates of the "philosophic Wanderer"— as Johnson would have called him—are unanswerable or not matters little to us now.  The poetry has outlived the purpose. What remains in Goldsmith's couplets is the beauty of the descriptive passages, the "curious" simplicity of the language, the sweetness and finish of the verse.  Where, in his immediate predecessors, are we to find the tender charm of such lines as

> Where'er I roam, whatever realms to see,
> My heart untravell'd fondly turns to thee;
> Still to my brother turns with ceaseless pain,
> And drags at each remove a lengthening chain.

> But me, not destin'd such delights to share,
> My prime of life in wand'ring spent and care,
> Impell'd, with steps unceasing, to pursue
> Some fleeting good, that mocks me with the view;
> That, like the circle bounding earth and skies,
> Allures from far, yet, as I follow, flies;
> My fortune leads to traverse realms alone,
> And find no spot of all the world my own.

It is characteristic both of Goldsmith, and of the mosaic of memories which the poetic theories of his day made legitimate, that, even in these few lines, there are happy recollections, and recollections, moreover, that he had already employed in prose.

*The Traveller* was an immediate and enduring success; and Newbery, so far as can be ascertained, gave Goldsmith £21 for it. Second, third and fourth editions quickly followed until, in 1774, the year of the author's death, a ninth was reached. Johnson, who contributed nine of the lines, declared it to be the best poem since the death of Pope, a verdict which, without disparagement to Goldsmith, may also be accepted as evidence of the great man's lack of sympathy with Gray, whose *Elegy* had appeared in the interval. Perhaps the most marked result of *The Traveller* was to draw attention to "Oliver Goldsmith, M. B.," whose name, for the first time, appeared on the title-page of Newbery's thin eighteen-penny quarto. People began to enquire for his earlier works, and thereupon came a volume of *Essays by Mr. Goldsmith*, which comprised some of the best of his contributions to *The Bee, The Public Ledger* and the rest, together with some fresh specimens of verse, *The Double Transformation* and *A new Simile*. This was in June, 1765, after which it seems to have occurred to the joint proprietors of *The Vicar of Wakefield*, that the fitting moment had then arrived for the production of what they apparently regarded as their bad bargain. The novel was accordingly printed at Salisbury by Collins for Francis Newbery, John Newbery's nephew, and it was published on 27 March, 1766, in two duodecimo volumes.

There is no reason for supposing that there were any material alterations in the MS. which, in October, 1762, had been sold by Johnson. "Had I made it ever so perfect or correct," said Goldsmith to Dr. Farr (as reported in the *Percy Memoir*), "I should not have had a shilling more "; and the slight modifications in the second edition prove nothing to the contrary. But it is demonstrable that there was one addition of importance, the ballad *The Hermit or Edwin and Angelina*, which had only been written, in or before 1765, for the amusement of the countess of Northumberland, for whom, in that year, it was privately printed. It was probably added to fill up chapter VIII, where, perhaps, a blank had been left for it, a conjecture which is supported by the fact that other *lacunae* have been suspected. But these purely bibliographical considerations have little relation to the real unity of the book, which seems to follow naturally on the character sketches of *The Citizen of the World*, to the composition of which it succeeded. In *The Citizen*, there is naturally more of the essayist than of the novelist; in *The Vicar*, more of the novelist than of the essayist. But the strong point in each is Goldsmith himself—Goldsmith's own thoughts and Goldsmith's own experiences. Squire Thornhill might have been studied in the pit at Drury lane, and even Mr. Burchell conceivably evolved from any record of remarkable eccentrics. But the Primrose family must have come straight from Goldsmith's heart, from his wistful memories of his father and his brother Henry and his kind uncle Contarine and all that half-forgotten family group at Lissoy, who, in the closing words of his first chapter were "all equally generous, credulous, simple, and inoffensive." He himself was his own "Philosophic Vagabond pursuing Novelty, but losing Content," as does George Primrose in chapter xx. One may smile at the artless inconsistencies of the plot, the lapses of the fable, the presence in the narrative of such makeweights as poetry, tales, political discourses and a sermon; but the author's genius and individuality rise superior to everything, and the little group of the Wakefield family are now veritable "citizens of the world." Only when some wholly new form has displaced or dispossessed the English novel will the Doctor and Mrs. Primrose, Olivia and Sophia, Moses (with the green spectacles) and the Miss Flamboroughs (with their red topknots) cease to linger on the lips of men.

It is a grave mistake, however, to suppose that this unique masterpiece, which still sells vigorously to-day, sold vigorously in 1766—at all events in the authorised issues. From the publisher's accounts, it is now known with certainty that, when the fourth edition of 1770 went to press, there was still a debt against the book. The fourth edition ran out slowly, and was not exhausted until April, 1774, when a fifth edition was advertised. By this time, Collins had parted with his unremunerative share for the modest sum of £5. 5s., and Goldsmith himself was dying or dead. These facts, which may be studied in detail in Charles Welsh's life of John Newbery, rest upon expert investigations, and are incontrovertible. They, consequently, serve as a complete answer to all who, in this respect, make lamentation over the lack of generosity shown by Goldsmith's first publishers. How could they give him a *bonus,* when, after nine years, they were only beginning to make a profit? They had paid what, in those days, was a fair price for the manuscript of a two volume novel by a comparatively unknown man; and, notwithstanding the vogue of his subsequent *Traveller,* the sale did not contradict their expectations. That, only as time went on, the book gradually detached itself from the rubbish of contemporary fiction, and, ultimately, emerged triumphantly as a cosmopolitan masterpiece—is its author's misfortune, but cannot be laid at the door of Collins, Newbery and Co. Johnson, who managed the sale of the manuscript, did not think it would have much success; they, who bought it, did not think so either, and the immediate event justified their belief. Goldsmith's appeal was not to his contemporaries, but to that posterity on whose fund of prospective praise he had ironically drawn a bill in the preface to his *Essays* of 1765. In the case of *The Vicar,* the appeal has been amply honoured; but, as its author foresaw, without being "very serviceable" to himself.

Meanwhile, he went on with a fresh course of that compilation which paid better than masterpieces. He edited *Poems for Young Ladies* and *Beauties of English Poesy;* he wrote *An English Grammar;* he translated *A History of Philosophy.* But, towards the close of 1766, his larger ambitions again began to bestir themselves, and, this time, in the direction of the stage, with all its prospects of payment at sight. Already we have seen, he had essayed a tragedy, which, if it were based or modelled on his favourite Voltaire, was, probably, no great loss. His real vocation was comedy; and, on comedy, his ideas were formed, having been, in great measure, expressed in the *Enquiry* and in other of his earlier writings. He held that comic art involved comic situations; he deplored the substitution for humour and character of "delicate distresses" and superfine emotion; and he heartily despised the finicking, new-fangled variation of the French *drame sérieux* which, under the name of "genteel" or "sentimental" comedy, had gradually gained ground in England. At this moment, its advocates were active and powerful, while the defenders of the old order were few and feeble. But, in 1766, *The Clandestine Marriage* of

Garrick and Colman seemed to encourage some stronger counterblast to the lachrymose craze; and Goldsmith began slowly to put together a piece on the approved method of Vanbrugh and Farquhar, tempered freely with his own gentler humour and wider humanity. He worked on his *Good-Natur'd Man* diligently at intervals during 1766, and, in the following year, it was completed. Its literary merits, as might be expected, were far above the average; it contained two original characters, the pessimist Croaker and the pretender Lofty; and, following the precedent of Fielding, it borrowed the material of one of its most effective scenes from those "absurdities of the vulgar" which its author held to be infinitely more diverting than the affected vagaries of so-called high life. The thing was to get it acted.

This was no easy matter, for it had to go through what Goldsmith had himself termed "a process truly chymical." It had to "be tried in the manager's fire, strained through a licenser, and purified in the Review, or the newspaper of the day." And he had said more indiscreet things than these. He had condemned the despotism of the monarchs of the stage, deplored the over-prominence of that "histrionic Daemon," the actor, and attacked the cheeseparing policy of vamping up old pieces to save the expense of "authors' nights." All these things were highly unpalatable to Garrick; but, to Garrick, owing to the confusion at Covent garden caused by the death of Rich, Goldsmith had to go. The result might have been foreseen. Garrick played fast and loose—finessed and temporised. Then came the inevitable money advance, which enabled him to suggest unwelcome changes in the MS., followed, of course, by fresh mortifications for the luckless author. Eventually, *The Good-Natur'd Man* was transferred to Colman, who, in the interval, had become Rich's successor. But, even here, difficulties arose. Colman did not care for the play, and the intrigues of Garrick still pursued its writer; for Garrick persuaded Colman to defer its production until after the appearance at Drury lane of a vapid sentimental comedy by Kelly called *False Delicacy*, which, under Garrick's clever generalship, had an unmerited success. Six days later, on 29 January, 1768, the ill-starred *Good-Natur'd Man* was brought out at Covent garden by a desponding

manager, and a (for the most part) depressed cast. Nor did
it derive much aid from a ponderous prologue by Johnson.
Nevertheless, it was by no means ill received. Shuter made
a hit with Croaker, and Woodward was excellent as Lofty, the
two most important parts; and though, for a space, a "genteel"
audience could not suffer the "low" scene of the bailiffs to come
between the wind and its nobility, the success of the comedy,
albeit incommensurate with its deserts and its author's expectations, was more than respectable. It ran for nine nights,
three of which brought him £400; while the sale in book form,
with the omitted scene, added £100 more. The worst thing
was that it came after *False Delicacy*, instead of before it.

During its composition, Goldsmith had lived much at
Islington, having a room in queen Elizabeth's old hunting lodge,
Canonbury tower. In town, he had modest lodgings in the
Temple. But £500 was too great a temptation; and, accordingly, leasing for three-fourths of that sum a set of rooms in
Brick court, he proceeded to furnish them elegantly with
Wilton carpets, moreen curtains and Pembroke tables. *Nil
te quaesiveris extra*, Johnson had wisely said to him when he
once apologised for his mean environment, and it would have
been well if he had remembered the monition. But Goldsmith was Goldsmith—*qualis ab incepto*. The new expense
meant new needs—and new embarrassments. Hence, we hear
of *Roman* and *English Histories* for Davies and *A History of
Animated Nature* for Griffin. The aggregate pay was more
than £1500; but, for the writer of a unique novel, an excellent
comedy and a deservedly successful poem, it was, assuredly,
in his own words, "to cut blocks with a razor." All the same,
he had not yet entirely lost his delight of life. He could still
enjoy country excursions—"shoemakers' holidays" he called
them—at Hampstead and Edgware; could still alternate
"The Club" in Gerrard street with the Crown at Islington and,
occasionally, find pausing-places of memory and retrospect
when, softening toward the home of his boyhood with a sadness
made deeper by the death of his brother Henry in May, 1768,
he planned and perfected a new poem, *The Deserted Village*.

How far Auburn reproduced Lissoy, how far *The Deserted
Village* was English or Irish—are surely matters for the seed-
splitters of criticism; and decision either way in no wise affects

the enduring beauty of the work. The poem holds us by the humanity of its character pictures, by its delightful rural descriptions, by the tender melancholy of its metrical cadences. Listen to the "Farewell" (and farewell it practically proved) to poetry:

> Farewell, and O, where'er thy voice be tried,
> On Torno's cliffs, or Pambamarca's side,
> Whether where equinoctial fervours glow,
> Or winter wraps the polar world in snow,
> Still let thy voice prevailing over Time,
> Redress the rigours of th' inclement clime;
> Aid slighted Truth, with thy persuasive strain
> Teach erring man to spurn the rage of gain;
> Teach him, that states of native strength possest,
> Though very poor, may still be very blest.

Here, Goldsmith ended, if we may rely on Boswell's attribution to Johnson of the last four lines. They certainly supply a rounded finish,[1] and the internal evidence as to their authorship is not very apparent. But, if they are really Johnson's, it is an open question whether the more abrupt termination of Goldsmith, resting, in Dantesque fashion, on the word "blest," is not to be preferred.

Report says that Goldsmith's more critical contemporaries ranked *The Deserted Village* below *The Traveller*—a mistake perhaps to be explained by the intelligible, but often unreasoning, prejudice in favour of a first impression. He was certainly paid better for it, if it be true that he received a hundred guineas, which, although five times as much as he got for *The Traveller*, was still not more than Cadell paid six years later for Hannah More's forgotten *Sir Eldred of the Bower*. *The Deserted Village* was published on 26 May, 1770, with an affectionate dedication to Reynolds, and ran through five editions in the year of issue. In the July following its appearance, Goldsmith paid a short visit to Paris with his Devonshire friends, Mrs. and the Miss Hornecks, the elder[2] of whom he had fitted with the pretty pet name "the Jessamy Bride," and who

---

[1] That trade's proud empire hastes to swift decay,
  As ocean sweeps the laboured mole away;
  While self-respecting power can Time defy,
  As rocks resist the billows and the sky.

[2] This has recently been established by reference to tablets in Weybridge church, and the researches of Sir Ernest Clarke and others.

is supposed to have inspired him with more than friendly feelings. On his return, he fell again to the old desk work, a life of Bolingbroke, an abridgment of his *Roman History* and so forth. But he still found time for the exhibition of his more playful gifts, since it must have been about this date that, in the form of an epistle to his friend Lord Clare, he threw off that delightful medley of literary recollection and personal experience, the verses known as *The Haunch of Venison*, in which the ease and lightness of Prior are wedded to the best measure of Swift. If the *chef d'œuvre* be really the equal of the *chef d'œuvre*, there is little better in Goldsmith's work than this pleasant *jeu d'esprit*. But he had a yet greater triumph to come, for, by the end of 1771, he had completed his second and more successful comedy, *She Stoops to Conquer*.

At this date, the worries and vexations which had accompanied the production of *The Good-Natur'd Man* had been more or less forgotten by its author; and, as they faded, Goldsmith's old dreams of theatrical distinction returned. The sentimental snake, moreover, was not even scotched; and "genteel comedy"—that "mawkish drab of spurious breed," as the opportunist Garrick came eventually to style it—had still its supporters: witness *The West Indian* of Cumberland, which had just been produced. Falling back on an earlier experience of his youth, the mistaking of squire Featherston's house for an inn, Goldsmith set to work on a new comedy; and, after much rueful wandering in the lanes of Hendon and Edgware, "studying jests with the most tragical countenance," Tony Lumpkin and his mother, Mr. Hardcastle and his daughter, were gradually brought into being, "to be tried in the manager's fire." The ordeal was to the full as severe as before. Colman accepted the play, and then delayed to produce it. His tardiness embarrassed the author so much that, at last, in despair, he transferred the piece to Garrick. But, here, Johnson interposed, and, though he could not induce Colman to believe in it, by the exercise "of a kind of force," prevailed on him to bring it out. Finally, after it had been read to "the Club," in January, 1773, under its first title *The Old House, a New Inn*, and, assisted to some extent by Foote's clever anti-sentimental puppet-show *Piety in Pattens; or, the Handsome Housemaid*, it was produced at Covent garden on 15 March, 1773, as *She Stoops to Conquer; or, the Mistakes of a Night*. When on the boards, supported by the suffrages of the author's friends, and enthusiastically welcomed by the public, the play easily triumphed over a caballing manager and a lukewarm company, and, thus, one of the best modern comedies was at once lifted to an eminence from which it has never since been deposed. It brought the author four or five hundred pounds, and would have brought him more by its sale in book form, had he not, in a moment of depression, handed over the copyright to Newbery, in discharge of a debt. But he inscribed the play to Johnson, in one of those dedications which, more, perhaps, than elsewhere, vindicate his claim to the praise of having touched nothing that he did not adorn.

Unhappily, by this time, his affairs had reached a stage of complication from which little short of a miracle could extricate him; and there is no doubt that his involved circumstances affected his health, as he had already been seriously ill in 1772. During the few months of life that remained to him, he did not publish anything, his hands being full of promised work. His last metrical effort was *Retaliation*, a series of epitaph-epigrams, left unfinished at his death, and prompted by some similar, though greatly inferior, efforts directed against him by Garrick and other friends. In March, 1774, the combined effects of work and worry, added to a local disorder, brought on a nervous fever which he aggravated by the unwise use of a patent medicine, James's powder, on which, like many of his contemporaries, he placed too great a reliance. On the 10th, he had dined with Percy at the Turk's Head. Not many days after, when Percy called on him, he was ill. A week later, the sick man just recognised his visitor. On Monday, 4 April, he died; and he was buried on the 9th in the burial ground of the Temple church. Two years subsequently, a memorial was erected to him in Westminster abbey, with a Latin epitaph by Johnson, containing, among other things, the oft-quoted *affectuum potens, at lenis dominator*. An even more suitable farewell is, perhaps, to be found in the simpler "valediction *cum osculo*" which his rugged old friend inserted in a letter to Langton: "Let not his frailities be remembered; he was a very great man."

Goldsmith's physical likeness must be sought between the

idealised portrait painted by Reynolds early in 1770, and the semi-grotesque "head" by Bunbury prefixed to the post-humous issue in 1776 of *The Haunch of Venison*. As to his character, it has suffered a little from the report of those to whom, like Walpole, Garrick, Hawkins and Boswell, his peculi-arities were more apparent than his genius; though certain things must be admitted because he admits them himself. Both early and late, he confesses to a trick of blundering, a slow and hesitating utterance, an assumed pomposity which looked like self-importance. He had also a distinct brogue which he cultivated rather than corrected. But as to "talking like poor Poll," the dictum requires qualification. It is quite intelligible that, in the dominating presence of Johnson, whose magisterial manner overrode both Burke and Gibbon, Gold-smith, who was twenty years younger, whose wit reached its flashing point but fitfully, and who was easily disconcerted in argument, should not have appeared at his best, though there were cases when, to use a colloquialism, he "got home" even on the great man himself—witness the happy observation that Johnson would make the little fishes of fable-land talk like whales. But evidence is not wanting that Goldsmith could converse delightfully in more congenial companies. With respect to certain other imputed shortcomings—the love of fine clothes, for instance—the most charitable explanation is the desire to extenuate physical deficiencies, inseparable from a morbid self-consciousness; while, as regards his extravagance, something should be allowed for the accidents of his education, and for the canker of poverty which had eaten into his early years. And it must be remembered that he would give his last farthing to any plausible applicant, and that he had the kindest heart in the world.

As a literary man, what strikes one most is the individuality —the intellectual detachment of his genius. He is a standing illustration of Boswell's clever contention that the fowls run-ning about the yard are better flavoured than those which are fed in coops. He belonged to no school; he formed none. If, in his verse, we find traces of Addison or Prior, of Lesage or Fielding in his novel, of Farquhar or Cibber in his comedies, those traces are in the pattern and not in the stuff. The stuff is Goldsmith—Goldsmith's philosophy, Goldsmith's heart,

Goldsmith's untaught grace, simplicity, sweetness. He was but forty-six when he died; and he was maturing to the last. Whether his productive period had ceased, whether, with a longer span, he would have gone higher—may be doubted. But, notwithstanding a mass of hackwork which his faculty of lucid exposition almost raised to a fine art, he contrived, even in his short life, to leave behind him some of the most finished didactic poetry in the language; some unsurpassed familiar verse; a series of essays ranking only below Lamb's; a unique and original novel; and a comedy which, besides being readable, is still acted to delighted audiences. He might have lived longer and done less; but at least he did not live long enough to fall below his best.

# CHAPTER X

# The Literary Influence of the Middle Ages

MACPHERSON'S OSSIAN.   CHATTERTON.   PERCY AND THE
WARTONS

I T is scarcely a paradox to say that the Middle Ages have
influenced modern literature more strongly through their
architecture than through their poems.   Gothic churches
and old castles have exerted a medieval literary influence on
many authors who have had no close acquaintance with old
French and German poets, and not much curiosity about
their ideals or their style.   Even in writers better qualified by
study of medieval literature, like Southey and Scott, it is
generally the historical substance of the Middle Ages rather
than anything in the imaginative form of old poetry or romance that attracts them.   Even William Morris, who is
much more affected by the manner of old poetry than Scott, is
curiously unmedieval in much of his poetry; there is nothing of
the old fashion in the poem The Defence of Guenevere, and the
old English rhythm of the song in Sir Peter Harpdon's End is
in striking contrast, almost a discord, with the dramatic blank
verse of the piece.   Medieval verse has seldom been imitated
or revived without the motive of parody, as, for instance, in
Swinburne's Masque of Queen Bersabe; the great exception is
in the adoption of the old ballad measures, from which English
poetry was abundantly refreshed through Wordsworth, Scott
and Coleridge.   And here, also, though the ballad measures
live and thrive all through the nineteenth century so naturally
that few people think of their debt to Percy's Reliques, yet, at
the beginning, there is parody in the greatest of all that race,

245

*The Ancient Mariner*—not quite so obvious in the established version as in the first editions (in the *Lyrical Ballads* of 1798 and 1800), but still clear enough.

The Middle Ages did much to help literary fancy long before the time of Scott; but the thrill of mystery and wonder came much more from Gothic buildings than from *Morte d'Arthur*, and it is found in writers who had paid little or no attention to old English romance, as well as in those who showed their interest in it. The famous passage in Congreve's *Mourning Bride* is romantic in spirit and intention, and its success is won from a Gothic cathedral, with no intermediary literature. So, also, the romantic ruin in the first version of Collins's *Ode to Evening*, "whose walls more awful nod," is pictorial, not literary, except in the conventional "nod," which is literary, indeed, but not at all medieval. This "nod," by the way, has been carefully studied in *Guesses at Truth;*[1] it is a good criterion of the eighteenth century romantic style; Collins, happily, got rid of it, and saved his poem unblemished.

Medieval literary studies undoubtedly encouraged the taste for such romantic effects as are beheld when abbeys or ruined castles are visited by twilight or moonlight; but the literary Gothic terror or wonder could be exercised without any more knowledge of the Middle Ages than Victor Hugo possessed, whose *Notre Dame de Paris* owes hardly anything of its triumph to medieval books. On the other hand, there was much literature of the Middle Ages known and studied in the earlier part of the eighteenth century without any great effect upon the aims or sensibilities of practising men of letters. There seems to have been no such prejudice against medieval literature, as there undoubtedly was, for a long time, against Gothic architecture. "Black letter" poetry and the books of chivalry were, naturally and rightly, believed to be old-fashioned, but they were not depreciated more emphatically than were the Elizabethans; and, perhaps, the very want of exact historical knowledge concerning the Middle Ages allowed reading men to judge impartially when medieval things came under their notice. Dryden's praise of Chaucer is, altogether and in every particular, far beyond the reach of his age in criticism; but it is not at variance with the common literary

[1] Pp. 44 ff. Eversley Series edn. 1897.

judgment of his time, or of Pope's.  The principle is quite
clear; in dealing with Chaucer, one must allow for his ignorance
of true English verse and, of course, for his old English phrasing;
but, then, he is to be taken on his merits, for his imagination
and his narrative skill, and, so taken, he comes out a better
example of sound poetical wit than Ovid himself, and more
truly a follower of nature.  Pope sees clearly and is not put
off by literary prejudices; the theme of *Eloisa to Abelard* is
neither better nor worse for dating back to the twelfth century,
and he appropriates *The Temple of Fame* from Chaucer because he finds that its substance is good enough for him.  Addison's estimate of *Chevy Chace* is made in nearly the same spirit;
only, here something controversial comes in.  He shows that
the old English ballad has some of the qualities of classical
epic; epic virtues are not exclusively Greek and Roman.  Yet,
curiously, there is an additional moral; the ballad is not used
as an alternative to the modern taste for correct writing, but,
on the contrary, as a reproof to the metaphysical school, an
example of "the essential and inherent perfection of simplicity
of thought."  It is significant that the opposite manner, which
is not simple, but broken up into epigram and points of wit,
is called "Gothick" by Addison; the imitators of Cowley are
"Gothick"; the medieval ballad, which many people would
have reckoned "Gothick," is employed as an example of classical
simplicity to refute them.  "Gothick" was so very generally
used to denote what is now called "medieval"—"the Gothick
romances," "the Gothick mythology of elves and fairies"—
that Addison's paradoxical application of the term in those
two papers can hardly have been unintentional; it shows, at
any rate, that the prejudice against Gothic art did not mislead
him in his judgment of old-fashioned poetry.  In his more
limited measure, he agrees with Dryden and Pope.  What is
Gothic in date may be classical in spirit.

Medievalism was one of the minor eccentric fashions of the
time, noted by Dryden in his reference to his "old Saxon
friends," and by Pope with his "mister wight"; but those
shadows of "The Upheaving of Ælfred" were not strong
enough, for good or ill, either to make a romantic revival or to
provoke a modern curse on paladins and troubadours.  Rymer,
indeed, who knew more than any one else about old French and

Provençal poetry, was the loudest champion of the unities and classical authority. Medieval studies, including the history of poetry, could be carried on without any particular bearing on modern productive art, with no glimmering of a medievalist romantic school and no threatening of insult or danger to the most precise and scrupulous modern taste. It would seem that the long "battle of the books," the debate of ancients and moderns in France and England, had greatly mitigated, if not altogether quenched, the old jealousy of the Middle Ages which is exemplified in Ben Jonson's tirade:

> No Knights o' the Sun, nor Amadis de Gauls,
> Primaleons, Pantagruels, public nothings,
> Abortives of the fabulous dark cloister.

This is the old scholarly contempt for the Middle Ages; it is coming to be out of date in Jonson's time. The books of chivalry recovered some of their favour, as they ceased to be dangerous distractions; those who laughed at *The Knight of the Burning Pestle* were not ashamed to read *The Seven Champions of Christendom*. There is a pleasant apology for the old romances by Chapelain in France, an author more determined than Ben Jonson in his obedience to literary rules. And it may be supposed that, later, when the extreme modern party had gone so far as to abuse Homer for his irregularities and barbarous want of taste, there would be less inclination among sensible men to find fault with medieval roughness; cavilling at superfluities in romance might be all very well, but it was too like the scandalous treatment of Homer by Perrault and his party; those, on the other hand, who stood up for Homer might be the less ready to censure *Amadis of Gaul*. There may be something of this motive in Addison's praise of *Chevy Chace;* at any rate, he has sense to find the classical excellences where the pedantic moderns would not look for anything of the sort.

Modern literature and the minds of modern readers are so affected by different strains of medieval influence through various "romantic" schools, through history, travel and the study of languages, that it is difficult to understand the temper of the students who broke into medieval antiquities in the seventeenth century and discovered much poetry by the way, though their chief business was with chronicles and state papers. It is safe to believe that everything which appeals to any reader as peculiarly medieval in the works of Tennyson or Rossetti was not apparent to Hickes or Hearne or Rymer, any more than it was to Leibniz (a great medieval antiquary), or, later, to Muratori, who makes poetry one of his many interests in the course of work resembling Rymer's, though marked by better taste and intelligence. The Middle Ages were studied, sometimes, with a view to modern applications; but these were generally political or religious, not literary. And, in literary studies, it is long before anything like *Ivanhoe* or anything like *The Defence of Guenevere* is discernible. Before the spell of the grail was heard again, and before the vision of Dante was at all regarded, much had to be learned and many experiments to be made. The first attraction from the Middle Ages, coming as a discovery due to antiquarian research and not by way of tradition, was that of old northern heroic poetry, commonly called Icelandic—"Islandic," as Percy spells it. Gray, when he composed *The Descent of Odin* and *The Fatal Sisters*, drew from sources which had been made known in England in the seventeenth century. These, in their effect on English readers, formed the first example of the literary influence of the Middle Ages, consciously recognised as such, and taken up with antiquarian literary interest.

Of course, the whole of modern literature is full of the Middle Ages; the most disdainful modern classicist owes, in France, his alexandrine verse to the twelfth century and, in England, his heroic verse to a tradition older still. The poet who stands for the perfection of the renascence in Italy, Ariosto, derives his stanza from the lyric school of Provence, and is indebted for most of his matter to old romances. Through Chaucer and Spenser, through *The Countess of Pembroke's Arcadia*, through many chapbooks and through the unprinted living folklore of England, the Middle Ages formed the minds of Dryden and Pope and their contemporaries. But, for a distinct and deliberate notice of something medieval found by study and considered to be available in translation or adaptation, one must go to Sir William Temple's remarks about *The Death-Song of Ragnar Lodbrok;* it is hard to find anything of the same sort earlier. What marks it out is not so much the literary curiosity which selects it, but the literary estimate which judges this ancient northern piece to have a present value. Thereby, Sir William Temple begins the modern sort of literary study which looks for suggestion in old remote and foreign regions, and he sets a precedent for the explorations of various romantic schools, wandering through all the world in search of plots, scenery and local colour.

Here, it may be objected that this kind of exploration was nothing new; that the Middle Ages themselves had collected stories from all the ends of the earth; that Elizabethans range as far as Southey or Victor Hugo; that Racine, too, calculates the effect of what is distant and what is foreign, in his choice of subjects for tragedy, *Iphigénie* or *Bajazet*. What, then, is specially remarkable in the fact that Scandinavian legend was noted as interesting and that Sir William Temple gave an hour of study to the death-song of Ragnar? The novelty is in the historical motive. *The Death-Song of Ragnar* is intelligible without much historical commentary; any one can understand the emphatic phrases: "we smote with swords" (*pugnavimus ensibus*); "laughing I die" (*ridens moriar*)—not to speak of the mistranslated lines which represent the heroes in Valhalla drinking ale out of the skulls of their enemies:

> *Bibemus cerevisiam*
> *Ex concavis crateribus craniorum.*

Those things caught men's fancy; and the honourable, courageous viking was launched to try his fortune in modern romantic literature. But there was the historical interest, besides; and Temple, in his essay *Of Heroic Virtue*, notices the song of Ragnar because it explains something in the past, and contributes something to the experience of the human race. He takes up "runic" literature again in his essay *Of Poetry;* he is working on the same lines as Sidney and attending the progress of poesy from its early life among the barbarians. He vindicates, like Daniel, the right of the Gothic nations to a share in the humanities. And he proves, by particulars, what Sidney and Daniel had left vague; he exhibits this specimen from a definite tract of country; and his quotation has a double effect; it touches those readers who may be looking for a new thrill and fresh sources of amazement; it touches those also who, besides this craving, are curious about the past; who are historically minded and who try to understand the various fashions of thought in different ages. Thus, one significance of this quotation from Ragnar's death-song is that it helps to alter the historical view of the world. Historical studies had suffered from the old prevalent opinion (still strong in the eighteenth century, if not later) that all ages of the world are very much alike. The *Death-Song of Ragnar* and other references to the heroic poetry of Norway were like distance marks which brought out the perspective.

Scandinavian suggestions did not lead immediately to any very large results in English poetry or fiction. Macpherson came in later and took their ground; the profits all went to Ossian. Students of northern antiquities were too conscientious and not daring enough; Percy's *Five Pieces of Runic Poetry* came out humbly in the wake of Macpherson; his book is like what the Icelanders, in a favourite contemptuous figure, call "the little boat towed behind."[1] But the history of Scandinavian studies is worth some notice, though Odin and his friends achieved no such sweeping victories as the heroes of Morven.

Temple's authorities are Scandinavian, not English, scholars; he conversed at Nimeguen on these subjects with count Oxenstierna, and he quotes from Olaus Wormius. But northern studies were already flourishing in England by means of the Oxford press, to which Junius had given founts of type from which were printed his Gothic and Old English gospels, and where the founts are still preserved and ready for use. Junius's type was used in printing Hickes's Icelandic grammar, which was afterwards included in the magnificent *Thesaurus Linguarum Veterum Septentrionalium*. It was used, also, for E. G.'s (Edmund Gibson's) Oxford edition of *Polemo-Middinia* and of *Christis Kirk on the Grene* (1691), which was brought out as a philological joke, with no detriment to philological science. Gothic, Icelandic, Old English and the languages of Chaucer and Gawain Douglas are all employed in illustration of these two excellent comic poems, for the benefit of the "joco-serious Commonwealth" to which the book is dedicated.

[1] "It would be as vain to deny, as it is perhaps impolitic to mention, that this attempt is owing to the success of the Erse fragments"(*Five Pieces*, 1763, Preface).

Hickes's *Thesaurus* is a great miscellaneous work on the antiquities of all the Teutonic languages. One page in it has now the authority of an original Old English document, for there he printed the heroic lay of *Finnsburh* from a manuscript at Lambeth which is not at present to be found. On the opposite page and immediately following is an Icelandic poem: Hervor at her father Angantyr's grave, calling upon him to give up the magic sword which had been buried with him. This poem is translated into English prose, and it had considerable effect on modern literature. It was thought good enough, and not too learned or recondite, to be reprinted in the new edition of Dryden's *Miscellany*, Part VI, in 1716, Icelandic text and all. It seems to have been an afterthought of the editor, or in compliance with a suggestion from outside which the editor was too idle to refuse—for the piece is printed with Hickes's heading, which refers to the preceding piece (*Finnsburh*) in the *Thesaurus* and compares the Icelandic with the Old English verse— quite unintelligible as it stands, abruptly, in the *Miscellany*.[1] But, however it came about, the selection is a good one, and had as much success as is possible to those shadowy ancient things. It is repeated, under the title *The Incantation of Hervor* by Percy, as the first of his *Five Runic Pieces;* and, after this, it became a favourite subject for paraphrase; it did not escape "Monk" Lewis; and it appears as *L'Épée d'Angantyr* in the *Poëmes barbares* of Leconte de Lisle.

Percy's second piece is *The Dying Ode of Ragnar Lodbrog*. This had not been left unnoticed after Temple's quotation from it. Thomas Warton the elder translated the two stanzas which Temple took from his authority, the *Literatura Runica* of Olaus Wormius; they appeared as "a Runic Ode," in the posthumous volume of his poems (1748). They counted for something in the education of Thomas the younger and Joseph Warton, together with the architecture of Winchester and Windsor, and the poetry of Spenser and Milton.

It will be observed that Old English poetry had none of this success—very slight success indeed, but still ascertainable— which attended *The Death-Song of Ragnar* and *The Incantation of Hervor*. Perhaps, if Hickes had translated *The Fight at Finnsburh*—but he did not, and so the Icelandic page was

[1] Part VI.

taken and the Old English left. Apart from that accident, there was good reason for the greater success of the "runic" or "Islandic" poems. They are much more compact and pointed than anything in Old English. The poem of Hervor is an intensely passionate lyrical drama; the song of Ragnar is an emphatic rendering of the heroic spirit of the north; the poem is itself the product of an early romantic movement which had learned the artistic use of heroic phrases, and makes the most of them in a loud metallic way. The literary artifice can be detected now; the difference from the older heroic style is as great as that between Burns and Barbour in their idea of the valiant king Robert and the eloquence of Bannockburn. But this calculated and brassy emphasis all went to establish *The Death-Song* as a remarkable proof of early poetical genius in the north, and a type of northern heroic virtue.

The other three pieces in Percy's volume had less *vogue* than Ragnar and the sword of Angantyr. One is *The Ransome of Egill the Scald*, taken from Olaus Wormius. It had been appreciated already by Temple, who calls the poet by the name of his father, but means Egil when he says "Scallogrim." The passage may be quoted; it follows immediately on *The Death-Song of Ragnar:*

I am deceived, if in this sonnet, and a following ode of Scallogrim (which was likewise made by him after he was condemned to die, and deserved his pardon for a reward) there be not a vein truely poetical, and in its kind Pindaric, taking it with the allowance of the different climates, fashions, opinions, and languages of such distant countries.

Unfortunately, the prose history of Egil Skallagrimsson was not printed as yet, and could not be used by Percy. There is a curious neglect of history in Percy's notes on the two poems that follow: *The Funeral Song of Hacon* and *The Complaint of Harold*. The selection of the poems is a good one; but it is clear that, with the editor, the mythological interest is stronger than the historical. His principal guide is *Introduction à l' histoire du Dannemarc* by Chevalier Mallet, as to which we read: "A translation of this work is in great forwardness, and will shortly be published." It is curious to see how the connection with the Oxford press and the tradition of Junius and

Hickes is still maintained; Percy here (as also in the preface to his *Reliques*) acknowledges the help of Lye, whose edition of the Gothic Gospels was published at Oxford in 1750. The "Islandic Originals," added by Percy after his translations, were plainly intended as a reminder to Macpherson that the original Gaelic of *Fingal* was still unpublished. The *Five Pieces*, it should be observed, were issued without Percy's name.

Gray's two translations from the Icelandic[1] are far the finest result of those antiquarian studies, and they help to explain how comparatively small was the influence of the north upon English poetry. How much Gray knew of the language is doubtful; but he certainly knew something, and did not depend entirely on the Latin translations which he found in Bartholinus or Torfaeus. He must have caught something of the rhythm in

> *Vindum, vindum*
> *Vef darradar,*

and have appreciated the sharpness and brilliance of certain among the phrases. His *Descent of Odin* and his *Fatal Sisters* are more than a mere exercise in a foreign language, or a record of romantic things discovered in little-known mythologies. The Icelandic poems were more to Gray than they were to any other scholar, because they exactly correspond to his own ideals of poetic style—concise, alert, unmuffled, never drawling or clumsy. Gray must have felt this. It meant that there was nothing more to be done with "runic" poetry in English. It was all too finished, too classical. No modern artist could hope to improve upon the style of the northern poems; and the subjects of northern mythology, good as they were in themselves, would be difficult and dangerous if clothed in English narrative or dramatic forms. Gray uses what he can, out of his Icelandic studies, by transferring some of the motives and phrases to a British theme, in *The Bard*.

In Hickes's *Thesaurus* may be found many curious specimens of what is now called Middle English: he quotes *Poema Morale*, and he gives in full *The Land of Cockayne*. He discusses versification, and notes in Old English verse a greater

---

[1] Cf. *ante*, Chap. VI, pp. 145 ff.

regard for quantity than in modern English (giving examples from Cowley of short syllables lengthened and long shortened); while, in discussing alliteration, he quotes from modern poets, Donne, Waller, Dryden. It might be said that the promise of the *History of English Poetry* is there; Hickes certainly does much in the ground later occupied by Warton. Gibson's little book may be mentioned again as part of the same work; and it had an effect more immediate than Hickes's "semi-Saxon" quotations. There was an audience ready for *Christis Kirk on the Grene*, and E. G. ought to be honoured in Scotland as a founder of modern Scottish poetry and one of the ancestors of Burns.[1] Allan Ramsay took up the poem, and, thus, E. G.'s new-year diversion (intended, as he says, for the Saturnalia) is related to the whole movement of that age in favour of ballads and popular songs, as well as specially to the new Scottish poetry of Ramsay, Fergusson and Burns.

If Percy's *Reliques* be taken as the chief result of this move-ment, then we may judge that there were in it two main interests —one, antiquarian; one, simply a liking for poetry, wherever found, with an inclination to find it in the "silly sooth" of popular rimes. Thus, the search for ballads is only partially and accidentally medieval. But it has a likeness to all "ro-mantic" schools, in so far as it turns away from fashionable and conventional literature, and it was natural that lovers of ballads should also be fond of old English poetry in general—a combination of tastes well exhibited in the famous folio MS. which was used by Percy and now bears his name.

Addison's essays on *Chevy Chace* and *The Children in the Wood* show how ballads were appreciated; and, in the last of these, he notes particularly how the late Lord Dorset "had a numerous collection of old English ballads and took a par-ticular pleasure in reading them." Addison proceeds: "I can affirm the same of Mr. Dryden, and know several of the most refined writers of our present age who are of the same humour." And then he speaks of Molière's thoughts on the subject, as he has expressed them in *Le Misanthrope*. Ballads, it is plain, had an audience ready for them, and they were provided in fair quantity long before Percy. The imitation of them began

---

[1] As to the publication of *Christis Kirk* in Watson's *Choice Collection* (1706–11) and Allan Ramsay's addition to the poem, cf. *ante*, Vol. IX, pp. 409 and 410.

very early; Lady Wardlaw's *Hardyknute* was published in 1719 as an ancient poem; and again in Ramsay's *Evergreen* (1724).

Between ballads and Scottish songs, which seem to have been welcome everywhere, and ancient "runic" pieces, which were praised occasionally by amateurs, it would seem as if old English poems, earlier than Chaucer, were neglected. But we know from Pope's scheme of a history of English poetry that they were not forgotten, though it was left for Warton to study them more minutely. Pope's liberality of judgment may be surprising to those who take their opinions ready made. He was not specially interested in the Middle Ages, but neither was he intolerant, whatever he might say about monks and "the long Gothic night." He never repudiated his debt to Spenser; and, in his praise of Shakespeare, he makes amends to the Middle Ages for anything he had said against them: Shakespeare, he says, is "an ancient and majestick piece of Gothick architecture compared with a neat modern building." But, before the medieval poetry of England could be explored in accordance with the suggestions of Pope's historical scheme, there came the triumph of Ossian, which utterly overwhelmed the poor scrupulous experiments of "runic" translators, and carried off the greatest men—Goethe, Bonaparte—in a common enthusiasm.

Ossian, like Ragnar Lodbrok, belongs to a time earlier than what is now generally reckoned the Middle Ages; it was not till after Macpherson that the chivalrous Middle Ages—the world of *Ivanhoe* or *The Talisman*, of *Lohengrin* or *Tannhäuser*—came to their own again. There was something in the earlier times which seemed to have been more fascinating. But Ossian did not need to concern himself much about his date and origin; there was no serious rivalry to be feared either from *The Descent of Odin* or *The Castle of Otranto*. Only a few vestiges of medieval literature contributed to the great victory, which was won, not unfairly, by rhythm, imagery and sentiment, historical and local associations helping in various degrees. The author or translator of Ossian won his great success fairly, by unfair means. To call him an impostor is true, but insufficient. When Ossian dethroned Homer in the soul of Werther, the historical and antiquarian fraud of Macpherson had very little to do with it. Werther and Charlotte mingle their tears over the "Songs of Selma"; it would be an insult to Goethe to suppose that he translated and printed these "Songs" merely as interesting philological specimens of the ancient life of Scotland, or that he was not really possessed and enchanted by the melancholy winds and the voices of the days of old. Blair's opinion about Ossian is stated in such terms as these:

> The description of Fingal's airy hall, in the poem called *Berrathon*, and of the ascent of Malvina into it deserves particular notice, as remarkably noble and magnificent. But above all, the engagement of Fingal with the Spirit of Loda, in *Carric-thura*, cannot be mentioned without admiration. I forbear transcribing the passage, as it must have drawn the attention of every one who has read the works of Ossian. The undaunted courage of Fingal opposed to all the terrors of the Scandinavian god; the appearance and the speech of the awful spirit; the wound which he receives, and the shriek which he sends forth, "as rolled into himself, he rose upon the wind," are full of the most amazing and terrible majesty, that *I know no passage more sublime in the writings of any uninspired author*.

Blair, as a doctor of divinity and professor of rhetoric and belles-lettres, was bound to be careful in his language, and, if it here seems extravagant, it is certainly not careless. His deliberate judgment as to the sublimity of Ossian must be taken as absolutely sincere, and it cannot be sincere if not founded on the text as it stands, if bribed or biassed in any measurable degree by antiquarian considerations. And the praise of Goethe and Blair was honestly won by Macpherson; his imagery, thoughts and sentences are estimated by these critics for the effect upon their minds. What they desire is beauty of imagination, thought and language; these, they find in Ossian, the published Ossian, the book in their hands; if Macpherson wrote it all, then their praise belongs to him. Nothing can alter the fact that sentences were written and published which were good enough to obtain this praise; all Macpherson's craft as a philological impostor would have been nothing without his literary skill. He was original enough, in a peculiar way, to touch and thrill the whole of Europe.

The glamour of Ossian is only very partially to be reckoned among the literary influences of the Middle Ages. It is romantic, in every acceptation of that too significant word. But "romantic" and "medieval" are not the same thing. The Middle Ages help the modern romantic authors in many ways, and some of these may be found in Ossian; the vague twilight of Ossian, and the persistent tones of lamentation, are in accordance with many passages of old Scandinavian poetry—of *The Lays of Helgi* and *The Lament of Gudrun*, in the elder *Edda*—with many old ballads, with much of the Arthurian legend. But those very likenesses may prove a warning not to take "medieval" as meaning the exclusive possession of any of those qualities or modes. If certain fashions of sentiment are found both in the elder *Edda* and in *Morte d'Arthur*, it is probable that they will be found also in ancient Babylon and in the South Sea islands. And, if the scenery and sentiment of Ossian are not peculiarly medieval, though they are undoubtedly romantic, the spell of Ossian, as we may fitly call it—that is, the phrases and rhythmical cadences —are obviously due to the inspired writings with which Blair, by a simple and well-known device of rhetoric, was willing to compare them. The language of Ossian is copied from David and Isaiah. It is enough to quote from the passage whose sublimity no uninspired author has outdone—the debate of Fingal and the "spirit of dismal Loda":

"Dost thou force me from my place?" replied the hollow voice. "The people bend before me. I turn the battle in the field of the brave. I look on the nations and they vanish; my nostrils pour the blast of death. I come abroad on the winds: the tempests are before my face. But my dwelling is calm, above the clouds; the fields of my rest are pleasant."

Another quotation may be taken from the other place selected by Blair (which, by the way, is close to Werther's last momentous quotation, following on "Selma"):

Malvina! where art thou, with thy songs, with the soft sound of thy steps? Son of Alpin, art thou near? where is the daughter of Toscar? "I passed, O son of Fingal, by Tor-lutha's mossy walls. The smoke of the hall was ceased. Silence was among the trees of the hill. The voice of the chase was over. I saw the daughters of the bow. I asked about Malvina, but they answered not. They turned their faces away: thin darkness covered their beauty. They were like the stars, on a rainy hill, by night, each looking faintly through her mist."

The last sentence is in a different measure from the rest of the passage. Most of it, and almost the whole of Ossian, is in parallel phrases, resembling Hebrew poetry. This was observed by Malcolm Laing, and is practically acknowledged by Macpherson in the parallel passages which he gives in his notes; his admirers dwelt upon the "uninspired" eloquence which reminded them of the Bible. It sometimes resembles the oriental manner satirised by Goldsmith in *The Citizen of the World:*[1] "there is nothing like sense in the true Eastern style, where nothing more is required but sublimity."

But Macpherson did not invent the whole of Ossian out of his own head: he knew a good deal of Gaelic poetry. If he had been more of a Celtic scholar, he might have treated Gaelic songs as Hickes did *The Incantation of Hervor*, printing the text with a prose translation, and not asking for any favour from "the reading public." But he wished to be popular, and he took the right way to that end—leaving Percy in the cold shade with his *Five Pieces of Runic Poetry* and his philological compilations.

The life of Macpherson has the interest of an ironical fable. Nemesis came upon him with a humorous cruelty; no detective romance ever worked out a more coherent plot. The end of the story is that Macpherson, long after his first successes, was compelled by the enthusiasm of his supporters to provide them with Gaelic originals. He laboured hard to compose the Gaelic Ossian, when he was weary of the whole affair. He would gladly have been allowed to pass with credit as the original composer of the English Ossian, which was all that he really cared for. But his ingenuity had brought him to this dilemma, that he could not claim what really belonged to him in the invention of Ossian without affronting his generous friends; and so, twenty years after his triumph, he had to sit down in cold blood and make his ancient Gaelic poetry. He had begun with

[1] Letter XXXIII.

a piece of literary artifice, a practical joke; he ended with deliberate forgery, which, the more it succeeded, would leave to him the less of what was really his due for the merits of the English Ossian.

James Macpherson was born in 1736 near Kingussie, the son of a small farmer. He did well at the university of Aberdeen and then, for some time, was schoolmaster in his native parish, Ruthven. His literary tastes and ambitions were keen, and, in 1758, he published a poem, *The Highlander*. About this date, he was made tutor to the son of Graham of Balgowan, and, in 1759, he went to Moffat with his pupil (Thomas Graham, the hero of Barrosa); from which occasion the *vogue* of Ossian began. At Moffat, Macpherson met John Home, the author of *Douglas*, who was full of the romantic interest in the Highlands which he passed on to Collins, and which was shared by Thomson. Macpherson really knew something about Gaelic poetry, and particularly the poems of Ossianic tradition which were generally popular in Badenoch. But his own literary taste was too decided to let him be content with what he knew; he honestly thought that the traditional Gaelic poems were not very good; he saw the chance for original exercises on Gaelic themes. His acquaintance Home, however, wanted to get at the true Celtic spirit, which at the same time, ought to agree with what he expected of it. Macpherson supplied him with *The Death of Oscar*, a thoroughly romantic story, resembling in plot Chaucer's *Knight's Tale*, but more tragical—it ended in the death of the two rivals and the lady also. This was followed by others, which Home showed to Blair in Edinburgh. In the next year, 1760, appeared *Fragments of Ancient Poetry collected in the Highlands of Scotland, and translated from the Gaelic or Erse language*.

Then, Macpherson went travelling in the Highlands and Western isles, persuaded by "several people of rank, as well as taste." The result was the complete epic of *Fingal: an ancient epic poem in six books*, which was published in 1762.

Several gentlemen in the Highlands and isles gave me all the assistance in their power, and it was by their means I was enabled to compleat the epic poem. How far it comes up to the rules of the epopoea, is the province of criticism to examine. It is only my business to lay it before the reader, as I have found it.

In the *Fingal* volume was also published among shorter pieces
*Temora, an epic poem:* "little more than the opening" is Macpherson's note. But, in 1763, this poem, too, was completed,
in eight books.

The "advertisement" to *Fingal* states that

there is a design on foot to print the Originals as soon as the translator
shall have time to transcribe them for the press; and if this publication shall not take place, copies will then be deposited in one of
the public libraries, to prevent so ancient a monument of genius
from being lost.

Nevertheless, it is clear that Macpherson, from the first, intended to take no more than was convenient from what he knew
of Gaelic verse. He did not wish to translate such poems as
captain Hector MacIntyre translated for Mr. Jonathan Old-
buck. He did not ask for help from Irish scholars. He spoke
slightingly of the Irish tales of Finn; the traditional name of
Finn MacCowl was not good enough, and Macpherson invented the name Fingal; he insisted that Fingal, Ossian, Oscar
and all the poems were not merely Scottish but "Caledonian";
in the glory of Ossian, the Irish have only by courtesy a share.
This glory, in Macpherson's mind, was not romantic like the tales
of chivalry, but heroic and political, like the *Iliad* and the *Aeneid*.
He might have been content, and he might have been successful, with the purely romantic elements as he found them in
Gaelic poems, whether of Scotland or of Ireland. But his
fabrications (like those of Geoffrey of Monmouth) are intended
to glorify the history of his native country, and Fingal and
Oscar (like king Arthur in *The Brut*) are victorious adversaries
of Rome. "Both nations" (Caledonia and Ireland), says Macpherson, "were almost the same people in the days of that
hero"; but they are not equal; and Fingal the Caledonian hero
comes to the relief of Ireland against the king of Lochlin, when
Cuchullin the Irish champion has been defeated. Macpherson thus provoked Irish scholars and English sceptics
equally, and in such a way that Irish scholars were generally cut
off from a hearing in England. Johnson did not care for them;
what he asked for was the original Gaelic of the "epopoea";
this the Irish Ossianic poems were not, and they were rejected
by Macpherson himself. They would have exploded his

history, and, with it, his epic scaffolding. Fingal, conqueror of
the Romans, and Ossian, rival of Homer, had become necessary
to Macpherson's scheme. And, as a literary man, Macpherson
was right—amazingly clever in his selections and rejections
and in the whole frame of his policy, so far as it was intended
to catch the greatest numbers of readers. Romance is to be
found there in its two chief modes—superficial variety of
scenes, and the opposite mode of intense feeling. There is
also enough to conciliate a severer taste, in the motives of
national heroism, and in the poet's conformity with the standards of epic. Thus, all sorts of readers were attracted—lovers
of antiquity, lovers of romance, hearts of sensibility and those
respectable critics who were not ashamed to follow Milton,
Dryden and Pope in their devotion to the epic ideal.

Macpherson's literary talent was considerable, and is not
limited to his ancient epic poems. Reference will be made
elsewhere[1] to his *History of Great Britain, from the Restoration
in* 1660 *to the Accession of the House of Hannover* (1775). In
1773, he had published a prose translation of the *Iliad*, which
was not highly appreciated. But it is interesting as an experiment in rhythm and as an attempt to free Homer from English
literary conventions. Macpherson died in 1796, in his native
Badenoch, in the house which he had built for himself and
named "Belleville"; he was buried in Westminster abbey, at his
own request. A Gaelic text, incomplete, was published from his
papers in 1807. Klopstock, Herder and Goethe, from specimens
published earlier by Macpherson, had tried to discover the laws
of Caledonian verse. In 1805, Malcolm Laing brought out an
edition of Ossian (and of Macpherson's own poems), in which
the debts of Macpherson were exposed, with some exaggeration.
Scott's article on Laing in *The Edinburgh Review* (1805) reaches
most of the conclusions that have been proved by later critical
research.

Percy's *Reliques* were much more closely related to the
Middle Ages than Ossian was; they revealed the proper medieval treasures of romance and ballad poetry. They are much
nearer than the "runic" poems to what is commonly reckoned
medieval. Percy's ballads are also connected with various

[1] Chap. XII, *post*.

other tastes—with the liking for Scottish and Irish music which had led to the publication of Scottish songs in D'Urfey's collection, in *Old English Ballads*, 1723–1727, in Thomson's *Orpheus Caledonius* and Ramsay's *Tea Table Miscellany*. But, though there was nothing peculiarly medieval in *Fy, let us all to the Bridal* or in *Cowden Knowes*, the taste for such country songs often went with the taste for "Gothic" romances.

The famous folio MS. which Percy secured from Humphrey Pitt of Shifnal had been compiled with no exclusive regard for any one kind. The book when Percy found it was being treated as waste paper and used for fire-lighting. When it was saved from total destruction, it was still treated with small respect; Percy, instead of copying, tore out the ballad of *King Estmere* as copy for the printers, without saving the original pages. But most of the book is preserved; it has been fully edited by Furnivall and Hales, with assistance from Child and Chappell; what Percy took or left is easily discerned. Ritson, the avenger, followed Percy as he followed Warton, and, in the introduction to his *Engleish Romanceës*, displayed some of Percy's methods, and proved how far his versions were from the original. But Percy was avowedly an improver and restorer. His processes are not those of scrupulous philology, but neither are they such as Macpherson favoured. His three volumes contain what they profess in the title-page:

*Old Heroic Ballads, Songs, and other Pieces of our earlier Poets (chiefly of the Lyric kind). Together with some few of later date.*

And there is much greater variety than the title-page offers; to take extreme cases, the *Reliques* include the song against Richard of Almaigne and the song on the false traitor Thomas Cromwell, the ballads of *Edom o' Gordon* and *Sir Patrick Spens*, "Gentle river" from the Spanish, *Old Tom of Bedlam* and *Lilliburlero, The Fairies Farewell* by Corbet and *Admiral Hosier's Ghost* by Glover. There are essays on ancient English minstrels, on the metrical romances, on the origin of the English stage, and the metre of *Pierce Plowman's Vision*, covering much of the ground taken later by Warton, and certainly giving a strong impulse to the study of old English poetry. Percy makes a strong and not exaggerated claim for the art of the old poets and, by an analysis of *Libius Disconius*, proves "their skill in distributing and conducting their fable." His opinion about early English poetry is worth quoting:

It has happened unluckily, that the antiquaries who have revived the works of our ancient writers have been for the most part men void of taste and genius, and therefore have always fastidiously rejected the old poetical Romances, because founded on fictitious or popular subjects, while they have been careful to grub up every petty fragment of the most dull and insipid rhymist, whose merit it was to deform morality, or obscure true history. Should the public encourage the revival of some of those ancient Epic Songs of Chivalry, they would frequently see rich ore of an Ariosto or a Tasso, tho' buried it may be among the rubbish and dross of barbarous times.

The public did not discourage this revival, and what Percy wanted was carried out by Ritson, Ellis, Scott and their successors. Perhaps the best thing in Percy's criticism is his distinction between the two classes of ballad; the one incorrect, with a romantic wildness, is in contrast to the later, tamer southern class, which is thus accurately described:

The other sort are written in exacter measure, have a low or subordinate correctness, sometimes bordering on the insipid, yet often well adapted to the pathetic.

As an example, Percy refers to *Gernutus:*

> In Venice town not long agoe
> A cruel Jew did dwell,
> Which lived all on usurie
> As Italian writers tell.

The difference here noted by Percy is the principal thing in this branch of learning, and it could hardly be explained in better words.

It was through Percy's *Reliques* that the Middle Ages really came to have an influence in modern poetry, and this was an effect far greater than that of Ossian (which was not medieval) or that of *The Castle of Otranto* (which was not poetical). The *Reliques* did not spread one monotonous sentiment like Ossian, or publish a receipt for romantic machinery. What they did may be found in *The Ancient Mariner*, and is acknowledged by the authors of *Lyrical Ballads:*

Contrast, in this respect, the effect of Macpherson's publication with the *Reliques* of Percy, so unassuming, so modest in their pretensions!—I have already stated how much Germany is indebted to this latter work; and for our own country its poetry has been absolutely redeemed by it. I do not think that there is an able writer in verse of the present day who would not be proud to acknowledge his obligations to the *Reliques;* I know that it is so with my friends; and for myself I am happy on this occasion to make a public avowal of my own [Wordsworth, 1815].

It is strange that there should be so little of *Reliques* in Chatterton. What one misses in the Rowley poems is the irregular verse of the ballads; the freest measures in the Rowley poems are borrowed from Shakespeare; the ballad called the *Bristowe Tragedie* is in Percy's second class, written with "a low or subordinate correctness sometimes bordering on the insipid," *e. g.,*

> I greeve to telle, before youre sonne
> Does fromme the welkinn flye,
> He hath upon his honour sworne,
> That thou shalt surelie die.

The real master of Chatterton is Spenser. Chatterton had a perfect command of the heroic line as it was then commonly used in couplets; he preferred the stanza, however, and almost always a stanza with an alexandrine at the end. He had learned much from *The Castle of Indolence*, but he does not remain content with the eighteenth century Spenserians; he goes back to the original. A technical variation of Chatterton's is proof of this: whereas the eighteenth century imitators of *The Faerie Queene* cut their alexandrines at the sixth syllable regularly, Chatterton is not afraid to turn over:

> Tell him I scorne to kenne hem from afar.
> Botte leave the vyrgyn brydall bedde for bedde of warre.
> *(Ælla, l.* 347.)
> And cries *a guerre* and slughornes shake the vaulted heaven.
> *(Hastings* 2, *l.* 190.)
> And like to them æternal alwaie stryve to be. *(Ibid. l.* 380.)

In following Spenser, he sometimes agrees with Milton: thus, *Elinoure and Juga* and the *Excelente Balade of Charitie* are in Milton's seven line stanza (rime royal, with the seventh line an alexandrine), thus:

> *Juga:*　Systers in sorrowe, on thys daise-ey'd banke,
> Where melancholych broods, we wyll lamente;
> Be wette wythe mornynge dewe and evene darke;
> Lyche levynde okes in eche the odher bente,
> Or lyche forlettenn halles of merriemente
> Whose gastlie mitches holde the traine of fryghte
> Where lethale ravens bark, and owlets wake the nyghte.
>
> *Elinoare:*　No moe the miskynette shall wake the morne
> The minstrelle daunce, good cheere, and morryce plaie;
> No moe the amblynge palfrie and the horne
> Shall from the lessel rouze the foxe awaic;
> I 'll seke the foreste all the lyve-longe daie;
> All nete amonge the gravde chyrche glebe wyll goe,
> And to the passante Spryghtes lecture mie tale of woe.

In the *Songe to Ælla*, again there are measures from Milton's *Ode:*

> Orr whare thou kennst fromm farre
> The dysmall crye of warre,
> Orr seest some mountayne made of corse of sleyne.

The poems attributed to Thomas Rowley are Elizabethan, where they are not later, in style; the spelling is freely imitated from the worst fifteenth century practice; the vocabulary is taken largely from Speght's glossary to Chaucer, from Kersey's *Dictionarium Anglo-Britannicum* (1708) and Bailey's *Universal Etymological Dictionary* (1737). Chatterton does not seem to have cared much for Chaucer except as an authority for old words; he studied the glossary, not the text, and does not imitate Chaucer's phrasing. His poetry and his medieval tastes are distinct; his poetry is not medieval, and his medieval fictions (like those of Scott, to a great extent) are derived from admiration of the life and manners, from architecture and heraldry, from the church of St. Mary Redcliffe, from the black-letter Bible in which he learned to read, and from the appearance of the old parchments which his father took from Canynge's coffer in the neglected muniment room of the church. His grandfather and great-grandfather had been

sextons there, and the church was the ancestral home of his
imagination, "the pride of Brystowe and the Westerne lande."
The child made an imaginary Bristol of the fifteenth century,
with personages who were seen moving about in it and distinctly known to him; the childhood of Sordello in Browning's
poem is the same sort of life as Chatterton's.   As he grew out
of childhood and became a poet with a mastery of verse, he
still kept up his fictitious world; his phantom company was not
dispersed by his new poetical knowledge and skill, but was
employed by him to utter his new poetry, although this was
almost wholly at variance with the assumed age and habit of
Thomas Rowley and his acquaintances.   The Rowley poems
are not an imitation of fifteenth century English verse; they
are new poetry of the eighteenth century, keeping wisely, but
not tamely, to the poetical conventions of the time, the tradition of heroic verse—with excursions, like those of Blake, into
the poetry of Shakespeare's songs, and one remarkable experiment (noted by Watts-Dunton) in the rhythm of *Christabel*,
with likeness to Scott and Byron:

> Then each did don in seemlie gear,
> What armour eche beseem'd to wear,
> And on each sheelde devices shone
> Of wounded hearts and battles won,
> All curious and nice echon;
> With many a tassild spear.

But this, *The Unknown Knight* (which is not in the early editions of the Rowley poems), is an accident.   Chatterton had
here for a moment hit on one kind of verse which was destined
to live in the next generation; but neither in the principal
Rowley poems nor in those avowedly his own does he show any
sense of what he had found or any wish to use again this new
invention.

Thomas Chatterton was born in November, 1752, and put
to school at Colston's hospital when he was nine; in 1765, he
was apprenticed to a Bristol attorney.   In April, 1770, his
master released him, and he came to London to try his fortune
as an author and journalist.   He had been a contributor to
magazines for some time before he left home, and possessed
very great readiness in different kinds of popular writing.   He

got five guineas for a short comic opera, *The Revenge* (humours of Olympus), and seems to have wanted nothing but time to establish a good practice as a literary man.   He does not seem to have made any mistake in judging his own talents; he could do efficiently the sort of work which he professed.   But he had come to a point of bad luck, and his pride and ambition would not allow him to get over the difficulty by begging or sponging; so he killed himself (24 August, 1770).

The nature of his impostures is now fairly well ascertained. They began in his childhood as pure invention and imaginary life; they turned to schoolboy practical joking (the solemn bookish schoolboy who pretends to a knowledge of magic or Hebrew is a well-known character); then, later, came more elaborate jokes, to impose upon editors—*Saxon Atchievements* is irresistible—and, then, the attempt to take in Horace Walpole with *The Ryse of Peyncteyning in Englande writen by T. Rowleie* 1469 *for Mastre Canynge*, a fraud very properly refused by Walpole.   The Rowley poems were written with all those motives mixed; but of fraud there was clearly less in them than in the document for the history of painting, because the poems are good value, whatever their history may be, whereas the document is only meant to deceive and is otherwise not specially amusing.

Chatterton was slightly influenced by Macpherson, and seems to have decided that the Caledonians were not to have all the profits of heroic melancholy to themselves.   He provided translations of Saxon poems:

The loud winds whistled through the sacred grove of Thor; far over the plains of Denania were the cries of the spirits heard.   The howl of Hubba's horrid voice swelled upon every blast, and the shrill shriek of the fair Locabara shot through the midnight sky.

There is some likeness between Macpherson and Chatterton in their acknowledged works: Macpherson, in his poems *The Hunter* and *The Highlander*, has great fluency with the heroic verse, and in prose of different sorts he was a capable writer. The difference is that Chatterton was a poet, with every variety of music, seemingly, at his command, and with a mind that could project itself in a hundred different ways—a true shaping mind.   Nothing in Chatterton's life is more wonderful than his impersonality; he does not make poetry out of his pains or sorrows, and, when he is composing verse, he seems to have escaped from himself. His dealing with common romantic scenery and sentiment is shown in the quotation above from *Elinoure and Juga;* he makes a poetical use of melancholy motives, himself untouched, or, at any rate, undeluded.

The Wartons were devoted to the Middle Ages through their appreciation of Gothic architecture. It began with Thomas Warton the elder, who let his sons Joseph and Thomas understand what he himself admired in Windsor and Winchester. But, as with Chatterton, and even with Scott, an admiration of the Middle Ages need not lead to a study of medieval philology, though it did so in the case of Thomas the younger. In literature, a taste for the Middle Ages generally meant, first of all, a taste for Spenser, for Elizabethans—old poetry, but not too old. Thomas Warton the father was made professor of poetry at Oxford in 1718, and deserved it for his praise of the neglected early poems of Milton. It was indirectly from Warton that Pope got his knowledge of *Comus* and *Il Penseroso.* Warton's own poems, published by his son Thomas in 1748, contain some rather amazing borrowings from Milton's volume of 1645; his paraphrase of Temple's quotation from Olaus Wormius has been already mentioned. The younger Thomas had his father's tastes and proved this in his work on Spenser, his edition of Milton's *Poems upon several occasions* and his projected history of Gothic architecture, as well as in his history of English poetry. His life, well written by Richard Mant, is a perfect example of the easy-going university man, such as is also well represented in the famous miscellany which Warton himself edited, *The Oxford Sausage.* Warton was a tutor of Trinity, distinguished even at that time for neglect of his pupils and for a love of ale, tobacco, low company and of going to see a man hanged. His works are numerous;[1] his poems in a collected edition were published in 1791, the year after his death. He was professor of poetry 1757 to 1767, Camden professor of history from 1785 and poet laureate in the same year. His appointment was celebrated by the *Probationary Odes* attached to *The Rolliad.*

[1] See bibliography.

The advertisement to Warton's *Poems* (1791) remarks that the author was "of the school of Spenser and Milton, rather than that of Pope." The old English poetry which he studied and described in his history had not much direct influence on his own compositions; the effect of his medieval researches was not to make him an imitator of the Middle Ages, but to give him a wider range in modern poetry. Study of the Middle Ages implied freedom from many common literary prejudices, and, with Warton, as with Gray and Chatterton and others, the freedom of poetry and of poetical study was the chief thing; metrical romances, Chaucer and Gower, Lydgate and Gawain Douglas, led, usually, not to a revival of medieval forms, but to a quickening of interest in Spenser and Milton. Nor was the school of Pope renounced or dishonoured in consequence of Warton's "Gothic" taste; he uses the regular couplet to describe his medieval studies:

> Long have I loved to catch the simple chime
> Of minstrel-harps, and spell the fabling rime;
> To view the festive rites, the knightly play,
> That deck'd heroic Albion's elder day;
> To mark the mouldering halls of barons bold,
> And the rough castle, cast in giant mould;
> With Gothic manners Gothic arts explore
> And muse on the magnificence of yore.[1]

Thomas Warton's freedom of admiration does not make him disrespectful to the ordinary canons of literary taste; he does not go so far as his brother Joseph. He is a believer in the dignity of general terms, which was disparaged by his brother; this is a fair test of conservative literary opinion in the eighteenth century.

The *History of English Poetry* (in three volumes, 1774, 1778, 1781) was severely criticised; not only, as by Ritson, for inaccuracy, but, even more severely, for incoherence. Scott is merciless on this head:

As for the late laureate, it is well known that he never could follow a clue of any kind. With a head abounding in multifarious lore, and a mind unquestionably imbued with true poetic fire, he wielded that most fatal of all implements to its possessor, a pen so

[1] *Verses on Sir Joshua Reynolds's painted window at New College, Oxford:* 1782.

scaturient and unretentive, that we think he must have been often astonished not only at the extent of his lucubrations, but at their total and absolute want of connection with the subject he had assigned to himself.[1]

This does not make allowance enough, either for the difficulties of Warton's explorations or for the various purposes of literary history. Warton certainly had no gift for historical construction. But the art of Gibbon is not required for every history, and the history of literature can spare a coherent plan, so long as the historian provides such plenty of samples as Warton always gives. Obviously, in literature, the separate facts may be interesting and intelligible, while the bare facts of political history can but rarely be such. The relation of book to book is not like the relation of one battle to another in the same war, or of one political act to the other events of a king's reign. In literary history, desultory reading and writing need not be senseless or useless; and Warton's work has and retains an interest and value which will outlast many ingenious writings of critics more thoroughly disciplined. Further, his biographer Mant has ground for his opinion (contrary to Scott's) that Warton

can trace the progress of the mind, not merely as exemplified in the confined exertions of an individual, but in a succession of ages, and in the pursuits and acquirements of a people.

There is more reasoning and more coherence in Warton's history than Scott allows.

Joseph Warton did not care for the Middle Ages as his brother did, but he saw more clearly than Thomas how great a poet Dante was; "perhaps the Inferno of Dante is the next composition to the Iliad, in point of originality and sublimity."[2] The footnote here ("Milton was particularly fond of this writer" etc.) shows, by its phrasing, how little known Dante was at that time to the English reading public. Though Joseph Warton was not a medievalist like Thomas, he had that appreciation of Spenser and Milton which was the chief sign and accompaniment of medieval studies in England. His

[1] See Scott's art. on Todd's *Spenser*, in *The Edinburgh Review*, 1805.
[2] *Essay on Pope*, sect. v.

judgment of Pope and of modern poetry agrees with the opinion expressed by Hurd in his *Letters on Chivalry and Romance* (1762: six years after the first part of Joseph Warton's *Essay*, eight years after Thomas Warton on *The Faerie Queene*).

> What we have gotten by this revolution, you will say, is a great deal of good sense. What we have lost, is a world of fine fabling; the illusion of which is so grateful to the *Charmed Spirit* that in spite of philosophy and fashion *Faery* Spenser still ranks highest among the Poets; I mean with all those who are either come of that house, or have any kindness for it.

Hurd's *Letters* are the best explanation of the critical view which saw the value of romance—"the Gothic fables of chivalry"—without any particular knowledge of old French or much curiosity about any poetry older than Ariosto. Not medieval poetry, but medieval customs and sentiments, were interesting; and so Hurd and many others who were tired of the poetry of good sense looked on Ariosto, Tasso and Spenser as the true poets of the medieval heroic age. It should be observed that the age of "good sense" was not slow to appreciate "the fairy way of writing"— the phrase is Dryden's, and Addison made it a text for one of his essays on Imagination.

At the same time as Thomas Warton, another Oxford man, Tyrwhitt of Merton, was working at old English poetry. He edited the *Rowley* poems. His *Essay on the Language and Versification of Chaucer* and his *Introductory Discourse to the Canterbury Tales* ("printed before Mr. Warton's book was published") are the complement of Warton's work. Warton is not very careful about prosody; his observations on the stanza of *The Faerie Queene* are dull and inaccurate. Tyrwhitt was interested in the history of verse, as Gray had been, and, from his grammatical knowledge and critical sense, he made out the rule of Chaucer's heroic verse which had escaped notice for nearly 400 years. No other piece of medieval scholarship in England can be compared with Tyrwhitt's in importance. Chaucer was popularly known, but known as an old barbarous author with plenty of good sense and no art of language. The pieces of Chaucer printed at the end of Dryden's *Fables* show what doggerel passed for Chaucer's verse, even with the finest judges, before Tyrwhitt found out the proper music of the line, mainly by getting the value of the *e* mute, partly by attending to the change of accent.

Tyrwhitt is the restorer of Chaucer. Though the genius of Dryden had discovered the classical spirit of Chaucer's imagination, the form of his poetry remained obscure and defaced till Tyrwhitt explained the rule of his heroic line and brought out the beauty of it. The art of the grammarian has seldom been better justified and there are few things in English philology more notable than Tyrwhitt's edition of Chaucer.

## CHAPTER XI

# Letter-Writers

I

HORACE WALPOLE is generally acknowledged as "the prince of letter-writers," and he is certainly entitled to this high literary rank in consideration of the extent and supreme value of his correspondence. Byron styled Walpole's letters "incomparable," and all who know them must agree in this high praise. English literature is particularly rich in the number and excellence of its letter-writers; but no other of the class has dealt with so great a variety of subjects as Walpole. His letters were, indeed, the chief work of his life.

As the beauty of the art largely depends on the spontaneity of the writers in the expression of their natural feelings, it would be futile to attempt to decide the relative merits of the great letter-writers in order to award the palm to the foremost or greatest of the class. We should be grateful for the treasures bequeathed to us and refrain from appraising their respective deserts. To weigh the golden words of such gracious spirits as Gray, Cowper or Charles Lamb, in order to decide which of them possesses the highest value, seems a labour unworthy of them all. Sincerity is the primary claim upon our respect and esteem for great writers of letters; and the lack of this rules out the letters of Pope from the place in literature to which they would otherwise be entitled. Now, in spite of the cruel criticism of Macaulay, we have no hesitation in claiming sincerity as a characteristic of Walpole's letters.

Walpole lives now and always will live in public esteem as a great letter-writer; but he was also himself a distinguished figure during his lifetime. Thus, his name attained to a fame which, in later years, has been considerably dimmed, partly by the instability which reflects itself in his writings, and, also, by the virulent censure to which he has been subjected by some critics of distinction. Macaulay's complete indictment of Horace Walpole as a man has left him with scarcely a rag of character. The charges brought against him are, however, so wholesale that the condemnation may be said to carry with it its own antidote; for it is not a mere caricature, but one almost entirely opposed to truth. To many of these unjust charges, any candid review of Walpole's career in its many aspects, exhibiting him as a man of quality, a brilliant wit, both in conversation and in writing, an author of considerable mark, a connoisseur of distinction and a generous and ready friend, will form a sufficient answer. A fuller reply, however, is required to those accusations which touch his honour and social conduct through life. Macaulay speaks of Walpole's "faults of head and heart," of his "unhealthy and disorganised mind," of his disguise from the world "by mask upon mask," adding that "whatever was little seemed great to him, and whatever was great seemed to him little." Now, Walpole placed himself so often at his reader's mercy, and, occasionally, was so perverse in his actions as to make it necessary for those who admire his character to show that, though he had many transparent faults, his life was guided by honourable principles, and that, though not willing to stand forth as a censor of mankind, he could clearly distinguish between the great and little things of life and, when a duty was clear to him, had strength to follow the call. His affectation no one would wish to deny; but, although this is an objectionable quality, it can scarcely be treated as criminal. In fact, Walpole began life with youthful enthusiasm and with an eager love of friends, but soon adopted a shield of fine-gentlemanly pretence, in order to protect his own feelings.

Horatio Walpole was born at the house of his father (Sir Robert Walpole) in Arlington street, on 24 September, 1717. After two years of study with a tutor, he went to Eton in April, 1727, where he remained until the spring of 1735, when he entered at King's college, Cambridge. He had many fast Etonian friends, and we hear of two small circles—"the triumvirate," consisting of George and Charles Montagu and

Walpole, and "the quadruple alliance," namely, Gray, West, Ashton and Walpole.[1] He left the university in 1739, and, on 10 March, set off on the grand tour with Gray, of which some account has already been given in this volume.[2] Of the quarrel between them, Walpole took the whole blame upon himself; but, probably, Gray was also at fault. Both kept silence as to the cause, and the only authentic particulars are to be found in Walpole's letter[3] to Mason, who was then writing the life of Gray—a letter which does the greatest credit to Walpole's heart. The friendship was renewed after three years and continued through life; but it was not what it had been at first, though Walpole's appreciation of the genius of Gray was always of the strongest and of the most enthusiastic character.

After Gray left Walpole at Reggio, the latter passed through a serious illness. His life was probably saved by the prompt action of Joseph Spence (who was travelling with Lord Lincoln) in summoning a famous Italian physician who, with the aid of Spence's own attentive nursing, brought the illness to a successful end. Walpole, when convalescent, continued his journey with Lord Lincoln and Spence; but, having been elected member of parliament for Callington in Cornwall at the general election, he left his companions and landed at Dover, 12 September, 1741. He changed his seat several times, but continued in parliament until 1768, when he retired from the representation of Lynn. He was observant of his duties, and a regular attendant at long sittings, his descriptions of which are of great interest. On 23 March, 1742, he spoke for the first time in the House, against the motion for the appointment of a secret committee on his father. According to his own account, his speech "was published in the Magazines, but was entirely false, and had not one paragraph of my real speech in it." On 11 January, 1751, he moved the address to the king at the opening of the session; but the most remarkable incident in his parliamentary career was his quarrel, in 1747, with the redoubtable speaker Onslow. More to his credit were his strenuous endeavours to save the life of the unfortunate admiral Byng.

[1] Cf. Chap. VI, p. 131, *ante*.          [2] Cf. *ibid.*, pp. 133–134.
[3] 2 March, 1773.

The turning-point of his life was the acquisition of Strawberry hill. The building of the house, the planning of the gardens and the collection of his miscellaneous artistic curiosities soon became of absorbing interest to Walpole. Much might be said of him as a connoisseur; his taste has been strongly condemned; but, although he often made much of what was not of great importance, he gradually collected works of enduring value, and the dispersion of his property in 1842 came to be regarded as a historical event.[1] Judge Hardinge was just when he wrote: "In his taste for architecture and vertu there were both whims and foppery, but still with fancy and genius."[2] The opening of the private press in 1757, the *Officina Arbuteana* or the *Elzevirianum*, as he called it, also, gave Walpole, with much additional work, a great deal of pleasure. He was enabled to print his light verses and present them to his distinguished visitors, and could make preparations for the printing of his projected works. Conway called his cousin "Elzevir Horace." Walpole was very proud to be able to begin the work of his press by printing two unpublished odes by Gray.[3]

Walpole's head was so full of Strawberry hill, and he mentioned it so frequently in his letters, that he sent a particular description to Mann (12 June, 1753) with a drawing by Richard Bentley, "for it is uncomfortable in so intimate a correspondence as ours not to be exactly master of every spot where one another is writing, reading or sauntering." He frequently produced guides to the "Castle"; but the fullest and final one is the *Description of the Villa* printed in 1784, and illustrated by

[1] The contents of Strawberry hill realised £33,450. 11s. 9d., and would be valued now at many times that amount.

[2] Nichols's *Literary Anecdotes*, vol. VIII, p. 525.

[3] They were published by Dodsley, out of whose hands the MS. was "snatched" by Walpole, in the presence of Gray. Several works of interest were printed at the press, such as Hentzner's *Journey into England* (a charming little book), *Mémoires de Grammont*, *The Life of Lord Herbert of Cherbury*, etc., and several of Walpole's own works. A bibliography of the Strawberry hill books is given by Austin Dobson as an appendix to his *Horace Walpole, a Memoir*. The output of the press was highly satisfactory, considering that the whole staff consisted of a man and a boy. In a letter to Sir David Dalrymple (23 February, 1764), Walpole makes some peevish remarks about his press: "The plague I have had in every shape with my own printers, engravers, the booksellers, etc., besides my own trouble, have almost discouraged me from what I took up at first as an amusement, but which has produced very little of it."

many interesting plates. Walpole was very generous in allowing visitors to see his house; but these visitors were often very inconsiderate, and broke the rules he made. He wrote to George Montagu (3 September, 1763):

My house is full of people and has been so from the instant I breakfasted, and more are coming—in short I keep an inn: the sign "The Gothic Castle." Since my gallery was finished I have not been in it a quarter of an hour together; my whole time is passed in giving tickets for seeing it and hiding myself while it is seen.

In December, 1791, Horace Walpole succeeded his nephew as earl of Orford. The prodigality, and then the madness, of the third earl forced his uncle to take upon himself the duties of a man of business, in order to keep the estate from dissolution. He had to undertake the management of the family estate, because there was no one else inclined to act. When he had put things into a better state, the earl's sudden return to sanity threw everything into confusion again, as he was surrounded by a gang of sharpers. Horace Walpole developed unexpected business qualities, and, according to his own account, was able to reduce the mismanaged estate to order and solvency.

In April, 1777, the nephew went mad again; and, on his recovery, in 1778, the uncle gave up the care of him. He was subjected to continual anxiety during the remainder of his nephew's life; but he did not again take charge of the estate. When he himself came into the property, there was little left to manage. The picture gallery at Houghton, which Horace greatly loved, was sold to the empress Catharine II of Russia; and, before Lord Orford died, in December, 1791, he had become practically bankrupt. Horace Walpole had thus to take up an earldom which had fallen on evil days. He was not likely, in his old age, to accept with pleasure a title whose credit he could not hope to retrieve. He refused to enter the House of Lords; but, however much he might wish to do so, he could not relieve himself of the title.[1] He died on 2 March, 1797, at the

---

[1] There is some misapprehension as to this. Within a few days of the death of his nephew, Walpole subscribed a letter to the duke of Bedford—"The Uncle of the late Earl of Orford"; but he did not refuse to sign himself "Orford," although Pinkerton printed in *Walpoliana* a letter dated 26 December, 1791, signed "Hor. Walpole"—but this was an answer to a letter of congratulation from Pinkerton himself on the succession, the advantages of which Walpole denied.

house in Berkeley square to which he had moved from Arlington street.

A rapid glance through Walpole's correspondence will soon reveal to us the secret of his life, which explains much for which he has been condemned. The moving principle of his conduct through life was love for, and pride in, his father. It is well, therefore, to insist upon the serious purpose of much of Horace's career, and to call to mind how signally his outlook upon affairs was influenced by the proceedings of his family. He was proud of its antiquity and of its history from the conquest downwards; but he knew that no man of mark had emerged from it until his father came to do honour to his race; so, with that father, the pride of his son began and ended. Sir Robert Walpole's enemies were his son's, and those of the family who disgraced their name were obnoxious to him in consequence. In a time of great laxity, Margaret, countess of Orford, wife of the second earl, became specially notorious, and the disgracefulness of her conduct was a constant source of disgust to him. His elder brother Robert, the second earl, was little of a friend, and mention has already been made of the misconduct of his nephew George, the third earl (who succeeded to the title in 1751 and held it for forty years).

The public came slowly into possession of Walpole's great literary bequest. A series of *Miscellaneous Letters* was published in 1778 as the fifth volume of the collected edition of his *Works*. In 1818, *Letters to George Montagu* followed, and, in subsequent years, other series appeared.[1] The first collected edition of *Private Correspondence* was published in 1820, and a fuller edition in 1840. But the reading world had to wait until 1857 for a fairly complete edition of the letters arranged in chronological order. This, edited in nine volumes by Peter Cunningham with valuable notes, held its own as the standard edition, until Mrs. Paget Toynbee's largely augmented edition appeared. The supply of Walpole's letters seems to be well-nigh inexhaustible, and a still fuller collection will, probably, appear in its turn.

We have here a body of important material which forms both an autobiography and a full history of sixty years of the eighteenth century. Although the letters contain Walpole's

[1] See bibliography.

opinions on events as they occurred day by day, he communicated them to his different correspondents from varied points of view. It is a remarkable fact, which proves the orderly and constructive character of the writer's mind, that the entire collection of the letters, ranging over a very long period, forms a well connected whole, with all the appearance of having been systematically planned.

The first letter we possess is to "My dearest Charles" (C. Lyttelton), and was written when Walpole was fifteen years of age (7 August, 1732). In it he says:

> I can reflect with great joy on the moments we passed together at Eton, and long to talk 'em over, as I think we could recollect a thousand passages which were something above the common rate of schoolboy's diversions.

In the last known letter from his hand,[1] written to the countess of Upper Ossory, to protest against her showing his "idle notes" to others, Walpole refers to his fourscore nephews and nieces of various ages, who are brought to him about once a year to stare at him "as the Methusalem of the family." He wants no laurels:

> I shall be quite content with a sprig of rosemary thrown after me, when the parson of the parish commits my dust to dust. Till then pray Madam accept the resignation of your ancient servant, Orford.

The same spirit runs through the entire correspondence. It constantly displays his affectionate feelings towards his friends and the lightness with which he is able to touch on his own misfortunes. Throughout his life, he was troubled by "invalidity"; yet he could repudiate any claim to patience, and ask Mann (8 January, 1786)

> if people of easy fortunes cannot bear illness with temper what are the poor to do, who have none of our alleviations? The affluent, I fear, do not consider what a benefit ticket has fallen to their lot, out of millions not so fortunate; yet less do they reflect that chance, not merit, drew the prize out of the wheel.

[1] 16 January, 1797.

He suffered from gout throughout his life; but he always made light of the affliction. He told Mason (Christmas day, 1779) that he had had a relapse, though a slight one, and "called it only a codicil to my gout. Mr. Gibbon said, 'Very well; but I fancy it is not in consequence of your *will*.'" There was no mistake about the reality of his attacks; for chalk-stones were continually breaking out from his fingers, and he told Lady Ossory that, if he could not wait upon her, he hoped she would have the charity "to come and visit the chalk-pits in Berkeley Square."

Walpole studied letter-writing as an art and understood its distinctive features. There is no violent change in his style from beginning to end of his correspondence; but a gradual growth may be observed in his artistic treatment of his matter. He could criticise other letter-writers with judgment and good taste; but there was one, above all, who was only to be worshipped, and that was Madame de Sévigné. He tells Richard Bentley[1] that

My Lady Hervey has made me most happy by bringing me from Paris an admirable copy of the very portrait [of Mme. de Sévigné] that was Madame de Simiane's [her granddaughter]. I am going to build an altar for it, under the title of *Notre Dame des Rochers!*

Walpole addresses the same Lady Hervey from Paris (8 October, 1765) to the effect that he had called upon Madame Chabot.

She was not at home, but the Hotel de Carnavalet was; and I stopped on purpose to say an *Ave Maria* before it. It is a very singular building, not at all in the French style, and looks like an *ex voto* raised to her honour by some of her votaries [Mme. de Sévigné's]. I don't think her honoured half enough in her own country.[2]

[1] 24 December, 1754.
[2] This interesting old house is now well known as the home of the Carnavalet museum. Eleven years after this, Madame Du Deffand hoaxed Walpole by sending him a snuffbox with a portrait of Mme. de Sévigné copied from one he greatly admired. This was sent with a letter signed "Rabutin de Sévigné" and beginning thus: "*Je connois votre folle passion pour moi; votre enthousiasme pour mes lettres, votre vénération pour les lieus que j'ai habités.*" In acknowledging the gift from judge Hardinge of four drawings of the *château* de Grignan, in a letter dated 4 July, 1779, Walpole wrote: "I own that Grignan is grander, and in a much finer situation than I had imagined; as I concluded the witchery of Madame de Sévigné's ideas and style had spread the same leaf-gold over places with which she gilded her friends." (See Nichols's *Literary Anecdotes*, vol. VIII, p. 526.)

Mrs. Toynbee's edition contains a total of three thousand and sixty-one letters, addressed by Walpole to one hundred and sixty correspondents, many of them men and women of mark. The number of letters to some of these personages are very few, but among them are seven, to each of whom over one hundred letters were written by him. Sir Horace Mann heads the list with 820, then comes the countess of Upper Ossory with 400. The other five have smaller numbers, as George Montagu 263, William Mason 217, William Cole 180, Henry Conway 179 and Mary Berry 159. The lifelong correspondence with Mann exhibits a unique instance of friendship, maintained without personal intercourse for forty-five years. Walpole might well say to his friend (4 December, 1785), "You and I have long out-friendshipped Orestes and Pylades."

Mann was an early friend of Walpole, and his appointment in 1737 as assistant to Charles Fane (afterwards second viscount Fane), envoy extraordinary at the court of Florence, by Sir Robert Walpole, was entirely owing to this intimacy. In 1740, Mann became Fane's successor, and Walpole visited him at Florence in the same year. After returning to England in September, 1741, Walpole never saw his friend again. Mann never left Italy, although, in 1755, he succeeded his elder brother in the possession of the family estate at Linton, Kent. His chief duties were to look after the two "pretenders" and to entertain distinguished English travellers in Italy. He was kept informed by Walpole of all that was going on in England, and he returned the favour by writing continuously in reply, though, it must be said, giving Walpole lead in return for his gold.[1] It should, however, not be overlooked, that, when writing to Mann and other friends abroad, Walpole always feared the opening of his letters at the post office. He complains to the earl of Hertford:[2]

As my letters are seldom proper for the post now I begin them at any time, and am forced to trust to chance for a conveyance. This difficulty renders my news very stale.

[1] Peter Cunningham described Mann's letters as "utterly unreadable." A selection of them was published by Doran in 1876, under the irritating title *Mann and Manners at the Court of Florence.*

[2] 3 August, 1764.

Walpole, writing to Lady Ossory,[1] praised women as far better letter-writers than men. When he wrote "I could lay down as an infallible truth in the words of my god-father, *Pennis non homini datis*, the English of which is, 'It was not given to *man* to write letters,'" it is just possible that it occurred to him how the dictum might apply to his friend Mann. Some of Walpole's best letters were addressed to his frequent correspondent Lady Ossory. Mary Berry would have stood higher in the numerical list; but Walpole did not become intimate with her and her father and sister until late in his life (in the winter of 1788). Madame Du Deffand's letters to Walpole were first printed by Miss Berry and afterwards reprinted in Paris.[2] A complete edition of these letters, edited by the late Mrs. Toynbee, was published in 1912. Walpole's letters to Madame Du Deffand were burnt at his particular request. It is supposed that he did not wish them to be published, lest his French should be criticised. He wrote to Mason:[3] "Mme. Du Deffand has told me that I speak French worse than any Englishman she knows." A little too much has been made of Walpole's gallicisms, although there certainly is a remarkable one in the preface to *Historic Doubts on Richard III:*

It is almost a question whether if the dead of past ages could revive, they would be able to *reconnoitre*[4] the events of their own times as transmitted to us.

Thomas Pitt, first Lord Camelford (nephew of the great Chatham), writing to judge Hardinge in 1789, refers to the translation of Walpole's *Essay on Gardening* by the duc de Nivernais:

I shall be glad to see the work of M. de Nivernois, if it answers at all to the specimens you have sent me. The truth is that, as Mr. Horace Walpole always thinks in French he ought never to write in English; and I dare be sworn Nivernois' translation will appear the more original work of the two.[5]

Did Hannah More venture to "chaff" Walpole when she sent him anonymously a clever letter dated "Alamode Castle,

[1] Christmas day, 1773.
[2] See bibliography.                    [3] 5 July, 1773.
[4] This use of the word "reconnoitre" in English was quite obsolete in Walpole's day.
[5] Nichols's *Literary Illustrations*, vol. VII, p. 118.

June 20, 1840" and headed it "A Specimen of the English language, as it will be written and spoken in the next century. In
a letter from a lady to her friend in the reign of George V"?
Walpole acknowledged this letter (5 April, 1785) with cordiality
and much praise, to show that "his withers were unwrung."
Walpole expressed to Lady Ossory (Christmas day, 1781) his
opinion that "Letters ought to be nothing but extempore
conversation upon paper," and, doubtless, his conversation was
much like his letters, and as excellent. His wit was ready and
brilliant in both forms of communication. He was himself
proud of the witty apophthegm which he seems to have first
imparted to Mann by word of mouth:

Recollect what I have said to you, that this world is a comedy
to those who think, a tragedy to those who feel. This is the quint-
essence of all I have learnt in fifty years![1]

At any rate, the saying has found its way into books of familiar
quotations.

Numerous instances might be given of the value of the
letters in illustration of history; but, in spite of the popular
notion as to the frivolity of a large part of their contents, it may
safely be said that matters of moment are dealt with throughout the series, and sidelights are to be found on every page.
There is, first, the Jacobite rising of 1745. Then, we have the
trials of the Jacobites, and, for a time, there is peace, broken by
the excitement of Wilkes's publication of *The North Briton* and
subsequent riots. Walpole was attacked in no. 2 of *The North
Briton;* and Wilkes was annoyed that he did not seem to mind
the attack. In a letter to Mann,[2] Walpole laments the state
of the nation, and, after giving instances of the grievous increase of gambling, he writes, "We are not a great age, but
surely we are tending to some great revolution." The American war was the next great event to supply Walpole with
material for invective and complaints of bad government. At
the end of his life came the great convulsion of the French
revolution and, in September, 1789, he congratulated Hannah
More on the demolition of the Bastille, the reform of which he
related fourteen years before.[3] The enormities of the revo-

[1] 5 March, 1772.          [2] 2 February, 1770.          [3] 25 October, 1775.

lutionaries changed his political views, as they did those of
the majority of Englishmen, and he welcomed with enthusiasm Burke's *Reflections*. He said that it painted the
queen "exactly as she appeared to me the first time I saw her
when Dauphiness."[1]

Many of Walpole's anecdotes are valuable as illustrations of
the manners of the time and contain information not to be
found elsewhere; but the chief interest of his correspondence
remains autobiographical. The first hundred pages of Mrs.
Toynbee's edition contain letters, from 1732 to 1741, to Charles
Lyttelton, Gray, West, George Montagu, Thomas Ashton and
Henry Conway, for the most part written during Walpole's
travels. The first letter to Mann was written on 11 September,
1741. From this time, the complete autobiography may be
said to begin, and it continues to the end. Walpole wrote an
interesting advertisement prefixed to the *Letters to Mann*,
explaining his reasons for preserving them, which is too long to
quote here, but will be found in a note to the first letter. For
the incidents of his early life we must search elsewhere, and he
has left us the main particulars in the *Short Notes of My Life*.

Walpole's character may be easily understood by any one
who studies his correspondence. In early life, he was not very
different from a large number of the highbred men of the
eighteenth century who took pride in their social position, for
it is necessary to remember that there were two classes of men
in the English society of this age—the jovial and the coarse, and
the reserved and refined. Sir Robert Walpole belonged to the
former, and his son Horace to the latter. Horace was never very
young, and his father said of himself that he was the younger
of the two. Horace adds:[2] "Indeed I think so in spite of his
forty years more." The son began life with a character for
frankness and enthusiasm; but, as he grew into the cynical man
of the world, he became colder in manner to mere acquaintances,
reserving his true self only for his bosom friends. He cultivated an extreme fastidiousness and severe refinement, which
caused him to exhibit a distaste for a robust humour that he
considered vulgar. This powerful prejudice caused him to

[1] See, also, his anecdote of Marie-Antoinette as queen, in his letter to Mary
Berry, 3 July, 1790.

[2] 22 January, 1742.

propound much absurd criticism. He could not admire Fielding because he kept "low company," and condemned the "vulgarity of his character." For the beautiful and pathetic *Voyage to Lisbon* he could find no praise, and he refers to "Fielding's Travels or rather an account of how his dropsy was treated," and how he was teased by an innkeeper's wife in the Isle of Wight.[1] He could not appreciate the genius of Richardson and refers to

> those tedious lamentations—*Clarissa*, and *Sir Charles Grandison*, which are pictures of high life as conceived by a bookseller, and romances as they would be spiritualised by a Methodist preacher.[2]

Sterne was no more fortunate in obtaining the good opinion of Walpole, who writes to Henry Zouch:

> The second and third volumes of *Tristram Shandy*, the dregs of nonsense, have universally met the contempt they deserve: genius may be exhausted;—I see that folly's invention may be so too.[3]

He could appreciate Johnson's great qualities; but he was repelled by his roughness. He said wittily:

> Johnson made the most brutal speeches to living persons, for though he was good-natured at bottom he was very ill-natured at top.

In considering Walpole's affected remarks on his own literary character, we should bear in mind the expressed opinions of so aristocratic an author as Byron, at a much later date. Walpole thought it would disgrace him to be known as a learned author, although, in his heart, he was proud of his books. He discloses his true character with a fine instinct more frequently when writing to Mann than to any other correspondent. At a quite early date, he takes Mann to task for over-estimating his abilities.

> I must answer for your brother a paragraph that he showed me in one of your letters "Mr. W.'s letters are full of wit; don't they adore them in England?" Not at all—and I don't wonder at them; for if I have any wit in my letters, which I do not at all take for granted,

[1] 27 March, 1755.　　　[2] 20 December, 1760.　　　[3] 7 March 1761.

it is ten to one I have none out of my letters. . . . Then as to adoring; you now see only my letters, and you may be sure I take care not to write you word of any of my bad qualities, which other people must see in the gross; and that may be a great hindrance to their adoration. Oh! there are a thousand other reasons I could give you, why I am not the least in fashion. I came over in an ill season: it is a million to one that nobody thinks a declining old minister's son has wit. At any time men in opposition have always most; but now it would be absurd for a courtier to have even common sense.[1]

The history of the growth of Walpole's works is fully detailed in the *Correspondence;* and, apparently, nearly all his books were written at high pressure. He particularly notes how long a time was occupied in their production. He was a dabbler in literature from his early life. He wrote, in 1742, a sermon on painting for the amusement of his father, which was afterwards published in *Ædes Walpolianæ*, and he was continually writing occasional verses, a practice in which he persevered when he possessed a private printing-press. It was not, however, until 1753 that he may be said to have begun his literary career with the writing of some clever papers in *The World*, a periodical written by men of fashion for men of fashion. His first substantive work was *A Catalogue of the Royal and Noble Authors of England*, printed at the Strawberry hill press in 1758. It is of no great value as a bibliography, but, dealing as it does with a distinctive subject, is of occasional use as well as of some interest. The next work, *Anecdotes of Painting in England*, also printed at the Strawberry hill press in 1762, is the only one of Walpole's works which has really held its position. It was reprinted several times by its author and twice re-edited. The publication originated in the purchase of Vertue's valuable collections from his widow in 1756. Walpole, ten years before, had visited Vertue with the purpose of learning something about the MSS., of the existence of which he had previously heard. Vertue's notes, which are now preserved at the British museum, are disjointed and difficult to decipher, and, therefore, it was much to Walpole's credit that he was able to produce from them a useful book, which has been constantly reprinted. Unfortunately, although a competent connoisseur, he had not sufficient knowledge to enable him to

[1] 7 January, 1742.

write a satisfactory history of painting, and his editors had not sufficient courage to correct his errors at all thoroughly, for he had a wonderful craze respecting the historical value of some old pictures which he had bought and incorrectly described in his *Anecdotes*.[1] It can hardly be doubted that the existence of Walpole's book has prevented the publication of a complete and trustworthy history of English painting.

Walpole's next works were *The Castle of Otranto* (1764–5) and *The Mysterious Mother* (1768). Byron affirmed that Walpole was "the father of the first romance and the last tragedy in our language," and he praised highly both romance and tragedy; but very few modern readers are likely to agree with him. *The Castle of Otranto* was originally published as a translation from an Italian original which appeared at Naples in 1529; but, when success was assured, it was acknowledged by its author. Of this story, which has become a sort of a classic of English literature, though few now care to read it, some account has been given in an earlier chapter.[2] *The Mysterious Mother* was printed at Strawberry hill in 1768; and, although Walpole perceived the unfitness for the stage of a tragedy with so repulsive a subject, he seems to have cherished a lingering hope of its production there, as he wrote an epilogue to it for Mrs. Clive to speak. In reading the play we see that the slowness of the action was of itself sufficient to exclude it from performance; for, even an eighteenth century audience could not be expected to sit out four acts of the ravings of a woman the cause of whose remorse and agony is not disclosed until the end of the fifth act. Fanny Burney, being on friendly terms with Walpole, was anxious to read the play; but, after reading it, she "felt a sort of indignant aversion rise" in her mind "against the wilful author of a story so horrible; all the entertainment and pleasure I had received from Mr. Walpole seemed extinguished." Fanny's friend Mr. Turbulent (Guiffardière) said: "Mr. Walpole has chosen a plan of which nothing can equal the abomination but the absurdity."

*Historic Doubts on the Life and Reign of Richard III*, written about the same time as *The Mysterious Mother*, offers a good

---

[1] Cf., for instance, his self-delusion as to his "suit of the house of Lancaster," long since corrected by Sir George Scharf.

[2] See Chap. III, pp. 67–68, *ante*.

example of Walpole's literary work. He chose an interesting subject and treated it with spirit. He was not, however, prepared to undertake the necessary research, and thus laid himself open to much severe criticism.[1] As two of his chief opponents were Milles, president, and Masters, a fellow, of the Society of Antiquaries, he resigned his fellowship of the society and swore hostility to most antiquaries, although a few, such as Cole and Gough, retained his favour. He never forgave his critics; but he had succumbed to their censures after a short fight.

Walpole's own feelings respecting his literary productions were very mixed. He wrote to Lady Ossory (15 September, 1787):

I have several reasons for lamenting daily that I ever was author or editor. . . . Were I to recommence my life, and thought as I do now I do not believe that any consideration could induce me to be an author. . . . It is pride not humility, that is the source of my present sentiments. I have a great contempt for middling authors. We have not only betrayed want of genius but want of judgment.

These confessions have been treated as untrue, and as an affected condemnation of his writings. But this is unjust. He valued them as containing his own opinions, well expressed, on subjects which required elucidation; but he knew that they were not sound enough to bear learned criticism—and he quite sincerely repudiated his possession of special learning.

From Horace Walpole's we pass to some other names of renown in the form of literature in which he excelled.

Philip, fourth earl of Chesterfield, was one of the foremost English statesmen of his age; but he was so unlike an ordinary Englishman that his character has been much misunderstood by his countrymen. He thoroughly appreciated the French, and was appreciated by them in return. Sainte-Beuve considers him to have united the good qualities of the two nations, and he describes the *Letters to his Son* as a rich book, which, in spite of some objectionable passages, contains not a page without some happy observation worthy of being kept in remembrance. In any case, Chesterfield must be considered a unique personality. He was particularly unfortunate in his relations

[1] Cf. as to this essay Chap. XII, *post*.

with Johnson, who was certainly not fair to him; and the cruel caricature in *Barnaby Rudge* of him as Sir John Chester, described "an elegant and polite, but heartless and unprincipled gentleman," must have seriously injured his fame among many of those unacquainted with history. He was not unprincipled or heartless, and selfishness was by no means a marked feature of his character. His shining mental qualities were universally acknowledged, and he was accepted as a shrewd man of the world, with engaging manners; but we can learn something more than this about him from his letters.

Of Chesterfield's abilities as a statesman, his country did not obtain the full benefit, largely in consequence of court intrigues; for, though the ablest statesman of his time, after Walpole (if Pitt be left out), he was persistently set aside. His time came when he was appointed lord lieutenant of Ireland in 1745. He held office for less than a year, but proved his power of governing in a dangerous time, by the measures which he took to prevent disturbances. He gained the gratitude of the people, and the memory of his rule during a critical period remained fresh for more than a century. He retained his interest in Ireland, and always considered the Irish as his countrymen, because he had ruled over them. He withdrew from public life, partly on account of ill health; and, in 1752, his deafness had become very serious. In 1757, he emerged from his retirement in order to effect a reconciliation between the duke of Newcastle and Pitt.

Chesterfield has the reputation of eloquence; but his was not unstudied. Horace Walpole denied that Chesterfield was an orator, because his speeches were written; yet, in a letter to Mann (15 December, 1743), he declared that "the finest oration [he] ever did hear" was one from Chesterfield—and this was delivered against Sir Robert Walpole. Chesterfield's wit, like his speeches, was, to a certain extent, prepared; but it was the kind of wit which is the most agreeable form of wisdom.

Although he had many enemies, he had a genius for friendship. His greatest friend was Richard, second earl of Scarborough, whose character he drew—a man held in so high a general esteem that Chesterfield declares:

He was the best man I ever knew, the dearest friend I ever had.

. . . We lived in intimate and unreserved friendship for twenty years, and to that I owe much more than my pride will let my gratitude own.

On Scarborough's melancholy death, Chesterfield wrote to his *protégé* Dr. Chenevix:[1] "We have both lost a good friend in Scarborough; nobody can replace him to me; I wish I could replace him to you; but as things stand I see no great hopes of it." Chesterfield appointed Chenevix to the first Irish bishop-ric in his gift (Killaloe) and, shortly afterwards, translated him to Waterford. He retained the bishop as a lifelong friend, and in the printed correspondence there are many bright letters to him which are full of kindly feeling, and to which he sub-scribed himself "with the greatest truth and affection." An-other lifelong friend was the diplomatist Solomon Dayrolles, a godson of Chesterfield, whose letters to him are of an intimate character and full of the most natural feelings, expressed in an altogether charming manner. The name of Dayrolles will always be associated with that of Chesterfield, because of the dying statesman's considerate order, "Give Dayrolles a chair." Many other interesting letters are to be found in the corre-spondence, such as those to the Dublin bookseller, alderman Faulkener, whose friendship Chesterfield secured when in Ireland and retained through life; and Lady Suffolk, a much esteemed friend. This general correspondence is extremely interesting and the letters it contains are models of what letters should be—natural, kindly and witty.

But Chesterfield's fame as a letter-writer must rest on his *Letters to his Son* and those *to his Godson*. His devotion to these two young men is a very remarkable indication of his true character. From 1737 (when his age was forty-three years) to the year of his death, it became little less than an obsession. He began writing letters of advice to his illegitimate son Philip Stanhope when the child was only five years old. When he had reached twenty-five, another Philip Stanhope (of Mans-field Woodhouse) was born. This was Chesterfield's godson and successor, whose education he undertook, and to whom he began to write educational letters when he was four years old. He, doubtless, was led to undertake these letters by the re-

[1] 13 Feburary, 1740.

collection of the neglect he had experienced from his own father, and his sense of its consequences.

When sitting in judgment on Chesterfield's letters to his son, we should not omit to remember that they were never intended for any eye but that of the receiver. He wrote (21 January, 1751):

> You and I must now write to each other as friends and without the least reserve; there will for the future be a thousand things in my letters which I would not have any mortal living but yourself see or know.

The *Letters* are written in English, Latin and French, and contain a large amount of valuable information on history, geography, and so forth, put in an easy and convenient form for the pupil. Philip Stanhope was censured for bad writing and bad spelling and for inattention. His father told him that nothing was too small for attentive consideration and that concentrated attention on one subject at a time was of paramount importance: "There is time enough for everything in the course of the day if you do one thing at once, but there is not time enough in the year if you will do two things at once."

Honour and morality, the need of which is strongly urged in the *Letters*, do not include sexual morality: the writer recommends his son to seek intimate association with married women of fashion, in order to improve his manners, which, by nature, were somewhat boorish. The general principles of good breeding continually urged in the *Letters* have been strangely misunderstood. The object of life is to be pleased, and, in order to attain this, we must please others; but it is quite evident that more than surface pleasing is here intended. Both respect for the feelings of others and sympathy with them are enjoined. The young man is told "never to be ashamed of doing what is right," but to use his own judgment instead of blindly following others in what the fashionable world considers to be pleasure. Such is a sample of Chesterfield's wise saws, many of which have become familiar quotations, and which show his recollection of his own bitterly repented mistakes in early life. When Philip Stanhope went out into the world and his early education was completed, his father continued to send him letters of advice; but, in 1768, the young man died, and the father learned that he had been married and had two sons. Chesterfield received this unexpected news with composure, and wrote kindly to the widow, Eugenia Stanhope, saying that he would undertake all the expenses connected with the bringing up of her boys. He did not remove them from her care, but took much interest in them, and became attached to them, observing their different characters and advising as to them.

Chesterfield's literary fame rests upon his *Letters to his Son*, which were never intended for publication; but, it has been augmented by his *Letters to his Godson*, which, also, were not intended to see the light of publicity. Fourteen of the letters on the art of pleasing, or, as the writer entitled them, "The Duty, Utility and Means of Pleasing," were first published in in 1774 in four numbers of *The Edinburgh Magazine and Review*. In 1776, they were added to a Dublin edition of *Letters to his Son*, and were incorrectly described as written to the son —instead of to the godson. In 1778, they were reproduced as a supplement to Maty's *Memoirs of Lord Chesterfield*. The complete series of Chesterfield's *Letters to his Godson* was not printed until 1890, when it was edited by the fourth earl of Carnarvon. Lord Carnarvon, by means of the charming *Life* which he prefixed to the *Letters*, placed Chesterfield's good name on a more substantial basis than that upon which it had hitherto rested.

These *Letters* follow very much the plan of their predecessors. They are sometimes in English, and more often in French. They contain the same form of instruction and anecdote, are written with the same mixture of wit and wisdom, and breathe the same affectionate interest of the writer in the doings of his correspondent. One of the letters may be specially mentioned, since it inculcates the spirit of two commandments, on which, according to the highest authority, "hang all the law and the prophets." Chesterfield writes:

I must from time to time remind you of two much more important dutys, which I hope you will never forget nor neglect. I mean your duty to God and your duty to Man. . . . Your duty to Man is very short and clear, it is only to do to him whatever you would be willing that he should do to you. And remember in all business of your life to ask your conscience this question *Should I be willing that this should be done to me?*   If your conscience which will always tell you truth answer No, do not do that thing.

Chesterfield took immense pains to show his two pupils how to live; and it evidently gave him great pleasure to watch over them, and to express to each of them his satisfaction in their progress.   He must, however, have suffered disappointment when he found that, in point of manners, neither of them did justice to his intentions.   His son, we learn from others, was "loutish," and Fanny Burney says of his godson that "with much share of humour, and of good humour also, [he] has as little good breeding as any man I ever met with."

Fanny Burney bore two surnames in succession; but her maiden name is that by which all true lovers know her, because it was when she had no right to any but this that she wrote and gained her fame.   She may be Madame d'Arblay on certain formal occasions; but the author of *Evelina* is far too English for a foreign name to sit easy upon her.[1]   The pictures of important events and the intimate records of Fanny's distinguished friends in her diaries and letters place these writings on a very high plane, entitling them to rank as reproductions of eighteenth century life not very far below the volumes of Walpole and Boswell.   She relates all she saw and did with so much spirit and vivacity, filling in the blanks of other writers, that the reading of the various incidents is an inexhaustible pleasure. It may, indeed, be said that she discloses the inner life of three different worlds.   In her *Early Diary* (1768–78), edited by Mrs. Ellis (1889), the doings of her family are fully displayed, and the professional world of Dr. Burney ("that clever dog," as Johnson called him) is brightly sketched; Garrick, too, is constantly gliding over the scene and playing the fool in his inimitable way.   But the most popular character of all is the eccentric "daddy" Crisp—Samuel Crisp, the recluse of Chessington hall near Epsom—who was the special friend and correspondent of his "Fannikin."   In the later *Diary and Letters* (1778–1840), edited by Mrs. Charlotte Barrett (1842–6), there is more about the larger literary and political world, including the great event of the Hastings trial.   The full and particular account of court

[1] As to Fanny Burney as a novelist, see Chap. III, pp. 70 ff. *ante*.

life is of the greatest interest and value. On 6 July, 1786, Fanny Burney was appointed second keeper of the robes to queen Charlotte, a position she held for five years. She received much kindness from the king and queen, who were fond of her; and, although, by reason of the rigid etiquette, the service was hard, she had much pleasant intercourse with her companions in the palace, whose portraits she painted with spirit. Her great and incessant trouble, however, was her inevitable long and close association with the terrible Mrs. Schwellenberg, otherwise *Cerbera*. In course of time, the confinement which Fanny had to undergo affected her health, and her friends cried out for her release, even Walpole uttering complaints. Windham threatened to set "The Club" on Dr. Burney to induce him to obtain her freedom, and Boswell threatened to interfere—much to Fanny's annoyance, for she did not love the "memorandummer" as she called him. Eventually, arrangements were made, and she finally left court in July, 1791, the queen granting out of her own privy purse a pension or retiring allowance.

A most interesting feature of these diaries and letters is the introduction of clear-cut portraits of the people whom the writer knew and met. Johnson alluded to her powers in this respect when he addressed her as ' You little character-monger"; and, here, her early novel writing stood her in good stead. The description of Boswell's persecution of her at Windsor, while pressing unsuccessfully for the use of Johnson's letters, and reading to her, at the gates of the castle which she would not let him enter, bits from the forthcoming *Life*, is a fine bit of high comedy. Among Fanny Burney's later friends were the Lockes, owners of Norbury park, above the vale of Mickleham. On her frequent visits to her hospitable friends, she became intimate with the French *émigrés* at Juniper hall; and, on 31 July, 1793 she was married to one of them—d'Arblay—at Mickleham church. The pair had but little upon which to set up house; but Locke gave them a site, and the handsome subscription of generous friends for the novel *Camilla* produced sufficient funds for building a cottage, which was named Camilla Lacey. The marriage was a happy one in spite of lack of means; but, in 1801, d'Arblay determined to return to France, and his wife followed him. The restoration of Louis XVIII brought better times, but, in July, 1815, general d'Arblay met with an accident and was placed on the retired list of the French army. Austin Dobson describes him as one of the most delightful figures in his wife's *Diary*. On 3 May, 1818, he died at Bath. This sad event virtually closes the work, and, although Madame d'Arblay lived until 1840, there are few letters left after her husband's death.

Mrs. Elizabeth Montagu was one of a bright company of brilliant women;[1] and, in spite of rivals, she reigned supreme for fifty years as the chosen hostess of the intellectual society of London. Mrs. Vesey, for a time, was a prominent rival, because, as wife of Agmondesham Vesey, a member of "The Club," she came forward as the special hostess of that select company. The fame of Mrs. Montagu has much waned, and, probably, her letters, published by her nephew Matthew Montagu in 1809–13, are little read now. This collection does not reach a date later than 1761; of the remainder of the correspondence from that date to the end of Mrs. Montagu's life, consisting, for the most part, of letters to Mrs. Robinson and a few other friends, Doran made a selection, which he printed with remarks of his own in biographical form, in 1873, under the title *A Lady of the last Century (Mrs. Elizabeth Montagu) illustrated in her unpublished Letters*. Although this lady was surrounded by the intellect of her time (she informed Garrick that she never invited idiots to her house), she did not succeed in emulating Fanny Burney in the portraiture of her friends. Windham praised her letters highly, but more for their style than for the particular interest of the subjects discussed. "The flow of her style," he writes, "is not less natural, because it is fully charged with shining particles, and sparkles as it flows." Her correspondent during fifty years was Lady Margaret Harley, daughter of the second earl of Oxford and wife of the second duke of Portland, who was also a lifelong friend of Mrs. Delany.

Elizabeth Robinson was the elder daughter of Matthew Robinson, a Yorkshire squire, and her early education was advanced by the instruction of Dr. Conyers Middleton, the

[1] For a general account of the Blue Stockings, see Vol. IX. The word first occurs in Mrs. Montagu's correspondence, in 1757.

second husband of her maternal grandmother, who lived at Cambridge. Her father, also, was fond of encouraging her to make smart repartees to his witty and caustic remarks, until he was beaten in these encounters and had to discontinue them. She became rather a formidable young lady and from her volatile disposition she acquired the sobriquet "Fidget." She married, in 1742, Edward Montagu, a grandson of the first earl of Sandwich, a quiet man who was contented that his wife should rule in her own drawing-room. Doran describes him as "a mathematician of great eminence and a coal-owner of great wealth." The match appears to have been a happy one, although the tastes of the two parties were very different.

Mrs. Montagu was fond of society, and the pleasures of the town had a great attraction for her; but she was also a great reader and somewhat of a student, so she was often glad to exchange the gaieties of London for the quiet pleasures of the country. She formed a sort of salon at her house in Hill street and gathered a brilliant company round her. Johnson was glad to be one of her honoured guests; but his feelings towards her seem to have been mixed. He acknowledged that she was "a very extraordinary woman," adding "she has a constant stream of conversation, and it is always impregnated, it has always meaning." At other times, he said some disagreeable things of her and to her. Something in her talk seems to have annoyed him—possibly her sharp repartees may not have pleased the dogmatic doctor. Lyttelton, Burke, Wilberforce and Reynolds were also among her favourite guests. Mrs. Montagu's husband died in 1775 and left all his property to his wife; but, though Horace Walpole at once jumped to the conclusion that she would marry again, she preferred to adopt a nephew, who succeeded to her possessions. She continued to be a hostess and built herself a mansion on the north-west corner of Portman square; but the glory had, to a great extent, departed, and the large parties that could be accommodated in the new house were dull compared with the smaller gatherings in Hill street. In her later letters, she gives much information respecting the management of her large estates, in which she proved herself a good economist. Her *Essay on the Writings and Genius of Shakespeare* with *Remarks upon the Misrepre-*

*sentations of Mons. De Voltaire* (1769) has been noticed elsewhere.[1]

David Garrick[2] was a brilliant and agreeable letter-writer, and, even when angry with those correspondents who worried him exceedingly, he continued to be bright and lively in his replies. His letters give an admirable idea of his mercurial disposition, and it has been said that he was never second in the keenest encounter of wits. The two quarto volumes of his correspondence, published by James Boaden in 1831–2, are of great value and interest, consisting of letters from many distinguished persons, and his answers to them. The miscellaneous letters were collected by Garrick himself, and copies of his own letters added to them. It has been suggested that he may have had the intention of using them as the groundwork of an autobiography; at any rate, he must have considered it important to keep the originals of his various controversies for his own justification. The correspondence is now preserved, together with family letters (not printed by Boaden) and some others, in the Forster collection at the Victoria and Albert museum. They form thirty-five bound volumes and are of considerable value. Boaden, however, arranged the letters carelessly, without putting his materials in a satisfactory chronological order or providing a much-needed index; but he added a good life of the actor, largely founded upon the materials printed by him. An improved, and more convenient, edition containing a fairly complete collection of Garrick's letters, while condensing those of his correspondents, would be a valuable addition to our literature. As it is, however, Boaden's collection shows how important a figure Garrick filled in the intellectual world of the eighteenth century.

The list of his correspondents contains the names of most of the distinguished men of his time, such as Lords Camden, Chatham and Lyttelton, Johnson, Burke, Reynolds, Goldsmith, Boswell, Burney, Hogarth, Hume, Sheridan and Steevens. Burke, who entertained the highest opinion of Garrick, was one of his best friends. He addressed him as "My dear David," "My dear Garrick" and sometimes "My dearest Garrick," and

---

[1] See *ante*, Vol. V, p. 326 and cf. Vol. XI.

[2] For Garrick as an actor, manager and dramatist, see Chap. IV, pp. 95–96, *ante.*

concluded his letters in terms of affection. Johnson and Garrick, notwithstanding their early relations, never got further than "Dear sir," and ended their letters in formal style. Mrs. Montagu was a frequent correspondent and the writer of some of the best letters in the collection. On one occasion, she is found entreating Garrick, on behalf of her friend Mrs. Vesey, to obtain the election of that lady's husband Agmondesham Vesey, into the select circle of "The Club." The bulk of the correspondence relates to theatrical affairs, as to which Garrick was in constant trouble, by reason of his strenuous attention to his duties as manager. The actors are constantly complaining, and the actresses, who were jealous of him and of each other, sometimes almost drove him mad. Mrs. Cibber, Mrs. Yates, Mrs. Abington and Mrs. Clive—all gave trouble in various ways; but Garrick's feelings were essentially different as to the last two ladies in the list. Mrs. Abington permanently annoyed him. He added to a letter, written by her in 1776: "The above is a true copy of the letter, examined word by word, of that worst of bad women Mrs. Abington, to ask my playing for her benefit, and why?" On the other hand, Kitty Clive and he were always quarrelling and making it up, since they thoroughly esteemed each other. In 1765, Kitty wrote an angry letter: "Sir, I beg you would do me the favour to let me know if it was by your order that my money was stopped last Saturday." In 1776, she wrote a letter which Garrick endorsed "My Pivy—excellent." It was not only the actors and actresses who annoyed Garrick—the playwrights were equally, if not more, troublesome. There is a long series of letters between Murphy and Garrick, which shows that they were continually at war with one another. The latter part of the second volume of Boaden's work is full of interesting letters from Frenchmen and Frenchwomen of distinction, proving how highly Garrick's genius was appreciated in France. Diderot, Marmontel, Mme. Necker, Fréron, Mlle. Clairon and Le Kain were among his correspondents.

The letters of Garrick do not throw much light upon his training for the stage. He seems to have been born an actor, with all the qualities of a first-rate comedian, while his achievements as a tragedian were the result of his genius and the powers of his imagination. He was of no school, and he had no master.

He was well educated and possessed a singular charm of manner; but he obtained his great position by incessant study, persistent practice and wide observation. Burke described him as one of the deepest observers of man. Well might Quin say that, if Garrick was right, he and his school were all wrong! He liked to astonish spectators by his sudden change from the all-inspiring tragedian to the laughter-forcing comedian. His Lear and his Abel Drugger were equally amazing. It was the freshness, the brightness and life of his style that made the instant acceptance of him as the greatest of living actors secure. At thirty, he was joint lessee of Drury lane theatre. In 1776, he retired from the stage and sold his moiety of the theatre to Sheridan, Linley and Ford. He kept up his interest in the stage; but he had little time to enjoy his well earned rest, and died in 1779, universally regretted. Burke wrote an epitaph, which unfortunately was rejected in favour of a foolish inscription by Pratt, for the monument in Westminster abbey. It was in a passage of the former that Garrick was said to have "raised the character of his profession to the rank of a liberal art."

It may not seem inappropriate to add in his place a few words concerning the series of *Discourses* delivered by Sir Joshua Reynolds, from 1769 to 1790, to the students of the Royal Academy. These *Discourses* have become a classic of our language, because they are justly regarded as a model of art criticism, devoted as they are to essentials and written in a style of great beauty and distinction, and exhibiting in every page Reynolds's love and knowledge of his art, as well as the literary powers of his mind. The advice of a master grounded on his own knowledge and practice must always possess a real value, and Reynolds is severe in his condemnation of the futility of much art criticism by amateurs.

"There are," he writes, "many writers on our Art, who not being of the profession and consequently not knowing what can or what cannot be done, have been very liberal of absurd praises in their descriptions of favourite works. They *always* find in them what they are resolved to find." And, again: "It has been the fate of *Arts* to be enveloped in mysterious and incomprehensible language, as if it was thought necessary that even the terms should correspond to the idea entertained of the instability and uncertainty of the rules which they expressed."

In urging the duty of industry and perseverance, he has been supposed to imply a doubt as to the existence of genius; but, when he affirms that the supposed genius must use the same hard means of obtaining success as are imposed upon others, a deeper scepticism than was really his need not be imputed to him. It was a false idea of genius which he desired to correct.

Genius is supposed to be a power of producing excellences which are out of the reach of the rules of art: a power which no precepts can teach, and which no industry can acquire.

In another place he says:

"The industry which I principally recommended is not the industry of the hands, but of the mind." Further, when advocating the duty of clear expression: "If in order to be intelligible, I appear to degrade art by bringing her down from the visionary situation in the clouds, it is only to give her a solid mansion upon the earth."

The first *Discourse* was delivered at the opening of the Royal Academy and deals with the advantages to be expected from the institution of that body. The ninth *Discourse* is, again, general, and was delivered on the removal of the Royal Academy from Pall Mall to Somerset place. The fifteenth and last contains the president's farewell to the students and members of the Royal Academy and a review of the scope of the *Discourses*, ending with an eulogium on Michel Angelo:

I reflect not without vanity that these Discourses bear testimony of my admiration of that truly divine man; and I should desire that the last words which I should pronounce in this Academy, and from this place, might be the name of MICHEL ANGELO.

Burke, who was in the president's chair, then descended from the rostrum, taking the lecturer's hand, and said, in Milton's words:

> The Angel ended, and in Adam's ear
> So charming left his voice, that he awhile
> Thought him still speaking, still stood fix'd to hear.[1]

[1] *Paradise Lost*, bk VIII, vv. 1–3.

The incident illustrates the deep interest taken by Burke in his friend's *Discourses;* and it has been suggested that he had much to do with their composition. But they so evidently contain Reynolds's own individual views, and the thoughts are expressed so naturally and clearly, that such an idea must be put aside as absurd. Reynolds was a highly cultured man, and, doubtless, he gained much in clearness of literary insight by his intimate association with such men as Johnson and Burke; but a careful study of the *Discourses* would prove to most readers that the language as well as the thoughts were Reynolds's own. He was, however, not the man to reject suggested improvement in style from his distinguished friends, and, doubtless, both Johnson and Burke proposed some verbal improvements in the proofs.

The general reception of the work was extremely favourable; and that it was appreciated abroad is evidenced by the empress Catharine of Russia's present to Reynolds of a gold snuff-box, adorned with her portrait in relief, set in diamonds, as an expression of her appreciation of the *Discourses*.

The plan of the *Discourses*, carried on through many years, is consistent throughout. The writer did not interfere with the teaching of the professors; but it was his aim to deal with the general principles underlying the art. He started by pointing out the dangers of facility, as there is no short path to excellence. When the pupil's genius has received its utmost improvement, rules may, possibly, be dispensed with; but the author adds: "Let us not destroy the scaffold until we have raised the building." In claiming the right to teach, he modestly says that his hints are in a great degree founded on his own mistakes.

The earlier half of the series dealt with the objects of study, the leading principles to be kept in view and the four general ideas which regulate every branch of the art—invention, expression, colouring and drapery. Much stress is laid upon the importance of imitation; but this word must be accurately defined:

Study Nature attentively but always with those masters in your company; consider them as models which you are to imitate, and at the same time as rivals with whom you are to contend.

The second half is appropriated to the consideration of more general points, such as genius and imagination. The tenth *Discourse*, on sculpture, is the least satisfactory of the series. The fourteenth *Discourse* is of special interest as relating to Gainsborough; and the particulars of the meeting of the two great painters at the death-bed of Gainsborough are charmingly related.

Although great changes have taken place in public opinion in the relative estimation of various schools of painting, most of Reynolds's remarks, dealing as they do with essentials, remain of value. The book is charming reading for all who love art, and the reader will close it with a higher appreciation of the character of the man and the remarkable insight of the great painter.

Hannah More's life was a remarkable one, and her fame as an author, at one time considerable, was kept alive until near the middle of the nineteenth century. It is at present nearly dead and is not likely to revive. But her correspondence is most undeservedly neglected, for she was a good letter-writer, and her accounts of the doings of the intellectual world are of great interest, and worthy to be read after Fanny Burney and Mrs. Thrale. We have full information respecting the doings of Johnson's circle from different points of view; but there is much fresh information in Hannah More's letters. Boswell was offended with the young lady and is often spiteful in his remarks about her. The story of the value of her flattery[1] has been made too much of, for there is plenty of evidence that Johnson highly esteemed the character of Hannah More. Sally More was a lively writer and she gives a vivid picture of her sister's intercourse with Johnson in 1775.

We drank tea at Sir Joshua's with Dr. Johnson. Hannah is certainly a great favourite. She was placed next him, and they had the entire conversation to themselves. They were both in remarkably high spirits; it was certainly her lucky night! I have never heard her say so many good things. The old genius was extremely jocular, and the young one very pleasant.

The scene had changed when Hannah More met Johnson

[1] See Boswell's *Life of Johnson*, ed. Hill, G. B., vol. III, p. 293.

at Oxford, in the year of his death, at dinner in the lodge at Pembroke. She wrote home:

Who do you think is my principal cicerone at Oxford? Only Dr. Johnson, and we do so gallant it about! You cannot imagine with what delight he showed me every part of his own college. . . . When we came into the Common room, we spied a fine large print of Johnson, framed and hung up that very morning with this motto: "And is not Johnson ours, himself a host?" Under which stared you in the face "From Miss More's *Sensibility*." This little incident amused us;—but alas! Johnson looks very ill indeed—spiritless and wan. However he made an effort to be cheerful and I exerted myself much to make him so.

The triumphant entrance into the great London world by Hannah More, a young Bristol schoolmistress, is difficult to account for except on the grounds of her remarkable abilities. An agreeable young lady of seven and twenty, fresh from the provinces, who gained at once the cordial friendship not only of Garrick, Reynolds, Johnson and Horace Walpole but of Mrs. Elizabeth Montagu and the literary ladies of the day, and who became herself one of the leaders of the Blue Stockings, must have been a woman very much out of the common. When Hannah More came first to London, she visited Reynolds, whose sister promised to introduce her to Johnson. She then met Garrick, who was first interested in her because of some intelligent criticism of his acting which he had seen. He and his wife became Hannah's dearest friends, and, on hearing of Mrs. Garrick's death, Hannah More wrote to a friend (21 October, 1822):

I spent above twenty winters under her roof, and gratefully remember not only their personal kindness, but my first introduction through them into a society remarkable for rank, literature and talents.

She kept up her correspondence with her distinguished London friends; but most of them had died before she had arrived at middle age. We then notice a considerable change in the subjects of her correspondence, and her letters are occupied with the progress of some of the great movements in which she was interested. Wilberforce was a constant correspondent, and he found her a warm helper in the anti-slavery cause. When she and her sisters gave up their school at Bristol and retired on a competence, she devoted all her time to philanthropic purposes. This is not the place for dealing with the subjects of her voluminous writings, and they are only referred to here as an indication of the more serious character of the later correspondence.[1]

Gilbert White's *Natural History and Antiquities of Selborne* (1789) holds a unique position in English literature as the solitary classic of natural history. It is not easy to give, in a few words, a reason for its remarkable success. It is, in fact, not so much a logically arranged and systematic book as an invaluable record of the life work of a simple and refined man who succeeded in picturing himself as well as what he saw. The reader is carried along by his interest in the results of far-sighted observation; but, more than this, the reader imbibes the spirit of the writer which pervades the whole book and endears it to likeminded naturalists as a valued companion.

For some twenty years or more (1767–87), White wrote a series of letters to Thomas Pennant and Daines Barrington, giving a remarkable account of the chief instances of the special habits of animals and of natural phenomena which he was daily observing. Although these correspondents asked him questions and remarked upon his observations, they learned much more from White than he from them. Pennant is severely criticised by Thomas Bell, one of the editors of White's work, who writes: "The man to whom the vain and self-seeking author of 'British Zoology' was so greatly indebted is almost entirely ignored." The late Alfred Newton, in his notice of Gilbert White in *The Dictionary of National Biography*, however, exonerates Pennant, noting that "In the preface he generally but fully acknowledges White's services." White's friendship with Barrington appears to have begun about the end of 1767, the first published letter to him being dated June, 1769. Barrington, in 1770, suggested the publication of White's observations; but, although White thought favourably of the advice, he was diffident and did not prepare his materials for press until January, 1788. Even then, there was more delay, so the book was not published until 1789.

[1] Cf., as to Hannah More, *post*, Vol. XI.

White seems to have collected largely, with the ultimate object of forming a naturalist's calendar; for, writing to Pennant on 19 July, 1771, he expresses his diffidence in respect to publishing his notes because

I ought to have begun it twenty years ago.—If I was to attempt anything, it should be somewhat of a Natural History of my native parish, an *Annus Historio-Naturalis*, comprising a journal for one whole year, and illustrated with large notes and observations.

Eventually, he did not make any considerable alteration in his letters but left all the vivid pictures in their original setting and *The Naturalist's Calendar* did not see the light until two years after his death—in 1795.

A *Quarterly* reviewer,[1] speaking of White, describes him as "a man the power of whose writings has immortalised an obscure village and a tortoise,—for who has not heard of Timothy—as long as the English language lives." The life history of Timothy may be read in White's letters, and in the amusing letter to Miss Hecky Mulso, afterwards Mrs. Chapone (31 August, 1784), written by him in the name of Timothy. The tortoise was an American, born in 1734 in the province of Virginia, who remembered the death of his great-great-grandfather in the 160th year of his age. Thomas Bell disputes the American origin and believes the animal to have belonged to a north African species, naming it *testudo marginata;* but Bennett held that it was distinct and he described and named it *T. Whitei*, after the man who had immortalised it.

Selborne may be obscure; but it is a beautiful village in a beautiful country eminently suited for the purpose of White in making it the centre of a life's work of zoological research and observation. The book was immediately popular both with the general public and with all naturalists, many of the most eminent of which class have successively edited it with additional and corroborative notes.

White's was an uneventful life as we usually understand the phrase; but it was also a full and busy one, the results of which have greatly benefited his fellow men. He was born and died at Selborne; and that delightful neighbourhood was the centre of his world. But it would be a mistake to forget that he was

[1] Vol. LXXI, no. 141, p. 8 note; art. on *The Honey-Bee*.

a man of capacity equal to the duties of a larger sphere. He
was for fifty years a fellow of Oriel college, Oxford, and, for
some of these years, dean of the college. In 1757, there was
an election for the provostship, when, although Musgrave was
chosen, White had many supporters. He quitted residence
at Oxford in the following year, with the intention of settling
permanently at Selborne. He refused several college livings
for this reason, although he held the living of Moreton
Pinckney in Northamptonshire as a non-resident incumbent.
Notwithstanding this apparent indifference to duty, he worked
successively in several curacies, the last being that of his
beloved Selborne.

## II

### THE WARWICKSHIRE COTERIE

Somewhat apart from the more famous letter-writers of
the age stood a circle of friends, some of whom might be described as in the great world while none were exactly of it, whose
correspondence, and more general literary work, are full of
interest. They were all, at one time or another, dwellers in
Warwickshire or on its borders, lived at no great distance from
each other and wrote frequently when they did not meet.
Perhaps the poet Shenstone is the most obvious link between
them: they all were acquainted with him, if they were not all
personally known to each other. The circle includes Henrietta
Lady Luxborough, of Barrels near Henley-in-Arden; Frances
duchess of Somerset, one of whose residence was Ragley near
Alcester; Richard Graves, who belonged to the family which
owned Mickleton, not actually in Warwickshire but not far
from Stratford-on-Avon; Richard Jago, who was vicar of
Harbury and held other cures in the county; William Somerville,
of Edstone near Henley; and it was completed by persons who
were not so much writers themselves as friends of men of
letters, such as Anthony Whistler (who had been at Pembroke
college, Oxford, with Graves and Shenstone), and Sanderson
Miller, antiquary and architect, the builder of the tower on
Edge-hill commemorated by Jago in his poem. Nearly all of
these wrote good letters, which were published, and most of
them at least dabbled in literature also, in light verse or easy

prose. And all were more or less in the net of the omnivorous publisher Robert Dodsley, who did a great deal to make Shenstone and the Leasowes famous.[1]

Of Somerville,[2] a scholar and a gentleman (though his writing does not always suggest it) some account has already been given in an earlier chapter:[3] his prose, in prefaces and letters, many of the latter still unpublished, is of the good, sonorous, somewhat pedantic kind which was beginning, even when he wrote, to be old-fashioned. Another country gentleman was Anthony Whistler of Whitchurch, an Eton boy, who imbibed "such a dislike to learning languages that he could not read the Classics, but no one formed a better judgment of them," and was "a young man of great delicacy of sentiment." As an undergraduate, he published anonymously, in 1736, a poem entitled *The Shuttlecock*. He died in 1754, aged forty. For many years he had corresponded with Shenstone and Graves, and, on his death, the former wrote to the latter "the triumvirate which was the greatest happiness and the greatest pride of my life is broken." Few of their letters, unfortunately, are preserved. Through Sanderson Miller, the squire of Radway at the foot of Edge-hill and the friend of all the noble builders and gardeners of the age (except Horace Walpole who rarely lost an opportunity of laughing at him), the Warwickshire coterie had links at once with the great world and with the greatest writer of the age. It was in his drawing-room that Fielding read the manuscript of *Tom Jones* to an admiring circle of ladies and gentlemen; and for an improvement which Pitt generously designed in his garden Miller happily thanked

> The Paymaster, well skilled in planting,
> Pleased to assist when cash was wanting,
> He bid my Laurels grow: they grew
> Fast as his Laurels always do.

It was no doubt as a refuge from domestic unhappiness that

---

[1] As to Robert Dodsley, see *ante*, Vol. IX, pp. 213–214 *et al.*

[2] This spelling has been continued in the present chapter for the sake of uniformity. The name was, however, always spelt *Somervile* in the autograph letters of its owner and in his works printed in his lifetime.

[3] See Chap. v, pp. 122 ff. *ante*. As to Jago, see *ibid.* pp. 125–127. As to Shenstone, see Chap. vii, pp. 168 ff., *ante*.

Lady Luxborough turned to literature and sought the friendship of lesser poets. Born about 1700, she was half-sister of Henry St. John, afterwards viscount Bolingbroke, to whom she was all her life devotedly attached.[1] In 1727, she married Robert Knight, son of the cashier of the South Sea company, whom Horace Walpole contemptuously calls a "transport." About nine years later, she was separated from her husband in consequence of some scandal which has never been verified. Horace Walpole, who disliked her and her friends, speaks of a "gallantry" in which Dalton, tutor to the son of Lady Hertford (afterwards duchess of Somerset) was concerned; but this is unlikely, for the friendship of the two ladies was unbroken, and Lady Hertford was a particularly upright and scrupulous person. Family tradition associates her rather with Somerville; but this, again, does not seem probable. Whatever the cause, Henrietta Knight was banished to Barrels in 1736, and never saw her husband (who became Lord Luxborough in 1746 and earl of Catherlough in 1763, seven years after her death) again.

At Barrels, she lived quietly, but made friends with her neighbours, and became the centre of a literary society which included Shenstone and Somerville, Graves, Jago and a number of Warwickshire clergy. She was the "Asteria" of their poems, which commemorated her love of letters, her library and her garden. Her letters to Shenstone were carefully preserved by him, and he described them as "written with abundant ease, Politeness, and Vivacity; in which she was scarce equalled by any woman of her time." She, certainly, wrote with simplicity and charm about trivial things, such as her friends' poetry and her own horticultural experiments—one of her letters contains a delightful defence of autumn; and, after the manner of ladies in society who have any knowledge of literature, she had an exaggerated appreciation of the literary achievements of her friends. Her adulation of Shenstone is so excessive that one almost begins to suspect her of a warmer feeling. The letters which he received from her between 1739 and 1756 were published by Dodsley in 1775, and three years later there appeared, under the editorship of Thomas Hull the actor, two more volumes of correspondence between them, with other

[1] Cf. *ante*, Vol. IX, p. 243 and note 2.

letters from the duchess of Somerset, Miss Dolman Shenstone's cousin), Thomas Percy (of the *Reliques*) who had himself connections with Warwickshire,[1] Dodsley, Whistler and others. They discussed public affairs sparingly, though, in later years, they were all, through the Lytteltons, much interested in Pitt; they talked a great deal about gardens, and waterfalls, statues and urns; and they cast a favourable eye upon contemporary literature, admiring Thomson (whose *Spring* was dedicated to Lady Hertford), thinking very well of Gray's *Elegy*, and being "highly entertained with the *History of Sir Charles Grandison*, which is so vastly above *Pamela* or *Clarissa*." Though the authors were students of the greater letter-writers, of Mme. de Sévigné, Pope and Lady Mary Wortley Montagu, their own interests were simple, only slightly tinged with the sentimental affectations of the shepherdesses and hermits with whom the poets played, genuinely delighting in out of door pleasures, but not averse from a good dinner and a glass of wine. They present a picture of English country life, in a literary circle, unsurpassed, if not unique, in its veracity and completeness. Hull's collection goes down to 1775, and is concluded by some rather tedious reflections from a "Miss N—" upon Venice and the residences and manners of John, third duke (and thirty-first earl) of Atholl, a benevolent personage who drowned himself in the Tay in 1774.

The *Correspondence between Frances Countess of Hertford (afterwards Duchess of Somerset) and Henrietta Louisa Countess of Pomfret*, which was not published till 1805, belongs to an earlier period, extending from 1738 to 1741. The two ladies were both of the bedchamber of queen Caroline, and it was Lady Hertford who obtained the pardon of Savage through the queen's influence. Johnson, who pays her a lofty compliment on this, is less polite towards her interests in literature, and tells us that it was her "practice to invite every summer some poet into the country, to hear her verses, and assist her studies," adding that this honour was one year conferred on Thomson, but he "took more delight in carousing with Lord Hertford and his friends than assisting her ladyship's poetical operations, and therefore never received another summons." Another poet who dedicated a volume to her was Issac Watts, and Shen-

---

[1] As to Percy, see Chap. x, *ante*.

stone's ode, *Rural Elegance*, was also, after her death, inscribed to her memory. Her correspondent Henrietta, countess of Pomfret, was granddaughter of lord chancellor Jeffreys, and her letters from France and Italy faintly recall the style of Lady Mary Wortley Montagu, with some details, not uninteresting, of life at foreign courts. Lady Hertford was a shrewd observer, and contributes opinions on the early methodists which represent the judgment of the quiet, cultivated, religious society to which, after her retirement from court, she belonged. Two smart poems in Dodsley's collection[1] refer to her supposed affection for Sir William Hamilton; and gossips made free with her name, but quite without reason. Her later years, at least, those of warm friendship with Lady Luxborough, were secluded and sad.

"After a Ball or Masquerade," she wrote, in language which well illustrates the style of these letters, "have we not come Home very well contented to pull off our Ornaments and fine Cloaths in order to go to rest? Such, methinks, is the Reception we naturally give to the Warnings of bodily Decays; they seem to undress us by Degrees, to prepare us for a Rest that will refresh us more powerfully than any Night's Sleep could do."

There is, indeed, in most of the members of this coterie, a pensive, even plaintive, tone. Jago found the country clergyman's quiet melancholy natural to him, and, if Shenstone began by being sad as night only for wantonness, his retirement at the Leasowes, in spite of the interest of his wilderness, his waterfall and his urns, and the polite appreciation of his fashionable neighbours, soon tinged his sedentary and self-indulgent life with sorrow and regret as well as with dyspepsia and fretfulness. But he could write a cheerful letter and a bright and ingenious essay to the last. His friend Graves, to whom a large number of his letters were addressed, in the *Recollection of some particulars* of his life (1788), perhaps the most interesting of his works, gives him not undeserved credit for

such a justness of thought and expression, and such a knowledge of human nature as well as of books that, if we consider how little [he] had conversed with the great world, one would think he had almost an intuitive knowledge of the characters of men.

[1] Vol. VI, pp. 230–1.

He had, indeed, all the acuteness of observation which belongs to the literary recluse, and he wrote with an entire absence of affectation and an easy grace which made his letters not unworthy to stand among the very best of those which the eighteenth century produced. Passages of pleasant fancy or humour, of description and of criticism, occur again and again in his correspondence, and, whatever may be said of his poetry, his prose style is eminently felicitous. Admirers of good writing have too long neglected him.

The same may be said of his intimate friend, Richard Graves, well known to all the Warwickshire coterie. He wrote so much that there is a natural temptation to regard him as a mere scribbler or a literary hack. Such a judgment would be most unjust. He lived to be nearly ninety, and in so many years it is no tedious achievement to have written some dozen books that are worth reading, besides a few more which, perhaps, are not. Graves was a fellow of All Souls, and there began a lifelong friendship with Blackstone. He was a poet, and a collector of poems: *Euphrosyne* and *The Festoon* bear witness. He was a translator of Marcus Aurelius and of many ancient epigrams. He was a correspondent of clever people, but better pleased to receive than to write letters and not one to copy and preserve those he had written. He was a diligent country parson (not to be confused with his nephew, sometime vicar of Great Malvern, whose boyish skill in Latin was commended by Shenstone), never away for a month at a time in all the fifty-five years he was rector of Claverton. In that delightful village, at an easy distance from Bath, by a charming country road, along which he walked almost every weekday for more than fifty years, he resided from 1749 to 1804, paying occasional visits to London, to Warwickshire and to the Leasowes. He was chaplain to the countess of Chatham, and became private tutor to several eminent persons, such as Prince Hoare and Malthus; and, at Bath, he was a popular figure, the intimate friend of "lowborn Allen" and his nephew-in-law, bishop Warburton. He had the knack of writing pleasing trivialities in the form of essays, which contained often curious information, entertaining anecdotes and sound morals. But his chief success, which should preserve his memory green, was as a novelist. He was unquestionably the most natural and effective writer of prose tales in his time, and might almost claim to be the originator of unemotional, impassionate romances of rural life and manners.

*The Spiritual Quixote* (1772), his most famous story, and the only one which, in his own time, achieved a second edition, is a tale of a young country squire who was influenced by the methodists and took a long tour of the midlands, suffering a number of mild adventures, as a follower of Whitefield. Graves had been at Pembroke, Oxford, and never quite overcame his disdain of the servitor. He makes great fun of the followers of methodism; but he always respects genuine piety. Descriptions of open air preaching and of the treatment of the preachers are frequent: he could never get rid of the conviction that, in spite of irregularities, methodism was showing the parish clergy how to do their duty. But this is only a small part of the interest of *The Spiritual Quixote:* its real attraction lies in the accounts of the social life and entertainments of the time, the ways of travellers and the customs of rustics and inn-keepers. So, again, *Columella, or the Distressed Anchoret* (1776), which, like its predecessor, has a detailed (this time faintly disguised) picture of Shenstone, records the travels of a lawyer and a college don and the placid, but not always proper, recreations of a sluggish country gentleman of small fortune and literary interest. There is a placid satisfaction in the outlook on life which represents not only the attitude of Columella's old friends but that of Graves himself. Thus, he speaks of the journey of Atticus the "solemn Head of a college," and Hortensius "the sage Counsel learned in the law":

> The consciousness of having punctually discharged every duty of their respective stations diffused an ease and chearfulness over their minds, and left them open to enjoyment, and at leisure to receive amusement from every object that presented itself in the way. The freshness of the morning, the serenity of the air, the verdure of the fields, every gentleman's seat, every farm-house, and every cottage they passed by, or every village they rode through, afforded some kind of pleasing reflections to persons of their happy disposition. . . . Thus if they overtook or were overtaken by any one on the road, even of the lowest rank, instead of passing by with a supercilious air, as if he were of a different species, they considered him in

the same light as a sportsman would a partridge or a woodcock, as one that might afford them either pleasure or instruction; and usually commenced a conversation.

This was the way in which Graves lived and wrote. Yet he was not blind, as *Columella* shows, to the seamy side of things.

More delicate than *Columella* are the two charming little volumes entitled *Eugenius or Anecdotes of the Golden Vale* (1785), which, from a description or two of scenery, suggest that the neighbourhood of the Wye was familiar to the writer and thus account, perhaps, for the reference in *The Spiritual Quixote* to Pope's "Man of Ross"—"What, old Kyrle! I knew him well; he was an honest old cock and loved his pipe and a Tankard of cider as well as the best of us."—They show, too, as do other of Graves's writings, in a touch here and there, a knowledge of the habits and sufferings of the poor almost as intimate as Crabbe's. *Plexippus or The Aspiring Plebeian*, published (anonymously as was *Columella*) in 1790, is a quiet tale of the love affairs of two young men, eminently sober and respectable, told in the pleasantest vein of Graves's quiet observation of mankind. Cheltenham, Wales and London are the scenes of the story, which is of the placid type that Graves loved. In his later years, he wrote essays and studies of character, with a few *vers de société*, all very gentle, unaffected and trivial; and he kept green, to the last, the memory of his friend Shenstone and the literary circle in which he had moved.

The venue was now changed to Bath, where everybody in the later eighteenth century (except poor Lady Luxborough, the terms of whose separation from her husband would not allow her even to go on the Bath road) came sooner or later. At Lady Miller's, of Bath Easton, the undoubted original Mrs. Leo Hunter, a company of poetasters and dilettantes met every week for some years; Graves, who was constantly present, records, with a little flutter of satisfaction, that on one occasion he met four duchesses. The results of their poetic contests were published in 1775 as *Poetical Amusements at a Villa near Bath*, increased to three volumes a year later, a sign of the popularity of this tepid form of literary dissipation. The verses themselves are often ingenious, and the "candid reader" is asked by their editor to

recollect that they were frequently the production of a few days—
most of them of as many hours; [and] that they originated amidst
the hurry of plays, balls, public breakfasts, and concerts, and all the
dissipations of a full *Bath Season*—alike unfriendly to contemplation
and the Muses.

By the time they were written, most of the earlier and much
more brilliant literary coterie to which Graves had belonged had
passed away, and he was the only survivor with any claim to be
a true man of letters. The Leasowes had received all the wit
and fashion of the earlier time, and lovers of good literature had
always been welcome at Barrels. It is, indeed, round Shenstone and Lady Luxborough, the poet and the letter-writer of
unaffected charm, that the memory of the Warwickshire
coterie lingers; but Richard Graves, who long survived them
both, won for himself a place in English letters, not lofty, but
secure, where none of his friends could excel him.

# CHAPTER XII

# Historians

## I

### HUME AND MODERN HISTORIANS

A S for good [English] historians," Voltaire wrote in 1734,
"I know of none as yet: a Frenchman [Rapin] has had
to write their history."[1] His criticism was just, and,
before him, both Addison and Bolingbroke had noted the
backwardness of English literature so far as history was concerned. Yet there was no lack of interest on the part of the
educated classes in the history of their own nation, for, during
the first half of the eighteenth century, several histories of
England appeared which, in spite of gross defects, found many
readers. Nor is this interest difficult to account for. Closely
connected with the conservatism of the national character,
it had been fostered by the conflicts through which the nation
had passed in the preceding century; for, in these conflicts,
great respect was shown for precedent; in the struggle with
Charles I, though it was temporarily subversive of ancient
institutions, the parliamentary party made constant appeals to
historic liberties, while the lawyers and judges on the king's
side found weapons in the same armoury and cited records in
support of the exercise of arbitrary authority. The process of
subversion was sharply checked, and reverence for the ancient
constitution was exhibited by the invitation to Cromwell to
assume the crown. More lately, the revolution of 1688 had been
a vindication of historic rights, conducted with a punctilious
observance of time honoured procedure. Principles involved in

[1] *Œuvres*, vol. XXIV, p. 137; see Gibbon's *Memoirs*, p. 295, ed. Hill, G. B

these conflicts still divided the nation into two opposing parties, and whigs and tories alike were eager to find such support for their opinions as might be derived from history. Whigs, for example, would turn to Oldmixon or Rapin, tories to the *History of England* by Thomas Carte, the nonjuror, which though written without literary skill, was superior, as regards the extent of the author's researches, to any English history of an earlier date than that of the appearance of his first two volumes (1747, 1750); his fourth and last volume, which goes down to 1654, was published in 1755, the year after his death; his *Life of James, Duke of Ormond* (1736), a tedious book, is of first-rate importance, especially as regards Irish history. The general interest in English history had been vastly strengthened by the appearance of Clarendon's *History*, which has been treated in a previous volume as belonging essentially to the class of contemporary memoirs, and it had been encouraged by the publication, at the expense of the state, of *Foedera et Conventiones* (1704–35), edited by Thomas Rymer and Robert Sanderson, in twenty volumes, a collection of public documents of great value for most periods of our history before the seventeenth century, the last document included in it being dated 1654. This work laid a new foundation for the writing of history on a scientific basis, from documentary authorities; its value was thoroughly appreciated by Rapin, who used it in his *History*, and, from time to time, published summaries of its contents which were translated into English under the title *Acta Regia* (1726–7).

Yet this interest did not, as has already been seen, call forth, before Hume wrote, any history of England by a native historian that is worthy to be classed as literature; indeed, it was in itself adverse to the appearance of such a work, for it caused English history to be written for party purposes, and, consequently, no effort was made to write it in a philosophic spirit, or to present it in well devised form or in worthy language; it fell into the hands of hacks or partisans. Only one Englishman of that time wrote history in a style that, of itself, makes his book valuable, and he did not write English history. Simon Ockley, vicar of Swavesey, Cambridgeshire, who had early devoted himself to the study of eastern languages and customs, was appointed professor of Arabic at Cambridge in

1711. The first volume of his *Conquest of Syria, Persia, and
Egypt by the Saracens*, generally known as *The History of the
Saracens*, appeared in 1708, the second in 1718, with an introduction dated from Cambridge gaol, where he was then imprisoned for debt: he had in past years received help from the
earl of Oxford (Harley); but that had ceased, and the poor
scholar had a large family. Gibbon, who admired and used
his work, speaks of his fate as "unworthy of the man and of
his country."[1] His *History* extends from the death of Mahomet, 632, to that of the fifth Ommiad caliph, 705; it was cut
short by the author's death in 1720, after a life of incessant and
ill-requited toil. The *Life of Mohammed* prefixed to the third
edition of his *History*, which was issued for the benefit of his
destitute daughter in 1757, is by Roger Long, master of Pembroke hall, Cambridge. Ockley based his work on an Arabic
manuscript in the Bodleian library which later scholars have
pronounced less trustworthy than he imagined it to be. His
English is pure, and simple, his narrative extraordinarily vivid
and dramatic, and told in words exactly suited to his subject—
whether he is describing how Caulah and her companions kept
their Damascene captors at bay until her brother Derar and
his horsemen came to deliver them, or telling the tragic story
of the death of Hosein. The book was translated into French
in 1748, and was long held to be authoritative. As a history,
its defects are patent, its account of the conquest of Persia, for
example, is so slight that even the decisive battle of Cadesia is
not mentioned; nor is any attempt made to examine the causes
of the rapid successes of the Saracen arms: it reads, indeed,
more like a collection of sagas than a history. Such defects,
however, do not impair its peculiar literary merit.

A change in the character of British historical writing began
in the middle of the century; it was raised by Hume to a foremost place in our prose composition; its right to that place was
maintained by Robertson, and, finally, in Gibbon's *Decline
and Fall of the Roman Empire*, it rose to the highest degree of
perfection that it has ever attained in this, or, perhaps, in any,
country. That its two earliest reformers should both have been
Scotsmen is one of many illustrations of the activity of the
Scots at that time in all the higher spheres of thought and of

[1] *Decline and Fall*, vol. VI, p. 4, note, ed. Bury, J. B.

literary production. When the failure of the Jacobite cause put an end to the struggle for Scottish national life as an independent political force, it would almost seem as though the educated class in Scotland consciously set themselves to endow their country with an independent life in the domains of philosophy, literature, science and art;[1] for their efforts were not made in isolation; they were made by men who constantly communicated with each other or consorted together, especially in Edinburgh, where, from 1754, they formed themselves into the "Select Society," of which both Hume and Robertson were members, and which met every week to discuss philosophical questions. While this intellectual life was distinctly national, its output was not marred by its local character. Political affairs had for centuries driven or led Scots abroad: the habit of resorting to other countries remained, and Scottish thinkers and writers kept in touch with the intellectual life of other peoples, and especially of the French, the ancient allies of Scotland. In their mode of expression, too, the desire to be widely read and the necessity of gaining a larger and richer market for their books than they could find at home made them careful to avoid local peculiarities, and write in such a way as would be acceptable to English readers. Though this movement attained its full development during the latter half of the century, it had been in progress for several years.

It was during those years that David Hume first became known as a philosopher and essayist; his earliest book, *A Treatise of Human Nature* (1739–40), written when he was not more than twenty-eight, met with a chilling reception which gave little promise of his future renown. His metaphysical opinions led him to put a special value on the study of history. As his scepticism limited mental capability to sensible experience, so he regarded past events as affording experience. Holding mankind to be much the same under all conditions, he considered that history, by exhibiting the behaviour of men in the past, enables us to discover the principles of human action and their results, and to order our conduct accordingly: its records are " so many collections of experiments by which the moral philosopher fixes the principles of his science," and man obtains a guide for his own conduct. Hume would therefore be

[1] Hume Brown, *History of Scotland*, vol. III, p. 371.

drawn to study history, and, believing that a knowledge of it would be of public utility by affording men experience, he would be inclined to record the experiments from which they could derive it. A three years' residence in France from 1734 to 1737, most of it spent "very agreeably" at La Flèche, on the Loir, then famous for its great Jesuits' college, probably strengthened this inclination and influenced his style. Historical study was being eagerly pursued in France. Among the religious orders, the Benedictines were preparing *Le Recueil des Historiens des Gaules et de la France*, issuing their *Gallia Christiana*, and beginning their histories of the French provinces, while the Dominicans had produced the *Scriptores* of their order, and the Jesuits were engaged on *Acta Sanctorum*. On the lay side, the *Académie des Inscriptions* was carrying on the publication of the royal ordinances, and gathering a store of historical erudition.[1] Count de Boulainvilliers had already treated French history in a philosophic spirit, and Voltaire, in his exquisite little *Histoire de Charles XII*, had shown that historical writing might be endowed with literary excellence. A strange contrast Hume must have seen in this activity and accomplishment to the condition of historical work in Great Britain. Elegance in the structure of sentences and an almost excessive purity of language, which marked contemporary French literature, were specially inculcated by the Jesuits, the masters of French education. Hume's *History* shows enough French influence to justify us in considering his long visit to La Flèche as an important factor in its character.

Some insight into the conduct of the great affairs of nations he gained as secretary to general St. Clair during his ineffectual expedition against Lorient in 1746, when Hume acted as judge advocate, and while attached to St. Clair's embassy to Vienna and Turin in 1748. By 1747, he had "historical projects." His appointment as librarian to the faculty of advocates at Edinburgh, in 1752, gave him command of a large library well stocked with historical works, and he forthwith set about his *History of England*. Intending to trace the steps by which, as he believed, the nation had attained its existing system of government, he had at first thought of beginning his work with the accession of Henry VII; for he imagined that the first

[1] Carré, H., *Histoire de France* (Lavisse), vol. VIII, ii., pp. 182-3.

signs of revolt against the arbitrary power of the crown were to be discerned during the Tudor period, and of carrying it down to the accession of George I. Finally, however, he began with the accession of James I, alleging, as his reason, that the change which took place in public affairs under the Tudor dynasty was "very insensible," and that it was "under James that the House of Commons first began to rear its head, and then the quarrel betwixt privilege and prerogative commenced."[1] The first volume of his *History of Great Britain*, containing the reigns of James I and Charles I, appeared in 1754. He was sanguine in his expectations of the success of the work; but, though for a few weeks it sold well in Edinburgh, it met with almost universal disapprobation and seemed likely to sink into premature oblivion. Its unfavourable reception was mainly due, as we shall see later, to political reasons. Hume was bitterly disappointed, and even thought of retiring to France and living there under an assumed name. His second volume, which ended with the revolution of 1688, and appeared in 1756, was less irritating to whig sensibilities: it sold well and helped the sale of the first. Then he worked backwards, and published two volumes on the Tudor reigns in 1759, ending, in 1761, with two on the history from the time of Julius Caesar to the accession of Henry VII. He did not carry out his original idea of bringing his work down to 1714. By that time, the sale of his *History* had become large, and had made him, he said, "not merely independent but opulent"; and it kept its place in popular estimation as the best comprehensive work on English history for at least sixty years. The first two published volumes were translated into French in 1760; and in Paris, where Hume resided from 1763 to 1766, during part of the time as secretary of legation, he received, both as historian and as philosopher, an amount of adulation which excited the spleen of Horace Walpole.[2]

Hume gave so little time to preparation for his task that it is evident that he had no idea of writing a scientific history. With all due allowance for the infinitely greater facilities which now exist for arriving at the truth, it cannot be contended that he took full advantage of such authorities as were then ac-

[1] Burton, J. H., *Life of Hume*, vol. I, p. 375.
[2] *Letters*, vol. VI, 301, ed. Toynbee.

cessible: he seems to have been content with those under his hand in the advocates' library; he was not critical as to their comparative value; and he was careless in his use of them. His *History*, consequently, contains many misstatements which he might have avoided—some of small importance, others of a serious kind, as they affect his conclusions. Of these, a typical instance, noticed by Hallam,[1] is, that he misstates the complaint of the Commons in 1396 that sheriffs were continued in office beyond a year, as a petition that they might be so continued, and uses this mistake in defence of the misgovernment of Richard II.

His later published volumes, on the history before the Tudor dynasty, become more and more superficial as he advances further into times which were obscure to him, in which he took no interest, regarding them as ages of barbarism, and on which he would scarcely have written save for the sake of completeness. What he set out to do was to write a history which would be generally attractive—for he appealed "*ad populum* as well as *ad clerum*"[2]—and would be distinguished from other histories alike by its style and by its freedom from political bias, a matter on which he was insistent in his correspondence. He approached his work, then, in a spirit of philosophic impartiality, or, at least, believed that he did so—a belief commonly dangerous to a historian—and, throughout its course, adorned it with judgments and reflections admirable in themselves though not always appropriate to facts as they really were. Here, his philosophical treatment ends: he shows no appreciation of the forces which underlay great political or religious movements. As a sceptic, he did not recognise the motives which led men to work for a common end, or the influences which guided them. Such movements were, to him, mere occurrences, or the results of personal temperament, of the ambition, obstinacy, or fanaticism of individuals. The advance of historical study is indebted to him; for his praiseworthy attempts at various divisions of his narrative to expound social and economic conditions were an innovation on the earlier conception of a historian's duty as limited to a record of political events.

[1] *Middle Ages*, vol. III, p. 75, ed. 1860.
[2] Hume to Clephane, Burton, vol. I, p. 397.

Hume's *History* occupies a high place among the few master-pieces of historical composition. His expression is lucid, conveying his meaning in direct and competent terms. It is eminently dignified, and is instinct with the calm atmosphere of a philosophic mind which surveys and criticises men and affairs as from an eminence. Its general tone is ironical, the tone of a man conscious of intellectual superiority to those whose faults and follies he relates. His sentences are highly polished; they are well balanced and their cadence is musical. They are never jerky, and they flow on in a seemingly inevitable sequence. Their polish does not suggest elaboration; their beauties, so easy is Hume's style, appear careless and natural. In fact, however, he made many corrections in his manuscript; he was anxious to avoid Scotticisms and, in a careful revision of the first edition of his earlier volumes, removed all he detected. Johnson, with his usual prejudice against Scotsmen, declared, he "does not write English, the structure of his sentences is French." Though this was a conversational exaggeration, it was more deliberately echoed by Lord Mansfield, and it is so far true that Hume's easy style indicates French influence, and, as Horace Walpole observed, the influence of Voltaire. The same may be said of the style of other contemporary Scottish writers, of Robertson, Adam Smith and Ferguson. While he never falls below dignity, he never rises to eloquence. The prose of his age was generally colourless, and his abhorrence of enthusiasm of every kind rendered this greyness of tone especially appropriate as a vehicle of his thoughts. Yet, though elegance rather than vigour is to be looked for in his writing, its irony gives it a force which, at the least, is as powerful as any which could be obtained by a more robust style. His excellences are not without their defects. Charmed, at first, by the polish of his sentences, the reader may, perhaps, soon find them cold, hard and monotonous; and since historical narrative will not excite sustained interest unless it appeals to the imagination and emotions as well as to the judgment, Hume's attitude of philosophic observer and dispassionate critic may become wearisome to him and, as he discovers that the philosopher is not free from prejudice, even irritating. In the composition of his *History*, Hume shows in a remarkable degree a skill which may be described as dramatic: when working up to some critical event, he selects and arranges his facts, so that each leads us a step further towards the climax that he has in view; he tells us nothing that is extraneous to his immediate purpose; there is no anticipation and no divagation in his narrative.

In spite of his belief in his own impartiality, Hume was justly accused of tory prejudice, and this caused the ill-success of his first published volume. He did not, of course, regard the royal authority as founded on divine appointment any more than on contract. As a utilitarian, he held that the end of government was the promotion of the public good, and that monarchy was based on the necessity of escape from lawless violence. While he admitted that resistance to sovereignty might be justifiable, he considered this doctrine so dangerous to society, as opening the door to popular excesses, that it should be concealed from the people unless the sovereign drove his subjects from their allegiance. This theory affected his view of the Stewart period. Ignorant of common law, as a Scotsman might well be, and of earlier English history, and inclined to scepticism, he failed to recognise the fundamental liberties of the nation. To him, they were "privileges," more or less dependent on the will and strength of the monarch; they had no common foundation in the spirit of the people, there was no general "scheme of liberty." He held that, at the accession of James I, the monarchy was regarded as absolute, and that, though Charles pushed the exercise of the prerogative too far, it was practically almost unlimited. The parliament made encroachments upon it: Charles defended his lawful position. Hume did not undervalue the liberties for which the parliamentary party contended, but he blamed them for the steps by which they asserted and secured them. His opinions were probably affected by his dislike of the puritans as much as by his erroneous theory of constitutional history: "my views of things," he wrote, "are more conformable to Whig principles, my representations of persons to Tory prejudices." His scepticism led him to sneer at a profession of religious motives. To the church of England in Charles's reign, he accorded his approval as a bulwark of order, and, possibly, because in his own day it afforded many examples of religious indifference; and, including all the sects under the common appellation of

puritans, he condemned them as "infected with a wretched
fanaticism" and as enemies to free thought and polite letters.
The extent to which his prejudices coloured his treatment of
the reign of Charles I may be illustrated by his remarks on
the penalties inflicted by the Star chamber and by his sneer
at the reverence paid to the memory of Sir John Eliot, "who
happened to die while in custody."

His second volume was not so offensive to the whigs, for he
held that limitations to the prerogative had been determined by
the rebellion, and that Charles II and James II tried to over-
ride them. In his treatment of the reign of Elizabeth, his
misconception of the constitution again came to the front and
again caused offence; for he regarded the queen's arbitrary
words and actions as proofs that it was an established rule that
the prerogative should not be questioned in parliament, and
that it was generally allowed that the monarchy was absolute.
The same theory influenced his treatment of some earlier reigns,
especially those of Henry III, Edward II and Richard II. His
contempt for the Middle Ages as a rude and turbulent period,
which he derived from, or shared with, Voltaire encouraged his
error. Quarrels between kings and their subjects might result
in diminutions of monarchical powers, but, in such barbarous
times, no system of liberty could have been established. No
one now reads Hume's *History*, though our more conscientious
and more enlightened historians might learn much from it as
regards the form in which the results of their labours should be
presented: its defects in matter, therefore, are of little consequence, while its dignity, its masterly composition and its
excellence of expression render it a literary achievement of the
highest order.

In 1759, William Robertson, a presbyterian minister of
Edinburgh, published his *History of Scotland during the Reigns
of Queen Mary and of James VI until his Accession to the Crown
of England*, in two volumes: it was received with general applause and had a large sale. Robertson was rewarded by his
appointment as principal of Edinburgh university in 1762, and
as historiographer royal. In 1769 appeared his *History of
Charles V* in three volumes, for which he received £4500, a
larger sum than had ever been paid for a historical work: it
brought him an European reputation; it was translated into

French in 1771; Voltaire declared that it made him forget his woes, and Catherine II of Russia, who sent him a gold snuff-box, that it was her constant travelling companion. His *History of America*, in two volumes, recording the voyages of discovery, conquests and settlements of the Spaniards, was published in 1771, and, in 1791, his *Disquisition concerning the Knowledge which the Ancients had of India*.

Robertson paid more attention to authorities than Hume did, but sometimes misunderstood them, besides being uncritical, and apt to be superficial. Like Hume, he comments on events in a philosophic strain; but his comments are often commonplace, and like Hume, too, he fails to appreciate the forces at work in great social or political movements. Nevertheless, he had the historic sense in a measure given to none of his contemporaries before Gibbon: he had some idea of the interdependence of events and of the unity of history as one long drama of human progress to which even checks in this direction or that contribute fresh forces. His *History of Scotland* is remarkably fair, though, here and elsewhere, he shows a strong protestant bias: his mistaken view of the character and aims of Esme Stewart, earl of Lennox, is probably connected with the earl's "firm adhesion to the protestant faith." In common with Hume, he did not satisfy the more ardent admirers of Mary, queen of Scots; and, in reply to both, William Tytler, a writer to the signet and a member of the Select Society, wrote his *Inquiry as to the Evidence* against her, in two volumes (1760), which passed through four editions and was twice translated into French. Before him, Walter Goodall, the advocates' sub-librarian, had defended her in his *Examination of the* [Casket] *Letters &c.*, in two volumes (1754), an ingenious book, proving that the French versions of the letters were translated; and so the endless dispute began.

Robertson's *Charles V* opens with a view of the "Progress of Society during the Middle Ages," which Hallam praises highly and Carlyle, in boyhood, found inspiring. His misrepresentation of the state of learning, especially among the clergy, from the eighth to the eleventh century, has been exposed by Maitland:[1] it illustrates the contempt with which he, in common with Hume, regarded the Middle Ages, his careless

[1] *Dark Ages, passim.*

use of authorities, his tendency to hasty generalisation and his religious bias. Other defects might be pointed out, but, though his review can no longer be regarded as authoritative, it is interesting and meritorious as the earliest attempt made by a British historian to present, on a large scale, a general view of history. In his work on the emperor's reign, his record of events, though insufficient and, occasionally, inaccurate, is, on the whole, more trustworthy than his estimate of their significance or of the characters and conduct of the chief actors in them. His erroneous description of the emperor's life at Yuste, as withdrawn from this world's affairs, is due to the authorities he used: in his day, access had not been allowed to the records at Simancas which have enabled later writers to give a very different account of it.

Robertson's style, in its lucidity, polish and signs of French influence, has a strong likeness to that of Hume: his sentences are well balanced, they lack Hume's ironic tone, but seem more alive than his. They are more sonorous, and often end with some word or words of weighty sound and Latin derivation, as when, speaking of the feeling of the English against queen Mary, he says, "they grasped at suspicions and probabilities as if they had been irrefragable demonstrations." Robertson's "verbiage" and use of big words, illustrated in this sentence, Johnson humorously declared to have been learnt from him.[1] Some development may be discerned in his writing: passages in his *Charles V* show that he was beginning to write history with an animation of which there is little sign in his *Scotland*, and this tendency ripened in his *America* into a faculty for rhetorical narrative finely displayed in his description of the voyage and landing of Columbus and some other passages. As history, his *America* is now of small value, for it is based on insufficient authorities, but, nevertheless, it is delightful to read. His books were, at least at first, more popular than Hume's *History:* as the work of a minister of religion, they did not alarm religious people, many of whom regarded all that Hume wrote as likely to be dangerous: his style was more attractive to simple folk, and they were impressed by the evidences of his learning in directions wholly beyond their knowledge. Hume's friendship with his younger rival,[2] and the cordial admiration

[1] Boswell, *Life*, vol. III, p. 173.   [2] Burton, *Life*, vol. II, *passim*.

which Gibbon expressed for both of them,[1] are among the pleasing incidents in our literary history.

The works of Hume and Robertson seem to have excited other Scotsmen to write history. "I believe," Hume wrote in 1770, "this is the true historical age and this the historical nation: I know no less than eight Histories on the stocks in this country."[2] The letter which begins with these words refers especially to a *History of England* by Robert Henry, an Edinburgh minister, in six volumes, of which the first appeared in 1771, and which ends with the death of Henry VIII. It is arranged under various headings, as political and military affairs, religion, commerce, and so forth; and its interest lies in the assertion, already, though not so strongly, made in Hume's *History*, that history is concerned with all sides of social life in the past. It is mainly written from second-hand authorities and is inordinately dull. Nevertheless, its comprehensiveness made it popular: it brought its author £3300 and a crown pension of £100 and was translated into French.

The character of the historical work of Sir David Dalrymple or Lord Hailes, the title he took as a Scottish judge (1766), was determined by professional instinct. He edited two small volumes of documents belonging respectively to the reigns of James I and Charles I, and compiled *Annals of Scotland from the Accession of Malcolm III to the Accession of the House of Stewart*, in two volumes (1776, 1779). This book contains an accurate and bare record of events, impartially stated, supported by references to authorities, and illustrated in footnotes and appendixes. Hailes, though one of the Select Society, was more closely connected with Johnson than with his fellow members. Johnson read the proofs of the *Annals* and praised its "stability of dates" and its "punctuality of citation," though it had not "that painted form which is the taste of the age" —a hit at Robertson—but also aptly described it as a "*Dictionary*" containing "mere dry particulars." Hailes's attack on Gibbon is noticed in the next chapter.[3]

Another Dalrymple, Sir John, of Cranstoun, a baronet, and, later, a judge, who was also a member of the Select Society,

---

[1] Gibbon, *Memoirs*, p. 122, ed. Hill, G. B.; Dugald Stewart, *Life of Robertson*, p. 367.

[2] Letters to Strahan, pp. 155 ff.              [3] See Chap. XIII, *post*

and had written an essay on feudal property, produced his *Memoirs of Great Britain and Ireland* from 1684 to 1692, in two parts (1771–8), beginning with a review of affairs from 1660. The appendixes to his chapters contain a mass of previously unpublished political correspondence of first-rate importance on which he based his work. His first volume caused much stir for it revealed the extent to which English politics, in the reign of Charles II, had been influenced by French intrigues, and disgusted the whigs by exhibiting Sidney's acceptance of money from Barillon. Dalrymple wrote in a pompous strain, and Johnson ridiculed his "foppery" and "bouncing style."[1] He continued his work, in a new edition (1790), to the capture of the French and Spanish fleets at Vigo.

Another history, which may have been "on the stocks" in Scotland in 1770, is Robert Watson's *History of the Reign of Philip II*, published in two volumes in 1777, the year of its author's promotion as principal of St. Salvator's college, St. Andrews. It contains a full and careful account of the revolt of the Netherlands, derived from van Meteren, Bentivoglio and Grotius, but its comparatively scanty notices of other Spanish affairs and of the foreign policy of Philip II are unsatisfactory.[2] Watson's style is similar, though inferior to Robertson's: his sentences are generally well balanced, but some are less skilfully constructed; he is verbose, and, though his narrative shows a perception of the things which appeal to the emotions, it lacks emotional expression. Horace Walpole greatly admired his book,[3] which passed through several editions and was translated into French, German and Dutch. At the time of his death in 1781, Watson was engaged on a *History of Philip III*, which was completed by William Thomson, a prolific Scottish writer.

Incursions into the field of history were made by two English authors of the governing class. Walpole's *Historic Doubts on the Life and Reign of Richard III* (1768) is an attempt to show that Richard was probably innocent of the crimes imputed to him by Lancastrian writers. Sir George Buck,[4]

---

[1] Boswell, *Life*, vol. II, pp. 210, 237; vol. V, p. 403.

[2] Forneron, H., *Histoire de Philippe II* (1881), vol. I, p. 392, says that, with Gregorio Leti, Watson contributed most to substitute legend for fact in the history of Philip II.

[3] *Letters*, vol. X, p. 224.

[4] Cf. *ante*, Vol. VII, p. 499.

Carte and William Guthrie, whose *History of England* to 1688 in four volumes (1744–51) was little read and is of no importance, had, in different degrees, anticipated him; but Walpole was the first to argue the case with skill. He got it up well, his points are clearly put, and his pleading is witty and readable. The question has been revived and adequately discussed in our own day. Some of the accusations which Walpole criticises are no longer maintained by competent historians, but Walpole could not (nor can any one) show sufficient cause for doubting that Richard had part, at least, in the murder of Henry VI, that he put Hastings to death without a trial and that he murdered his nephews. Walpole was much pleased with his own book and bitterly resented adverse criticism from Hume[1] and others.[2]

George, first baron Lyttelton, a second rate whig statesman, whose active interest in other departments of literature is noticed elsewhere,[3] worked intermittently for some thirty years at his *History of the Life of Henry II*, which he produced, in three volumes, in 1767. The whole work, Johnson records, was printed twice over and a great part of it three times, "his ambitious accuracy" costing him at least £1000.[4] He used the best authorities he could find, and gives a minute and accurate account of the political events of Henry's reign, together with remarks not always according to knowledge on its constitutional and legal aspects. His style is clear, but remarkably flat, his narrative inanimate, and his reflections, in which "Divine Providence" frequently appears, are often almost childish. His opinions on the constitution in the twelfth century flattered whig sentiment. Hume jeered at his whiggery and his piety; Johnson was offended by his whiggery; and Gibbon, referring to a review of the book which he had written in *Mémoires Littéraires de la Grande Bretagne*, declared that the public had ratified his judgment that the author's "sense and learning were not illuminated by a single ray of genius."[5] Horace Walpole's remark, "How dull one may be if one will but take pains for six or seven and twenty years together![6]", is

---

[1] In *Mémoires Littéraires de la Grande Bretagne*. See Walpole, *Short Notes of My Life*.

[2] See bibliography.　　　[3] See Chap. v, *ante*.　　　[4] *Lives of the Poets*.

[5] *Memoirs*, pp. 173–4, ed. Hill, G. B.　　　　　[6] *Letters*, vol. VII, p. 122.

just, though, as work conscientiously and, to some extent, efficiently done, the book deserves some kinder comment. Lyttelton was a patron of poorer authors, and among those he befriended was Archibald Bower, a Scot, who wrote for booksellers. Bower asserted that he had been a Jesuit and a counsellor of the inquisition in Italy, that he had escaped and had become a protestant. Between 1748 and 1753, he issued to numerous subscribers three volumes of a *History of the Popes* written with a great show of learning and ending at 757. Through Lyttelton's influence, he was appointed librarian to the queen (1748), and clerk of the buck-warrants (1754). In 1756–8, however, John Douglas, afterwards bishop of Salisbury, published proofs that Bower's account of himself was false, and that his volumes, text and references, were stolen from other authors, two-thirds of his first volume being practically translated from Tillemont.[1] He defended himself vigorously so far as his own story was concerned, and gradually completed his *History* in seven volumes, the seventh going down to 1758, but disposing of the history from 1600 onwards in twenty-six pages. The book, which was avowedly written against the claims of the see of Rome, has no literary merit. Bower, though an impudent impostor, had some learning, but his last four volumes are not of historical importance, and the reputation of his *History* did not survive Douglas's attack.

History was written as hackwork by two authors of eminent genius. Tobias George Smollett was hired to write a history to rival Hume's work, of which the first two volumes had then appeared, and, in 1757, he produced his *Compleat History of England* to 1748, in four volumes, written in fourteen months. He boasts of having consulted over three hundred books. When he began to write, he had "a warm side" to whig principles; but he changed his opinions as he proceeded. The *History* sold well, and Hume, while contemptuous, was annoyed at his rivalry.[2] Smollett wrote a continuation; the part from the revolution was revised and republished as a continuation of Hume's *History* and, as such, passed through several editions. It favours the tory side and is written in a robust and unaffected style. Oliver Goldsmith, in the preface to his *History*

---

[1] See bibliography as to Gibbon's debt to Tillemont, cf. Chap. XIII, *post.*
[2] Burton, J. H., *Life*, vol. II, p. 53.

*of England* to 1760, in four volumes (1771), disclaims any attempt at research, and says that he wrote to instruct beginners and to refresh the minds of the aged, and "not to add to our historical knowledge but to contract it." In matter, his *History* is indebted to Hume. Both it and his two smaller books on the same subject are written in the charming and graceful style which makes all his prose works delightful. The smaller books, at least, were extensively used in education within the last seventy years. Neither Smollett, though he took his *History* seriously, nor Goldsmith should be considered as a historian.

Ireland found its historian at home. Thomas Leland, senior fellow of Trinity college, Dublin, wrote a *History of Ireland from the Invasion of Henry II*, ending with the treaty of Limerick (1691), which was published in 1773 in three volumes. Though he consulted some original authorities, he founds his work, after losing the guidance of Giraldus, mainly on those of Ware, Camden, Stanihurst, Cox and Carte, noting his authorities in his margins though without precise references. He writes in a lucid, straightforward, but inanimate style, and, though some of his statements and comments are capable of correction by modern scholars, his narrative, as a whole, is accurate, sober and impartial. *The History of the Military Transactions of the British Nation in Indostan*, from 1745 to 1761, by Robert Orme, published in two volumes (the second in two "sections") in 1763–78, is a contemporary memoir, for Orme was in India in the company's service during practically the whole time of which he wrote. It is a record of noble deeds written with picturesque details, and in dignified and natural language appropriate to its subject. Its accuracy in all important matters is unquestionable.[1] It is too full of minor events which, however interesting in themselves, bewilder a reader not thoroughly acquainted with the history. Nor does it lay sufficient stress on events of the first magnitude. To this defect, all contemporary memoirs are, relatively, liable, and, in Orme's case, it is heightened by his excessive minuteness. It has been observed that he errs in treating the native princes rather than the French "as principals in the story." This, which would be a fault in a later history, is interesting in

[1] Macaulay, *Essay on Clive*.

Orme's book, as it shows the aspect under which affairs appeared to a competent observer on the spot. William Russell's *History of Modern Europe*, from the time of Clovis to 1763, in five volumes (1779–86), is creditable to its author, who began life as an apprentice to a bookseller and printer, and became "reader" for William Strahan, the publisher of the works of Gibbon, Hume, Robertson and other historians. Its sole interest consists in Russell's idea that Europe, as a whole, has a history which should be written by pursuing what he calls "a great line." He was not the man to write it: his book is badly constructed; far too large a space is given to English history; there are strange omissions in his narrative and several blunders.

Together with the development of historical writing, this period saw a remarkable increase in the publication of materials for it in the form of state papers and correspondence. The share taken by Lord Hailes and Sir John Dalrymple in this movement is noticed above. A third volume of Carte's *Ormond*, published in 1735, the year before the publication of the two containing the duke's *Life*, consists of a mass of original letters to which he refers in the *Life*. A portion of the *State Papers of the Earl of Clarendon* was published in three volumes by the university of Oxford in 1767. The publication of the *Thurloe Papers* by Thomas Birch has already been noted in his work.[1] Birch, rector of St. Margaret Pattens, London, and Depden, Suffolk, did much historical work, scenting out manuscript authorities with the eagerness of "a young setting dog." His more important productions are *An Inquiry into the Share which Charles I had in the Transactions of the Earl of Glamorgan* (1747), in answer to Carte's contention in his *Ormond* that the commission to the earl was not genuine; *Negotiations between the Courts of England, France, and Brussels, 1592–1617* (1749); *Memoirs of the Reign of Elizabeth* from 1581 (1754), mainly extracts from the papers of Anthony Bacon at Lambeth; and *Lives* of Henry, prince of Wales and archbishop Tillotson. At the time of his death (1766), he was preparing for press miscellaneous correspondence of the times of James I and Charles I. This interesting collection presenting the news of the day has been published in four

[1] See Vol. VII, p. 214.

volumes, two for each reign, under the title *Court and Times* etc. (1848). Birch, though a lively talker was a dull writer; but his work is valuable. He was a friend of the family of lord chancellor Hardwicke, who presented to him seven benefices.

The second earl of Hardwicke shared Birch's historical taste, and, in 1778, published anonymously *Miscellaneous State Papers, from 1501 to 1726*, in two volumes, a collection of importance compiled from the manuscripts of lord chancellor Somers. In 1774, Joseph Maccormick, a St. Andrews minister, published the *State Papers and Letters* left by his great-uncle William Carstares, private secretary to William III, material invaluable for Scottish history in his reign, and prefixed a life of Carstares. The manuscripts left by Carte were used by James Macpherson, of Ossianic fame, in his *Original Papers*, from 1660 to 1714, in two volumes (1775). In the first part are extracts from papers purporting to belong to a life of James II written by himself, Carte's extracts being supplemented by Macpherson from papers in the Scottish college in Paris. The second part contains Hanover papers, mostly extracts from the papers of Robethon, private secretary to George II, now in the British Museum; the copies are accurate, but some of the translations are careless.[1] Also, in 1775, he produced a *History of Great Britain* during the same period, in two volumes, which is based on the papers, and is strongly tory in character. For this, he received £3000. His style is marked by a constant recurrence of short and somewhat abrupt sentences. Both his *History* and his *Papers* annoyed the whigs, especially by exhibiting the intrigues of leading statesmen of the revolution with the court of St. Germain.[2] His *Introduction to the History of Great Britain and Ireland* (1771) contains boldly asserted and wildly erroneous theories, particularly on ethnology, inspired by a spirit of excessive Celticism.

Much interest was excited by the speculations of the French *philosophes*, in some measure the literary offspring of Locke and enthusiastic admirers of the British constitution. Influenced by Montesquieu's famous *Esprit des Lois* (1748),

[1] For the James II papers and their relation to the *Life of James II*, ed. Clarke, J. S., 1816, see Ranke, *History of England* (Eng. trans.), vol. VI, pp. 29 ff., and, for the Hanover papers, Chance, J. F., in *Eng. Hist. Rev.*, vol. XIII (1898), pp. 55 ff. and pp. 533 ff.

[2] Horace Walpole, *Last Journals*, vol. I, pp. 444–5. ed. Steuart, A. F.

Adam Ferguson, Hume's successor as advocates' librarian (1757) and then a professor of philosophy at Edinburgh, published his *Essay on the History of Civil Society* (1767). Hume advised that it should not be published, but it was much praised, was largely sold and was translated into German and French. Nevertheless, Hume's judgment was sound; the book is plausible and superficial.[1] It is written in the polished and balanced style of which Hume was the master.[2] The admiration expressed on the continent for the British constitution led Jean Louis Delolme, a citizen of Geneva, who came to England about 1769, to write an account of it in French which was published at Amsterdam in 1771. An English translation, probably not by the author, with three additional chapters, was published in London in 1775, with the title *The Constitution of England;* it had a large sale both here and in French and German translations abroad, and was held in high repute for many years. Delolme was a careful observer of our political institutions and, as a foreigner, marked some points in them likely to escape the notice of those familiar with them from childhood. The fundamental error of his book is that it regards the constitution as a nicely adjusted machine in which the action of each part is controlled by another, instead of recognising that any one of the "powers" within it was capable of development at the expense of the others;[3] though, even as he wrote, within hearing of mobs shouting for "Wilkes and Liberty," one of them, the "power of the people," was entering on a period of development. To him, the outward form of the constitution was everything: he praised its stability and the system of counterpoises which, he believed, assured its permanence, so long as the Commons did not refuse supplies; he failed to see that it was built up by living forces any one of which might acquire new power or lose something of what it already had, and so disturb the balance which he represented as its special characteristic and safeguard.

[1] Stephen, Sir L., *English Thought in the Eighteenth Century*, vol. II, p. 215.
[2] Ferguson's *History of the Progress and Termination of the Roman Republic* is noticed in the following chapter.
[3] Stephen, *u. s.* 209–214.

# CHAPTER XIII

# Historians

## II

### GIBBON

THE mind of Gibbon, like that of Pope, from which, in many respects, it widely differed, was a perfect type of the literary mind proper. By this, it is not meant that either the historian or the poet was without literary defects of his own, or of weaknesses—one might almost say obliquities— of judgment or temperament which could not fail to affect the character of his writings. But, like Pope and very few others among great English men of letters, Gibbon had recognised, very early in his life, the nature of the task to the execution of which it was to be devoted, and steadily pursued the path chosen by him till the goal had been reached which he had long and steadily kept in view.[1] Like Pope, again, Gibbon, in the first instance, was virtually self-educated; the intellectual education with which he provided himself was more con- scientious and thorough, as, in its results, it was more pro- ductive, than that which many matured systems of mental training succeed in imparting. The causes of his extraordinary literary success have to be sought, not only or mainly in the activity and the concentration of his powers—for these elements of success he had in common with many writers, who remained half-educated as well as self-educated—but, above all, in the discernment which accompanied these qualities. He was

[1] His statement (*Memoirs*, ed. Hill, G. Birkbeck—the edition cited through- out this chapter—p. 195) that "he never presumed to accept a place," with Hume and Robertson, "in the triumvirate of British historians" may be taken *cum grano*.

endowed with an inborn tendency to reject the allurements of hand-to-mouth knowledge and claptrap style, and to follow with unfaltering determination the guidance which study and reason had led him to select. Thus, as culminating in the production of his great work, Gibbon's literary labours were very harmonious, and, so far as this can be asserted of any performance outside the field of pure literature, complete in themselves. While carrying them on, he experienced the periods of difficulty and doubt which no worker is spared; but, though the flame flickered at times, it soon recovered its steady luminosity. After transcribing the caliph Abdalrahman's reflection, how, in a reign of fifty years of unsurpassed grandeur, he had numbered but fourteen days of pure and genuine happiness, he adds in a note:

> If I may speak of myself (the only person of whom I can speak with certainty) *my* happy hours have far exceeded the scanty numbers of the caliph of Spain; and I shall not scruple to add, that many of them are due to the pleasing labour of the present composition.[1]

Thus, while he was continuously engaged in occupations which never ceased to stimulate his energies and to invigorate his powers, he was also fortunate enough to achieve the great work which proved the sum of his life's labours, to identify himself and his fame with one great book, and to die with his intellectual task done. Macaulay, the one English historian whose literary genius can be drawn into comparison with Gibbon's, left the history of England which he had "purposed to write from the accession of King James II down to a time which is within the memory of men living" a noble fragment. Gibbon could lay down his pen, in a summer-house in his garden at Lausanne, "in the day, or rather night, of the 27th of June, 1787," after writing this final sentence of his completed book:

> It was among the ruins of the Capitol, that I first conceived the idea of a work which has amused and exercised near twenty years of my life; and which, however inadequate to my own wishes, I finally deliver to the curiosity and candour of the public.[2]

[1] *Decline and Fall*, chap. LII.  [2] Cf. *Memoirs*, p. 225.

Though what Gibbon calls "the curiosity of the public" may have exhausted itself long since, the candid judgment of many generations and of almost every class of readers has confirmed the opinion formed at once by Gibbon's own age. His great work remains an enduring monument of research, an imperishable literary possession and one of the highest encouragements to intellectual endeavour that can be found in the history of letters.

The facts of Gibbon's life—in themselves neither numerous nor startling—are related by him in an autobiography which, by general consent, has established itself as one of the most fascinating books of its class in English literature. This is the more remarkable, since the *Memoirs of My Life and Writings*, as they were first printed by Gibbon's intimate friend the first earl of Sheffield (John Baker Holroyd), who made no pretence of concealing his editorial method, were a *cento* put together out of six, or, strictly speaking, seven, more or less fragmentary sketches written at different times by the author.[1] Lord Sheffield was aided in his task (to what extent has been disputed) by his daughter Maria Josepha (afterwards Lady Stanley of Alderley), described by Gibbon himself as "a most extraordinary young woman," and certainly one of the brightest that ever put pen to paper. The material on which they worked was excellent in its way, and their treatment of it extraordinarily skilful; so that a third member of this delightful family, Lord Sheffield's sister "Serena," expressed the opinion of many generations of readers in writing of the *Memoirs:* "They make me feel affectionate to Mr. Gibbon."[2] The charm of Gibbon's manner as an autobiographer and, in a lesser degree, as a letter-writer, lies not only in his inexhaustible vivacity of mind, but, above all, in his gift of self-revelation,

---

[1] For details, see bibliography. Frederic Harrison, in *Proceedings of the Gibbon Commemoration* (1895), describes the whole as "a *pot-pourri* concocted out of the MS. with great skill and tact, but with the most daring freedom." He calculates that possibly one-third of the MS. was not printed at all by Lord Sheffield. The whole series of autobiographical sketches are now in print. Rowland Prothero, in a note in his edition of *Private Letters of Edward Gibbon* (1753–94) —the edition cited throughout this chapter as *Letters*—vol. I, p. 155, shows, by the example of a letter (no. XXXIII) patched together by Lord Sheffield out of five extending over a period of six months, that he applied the same method to the *Letters* published by him in 1814.

[2] *The Girlhood of Maria Josepha Holroyd*, ed. Adeane, Jane, p. 372.

which is not obscured for long either by over-elaboration of
style or by affectation of *chic* (such as his more than filial effusions to his stepmother or his facetious epistles to his friend
Holroyd occasionally display). Out of all this wealth of
matter, we must content ourselves here with abstracting only
a few necessary data.

Edward Gibbon, born at Putney-on-Thames on 27 April,
1737, came of a family of ancient descent,[1] tory principles and
ample income. His grandfather, a city merchant, had seen his
wealth engulfed in the South Sea abyss—it was only very wise
great men, like Sir Robert Walpole, or very cautious small men,
like Pope, who knew when to withdraw from the brink; but
he had realised a second fortune, which he left to a son who,
in due course, became a tory member of parliament and a
London alderman. Edward, a weakly child—so weakly that
"in the baptism of each of my brothers my father's prudence
successively repeated my Christian name . . . that, in case of
the departure of the eldest son, this patronymic appellation
might still be perpetuated in the family,"[2] was, after two years
at a preparatory school at Kingston-upon-Thames, sent to the
most famous seminary of the day, Westminster school. But,
though he lodged in College street at the boarding-house of his
favourite "Aunt Kitty" (Catherine Porten), the school, as
readers of Cowper do not need to be reminded, was ill-suited
to so tender a nursling; and Gibbon remained a stranger to its
studies almost as much as to its recreations. More than this
—he tells us, in words that have been frequently quoted, how
he is

tempted to enter a protest against the trite and lavish praise of the
happiness of our boyish years, which is echoed with so much affectation in the world. That happiness I have never known, that time
I have never regretted.[3]

Yet, even his boyhood had its enjoyments, and the best of
these was, also, the most enduring. His reading, though
private, was carried on with enthusiasm, and, before he was

[1] The Gibbons were connected, among others, with the Actons, and Edward
Gibbon, the historian's father, was a kinsman of the great-grandfather of the late
Lord Acton.

[2] As a matter of fact, all his five brothers died in infancy.

[3] *Memoirs*, p. 216.

sixteen, he had, in something more than outline, covered at
least a large part of the ground which he afterwards surveyed
in *The Decline and Fall*.[1] Before, however, his boyhood was
really over, his studies were suddenly arrested by his entry, as
a gentleman-commoner, at Magdalen college, Oxford, on 3
April, 1752. No passage of his *Memoirs* has been more frequently quoted than his account of his *Alma Mater*, whom,
if not actually "dissolved in port," he found content with the
leavings óf arí obsolete system of studies, varied by prolonged
convivialities, tinged, in their turn, by way of sentiment, with
a futile Jacobitism.[2] The authorities of his college made no
pretence of making up by religious training for the neglect of
scholarship. He was, he says, forced by the "incredible
neglect" of his tutors to "grope his way for himself"; and the
immediate result was that, on 8 June, 1753, he was received into
the church of Rome by a Jesuit named Baker, one of the chap-
lains to the Sardinian legation, and that, in the same month,
his connection with Oxford came to an abrupt close. He had,
at that time, barely completed his sixteenth year; but he tells
us that, "from his childhood, he had been fond of religious
disputation."

No sooner had Gibbon left Oxford than his taste for study
returned, and he essayed original composition in an essay on
the chronology of the age of Sesostris. But the situation had
another side for a "practical" man like the elder Gibbon, who
might well view with alarm the worldly consequences entailed,
at that time, by conversion to Roman catholicism. He seems
to have tried the effect upon his son of the society of David
Mallet, a second-rate writer patronised in turn by Pope,
Bolingbroke and Hume. But Mallet's philosophy "rather
scandalised than reclaimed" the convert, and threats availed
as little as arguments. For, as he confesses, in his inimitable
way, he "cherished a secret hope that his father would not
be able or willing to effect his menaces," while "the pride of
conscience" encouraged the youth "to sustain the honourable
and important part which he was now acting." Accordingly,

---

[1] Morison, J. C., *Gibbon* (English Men of Letters), pp. 4–5.

[2] For comparison pictures of the intellectual barrenness of Oxford in the
period 1761–92, see *Memoirs*, appendix 15, where Sir James Stephen's account
of Cambridge in 1812–16 is also cited.

change of scene (and of environment) was resolved upon as the only remedy left. In June, 1753, he was sent by his father to Lausanne, where he was settled under the roof and tuition of a Calvinist minister named Pavillard, who afterwards described to Lord Sheffield "the astonishment with which he gazed on Mr. Gibbon standing before him: a thin little figure" (time was to render the first epithet inappropriate), "with a large head, disputing and urging, with the greatest ability, all the best arguments that had ever been used in favour of Popery."[1]

To Lausanne, Gibbon became so attached that, after he had returned thither in the days of his maturity and established reputation, it became, in Byron's words[2] one of

> the abodes
> Of names which unto [them] bequeath'd a name.

His Swiss tutor's treatment of him was both kindly and discreet, and, without grave difficulty, weaned the young man's mind from the form of faith to which he had tendered his allegiance. In matters spiritual, Gibbon inclined rather to frivolity than to deliberate change; nor was this the only illustration of a disposition of mind "clear" as the air and "light" like the soil of Attica, and one in which some of the highest and of the deepest feelings alike failed to take root. It is, at the same time, absurd to waste indignation (as, for instance, Schlosser has done) upon his abandonment of an early engagement to a lady of great beauty and charm, Suzanne Curchod, who afterwards became the wife of the celebrated Necker. The real cause of the rupture was the veto of his father, upon whom he was wholly dependent, and whose decision neither of the lovers could ignore.[3]

[1] *Letters*, vol. I, p. 2, note.

[2] *Childe Harold*, canto III, st. 105. For an account of Lausanne and the Gibbon relics there and elsewhere, see Read, Meredith, *Historic Studies in Vaud, Berne and Savoy*, 2 vols., 1897: vol. II in especial.

[3] A full account of their relations from first to last, characteristic of both the man and the age, will be found in an editorial note to *Letters*, vol. I, p. 40, and cf. *ibid.*, vol. I, p. 81, note, as to "the last phase." In June, 1794, Maria Josepha wrote: "I thought I had told you that Madame Necker had the satisfaction of going out of the world with the knowledge of being Mr. Gibbon's First and Only love" (*Girlhood*, p. 288). The passage in the *Memoirs* referring to Gibbon's renunciation of his engagement, was, as F. Harrison shows, unscrupulously recast by Lord Sheffield.

Gibbon did not leave Lausanne till April, 1758.  During his five years' sojourn there, his life had been the very reverse of that of a recluse—a character to which, indeed, he never made any pretension.  As yet, he had not reached his intellectual manhood; nor is it easy to decide in what degree a steadfast ambition had already taken possession of him.  Though his reading was various, it was neither purposeless nor unsystematic.  He brought home with him, as the fruit of his studies, a work which was in every sense that of a beginner, but, at the same time, not ill calculated to attract the public.  Before sending it to the printer, however, he cheerfully took the experienced advice of Paul Maty, editor of *The New Review*, and entirely recast it.  The very circumstance that Gibbon's *Essai sur l'Étude de la Littérature*, published in 1761, was written in French shows under what influences it had been composed and to what kind of readers it was primarily addressed. Its purpose is one more defence of classical literature and history, the study of which was then out of fashion in France; but, though the idea is good, the style lacks naturalness—a defect due to the youthfulness of the writer far more than to the fact of his having written his treatise in a foreign tongue; for he had already acquired a mastery over French which he retained through life.

Before, however, he had entered the lists as an English author, he had passed through a different, but by no means barren, experience of life.  A few days before the publication of his essay, he joined the Hampshire militia, in which, for two years, he held in succession the rank of captain, major and colonel, and became, practically, the commander of a smart "independent corps of 476 officers and men," whose encampment on Winchester downs, on one occasion, at least, lasted four months, so that for twice that period he never took a book into his hands.  His predilection for military history and the accounts of marches and campaigns was of old standing, and afterwards reflected itself in many passages of his historical masterpiece.

There cannot be any reason for doubting his statement that, during all this time, he was looking to the future rather than to the present, and that the conviction was gaining upon him of the time having arrived for beginning his proper career in life.

It was in the direction of history that Gibbon's reading had lain almost since he had been able to read at all; and, by 1760 or thereabouts, Hume and Robertson were already before the world as historical writers who commanded its applause, and the reproach of having failed to reach the level of Italian and French achievement in this branch of literature could no longer be held to rest upon English writers.  Gibbon, as a matter of course, was familiar with the chief historical productions of Voltaire, and, during his visit to Paris, in 1763, became personally acquainted with more than one French historian of note.[1] Thus, he could not fail to agree with Hume that "this was the historical age.[2]"  But, though he had no doubt as to the field of literature in which it behoved him to engage, he hesitated for some time with regard to the particular historical subject upon which he should fix his choice.  Charles VIII's Italian expedition (which subject he rejected for the good reason that it was rather the introduction to great events than important in itself), the English barons' war, a Plutarchian parallel between Henry V and Titus and the biographies of more than one British worthy—that of Sir Walter Ralegh in especial— attracted him in turn.  Gradually, he arrived at the conclusion that the theme chosen by him must not be narrow, and must not be English.  The history of Swiss liberty, and that of Florence under the Medici, hereupon, for a time, busied his imagination—the former, he afterwards actually began, in French, but abandoned after, in 1767–8, the first book of it had been read to "a literary society of foreigners in London," and unfavourably received by them.[3]  But if, like Milton, he was embarrassed by the wealth of themes which presented themselves to his literary imagination, he ended, again like Milton, by choosing what, in its development, proved the grandest and noblest of them all.

Soon after the disbandment of the militia on the close of the war in 1763, he paid a long visit to the continent, spending some

---

[1] *Memoirs*, pp. 135 ff., cf. appendix 24.

[2] *Letters of Hume to Strachan*, p. 155, cited *ibid.*, appendix 21.

[3] Cf. Morison, J. C., *Gibbon*, pp. 38–40; and see, as to *Introduction à l'Histoire Générale de la République des Suisses*, *Memoirs*, pp. 171–2.  This fragment, on a theme which has more fitfully than enduringly attracted the attention of English historians, is largely based on Tschudi.  It is printed in vol. iii of *The Miscellaneous Works of Edward Gibbon* (1814 ed.).

time in Paris and then in Lausanne, where, during the better part of a year, he prepared himself for a sojourn in Italy by a severe course of archaeological study.[1]  He crossed the Italian frontier in April, 1764, and reached Rome in October.  Here, on the 15th of that month, as he records in a passage which is one of the landmarks of historical literature, it was

—as I sat musing amidst the ruins of the Capitol, while the bare-footed fryars were singing vespers in the Temple of Jupiter, that the idea of writing the decline and fall of the city first started to my mind.[2]

For, as he adds, the conception of his life's work was, at first, confined within these limits, and only gradually grew in his mind into the vaster scheme which he actually carried into execution.  We shall, perhaps, not err in attributing a direct incitement towards this expansion to the title, if not to the substance, of Montesquieu's *Considérations sur les causes de la grandeur des Romains et leur décadence* (1734), which, to a mind like Gibbon's, already occupied with part of the theme, could hardly fail to suggest such an achievement as that to which, in the end, his genius proved capable of rising.[3]

Still, a long interval separates the original conception of Gibbon's *Decline and Fall* from the execution of even its first instalment.  During the years 1756 to 1764, he produced a series of miscellaneous historical writings, which, in part, may be described as preliminary studies for the great work of which the design had now dawned upon him.  Some of them were in the synoptical form for which he always had a special predilection, characteristic of a mind desirous, with all its inclination to detail, of securing as wide as possible a grasp of the theme on which it was engaged—*e. g.* the first of the whole series, *Outlines of the History of the World—The Ninth Century to the Fifteenth inclusive.*  Others were of the nature of small monographs, showing Gibbon's complementary interest in close and accurate investigations—such as *Critical Enquiries concerning the Title of Charles the Eighth to the Crown of*

[1] Morison, J. C., *Gibbon*, p. 51.  [2] *Memoirs*, p. 167.
[3] The similarity in title, and the difference in design, are well pointed out in the preface to the 1776 edition of the German translation of *The Decline and Fall* by Wenck, F. A. W.

*Naples* (1761).[1] To a rather later date belongs the review (in French) (1768) of Horace Walpole's *Historic Doubts*,[2] which treats this celebrated *tour de force* politely, but as a striking, rather than convincing, piece of work and ends with arguments derived from Hume, showing that the *sentiment général* on the subject represents the better grounded conclusion.[3] We pass by the classical studies belonging to the same period (1762 to 1770),[4] noting only the long collection of French "minutes" taken from the *magnum opus* of Cluverius in 1763 and 1764, as a preparation for his Italian tour, and entitled *Nomina Gentesque Antiquae Italiae*, and the well-known *Observations on the Design of the VIth Book of the Aeneid*, Gibbon's first larger effort in English prose. The attack which the latter piece makes upon Warburton's hypothesis, that Vergil's picture symbolises the mystic conception of ancient religion, is very spirited; but modern scholarship is in this instance in sympathy with the theory denounced.[5] During the greater part of the year 1770, in which these *Observations* appeared (and in which Gibbon also put to paper some *Remarks on Blackstone's Commentaries*), Gibbon's father was afflicted by an illness which, in November, proved fatal; yet the coincidence of this illness with a long interval of silence in the letters addressed by "Junius" to *The Public Advertiser* and to its printer has been made the starting-point of a theory that Gibbon was the author of the famous *Letters!*[6]

The death of Gibbon's father involved the son in a mass of uncongenial business, and, in the end, he found himself far from being a wealthy man. Still, he had saved enough from the wreck to be able, in the autumn of 1772, to establish himself in London, where he found easy access to the materials which he needed for the progress of his great work, together with the stimulus, which he could ill spare, of intellectual society in club and drawing-room.[7] In 1774, he entered the

[1] The French introduction to the intended Swiss *History* has been already noted.

[2] Cf., as to this, Chap. XII, *ante*.

[3] For all these, see vol. III of *Miscellaneous Works*.

[4] For all these, see *ibid.*, vol. IV.

[5] Cf. Morison, J. C., *Gibbon*, p. 29. The *Observations* are printed in vol. IV, the *Remarks* on Blackstone in vol. V, of *Miscellaneous Works*.

[6] See Smith, James, *Junius Unveiled* (1909).

[7] "I never found my mind more vigorous, nor my composition more happy, than in the winter hurry of society and parliament." *Memoirs*, p. 201.

House of Commons, and, two years later, the first volume of
*The Decline and Fall* was published.

The success of his political venture, in itself, was moderate;
but he has recorded that "the eight sessions that I sat in parliament were a school of civil prudence, the first and most essential
virtue of an historian."[1]   Although, while sitting for Liskeard
till 1781 and then for Lymington till 1783, he remained a silent
member, he voted steadily for Lord North's government and,
afterwards, adhered to him in his coalition with Fox.   In 1779,
he was rewarded for his public fidelity by a commissionership
of trade and plantations,[2] which he held till its abolition in
1782.   The salary of the office was of much importance to
him;[3] indeed, he thought himself unable to live in England
without it, and when, on its suppression, he was disappointed
in his hopes of other official employment, he, in the year before
the downfall of the coalition, "left the sinking ship and swam
ashore on a plank."[4]   In truth, Gibbon was so conscious of
his complete lack of the requisite gifts that (as he apologetically
confesses) he rapidly relinquished the "fleeting illusive hope of
success in the parliamentary arena."   He was, however, persuaded, by Lords Thurlow and Weymouth, to indite, in the
shape of a *Mémoire Justificatif* (1778), a reply to an official
vindication by the government of Louis XVI of its conduct
towards Great Britain.   This paper, which denounces the intervention of the French government in Great Britain's quarrel
with her American colonies, and the delusive Spanish offer of
mediation, is a state manifesto rather than a diplomatic document, and resembles some of the publicistic efforts put forth a
generation later by Gentz—if not the productions of Gentz's
model, Burke.[5]

While the political phase of his career, as a whole, was lame
and self-ended, the first instalment of his great historical work,
of which vol. I was published on 17 Feburary, 1776, took the
town by storm; nor has *The Decline and Fall of the Roman*

[1] *Memoirs*, p. 193.

[2] For the doggerel, attributed to Fox, commenting on this appointment, see
*Letters*, vol. I, p. 354.

[3] See his letter to Edward (afterwards Lord) Elliot (1779) in *Memoirs*, appendix
43.

[4] See *ibid.*, appendix 47 (*Letters*, vol. II, p. 92).

[5] It is printed in *Miscellaneous Works*, vol. V.

*Empire* ever ceased to hold the commanding position in the world of letters which it occupied at the outset.

He had produced the first portion of his work in a more leisurely way than that in which he composed the five succeeding volumes, on each of which he spent about a couple of years; and everything in the circumstances of its publication pointed to a fair success. But the actual reception of the volume very far surpassed the modest expectations entertained by him just before its issue, when, as he avers, he was "neither elated by the ambition of fame, nor depressed by the apprehension of contempt."[1] He felt conscious of his essential accuracy, of the sufficiency of his reading, of his being in accord with the spirit of enlightenment characteristic of his age and of the splendour, as well as the attractiveness, of his theme. Yet the triumph was not the less sweet; and he confesses himself "at a loss to describe the success of the work without betraying the vanity of the writer." Three editions were rapidly exhausted; Madame Necker brought him her congratulations in person; and when, in the following year, he returned her visit at Paris, the world of fashion (which, more entirely here than in London, covered the world of letters) was at his feet. At home, Hume wrote him a letter which "overpaid the labour of ten years," and Robertson's commendations were equally sincere. Other historians and scholars added their praise; and, when it proved, for a time, that he had provoked the susceptibilities of religious orthodoxy, without calling forth the cavils of "profane" critics, he was satisfied.

It will be most convenient to enumerate at once the chief attacks to which *The Decline and Fall* gave rise, without separating the earlier from the later. In a scornful review of antagonists, victory over whom he professes to regard as a sufficient humiliation, and whose "rewards in this world" he proceeds to recite,[2] Gibbon declares that "the earliest of them was, in this respect, neglected." Although this was not strictly true,[3] it suggests a just estimate of James Chelsum's *Remarks on the*

---

[1] Cf., as to the reception of vol. 1, *Memoirs*, pp. 194–9, where Hume's letter is printed at length.

[2] *Ibid.*, pp. 202 ff.

[3] Chelsum held three benefices and was chaplain to two bishops, besides being preacher at Whitehall. See *ibid.*, appendix 39, which contains a notice of several of Gibbon's censors.

*Two Last Chapters of Mr. Gibbon's History* (1776), a pamphlet
not discourteous in tone, but devoid of force. Gibbon was
probably less touched by this tract and by the sermons of
Thomas Randolph, another Oxford divine, directed against his
fifteenth chapter, than by *An Apology for Christianity in a
Series of Letters to Edward Gibbon* (1776), by Richard Watson,
regius professor of divinity at Cambridge, afterwards bishop of
Llandaff, the polished character of whose style he feels himself
bound to acknowledge. What is even more notable in Watson's
*Apology* (which was afterwards reprinted with a companion
*Apology for the Bible*, in answer to Thomas Paine), is the tolerance of tone observable in the general conduct of his argument,
as well as in such a passage as that acknowledging Voltaire's
services to Christianity in the repression of bigotry. The
criticism of Gibbon's use of insinuation is telling, and in the
last letter the appeal, not to Gibbon, but to that section of
the public which, so to speak, was on the look-out for religious
difficulties obstructing the acceptance of the Christian faith—
is both skilful and impressive. Passing by *Letters on the Prevalence of Christianity before its Civil establishment* by East
Apthorpe (on whom archbishop Cornwallis promptly bestowed
a city living), and Smyth Loftus's *Reply to the Reasonings of Mr.
Gibbon* (whose mention of "a Theological answer written by
a *mere* Irish parson" seems to apply to this effort), both printed
in 1778,[1] we come to a publication of the same year, which at
last moved Gibbon to break the silence hitherto opposed by
him to the assailants of his first volume, or, rather, of the
portion of it which had treated of the progress of early Christianity. Henry Edwards Davis, a young Oxonian, in his
*Examination of the Fifteenth and Sixteenth Chapters of Mr.
Gibbon's History etc.* (1778), set about his task in the ardent
spirit of a reviewer fresh to the warpath, and, after attempting
to convict the author of *The Decline and Fall* of misrepresentation (including misquotation) of a number of—mainly Latin—
writers, launched forth into the still more nebulous sphere of
charges of plagiarism from Middleton, Barbeyrac, Dodwell and
others—curiously enough tracing only a s'ngle passage to Tille-

[1] *An Enquiry into the Belief of the Christians of the first three centuries respecting the Godhead* by William Burgh, author of three volumes of *Political Disquisitions* (1773-5), belongs to the same year.

mont[1] as its source. Davis's *Examination* is of the sort which small critics have at all times applied to writers whether great or small, and, in this as in other instances, it succeeded in stinging. In *A Vindication of some Passages in the Fifteenth and Sixteenth Chapters* (1779),[2] after declaring that Davis's accusations, as touching the historian's honour, had extorted from him a notice which he had refused to more honourable foes, he defended himself, with indisputable and, in point of fact, undisputed success, against the indictment preferred against him, and took advantage of the occasion to reply, without losing his temper, to "the theological champions who have signalized their ardour to break a lance against the shield of a *Pagan* adversary." The defence served its purpose, and he did not find any necessity for renewing it. As his great work progressed, a second series of censors took up their parable against it. In 1781, Henry Taylor, a divine of the "intellectual" school, in his *Thoughts on the Nature of the Grand Apostacy and Observations* on Gibbon's still-vext fifteenth chapter, sought, while deprecating the historian's sneers, to show that he aimed not at the essence, but only at the particulars of his subject; and Joseph Milner, a mystically disposed evangelical who wrote ecclesiastical history with the intent of illustrating the display of Christian virtues, and whom Gibbon set down as a fool, published his *Gibbon's Account of Christianity considered etc.* In the following year, Joseph Priestley, in the second volume of his *History of the Corruptions of Christianity* joined issue with Gibbon, whom he charged with representing the immediate causes of the spread of the Christian religion as having been themselves effects.[3] In 1784, Joseph White, in the third of a set of Bampton lectures delivered at Oxford, returned to the subject of Gibbon's "five causes," which the critic conceived to be "in reality unconnected with any divine interposition"; in the same year, a special point—intended, of course, as a test-point—concerning Gibbon's trustworthiness was raised by George Travis, archdeacon of Chester, in his *Letters to Edward Gibbon* in defence of the disputed verse (St. John's *First Epistle*, chap. V, v. 7) introducing the three heavenly witnesses. The

---

[1] Cf. *ante*, Chap. XII and *post*, p. 354, note 4.
[2] Reprinted in vol. IV of *Miscellaneous Works*.
[3] As to Priestley and his point of view, see Vol. XI.

attack drew down upon its unfortunate author a series of replies
by Richard Porson, which have been classed with the controversial criticism of Bentley; but, although satisfactorily vindicated as to the main issue of the dispute, Gibbon cannot have
regarded his champion's intervention with feelings of unmixed
gratitude. Travis's arguments were confounded; but Porson's
criticism of the writer whom Travis had attacked has survived:

> I confess I see nothing wrong in Mr. Gibbon's attack upon
> Christianity. It proceeded, I doubt not, from the purest and
> most virtuous motives. We can only blame him for carrying on
> the attack in an insidious manner, and with imperfect weapons,[1]

and there follows a literary judgment of the great historian's
style—and, incidentally, of his ethics—to which further reference must be made below, and which, while full of wit, is, in
some respects, not more witty than true. A more formidable
censor than archdeacon Travis appeared, in 1782, in the person
of Lord Hailes (Sir David Dalrymple), of whose own contributions to historical literature some mention was made in the
previous chapter of this work. Much of the logic of *An Inquiry into the Secondary Causes which Mr. Gibbon has assigned
for the Rapid Growth of Christianity* (1778)—which is at once
straightforward in form and temperate in tone—is irrefutable;
and Gibbon was sagacious enough to allow that, possibly,
some flaws were discovered in his work by his legal critic, to
whose accuracy as a historian he goes out of his way to pay a
compliment.[2] Finally, after, in a university sermon at Cambridge (1790), Thomas Edwards had referred, as to a formidable
enemy, to a writer whose work "can perish only with the
language itself," John Whitaker, of whose *History of Manchester*
notice will be taken below, and who seems to have been actuat-
ed by recent private *pique*,[3] published, in 1791, a series of criticisms begun by him in *The English Review*, in October, 1788,
under the title *Gibbon's History etc., in Vols. IV. V. and VI.
reviewed*. In this tractate, Gibbon's supposed lack of veracity

---

[1] *Letters to Mr. Archdeacon Travis* (1790), preface, p. XXIX.

[2] *Memoirs*, p. 204.

[3] See Lord Sheffield's note in *Misc. Works*, vol. I, p. 243, where it is stated that
Whitaker had written very amiable letters to Gibbon *after* perusing chapters XV
and XVI.

is traced back to the lack of probity stated to be shown by him
already in the earlier portions of his work; and his absorption of other writers' materials is held up to blame together
with the frequent inelegance of his style.   The general method
of Whitaker's attack can only be described by the word
"nagging"; at the close, he gathers up the innumerable charges
into a grand denunciation of the historian as another Miltonic
Belial, imposing but hollow, pleasing to the outward sense
but incapable of high thoughts.

This summary account of the attacks upon *The Decline and
Fall* published in the lifetime of its author at least illustrates
the narrowness of the limits within which the sea of criticism
was, after all, almost entirely confined.   Gibbon's treatment of
them, on the other hand, shows how little importance he
attached to such censure except when it impugned his general
qualifications as a historian.   How little he cared for immediate applause is shown by the fact that, though the popular
welcome extended to his second and third volumes (1781) was,
at first, fainter, it was only now that he finally resolved to carry
on the work from the fall of the western to that of the eastern
empire—an interval of about a thousand years.   Not long
afterwards, he at last made up his mind to exchange conditions
of existence which, as he asserts, had become wearisome to him
and which he, certainly, could no longer afford to meet, for
the freedom of a purely literary life; and, in the autumn of
1783, he broke up his London establishment and carried out
the long-cherished plan of settling with his tried friend George
Deyverdun[1] at Lausanne.   Here, in a retirement which was
anything but "cloistered," he, by the end of 1787, brought to a
close the main work of his life, of which the three concluding
volumes (IV–VI) were carried by him to England and published
in April, 1788.   The passage in the *Memoirs* relating the historian's actual accomplishment of his task is one of the commonplaces of English literature, and records one of the golden
moments which redeem the endless tale of disappointments
and failures in the annals of authorship.

[1] It was with Deyverdun that, in 1768, Gibbon had brought out in London the
French literary annual called *Mémoires Littéraires de la Grande Bretagne pour les
Années 1767 et 1768*, to which he contributed, with other articles, a review of
Lyttelton's *History of Henry II*, "that voluminous work, in which sense and learn-
ing are not illuminated by a ray of genious." (*Memoirs*, pp. 173–4.)

After, in 1788, Gibbon had again returned to Lausanne, where, in the following year, he lost the faithful Deyverdun, he made up his mind—once more setting an example which but few men of letters have found themselves able to follow—to undertake no other great work, but to confine himself henceforth to essays or "Historical excursions."[1] It was as one of these that he designed his *Antiquities of the House of Brunswick*. What he wrote of this work amounts to more than a fragment;[2] for, of the three divisions contemplated by him, the first (*The Italian Descent*) and part of the second (*The German Reign*), were actually carried out, though the third (*The British Succession of the House of Brunswick*), for which Gibbon could have but very imperfectly commanded the material preserved in Hanover and at home, was not even approached by him. Whatever temporary value Gibbon's treatment of the material amassed by Leibniz and Muratori might have possessed vanished with the tardy publication, in 1842, of Leibniz's own *Annales imperii occidentis Brunsvicenses*. But Gibbon's narrative has a few purple patches, nor would posterity willingly forego the tribute which, near its opening, he pays to "the genius and unparalleled intellect" of Leibniz as well as to the industry and critical ability of the indefatigable Italian scholar with whom the great German was associated in his researches.

In 1791, Gibbon bade farewell to Lausanne, and the rest of his life was spent in England, where he almost continuously enjoyed the paternal hospitality of his most intimate English friend, the earl of Sheffield (John Baker Holroyd), at Sheffield place, Sussex, and in London. Lord Sheffield's name is as enduringly associated with that of the great historian as Boswell's is with Johnson's, but in a more equal way—as is shown by Lord Sheffield's unique treatment of Gibbon's *Memoirs* and by his admirable posthumous editions of the *Miscellaneous Works*. The last addition which Gibbon lived to make to these, the *Address* recommending the publication of *Scriptores Rerum Anglicanarum*, under the editorship of the Scottish antiquarian and historian John Pinkerton—a noble design which was to remain long unaccomplished—was interrupted

[1] See the letter to Langer in *Letters*, p. 229.
[2] See *Miscellaneous Works*, vol. III.

by death.[1]   Thus, his last literary effort appropriately directed itself to the promotion of historical research.   He died on 16 January, 1794, and was buried in the Sheffield mausoleum in Fletching church, by the side "of his dear friend, we may almost say, of his brother by adoption."[2]   In the *Memoirs*, which he left behind him as the best monument of his long literary life, he confesses himself "disgusted with the affectation of men of letters, who complain that they have renounced a substance for a shadow; and that their fame (which sometimes is no insupportable weight) affords a poor compensation for envy, censure, and persecution."[3]   Whatever crowning grace Gibbon's life may have missed, it brought him a long intellectual triumph and a fame which the course of time has left undimmed.

Gibbon declared, as has been seen, that he "never presumed to accept a place in the British triumvirate of historians"; but succeeding generations have concurred in assigning to *The Decline and Fall* the primacy, which it still holds, among historical works in our literature, and in esteeming its author the most brilliant example known of "the union of the historian and the man of letters."[4]   From the ancients, he had taken over the rhetorical side of the historian's task; from the French, he had derived the treatment of historical materials by a scientific method of criticism and selection; from the French, too, with the assistance of Hume and Robertson, he had learnt how to combine scientific method with artistic effect.   His literary art may suffer from mannerisms, which were those of his age, as well as from foibles, which were his own, and, as a scientific history, his work has, in many respects, become superannuated; but its main and distinctive qualities continue unimpaired. Is it possible to indicate, in a few words, of which, among these qualities, the importance seems paramount?

In the first place, his choice of subject—as it gradually developed itself in the progress of the work—was supremely felicitous; for it is the greatest theme furnished by profane history.   Even before Gibbon could feel assured that the

---

[1] It is printed, with an explanatory appendix by Pinkerton, in vol. III of *Miscellaneous Works*.       [2] Harrison, Frederic, *u.s.*       [3] *Memoirs*, p. 241.
[4] Bury, J. B., preface to the 1909 edn., p. viii.

complete treatment of the whole subject would be compassed by himself, he already contemplated it in its unity.[1]  What the Roman empire was, after it had attained to its full strength and maturity, and how its western division verged gradually to its decline and downfall, is only half the story; the other and much longer half shows how its fall was followed by long centuries of life in the eastern, and a revival, in new conditions, of its existence in the western, world.  And more than this: Janus-like, the historian is constrained to turn, with one face, to the Roman commonwealth out of which the empire grew and of which it never lost the impress; while, with his other face, he looks forward to modern times.  He bids us consider, not only what it was that declined and fell, but, also, what grew into life.  The new elements of movement, the rise of new national, and that of new religious, powers must all be reviewed in their twofold relation to what they superseded and to what they prepared.  The migration and settlements of the Teutonic tribes, and the spread and establishment of the Christian, and, after it, of the Mohammedan, religion, must be treated not only as helping to break up the Roman empire, but, also, as co-operating in the new order of things.  The principle of the continuity of history, Freeman's favourite theme, is, as the latest editor of Gibbon reminds us,

not the least important aspect of *The Decline and Fall*. . . . On the continuity of the Roman Empire depended the unity of Gibbon's work . . . whatever names of contempt he might apply to the institution in the days of the decline.[2]

Thus, the historian essays to narrate how the ancient world became the modern, just as the mausoleum of Hadrian became the papal fastness of St. Angelo—or, in his own characteristic words,[3] to "describe the triumph of barbarism and religion."

The capabilities of the subject, then, are of surpassing greatness; yet the mind is able to grasp it as a whole.  Here, we have no mere series of annals, such as were presented even by the excellent Tillemont, to whom Gibbon was indebted for much of his material,[4] but a complete work.  Its opening

[1] See the outline of the scheme in the preface to vol. I dated I February, 1776.
[2] Bury, *u.s.*                                              [3] Bury, p. vii.
[4] Tillemont, Le Nain de, *Histoire des Empereurs*, etc., treats each successive reign in a series of short chapters or headed articles, with notes appended on a wide

chapters may fall short of the results of modern numismatical and epigraphical research; its later portions, which cover a relatively far larger ground, may show an inadequate command of the political life of the Byzantine empire and all but ignore much of the Slavonic side of its history, may inadequately appreciate the historic significance, or the individual grandeur, of the figure of Charles the great and may fail in the narration of the second and third crusades[1]—in a word, it may need to be supplemented, repaired or changed here and there, and again and again. But it is complete even though it is imperfect. Eminent historians—Guizot, Milman, Bury—have, therefore, been willing to become Gibbon's editors and commentators; but they have not dealt with him as he dealt with Tillemont. It is as a whole that his work has maintained the position which it conquered for itself at once in historical literature.

Inspired, as it were, by the muse of history herself in the magnificence of his choice of subject and in the grandeur of his determination to treat it with a completeness in harmony with its nature, Gibbon displayed a breadth of grasp and a lucidity of exposition such as very few historians have brought to the performance of a cognate task. Whether in tracing the origin and growth of a new religion, such as Mohammedanism, or in developing in comprehensive outline the idea of Roman jurisprudence,[2] the masterly clearness of his treatment is equal to the demands of his philosophic insight; nor does the imaginative power of the historian fall short of the consummate skill of the literary artist.

But there is another requirement which the historian, whatever may be his theme, is called upon to satisfy, and which, in plain truth, is antecedent to all others. Any work claiming to be a contribution to historical knowledge should, within the limits of human fallibility and the boundaries at different times confining human knowledge, be exactly truthful. It was on this head only that Gibbon avowed himself sensitive, and on this alone that he condescended to reply to antagonists of any sort. It is worse than needless to attempt to distinguish

---

variety of points, in the way that Gibbon loved. It reaches to the death of the emperor Anastasius, A.D. 518. His *Mémoires Ecclésiastiques* cover the first six centuries of the Christian era. As to Gibbon's debt to him, see Bury, *u.s.* p. ix.

[1] Cf. *ibid.*, pp. xix–xxi; Morison, *Gibbon*, pp. 162–5.

[2] Cf. Bury, pp. xiii and xiv.

between the infinitely numerous shades of inveracity; and Gibbon would have scorned any such endeavour. His defence, of which, in the opinion of those capable of rising above the method adopted by more than one of his censors, the validity is indisputable, is a real vindication. He allows that a critical eye may discover in his work some loose and general references. But he fairly asks whether, inasmuch as their proportion to the whole body of his statements is quite inconsiderable, they can be held to warrant the accusation brought against him. Nor is he unsuccessful in explaining the circumstances which, in the instances impugned, rendered greater precision of statement impossible. The charge of plagiarism—the last infirmity of sagacious critics—he rebuts with conspicuous success, and courageously upholds his unhesitating plea of *not guilty:*

If my readers are satisfied with the form, the colours, the new arrangement which I have given to the labours of my predecessors, they may perhaps consider me not as a contemptible thief, but as an honest and industrious manufacturer, who has fairly procured the raw materials, and worked them up with a laudable degree of skill and success.[1]

The verdict of modern historical criticism has approved his plea. "If," writes Bury, "we take into account the vast range of his work, his accuracy is amazing, and, with all his disadvantages, his slips are singularly few."[2] It is an objection of very secondary importance, though one to which even experienced writers are wont to expose themselves, that Gibbon is apt to indulge in what might almost be called a parade of authorities.

Complete, lucid and accurate, Gibbon, finally, is one of the great masters of English prose. His power of narrative is at least equalled by his gift of argumentative statement, and, in all parts of his work, his style is one which holds the reader spellbound by its stately dignity, relieved by a curious subtlety of *nuance*, and which, at the same time, is the writer's own as much as is that of Clarendon, Macaulay or Carlyle. Gibbon's long sentences, which, at times, extend over a whole paragraph or page, but are never involved, resemble neither those of Johnson nor those of Robertson; if his style is to be compared to

[1] *Vindication* (*Miscellaneous Works*, vol. IV, p. 588).
[2] *u.s.*, p. ix.

that of any other master of English prose, it is to Burke's.
Built with admirable skill and precision, his sentences are
coloured by a delicate choice of words and permeated by a
delightful suggestion of rhythm in each case—too pleasing to
seem the effect of design.  Gibbon's irony differs greatly from
that of Swift, who deliberately fools his reader and, thereby, in-
creases the enjoyment that arises from the perception of his
real meaning, and still more from that of Carlyle, the savage
purpose of whose sarcasm never leaves the reader in doubt.
The irony of Gibbon is almost always refined, but not at any
time obscure.  It reveals itself in the choice of an epithet, in
the substitution of a noun of more ordinary usage for another
of a more select class; it also appears in the inversion of the order
in which, commonly, reasons are assigned or motives suggested,
and often makes use of that most dangerous of all rhetorical devices—insinuation.  This, however, already carries us
beyond mere questions of style.  Where this insinuation
is directed against assumed ethical principles, it has been
admirably characterised[1] "as sub-cynical."

Gibbon's diction, it may be added, was not formed on
native models only; yet it would be in the highest degree unjust
to describe it as Gallicising.  His fine taste preserved him from
the affectation of special turns or tricks of style not due to the
individuality of a writer, but largely consisting in idioms
borrowed from a tongue whose genius is not that of ours.
Much as Gibbon, who, from an early date, wrote French with
perfect ease and clearness, owed to that language and literature
in the formation of his style as well as in his general manner
as a historian, he merely assimilated these elements to others
which he could claim as native.  Notwithstanding the powerful presentment of the case by Taine,[2] the influence of French
works upon the style of English historians has probably been
overrated.  In the first place, the "triumvirate" Hume,
Robertson and Gibbon should not be "lumped" together from
the point of view of style any more than from other more or
less adjacent points of view.  The style of Hume, in some

[1] By Frederic Harrison, *u.s.*   Horace Walpole paid to Gibbon's style the compliment: "he never tires me."   Coleridge thought it "detestable."   (*Memoirs*,
appendix 27.)

[2] *Histoire de la Littérature Anglaise*, vol. IV, p. 230 (edn. 1866).

measure, was influenced by his reading of French philosophers, and that of Gibbon by his reading of the works of this and of other French literary schools—the sequence of great pulpit orators among them; in the style of Robertson, it is difficult to see much influence of French prose of any sort. And, if we are to trace the genesis of Gibbon's prose style, we should take care, while allowing for French, not altogether to disregard native influences. Gibbon, as is well known, was a great admirer of Fielding, to whom (as it would seem, erroneously) he ascribed kinship with the house of Habsburg; and, though there can be no question of comparing the style of the great novelist to that of the great historian, it may be pointed out how Fielding, like Gibbon, excels in passages holding the mean between narrative and oratorical prose, and how, among great writers of the period, he alone (except, perhaps, in a somewhat different fashion, Goldsmith) shares with Gibbon that art of subdued irony which it was sought alone to characterise. Gibbon, then, has much of the magnificence of Burke, of the incisiveness of Hume and of the serene humour of Fielding, in addition to the ease and lucidity of the French writers who had been the companions of his youthful studies. The faults of his style have been summarised, once for all, in the celebrated passage in Porson's exposure of Travis which has already been cited;[1] they consist, in the first instance, of a want of terseness, and, at the same time, a want of proportion, to which our age is more sensitive than was Gibbon's; he sometimes, says Porson, in Shakespearean phrase, "draws out the thread of his verbosity finer than the staple of his argument"; while, on other occasions, he recalls Foote's auctioneer,"whose manner was so inimitably fine that he had as much to say upon a ribbon as a Raphael." The other fault reprehended by Porson we may imitate Gibbon himself in veiling under the transparent cover of a foreign tongue—it is, in the scathing words of Sainte-Beuve,[2] *une obscénité érudite et froide.*

Concerning yet another, and more comprehensive charge against Gibbon, on which, as has been seen, critic after critic, returning again and again to the fifteenth and sixteenth chapters, thought it necessary to insist, we need, in conclusion, say

---

[1] It is reprinted in Watson, J. S., *Life of Porson* (1861), p. 85.

[2] Cited by Birkbeck Hill in preface to *Memoirs*, p. xi.

little or nothing. The day has passed for censuring him because, in this part of his work, he chose to dwell upon what he described as the secondary causes of the progress of the Christian religion, and the community which professed it, from the days of Nero to those of Constantine. Such a selection of causes he had a right to make; nor did he ask his readers to shut their eyes to the cardinal fact, as stated by Milman,[1] that, "in the Christian dispensation as in the material world, it is as the First Great Cause that the Deity is most undeniably present." Even the manner in which, in his first volume, at all events, he chose to speak of men and institutions surrounded by traditional romance cannot be made the basis of any charge against him as a historical writer. But it is quite obvious to any candid student of *The Decline and Fall* that its author had no sympathy with human nature in its exceptional moral developments—in a word, that his work was written, not only without enthusiasm, but with a conscious distrust, which his age shared to the full, of enthusiasts. Unlike Hume, who was at one with Gibbon in this distrust, the latter remained, in this respect, master of himself, and did not allow antipathies against those who stood on one side to excite his sympathies with those on the other. He would have treated the puritan movement in the spirit in which Hume treated it, and have had as little wish to penetrate into its depths, as, in contemporary politics, he tried to understand the early aspirations of the French revolution. But he would not, it may be supposed, have drawn a sympathetic picture of king Charles I—for it would be unjust to him to ascribe to any such mental process the conception of Julian the apostate, whereby he scandalised the orthodox. Nothing in the historian's own idiosyncrasy responds to the passions which transform the lives of men and nations; and, to him, history, in his own words,[2] is "little more than the crimes, follies and misfortunes of mankind." This limitation deprives the greatest of English historical works of a charm which is more than a charm, and the absence of which, however legitimate it seemed to the historian himself, cannot be ignored by his readers.

Though Gibbon overtops all contemporary English histori-

[1] Preface to edition of 1872, with notes by Milman and Guizot, p. xiii.
[2] Cited by Bury, *u.s.*, p. xxi.

cal writers who concerned themselves with ancient history—
in the sense in which it long remained customary to employ the
term—it may be well to note in this place a few of the more
important productions in this field by lesser writers. The
general public was not supplied with many nutritious droppings
from academical tables, still largely supplied with the same
"classical" fare; and, in the field of ancient history in particular,
its illpaid labourers had, like Oliver Goldsmith, to turn out as
best they might a "popular" history of Greece or of Rome.
Meanwhile, the demands of a more fastidious section of readers
for more elaborate works on ancient history were by no means
clamorous. The great success of Conyers Middleton's *History of the Life of Marcus Tullius Cicero* (1741) had proved, as
an exception, how barren this branch of classical work had
hitherto remained, and, albeit he was a voluminous writer,[1]
his other publications of this class had been, in the main,
ancillary to his historical *magnum opus*. Though he describes
it in his preface as a "life and times" rather than a "life" of his
hero, it is constructed on biographical lines, and contributed in
its way to nourish the single-minded devotion to Cicero, as a
politician hardly less than as a writer, which, at a later date,
was to suffer ruthless shocks. Nor should another production
be passed by, which was directly due to its author's unwilling-
ness to remain content with the French Jesuit history of Rome
that had hitherto commanded the field, supplemented by the
more discursive writings of Aubert de Vertot and Basil Kennett.
Nathaniel Hooke, the friend of Pope from his youth to the
hour of his death, dedicated to the poet the first volume of his
*Roman History from the Building of Rome to the Ruin of the
Commonwealth*, which appeared in 1738, though the fourth
and concluding volume was not published till 1771, eight years
after the author's death. Hooke also wrote *Observations on the
Roman Senate* (1758); but he is best known as the literary editor
of the famous *Account of the Conduct of the Dowager Duchess
of Marlborough* (1742). His *Roman History*, though, of course,
obsolete, especially in its earliest sections (as to the chronology
of which he falls in with the chronological conclusions of New-

---

[1] A full bibliography of Middleton will be found in vol. 1 of his *Miscellaneous
Works* (2nd edn., 1755). Cf., as to his place among scholars, *ante*, Vol. IX, Chap.
XIII.

ton), is written clearly and simply; moreover, his sympathies are broad, and, though his narrative may, at times, lack proportion, it shows that he had a heart for the *plebs* and could judge generously of Julius Cæsar.

It was in far broader fashion, as became a Scottish professor of moral philosophy, that Adam Ferguson proved his interest in the more extended view of historical study which was engaging the attention of British, as well as French, writers. Something was said in our previous chapter of his *Essay on the History of Civil Society* (1767). Thus, when, in 1783, Ferguson published his chief work, *The History of the Progress and Termination of the Roman Republic*, it was with no narrow conception of his task that he undertook what, as its title indicates, was designed as a sort of introductory supplement to Gibbon's masterpiece. The preliminary survey of the course of Roman history from the origins, though done with care and with due attention to historical geography, is, necessarily, inadequate, and some portions of what follows, avowedly, serve only to inform us as to what the Romans themselves believed to be a true narrative. His sketches of character are the reverse of paradoxical, though after recounting the enormities of Tiberius, he grieves "to acknowledge that he was a man of considerable ability."[1]

In the year (1784) following that of the publication of Ferguson's Roman *History* appeared the first volume of William Mitford's *History of Greece*, a venture upon what was then, in English historical literature, almost untrodden ground. Gibbon had suggested the enterprise to Mitford, who was his brother-officer in the south-Hampshire militia and had published a treatise on the military force of England, and the militia in particular. Mitford's *History*, which was not completed till 1810, long held the field, and only succumbed to works of enduring value. It is only necessary to glance at Macaulay's early article on the work,[2] in order to recognise that, in the midst of his partisan cavils[3]—in spite, too, of shortcomings of historical criticism particularly obvious in the account of the heroic age—Mitford displays an apprehension

[1] Vol. III, p. 551.   [2] *Knight's Quarterly Magazine*, November, 1824.
[3] Mitford, who has the courage of his opinions, states (vol. I, p. 278) that "the House of Commons properly represents the Aristocratical part of the constitution."

of the grandeur of the theme on which he is engaged. He is prejudiced, but not unconscientious; and, from his frequently perverse conclusions, many an English student has been able to disentangle his first conception of Greek free citizenship.

Finally, John Whitaker, who plays a rather sorry part at the fag-end of the list of Gibbon's assailants, is more worthily remembered as author of *The History of Manchester*. Of this he produced only the first two books (1771–5)—dealing respectively with the Roman and Roman-British, and with the English period to the foundation of the heptarchy, and, therefore, belonging in part to the domain of ancient history. Though it has been subjected to criticism at least as severe as that poured by Whitaker and others upon Gibbon's great work, the *History* survives as a notable product of learning, albeit containing too large an imaginative element. Whitaker carried on the same line of research and conjecture in his *Genuine History of the Britons* (1772), intended as a refutation of Macpherson's treatise on the subject. In 1794 he published *The Course of Hannibal over the Alps ascertained*, which has not proved the last word on the subject.

# CHAPTER XIV

# Philosophers

## HUME AND ADAM SMITH

OF the two friends whose names give a title to this chapter, it has been truthfully said that "there was no third person writing the English language during the same period, who has had so much influence upon the opinions of mankind as either of these two men."[1] There were many other writers on the same or cognate subjects, who made important contributions to the literature of thought; but Hume and Adam Smith tower above them all both in intellectual greatness and in the permanent influence of their work.

## I. DAVID HUME

In the sketch of his *Own Life*, which he wrote a few months before his death, Hume says that he was "seized very early with a passion for literature, which has been the ruling passion of my life, and the great source of my enjoyments." Another document of much earlier date (1734), which Hume himself revealed to no one, but which has been discovered and printed by his biographer,[2] gives us a clear insight into the nature of this literary ambition and of the obstacles to its satisfaction.

As our college education in Scotland, extending little further than the languages, ends commonly when we are about fourteen or fifteen years of age, I was after that left to my own choice in my reading, and found it incline me almost equally to books of reasoning and philosophy, and to poetry and the polite authors. Every one who is acquainted either with the philosophers or critics, knows

[1] Burton, J. H., *Life and Correspondence of David Hume*, vol. 1, p. 117.
[2] *Ibid.* vol. 1, pp. 30–39.

that there is nothing yet established in either of these two sciences, and that they contain little more than endless disputes, even in the most fundamental articles.  Upon examination of these, I found a certain boldness of temper growing in me, which was not inclined to submit to any authority in these subjects, but led me to seek out some new medium by which truth might be established.  After much study and reflection on this, at last, when I was about eighteen years of age, there seemed to be opened up to me a new scene of thought, which transported me beyond measure, and made me, with an ardour natural to young men, throw up every other pleasure or business to apply entirely to it. . . .  Having now time and leisure to cool my inflamed imagination, I began to consider seriously how I should proceed in my philosophical inquiries.  I found that . . . every one consulted his fancy in erecting schemes of virtue and of happiness, without regarding human nature, upon which every moral conclusion must depend.  This, therefore, I resolved to make my principal study, and the source from which I would derive every truth in criticism as well as morality.

These passages show, not only that Hume's ambition was entirely literary, but, also, that his literary ambition was centred in philosophy and that he was convinced he held in his grasp a key to its problems.  Literary ambition never ceased to be Hume's ruling passion, and it brought him fame and even affluence.  But his early enthusiasm for the discovery of truth seems to have been damped by the reception of his first and greatest work, or by the intellectual contradiction to which his arguments led, or by both causes combined.  In philosophy, he never made any real advance upon his first work, *A Treatise of Human Nature;* his later efforts were devoted to presenting its arguments in a more perfect and more popular literary form, or to toning down their destructive results, and to the application of his ideas to questions of economics, politics and religion, as well as to winning a new reputation for himself in historical composition.

His career contained few incidents that need to be recorded beyond the publication of his books.  He was born at Edinburgh on 26 April, 1711, the younger son of a country gentleman of good family, but small property.  His "passion for literature" led to his early desertion of the study of law; when he was twenty-three, he tried commerce as a cure for the state of morbid depression in which severe study had landed him, and also, no doubt, as a means of livelihood. But, after a few months in a merchant's office at Bristol, he resolved to make frugality supply his deficiency of fortune, and settled in France, chiefly at La Flèche, where, more than a century before, Descartes had been educated at the Jesuit college. But he never mentions this connection with Descartes; he was occupied with other thoughts; and, after three years, in 1737, he came home to arrange for the publication of *A Treatise of Human Nature*, the first two volumes of which appeared in January, 1739. If the book did not literally, as Hume put it, fall "dead-born from the press," it excited little attention; the only literary notice it received entirely failed to appreciate its significance. He was bitterly disappointed, but continued the preparation for the press of his third volume, "Of Morals." This appeared in 1740; and, in 1741, he published a volume of *Essays Moral and Political*, which reached a second edition and was supplemented by a second volume in 1742. The success of these essays gratified Hume's literary ambition and, perhaps, had a good deal to do with the direction of his activity towards the application and popularisation of his reflections rather than to further criticism of their basis. About this time, Hume resided, for the most part, at the paternal estate (now belonging to his brother) of Ninewells in Berwickshire; but he was making efforts to secure an independent income: he failed twice to obtain a university professorship; he spent a troublesome year as tutor to a lunatic nobleman; he accompanied general St. Clair as his secretary on his expedition to France in 1746, and on a mission to Vienna and Turin in 1748. In the latter year was published a third volume of *Essays Moral and Political*, and, also, *Philosophical Essays concerning Human Understanding*, afterwards (1758) entitled *An Enquiry concerning Human Understanding*, in which the reasonings of book I of *A Treatise of Human Nature* were presented in a revised but incomplete form. A second edition of this work appeared in 1751, and, in the same year, *An Enquiry concerning the Principles of Morals* (founded upon book III of the *Treatise*) which, in the opinion of the author, was of all his "writings, historical, philosophical, or literary, incomparably the best." A few months later (February, 1752), he published a volume of

*Political Discourses* which, he said, was "the only work of mine that was successful on the first publication." According to Burton, it "introduced Hume to the literature of the continent." It was translated into French in 1753 and, again, in 1754. In 1752, he was appointed keeper of the advocates' library—a post which made a small addition to his modest income and enabled him to carry out his historical work. In 1753-4 appeared *Essays and Treatises on several subjects;* these included his various writings other than the *Treatise* and the *History*, and, after many changes, attained their final form in the edition of 1777. The new material added to them in later editions consisted chiefly of *Four Dissertations* published in 1757. The subjects of these dissertations were the natural history of religion, the passions (founded on book II of the *Treatise*), tragedy and taste. Essays on suicide and on immortality had been originally designed for this volume, but were hurriedly withdrawn on the eve of publication.

For more than two years, 1763 to 1765, Hume acted as secretary to the English embassy at Paris, where he was received with extraordinary enthusiasm by the court and by literary society. "Here," he wrote, "I feed on ambrosia, drink nothing but nectar, breathe incense only, and walk on flowers." He returned to London in January, 1766, accompanied by Rousseau, whom he had befriended and who, a few months later, repaid his kindness by provoking one of the most famous of quarrels between men of letters. Before the close of the year, he was again in Scotland, but, in the following year, was recalled to London as under-secretary of state, and it was not till 1769 that he finally settled in Edinburgh. There, he rejoined a society less brilliant and original than that he had left in Paris, but possessed of a distinction of its own. Prominent among his friends were Robertson, Hugh Blair and others of the clergy—men of high character and literary reputation, and representative of a religious attitude, known in Scotland as "moderatism,"[1] which did not disturb the serenity of Hume. He died on 25 August, 1776.

After his death, his *Own Life* was published by Adam Smith (1777), and his *Dialogues concerning Natural Religion* by his

---

[1] For a definition of "moderatism" by an observer of its decline, see Lord Cockburn's *Journal*, vol. II, pp. 289–291.

nephew David (1779). We hear of these *Dialogues* more than twenty years earlier; but he was dissuaded from publishing them at the time, though he was concerned that they should not be lost and subjected the manuscript to repeated and careful revision. His philosophical activity may be said to have come to an end in 1757 with the publication of *Four Dissertations*, when he was forty-six years old. In spite of many criticisms, he refused to be drawn into controversy; but, in an "advertisement" to the final edition of *Essays and Treatises*, he protested, with some irritation, against criticisms of *A Treatise of Human Nature*—"the juvenile work which the Author never acknowledged."

This disclaimer of his earliest and greatest work is interesting as a revelation of Hume's character, but cannot affect philosophical values. If he had written nothing else, and this book alone had been read, the influence of his ideas on general literature would have been less marked; but his claim to rank as the greatest of English philosophers would not be seriously affected: it would be recognised that he had carried out a line of thought to its final issue, and the effect upon subsequent speculation would have been, in essentials, what it has been.

Hume is quite clear as to the method of his enquiry. He recognised that Locke and others had anticipated him in the "attempt to introduce the experimental method of reasoning into moral subjects." Locke had, also, opened the way for deriving a system of philosophy from the science of the human mind; but Hume far excelled him in the thoroughness and consistency with which he followed this way. Locke's express purpose was to examine the understanding, that he might discover "the utmost extent of its tether." He does not doubt that knowledge can signify a reality outside the mind; but he wishes to determine the range of this cognitive power. From the outset, Hume conceives the problem in a wider manner. All knowledge is a fact or process of human nature; if we are able, therefore, "to explain the principles of human nature," we shall "in effect propose a complete system of the sciences." Without doubt, this utterance points back to his early discovery of a "new medium by which truth might be established"— a discovery which, at the age of eighteen, had transported him beyond measure. In saying that "a complete system of the sciences" would result from "the principles of human nature," Hume did not mean that the law of gravitation or the circulation of the blood could be discovered from an examination of the understanding and the emotions. His meaning was that, when the sciences are brought into system, certain general features are found to characterise them; and the explanation of these general features is to be sought in human nature—in other words, in our way of knowing and feeling. His statement, accordingly, comes simply to this, that mental science, or what we now call psychology, takes the place of philosophy—is itself philosophy.

Hume is commonly, and correctly, regarded as having worked out to the end the line of thought started by Locke. But, in the width of his purpose, the thoroughness of its elaboration and his clear consciousness of his task, he may be compared with Hobbes—a writer who had little direct effect upon his thought. For Hume is Hobbes inverted. The latter interprets the inner world—the world of life and thought—by means of the external or material world, whose impact gives rise to the motions which we call perception and volition. Hume, on the other hand, will assume nothing about external reality, but interprets it by means of the impressions or ideas of which we are all immediately conscious. And, as Hobbes saw all things under the rule of mechanical law, so Hume, also, has a universal principle of connection.

"Here," he says, that is to say, among ideas, "is a kind of *Attraction*, which in the mental world will be found to have as extraordinary effects as in the natural, and to shew itself in as many and as various forms.

The law of gravitation finds its parallel in the law of the association of ideas; as the movements of masses are explained by the former, so the latter is used to account for the grouping of mental contents.

In enumerating these contents, he modifies the doctrine of Locke. According to Locke, the material of knowledge comes from two different sources—sensation and reflection. The view hardly admitted of statement without postulating both a mental and a material world existing over against one another. Hume tries to avoid any such postulate. His primary data are all of one kind; he calls them "impressions," and says that they arise "from unknown causes." . Ideas are distinguished from impressions by their lesser degree of "force and liveliness." Hume makes the generalisation that "every simple idea has a simple impression which resembles it"; an idea is thus the "faint image" of an impression; and there are degrees of this faintness: the "more lively and strong" are ideas of memory, the weaker are ideas of imagination. Further, certain ideas, in some unexplained way, reappear with the force and liveliness of impressions, or, as Hume puts it, "produce the new impressions" which he calls "impressions of reflection" and which he enumerates as passions, desires and emotions. Reflection is, thus, derived from sensation, although its impressions in their turn give rise to new ideas. All mental contents (in Hume's language, all "perceptions") are derived from sense impressions, and these arise from unknown causes. Simple ideas are distinguished from simple impressions merely by their comparative lack of force and liveliness; but these fainter data tend to group themselves in an order quite different from that of their corresponding impressions. By this "association of ideas" are formed the complex ideas of relations, modes and substances.

Such are the elements of Hume's account of human nature; out of these elements, he has to explain knowledge and morality; and this explanation is, at the same time, to be "a complete system of the sciences." He is fully alive to the problem. In knowledge, ideas are connected together by other relations than the "association" which rules imagination; and he proceeds at once to an enquiry into "all those qualities which make objects admit of comparison." These, he calls "philosophical relations," and he arranges them under seven general heads: resemblance, identity, space and time, quantity, degree of quality, contrariety, cause and effect.

All scientific propositions are regarded as expressing one or other of these relations. Hume regards the classification as exhaustive; and, at least, it is sufficient to form a comprehensive test of his theory. Since we have nothing to go upon but ideas and the impressions from which ideas originate, how are we to explain knowledge of these relations? Hume's enquiry did not answer this question even to his own satisfaction; but it set a problem which has had to be faced by every subsequent thinker, and it has led many to adopt the sceptical conclusion to which the author himself was inclined.

The "philosophical relations," under his analysis, fall into two classes. On the one hand, some of them depend entirely on the ideas compared: these are resemblance, contrariety, degrees in quality and proportions in quantity or number. On the other hand, the relations of identity, space and time, and causation may be changed without any change in the ideas related; our knowledge of them thus presents an obvious difficulty, for it cannot be derived from the ideas themselves. Hume does not take much trouble with the former class of relations, in which this difficulty does not arise. He is content to follow on Locke's lines and to think that general propositions of demonstrative certainty are, obviously, possible here, seeing that we are merely stating a relationship clearly apparent in the ideas themselves. He does not ask whether the relation is or is not a new idea, and, if it is, how it can be explained—from what impression it took its rise. And he gives no explanation of the fixed and permanent character attributed to an idea when it is made the subject of a universal proposition. It is important to note, however, that he does not follow Locke in holding that mathematics is a science which is at once demonstrative and "instructive." The propositions of geometry concern spatial relations, and our idea of space is received "from the disposition of visible and tangible objects"; we have "no idea of space or extension but when we regard it as an object either of our sight or feeling" (*i.e.* touch); and, in these perceptions, we can never attain exactness: "our appeal is still to the weak and fallible judgment which we make from the appearance of the objects, and correct by a compass or common measure." Geometry, therefore, is an empirical science; it is founded on observations of approximate accuracy only, though the variations from the normal in our observations may be neutralised in the general propositions which we form. Hume does not apply the same doctrine to arithmetic, on the ground (which his principles do not justify) that the unit is something unique. He is thus able to count quantity and number in his first class of relations and to except algebra and arithmetic from the effect of his subtle analysis of the foundations of geometry. In his *Enquiry concerning Human Understanding*, however, he deserts, without a word of justification, the earlier view which he had worked out with much care and ingenuity, and treats mathematics generally as the great example of demonstrative reasoning. In this later work, in which completeness is sacrificed to the presentation of salient features, he speaks, not of two kinds of relations, but of "relations of ideas" and "matters of fact"; and, in each, he seeks to save something from the general ruin of the sciences to which his premises lead. The last paragraph of the book sets forth his conclusion:

When we run over our libraries, persuaded of these principles, what havoc must we make? If we take in our hand any volume; of divinity or school metaphysics, for instance; let us ask, *Does it contain any abstract reasoning concerning quantity or number?* No. *Does it contain any experimental reasoning concerning matter of fact and existence?* No. Commit it then to the flames; for it can contain nothing but sophistry and illusion.

This passage, startling and ruthless as it sounds, is chiefly remarkable for its reservations. It was easy to condemn "divinity or school metaphysics" as illusory; they had for long been common game. But to challenge the validity of mathematics or of natural science was quite another matter. Hume did not temper the wind to the shorn lamb; but he took care that it should not visit too roughly the sturdy wethers of the flock. Yet we have seen that, according to his principles, mathematics rests upon observations which fall short of accuracy, while natural science, with its "experimental reasoning concerning matter of fact," depends upon the relation of cause and effect.

The examination of this relation occupies a central position in both his works; and its influence upon subsequent thought has been so great as, sometimes, to obscure the importance of other factors in his philosophy. He faced a problem into which Locke had hardly penetrated, and of which even Berkeley had had only a partial view. What do we mean when we say that one thing is cause and another thing its effect, and what right have we to that meaning? In sense perception, we have impressions of flame and of heat, for instance; but why do we say that the flame causes the heat, what ground is there for asserting any "necessary connection" between them? The connection cannot be derived from any comparison of the ideas of flame and of heat; it must come from impression, therefore; but there is no separate impression of "cause" or "causation" which could serve as the link between two objects. What, then, is the origin of the connection? To use the terminology of the *Enquiry*, since cause is not a "relation of ideas," it must be a "matter of fact"—an impression. But it is not itself a separate or simple impression; it must, therefore, be due to the mode or manner in which impressions occur. In our experience, we are accustomed to find flame and heat combined; we pass constantly from one to the other; and the custom becomes so strong that, whenever the impression of flame occurs, the idea of heat follows. Then, we mistake this mental or subjective connection for an objective connection. Necessary connection is not in the objects, but only in the mind; yet custom is too strong for us, and we attribute it to the objects.

This is a simple statement of the central argument of Hume's most famous discussion. The "powers" which Locke attributed to bodies must be denied—as Berkeley denied them. The consciousness of spiritual activity on which Berkeley relied is equally illusory on Hume's principles.

"If we reason *a priori*," says Hume, "anything may appear able to produce anything. The falling of a peeble may, for aught we know, extinguish the sun, or the wish of a man control the planets in their orbits."

This striking utterance is, strictly, little better than a truism. No philosopher ever supposed that such knowledge about definite objects could be got in any other way than by experience. But Hume's negative criticism goes much deeper than this. We have no right to say that the extinction of the sun needs any cause at all, or that causation is a principle that holds of objects; all events are loose and separate. The only connection which we have a right to assert is that of an idea with an impression or with other ideas—the subjective routine which is called "association of ideas." Hume's constructive theory of causation is an explanation of how we come to suppose that there is causal connection in the world, although there is really nothing more than customary association in our minds.

If we admit Hume's fundamental assumption about impressions and ideas, it is impossible to deny the general validity of this reasoning. Any assertion of a causal connection—the whole structure of natural science, therefore—is simply a misinterpretation of certain mental processes. At the outset, Hume himself had spoken of impressions as arising from "unknown causes"; and some expressions of the sort were necessary ·to give his theory a start and to carry the reader along with him; but they are really empty words. Experience is confined to impressions and ideas; causation is an attitude towards them produced by custom—by the mode of sequence of ideas; its applicability is only within the range of impressions or ideas; to talk of an impression as caused by something that is neither impression nor idea may have a very real meaning to any philosopher except Hume; but to Hume it cannot have any meaning at all.

The discussion of causation brings out another and still more general doctrine held by Hume—his theory of belief. When I say that flame causes heat, I do not refer to a connection of ideas in my own mind; I am expressing belief in an objective connection independent of my mental processes. But Hume's theory of causation reduces the connection to a subjective routine. Now, some other impression than "flame" might precede the idea of heat—the impression "cold," for instance. How is it, then, that I do not assert "cold causes heat"? The sequence "cold—heat" may be equally real in my mind with the sequence "flame—heat." How is it that the former does not give rise to belief in the way that the latter does? Hume would say that the only difference is that the association in the former case is less direct and constant than in the latter, and thus leads to an idea of less force and liveliness. Belief, accordingly, is simply a lively idea associated with a present impression. It belongs to the sensitive, not to the rational, part of our nature. And yet it marks the fundamental distinction between judgment and imagination.

In the *Treatise*, at any rate, there is no faltering of purpose or weakening of power when the author proceeds to apply his principles to the fabric of knowledge. It is impossible, in this place, to follow his subtle and comprehensive argument; but its issue is plain. With objections not unlike Berkeley's, he dismisses the independent existence of bodies, and then he turns a similar train of reasoning against the reality of the self:

> When I enter most intimately into what I call *myself*, I always stumble on some particular perception or other, of heat or cold, light or shade, love or hatred, pain or pleasure. I can never catch *myself* at any time without a perception, and never can observe anything but the perception. When my perceptions are removed for any time, as by sound sleep, so long am I insensible of *myself*, and may truly be said not to exist.

According to Hume's own illustration, the mind is but the stage on which perceptions pass and mingle and glide away. Or, rather, there is no stage at all, but only a phantasmagory of impressions and ideas.

Hume's purpose was constructive; but the issue, as he faces it, is sceptical. And he is a genuine sceptic; for, even as to his scepticism, he is not dogmatic. Why should he assent to his own reasoning? he asks; and he answers, "I can give no reason why I should assent to it, and feel nothing but a *strong* propensity to consider objects *strongly* in that view." The propensity, however, is strong only when the "bent of mind" is in a certain direction; a dinner, a game of backgammon, makes such speculations appear ridiculous; and "nature" suffices to "obliterate all these chimeras." A year later, Hume referred again to this sceptical *impasse*, in an appendix to the third volume of his *Treatise;* and there, with remarkable insight, he diagnosed the causes of his own failure. The passage deserves quotation, seeing that it has been often overlooked, and is, nevertheless, one of the most significant utterances in the history of philosophy.

> In short there are two principles, which I cannot render consistent; nor is it in my power to renounce either of them, viz. *that all our distinct perceptions are distinct existences,* and *that the mind never perceives any real connexion among distinct existences.* Did our perceptions either inhere in something simple and individual, or did the mind perceive some real connexion among them, there would be no difficulty in the case. For my part, I must plead the privilege of a sceptic, and confess that this difficulty is too hard for my

understanding. I pretend not, however, to pronounce it absolutely insuperable. Others, perhaps, or myself, upon more mature reflexions, may discover some hypothesis that will reconcile those contradictions.

Hume seems himself to have made no further attempt to solve the problem. His followers have been content to build their systems on his foundation, with minor improvements of their own, but without overcoming or facing the fundamental difficulty which he saw and expressed.

The logical result of his analysis is far from leading to that "complete system of the sciences" which he had anticipated from his "new medium"; it leads, not to reconstruction, but to a sceptical disintegration of knowledge; and he was clear-sighted enough to see this result. Thenceforward, scepticism became the characteristic attitude of his mind and of his writings. But his later works exhibit a less thorough scepticism than that to which his thinking led. Even his *Enquiry concerning Human Understanding* shows a weakening of the sceptical attitude, in the direction of a "mitigated scepticism" which resembles modern positivism and admits knowledge of phenomena and of mathematical relations.

When he came to deal with concrete problems, his principles were often applied in an emasculated form. But the "new medium" is not altogether discarded: appeal is constantly made to the mental factor—impression and idea. This is characteristic of Hume's doctrine of morality. "Here is a matter of fact; but 't is the object of feeling not of reason. It lies in yourself not in the object." And from this results his famous definition of virtue: "every quality of the mind is denominated virtuous which gives pleasure by the mere survey; as every quality which produces pain is called vicious." The "sentiments of approbation or blame" which thus arise depend, in all cases, on sympathy; sympathy with the pleasures and pains of others is, thus, postulated by Hume as an ultimate fact; the reasonings of Butler and Hutcheson prevented him from seeking to account for it as a refined form of selfishness, as Hobbes had done; and yet, upon his own premises, it remains inexplicable. In his *Enquiry concerning the Principles of Morals*, his differences from Hobbes, and even from Locke, are still more clearly shown than in the *Treatise;* he defends the reality of disinterested benevolence; and the sentiment of moral approbation is described as "humanity," or "a feeling for the happiness of mankind," which, it is said, "nature has made universal in the species." This sentiment, again, is always directed towards qualities which tend to the pleasure, immediate or remote, of the person observed or of others. Thus, Hume occupies a place in the utilitarian succession; but he did not formulate a quantitative utilitarianism, as Hutcheson had already done. He drew an important distinction, however, between natural virtues, such as benevolence, which are immediately approved and which have a direct tendency to produce pleasure, and artificial virtues, of which justice is the type, where both the approval and the tendency to pleasure are mediated by the social system which the virtue in question supports.

Hume exerted a profound influence upon theology, not only by the general trend of his speculation but, also, through certain specific writings. Of these writings, the most important are the essay "Of Miracles" contained in *An Enquiry concerning Human Understanding*, the dissertation entitled "The Natural History of Religion," and *Dialogues concerning Natural Religion*. The first-named is the most famous; it produced a crowd of answers, and it had a good deal to do with public attention being attracted to the author's works. It consists of an expansion of a simple and ingenious argument, which had occurred to him when writing his *Treatise of Human Nature*, but which, strangely enough, is inconsistent with the principles of that work. It regards "laws of nature" as established by a uniform experience, "miracles" as violations of these laws and the evidence for these miracles as necessarily inferior to the "testimony of the senses" which establishes the laws of nature. Whatever validity these positions may have on another philosophical theory, the meaning both of laws of nature and of miracles as conflicting with these laws evaporates under the analysis by which, as in Hume's *Treatise*, all events are seen as "loose and separate." "The Natural History of Religion" contains reflections of greater significance. Here, Hume distinguishes between the theoretical argument which leads to theism and the actual mental processes from which religion has arisen. Its "foundation in reason" is not the same thing as its "origin in human nature"; and he made an important step in advance by isolating this latter question and treating it apart. He held that religion arose "from a concern with regard to the events of life, and from the incessant hopes and fears which actuate the human mind," and, in particular, from the "melancholy" rather than from the "agreeable" passions; and he maintained the thesis that polytheism preceded theism in the historical development of belief.

"The whole is a riddle, an enigma, an inexplicable mystery." Such is the concluding reflection of this work. But a further and serious attempt to solve the riddle is made in *Dialogues concerning Natural Religion*. This small book contains the author's mature views on ultimate questions. It is written in his most perfect style, and shows his mastery of the dialogue form. There is none of the usual scenery of the dramatic dialogue; but the persons are distinct, the reasoning is lucid, and the interest is sustained to the end. The traditional arguments are examined with an insight and directness which were only equalled afterwards by Kant; but, unlike Kant, and with insight more direct if not more profound, Hume finds the most serious difficulties of the question in the realm of morals. The form of the work makes it not altogether easy to interpret; and some commentators have held that Hume's own views should not be identified with those of the more extreme critic of theism. Hume himself says as much at the close of the work; but his habitual irony in referring to religious topics is part of the difficulty of interpretation. All the speakers in the *Dialogues* are represented as accepting some kind of theistic belief; and it is not necessary to attribute expressions of this kind simply to irony. The trend of the argument is towards a shadowy form of theism—"that the cause or causes of order in the universe probably bear some remote analogy to human intelligence"; and, in a remarkable footnote, the author seems to be justifying his own right to take up such a position:

No philosophical Dogmatist denies, that there are difficulties both with regard to the senses and to all science; and that these difficulties are in a regular, logical method, absolutely insolvable. No Sceptic denies, that we lie under an absolute necessity, notwithstanding these difficulties, of thinking, and believing, and reasoning with regard to all kind of subjects, and even of frequently assenting with confidence and security.

In other words, his logic leads to complete scepticism; but, just because the "difficulties" are insoluble, he claims a right to disregard them, and to act and think like other men, when action and thought are called for.

For this reason, his theory of knowledge has little effect upon his political and economical essays, although they are closely connected with his ethical and psychological views. The separate essays were published, in various volumes, between 1741 and 1777; and, in the interval, political philosophy was profoundly influenced by the works of Montesquieu and Rousseau. The essays do not make a system, and economics is in them not definitely distinguished from politics; but both system and the distinction are suggested in the remarks on the value of general principles and general reasonings which he prefixed to the essays on commerce, money and other economical subjects. "When we reason upon *general* subjects," he says, "our speculations can scarcely ever be too fine, provided they be just."

In both groups of essays, Hume was not merely a keen critic of prevailing theories and conceptions; his knowledge of human nature and of history guided his analysis of a situation. A growing clearness of doctrine, also, may be detected by comparing his earlier with his later utterances. In later editions, he modified his acceptance of the traditional doctrines of the natural equality of men, and of consent as the origin of society. The essay "Of the Origin of Government," first published in 1777, makes no mention either of divine right or of original contract. Society is traced to its origin in the family; and political society is said to have been established "in order to administer justice"—though its actual beginnings are sought in the concert and order forced upon men by war. Again, whereas, in an earlier essay, he had said that "a constitution is only so far good as it provides a remedy against maladministration," he came, later, to look upon its tendency to liberty as marking the perfection of civil society—although there must always be a struggle between liberty and the authority without which government could not be conducted. His political thinking, accordingly, tends to limit the range of legitimate governmental activity; similarly, in economics, he criticises the doctrine of the mercantilists, and on various points anticipates the views of the analytical economists of a later generation. Perhaps, however, nothing in these essays shows better his insight into the principles of economics than the letter which, shortly before his death, he wrote to Adam Smith upon receipt of a copy of *The Wealth of Nations*. In this letter, after a warm expression of praise for, and satisfaction with, his friend's achievement, he makes a single criticism—"I cannot think that the rent of farms makes any part of the price of the produce, but that the price is determined altogether by the quantity and the demand"—which suggests that he himself had arrived at the theory of rent commonly associated with the name of Ricardo.

## II.  ADAM SMITH

Adam Smith was born at Kirkcaldy on 5 June, 1723. He was educated at the university of Glasgow, where he had Hutcheson as one of his teachers, and, in 1740, he proceeded to Oxford, where he resided continuously through term and vacation for more than six years. Like Hobbes in the previous century, and Gibbon and Bentham shortly after his own day, he has nothing that is good to say of the studies of the university. His own college of Balliol gave small promise of its future fame: it was, then, chiefly distinguished as a centre of Jacobitism, and its authorities confiscated his copy of Hume's *Treatise of Human Nature;* but its excellent library enabled him to devote himself to assiduous study, mainly in Greek and Latin literature. After some years spent at home, he returned to Glasgow as professor of logic (1751) and, afterwards (1752), of moral philosophy. In 1759, he published his *Theory of Moral Sentiments*, which brought him immediate fame. Early in 1764, he resigned his professorship in order to accompany the young duke of Buccleuch on a visit to France which lasted over two years. This marks the beginning of the second and more famous period of his literary career. He found Toulouse (where they first settled) much less gay than Glasgow, and, therefore, started writing a book "in order to pass away the time."[1] This is probably the first reference to the great work of his riper years. But it does not mark the beginning of his interest in economics. By tradition and by his own preference, a comprehensive treatment of social philosophy was included in the work of the moral philosophy chair at Glasgow; and there is evidence to show that some of his most characteristic views had been written down even before he settled there.[2] When, in 1765–6, Smith resided for many months in Paris with his pupil, he was received into the remarkable society of "economists" (commonly known as the "physiocrats"[3]). Quesnay, the leader of the school, had published his *Maximes générales de gouvernement économique* and his *Tableau économique* in 1758; and Turgot, who was soon to make an effort to introduce their common principles into the national finance, was, at this time, writing his *Réflexions sur la formation et la distribution des richesses*, although it was not published till some years later. Smith held the work of the physiocrats, and of Quesnay in particular, in high esteem; only death robbed Quesnay of the honour of having *The Wealth of Nations* dedicated to him. The exact extent of Smith's indebtedness to the school is matter of controversy. But, two things seem clear, though they have been sometimes overlooked. He shared their objection to mercantilism and their approval of commercial freedom on grounds at which he had arrived before their works were published; and he did not accept their special theory that agriculture is the sole source of wealth, or the practical consequence which they drew from the principle that the revenue of the state should be derived from "a single tax" on land. After his return from France, Smith settled down quietly with his mother and cousin at Kirkcaldy and devoted himself to the composition of *The Wealth of Nations*, which was published in 1776. In 1778, he removed to Edinburgh as commissioner of customs; he died on 17 July, 1790.

Apart from some minor writings, Adam Smith was the author

---

[1] Cf. Rae, J., *Life of Adam Smith*, p. 179.
[2] Cf. Stewart, Dugald, *Life and Writings of Adam Smith*, in *Works*, vol. x, pp. 67, 68.
[3] This term was invented by Dupont de Nemours (1739–1817), a younger member of the school.

of two works of unequal importance. These two works belong to different periods of his life—the professorial, in which he is looked upon as leading the ordinary secluded life of a scholar, and the later period, in which he had gathered wider knowledge of men and affairs. And the two works differ in the general impression which they are apt to produce. According to the earlier, sympathy, or social feeling, is the foundation of morality; the ideal of the later work is that of a social system in which each person is left free to pursue his own interest in his own way, and the author throws gentle ridicule upon the "affectation" of "trading for the public benefit." Undue stress has, however, been laid upon the difference; it is superficial rather than fundamental, and results from the diversity of subject and method in the two works rather than from an opposition between their underlying ideas. Indeed, it may be argued that the social factor in the individual, which is brought out in the ethical treatise, is a necessary condition of that view of a harmony between public and private interests which underlies the doctrine of "natural liberty" taught in *The Wealth of Nations*.

   *The Theory of Moral Sentiments* covers much ground already traversed by preceding British moralists. It is an elaborate analysis of the various forms and objects of the moral consciousness. It is written in a flowing and eloquent, if rather diffuse, style; it is full of apt illustration; and the whole treatise is dominated by a leading idea. Smith's central problem, like that of his predecessors, is to explain the fact of moral approval and disapproval. He discards the doctrine of a special "moral sense," impervious to analysis, which had been put forward by Shaftesbury and Hutcheson. Like Hume, he regards sympathy as the fundamental fact of the moral consciousness; and he seeks to show, more exactly than Hume had done, how sympathy can become a test of morality. He sees that it is not, of itself, a sufficient test. A spectator may imaginatively enter into the emotional attitude of another man, and this is sympathy; but it is not a justification of the man's attitude. The spectator may have misunderstood the circumstances, or his own interests may have been involved. Accordingly, the only sympathy that has ethical value is that of an "impartial and well-informed spectator." But this impartial and well-informed spectator, whose sympathy with our passions and affections would be their adequate justification, is not an actual but an ideal person; and, indeed, Smith recognises as much when he says that we have to appeal from "the opinions of mankind" to "the tribunal of [our] own conscience"—to "the man within the breast." The great merit of the theory, as worked out by Smith, is its recognition of the importance of the social factor in morality, and of sympathy as the means by which this social factor operates. The individual man, in his view, is a being of social structure and tendencies. But the social side of his nature is not exaggerated: if man "can subsist only in society," it is equally true that "every man is by nature first and principally recommended to his own care." These points modify the contrast between the teaching of his first work and the "individualism" of his economic theory.

Adam Smith is frequently spoken of as the founder of political economy. By this is meant that he was the first to isolate economic facts, to treat them as a whole, and to treat them scientifically. But, nine years before the publication of *The Wealth of Nations*, another work appeared which may be regarded as having anticipated it in this respect—Sir James Steuart's *Inquiry into the Principles of Political Economy*. Steuart was a Jacobite laird, who, in 1763, returned from a long exile abroad. He had travelled extensively, and his work contains the result of observation of different states of society as well as of systematic reflection; but it is without merit in respect of literary form. It is presented to the public as "an attempt towards reducing to principles, and forming into a regular science, the complicated interests of domestic policy." It deals with "population, agriculture, trade, industry, money, coin, interest, circulation, banks, exchange, public credit, and taxes"; and the author has a definite view of scientific method. He speaks, indeed, of "the art of political economy," using the term "political economy" in much the same sense as that in which Smith used it in dealing with "systems of political economy" in the fourth book of his great work. But this art is the statesman's business; and behind the statesman stands "the speculative person, who, removed from the practice, extracts the principles of this science from *observation* and *reflection*." Steuart does not pretend to a system, but only to "a clear deduction of principles." These principles, however, are themselves gathered from experience. His first chapter opens with the assertion, "Man we find acting uniformly in all ages, in all countries, and in all climates, from the principles of self-interest, expediency, duty and passion." And, of these, "the ruling principle" which he follows is "the principle of self-interest." From this point, the author's method may be described as deductive, and as resembling that of Smith's successors more than it does Smith's own. Further, he recognises that the conclusions, like the principles from which they proceed, are abstract and may not fit all kinds of social conditions, so that "the political economy in each [country] must necessarily be different." How far Smith took account of Steuart's reasonings we cannot say; he does not mention his name: though he is reported to have said that he understood Steuart's system better from his talk than from his book.

Adam Smith does not begin with a discourse on method; he was an artist in exposition; and he feared, perhaps unduly, any appearance of pedantry. He plunges at once into his subject: "The annual labour of every nation is the fund which originally supplies it with all the necessaries and conveniences of life which it annually consumes." These first words suggest the prevailing theme. Wealth consists not in the precious metals, but in the goods which men use or consume; and its source or cause is labour. On this foundation, he builds the structure of his science; and—although he says nothing about it—we can trace the method which he regarded as appropriate to his enquiry. It may be described shortly as abstract reasoning checked and reinforced by historical investigation. The main theorems of the analytical economics of a later period are to be found expressed or suggested in his work; but almost every deduction is supported by concrete instances. Rival schools have, thus, regarded him as their founder, and are witnesses to his grasp of principles and insight into facts. He could isolate a cause and follow out its effects; and, if he was apt sometimes to exaggerate its prominence in the complex of human motives and social conditions, it was because the facts at his disposal did not suggest the necessary qualifications of his doctrine, although more recent experience has shown that the qualifications are needed.

Adam Smith isolates the fact of wealth and makes it the subject of a science. But he sees this fact in its connections with life as a whole. His reasonings are grounded in a view of human nature and its environment, both of which meet in labour, the source of wealth and also, as he thinks, the ultimate standard of the value of commodities. In the division of labour, he sees the first step taken by man in industrial progress. His treatment of this subject has become classical, and is too well known for quotation; it is more to the purpose to point out that it was an unerring instinct for essentials which led him, in his first chapter, to fix attention on a point so obvious that it might easily have been overlooked and yet of far-reaching importance in social development generally. The division of labour, according to Smith, is the result of "the propensity to truck, barter, and exchange one thing for another." But his analysis of motives goes deeper than this; and, so far as they are concerned with wealth, human motives seem to be reduced by him to two: "the passion for present enjoyment" which "prompts to expense," and "the desire of bettering our condition" which "prompts to save." Both are selfish; and it is on this motive of self-interest, or a view of one's own advantage, that Smith constantly relies. He constructs an economic commonwealth which consists of a multitude of persons, each seeking his own interest and, in so doing, unwittingly furthering the public good—thus promoting "an end which was no part of his intention."

"The natural effort of every individual to better his own condition," he says, "when suffered to exert itself with freedom and security, is so powerful a principle, that it is alone, and without any assistance, not only capable of carrying on the society to wealth and prosperity, but of surmounting a hundred impertinent obstructions with which the folly of human laws too often encumbers its operations."

Smith, like many other philosophers of the time, assumed that there was a natural identity of public and private interest. It is a comfortable belief that society would be served best if everybody looked after his own interests; and, in an economist, this belief was, perhaps, an inevitable reaction from a condition in which state regulation of industry had largely consisted in distributing monopolies and other privileges. In Smith's mind, the belief was also bound up with the view that this identity of interests resulted from the guidance of "the invisible hand" that directs the fate of mankind. But the belief itself was incapable of verification, and subsequent industrial history refutes it. Indeed, in various places in his work, Smith himself declines to be bound by it. He thinks that the interests of the landowners and of the working class are in close agreement with the interest of society, but that those of "merchants and master manufacturers" have not the same connection with the public interest. "The interest of the dealers," he says, "is always in some respects different from, and even opposite to, that of the public." The harmony of interests, therefore, is incomplete. Nor would it be fair to say that Smith had relinquished, in *The Wealth of Nations*, his earlier view of the social factor in human motive. What he did hold was, rather, that, in the pursuit of wealth, that is to say, in industry and commerce, the motive of self-interest predominates; in famous passages, he speaks as if no other motive need be taken into account; but he recognises its varying strength; and it is only in the class of "merchants and master manufacturers" that he regards it as having free course: they are acute in the perception of their own interest and unresting in its pursuit; in the country gentleman, on the other hand, selfish interest is tempered by generosity and weakened by indolence.

From the nature of man and the environment in which he is placed, Smith derives his doctrine of "the natural progress of opulence." Subsistence is "prior to conveniency and luxury"; agriculture provides the former, commerce the latter; the cultivation of the country, therefore, precedes the increase of the town; the town, indeed, has to subsist on the surplus produce of the country; foreign commerce comes later still. This is the natural order, and it is promoted by man's natural inclinations. But human institutions have thwarted these natural inclinations, and, "in many respects, entirely inverted" the natural order. Up to Adam Smith's time, the regulation of industry had been almost universally admitted to be part of the government's functions; criticism of the principles and methods of this regulation had not been wanting; the theory of "the balance of trade," for instance, important in the doctrine of the mercantilists, had been examined and rejected by Hume and by others before him. But Smith made a comprehensive survey of the means by which, in agriculture, in the home trade and in foreign commerce, the state had attempted to regulate industry; these attempts, he thought, were all diversions of the course of trade from its "natural channels"; and he maintained that they were uniformly pernicious. Whether it acts by preference or by restraint, every such system "retards, instead of accelerating, the progress of the society towards real wealth and greatness; and diminishes, instead of increasing, the real value of the annual produce of its land and labour." When all such systems are swept away, "the obvious and simple system of natural liberty establishes itself of its own accord."

The ideas and arguments of Adam Smith were influential, at a later date, in establishing the system of free trade in Great Britain; and, perhaps, it would be not far wrong to say that a generation of economists held his views on this question to be his most solid title to fame. He regarded liberty as natural in contrast with the artificiality of government control; and the term "natural" plays an ambiguous part in his general reasonings, changing its shade of meaning, but always implying a note of approval. In this, he only used the language of his time—though Hume had pointed out that the word was treacherous. But it has to be borne in mind that, while he extolled this "natural liberty" as the best thing for trade, he did not say that it was in all cases the best thing for a country. He saw that there were other things than wealth which were worth having, and that of some of these the state was the guardian. Security must take precedence of opulence, and, on this ground, he would restrict natural liberty, not only to defend the national safety, but, also, for the protection of individual traders.

### III. OTHER PHILOSOPHICAL WRITERS

As we look back upon the development of philosophical problems, it might seem that, for a philosophical writer after Hume, there was but one thing worth doing—to answer him, if possible; and, if that were not possible, to keep silent. But the issue was not quite so clear to his contemporaries. Indeed, his own example did not press it home. It showed, on the contrary, that work of importance might be done in certain departments even when the contradiction was ignored to which Hume had reduced the theory of knowledge. Soon after the publication of *A Treatise of Human Nature*, valuable writings appeared on psychology, and on moral and political theory; there were also critics of Hume in considerable number; and one of that number had both the insight to trace Hume's scepticism to its logical origin and the intellectual capacity to set forth a theory of knowledge in which the same difficulty should not arise.

Among the psychologists, the most important place belongs to David Hartley, a physician, and sometime fellow of Jesus college, Cambridge, whose *Observations on Man: his frame, his duty, and his expectations* appeared in 1749. The rapid march of philosophical thought in the previous forty years was ignored by, and probably unknown to, the author. The whole second part of his book in which he works out a theological theory may be regarded as antiquated. He does not mention Berkeley; he seems never to have heard of David Hume. But the first or psychological part of the book has two striking features: it is a systematic attempt at a physiological psychology, and it developed the theory of the association of ideas in a way which influenced, far more than Hume did, the views of the later associational school of James Mill and his successors. The physiological doctrine was suggested by certain passages in Newton's *Optics*. Hartley supposes that the contact of an external object with the sensory nerves excites "vibrations in the æther residing in the pores of these nerves"; these vibrations enter the brain, are "propagated freely every way over the whole medullary substance," and sensations are the result; further, they leave vestiges or traces behind them, and this is the origin of ideas which depend on minute vibrations or "vibratiuncles." Motor activity is explained in a similar way. This physiological view is the basis of his whole doctrine of mind, and, more particularly, of the doctrine of association. In respect of the latter doctrine, Hartley wrote under the influence of Locke; but he has left it on record that the suggestion to make use of association as a general principle of psychological explanation came from John Gay, who had written *A Dissertation* prefixed to Law's English translation of archbishop King's *Origin of Evil* (1731), in which the doctrine was used to explain the connection of morality with private happiness. Hartley offered a physiological explanation of association itself, gave a generalised statement of its laws and applied it to the details of mental life. He did not see, as Hume had seen, the special difficulty of applying it so as to explain judgment, assent, or belief.

Abraham Tucker was a psychologist of a different temper from Hartley. He was a constant critic of Hartley's physiological doctrines, and he excelled in that introspective analysis which has been practised by many English writers. Tucker was a country gentleman whose chief employment was a study of the things of the mind. The first fruit of his reflection was a fragment *Freewill, Foreknowledge and Fate* (1763), published under the pseudonym of Edward Search; certain criticisms of this piece produced, also in 1763, *Man in quest of Himself: or a Defence of the Individuality of the Human Mind*, "by Cuthbert Comment." Thereafter, he did not turn aside from his great work, *The Light of Nature pursued*, of which the first four volumes were published by himself (again under the name of Search) in 1765, and the last three appeared after his death (1774). The author was a man of leisure himself, and he wrote for men of leisure; he was not without method; but his plan grew as he proceeded; when new fields of enquiry opened, he did not refuse to wander in them; and he liked to set forth his views *de omnibus rebus et quibusdam aliis*. Indeed, it is a work of inordinate length, and the whole is of unequal merit. Many of the long chapters have lost their interest through lapse of time and the changes which time has brought. Others, perhaps, may appeal to us only when we can catch the author's mood. Such are the speculations—put forward as purely hypothetical—concerning the soul's vehicle, the mundane soul and the vision of the disembodied soul. Mysticism is apt to appear fantastic when expressed in language so matter of fact; but the writer has a rare power of realising his fancies. The chapters, however, which deal more specifically with human nature are a genuine and important contribution to the literature of mind and morals. The writer was as innocent of Hume as was Hartley; he criticised Berkeley, though seldom with insight and never with sympathy; and he took Locke as his master. But he was not a slavish follower; it would be difficult to instance finer or more exhaustive criticism than his examination of the Lockean view that all action has for its motive the most pressing uneasiness. His moral doctrine is, perhaps, still more remarkable for the candour and elaboration with which he discussed the problem which faced all followers of Locke—the consistency of an analysis of action in terms of personal pleasure and pain with a theory of morality in which benevolence is supreme. Herein, he provided most of the material afterwards made use of by Paley. Into the details of his teaching it is impossible to enter. But, perhaps, it is not too much to say that only his diffuseness has prevented him from becoming a classic. The mere mass of the book is deterrent. Yet he would be an unlucky reader who could spend half-an-hour over its pages without finding something to arrest his attention and even to enthral his interest. The author sees mankind and the human lot with a shrewd but kindly eye; his stores of illustration are inexhaustible and illuminate subjects which in other hands would be dull; even the subtlest points are made clear by a style which is free and simple and varied; there is never any trace of sentimentality; but there are passages of humour and of pathos worthy of Goldsmith.

Richard Price, a native of Glamorgan, who became a unitarian minister in London, left his mark on more than one department of thought. His *Observations on Reversionary Payments* (1771) made a distinct advance in the theory of life assurance. His *Appeal to the Public on the Subject of the National Debt* (1772) is said to have contributed to the reestablishment of the sinking fund. He was drawn into the current of revolutionary politics and became a leading exponent of their ideas. His *Observations on the Nature of Civil Liberty, the Principles of Government, and the Justice and Policy of the War with America* made him famous in two continents. The preface to the first edition was dated 8 February, that to the fifth edition 12 March, 1776. *Additional Observations* on the same subject appeared in 1777, and a *General Introduction and Supplement* to the two tracts in 1778. The revolution in France was the occasion for *A Discourse on the Love of our Country, delivered on Nov.* 4, 1789; and this he closed with a *Nunc dimittis:* "After sharing in the benefits of one Revolution, I have been spared to be a witness to two other Revolutions, both glorious." This *Discourse* had the further distinction of provoking Burke's *Reflections on the Revolution in France.* But, famous as his political partisanship made him at the time, Price has a better title to be remembered for his first work, *A Review of the Principal Questions in Morals* (1757; 3rd edn., revised and enlarged, 1787).

Price has the mathematician's interest ·in intellectual concepts and his power of dealing with abstractions. In philosophy, he is a successor of Cudworth and Clarke, and the theories of knowledge of both Locke and Hume are attacked at the roots. The understanding or reason (he argues) has its own ideas, for which it does not depend upon sense-impression. Necessity, possibility, identity, cause are instances of such abstract ideas. They are "intelligible objects" discovered by "the eye of the mind." Reason is thus "the source of new ideas"; and among them are the ideas of right and wrong; these are simple ideas and perceived by an immediate "intuition" of the understanding: "morality is a branch of necessary truth." The system which Price bases on this view has become, more than any other, the type of modern intuitional ethics.

Joseph Priestley had many points of sympathy with Price. They belonged to the same profession—the unitarian ministry —and they were prominent on the same side in the revolutionary politics of the day. But, in spite of this similarity and of their personal friendship, they represent different attitudes of mind. Price was a mathematician, familiar with abstract ideas, and an intellectualist in philosophy. Priestley was a chemist, busied in experiments, a convinced disciple of the empirical philosophy and a supporter of materialism. He was the author of *The History and present State of Electricity* (1767), and, afterwards, of numerous papers and treatises on chemical subjects, which recorded the results of his original investiga-

tions and have established his fame as a man of science.  He
came early under the influence of Hartley and published a
simplification of his book—omitting the doctrine of vibrations
and laying stress solely on the principle of the association of
ideas; but he rejected Hartley's view of mind as an immaterial
principle and held that the powers termed mental are the
result "of such an organical structure as that of the brain."
His philosophical views were expressed and defended in *Disquisitions relating to Matter and Spirit* (1777), in *The Doctrine
of Philosophical Necessity* (1777) and in *A Free Discussion*
(1778) on these topics with Price; and he also published (1774)
*An Examination* of the doctrines of Reid and others of the
new school of Scottish philosophers.  Of greater interest than
these, however, is the short *Essay on the First Principles of
Government* (1768).  This forms a contrast to the *a priori*
arguments in which Price delighted—although its practical
tendency is the same.  It propounds "one general idea,"
namely, "that all people live in society for their mutual advantage," and draws the conclusion that their happiness is
"the great standard by which every thing relating to that state
must finally be determined."  Priestley thus set the example,
which Bentham followed, of taking utilitarian considerations
for the basis of a philosophical radicalism, instead of the dogmas
about natural rights common with other revolutionary thinkers
of the period.  He did not anticipate Bentham in using the
famous utilitarian formula (as he is often said to have done[1]),
but he did precede him in taking the happiness of the majority
as the test in every political question, and he made it easier for
Bentham to use the same standard in judging private conduct.

In a somewhat similar way, the exhaustive analyses of
Tucker led to the theological utilitarianism of William Paley,
sometime fellow of Christ's college, Cambridge, and senior
wrangler in 1763.  Paley was not a writer of marked originality.  If, in his *Principles of Moral and Political Philosophy*
(1785), he owed much to Tucker, in his *View of the Evidences
of Christianity* (1794), he depended on the *Criterion* (1752) of
John Douglas, bishop of Salisbury—a reply to Hume's argument against miracles—and on Nathaniel Lardner's *Credibility*

[1] See *ante*, Vol. IX, p. 337 note.

*of the Gospel History* (1723–55); and, in his *Natural Theology*
(1804), he drew much material from John Ray's *The Wisdom
of God manifested in the Works of the Creation* (1691), from
William Derham's *Physico-Theology* (1713) and from the work
of the Dutchman Nieuwentyt, which had been translated into
English in 1730 as *The Religious Philosopher*. His *Horæ Paulinæ*
(1790) is said to be the most original, and to have been the
least successful, of his publications.    These four books form a
consistent system.    Probably, no English writer has ever
excelled Paley in power of marshalling arguments or in clearness of reasoning; and these merits have given some of his
works a longer life as academic text-books than their other
merits can justify.    Paley was, essentially, a man of his time
and his views were its views, through expressed with a skill
which was all his own.

In his *Moral Philosophy*, there is no trace of the vacillation
at critical points which marks most of his empirical predecessors.    The only criticism to which it lies open is that morality
vanishes when reduced to a calculation of selfish interests.
A man's own happiness is always his motive; he can seek
the general happiness only when that way of acting is made
for his own happiness also; and this can be done only by the
rewards and punishments of a lawgiver.    Locke distinguished
three different sorts of law, and Paley followed him rather
closely.    But the law of honour is insufficient, as having little
regard to the general happiness; and the law of the land is
inadequate for it omits many duties as not fit objects for com-
pulsion, and it permits many crimes because incapable of
definition; there remains, therefore, only the law of Scripture
(that is, of God) which, alone, is obviously sufficient.    Hence,
the famous definition, "Virtue is the doing good to mankind,
in obedience to the will of God, and for the sake of everlasting
happiness."

This conclusion leads up to the argument of his later works.
His *Horæ Paulinæ* and *Evidences* have to demonstrate the
credibility of the New Testament writings and the truth of the
Christian revelation; and this position assumes the existence
of God which, in his *Natural Theology*, he proves from the marks
of design in the universe and, in particular, in the human
body.    In these works, we see how complete is the shifting of

interest to which reference has previously been made.[1]  Attention is concentrated on the question of external evidences, and the content of religion is almost entirely overlooked.  God is the superhuman watchmaker who has put the world-machine together with surprising skill, and intervenes miraculously, on rare occasions, when the works are getting out of order. Paley developed a familiar analogy with unequalled impressiveness; he should not be blamed for failing to anticipate the effect upon his argument which has been produced by the biological theory of natural selection; but he did not pause to examine the underlying assumptions of the analogy which he worked out; he had no taste for metaphysics; and his mind moved easily only within the range of the scientific ideas of his own day.

The most powerful reply to Hume—indeed, the only competent attempt to refute his philosophy as a whole—came from a group of scholars in Aberdeen who had formed themselves into a philosophical society.  Of this group, Thomas Reid, a professor in King's college, was the most notable member, and he was the founder of the school of Scottish philosophy known as the common-sense school.  With him were associated George Campbell and James Beattie,[2] professors (the former afterwards principal) in Marischal college, as well as other men of mark in their day.  The earliest contribution to the controversy —Campbell's *Dissertation on Miracles* (1763)—dealt with a side issue; but it is of interest for its examination of the place of testimony in knowledge; whereas experience (it is argued) leads to general truths and is the foundation of philosophy, testimony is the foundation of history, and it is capable of giving absolute certainty.  Campbell's later work, *The Philosophy of Rhetoric* (1776), contains much excellent psychology. Beattie's *Essay on the Nature and Immutability of Truth* (1770) is not a work of originality or of distinction; but it is a vigorous polemic; it brought him great temporary fame, and he has been immortalised by the art of Reynolds as serenely clasping his book whilst Hume and other apostles of error are being hurled into limbo.  About the same time, James Oswald, a Perthshire

---

[1] See *ante*, Vol. IX, p. 323.
[2] As to Beattie's poetry cf. Chap. VII, pp. 174 f., *ante*.

clergyman, published *An Appeal to Common Sense in behalf of Religion* (1766–72). Reid, Beattie and Oswald were placed together by Priestley for the purpose of his *Examination;* and the same collocation of names was repeated by Kant; but it is entirely unjust to Reid.

Reid's *Inquiry into the Human Mind on the Principles of Common Sense* was published in 1764; shortly afterwards, he removed to Glasgow, to fill the chair vacated by Adam Smith. His later and more elaborate works—*Essays on the Intellectual Powers of Man* and *Essays on the Active Powers of Man*—appeared in 1785 and 1788 respectively. In his philosophical work, Reid has the great merit of going to the root of the matter, and he is perfectly fair-minded in his criticism. He admits the validity of Hume's reasonings; he does not appeal to the vulgar against his conclusions; but he follows the argument back to its premises and tests the truth of these premises. This is his chief claim to originality. He finds that the sceptical results of Hume are legitimate inferences from "the ideal theory" which Locke took over from Descartes, and he puts to himself the question, "what evidence have I for this doctrine, that all the objects of my knowledge are ideas in my own mind?" He points out (what is undoubtedly true) that neither Locke nor Berkeley nor Hume produced any evidence for the assumption. They started with the view that the immediate object of knowledge is something in the mind called ideas; and they were consequently unable to prove the existence of anything outside the mind or even of mind itself. "Ideas," says Reid, "seem to have something in their nature unfriendly to other existences." He solves the difficulty by denying the existence of ideas. There are no such "images of external things" in the mind, but sensation is accompanied by an act of perception, and the object of perception is the real external thing.

Hume had said that his difficulties would vanish if our perceptions inhered in something simple and individual, or if the mind perceived some real connection among them; and Reid proposes a positive theory of knowledge which will give the required assurance on this point. Every sensation is accompanied by a "natural and original judgment" which refers the sensation to mind as its act. We do not need, first of all, to get the two things "mind" and "sensation" and then to connect them; "one of the related things—to wit sensation—suggests to us both the correlate and the relation." Reid's terminology is not happy. The word "suggests" is badly chosen, though he distinguishes this "natural suggestion" from the suggestion which is the result of experience and habit. And his term "common sense" has given rise to more serious misunderstandings, for which he is by no means blameless. Even his doctrine of immediate perception is far from clear. But, if we read him sympathetically, we may see that he had hold of a truth of fundamental importance. The isolated impressions or ideas with which Locke and Hume began are fictions; they do not correspond to anything real in experience. The simplest portion of our experience is not separate from its context in this way; it implies a reference to mind and to an objective order, and thus involves the relations which Reid ascribed to "natural suggestion" or "common sense."

# CHAPTER XV

## Divines

WITH the beginning of the eighteenth century, we reach a period in English theological literature of which the character is not less definite because there were individual writers who struggled against it. The matter and the style alike were placid and unemotional, rational rather than learned, tending much more to the commonplace than to the pedantic, and, above all, abhorrent of that dangerous word, and thing, enthusiasm. Johnson's definition gives a significant clue to the religious literature in which his contemporaries had been educated. Enthusiasm, in his *Dictionary*, is (from Locke) "a vain belief of private revelation, a vain confidence of divine favour," to which even the nonconformists, if one may judge by the subjects of their books, had, in the early eighteenth century, abandoned all special claim; and, also, it implied, in Johnson's own view, "heat of imagination" and "violence of passion." From this, the main current of theological writing, for more than fifty years, ran conspicuously away. The mystics, such as William Law, as has been shown in an earlier chapter,[1] were strange exceptions, *rari nantes in gurgite vasto* of this decorous self-restraint or complacency. It was not till count Zinzendorf and the Moravians completed the impression which *A Serious Call* had made on the heart of John Wesley that the literature of religion received a new impetus and inspiration; and the old school fought long and died hard. It was not till the word enthusiasm could be used in their condign praise that English theologians began to feel again something of the fire and poetry of their subject, and,

[1] See Vol. IX, Chap. XII, *ante*, and cf. Byrom's poem "Enthusiasm," with introduction on the use of the word, in *The Poems of John Byrom*, ed. Ward, A. W., vol. II (1895). See, also, *Ibid.*, vol. III (1912), p. 113 and note.

once more, to scale its heights and sound its depths. And yet, as we say this, we are confronted by evident exceptions. No one can deny the power of Butler's writing, whatever it may be the fashion to assert as to the depth of his thought; and, while there was fire enough in Atterbury, in Wilson there was certainly the delicate aroma of that intimate sincerity which has in all literature an irresistible charm. Some earlier writers may be left aside, such as Richard Cumberland, who, though a bishop, was rather a philosopher than a theologian, and Samuel Johnson, the Ben Jochanan of Dryden, whose divinity was not more than an excrescence on his fame as a whig pamphleteer who suffered excessively for his opinions. His manner of writing was unquestionably savage. *Julian the Apostate: Being a Short Account of his Life; the sense of the Primitive Christians about his Succession; and their Behaviour towards him. Together with a comparison of Popery and Paganism* (1682), is more vehement and obnoxious than most of those bitter attacks on James duke of York with which the press groaned during the last years of Charles II; yet its author hardly deserved degradation from the priesthood, the pillory and whipping from Newgate to Tyburn. As the chaplain of Lord William Russell, Johnson might be expected to speak boldly: and his writing was full of sound and fury, as a characteristic sentence—a solitary one, be it observed—from his *Reflections on the History of Passive Obedience* may show.

I have reason to enter a just Complaint against the pretended Church-of-England Men of the two last Reigns, who not only left me the grinning Honour of maintaining the establish'd Doctrine of the Church all alone, (which I kept alive, till it pleased God to make it a means of our Deliverance, with the perpetual hazard of my own life for many years, and with suffering Torments and Indignitys worse than Death) but also beside this, were very zealous in running me down, and very officious in degrading me, as an Apostate from the Church of England for this very Service: While at the same time, they themselves were making their Court with their own Renegado Doctrine of Passive Obedience; and wearing out all Pulpits with it, as if it had been, not only the First and Great Commandment, but the Second too; and cramming it down the reluctant throats of dying Patriots, as the Terms of their Salvation.

We may begin the tale with Francis Atterbury. He was born in 1663, and his upbringing, at the quiet Buckinghamshire rectory of Milton Keynes, by a father who had been suspect of disloyalty for his compliance with the commonwealth and, probably, atoned for it by an exaggerated attachment to the restored Stewarts, was in the strictest principles of the establishment in church and state. A Westminster boy and student of Christ Church, he became prominent among the scholars of his day, and his contribution to the Phalaris controversy[1] made him famous. He took holy orders in 1687, and, before long, reached high preferment. Soon after the beginning of the century, he was archdeacon of Totnes and chaplain in ordinary to queen Anne. He became dean of Carlisle (1704), of Christ Church (1712) and of Westminster and bishop of Rochester (1713). Seven years later, he was imprisoned in the Tower, without much evidence against him, for having been concerned in a plot to restore the Stewarts. Banishment followed, and he definitely threw in his lot with the exiled family. He lived till 1732. For fifty years, he was an influential, though not a voluminous, writer. Politically, he was vehement; in religion, he was wholehearted; and the two interests seemed to him inseparable. What weighed most with him in politics, truly says his latest biographer,[2] was "the consequence that the Whigs' latitudinarianism would have, and as a matter of fact did have, on the Church of England." He was, indeed, from first to last, a "church of England man," of the type which the sunshine of queen Anne's favour ripened. The Hanoverian type of protestantism was uncongenial to him: he distrusted and feared its rationalising influence. In his view, as he said in the dedication of his sermons to Trelawny (famous as one of the seven bishops), "the Fears of Popery were scarce remov'd, when Heresy began to diffuse its Venom." Thus, he came to the position which Addison expressed in an epigram, but which, perhaps, was not so inconsistent as it seemed— "that the Church of England will always be in danger till it has a Popish king for its defender."

If his contribution to the Phalaris controversy best exhibits his wit, and his political writing his trenchant diction, his

---

[1] See Vol. IX, Chap. XIII, p. 372, *ante.*

[2] Beeching, H. C., *Francis Atterbury* (1909), p. 263.

sermons may, perhaps, be regarded as his permanent contributions to English literature. There is no conspicuous merit in their style or in their argument; but they are lucid, argumentative and, on occasion, touched by real feeling. Perhaps, his sincerity never appeared to more advantage than in the quiet pathos of his *Discourse on the death of the Lady Cutts* (1698), the opening passage of which gave at least a hint to Sterne for a very famous sermon.

Much the same may be said of Atterbury's friend George Smalridge, who succeeded him as dean of Christ Church. Smalridge was a less active Jacobite and a less vehement man, and died peaceably, though in disgrace, as bishop of Bristol. He

toasted the Pretender in the privacy of his rooms at Christ Church, but gave him no other support; recognising, no doubt, that anything but a Platonic affection was incompatible with the Church principles of non-resistance to established authority, of which he and Atterbury had been among the foremost champions.

Some of this quietude gives tone to his sermons, which Johnson praised for their elegant style; and Addison wrote in 1718 "he is to me the most candid and agreeable of all the bishops." Dedicated to Caroline princess of Wales—who, as queen, had a striking talent for the discovery of clever clergymen—and produced in print for an extraordinarily large number of subscribers, the sermons are more remarkable for sound sense than for eloquence or argument. The English is pure and unaffected; Addison, perhaps, is the model; but his excellence is far from being attained. Smalridge was indignant when some one thought to flatter him by suggesting that he wrote *A Tale of a Tub:* a very moderate knowledge of his style should have convinced the most obtuse that he could not have written the *Tale* if he would. In truth, he is typical of his period. The theological writings of the day had none of the learning, or the attempt at it, which had marked the Caroline epoch; they had no charm of language, no eloquence or passion. The utmost they aimed at was lucidity, and, when this was achieved, we are left wondering whether what could be so expressed was worth expressing at all. Atterbury had stood alone against the benumbing influence of Tillotson.

It needed controversy to stir the placid contentment of the early Hanoverian dignitaries. And, of controversy, vehement enough, they had their share. If Sacheverell did not contribute anything of value to English literature, the same cannot be said of Wake or even, perhaps, of Hoadly. In 1715, William Wake succeeded Tenison as archbishop. His predecessor had possessed a certain skill in anti-Roman controversy, and he had the very rare accomplishment of being able to write a good collect; but Wake was altogether his superior. In history, his translation of the Apostolic Fathers and his very important contributions to the discussion on the powers of convocation give him a place in the short list of English archbishops who have been learned men. Nor was his learning anglican only; he was better known in Germany and France, as well as in the eastern church, than any of his successors till quite modern times. As a controversialist, he was lucid and graceful; but when he hit he could hit hard. The convocation controversy, though it employed the powers of Atterbury, Burnet, Hody, Kennett, and Matthew Hutton of Aynho, hardly belongs to the history of literature. But it gave great opportunity for the display of that kind of antiquarian knowledge in which many of the English clergy of the time excelled. Few of those who joined in it were not, at the same time, writers of eminence in their own fields: Wake was distinguished for his studies of the Apostolic Fathers, Hody as a Hebraist, Kennett, in that admirable book *The Parochial Antiquities of Ambrosden*, a very model for local historians. And the convocation controversy was soon merged in the discussion as to the orthodoxy of certain ecclesiastics, some prominent, some undistinguished, which began with Hoadly and his views of church authority.

Benjamin Hoadly was a clergyman in whom the objectionable features of Gilbert Burnet were exaggerated to the verge of caricature. He was a whig and a follower of the government in power first of all, a controversialist in consequence, and only after that was he an ecclesiastic. As a political writer, he opposed Atterbury and Blackall in 1709–10; on the Hanoverian succession being accomplished, he was rewarded by the see of Bangor, which he hardly ever visited. In 1717, his famous sermon entitled *The Nature of the Kingdom or Church of Christ* caused the acid controversy which was named after him; *A Preservative against the Principles and Practices of the Nonjurors*, a treatise published by him in 1716, called forth the drastic criticism of William Law; and *A Plain Account of the Nature and End of the Sacrament* (1735), the massive treatise of Waterland on the doctrine of the Eucharist. He seemed to live for dispute and preferment; and he accepted both with the placid dignity which is inimitably rendered in Hogarth's immortal portrait. As a writer, he carries the sobriety of Tillotson to the extreme of pompous dulness; it is safe to say that the volumes of his sermons and other argumentative works which line many old libraries have rested for a century and a half undisturbed by any reader's hand. Their manner, which is devoid of any original touch, contrasts strangely with their matter. Hoadly's theory of churchmanship reduced itself to pure individualism tempered by toleration. He was a conscientious advocate for the repeal of the whole range of test acts. He was, in fact, a much better thinker in matters of state than in those which belonged more directly to his own profession. From under the cloud of words and the skilful tangle of qualifications in which his thought is enveloped, there emerges the certainty that he had no coherent idea of a religious society at all. If he had points of affinity with Thomas Arnold, he is, perhaps, not very far away from the reforming theologians or even the theorists of the Middle Age. Church and state are one in his mind; but it is the state which turns church communion into something quite vague, general and ultimately unmeaning; yet he has not risen to the idea of a federation; he remains in a conception of essential fluidity. On the other hand, his advocacy of toleration, on true principles, was, if not an advance in theory on the position of several earlier English writers, of different parties, at least one in actual practice, before whig statesmen as well as anglican bishops were prepared to accept it. Hoadly became bishop of Winchester in 1734 and held the see till his death in 1761. It cannot be said that he rendered any service to the church, and the controversies of which he was the centre had no small share in that eclipse of her literary glory, which was the conspicuous characteristic of the Hanoverian, as opposed to the Stewart, age.

If Hoadly typifies the comfortable Erastianism of the leaders of the establishment, William Law's enthusiasm and depth were reproduced in not a few of the later nonjurors. It was some time before the inspiring self-sacrifice of Sancroft and Hickes and their colleagues died down into the sordid, insignificance which Johnson professed to have witnessed. The spirit of literary audacity which had fled the established church was still to be found among the nonjurors. The two Thomas Wagstaffes—the father (1645–1712) nonjuring bishop of Ipswich, the son (1692–1770) English chaplain to the banished Stewarts—were writers of considerable power. The *Vindication*, by the pen of the elder, of Charles I's authorship of *Eikon Basilike*, followed by *A Defence of the Vindication*, is a work of considerable, though not of convincing, force. Both were noted as antiquaries, and belong, indeed, to the school, as we may call it, of Carte, Leslie, Rawlinson and Hearne. Thomas Deacon, again, was a scholar of no mean order with a range of theological knowledge unusual in his day. By profession a physician, he was ordained by the nonjuring bishop Gandy in 1716, and consecrated, probably in 1733, by Archibald Campbell, bishop of Aberdeen, whom Dr. Johnson described as "very curious and inquisitive but credulous." The nonjurors (as has been seen in the case of Hickes) were close students of liturgiology, and the revised communion office of the "Usagers," with the *Compleat Devotions* of 1734, bear witness to the accuracy of Deacon's study and influenced the important liturgies of the Scottish and American churches of the present day.

As may seem natural for men who found themselves compelled to live more and more apart from the general religious and even the social life of their day, the nonjurors turned to antiquarianism as a solace for their seclusion as well as a support for their doctrines. The older race of those who withdrew from communion with the national church were often men of great learning as well as steadfast principle. Henry Dodwell is a typical example. He held a fellowship at Trinity college,

Dublin, but resigned it, being unwilling to take holy orders. He then resided in England, in London or Oxford at first, in later years in Berkshire. From 1688 to 1691, he was Camden professor of history at Oxford. He was deprived because he would not take the oaths; but William III is said to have declared that he would not make him a martyr—"He has set his heart on being one and I have set mine on disappointing him." Hearne considered him "the greatest scholar in Europe when he died," and even such an opponent as White Kennett respected his learning. His writings are partly "occasional" and vehement, partly deliberate and scholastic. To the former class belongs what he wrote about the schism; to the latter, his work on Irenaeus and on ancient history in general. It cannot be said that he left any permanent impression on English literature or scholarship, though his writings were long remembered and utilised by lesser men. His friends Nelson, Hearne, Cherry and the rest preserved his memory in their circle of devout ecclesiasticism. But the whole mass of the nonjurors' literary output, even work so good as that of Brett and Leslie, belongs to a backwater in English letters. One fragrant survival, however, may be mentioned here for its exquisite and simple pathos, *A Pattern for Young Students in the University, set forth in the Life of Mr. Ambrose Bonwicke, sometime Scholar of St. John's College in Cambridge* (1729).[1] It is the record of a young nonjuror's life, told by his father, in an unaffected, but deeply touching, manner which no man of letters of the day could have surpassed. One is tempted to put beside it, for their record of devotion to duty in circumstances very different, the *Journals* of the Scottish bishop Robert Forbes (in 1762 and 1770),[2] a divine whose "primitive piety" and ecclesiastical principles were supported by the same doctrines of church obedience as directed the life of the young Cambridge scholar. Men such as these must in all ages live remote from public haunt. Joseph Bingham, the greatest ecclesiastical antiquary of his time and for long after it, was incessantly active as a writer, but (save that he was unjustly stigmatised as a heretic and had to resign his fellowship at Oxford in consequence) was entirely neglected by those

[1] Edited by Mayor, J. E. B., Cambridge, 1870.
[2] Edited by Craven, J. B., 1876.

whose business it should have been to know what scholars wrote. His *Origines Ecclesiasticae*, or *The Antiquities of the Christian Church* (published in successive volumes from 1708 to 1722) is a mine of learning, to which writers everywhere had recourse till the Cambridge scholars of the later nineteenth century began the critical rewriting of the history of the early church. Bingham, it may be said, did for church history what Pearson did for the creed. He showed what it meant at the time of its beginning and he illustrated its growth by a store of learning which none in his own time could rival, and few since have surpassed. At the beginning of the eighteenth century it was, certainly, in learning rather than in pure letters that the *clerus Angliae* preserved its reputation.

Returning from this interesting by-path, we find the main field of theology in possession of writers of scarcely a single literary merit. *The Annual Register*, when it commemorated Hoadly on his death, allowed him the virtue that, in all his controversies with his brethren ("and no one surely ever held more"), he never lost his equanimity of temper or descended to any railing accusation. In the same way, Thomas Sherlock, bishop of London, was praised in that

he too had his controversies, and those carried on with warmth and spirit, but without any injury to his temper, or any interruption to his thoughts and mind.

He was, indeed, an opponent of Hoadly even more persistent than Law. He was chairman of the committee of the lower house of convocation which considered the book that was the *fons et origo mali;* and, though, owing to the suspension of the sessions of convocation, the report was never published, its substance, no doubt, appeared in *Remarks on the Bishop of Bangor's treatment of the Clergy and Convocations*, issued by him anonymously in 1717, and in other pamphlets. Sherlock's politics, in early life, were, like those of his more famous father (master of the Temple and dean of St. Paul's), not above suspicion with those in power: the wits compared the two thus:

As Sherlock the elder with *jure* divine
Did not comply till the battle of Boyne;

So Sherlock the younger still made it a question
Which side he should take till the battle of Preston.

But, in later life, he was a steady supporter of Walpole, and
his politics even more than his preaching brought him to high
place.   He was appointed bishop of London in 1748, and it is
said that he had declined even higher preferment.   Before
this, nearly all his important literary work had been done.   He
had engaged in the deist controversy in 1725, and his *Trial of
the Witnesses of the Resurrection of Jesus* (1729) was a very
notable apologetic, on quite modern lines, in answer to Wool-
ston.   Next to Butler, he was the most powerful opponent,
and the most rational, whom the deists encountered.   His
last work, which enjoyed the popularity of a modern novel,
was *A Letter to the Clergy and People of London and Westminster
on occasion of the late Earthquake* (1750).   Nichols, the bookseller, tells that 100,000 copies were sold in less than a month;
and the trenchant vigour of its denunciation of vice and appeal
for amendment make it still worthy of perusal.

But books and pamphlets such as Sherlock's are at least
on the fringe of that sad class of writings which Lamb stigmatised as *biblia abiblia*.   We rise far above it when we come
to the work of men so different as bishop Wilson, bishop
Butler and Daniel Waterland.   The three men were profoundly
different.   Wilson, in much of his thought and life, was a
survival of the early seventeenth century and, indeed, of far
earlier times.   Waterland, in many respects, was typical of the
early eighteenth century.   Butler had affinities with the
nineteenth—with Newman, for example, and Gladstone.   The
life of Wilson was uneventful.   He took his degree from Trinity
college, Dublin, and was ordained in the church of Ireland,
served a Lancashire curacy, became chaplain to the earl of
Derby and preceptor to his son at the salary of thirty pounds a
year, to which was added the mastership of the Lathom alms-
house, twenty pounds more—whereupon he had "an income
far beyond his expectations, far beyond his wishes, except as
it increased his ability to do good"—and, in 1697, was appointed
by his patron to the bishopric of Sodor and Man, in spite of his
refusal.   At Bishop's court, Kirk Michael, he lived, for nearly
sixty years, the life of a primitive saint, devoted entirely to

works of piety, the father of his people, not neglecting to punish as well as to protect. His collected works were not published till 1781; but many of them had long achieved a remarkable popularity. Of the eight volumes, four contain sermons, of a directness of appeal and simplicity of language unusual for the time. The English is forcible and unaffected; there are no pedantic expressions, or classical phrases, or lengthy words. Everyone could understand what Wilson said, and everyone might profit by it. He wrote, not to astonish, but to convince; yet the simplicity of his manner avoids the pit of commonplace into which such writers as Tillotson not rarely fall. No one could call the good bishop a great writer; but no one could call him a poor one. In his *Maxims* and his *Parochialia*, he shows a knowledge of human nature not very common among clergymen; while his *Sacra Privata*, which explains (to an intelligent reader) how this knowledge was obtained, places him with bishop Andrewes among the masters of English devotional literature.

Very different is the ponderous solidity of Daniel Water-land. He was a controversialist, a scholar and an archdeacon —callings which tend to dryness and pomposity and seldom encourage literary excellence. Master of Magdalene college, Cambridge, and vice-chancellor, he was recommended, says his biographer, "to the favour of the government" by his "wise and moderate sentiments," but he did not attain to any great position in the church. He preferred, it may well be, to remain an adept in university business and a wielder of the cudgel against the heretics of his age, among whom several, such as Biddle, Firmin and Gilbert Clerke (to repeat the phrase used by bishop van Mildert nearly a century ago) "now scarcely retain a place in our recollection." Samuel Clarke's *Scripture Doctrine of the Trinity* (1712), amid all the heavy literature which it evoked, had no more successful rival than Waterland's *Vindication of Christ's Divinity*, which is almost worthy to be placed beside the work of bishop Bull; and this was but one of the writings of the Cambridge scholar which dealt with the subject. Waterland had long given attention to the claims of semi-Arians to hold office in the church of England, and, in a famous disputation, when he "kept a Divinity Act for his

Bachelor of Divinity," had had for his opponent (who was, of course, merely assuming the post of *advocatus arianismi*) Thomas Sherlock,

"one of the greatest ornaments of the Church, and finest writers of the age, who gave full play to his abilities, and called forth," says a contemporary, "all that strength of reason of which he was the master."

Here, in spite of a certain favour which royalty was inclined to bestow upon Arianism, Waterland was safe from censure by great personages of the day. His moderation appears less favourably in his abstention from action throughout the long period during which Bentley was unjustly suspended. His learning, on the other hand, in his treatise on the Athanasian creed, a vindication of that much-contested symbol, which is even now not out of date, appears in its most favourable aspect, and the book deserved the eulogy of archbishop Dawes of York, a prelate who did not fear, even when suspected of Jacobitism, to express his opinions:

"With great pleasure I read it," wrote the primate of England, "both on account of the subject matter of it, and the manner in which you have treated it; the one, of the greatest importance to the Christian faith; the other, a pattern to all writers of controversy in the great points of religion."

In 1727, he became canon of Windsor; in 1730, vicar of Twickenham and archdeacon of Middlesex; and he enjoyed "his retirement at Twickenham," his visits to Cambridge and the honour of being prolocutor of the lower house of the convocation of Canterbury, till his death in 1740, when an opponent offered the curious testimony to his merits that

notwithstanding his being a contender for the Trinity yet he was a benevolent man, an upright Christian and a beautiful writer; exclusive of his zeal for the Trinity, he was in everything else an excellent clergyman and an admirable scholar.

But the most famous of his writings is, undoubtedly, his *Review of the Doctrine of the Eucharist*, which was for long regarded as the classic work of anglican theology on its subject. It is only necessary to say of the doctrine, as stated by Waterland, that it does not proceed beyond the qualified statement of the judicious Hooker and would not have satisfied Andrewes, Jeremy Taylor, or Cosin—not to mention so typical an anglican as George Herbert—among his predecessors; still less does it rise to the views which found expression in the notable work of John Johnson, *The Unbloody Sacrifice.* In his own words, Waterland advocates not a sacrificial, but a federal, view of the Eucharist. As a writer, he is lucid without being common-place and learned without being pedantic. His prose is better than Tillotson's, easier than Butler's; but no one would quote it for its excellence, as, in his day, men quoted the archbishop, or remember it for its massive power, as Butler must always be remembered.

Joseph Butler is, indeed, even as a master of English, con-spicuously the greatest of the three writers whom we have chosen to illustrate the character of English theology during this period. The explanation is that Butler was, what the others were not, a great writer and a great man. His prose has a massive force, a sheer weight, to which no English writer of his time approaches. Under its severe restraint burns the fire of a deep and intense conviction. He has been but poorly under-stood by those who have regarded him as a convincing critic, a master of logical acuteness. He was far more; and what he was is revealed in every paragraph of his writing. On the one hand, his view of life and thought was synthetical, not merely inquisitive or analytic: on the other, he was inspired with a supreme belief, a mastering optimism, a triumphant faith. In the cold marble of his prose, there are veins of colour, touches of rich crimson, caerulean blue, or sunny gold, such as one sees on some beautiful ancient sarcophagus. He is a master of calm exposition, as well as of irony; but he is, even more notably, a writer of profound and unquenchable passion. His heart no less than his head is in what he has written; and it is this which gives him his place among the masters of English prose. Butler has enriched English literature with many a striking apophthegm; but his use of the language can only be adequately tested by long passages. It is difficult to select from him; he has no purple patches; page after page shines with the same massive splendour. The manner of the *Sermons* is

as admirable as the matter: it is typical of the prose of his age
at its very best. The style of the *Analogy* is more difficult,
more compressed and concise, so that it seems at first sight to
be stiff and involved; but a little study of it shows that it is
intentionally, and admirably, adapted to its matter. The steps,
as Gladstone said, are as carefully measured out as if we were
climbing the hill of the *Purgatorio;* and each single sentence
has been well compared to "a well-considered move in chess."
From another point of view, we may again adopt the statesman's quaint retort to the criticism of Matthew Arnold:

The homely fare, upon which Butler feeds us, cannot be so gratifying to the palate as turtle, venison, and champagne. But it has
been found wholesome by experience: it leads to no doctor's bills;
and a perusal of this "failure" is admitted to be "a most valuable
exercise for the mind."

No religious book of the eighteenth century, save only
Law's *Serious Call*, had so much influence as the *Analogy*, and
the influence of each, different though they were, has proved
abiding in English literature as well as English religion. It
came without question from the same source. It has been
said of Joseph Butler, that he was known to be given to religious
retirement and to reading the biographies of holy persons; and,
though the one was a bishop and the other a nonjuror, the
words are equally applicable to William Law.[1]

The work of Butler is the high-water mark of English theology in the middle of the eighteenth century. The descent
from it is almost abrupt. Two names only remain to be
specially noticed before we pass to a new period—those of
Thomas Herring and Thomas Secker, both archbishops of
Canterbury, who were born in the same year 1693, and died,
the former in 1757, the latter in 1768. Archbishop Herring
was a complete contrast to the leading prelates of his day.
His sermons at Lincoln's inn gave him fame, and he passed, in
a career of unemotional benevolence, from the deanery of
Rochester to the sees of Bangor, York and Canterbury. He
did not contend with deists or Arians, and the Athanasian

---

[1] Cf., as to Butler's *Fifteen Sermons* and *Analogy*, *ante*, Vol. IX, pp. 338 ff. As
to Law, see *Ibid.*, Chap. XII.

controversy had for him no charms. He was prepared to re-
vise the *Prayer-Book* and the Articles, and to exchange pulpits
with dissenters. He befriended the Jews, and Hume tells us,
in his *Essays*, that the archbishop praised him for his *History*.
He raised a large sum for the government during the '45. But
his literary work, save his rather pleasing letters, is uninteresting and ineffective. His successor at York and Canterbury,
Matthew Skelton, was little thought of and soon forgotten.
But with Thomas Secker, bishop in turn of Bristol and of
Oxford, and archbishop of Canterbury for ten years, from 1758,
we reach a higher grade. Like Butler, with whom he had been
at school, and like not a few in the list of English primates, he
was not till manhood converted to the English church, and,
to the delicate taste of Horace Walpole, he seemed to retain
to the last something of the "tone of fanaticism" which had
belonged to his early training. Yet the beginning of methodism filled him with alarm: whatever he may have shown of
"fanaticism," he was certainly no "enthusiast." On his
sermons, which, with his *Lectures on the Church Catechism*, were
his chief work, the opinion of his contemporaries, for once, very
fairly represents what would be thought to-day. Hurd, the
favourite bishop of George III, said that they had "a certain
conciliatory calmness, propriety, and decency of language,
with no extraordinary reach of thought, vigour of sentiment,
or beauty of expression." And Christopher Pitt, when, in *The
Art of Preaching*, he advises young preachers, describes the
impression made by the archbishop, in words that no doubt
sum up his merits:

> Speak, look, and move with dignity and ease
> Like mitred Secker, you'll be sure to please.

Secker, however, did not wear a mitre—he only wore a wig,
and the literary style in which he excelled has passed away with
his headgear. It was the methodist movement which swept
away what seemed to it to be solemn trifling. From the middle
of the eighteenth century, the new influence which passed over
English religion had its effect, gradual and much contested,
upon English literature also. The age of Wesley and Whitefield introduced what may be called a new romanticism in
religion, just as the Lake school, half a century later, may be

said to have destroyed the classic tradition of the older poetry.
A word is needed as to the historical setting of this new departure in English theology.

The methodist movement was a reaction against the calmness with which English theologians had accepted, and suppressed, many of the vital elements of the Christian creed.
Divinity is the most progressive of the sciences, and no literature becomes so rapidly out of date as theology—all but the
highest. Admirably straightforward though much of the
writing of English divines in the early eighteenth century was,
it had fewer of the elements of permanence than any of the
systems that had preceded it; to appropriate words of Johnson,
it had not sufficient vitality to preserve it from putrefaction.
A new theology, or, at least, a revival of the old, was needed,
which should base its appeal on the verities of the Christian
life. The young Oxford students who founded methodism
were, above all things, anxious to rule their daily doings by the
standard, ascetic and devotional, of the English church. It
has been, in recent years, generally believed that the tendency
of the movement was from the first towards separation. This
is hardly true. In practice, no doubt, much that Wesley
did tended to separatism; but, in theory, never. The movement which now bears his name was at first, distinctly, a
church movement, owing its impetus to long neglected doctrines
of the church; and Wesley's own first direction of life came from
Jeremy Taylor. The story of the movement, during the period
now under survey, may be briefly told. John Wesley, son of
the rector of Epworth, went to Charterhouse in 1713 and to
Christ Church in 1720, and became a fellow of Lincoln college
in 1726. The society founded, very soon after, by his brother
Charles, a student of Christ Church, was composed of a few
pious young men who desired to live by the church's rules of
fasting, almsgiving and prayer, and received the holy communion weekly. Southey, writing nearly a century later, thought
that "such conduct would at any time have attracted observation in an English university." Unpopular, these beginnings
certainly were, but it was not long before they passed beyond
the petty criticisms of Oxford. John Wesley joined this
"Holy Club" on his return to college in 1729, and he

remained at Oxford for some years, actively engaged in works of piety.

Among the earlier members of the society were two destined for great public fame. The first was George Whitefield, perhaps the greatest popular orator of the eighteenth century. He had traced in himself, he tells, from cradle to manhood, nothing but "a fitness to be damned"; but the fiery enthusiasm of his nature seems always to have been turned toward the light, and, from his entrance into the methodist company, he became a devoted worker and preacher. John Wesley went to America in 1735, Charles in 1736, Whitefield in 1738. The freedom of missionary work rendered each of them disposed to new religious influences, and John Wesley and George Whitefield gradually drifted apart from each other and from the accepted theology of the English church. Wesley was greatly influenced by the Moravians and especially by their very attractive apostle count Zinzendorf, Whitefield by the Calvinism which seemed to be dying a natural death in the church of England till his influence revived it. Wesley dated his conversion from 24 May, 1738; and, soon afterwards, he began his wonderful journeys, which lasted almost to his death. During the half-century, he preached forty thousand sermons, and travelled (it is said) a quarter of a million of miles. His brother Charles equalled him in devotion, if not in tireless health, and Whitefield in enthusiasm. In 1740, Wesley severed his connection with the Moravians, and, in 1743, the followers of Whitefield became distinguished as Calvinistic methodists. In 1764, the separation between the two methodist bodies became permanent, and, from that time, perhaps, it may be correct to date the creation, from the original movement, of a newly organised dissent. Though Wesley himself passionately desired, to the end, to belong to the church of his baptism and ordination and vigorously denounced all who separated from it, in 1784 (when his brother Charles, who deeply regretted the act, thought him to be in his dotage) he ordained ministers, and, from that moment, the separation was complete. Whitefield, who was the founder of the Calvinistic methodists, Lady Huntingdon's connection, died in 1770. At that date, it may be well to conclude our brief survey. The prominent names which belong especially to this earlier period, when what came to be called evangelicalism was hardly distinguishable from methodism, are those of the two Wesleys, Whitefield, Hervey, Toplady and Fletcher of Madeley.   The influence of Newton, Venn, Romaine and others, more definitely evangelical than methodist, belongs chiefly to a later period.

Whitefield was not a man of letters, but an orator.  His literary work is negligible, though not uninteresting; but it marks more decisively than that of any of his contemporaries the earliest reaction against the common-sense religious writing of the age.  Whitefield wrote plain English, the vernacular of his day, with a touch of the university added, just as Latimer did two hundred years before.  But he was not nearly so great a writer as was the reformer, probably because of his being a far greater preacher.  To quote from his sermons or his controversial writings would be useless: he began a venture rather than led a school.  And not all his friends followed his style.

The first to be mentioned after Whitefield was almost a complete contrast to him.  There can be no doubt that the most popular writer among those who were influenced by the earlier stages of the methodist movement was James Hervey, who was at Lincoln college, Oxford, as an undergraduate when John Wesley was a fellow and, after serving in Cornwall, became rector of two parishes, not adjoining each other, Collingtree and Weston Favell, in Northamptonshire.  He was a most excellent man and an exemplary parish priest, but he escaped controversy as little as did any other of the evangelical company.  His disputes with Wesley are of no importance in literary history, and his curious dialogues, on his favourite doctrine of "imputed righteousness" and other opinions which he extracted from the Gospels, entitled *Theron and Aspasia*, have long ceased to interest even the most assiduous student. But his *Meditations Among the Tombs, Reflections on a Flowergarden* and *Contemplations on the Night*, which met with extraordinary success in their day, illustrate most effectively the fantastic and affected style which the most sincere writers of the time, save the robust John Wesley himself, seemed to assume with their "pulpit manner," till it became a second nature to them.  A passage from Hervey's *Contemplations on the Night* may be quoted here, since it would be difficult to find a more striking example of the descent of popular taste in the darkest period of English letters. The thoughts might be found in Jeremy Taylor; but how different is the pompous and posturing performance with which Hervey seeks to impress the reader from the plangent feeling which inspires Taylor even in his richest and most gorgeous prose! In Hervey, the ideas are impoverished and the expression is at once affected and commonplace.

We need not go down to the charnel house, nor carry our search into the repositories of the dead, in order to find memorials of our impending doom. A multitude of these remembrancers are placed in all our paths, and point the heedless passengers to their long home. I can hardly enter a considerable town but I meet a funeral procession, or the mourners going about the streets. The hatchment suspended on the wall, or the crape streaming in the air, are silent intimations that both rich and poor have been emptying their houses, and replenishing their sepulchres. I can scarce join in any conversation, but mention is made of some that are given over by the physician, and hovering on the confines of eternity; of others that have just dropt their clay among weeping friends, and are gone to appear before the Judge of all the earth. There's not a newspaper comes to my hand, but, amidst all its entertaining narrations, reads several serious lectures of mortality. What else are the repeated accounts—of age, worn out by slow-consuming sicknesses—of youth, dashed to pieces by some sudden stroke of casualty—of patriots, exchanging their seats in the senate for a lodging in the tomb—of misers, resigning their breath, and (O relentless destiny!) leaving their very riches for others! Even the vehicals of our amusement are registers of the deceased! and the voice of Fame seldom sounds but in concert with the knell!

From this, the transition to John William Fletcher is agreeable. He is one of the examples, more common in the seventeenth, than in the eighteenth, century, of the attractive power of the English church, its system and its theology, for he was born in Switzerland (his name was de La Flechère); but he became a priest of the English church and gave his life to the work of an English village. His anti-Calvinist views severed him from Lady Huntingdon's connection, with which, for a time, he was associated as superintendent of her training college at Trevecca, but endeared him the more to Wesley, who preached his funeral sermon from the text "Mark the perfect man, and behold the upright, for the end of that man is peace." Never was there a controversialist more honest or more gentle. The title of his *Zelotus and Honestus Reconciled; or an Equal Check to Pharisaism and Antinomianism*, which includes parts I and II of *Scriptures Scales to weigh the gold of Gospel truth, and to balance a multitude of opposite Scriptures*, gives a misleading idea of the wit and charm of its contents.  Fletcher writes gracefully and truthfully.  He has the tendency to gloom in which Hervey revelled; but he does not parade it.  He has a wholesome detestation of his opponent's Calvinism; but it leads him, not to sound and fury, but to placid and conciliatory argument.  Southey well summed up the character of Fletcher's writing when he said that

his talents were of the quick mercurial kind; his fancy was always active, and he might have held no inconsiderable rank, both as a humourous and as an empassioned writer, if he had not confined himself wholly to devotional subjects.

He was the St. Francis of early methodism, and it seems the most natural thing in the world to be told that, one day, he took a robin for his text.  If other leaders of the movement were stern, his was always the voice of tenderness and charity. By way of contrast, we may, like Southey, take the vehement denunciations of Augustus Toplady, who deserves to be remembered for the immortal hymn "Rock of Ages," while his *The Historic Proof of the Doctrinal Calvinism of the Church of England* best remains buried in oblivion.  He wrote with coarse vigour, smartness and *abandon*, in complete contrast alike to the preciousness of Hervey and to the calm of Fletcher. His quarrel with John Wesley, which from theological became personal, makes curious reading to-day.  Wesley declared that Toplady's doctrine might be summed up thus—

One in twenty of mankind is elected; nineteen in twenty are reprobated.  The elect shall be saved, do what they will; the reprobate shall be damned, do what they can.  Reader, believe this, or be damned.

Toplady replied by accusing his critic of satanic guilt and

shamelessness in thus describing his opinion and answered him, after the manner of Martin Marprelate, with *An Old Fox tarred and feathered* and suchlike pamphlets. Wesley, he declared, was an Arminian, which meant that he had

an equal portion of gross Heathenism, Pelagianism, Mahometanism, Popery, Manichaeism, Ranterism and Antinomianism, culled, dried, and pulverised, and mingled with as much palpable Atheism as you can scrape together.

Literary squabbles do not lose their bitterness when they become theological.

Of John Wesley himself, as a writer, it need only be said that he was, with the pen as with the tongue, a master of direct English and simple strength. Southey chose a passage in which he summed up his chief answer to the Calvinists, as "the most remarkable and powerful in all his works" to illustrate his theology. It, also, illustrates his style. A few sentences will suffice to show the kind of writer he was. His manner is eminently that of an orator. The sentences are short, the points clear, the assertion incisive, the repetition emphatic: "Here I fix my fort"—"Let it mean what it will it cannot mean that"—"Hold! what will you prove by Scripture? That God is worse than the devil? It cannot be." Here we have the familiar trick of the special pleader. He asks his opponent a question, supplies an answer on his behalf, and then knocks him on the head for it. This manner has the appearance of logic; but, often, a fallacy lurks behind. As a theologian, whatever else he is, he is smart, direct, deeply serious and utterly uncompromising.

But Wesley is not only remembered by his theological writings and his work as an evangelist. His *Journal* has all the charm of a pious Pepys, and, now that it is being published as it was written, the world can see through it closely into the writer's heart, as in the curious account of his love for Grace Murray.[1] In pathos and descriptive power, its simple narrative shows the rugged force of Walt Whitman: the word is not sought for, it comes naturally, and, one feels, is inevitable. Whether one reads the Savannah journal, with its marvellous

[1] See Leger, Augustin, *John Wesley's Last Love* (1910).

record of faith, inconsistency and courage, or the unvarnished record of the long years of laborious ministry, one meets the same straight-forward, clear-eyed observer, enthralled by the Divine vision which he saw and tried to make known among men, yet full of humour and observant, to the very minutest detail, of everything that concerns the daily life of mankind. When he scolded or denounced, he thought that he was showing "that childlike openness, frankness, and plainness of speech manifest to all in the Apostles and first Christians." He had no doubt of himself, nor any of God's constant guidance and protection. This gives to his everyday life, in all its realism, a touch of romance, which shines through the stupendous record of what he did and said. In the *Journal*, we see how English divinity was breaking from the trammels of its literary convention, and the deliverer was John Wesley. If we judge the *Journal* with the life which it lays bare, it is one of the great books of the world.

No one would call John Wesley a man of letters. He had no horror, such as Hervey's, of literature which was not spiritual. He read Prior, and Home (of *Douglas* fame), Thomson, Lord Chesterfield and Sterne: he delighted to quote the classics. But he had not the taste for "style" which was born in his brother Charles. John was no poet; but Charles, among his six thousand hymns, has left some verses that will never die. In his case, we see that, after all, methodism was not entirely apart from the literature of its day. He reminds us, again and again, of his contemporaries, especially, perhaps, of Shenstone, for whose rather thin sentiment he substitutes a genuine piety. He can be virile, felicitous, vivid; if his sweetness often cloys, he has a depth of feeling which frequently brings him within the ranks of the poets. Though he might feel strange in the company of Crashaw or George Herbert, of Newman or Keble, Christina Rossetti would take him by the hand. In English literature, so long as the hymns of Charles, and the *Journal* of John, Wesley are read, methodism will continue to hold an honoured place.

## CHAPTER XVI

# The Literature of Dissent

## 1660–1760

THE narrowness of intellectual life and sterility of spiritual life which fell upon the dissenting churches after the exclusion of 1662 were the outcome of a long chain of historical development. When dissent succumbed, yielding itself, body and soul, to the dehumanising genius of Calvin, it entered upon two—indeed, nearer three—centuries of wandering in a stony wilderness. During its birthtime in the middle and latter part of the sixteenth century, during the period of its trial in the early seventeenth century and during the short span of its chequered and flickering triumph under the commonwealth, the main concern and preoccupation of dissent was with the mere question of church membership. The arid discussions on church polity centred in this idea; the still more arid discussions on doctrine were aroused simply by the demand for a standard of the church member's doctrinal purity, and the chief contention with the state was waged round the demand for a church control of admission to the sacrament—the wielding of the wooden sword of excommunication. The rock upon which this inveterate purpose split was not so much Erastianism as the national consciousness of the English race itself; and when, as the logical result of a century of historical development, dissent was driven out in 1662, it was pitting itself not so much against the church of England as against this English national consciousness. Throughout the remainder of the seventeenth century, and nearly through the whole of the eighteenth century, dissent remained true to the cramped and narrow basis on which it had been reared. If the church of England was sunk in lethargy, dissent was sunk in puny congregational and individual selfishness. Of any true missionary sense, of any conception of humanity as apart from religious system, dissent was even more devoid—because more deliberately devoid—than was the established church. With the one noble exception of Philip Doddridge (and, possibly, a generation earlier, of Richard Davis of Rothwell), it was not until the missionary fervour, the wide and intense humanity, of the methodist movement had revivified the church, that it, also, and in the last instance, revivified dissent. From that moment—towards quite the close of the eighteenth century, and with gathering force in the nineteenth—dissent has deserted its historical basis of dogma and polity, has ceased to war with the national consciousness, and has taken up the burden of Christ.

This main aspect of the historical evolution of dissent will be found mirrored in its literature. But there are two other aspects of that evolution which, also, demand attention, and these are aspects which found relatively much greater expression in that literature. The free churches claim the credit of the assertion of the principle of toleration. Historically, the claim is untenable, for, during its transient triumph under the commonwealth, dissent was intolerant and persecuting, or tried to be. The enunciation of the principle came from laymen, and from those sectaries whom the entrenched and enthroned presbyterian wished to persecute. Dissent was converted to the principle only by itself passing under the fiery sword; and, when, in the eighteenth century, it became the mouthpiece of the demand for toleration, it was such merely as asserting for itself a principle, and claiming for itself the protection and benefit of that principle, which was in the air, and which grew organically with the self-consciousness of the nation. But, in so far as they put forth these claims, the free churches gave birth to a considerable literature, which, though controversial in purpose, is not the less of account in any record of English eighteenth century literature at large.

Secondly—and this is most important of all—the process of disintegration, which, after 1662, overtook all three dissenting bodies—presbyterians, congregationalists and baptists—alike loosened the bands of doctrinal narrowness. One and all, they took the path which led through Arianism to unitarianism. To tell the story of that development is to recount not merely the general history of the three bodies themselves, but, also, the particular history of a very large proportion of the individual congregations nominally composing those bodies. Such a survey would, of course, be out of place here. But the literature which grew out of that development is of the greatest importance on a higher plane, as literature pure and simple, as a contribution to human thought, as well as on the lower plane of mere theological controversy.

Professedly, the three denominations of protestant dissenters are the presbyterians, the congregationalists and the baptists. But, as a matter of fact, after the secession of 1662, these terms—or the churches they profess to designate—are in a state of incessant flux; and it is dangerous to use the names in a general sense as applicable to three bodies with defined boundaries. The presbyterian churches became, perforce, congregational; some of the congregational churches became, of choice, baptist, or *vice versa;* and all three types took on Arianism as a garb. According to the particular bias or intellectual momentum of a particular pastor, a congregation might pass from one extreme limit to the other. In dealing, therefore, with the mere personal side of dissenting literature, we shall find it unsafe and difficult to employ the ordinary terminology of dissent.

Although a theological literature of a certain sort, originating in separation and directed against secular rule in spiritual things, was in existence even before the period under present consideration, it may be safely asserted that the ultimate basis of the conception of toleration rested on the unadulterated Erastianism of the English reformation settlement. Such a literature,[1] on the one side, and, equally, Jeremy Taylor's *Liberty of Prophesying* (1646), on the other, alike betray their genesis by their birthtime. Those who were not tolerated pleaded for toleration; and from this necessity sprang the bare assertion of the principle of liberty of conscience. Their advocacy, therefore, has not the value in the history of human thought which the pure and naked assertion of the principle possesses in the mouth of Henry Robinson, merchant and

[1] For some of the productions belonging to it, see bibliography.

economist, of Hobbes,[1] of Milton[2] or of Locke.[3] But the final achievement of the pure principle of toleration and freedom of conscience came neither from the theologian nor from the philosopher. It came from the social secular sense of the race, and fought its way to victory through the mere mechanism and clash of church and state politics. And, so far as the result achieved is concerned, the only difference between the enforced, if restricted, tolerance established by Cromwell, and the gradually won legislative tolerance of eighteenth and nineteenth century dissent, consists in the fact that, under Cromwell, the executive constrained and led the social sense, while, in later ages, the social sense constrained and led the legislature. With the mere political history of the principle we are, however, not concerned, but only with the expression which that history found in dissenting literature.

Broadly speaking, the literary battle about the principle of toleration passes through two quite distinct phases in the period here under review. If we pass by the earlier toleration controversy in Charles II's reign, as not possessing any permanent importance either in literature or in ecclesiastical history, its first real phase covers the episodes of the Toleration act of William III's reign, the Occasional Conformity bill and the Schism act. In this phase, dissent is on the defensive and concerned merely with vindicating its claim to civil and religious rights and freedom. In the second and later phase, it boldly challenges the very principle of an established church, or, as we should say to-day, raises the question of disestablishment.

Naturally enough, the earlier phase of this battle, from the point of view of literature, lacks the high ethical quality that marks the later phase. For, in the various skirmishes concerning the Toleration and Schism acts, the attitude of dissent was paltering and opportunist. In truth, the achievement of the Toleration act of 1689 was rather the work of such exponents of the secular or civil sense of the nation as Burnet, Somers, Maynard and Sir Isaac Newton; and the dissenters, who, because of their hatred of Rome, had refused the indulgences of Charles II and James II, were content to accept meekly the state-given toleration of 1689, while, as a body,

---

[1] *Leviathan*, pt. III., chaps. 41 and 42.

[2] *Areopagitica.*

[3] *Letters on Toleration.*

supinely looking on at the legislative interment of the comprehension scheme of the same year. Only Baxter and Calamy and Howe could see far enough, and high enough, to deplore the failure of that scheme, remaining, in this respect, true to their unwavering attitude in the comprehension scheme of 1667–8, as well as in the controversy with Stillingfleet of 1680. And, during the interval between the Toleration act and the Schism act, dissent showed its mettle and its conception of the pure principle of toleration, by intolerantly attacking Socinianism, as if all the intervening years, from the Westminster assembly to the Exeter meetings, had gone for nothing.

Out of this limited conception and attitude of mere political opportunism, dissent was rudely awakened by a layman. From the point of view of consistency and principle—of logic and morality—Defoe condemned the practice of occasional conformity.[1] His completely unanswerable *Inquiry into the occasional Conformity of Dissenters in Cases of Preferment* (1697) drew from John Howe a deplorably ill-tempered and futile reply, *Some Considerations of a Preface to an Inquiry* (1701). With Defoe's rejoinder to this in the same year, *A Letter to Mr. Howe by way of Reply*, the controversy temporarily closed. But, unintentionally, Defoe had delivered his friends into the hands of the enemy. The tory reactionaries of Anne's reign seized with avidity the weapon he had forged, and, coupling the subject of dissenting academies with the subject of occasional conformity, delivered a furious onslaught on the whole front of dissent. The scurrilous and rabid attack on dissent generally, and on dissenting academies in particular, which was opened by Sacheverell and Samuel Wesley, was met, on the one hand, by Defoe's *Shortest Way with the Dissenters* (1702)[2] and, on the other hand, by Samuel Palmer's *Vindication* (1705). But, neither matchless sarcasm nor sober logic could avail. The theological torrent became a popular tory avalanche. The publication of Calamy's *Abridgment of the Life of Baxter* (1702) only added fuel to the fire. It was answered by Olyffe, and, again, by Hoadly (in *The Reasonableness of Conformity*, 1703), to whom Calamy replied in his *Defence of Moderate Nonconformity* (1703). Other tracts on both sides

[1] Cf. *ante*, Vol. IX, Chap. I, p. 8.
[2] Cf. *ibid.*, p. 9.

followed; but the mere literary strife was quickly swallowed up in the popular agitation about Sacheverell's case.

The Hanoverian succession broke the storm; and, with the reversal of the Schism act and the Occasional Conformity act, the religious existence and civil freedom of dissent were safe. But the paltering and merely opportunist attitude of the leaders of the free churches was responsible for the failure to secure the repeal of the Test and Corporation acts. Accordingly, for the remainder of our period, dissent went halting, content with the *regium donum* and with a religious tolerance tempered by partial civil disability. Samuel Chandler's *History of Persecution* (1736) and *The Case of Subscription* (1748) are fairly typical of this attitude. Had it not been for the genius of Watts and Towgood, eighteenth century dissent would appear to have exhausted its zeal for freedom of conscience in the mere selfish assertion of its own right to existence; for, so far as the purely political battle for freedom is concerned, it did not achieve any further triumph until the dawn of the nineteenth century. But, in 1731, a completely new turn was given to the old controversy by Isaac Watts's *Humble attempt towards the Revival of Practical Religion among Christians*. In this work, and in his later *Essay on Civil Power in Things Sacred*, Watts defended the general position of dissenters by arguing on lofty grounds against any civil establishment of a national church. While thus, in one sense, reverting to the standpoint of seventeenth century philosophy, Watts, in another sense, opens a new era in these publications. They foreshadow the claim of dissent for the achievement of equality by the way of disestablishment. The cause of a national church —of the connection between the episcopal church and the English state—was taken up by William Warburton in his *Alliance between Church and State* (1736), written from the point of view of the state rather than of the church, and presenting, surely, the most utilitarian theory of the English church ever produced by a representative churchman.[1]

From the lower ground of mere hand to mouth polemics, Watts's treatises were also answered by John White in his *Three Letters to a Gentleman Dissenting from the Church of England*—letters which, in spite of the popularity which they

[1] As to Warburton, cf. *ante*, Vol. IX, p. 331.

enjoyed with the church party, would be otherwise inconsiderable, were it not that they gave birth to one of the most enduring monuments of the polemics of dissent. White's *Letters* were demolished by Michaijah Towgood, presbyterian minister at Crediton. In *The Dissenting Gentleman's Answer to the Reverend Mr. White's Letter* (1746–8), Towgood gave to the world one of the most powerful and widely read pleas for disestablishment that dissent ever produced. So far as the literature of dissent on the subject of toleration and freedom of conscience is concerned, this monumental work is the last word spoken in the period here treated; for the activity of the dissenters' committee of deputies (a dissenters' defence board in the matter of civil disabilities) was entirely legal and secular in its motive and expression.[1]

The controversial literature of dissent on the subjects of church polity and dogma covers the field of a whole series of successive disputes. Although, in these disputes, there is a constant shifting of the ground, yet the driving impulse, at bottom, is only one of freedom. At the outset, this freedom is purely ecclesiastical, the irresponsibility of a congeries of churches now, at last, cut asunder from the establishment. But it was inevitable that, in the end, such ecclesiastical freedom should loosen the bonds of dogmatic authority also, and so pave the way for pure free thought. Although the two paths of development often ran side by side, and crossed and recrossed, yet, historically, the ecclesiastical is the precedent and necessary condition of dogmatic freedom. By ecclesiastical freedom is here meant, not merely that, after the ejection of 1662, dissent was, or was to become, free of the yoke of the episcopal church, but that, within the limits of dissent itself, all bonds of authority had been destroyed. In the seventeenth century, a presbyterian system which had not the sanction of the state behind it was left without any compulsory force at all; and, as a system, it instantly fell to pieces. In addition, dissent had inherited from the commonwealth days the heritage of the curse of Cain—the internecine warfare of independ-

---

[1] This is shown, for instance, by such cases as the corporation of London *v.* Sheafe, Streatfield and Evans (1754–67). Lord Mansfield's judgment in this important case is only another proof—if further proof were needed—that freedom was achieved not so much by dissent leading the national civic sense as by the national civic sense leading church and dissent alike.

cnt and presbyterian. In the later days of the commonwealth, feeble attempts had been made to heal that strife, and, when thirty years of later persecution had chastened their mood, the attempts were revived with the passing of the Toleration act. In the so-called "happy union," which was established in London in 1691 by agreement between the independent and presbyterian bodies, it was fondly hoped that, at last, the foundation had been laid for a church polity of dissent. But the disintegrating force of irresponsibility soon laid low these builded hopes. In London, the association of the two bodies endured only a brief four years, and, although in the country "the heads of the agreement" of this union became somewhat widely adopted, and were worked out into the scheme of county or provincial associations and unions, these lived but a palsied and flickering life, and possess little true organic connection with modern county unions.

Although the deep underlying causes of this disruption were inherent in the life history of dissent, it was natural that the actual expression which the disintegrating principle took on should be one of controversy. The first form which this took was the so-called neonomian controversy. In 1690, the sermons of Tobias Crisp, a royalist but Calvinistic divine, were republished by his son with certain additional matter, to which he had obtained the *imprimatur* of several London dissenting ministers. The popularity of the book revived the spirit of thc ultra-Calvinist section of dissent, at a time when Calvinism was losing its hold. To check the rising spirit of antinomianism which Crisp's fantastic Calvinism encouraged, the presbyterian ministers of London deputed Daniel Williams to reply to the book. His reply, *Gospel Truth stated and vindicated* (1692), though moderate and non-partisan in tone, and aiming only at the establishment of a *via media* between legalism and antinomianism, merely increased the storm. Williams's own orthodoxy was impeached, charges of neo-nomianism, of Arminianism and Socinianism were hurled against him by Stephen Lobb and by Isaac Chauncy, an independent, in his *Neo-Nomianism Unmasked* (1693), and Williams's *Defence* (1693) failed to still the commotion.[1] In the following year,

[1] See Calamy, *Account*, vol. I, p. 337, where "the one side" may be roughly read as independents and "the other side" as presbyterians.

Williams was prohibited from preaching his "turn" to the united ministers at the merchants' lecture in Pinners' hall. The presbyterians, accordingly, withdrew and established their own lecture at Salters' hall, leaving the independents in possession of the Pinners' hall lectures.  In spite of all attempts at reconciliation, the dispute wrecked the "happy union" to which the independents' self-defence, in their *History of the Union* (1698), and Williams's own *Peace with Truth, or an end to Discord* (1699) only served as funeral elegies.

To this controversy succeeded that concerning occasional conformity which has been already mentioned above.  But all these pale in their significance before the Subscription controversy—the doctrinal dispute aroused by the spread of Arianism. Under the commonwealth, Socinianism (represented by Paul Best and John Biddle), Sabellianism (by John Fry), Arianism (by John Knowles, Thomas Collier and Paul Hobson) and universalism (by Richard Coppin, John Reeve and Ludowicke Muggleton), had been alike banned and persecuted.  The intolerant attitude of both presbyterians and independents was continued after the restoration; and to this was now added the rigour of the re-established English church.  To Richard Baxter, not less than to John Owen or to Stillingfleet, the Socinians were on a par with Mohammedans, Turks, atheists and papists.  But, in spite of persecution, the discrete strands of varying anti-Trinitarian thought remained unbroken.  Gilbert Clerke of Northamptonshire, a mathematician and, in a sense, a teacher of Whiston, Noval of Tydd St. Giles near Wisbech, Thomas Firmin (Sabellian), William Penn, Stephen Nye (Sabellian), William Freke (Arian), John Smith, the philomath, of St. Augustine's, London (Socinian), Henry Hedworth, the disciple of Biddle, and William Manning, minister of Peasenhall (1630–1711) (independent), form a direct and unbroken, though irregular, chain of anti-Trinitarian thought, extending from the commonwealth days to those of toleration —not to mention the more covert but still demonstrable anti-Trinitarianism of Milton and Locke.

With the passing of the Toleration act of 1689, the leaven of this long train of anti-Trinitarian thought made itself strongly felt.  It first appeared in the bosom of the church of England itself, in the so-called Socinian controversy.  In 1690,

Arthur Bury, a latitudinarian divine, was deprived of the rectorship of Lincoln college, Oxford, for publishing his *Naked Gospel*. The proceedings gave rise to a stream of pamphlet literature on both sides. In the same year, 1690, John Wallis, Savilian professor of mathematics at Oxford, was involved in a controversy with a succession of anonymous Arian and Socinian writers (among them William Jones) by the publication of his *Doctrine of the Blessed Trinity briefly Explained*. Simultaneously, Sherlock's *Vindication of the Holy and ever Blessed Trinity*, although directed against the same group of writers, called forth another outburst of pamphleteering from quite another quarter, South leading the attack with his *Animadversions upon Dr. Sherlock's Vindication*. The first portion of the anti-Trinitarian literature produced in this triangular contest is collected in *The Faith of one God Who is only the Father* (1691). In the ranks of dissent, the same controversy manifested itself in the disputes which wrecked the independent and presbyterian "happy union" and, contemporaneously, it appeared in the baptist body. In 1693, Matthew Caffyn, baptist minister at Horsham, Sussex, was for a second time accused before the "Baptist General Assembly" of denying Christ's divinity; and, when the assembly refused to vote his expulsion, a secession took place, and the rival "Baptist General Association" was formed. In the same year, the anti-Trinitarians published a *Second collection of tracts proving the God, and Father of our Lord Jesus Christ, the only true God* (1693). The tenth, and last, tract in this volume was a reply to South's *Animadversions* on Sherlock's *Vindication*. In the following year (1694), the presbyterian John Howe entered the field with his *Calm and sober Inquiry* directed against the above tract, and, to make the fight triangular, Sherlock replied to South and Howe together in *A Defence of Dr. Sherlock's notion of a Trinity in Unity*. The anti-Trinitarians' *Third collection of Tracts*, which followed immediately, was a reply at once to Howe, on the one hand, and to Sherlock, on the other.

This first Trinitarian or so-called Socinian controversy, practically, came to an end in 1708. It received its deathblow, in 1698, by the act for the more effectual suppression of blasphemy and profaneness, which remained on the statute book till 1813. With the exception of John Smith's *Designed End to the Socinian Controversy* (1695), the whole of the anti-Trinitarian contributions to it had been anonymous (both Locke and Sir Isaac Newton are supposed to have contributed under the cover of this anonymity); and, with the exception of Howe, no representatives of the professed dissenting denominations had joined in the fray. It is therefore to be regarded, primarily, as a church of England controversy, in which the churchmen had weakened the Trinitarian cause by a triangular and virtually conflicting defence: Sherlock *versus* South *versus* Tillotson and Burnet, and all four *versus* the enemy. The agitation which the controversy produced among the dissenters was mainly reflex, and is apparent more in their domestic quarrels, noted above, than in their published literature. But, disproportionately small as was the dissenting share of the combatants in mere point of literature, the intellectual ferment which ensued in following years showed itself more in the bosom of dissent than in the life and thought of the church of England. Thomas Emlyn, a presbyterian, who was tried at Dublin, in 1693, for publishing his *Humble Inquiry into the Scripture account of Jesus Christ*, attributed his own Arianism to Sherlock's *Vindication of the Doctrine of the Trinity*.

But the Arian controversy, properly so-called, does not owe anything to Emlyn. It was, rather, opened by William Whiston's *Historical Preface* (1710), prefixed to his *Primitive Christianity* (1711), and Samuel Clarke's *Scripture Doctrine of the Trinity* (1712). Although, however, Whiston finally joined the general baptists and claimed to have influenced Peirce of Exeter, the importance of this second controversy is, so far as dissent is concerned, rather practical or constitutional than literary. Among the dissenters, it assumed a particularly accentuated form of the subscription controversy. In 1717, James Peirce and Joseph Hallett, presbyterian ministers of Exeter, were taken to task locally for Arianism. In the Exeter assembly of May, 1719, an attempt to enforce subscription to the first of the thirty-nine articles brought about a split. In the same year, the matter came before the committee of the deputies of the three denominations of protestant dissenters at Salters' hall meeting-house, London—the so-called Salters' hall synod. Here, the question of subscription followed a clean-cut line of cleavage. The congregationalists, in the main, under the lead of Thomas Bradbury, insisted on subscription; the presbyterians, in the main, under the lead of John Shute Barrington, afterwards viscount Barrington, resisted the proposal as an unnecessary imposition of a creed. As a result, the whole body of dissent was divided into three parties—non-subscribers, subscribers and neutrals. The minority of subscribers, being defeated, withdrew from the synod and formed a distinct meeting under Bradbury, while the majority of non-subscribers despatched a letter of advice to Exeter, which, by virtue of its statement of reasons for non-subscribing, is regarded by unitarians as their charter of dogmatic freedom. The mere momentary controversy concerning these synod proceedings gave birth to more than seventy pamphlets.

It is claimed by presbyterian writers that there was no avowed heterodoxy among the London ministers for half a generation after Salters' hall. This means little more than that the great luminaries of dissent of the era following on the Toleration act had passed away, and that, between 1720 and 1740, no successors had arisen worthy of the memory of those giants—outside, that is to say, of the world of academic teaching. But, underneath the surface deadness and mental lethargy of this later period, the leaven of anti-Trinitarian thought continued incessantly at work, and, when the interim of quiescence had ended, it was found to have been merely a phase of growth, an intermediate stage between the Arianism of 1720 and the later unitarianism. In matter of literature, the intermediate phase was distinguished by the writings of John Taylor of Norwich, a professed presbyterian (*Defence of the Common rights of Christians*, 1737; *The Scripture doctrine of Original Sin*, 1740), and of Samuel Bourn (*Address to Protestant Dissenters*, 1737).

In itself, the literary importance of this period of nonconformist history is not great, save and in so far as it marks the stepping-stone to the latest phase of the development of unitarian thought—that phase, namely, which is distinguished by the names of Nathaniel Lardner, Richard Price, Joseph Priestley and Theophilus Lindsey—a movement which lies outside the scope of the present chapter.[1]

[1] As to Price and Priestley cf. Chap. XIV, pp. 389–391, *ante*.

It is not to be supposed that the evolution of a distinctively unitarian church was the sole outcome of the train of development which has been briefly sketched above. The sections of dissent—in all its three denominations—which stood aloof from the distinctively unitarian development, yet remained profoundly affected by the spirit of it. The presbyterian, independent and baptist churches alike showed, in their loose internal organisations, the disintegrating force of the unitarian movement. Both in individual congregations and in the loose and feeble associations, the spirituality of dissent, which had been its glory and motive force in the seventeenth century, had sunk into atrophy; and, had it not been for the reviving influence of methodism, all three denominations would probably, at the close of the eighteenth century, have offered a melancholy spectacle    The intellectual gain to English thought generally, quite apart from dissenting theology in particular, was incalculable: but the spiritual loss was none the less to be deplored.

In emphasising, however, the free thought side, or effect of the unitarian movement within dissent, it is not to be understood that this was a free thought movement in the sense of twentieth century science or philosophy. The eighteenth century unitarian movement was, in the main, theological, not rationalistic. If any comparison were called for, it should rather be with the spread of Arminianism in the English church in the seventeenth century. Both movements had for their motive springs one impulse, that is to say, a protest against Calvinism, and, when dissent, by means of unitarian thought, had thrown off the fetters of that Calvinism, it remained, on the whole, during the period here surveyed, quiescent and content. And, as a result, when the deistic controversy, a purely rationalistic movement, engaged the English church and English thought in the first quarter of the eighteenth century, the leading exponents of dissent, whether orthodox or Arian, are to be found on the conservative side. James Foster, baptist minister of the Barbican chapel, and Nathaniel Lardner, then presbyterian minister in Poor Jewry lane, the accomplished presbyterians William Harris, Joseph Hallett, Isaac Watts and Philip Doddridge—all these dissenting writers[1] contributed

[1] For a list of nonconformist contributions to the deistic controversy, and of works of other nonconformist writers, see bibliography.

not less powerfully, if less sensationally and attractively, to the rout of the deists than did Butler and Berkeley themselves.

Finally, outside and apart from the field of pure thought, eighteenth century England owes a heavy debt to dissent for its educational system, to which reference has already been made in an earlier volume,[1] but which seems to deserve further notice here in its connection with the influence of nonconformity upon literature. Although the presbyterians had but one or two free schools (public charity schools) in London before 1714, and, although the baptists and independents joined forces in that and the succeeding year to establish a similar free school at Horsleydown (subsequently the Maze Pond school), the academy system of the dissenters, in the main, had reference only to the private and domestic problem of the supply of educated ministers for their respective denominations. Accordingly, each one of the more widely recognised academies, during some period of its generally chequered and brief career, takes on a denominational colour. As a system, these academies date entirely from the era of the Toleration act. Prior to that date, dissenting ministers engaged in education acted as private tutors in families or contented themselves with opening small private schools in their own houses. After the Toleration act, however, individual ministers started private schools of their own of which it is now impossible to ascertain the number or, in many instances, the circumstances of origin and growth. Where the minister was a man of learning and power, these schools endured for a generation and sometimes longer, and linked their names with the history of dissent through the personality alike of pupils and of tutors. And it is herein that they claim special recognition; for, in their totality, they present a brilliant galaxy of talent in fields of learning far removed from mere theological studies. Such a result could not have been achieved, had it not been for the powerful solvent of intellectual freedom which the unitarian movement brought in its train. Few of the academies, whatever their denominational colour at the outset, escaped contact with it, and those of them which assimilated the influence most freely produced great tutors and scholars. In this matter, the academies trod the same historical path as that followed by the individual

[1] See *ante*, Vol. IX., Chap. xv.

dissenting churches. Their intellectual activity blazed so fiercely that it tended to burn up the spiritual life; and herein lies the secret at once of their first success, their chequered and bickering career and, in most cases, their ultimate atrophy.

The attitude of the church of England towards these academies has already been detailed.[1] But the fear which the establishment entertained that these academies would starve the universities proved baseless. In their early days, indeed, they attracted a lay *clientela* as well as candidates for the ministry. But the bent towards unitarianism which provided the intellectual stimulus to tutors and ministerial candidates frightened off the layman, and effectually prevented the dissenting academies from leaving the deep mark on the English race and on the English educational system that might have been expected from the individual talent and prestige of their tutors.[2]

Whatever the theological basis of the three denominations of which this chapter has mainly treated, there is one general field of literary activity which they cultivated in common— that of hymn-writing and religious poetry. A list of their chief contributors to this branch of literature will be found elsewhere.[3] But, apart from this phase, in so far as the devotional literature of dissent is merely devotional, whether it be "practical" or "theological," it does not enter into the wider subject of English literature as such. All the same, there are certain outstanding products of this portion of the writings of dissent (Baxter's *Saints' Everlasting Rest*, 1650; Doddridge's *Rise and Progress of Religion in the Soul*, 1745) which, by their mere literary, as well as spiritual, quality, challenge a place in the annals of our literature by the side of the masterpieces of Bunyan and Milton. Broadly speaking, however, the course of the history of dissent, from 1660 to 1760, militated against the production of purely devotional literature. The race of giants who had seen the great commonwealth days, and who went out in 1662, were mainly preachers. The succeeding

[1] See *ante*, Vol. IX., p. 440. A reference might have been added to the later important and illuminating case of the strife between chancellor Reynolds and Philip Doddridge concerning the academy of Northampton.

[2] For a list of some of the chief of these academies, in the period under survey, see appendix to the present chapter.

[3] See bibliography.

generation, likewise one of giants, was occupied with dogmatic wrangles, practical questions of church organisation, or actual political dealings with the state. From 1720 to 1740, there followed a period of almost unbroken spiritual deadness; and, when this partially came to an end with the advent of Doddridge, the spiritual impress is from without, from methodism, rather than from within, from the inherent spirituality of dissent itself. During this period, therefore, English nonconformity rather looks forward, as anticipating that later general revival of the national religious life which was born of methodism, than backward to that stern spirituality of Calvinistic dissent which had puritanised the great revolution.

# APPENDIX TO CHAPTER XVI

## LIST OF NONCONFORMIST ACADEMIES (1680–1770)

Within the period here treated, the following are some of the chief of these academies. The publication in the *Calendar of State Papers Domestic*, 1672–3, and in C. L. Turner's *Original Records*, 2 vols., 1911, of the whole series of dissenters' licences, has revealed the astonishing extent to which the ejected ministers applied themselves to the work of teaching. This material still needs to be worked up, and it is obviously impossible to quote the licences here. The following list, therefore, contains only such academies as are referred to in sources other than, or extraneous to, the Entry Book of licences—in other words, in the general sources of the history of dissent. The classification among the three denominations must be taken as very loose and uncertain, except in certain well-known cases. It need only be added that many of the tutors briefly mentioned here were men of great intellectual power, who had held high academic positions under the commonwealth.

*Independent academies*

Exeter a. (Opened by Joseph Hallett, sen., who was orthodox. Under his son, who was an avowed Arian, the a. became a nursery of Arianism. It dwindled away after his death and was reopened in 1760 by Michaijah Towgood.)

Moorfields (Tenter alley) a. (Started by the independent fund, about 1700, under Isaac Chauncy. After 1712, under Dr. Ridgeley and John Eames, F.R.S., friend of Sir Isaac Newton, to whom succeeded Dr. David Jennings and Dr. Morton Savage, 1744.)

King's Head society a. (Started in 1732 by the King's Head society, as a protest against the freedom of thought prevailing in the fund a. It was at first under Samuel Parsons, and from 1735 under Abraham Taylor, and then John Hubbard and Zephaniah Marryat; after several changes of place, it settled at Homerton in 1772.)

Kibworth a. (Started by John Jennings, 1715–22, with the help of the Coward trustees. This school was continued at Northampton by Philip Doddridge with the help of William Coward, 1729–51. It removed to Daventry, and after 1751 became Arian in tone, under Dr. Caleb Ashworth, tutor of Joseph Priestley. Dissolved 1798.)

Dr. David Jennings' private a. in Well Close square. (After his death in 1762, it changed its theological character under Dr. Samuel Morton Savage, Dr. Andrew Kippis and Dr. Abraham Lees and was moved to Hoxton, becoming Arian. Dissolved 1785, and succeeded by a fresh orthodox a. there.)

Ottery a. (Started under John Lavington in 1752 by the joint endeavour of the fund board and the King's Head society.)

Heckmondwike a. (Started in 1756, as anti-Socinian in character, by the Education society of the Northern counties—or rather of the West riding of Yorkshire. At first under James Scott, Timothy Priestley (the brother of Dr. Joseph Priestley), and Timothy Waldegrave. It is to-day represented by the Yorkshire United college, Bradford.)

Warrington a. (Started in 1757 on the extinction of an a. at Kendal. It was from the outset frankly rationalistic in purpose, being promoted by "rational" dissenters on their own principles under Dr. John Taylor of Norwich. John Seddon of Warrington provided it with a "rational" liturgy. Among its tutors were Dr. J. Aikin, Gilbert Wakefield, Joseph Priestley, and Dr. Enfield—all Arians. Priestley himself left in 1767.)

Bedworth (co. Warwick) a. (Under Julius Saunders, ? 1730–40; who was succeeded by John Kirkpatrick.)

Saffron Walden a. (Under John (or Thomas) Payne, 1700 c.)

Pinner (co. Middlesex) a. (Under Thomas Goodwin, jun., from 1699. Theophilus Lobb was one of his pupils.)

Hackney (London) a. (Under Thomas Rowe, 1681–3, removed to London and then to Jewin street; from 1703 in Ropemakers' alley in Moorfields.)

Newington Green a. (Under Theophilus Gale, 1665 to his death in 1678. Succeeded by Thomas Rowe; but closed on his death, 1705, after having been removed to Clapham and again to Little Britain, London. Dr. Watts and Josiah Hort were pupils.)

Wapping a. (Under Edward Veal, before 1678 to ?1708; closed shortly before his death, having been temporarily broken up in 1681. Nathaniel Taylor, John Shower and Samuel Wesley were among his pupils.)

Nettlebed (co. Oxford) a. (Under Thomas Cole, 1662–72. John Locke and Samuel Wesley were his pupils.)

*Presbyterian academies*

London: Hoxton square a. (Its first origin appears to be traceable in the city of Coventry, where Dr. John Bryan and Dr. Obadiah Grew founded an a. To them succeeded Dr. Joshua Oldfield (the friend of Locke). Oldfield, with Mr. Tong, transferred it to London. Elsewhere the Hoxton square a. is stated to have been founded by John Spademan, Joshua Oldfield and Lorimer. Spademan was succeeded by Capel: but the a. became extinct after Oldfield's death in 1729.)

Bridgnorth a. (Started in 1726 by Fleming, with whom it died. Possibly this was the John Fleming who conducted an a. at Stratford-on-Avon.)

Highgate a., afterwards removed to Clerkenwell. (Under John Kerr or Dr. Ker, ? presbyterian.)

Colyton (co. Devon) a. (Under John Short till 1698; then under Matthew Towgood, till his removal in 1716.)

Alcester (co. Warwick) a. (Under Joseph Porter: removed to Stratford-on-Avon under John Alexander, who died 1740 c.)

Manchester a. (Opened in 1698, after Henry Newcome's death, under his successor, John Chorlton. Dissolved under his successor, James Coningham.)

Islington a. (Under Ralph Button, at Brentford after 1662: from 1672 at Islington. He died in 1680. Sir Joseph Jekyll was a pupil.)

Coventry a. (Started 1663 by Dr. Obadiah Grew and Dr. John Bryan. After Grew's death it was continued by Shewell (d. 1693) and Joshua Oldfield. In 1699, William Tong took over a few of Oldfield's pupils; but on his removal to London, 1702, the a. came to an end.)

**Rathmell** (Yorks.) a. (Under Richard Frankland. Opened at Rathmell, March. 1669–70; removed, 1674, to Natland near Kendal; 1683, to Calton in Craven; 1684, to Dawsonfield near Crosthwaite in Westmorland; 1685, to Hartleborough in Lancs.; 1685–6, suspended; 1686–9, reopened at Attercliffe near Sheffield; 1689, at Rathmell. Frankland died in 1698, and his a. was then dissolved. Of his pupils left at his death, some went to John Chorlton at Manchester and some to Timothy Jollie at Attercliffe.)

**Attercliffe** a. (Under Timothy Jollie, 1691, who rented Attercliffe hall and called his a. Christ's college; among his many pupils, was Dr. Thomas Secker. J. died in 1714, when he was succeeded by Wadsworth. The a. died out long before W.'s death in 1744.)

**London** a. (Under Dr. George Benson, about 1750. Arian.)

**Sheriff Hales** (co. Salop) a. (Under John Woodhouse, 1676; broken up about 1696. In this a. there were many lay students, among them Robert Harley, afterwards earl of Oxford, and Henry St. John (afterwards viscount Bolingbroke). Matthew Clarke and Benjamin Robinson were also pupils.)

**Hungerford** (co. Berks.) a. (Under Benjamin Robinson, 1696, having been open, three years earlier, at Findern in Derbyshire as a grammar school only.)

**Islington** a. (Thomas Doolittle: started in 1662 as a boarding-school in Moorfields, Doolittle being assisted by Thomas Vincent; in 1665 removed to Woodford Bridge, Essex; in 1672 removed to Islington; closed under the persecution, 1685–8; reopened 1688, but died out before Doolittle's death in 1707. Edmund Calamy and Thos. Emlyn were his pupils.)

**Oswestry and Shrewsbury** a. (Connected principally with the name of James Owen, 1679 onwards, but actually started by his predecessor, Francis Tallents. After Owen's death continued by Samuel Benion and John Reynolds. Under the latter it was dissolved, before 1718.)

**Taunton** a. (Started by Matthew Warren and others after 1662. After Warren's death, 1706, it was carried on by joint efforts of Stephen James (d. 1725), Robert Darch and Henry Grove (d. 1738). After 1738 Thomas Amory became head of the whole a.; but, under his Arian tendencies, it collapsed before his removal to London in 1759.)

**Gloucester and Tewkesbury** a. (Under Samuel Jones, 1712–20. Archbishop Secker, bishop Butler and Samuel Chandler were students here together. After Jones's death the a. was removed to Carmarthen, and there remained under Thomas Perrot till 1733. Then it was under Vavasor Griffiths at Llwynllwyd (co. Brecknock) till 1741; then at Haverfordwest under Evan Davies; then again at Carmarthen under Samuel Thomas and Dr. J. Jenkins. Under Samuel Thomas the independents withdrew and formed a new a. at Abergavenny under David Jardine.)

**Stoke Newington or Newington Green** a. (Under Charles Morton, 1667–85. Defoe, Samuel Wesley and Samuel Palmer were students here. Discouraged by persecution in 1685, Morton went to New England and became vice-president of Harvard. His a. was continued by William Wickens and Stephen Lobb, both of whom died in 1699, and by Thomas Glasscock (d. 1706); but it probably died out not long after 1696.)

Kendal a. (Under Dr. Caleb Rotherham, 1733–52: possibly as a continuation of the extinct Attercliffe a.)

Brynllywarch (Llangynwyd, co. Glamorgan) a. (Commonly regarded as the germ of the Carmarthen Presbyterian college; but this is impossible. Started by Samuel Jones, 1672. After his death in 1697, Roger Griffith opened an a. at Abergavenny, which is regarded as a continuation of Brynllywarch. It lasted only three or four years. At Brynllywarch, Rees Price continued either Jones's or Griffith's school but gave up between 1702 and 1704 when the a. was united with a grammar school at Carmarthen started by William Evans, who died 1718. To this school Dr. Williams left an annuity. William Evans is considered the founder of the Welsh a. system.)

Stourbridge and Bromsgrove (co. Worcester) a. (Under [? Henry] Hickman, 1665. He was disabled by age, ? 1670 c.)

Tubney (Berks.) a. (Under Dr. Henry Langley, 1662–72.)

Bridgwater a. (Started by John Moore 1676: became Arian under his son, who died 1747.)

Sulby (co. Northampton) a. (Under John Shuttlewood, about 1678; died 1689.)

Alkington (Whitchurch, co. Salop) a. (Under John Malden, 1668–80.)

Wickham Brook (co. Suffolk) a. (Under Samuel Cradock, from after 1672 to his removal in 1696. Edmund Calamy was one of his pupils.)

Tiverton a. (Under John Moor, 1688 c., or possibly after.)

Shaftesbury (and afterward Semly) (co. Wilts.) a. (Under Matthew Towgood, after 1662. He was the grandfather of Michaijah Towgood.)

Besides the above, there are stray references to private schools kept by John Flavel of Dartmouth, [John, son of] Edward Rayner of Lincoln, John Whitlock and Edward Reynolds of Nottingham, Ames Short of Lyme Dorset, Samuel Jones of Llangynwydd, John Ball of Honiton.

*Baptist academies*

In 1702 the General Baptist association resolved to erect a school of universal learning in London, with a view to training for the ministry. It is not known what followed. In 1717 the Particular Baptist fund was started for the support of ministers and for supplying a succession of them.

Trowbridge a. (Opened by John Davisson, who died in 1721. His successor was Thomas Lucas, who died in 1740.)

Bristol a. (In its earliest form, founded by several London baptists in 1752 as an education society for assisting students. It was, at first, under Dr. Stennett, Dr. Gill, Wallin and Brine. Subsequently it was under Bernard Foskett and Hugh Evans; it was taken in hand, in 1770, by the Baptist education society, and firmly established by Dr. Caleb Evans. This a. became, subsequently, the Baptist Rawdon college.)

# CHAPTER XVII

# Political Literature

## (1755-75)

THE death of Henry Pelham in 1754 destroyed the equilibrium of English politics. "Now," said King George II, regretting, possibly, the minister more than the man, "Now, I shall have no peace." And he was right, for the leading whigs entered on an angry struggle for supreme power which only ended when, in 1757, the domination of the elder Pitt was, virtually, established. Round the duke of Newcastle, formidable by his phalanx of obedient votes, Pitt, the man of genius and of the public confidence, and the shrewd, but far from high-minded, Henry Fox arose a dense dust of controversy.

It was not merely the conflict of personal ambitions that was in question. Great public issues were rapidly raised and discussed, if, as rapidly, let fall again. The sober middle class were weary of the prevailing corruption which handed over the country's government to glaring incompetence. Tories, abandoning their vain hopes of a revolution, were eager to loose England from the Hanoverian tether which involved her in the intricacies of German politics, and to have done with the long feud with France. And both parties were anxious to see power held by men more representative than were the members of the existing narrow whig oligarchy, who, on their side, still believed in their hereditary mission to rule. Material for honest discussion there was in plenty.

At first, it seemed as if this kind of discussion would hold the field. In August, 1755, *The Monitor* was founded by a London merchant, Richard Beckford, and was edited, and part written, by John Entick, of dictionary fame.[1] Like its predecessors in political journalism, it consisted of a weekly essay on current events and topics: it was all leading article. The maintenance of whig principles and the uprooting of corruption formed its policy: good information, good sense and a kind of heavy violence of style were its characteristics. Soon, it was supplemented by a series of tory pamphlets, under the title *The Letters to the People of England*, written by John Shebbeare, a physician of some literary celebrity. They were not his first production; he had for some time been eminent in "misanthropy and literature"; but they were distinguished beyond his other efforts by bringing him to the pillory. His politics, not the scurrility that tinged them, were in fault. He was a virulent tory, and in his *Sixth Letter* held up the reigning dynasty to public scorn. His highest praise is that he still remains readable. Logical, rhetorical, laboriously plain and, occasionally, cogent, his short paragraphs pretty generally hit the nail—often, no doubt, a visionary nail—on the head. Later, he was to enjoy court favour and be a capable pamphleteer on the side of George III; but his time of notoriety was gone.

Soon, however, the personal conflict asserted itself. In November, 1756, Arthur Murphy, the dramatist, started *The Test*, with a view to capturing public favour for Henry Fox. But his amiable prosing and feeble giggle were soon overcrowed by the Pittite *Con-Test*, a far more able, and, also, more scurrilous, print, in some of the better essays of which we detect the pith and point of Shebbeare.

Save the honest *Monitor*, these Grub-street railers vanished with the whig feud which called forth their exertions, and the splendid success of the great commoner's ministry almost succeeded in silencing criticism. It required a new ferment of public opinion, a new conflict of principles and a renewed struggle for the possession of power to reawaken the fires of controversy, which, this time, were not to be quenched. George III's accession and his personal policy gave the signal. The new king was determined to choose his own ministers and break up the band of ruling whigs. The now loyal tories were to

---

[1] His extremely popular *Spelling Dictionary* (1764) was followed by his *Latin and English Dictionary* (1771) and by other useful works.

share in the government, and the system of king William's
time was to be revived. The first literary sign of the change
was a rally of pamphleteers for the defence and propagation of
the royal views. In 1761, Lord Bath—the William Pulteney
who, in the last reign, had led the opposition to Walpole and
helped to set on foot *The Craftsman*—published his *Seasonable
Hints from an Honest Man*, which contained an able exposition
of the whig system and its vices, and outlined the new pro-
gramme. Others followed, professional writers for the most
part, such as the veteran Shebbeare and the elder Philip
Francis—in his *Letter from the Cocoa-Tree*[1] *to the Country
Gentlemen*, which was not devoid of skill—and Owen Ruffhead,
formerly editor of *The Con-Test*. But, in spite of the real
ability displayed by these writers, their frequent ignorance of
the true course of events and the lack of good faith habitual
to them prevented them from attaining to any real excellence.

Meanwhile, events were moving rapidly. George III had
been able to oust Pitt and Newcastle from power and to promote his Scottish favourite, Lord Bute, to the office of prime
minister. Bute had seen, from the first, that something beyond sporadic pamphlets was needed for converting public
opinion to the new *régime*, discredited as it was by the dismissal
of Pitt. For this, an imitation of *The Monitor* was the only
means, a steady drumming of the same views and sentiments
into the popular ear. It was all the more necessary, at the
moment of Bute's accession to power, to set up a rival weekly
journal, since *The Monitor* (in this representing the public)
was a bitter opponent of the Scottish minister. Bute, however,
cannot be called happy in his choice of means. Eminent
literary talent was required, but not any sort of literary talent,
and Tobias Smollett, famous as a novelist, was only to earn
humiliation as a political controversialist. In vain his sheet,
*The Briton*, discharged a weekly broadside of ferocious epithets
on the opposition and its journalistic defenders. His persuasive
powers were small, and he was fairly distanced in argumentative skill, raillery and vituperation. Arthur Murphy, writer
of the dead *Test*, was soon summoned to Smollett's aid with a
new paper, *The Auditor;* but, although more bitter than of old,
he was not less feeble. The public judgment was only too clear.

[1] The celebrated tory club described by Gibbon in his letters.

Neither of the ministerial papers would sell. Of course, Bute's unpopularity was partly at fault; but the scanty merit of the two champions was unable to surmount the weakness of their case.

The publication of *The Briton* provoked the appearance of the only one of these fugitive periodicals which has any reputation, *The North Briton*, edited by John Wilkes. That demagogue, on whom the mob-ruling mantle of Sacheverell descended, was sprung from a middle class family, typical of a respectability alien to the manners of its celebrated scion. He was born in 1727, and was the son of a maltster of Clerkenwell. He received a good education from a presbyterian minister and at the university of Leyden; and, before he was twenty-one, married, by his father's desire, an heiress much his senior in years. His wife and her mother were dissenters, and he was gallant and gay. Wilkes grew steadily estranged from his home and soon exceedingly dissipated. A separation from his wife was arranged, and he plunged into a course of profligate living in town. He became a member of the Hellfire club, which met at Medmenham abbey and included the most noted rakes of the day. It was in the midst of these wild orgies that he took up politics. In 1755, he obtained a seat in the commons as a member for Aylesbury, where his wife's estate lay. He was a follower of Pitt and hoped for some promotion—the embassy in Constantinople would have been most congenial to him—from his patron. But George III was king, and Bute intervened. His hopes of repairing his shattered fortunes having thus vanished, Wilkes turned to journalism for his revenge upon the favourite, whose incompetence filled him with indignation. After producing a successful pamphlet concerning the breach with Spain, he proceeded to send contributions to *The Monitor*, in which he developed with much ingenuity the history of contemporary foreign favourites, and left his readers to point the obvious moral. Then, on the appearance of *The Briton*, he, in June, 1762, started his rival print, *The North Briton*. Week by week, the new periodical continued its attacks on the government. It showed itself bold, to start with, in printing the ministers' names in full, without the usual subterfuges of dashes and stars; and it grew bolder as it went on, and as the odium into which Bute had

fallen became more obvious.   Nothing, however, gave a handle
to the authorities by which, even under the existing law of
libel, the writers could be brought to book, although *The
Monitor* was subjected to lengthy legal proceedings.   At last,
Wilkes overstepped the line in No. 45, which bitterly impugned
the truthfulness of the speech from the throne regarding the
peace of Paris.   The long government persecution of the libeller,
which followed the publication of No. 45, and which finally
resulted in the abolition of the tyrannic system of general
warrants, also snuffed out *The North Briton*.   The paper was
subsequently revived; but it proved only the ghost of its
former self.   Wilkes, on the other hand, had yet to play the
part of a full-fledged demagogue in his contest with king and
parliament concerning the Middlesex election of 1768.   Triumphant at last, he ended his life in 1797 as chamberlain of
London and a *persona grata* with George III.   In all his vicissi-
tudes, he had kept in touch with public opinion.

It is not easy to describe the blackguard charm of Wilkes.
Notoriously self-interested and dissolute, ugly and squinting,
he enjoyed a popularity by no means confined to the mob.
Much may be ascribed to the singular grace of his manners.
Even Johnson fell a victim to these.   But he, also, possessed
some very obvious virtues.   He was brave, good-humoured and
adroit.   He had a sort of selfish kindliness.   He was, moreover,
manifestly on the right side: few people had any love for general
warrants or for the infringement of the liberty of election.
And he turned all these advantages to account.

His paper, *The North Briton*, may be regarded as the best
example of its kind, the brief periodical pamphlet.   It represents the type at which *The Briton* and the rest aimed, but
which they could not reach.   Like its congeners, it consisted
of a weekly political essay.   It was directed entirely to the
object of overthrowing Bute and of reinstating the old group
of whig families in alliance with Pitt.   We notice at once in its
polemic the scantiness of serious argument.   Satire, raillery,
scandal and depreciation in every form are there; but a real
tangible indictment does not readily emerge from its effusions.
In part, this peculiarity was due to the difficulty under which
an opposition writer then lay in securing information and in
publishing what information he possessed.   When the prelimin-

aries of peace or the jobbery of Bute's loan issues gave Wilkes his opportunity, he could be cogent enough. But a more powerful reason lay in the main object of the paper. Bute was safe so long as he was not too unpopular: he had the king's favour and a purchased majority in parliament. Therefore, he had to be rendered of no value to king and parliament. He was to be written down and to become the bugbear of the ordinary voter, while his supporters in the press were to be exposed to derision and thus deprived of influence. Wilkes and his allies in *The North Briton* were well equipped for this task. They were interesting and vivacious from the first, making the most of the suspicions excited by Bute. As the heat of battle grew and their case became stronger, the violence and abusiveness of their expressions increased till it reached the scale of their rivals. Still, even so, they continued to display an apt brutality wanting in the latter. In the earlier numbers, too, *The Briton* and *The Auditor* fell easy victims to the malicious wit of Wilkes. Perhaps the best instance of his fun is the letter which he wrote under a pseudonym to the unsuspecting *Auditor*, descanting on the value of Floridan peat, a mythical product, for mitigating the severity of the climate in the West Indies. An exposure followed in *The North Briton;* and poor Murphy could only refer to his tormentor afterwards as " Colonel Cataline."

But the scheme of *The North Briton* gave an easy opportunity for ironic satire. The editor was supposed to be a Scot exulting over the fortune of his countryman, and very ingenuous in repeating the complaints of the ousted English. There was nothing exquisite in this horseplay; but it was not badly done, and it had the advantage of appealing to strong national prejudice. The antipathy to the Scots, which was to disappear with startling suddenness during the American war of independence, had not yet undergone any sensible diminution. At root, perhaps, it was the dislike of an old-established firm for able interlopers. Scots were beginning to take a leading share in the common government, and their nationality was always unmistakable. Accordingly, old legends of their national character and a purse-proud contempt for their national poverty lived obstinately on; and *The North Briton* worked the vein exhaustively.

In the composition of his journal and in his whole campaign against the minister, Wilkes had for his coadjutor a more eminent man, who, unlike himself, is to be conceived of, not as a pleasant adventurer, but as a principal literary figure of the time, the poet and satirist Charles Churchill. The two men were fast friends, although their lives had flowed in very different streams until they became acquainted in 1761. Churchill was the son of a clergyman, who was curate and lecturer of St. John's, Westminster, and vicar of Rainham in Essex. The younger Charles was born in 1731 and early distinguished himself by his ability at Westminster school. Thence, he proceeded, in 1748, to St. John's college, Cambridge;[1] but his residence there was not for long. With characteristic impulsiveness, when only 18 years of age, he contracted a marriage in the Fleet with a girl named Martha Scott, and his university education had to be discontinued. His kindly father took the young couple into his house and had his son trained, as best he might, for holy orders. In 1754, Churchill was ordained deacon and licensed curate of South Cadbury in Somerset, whence, as priest, he removed, in 1756, to act as his father's curate at Rainham. Two years later, the father died, and the son was elected to succeed him as incumbent of St. John's in Westminster, where he increased his income by teaching in a girls' school.

Such is the outline of Churchill's earlier life—bald enough, if stripped of the malicious inventions which gathered round it. His later career is full of evidence both of his good and of his bad qualities. Burdened with two children and an extravagant wife, himself completely unsuited for his clerical profession and inclined to the pleasures of the town, in two years he became bankrupt, and owed the acceptance by his creditors of a composition to the generosity of his old schoolmaster, Pierson Lloyd. Afterwards, Churchill was to show his natural honesty and good feeling, not only by a constant friendship to his benefactor's son, Robert Lloyd, a poet of secondary rank, but, also, by paying his own debts in full, in disregard of his bankruptcy. That he was able to do this was due to his own new profession of poetry. He began, unluckily, with a Hudi-

---

[1] See *Admissions to the College of St. John the Evangelist*, pt. II, ed. Scott, R. F., p. 580.

brastic poem, *The Bard*, in 1760, which could not find a publisher. His second effort, *The Conclave*, contained matter against the dean and chapter of Westminster so libellous that the intending publisher dared not bring it out. A more interesting subject of satire presented itself in the contemporary stage, and, in March, 1761, there appeared, at the author's own risk, *The Rosciad*. Its success was immediate and extraordinary; Churchill was enabled to pay his debts, to make an allowance to his wife, from whom he had now been for some time estranged, and to set up in glaringly unclerical attire as a man about town. But the penalty, too, for indulging in bitter criticism—a penalty, perhaps, welcome to the combative poet —was not long in coming; and, for the rest of his life, he was involved in an acrid literary warfare. Yet, in these tedious campaigns he was a constant victor. Few escaped unbruised from the cudgel of his verse, and, vulnerable though his private life made him to attack, the toughness of his fibre enabled him to endure.

In consequence of this literary celebrity, Churchill made the acquaintance of Wilkes, whose friendship was responsible for the turn his life took in his few remaining years. The last shred of the poet's respectability was soon lost in the Medmenham orgies; yet, his political satires, which, unlike those of his friend Wilkes, do not admit doubt of their sincerity, gave him a permanent place in English literature. Quite half of *The North Briton* was written by him; his keenest satiric poem was *The Prophecy of Famine*, which, in January, 1763, raised the ridicule of Bute and his countrymen to its greatest height. Thanks to Wilkes's adroitness, Churchill escaped the meshes of the general warrant, and was afterwards let alone by government: he had not written No. 45. But he ceased to reside permanently in London. We hear of him in Wales in 1763, and, later, he lived at Richmond and on Acton common. The stream of his satires, political and social, continued unabated throughout. His days, however, were numbered. He died at Boulogne, on 4 November, 1764, while on his way to visit Wilkes at Paris, and was buried at Dover.

"Life to the last enjoyed, here Churchill lies." This line of his own was placed on his gravestone, and not inaccurately sums up the man. The burly poet's faults are too manifest to need insisting upon. It is pleasanter to remember that, as already stated, he supported his brother rake, Robert Lloyd, when the unlucky man was dying beggared in the Fleet. His devotion to Wilkes, like the rest of him, was unbounded and whole-hearted. Nor is any mean action recorded of him.

There is no denying that his verse is truculent and loud. What most distinguishes it from contemporary couplets is its spirit and strength. He may ramble, he may prose; but he never exhibits the neat, solemn tripping which tires us in his contemporaries. *The Rosciad*, with which he first won reputation, consists chiefly of a series of severe sketches of the leading actors in 1761. Few, save Garrick, escape unblamed; but the poet, although censorious, can hardly be called unfair. His verse maintains a steady level of force and skill, just within the bounds of poetry, lighted up, now and then, by such shrewd couplets as:

> Appearances to save his only care;
> So things seem right, no matter what they are;

and, occasionally, phrases of stinging wit intensify the ridicule.

*The Rosciad* called forth many enemies, and, in reply to an attack in *The Critical Review*, Churchill published *The Apology*, under the impression that the critique was Smollett's. It cannot be called an advance on its forerunner, although sufficiently tart to make Garrick, who was victimised in it, almost supplicate his critic's friendship. As a poem, it is much surpassed by Churchill's next composition, *Night*, which appeared in October, 1761. The versification has become easier, the lines more pliant, without losing vigour. There is a suggestion of a poetical atmosphere not to be found in the hard, dry outlines of his earlier work. The substance is slight; it is merely a defence of late hours and genial converse over "the grateful cup." Churchill was, in this instance at all events, too wise to defend excess.

A year's rest given to the prose of *The North Briton* seems to have invigorated Churchill for the production of his best satire, *The Prophecy of Famine*. Its main object was to decry and ridicule Bute and the Scots, although there is an undercurrent of deserved mockery at the reigning fashion of pastoral.

Churchill, as he owns, was himself half a Scot;[1] but the circumstance did not mitigate his national and perfectly sincere prejudice against his northern kinsfolk. The probable reason was that Bute was Wilkes's enemy, and the warmhearted poet was wroth, too, in a fascinated sympathy with his friend. The wit and humour of the piece are in Churchill's most forcible and amusing vein. His hand is heavy, it is true; more dreary irony was never written; and he belabours his theme like a peasant wielding a flail; but the eighteenth century must have found him all the more refreshing. Compare him with the prose polemics of his day, and he is not specially venomous. He only repeats in sinewy verse the current topics of reproach against the Scots.

The painter Hogarth now crossed Churchill's path. A satiric print of Wilkes by Hogarth roused the poet's vicarious revenge. The savage piece of invective, *The Epistle to William Hogarth*, was the result, which, if it has not worn so well as Hogarth's pictures, yet, here and there, strikes a deeper note than is usual with its author. Take, for instance, the couplet:

> With curious art the brain, too finely wrought,
> Preys on herself, and is destroy'd by thought;

although his own fertility shows no sign of exhausting the soil. He was beginning, however, in his own metaphor, to vary the crop. *The Duellist*, published in January, 1764, was written, not in the stock heroic couplet, but in octosyllabics suggestive of *Hudibras*. This was an attack on Samuel Martin, one of Wilkes's ministerial enemies, with a few satirical excursions like that on Warburton. The adoption of a new metre was not a success; its straggling movement doubled the risk which Churchill always ran of being tedious, and the extravagance of his vituperation is no antidote. In compensation, the poem contains some of his finest lines. The curse on Martin reveals an old and clearsighted pupil in the school of life:

> Grant him what here he most requires,
> And damn him with his own desires!

while the malicious criticism of Warburton's defence of Scrip-

[1] *The Prophecy of Famine*, ll. 221-2.

ture suggests a literary experience which approves itself to the instincts of human nature:

> So long he wrote, and long about it,
> That e'en believers 'gan to doubt it.

Contemporaneously with *The Duellist*, Churchill was writing, in the heroic couplet, *Gotham*, a curious farrago, in the three books of which a Utopian realm ruled by himself, a long denunciation of the Stewart dynasty and a description of an ideal king jostle one another. He does not appear at his best in this attempt at non-satiric poetry. The usual mannerisms of eighteenth-century poetry, the personifications, the platitudinous moralising, the hackneyed, meaningless descriptions are all to be found here. That entire absence of any taste for nature outside Fleet street which was characteristic of Churchill as fully as it was of Johnson places him at peculiar disadvantage when he imitates Spenser in a hasty catalogue of flowers, trees, months and other poetic properties. Not less did the straightforward vigour of his usual metre and style disqualify him for the prophet of the ideal. In short, in spite of Cowper's praise, he was off his track.

Only a few months before *Gotham* was printed, Churchill had published a very different poem, *The Conference*. He was accused of merely making his profit out of political satire, and he here, in words of obvious sincerity, repudiates the charge that he was looking for office or pension. At the same time, he refers to a better-grounded cause of censure—his seduction of a girl, whose father is said to have been a stone-cutter of Westminster. Instead of pleading extenuating circumstances, such as, in this case, certainly existed, he only confesses his fault and avows his remorse. On the other hand, his personal conduct throughout this miserable affair must be described as callous.

The rest of Churchill's poems are of less interest. *The Author* is a slashing attack on Smollett and other ministerial publicists and agents. *The Ghost*, in octosyllabics, derives its only interest from being, in part, his earliest work; it is tedious and rambling to a degree. We may allow *The Candidate*, directed against Lord Sandwich, to have deserved its share of

praise for the defeat of "Jemmy Twitcher,"[1] as he was nick-
named, in the election for the high stewardship of Cambridge
university; but its appeal was merely temporary. There is
little to remark on any of the other poems—*The Farewell,
Independence* and *The Journey*—produced by the prolific poet
in 1764. They showed an increasing metrical skill, and maintained his reputation, but they did not add to it. *The Times,*
which, from its greater fire, might have taken high place among
his works, was, unfortunately, both hideous in subject and
extravagantly exaggerated in execution.

We find, in fact, that Churchill's talent remained almost
stationary during the four years of his poetic industry. Crab-
apples, according to Johnson, he produced from the first; and
such his fruits remained to the end. He never shows the
greater qualities of either of his two chief English predecessors
in satire—either those of Pope whom he underrated, or those
of Dryden whom he admired. His wit, though strong, is
never exquisite. His characters are vividly and trenchantly
described; but they do not live to our imagination. His good
sense cannot be said to rise to wisdom; and he is deficient in
constructive skill. *The Prophecy of Famine* is, after all, an
ill-proportioned mixture of satiric epistle and satiric eclogue;
while his other satires have little unity except what is provided
by the main object of their attack. Although he justly ridicules
some of the current phrases of contemporary lesser poetry, he
cannot be said himself to rise superior to eighteenth-century
conventions. His incessant personifications, "Gay Description," "Dull Propriety," are, in the end, wearisome; and
many of his humorous couplets, constructed after the fashion
of the time, rather seem like epigrams than are such. His
real *forte* consisted in a steady pommelling of his adversary;
with all his fierceness and prejudice, acidity and spite were
foreign to his nature.

As a metrist, Churchill can claim some originality. He
uses the heroic couplet of the day with fresh freedom and
effectivity. At first, in *The Rosciad,* he can hardly be said to
form his paired lines into periods. Then, in *The Epistle to*

---

[1] "That Jemmy Twitcher should peach, I own surprises me." Sandwich, the
completest rake of the day, had brought Wilkes's obscene *Essay on Woman* before
the House of Lords in a speech of extraordinary hypocrisy.

*William Hogarth*, the last line of his paragraph has a closing sound and really ends a period. Perhaps, it was his long involved sentences, compiled of many clauses, which led him, in later pieces, to a further change. From time to time, he uses *enjambement*, and even, by means of it, breaks up his couplets.[1]

Churchill so overtops his rivals in political verse that they scarcely seem worth mentioning. Mason, his frequent butt as a writer of pastorals—"Let them with Mason bleat and bray and coo"—shrouded himself in political satire under the name Malcolm Macgregor.[2] Falconer, a naval officer, attacked Pitt from the court point of view.[3] But both of these, and even Chatterton in his *Consuliad*,[4] merely illustrate their inferiority to Churchill.

Prose was far more effective than verse in the political controversies which followed Bute's resignation. The weekly essay, in its old form, died out gradually; but the flood of pamphlets continued. They were in a more serious vein than formerly. Measures rather than men were in dispute, not so much because the public taste had changed, as because the more prominent politicians, with the exception of Pitt, presented few points of interest. The ability of many of these numerous pamphlets is undeniable. Some leading statesmen had a share in them. We find such men as George Grenville, an ex-prime minister, and Charles Townshend, leader of the House of Commons, defending or attacking current policy in this fashion. Others were written by authors of literary eminence. Edmund Burke published a celebrated tract in defence of the first Rockingham ministry;[5] Horace Walpole was stirred to address the public concerning the dismissal of general Conway in 1764; latest of all, Johnson took part as a champion of the government during the agitation about the Middlesex election, and in opposition to the accusations of Junius. Perhaps, however, the more effective among these pamphlets were due to political understrappers. Charles Lloyd,

---

[1] Cf., for the effect gained by this occasional variation, *Independence*, ll. 199–206.

[2] As to Mason, cf. *ante*, Chap. VI.

[3] As to Falconer, cf. *ante*, Chap. VII.  [4] Cf. *ante*, Chap. X.

[5] *A Short Account of a Short Administration*, 1766. (See bibliography.)

Grenville's secretary, wrote a series in support of his patron's policy, including a clever reply to Burke.  Thomas Whateley, secretary to the treasury, defended the same minister's finance. These and their fellows worked with more or less knowledge of the ground, and, if their special pleading be conspicuous, they also dispensed much sound information.

Two pamphlets, which appeared in 1764, and dealt with the constitutional questions raised by the prosecution of Wilkes, stand well above their fellows in ability and influence.  The first appeared, originally, as *A Letter to The Public Advertiser*, and was signed "Candor."  It was an attack on Lord Mansfield for his charge to the jury in the Wilkes case and on the practice of general warrants.  With a mocking irony, now pleasant, now scathing, the author works up his case, suiting the pretended moderation of his language to the real moderation of his reasoning.  The same writer, we cannot doubt, under the new pseudonym "The Father of Candor," put a practical conclusion to the legal controversy in his *Letter concerning Libels, Warrants, etc.*, published in the same year.  This masterly pamphlet attracted general admiration, and its cool and lucid reasoning, varied by an occasional ironic humour, did not meet with any reply.  Walpole called it "the only tract that ever made me understand law."  The author remains undiscovered.  The publisher, Almon, who must have known the secret, declared that "a learned and respectable Master in Chancery" had a hand in it.[1]  Candor's handwriting has been pronounced that of Sir Philip Francis;[2] but, clearly, in view of Almon's evidence, he can only have been part author; and the placid, suave humour of the pamphlets reads most unlike him, and, we may add, most unlike Junius.

Candor's first letter had originally appeared in *The Public Advertiser*, and there formed one of a whole class of political compositions, which, in the next few years, were to take the

---

[1] *Anecdotes of Eminent Persons*, vol. I, pp. 79, 80.  Almon's words obviously imply that the master in chancery was still living in 1797.  He wrote again, in 1770, both anonymously and under the name Phileleutherus Anglicanus (*Grenville Correspondence*, vol. III, pp. clxxvi *sqq.*, where the resemblance in manner to the Candor pamphlets is made obvious by extracts).

[2] Parkes, *Memoirs of Sir Philip Francis*, vol. I, pp. 74–81 and 99–101.  A facsimile of Candor's handwriting is given in vol. II, plate 5.

foremost place in controversy. Their existence was due to the shrewd enterprise of the printer Henry Sampson Woodfall, who had edited *The Public Advertiser* since 1758. In addition to trustworthy news of events at home and abroad, Woodfall opened his columns to correspondence, the greater part of which was political. He was scrupulously impartial in his choice from his letter-bag. Merit and immunity from the law of libel were the only conditions exacted. Soon, he had several journals, such as *The Gazetteer*, competing with his for correspondents; but *The Public Advertiser's* larger circulation, and the inclusion in it of letters from all sides in politics, enabled it easily to distance the rival prints in the quality and quantity of these volunteer contributions. George III himself was a regular subscriber; it gave him useful clues to public opinion. The political letters are of all kinds—denunciatory, humorous, defensive, solemn, matter-of-fact, rhetorical and ribald. Their authors, too, were most varied, and are now exceedingly hard to identify. Every now and then a statesman who had been attacked would vindicate himself under a pseudonym; more frequently, some hanger-on would write on his behalf, with many professions of being an impartial onlooker. There were independent contributors; and small groups of minor politicians would carry on a continuous correspondence for years. But neither single authors nor groups can be easily traced through their compositions. As is natural, their style seldom helps us to identify them. They wrote the current controversial prose, and, after 1770, their prose is tinged with a Junian dye. The pseudonyms throw little light on the matter. There was no monopoly in any one of them, and the same author would vary his pseudonyms as much as possible, chiefly with intent to avoid discovery and the decrease of credit which his communications might undergo if he were known, but, also, to provide sham opponents as a foil to his arguments and to create an illusion of wide public support for his views.

A good instance of the letter-writers was James Scott, a preacher of repute. In 1766, he contributed a series of letters to *The Public Advertiser*, signed "Anti-Sejanus." They were written in the interests of Lord Sandwich, and assailed, with much vehemence, the supposed secret intrigues of Bute. Scott used many other pseudonyms, and wrote so well that his later letters, which show Junius's influence in their style, were re-published separately. From a private letter written by him to Woodfall,[1] we learn that he, too, was a member of a group who worked together. Another writer we can identify was John Horne, later known as John Horne Tooke and as the author of *The Diversions of Purley*. He began to send in correspondence to the newspapers about 1764; but his celebrity only began when he became an enthusiastic partisan of Wilkes in 1768. Under the pseudonym "Another Freeholder of Surrey," he made a damaging attack on George Onslow,[2] and, on being challenged, allowed the publication of his name. The legal prosecution which followed the acknowledgment of his identity, in the end, came to nothing, and Horne was able to continue his career as Wilkes's chief lieutenant. But the cool un-scrupulousness with which Wilkes used the agitation as a mere instrument for paying off his own debts and gratifying his own ambitions disgusted even so warm a supporter as Horne. A quarrel broke out between them in 1771 concerning the dis-posal of the funds raised to pay Wilkes's debts by the society, The Supporters of the Bill of Rights, to which both belonged. Letter after letter from the two former friends appeared in *The Public Advertiser*. Horne, who, perhaps, had the better case, allowed himself to be drawn off into long petty recrimina-tions on Wilkes's private life. Indiscreet expressions of his own were brought up against him, and the popularity of Wilkes, in any case, made the attempt to undermine him impossible. Yet "parson Horne" had his triumph, too. The redoubtable Junius entered the controversy on Wilkes's side; Horne retorted vigorously, and proved the most successful critic of the greater libeller's productions. In truth, Junius's letters owed much of their success to his victims' inability to rebut his insinuations by giving the real facts in transactions which were necessarily secret. Horne's record was clear; he had no dignity to lose; he could pin Junius down by a demand for proof. Yet, even allowing for these advantages, his skill

[1] Parkes, *Memoirs of Sir Philip Francis*, vol. I, pp. 130–1. Parkes, as usual with him in the case of the abler letters previous to 1769, attributes "Anti-Sejanus" to Sir P. Francis. "Anti-Sejanus" should probably be distinguished from "Anti-Sejanus junior," in 1767, who is likely to be Junius.

[2] Celebrated as the single member of the House of Commons who "said that No. 45 was not a libel."

in dissecting his adversary's statements and his courage in defying the most formidable libeller of the day are much to his credit as a pamphleteer. Before long, Junius was glad to beat a retreat.

It was in the autumn of 1768 that the political letters of the unknown writer who, later, took the pseudonym of Junius, gained the public ear. But we know from his own statement[1] that, for two years before that date, he had been busy in furtive, assassinating polemic; and it is possible that a careful search of newspaper files would result in the discovery of some of his earlier performances of 1766 and 1767. The time when he appears to have begun letter-writing tallies well with the objects pursued by him during the period of his known writings. He was an old-fashioned whig, and a warm, almost an impassioned, adherent of the former prime minister, George Grenville. Thus, the accession to power, in July, 1766, of the elder Pitt, now Lord Chatham, with his satellite, the duke of Grafton, after a breach with Lord Temple, Grenville's brother, and their adherents, most likely, gave the impulse to Junius's activity. It was not, however, till October, 1768 that he became clearly distinguishable from other writers in *The Public Advertiser*. By that time, Chatham's nervous prostration had rendered him incapable of transacting business, and the duke of Grafton was acting as prime minister in an administration which had become mainly tory. For some reason or other, Junius nursed a vindictive and unassuageable hatred against the duke, which it seems difficult to attribute only to the rancour of a partisan. The weakness of the loosely constructed ministry, too, would tempt their adversary to complete their rout by a storm of journalistic shot and shell. So, Junius, sometimes under his most constant and, perhaps, original signature "C.," sometimes under other disguises, continued to add to the fury and cruel dexterity of his attacks. "The Grand Council" ridiculed the ministers' Irish policy and their methods of business. A legal job which was attempted at the duke of Portland's expense furnished another opportunity. Nor was Junius content with these public efforts to discredit his foes. In January, 1768, he sent Chatham an unsigned letter, full of flatteries for the sick man and of suggestions of

[1] *Grenville Correspondence*, vol. IV, p. 380.

disloyalty on the part of his colleagues. For the time being, however, Chatham continued to lend his name to the distracted ministry, which staggered on from one mistake to another. Those on which Junius, under his various *aliases*, seized for animadversion were small matters; but they were damaging, and his full knowledge of them, secret as they sometimes were, gave weight to his arguments. His ability seemed to rise with the occasion: the 'prentice hand which may have penned "Poplicola's" attacks on Chatham in 1767 had become a master of cutting irony and merciless insinuation, when, as "Lucius," he, in 1768, flayed Lord Hillsborough. The time was ripe for his appearance as something better than a skirmisher under fleeting pseudonyms, and the series of the letters of Junius proper began in January, 1769. They never, however, lost the stamp of their origin. To the last, Junius is a light-armed auxiliary, first of the Grenville connection, then, on George Grenville's death in 1770, of the opponents of the king's tory-minded ministry under Lord North. He darts from one point of vantage to another. Now one, now another, minister is his victim, either when guilty or when unable to defend himself efficiently. Ringing invective, a deadly catalogue of innuendoes, barbed epigrams closing a scornful period, a mastery of verbal fencing and, here and there, a fund of political good sense, all were used by the libeller, and contributed to make him the terror of his victims. The choice and the succession of the subjects of his letters were by no means haphazard. His first letter was an indictment of the more prominent members of the administration. It created a diversion which made the letter-writer's fortune, for Sir William Draper, conqueror of Manilla, rushed into print to defend an old friend, Lord Granby. Thoroughly trounced, ridiculed, humiliated and slandered, he drew general attention to his adversary, who then proceeded to the execution of his main design. In six letters, under his customary signature or the obvious alternative Philo-Junius, he assailed the duke of Grafton's career as man and minister. Meanwhile, the agitation provoked by Wilkes's repeated expulsion from the commons, and his repeated election for Middlesex, was growing furious; and, in July, 1769, Junius, following the lead of George Grenville, took up the demagogue's cause. For two months, in some of his most

skilful compositions, he urged the constituency's right to elect
Wilkes. Then, as the theme wore out, he chose a new victim.
Grafton's administration depended on his alliance with the
duke of Bedford, one of the most unpopular men in England.
Junius turned on his foe's ally with a malignity only second to
that which he displayed against Grafton himself. A triumphant tone begins to characterise the letters, for it was obvious
that the Grafton ministry was tottering to its fall; and Junius
decided on a bolder step. His information was of the best,
and he was convinced that the king had no intention of changing his ministerial policy, even if Grafton resigned. The king,
then, must be terrorised into submitting to a new consolidated
whig administration. The "capital and, I hope, final piece,"
as it was called by Junius, who was conscious of his own influence with the public though he much overrated it, was an
address to the king which contained a fierce indictment of
George III's public action since his accession. It was an attempt to raise popular excitement to a pitch which would
compel George to yield. But the libeller placed too much
trust in his power over the ruling oligarchy and gave too little
credit to the dauntless courage and resolution of the king.
Lord North took up the vacant post of prime minister; and
his talent and winning personality, assisted by the all-prevail-
ing corruption and by the very violence of the opposition in
which Junius took part, carried the day. It was the House of
Commons which kept Lord North in power, and to its conquest
the angry opposition turned. Junius now appears as one of
the foremost controversialists on Wilkes's election, and as
champion of the nascent radical party forming under Wilkes's
leadership in the city of London. Other matters, also, were
subjects of his letters, such as the dispute with Spain concerning the Falkland islands, and the judicial decisions of Lord
Mansfield; but they are all subordinate to his main end. Ever
and anon, too, he returns, now with little public justification,
to the wreaking of his inexplicable hatred on the duke of
Grafton, "the pillow upon which I am determined to rest all
my resentments." But the game was up. Clearly, neither
king nor commons could be coerced by an outside agitation,
which, after all, was of no great extent. The quarrel of Wilkes
and Horne wrecked the opposition in the city. Junius saw

his scale kick the beam, and it was only the too true report conveyed by Garrick to the court, in November, 1771, that he would write no more, which induced him to pen his final attack on Lord Mansfield, with which the collected letters close.

Junius vanishes with the publication of the collected edition of his letters. It was far from complete. Not only are the letters previous to 1769 omitted, but many of inferior quality or of transient interest, written during the continuance of the great series, usually under other pseudonyms, are absent. And, more remarkable still, there are certain letters of 1772, after the Junian series had closed, which he very anxiously desired not to be known as his, and which passed unidentified for years. Under fresh pseudonyms, such as "Veteran," he poured forth furious abuse on Lord Barrington, secretary at war. The cause, in itself, was strangely slight. It was only the appointment of a new deputy secretary, formerly a broker, Anthony Chamier, and the resignations of the preceding deputy, Christopher D'Oyly, and of the first clerk, Philip Francis. But, trifling as the occasion might be, it was sufficient to make the cold and haughty Junius mouth with rage.

Junius follows the habit of his fellow-correspondents in dealing very little with strictly political subjects. Personal recrimination is the chief aim of his letters, and it would hardly be fair to contrast them with those of a different class of authors, such as Burke, or even with the product of the acute legal mind of Candor. Yet, when he treats of political principles he does so with shrewdness and insight. He understood the plain-going whig doctrine he preached, and expounded it, on occasion, with matchless clearness. What could be better as a statement than the sentences in the dedication of the collected letters which point out that the liberty of the press is the guarantee of political freedom and emphasise the responsibility of parliament? And the same strong common-sense marks an apophthegm like that on the duke of Grafton—

Injuries may be atoned for and forgiven; but insults admit of no compensation. They degrade the mind in its own esteem, and force it to recover its level by revenge.

Yet these sentences betray in their sinister close the cast of Junius's mind. There is an evil taint in his strength, which could not find satisfaction in impartial reasoning on political questions. This partisanship merges at once into personal hatred, and his rancour against his chief victim, Grafton, can hardly be accounted for on merely political grounds. His object is to wound and ruin, not only to overthrow. Scandal, true or false, is the weapon of his choice. "The great boar of the forest," as Burke called him, loved the poison in which he dipped his tusks, and took a cruel pleasure in the torture he inflicted. Secure in his anonymity, no insult or counter-thrust could reach him. With frigid glee, he retorts upon accusations, which, of necessity, were vague and wide, by plausible insinuations against his opponents. "To him that knows his company," said Dr. Johnson, "it is not hard to be sarcastic in a mask." And Junius, thus gripped with the obvious realities of his position, found no reply to this sarcasm.

But, however much he owed to his concealment and to his remarkable knowledge of the vulnerable points of his quarry (and, be it added, to the cunning with which he selected for his attack men who could not produce their defence), Junius holds a high position on his own literary merits. He was the most perfect wielder of slanderous polemic that had ever arisen in English political controversy. Not lack of rivals, but eminent ability, made him supreme in that ignoble competition. In invective which is uninformed by any generosity of feeling he stands unequalled. His sentences, brief, pithy and pungent, exhibit a delicate equilibrium in their structure. Short as they are, their rhythm goes to form the march of a period, and the cat-like grace of their evolution ends in the sudden, maiming wit of a malign epigram. Direct invective, lucid irony, dry sarcasm mingle with one another in the smooth-ranked phrases. A passage on George III and Grafton will show to what excellence Junius can rise:

There is surely something singularly benevolent in the character of our sovereign. From the moment he ascended the throne there is no crime of which human nature is capable (and I call upon the recorder[1] to witness it) that has not appeared venial in his sight. With any other prince, the shameful desertion of him in the midst

---

[1] Jas. Eyre, later chief justice, in whose court there had lately been condemned for murder two or three persons, who received the royal pardon.

of that distress, which you alone had created, in the very crisis of danger, when he fancied he saw the throne already surrounded by men of virtue and abilities, would have outweighed the memory of your former services. But his Majesty is full of justice, and understands the doctrine of compensations; he remembers with gratitude how soon you had accommodated your morals to the necessities of his service; how cheerfully you had abandoned the engagements of private friendship, and renounced the most solemn professions to the public. The sacrifice of Lord Chatham was not lost upon him. Even the cowardice and perfidy of deserting him may have done you no disservice in his esteem. The instance was painful, but the principle might please.

Junius possessed to perfection the art of climax.

The anonymity which he marvellously preserved enabled Junius to maintain that affectation of superiority which distinguished him. Never before were mere scandals and libellous diatribes presented with such an air of haughty integrity and stern contempt for the baseness of jacks-in-office. We have to make an effort in order to remember that this lofty gentleman, above the temptation of "a common bribe," is really engaged in the baser methods of controversy, and cuts a poor figure beside Johnson and Burke. But, from his impersonal vantage ground, he could deliver his judgments with more authority and more freely display the deliberate artifice of his style. Its general construction will appear from the passage on Grafton which has been quoted above. But he also uses a more shrouded form of innuendo than he there employs. He was very ingenious in composing a sentence, or even a whole period, of double meaning, and in making his real intent peculiarly clear withal. Perfect lucidity, indeed, is one of his chief literary qualities. In his most artificial rhetoric, his meaning is obvious to any reader. His wit, too, is of high quality, in spite of his laboured antitheses. It has outlived the obsolete fashion of its dress. It far transcends any trick of words; as often as not, it depends on a heartless sense of comedy. "I should," he wrote to the unhappy Sir William Draper, "justly be suspected of acting upon motives of more than common enmity to Lord Granby, if I continued to give you fresh materials or occasion for writing in his defence." He needs, we feel, defence himself. The best apology, perhaps, that can be offered for him is that he was carrying on an evil tradition and has to be condemned chiefly because of his excellence in a common mode.

Something, too, of his celebrity is due to the mystery he successfully maintained. The wildest guesses as to his identity were made in his own day and after. It was thought at first that only Burke could write so well, and most of the eminent contemporaries of Junius have, at one time or another, been charged with the authorship of the letters. Fresh light was cast on the problem by the publication, in 1812, of his private letters to Woodfall, with specimens of his handwriting, and subsequent research has at least laid down some of the conditions which must be satisfied if his identity is to be proved. Among them, we may take it that a coincidence of the real life of the author with the hints regarding himself thrown out in the letters is not to be expected. It was part of Junius's plan to avoid giving any real clue, and he was anxious to be thought personally important. But there are more certain data to go upon. The very marked handwriting of Junius is well known, although, to all seeming, it is a feigned hand. The dates of the letters show when the author must have been in London. His special knowledge is of importance. He had an inner acquaintance with the offices of secretary at war and secretary of state, and he was very well informed on much of the doings of contemporary statesmen and on the court. His politics show him to have been an adherent of George Grenville, who was anxious to draw Lord Chatham into alliance with the thoroughgoing whigs, and turn out the king's chosen ministers. The latter he hated to a man; but he had a singular antipathy to Grafton and Barrington.[1] His power of hating is characteristic. We must find a man proud and malignant, yet possessed of considerable public spirit and of a desire for an honest, patriotic administration. Finally, we require a proof of ability, in 1770, to write the letters with their merits and defects. Later writings, even when tinged with the admired Junian style, are but poor evidence. Nor is the inferior quality of a man's later productions an absolute bar to his claims. He may have passed his prime.

Perhaps it is not too bold to say that the only claimant who

[1] "Next to the Duke of Grafton, I verily believe that the *blackest heart* in the kingdom belongs to Lord Barrington." Junius to Woodfall, Letter 61.

fulfils the majority of these conditions is Sir Philip Francis. In his case, also, there are corroborative circumstances of weight; and, although, with our present knowledge, we cannot definitely state that he was the author of the letters, yet it is pretty clear that he was concerned in their production. Sir Philip was an Irishman, the son of that elder Philip Francis who was also a pamphleteer. He was born in Dublin on 22 October, 1740, but was bred in England at St. Paul's school. In 1756, he obtained a clerkship in the secretary of state's office, and accompanied Lord Kinnoul on his embassy to Portugal in 1760. From 1762 to 1772, he held the post of first clerk at the war office, which he resigned in obscure circumstances only to be appointed a member of the governor-general's council in India next year. His long feud there with Hastings brought him into public notice, and, after his return to England in 1781, he became the relentless engineer of the prosecution of his enemy. Failure, however, alike attended these efforts and his hopes of political office. He gave up, in 1807, the seat in parliament which he had held from 1784. He survived to see the claim put forward that he was the author of Junius; but he died, without either admitting or denying the fact, on 23 December, 1818. He had married twice and left descendants by his first wife.

Though this career was not humdrum, yet the earlier part of it by no means corresponded with the fancied importance of Junius, and John Taylor, who declared for Francis's authorship in 1814, showed an adventurous spirit in his thesis. Nevertheless, the arguments he collected then, and those since added by his adherents, form a strong array. The all-important handwriting has been assigned to Francis by expert evidence; 4 out of the 5 Junian seals were used by him, and, since Francis's undisguised hand appears in a dating on the Junian proofs along with the feigned, while the feigned hand directs the envelope of a copy of verses dated 1771 and shown, by absolutely independent evidence,[1] to be of Francis's composition, it seems

---

[1] The verses, copied out by Francis's cousin, Tilghman, and addressed in the feigned Junian hand, were sent to a Miss Giles at Bath, in the winter of 1770-1. Later, before this copy was the subject of investigation, Sir P. Francis gave his second wife another copy, in his own hand and on a portion of the same sheet of paper as Miss Giles's copy, among other specimens of his early verses.

impossible to avoid the conclusion that Francis was Junius's collaborator, if not Junius himself.  The same result is obtained from the facts that Junius used, and vouched for, a report made by Francis of one of Chatham's speeches in December, 1770, and that an unacknowledged Junian letter signed "Phalaris" can hardly have been written without Francis's co-operation, employing, as it does, Francis's very words in a letter to Chatham.[1]  Again, Francis's presence in London tallies remarkably with the dates of the letters.[2]  When he is absent, Junius is silent.  In less external matters, Francis had that experience of the offices of war and state which is marked in Junius.  His politics were identical with those of the libeller and he was at the time engaged as a jackal of the declining politician Calcraft, in the labour of effecting a junction of Chatham and the Grenvilles.  Calcraft and Lord Temple, the latter a veteran patron of libellers, may well have given him court intelligence not otherwise obtainable.  Calcraft, again, at the time of his death in 1772, was, obviously, under great obligations to Francis for services rendered: he leaves him a legacy and prescribes his nomination to a pocket-borough of his own.  If Junius's remorseless hatred of the duke of Grafton remains unexplained[3]—though some insult received by Francis in the course of his official duties is an easy supposition—the fury he manifests against Barrington in 1772 is in precise harmony with the mysterious retirement of D'Oyly and Francis which partly forms the theme of that attack.  Then, the characters of Junius and Francis markedly coincide.  The same pride, the same fierce hatreds, the same implacable revenge and the same good intention towards the public interest meet us in both.  Even the seeming improbability of Junius's hostile reference to Calcraft is paralleled by Francis's readiness, when piqued, to put the worst construction on his friends.  At the same time, a difficulty arises in the question as to Francis's ability to write the letters.  True, there are Junian turns in

[1] See the article by Sir Leslie Stephen in *The English Historical Review*, April 1888.  The letter to Chatham was sent through Calcraft.

[2] Yet the evidence here is rather negative than positive.  See Hayward, *More about Junius*.

[3] The explanation may lie hid in the lost Junian letter to the duke, signed "Lucius," and seen by Henry Bohn (Lowndes's *Bibliographer's Manual*, see bibliography).

his productions of later date.   He shares that trait with many writers, and, high though his reputation as a pamphleteer was, we must admit that, if he was Junius in 1770, under his own name in 1780 he was a cooling sun.

To sum up, the letters of Junius seem to be brought home to a small group which included Calcraft, Francis and, perhaps, Lord Temple.[1]   They passed through Francis's hands, and he is their most likely author.   He evidently wished to be thought so; but, if he was, the malignant talent they displayed could only develop in secrecy, or, perhaps, his prime was short. He remains in his real character a pretender only, in his assumed, a shade: *stat nominis umbra.*

In Junius, we have the culmination of a series of political writings; but his merits and defects do not exhaust theirs. Abuse and slander and political hatred are continually to be found in all.   These blameworthy features should not obscure the quantity of solid facts and serious argument put forward for the public information, in many able and honest pamphlets and letters.   It is easier for posterity than it was for the writers to judge of their fairness and accuracy; not so easy, perhaps, to perceive that, with their open discussion and criticism, they were the chief safeguards of the responsibility of government to public opinion.

[1] Temple has even been claimed as the author of the *Letters* (Smith, W. J., *Grenville Papers*, see bibliography); but, beyond the facts that he, doubtless, approved their purpose and was a patron of virulent pamphleteers and himself a pamphleteer, there does not seem to be corroboration of this theory.   It is true that Lady Temple's handwriting had a strong resemblance to that of Junius. But Temple would hardly have sent anonymous letters to his brother-in-law, Chatham, written in a hand which the latter must have known well.

# Bibliographies

## CHAPTER I

## RICHARDSON

### I. Collected Editions

Works, with a sketch of his life and writings by Mangin, E. 19 vols. 1811.
Novels. In Ballantyne's Novelists' Library, with a life by Sir Walter Scott.
3 vols. Edinburgh, 1824.
—— Ed. Stephen, L., with a prefatory chapter of biographical criticism. 12 vols.
1883.
—— With introduction by McKenna, E. M. M. 20 vols. 1902.
Complete Novels. With life by Phelps, W. L. 18 vols. New York, 1901–3.

A Collection of the Moral and Instructive Sentiments, Maxims, Cautions, and
Reflections, contained in the Histories of Pamela, Clarissa Harlowe, and
Sir Charles Grandison, digested under proper heads. 1755.

### II. Separate Novels

Pamela, or Virtue rewarded. In a series of familiar letters from a beautiful
young damsel to her parents. 2 vols. 1740. 4 vols. 1741–2. 10th edn.
1771. Abridged 1817. Rptd. 1891. Transl. into French by Prévost
d'Exiles, A. F. 4 vols. Amsterdam, 1742–3. Another version, 1771.
    The following are the direct adaptations of Pamela for the French stage:
Boissy, Louis de, Paméla en France, ou La Vertu mieux éprouvée, Paris,
1745. Voltaire, Nanine, Paris, 1749. Neufchâteau, François de, Paméla,
Paris, 1795. Goldoni's adaptations for the Italian stage, Pamela Fanciulla
and Pamela Maritata, both appeared in 1750.
    An Apology for the life of Mrs. Shamela Andrews, in which the many
notorious falsehoods and misrepresentations of a book called Pamela
are exposed. By Conny Keyber. 1741.
    As to Fielding's Joseph Andrews, see bibl. to Chap. II, *post*.
Pamela censured in a letter to the Editor, shewing that under the specious
pretence of cultivating the principles of virtue . . . the most artful
and alluring amorous ideas are conveyed. . . . 1741.
Pamela's conduct in high life. (Sequel to Richardson's novel.) 1741.
Povey, C. The Virgin in Eden. To which are added Pamela's Letters
proved to be immodest romances. 1741.

Clarissa; or the History of a young Lady, comprehending the most important concerns of private life, and particularly shewing the distresses that may attend the misconduct both of parents and children in relation to marriage, published by the Editor of Pamela. 7 vols. 1748. 2nd edn., 8 vols., 1749–51; 7th edn., 8 vols., 1774. In Mrs. Barbauld's British Novelists, with prefaces biographical and critical. 1810. Abridged by Dallas, E. S. 1868. Rptd. 1890. Transl. into French by Le Tourneur, P. 10 vols. Geneva, 1785–6. Transl. into French by Prévost d'Exiles, A. F. 2 vols. Paris, 1845–6. Transl. into French by Janin, J. 2 vols. Brussels, 1846. Transl. into Italian. 5 vols. Venice, 1783–6. Transl. into Dutch by Stinstra, John. 8 vols. Harlingen, 1752–3. Stinstra's correspondence with Richardson is printed in vol. v of Mrs. Barbauld's edition of Richardson's correspondence (see sec. III, post).

Remarks on Clarissa addressed to the author. 1749.

The History of Sir Charles Grandison in a series of Letters published from the originals by the Editor of Pamela and Clarissa. 7 vols. 1754. 2nd edn. to which is added a brief history of the treatment which the author has met with from certain booksellers and printers in Dublin, 1754; 3rd edn. 1755; 7th edn. 1776; 8th edn. 1796. In Mrs. Barbauld's British Novelists, with prefaces biographical and critical. 1810. New and abridged edition by Howitt, M. 1873.

Letters from Sir Charles Grandison. Selected with a biographical introduction and connecting notes by Saintsbury, G. 2 vols. 1895. Transl. into French by Prévost d'Exiles, A. F. 4 vols. Amsterdam, 1784. Imitated in German. Eisenach, 1760–2. Transl. into Italian. 4 vols. Venice, 1784–9. Transl. into Spanish. 6 vols. Madrid, 1798.

A candid examination of The History of Sir Charles Grandison. 1754. Critical remarks on Sir Charles Grandison, Clarissa, and Pamela, enquiring whether they have a tendency to corrupt or improve the public taste and morals. In a letter to the author by a Lover of Virtue. 1754.

For a list of plays in English, French, German and Italian, founded on Richardson's novels, see, also, the bibliography in Samuel Richardson, by Thomson, Miss C. L., mentioned under sec. v, post.

### III. Correspondence

Correspondence, to which are prefixed a biographical account of the author, and observations on his writings, by Barbauld, A. L. 6 vols. 1804. Mrs. Barbauld's life transl. into French, 1808.

For an account of the Forster collection of Richardson's correspondence preserved in the South Kensington Museum, see the bibliography in Miss Thomson's work mentioned below.

### IV. Edited Matter

The negociations with the Ottoman Porte from 1621 to 1628. By Sir Thomas Roe. Ed. by S. Richardson. 1740.

Tour through the whole Island of Great Britain. (By Defoe.) With considerable additions [by Richardson]. 4 vols. 1742. Other edns.: 1753, 1769; 8th edn., 1778; 9th edn., Dublin, 1779.

## V. Biography and Criticism

Boas, F. S. Richardson's novels and their influence. Essays and studies by members of the English Association. Vol. II. Oxford, 1911.

Cross, W. The Development of the English Novel. (Chap. II. The 18th century realists.) New York, 1899.

Dibelius, W. Englische Romankunst. Die Technik d. engl. Romans im 18. u. zu
> Angfang d. 19. Jahrh. Vol. I. Berlin, 1910.

Diderot, D. Éloge de Richardson. 1761. Rptd. in Œuvres complètes, vol. v. Paris, 1875.

Dobson, A. Richardson at home. Eighteenth Century Vignettes. 2nd series. 1894.

—— Richardson. (English Men of Letters.) 1902.

Donner, J. O. E. Richardson in der deutschen Romantik. Weimar [1896].

Hazlitt, W. On the English novelists. English Comic Writers, v. Works, edd. Glover, A., and Waller, A. R., vol. VIII. 1903.

Hettner, H. Litteraturgesch. d. 18. Jahrh.: I. Gesch. d. Engl. Literatur, 1660–1770. 2nd edn. Brunswick, 1865. (Bk. III, part II, chap. I, sec. I, Richardson u. der moralisirende Familienroman.)

Jeffrey, Francis, Lord. Samuel Richardson. Edinburgh Review. Oct., 1804. Rptd. 1853.

Jusserand, J. Le Roman Anglais. Origines et Formation des Grandes Écoles de Romanciers du 18me siècle. Paris, 1886.

Nichols, J. Samuel Richardson. Literary Anecdotes, IV, 578–598. 1812.

Poetzsche, E. Samuel Richardson's Belesenheit. Kieler Studien zur englischen Philologie. Kiel, 1908.

Schmidt, E. Richardson, Rousseau, und Goethe. Ein Beitrag zur Geschichte des Romans im 18. Jahrhundert. Jena, 1875.

Texte, J. Jean-Jacques Rousseau et les Origines du Cosmopolitisme Littéraire. (Bk. II, chap. II: Popularité européenne du Roman Anglais; chap. III: L'œuvre de Samuel Richardson; chap. IV: Rousseau et le Roman Anglais.) Paris, 1895. Eng. trans. by Matthews, J. W. 1899.

Thomson, C. L. Samuel Richardson: a biographical and critical study. 1900. [Contains a useful bibliography.]

A. T. B.

## CHAPTER II

## FIELDING AND SMOLLETT

### I. Fielding

#### A. Collected Works

Works, with The Life of the Author. 4 vols. 1762.
Vol. I: An Essay on the Life and Genius of Henry Fielding, Esq.[ by Arthur Murphy]. Plays. Vol. II: Plays—Life of Jonathan Wild. Journey from this world to the next. History of the Adventures of Joseph Andrews. Preface to David Simple. Preface to Familiar Letters between Principal Characters. Vol. III: The history of Tom Jones. Vol. IV: The history of Amelia.
Of later editions, that of 1783 is the first containing The Fathers. 1806 (ed. Chalmers, A.); 1871 (ed. Browne, J. P.).

Dobson, A. A New Dialogue of the Dead, in National Review. December, 1912. Rptd. in At Prior Park and other Papers. 1912.
[A rectification of Errors in the Essay in vol. I of the above in the form of a dialogue between the shades of Fielding and Murphy.]

Works. Ed. Roscoe, T. (with Memoir). 1840.
—— Ed. Stephen, L. (with biographical essay). 10 vols. 1882.
—— Ed. Saintsbury, G. (with introduction). 12 vols. 1893.
—— Ed. Gosse, E. (with introduction). 12 vols. 1898–9.

## B. *Collected Novels*

Novels. Complete in one volume. To which is prefixed a Memoir of the Life
of the Author (by Sir W. Scott). London. . . . Edinburgh, 1821.
—— Ed. Roscoe, T., illustrated by Cruikshank, G. 1831–2.
The writings of Henry Fielding. Comprising his celebrated works of fiction.
Ed., with memoir, by Herbert, D. 1872.
Also in Bohn's Novelists' Library, 1876–7.

## C. *Separate Novels*

The History of the Adventures of Joseph Andrews and his friend Mr. Abraham
Adams, Written in Imitation of the Manner of Cervantes, Author of Don
Quixote. 2 vols. 1742. The number of later editions exceeds a score.
*See, also, under* secs. A and B, *ante.*
Translations: French, 1750, 1755.
The History of Tom Jones, a Foundling. 6 vols. By Henry Fielding, Esq.
1749. The number of later editions is even greater than in the case of the
previous work. *See, also, under* secs. A and B, *ante.*
Translations: French, 1750, and of many later dates; German, 1786,
1787, 1853; Dutch, 1862; Bohemian, 1873; Polish, 1783; Russian, 1849;
Spanish, 1846.
Amelia. By Henry Fielding, Esq. 4 vols. 1752. *See, also, under* secs. A and
B, *ante.*
Translations: French, 1762, 1782.
For Jonathan Wild, *see under* sec. D, *post.*

## D. *Miscellaneous*

Miscellanies, by Henry Fielding, Esq. 3 vols. Printed for the Author. 1743.
Contents. Vol. 1: Poems. Essay on Conversation. Essay on the know-
ledge of the characters of men. Essay on Nothing. Some papers proper to
be read before the R——l Society, Concerning the Terrestrial Chrysipus . . .
by Petrus Gualterus. . . . The First Olynthiacs of Demosthenes. Of
the Remedy of Affliction for the Loss of our Friends. A Dialogue between
Alexander the Great and Diogenes the Cynic. An interlude between Jupiter,
Juno, Apollo and Mercury.
Vol. 11. A journey from this World to the Next. Eurydice, a Farce.
The Wedding-day, a Comedy.
Vol. 111. The Life of Mr. Jonathan Wild the Great.
Jonathan Wild was reissued separately in 1775, 1782, 1840 (with a con-
temporary Life of J. W. by H. D.). *See, also, under* secs. A and B, *ante.*
Translations: French, 1763, 1784; Dutch, 1757; German, 1790.
An Essay on Nothing and The Chrysipus were reprinted separately in
The Repository, ed. Reed, I., vol. iv, 1783.
Miscellanies and Poems. Ed., with preface, Browne, J. P. 1882.

## E.  *Pamphlets and Fugitive Pieces*

Epilogue to Caelia: Or, The Perjur'd Lover.  A Play.  [By Johnson, Charles.]
1733.

Prologue to Fatal Curiosity: A True Tragedy of Three Acts.  By Mr. Lillo.
1737.

THE ΟΜΗΡΟΥ ΤΕΡΠΝΟΝ-ΙΑΔΟΣ, ΡΑΨΩΙΔΙΑ ἤ ΓΡΑΜΜΑ Α'.  The Vernoniad.
Done into English, from the original Greek of Homer.  Lately found at
Constantinople. . . . Book I.  1741.

The Opposition.  A Vision.  1742.

The Crisis: A Sermon on Rev. 14. 9-11 (ascribed to Fielding—see Nichol's
Anecdotes, vol. VIII, 8. 4 (6) ).

A Review of a Late Treatise entitled An Account of the Conduct of the Dowager
D—— of M——, &c.  In which Many Misrepresentations are detected,
several Obscure Passages searched into and explained, and Abundance of
False Facts set in their true Light; Especially such as relate to the Reigns
of K. William and Q. Mary.  In a Letter to a Person of Distinction.  1742.

Plutus, The God of Riches.  A Comedy.  Translated from the Original Greek
of Aristophanes.  With Large Notes Explanatory and Critical.  By Henry
Fielding, Esq., and the Revd. Mr. Young.  1742.

A Letter to a Noble Lord, To whom alone it Belongs.  Occasioned by a Representation at the Theatre Royal in Drury Lane, of a Farce called Miss Lucy
in Town.  1742.

Preface to The Adventures of David Simple.  By a Lady [Sarah Fielding].  1744.

Preface (anonymous) to Familiar Letters between the principal characters in
David Simple. . . . By the author of David Simple.  1747.

A True State of the Case of Bosavern Penley, who suffered on account of the
late Riot in the Strand.  In which the Law regarding these Offenses, and
the Statute of George the First, commonly called the Riot Act, are fully
considered.  By Henry Fielding, Esq.  1749.

A Charge delivered to the Grand Jury at the Sessions . . . held for the City
and Liberty of Westminster, etc., the 29th of June, 1749.  1749.

An Enquiry Into the Causes of the late Increase of Robbers, etc.  With some
Proposals for Remedying this Growing Evil.  In which the Present reigning
Vices are impartially exposed; and the Laws that relate to the Provision
for the Poor, and to the Punishment of Felons are eagerly and freely examined.
By Henry Fielding, Esq.  1751.

Examples of the Interposition of Providence in the Detection and Punishment
of Murder.  Containing above thirty Cases, in which this dreadful Crime
has been brought to Light in the most extraordinary and miraculous manner;
collected from various authors, ancient and modern.  With an Introduction
and conclusion.  Both written by Henry Fielding, Esq.  1752.

A proposal for Making an Effectual Provision for the Poor, for Amending their
morals, and for rendering them useful Members of the Society.  To which
is added, A Plan of the Buildings proposed, with proper Elevations.  Drawn
by an Eminent Hand.  By Henry Fielding, Esq.  1753.

A Clear State of the Case of Elizabeth Canning, Who hath sworn that she was
robbed and almost starved to Death by a Gang of Gipsies and other Villains
in January last, for which one Mary Squires now lies under Sentence of Death.
By Henry Fielding, Esq.  1753.

The Lover's Assistant; or New Year's Gift; Being a New Art of Love Adapted to
the Present Times.  Translated from the Latin with Notes, By the Late

Ingenious Henry Fielding of Facetious Memory. 1759. [On page 1: Ovid's Art of Love Paraphrased.]

### F. *A Voyage to Lisbon*

The Journal of a Voyage to Lisbon, By the late Henry Fielding, Esq. With A Fragment of a Comment on L. Bolingbroke's Essays. 1755. Later edns.: 1755, 1892 (introd. by Dobson, A.); 1907 (introd. by Dobson, A., in The World's Classics).
> As to the two editions of 1755, *see* Dobson, A., Introd. and Notes to World's Classics edn. 1907.

Dobson, A. At Prior Park and other Papers. 1912. P. 128: A Fielding Find.
> [Contains selections from previously unpublished letters written by Fielding from Lisbon, which throw light upon his life there.]

### G. *Plays*

Love in Several Masques. A Comedy as it is Acted at the Theatre Royal, by His Majesty's Servants. Written by Mr. Fielding. 1728. German trans., 1782.

The Temple Beau. A Comedy. As it is Acted at the Theatre in Goodman's Fields. Written by Mr. Fielding. 1730.

The Author's Farce; And the Pleasures of the Town. As Acted at the Theatre in the Hay-Market. Written by Scriblerus Secundus. 1730.

The Author's Farce; With a Puppet Show called The Pleasures of the Town. As Acted at the Theatre Royal in Drury Lane. Written by Henry Fielding, Esq.: The Third Edition. This Piece was Originally Acted at the Hay Market and Revived some Years after at Drury Lane, when it was Revis'd and partly Alter'd by the Author, as now Printed. 1750.

Rape upon Rape, Or The Justice Caught in his own Trap. A Comedy, As it is Acted at the Theatre in the Hay-Market. The Coffee-House Politician; or, the Justice Caught in his own Trap. A Comedy. As it is Acted at the Theatre Royal in Lincoln's Inn Fields. Written by Mr. Fielding. 1730.

Tom Thumb. A Tragedy. As it is Acted at the Theatres in London. Dublin; Printed and sold by S. Powell. 1730.
> Many other editions: 1730, etc.; 1830 (with designs by Cruikshank, G.). German trans., 1899.

The Welsh Opera: Or, The Grey Mare the better Horse. As it is Acted at the New Theatre in the Hay Market. Written by Scriblerus Secundus, Author of the Tragedy of Tragedies. 1731. Re-issued 1731 under the title of The Grub-street Opera, with The Masquerade, a Poem.

The Letter-writers: Or, a New Way to keep a wife at Home. A Farce, in Three Acts. As it is Acted at the Theatre in the Hay Market. Written by Henry Fielding, Esq. 1750. German trans., 1781.

The Lottery. A Farce. As it is Acted at the Theatre-Royal in Drury Lane, With the Musick prefix'd to each Song. 1732.

The Modern Husband. A Comedy. As it is Acted at the Theater-Royal in Drury Lane. Written by Henry Fielding, Esq. 1732. German trans. 1781.

The Covent Garden Tragedy. As it is Acted at the Theatre-Royal in Drury Lane. 1732.

The Old Debauchees. A Comedy. As it is Acted at the Theater-Royal in Drury Lane. By the Author of the Modern Husband. Dublin. 1732. 3rd edn. 1750, under the title: The Debauchees, or, The Jesuit Caught.

The Mock Doctor: or The Dumb Lady Cur'd. A Comedy. Done from Molière. As it is Acted at the Theatre Royal in Drury Lane. With the Musick prefix'd to each Song. 1732.

The Miser. A Comedy. Taken from Plautus and Molière. As it is Acted at the Theatre-Royal in Drury Lane. By Henry Fielding, Esq. 1733.

The Intriguing Chambermaid. A Comedy of Two Acts. As it is Acted at the Theatre Royal in Drury Lane. Taken from the French of Regnard, by Henry Fielding, Esq. 1750.

Don Quixote in England. A Comedy. As it is Acted at the New Theatre in the Hay-Market. By Henry Fielding, Esq. 1734.

An Old Man taught Wisdom: or, The Virgin Unmask'd. A Farce. As it is Perform'd at the Theatre Royal. By Henry Fielding, Esq.: With the Musick prefix'd to each Song. 2nd edn. 1735.

The Universal Gallant: or, The Different Husbands. A Comedy. As it is Acted at the Theatre Royal in Drury Lane, By His Majesty's Servants. By Henry Fielding, Esq. 1735.

Pasquin. A Dramatick Satire on the Times: Being the Rehearsal of Two Plays, viz. A Comedy call'd The Election; and a Tragedy call'd The Life and Death of Common-Sense. As it is Acted at the Theatre in the Hay-Market. By Henry Fielding, Esq. 1736. Other edns.: 1736, 1740.

The Historical Register for the Year 1736. As it is Acted at the New Theatre in the Hay-Market. To which is added a very merry Tragedy call'd Eurydice Hiss'd; or, A Word to the Wise. Both written by the Author of Pasquin. To these are prefixed a long Dedication to the publick, and a Preface to that Dedication. Dublin: Printed by and for J. Jones. 1737. Other edns.: 1741, 1744.

Eurydice, a Farce: As it was d—mned At the Theatre Royal in Drury-Lane. [1735.]

Tumble-Down Dick: Or, Phaethon in the Suds. A Dramatick Entertainment of Walking, in Serious and Foolish Characters; Interlarded with Burlesque, Grotesque, Comick Interludes, Call'd Harlequin a Pick-Pocket. As it is Perform'd at the New Theatre in the Hay Market. Being (tis hop'd) the last Entertainment that will ever be exhibited on any Stage. Invented by the Ingenious Monsieur Sant Esprit. The Musick compos'd by the Harmonious Signior Warblerini, And the Scenes Painted by the Prodigious Mynheer Van Bottom-feet. 1744. (1st edn. 1737.)

Miss Lucy in Town. A Sequel to The Virgin Unmasqued. A Farce; With Songs. As it is Acted at the Theatre-Royal, in Drury-lane. 1742.

The Wedding-Day. A Comedy, As it is Acted at the Theatre-Royal in Drury Lane. By Henry Fielding, Esq. 1743.

The Fathers: Or, The Good Natur'd Man. A Comedy, As it is Acted at the Theatre Royal, In Drury Lane. By the late Henry Fielding, Esq., Author of Tom Jones, etc. 1778.

## H. *Periodicals*

The Champion: Containing a Series of Papers, Humorous, Moral, Political and Critical, to each of which is added A popular Index to the Times. [2 vols.] 1741. Another edn. 1766.

The True Patriot: And the History of Our Own Times (To be continued Every Tuesday). 5 November, 1745—10 June, 1746.

The Jacobite's Journal. By John Trott-Plaid, Esq. [Saturdays]. 5 December, 1747—5 November, 1748.

The Covent Garden Journal. By Sir Alexander Drawcansir, Knt. Censor of Great Britain, Saturday, January 4, 1752. To be continued every Tuesday and Saturday. Last number 70, 11 November, 1752. (In Burney Collection in B. M. some numbers missing and some seemingly not issued.)

### I.  Selections

Illustrations of Smollett, Fielding and Goldsmith, in a series of forty-one plates, designed and engraved by Cruikshank, G. Accompanied by descriptive extracts.  1832.

Fielding. Edited by Saintsbury, G. (with introduction). (Masters of Literature.) 1905.

### J.  Biography and Criticism

Besides the introductions and notes mentioned above the following may be consulted:

A Catalogue of the entire and valuable library of books of the late Henry Fielding, Esq., which will be sold by auction by Samuel Baker . . . on Monday, Feb. the 10th, and the three following evenings, etc. [British Museum copy, with MS. prices.]  [1755.]

An Essay on the New Species of writing founded by Mr. Fielding: With a word or two upon the Modern State of Criticism.  1751.

Dobson, Austin.  Art. Fielding, Henry, in Encyclopaedia Britannica, 11th edn.
—— Henry Fielding.  A Memoir.  1900.
—— Fielding.  (English Men of Letters.)  1907.

Fraser's Magazine.  January and February, 1858.

Godden, G. M.  Henry Fielding: a memoir.  1910.  [Contains previously unpublished facts and a chronological list of Fielding's writings.]

Green, Emanuel.  Henry Fielding, his works.  An independent criticism.  1909.

Hazlitt, William.  Lectures on the English Comic Writers.  1819.
        [Waller and Glover's Hazlitt, vol. VIII, p. 106 et al.  For further references by Hazlitt, see the Index to this edn.]

Jesse, J. Heneage.  Memoirs of celebrated Etonians, vol. I.  1875.

Lawrence, F.  The Life of Henry Fielding, with notices of his writings, his times and his contemporaries.  1855.

Quarterly Review, The, vol. XXXIV, no. 68, p. 349.  September, 1826.
—— Vol. XCVIII, No. 195, p. 100.  December, 1855.
—— Vol. CIII, No. 205, p. 66.  January, 1858.
—— Vol. CLXIII, No. 325, p. 34.  July, 1886.

Raleigh, Sir Walter.  The English Novel.  1894.

Stephen, Sir Leslie.  Art. Fielding, Henry, in D. of N. B. vol. XVIII.  1889.

Thackeray, W. M.  The English Humourists of the XVIII Century.  1853.

Times, The, Literary Supplement, no. 423.  17 February, 1910.

### II.  Smollett

### A.  Collected Works

The Miscellaneous Works of Tobias Smollett M.D.  6 vols.  1790.
—— with memoirs of his life and writings by Robert Anderson.  6 vols.  1796.
—— Edited, with memoir, by Roscoe, T.  1841.
—— with memoir of his life, to which is prefixed a view of the commencement and progress of romance by Moore, J.  1797.  Re-issue, ed. Browne, J. P. 8 vols.  1872.

The Miscellaneous Works of Tobias Smollett, M.D. Edited by Saintsbury, G. 12 vols. 1895.
—— With an introduction by Henley, W. E. 12 vols. 1899–1901.

### B. *Collected Novels*

Cooke's Select British Novels. 1793–5. Walker's British Classics. 1815. Ballantyne's Novelists' Library (with life by Sir Walter Scott). 1821. Roscoe's Novelists' Library. 1831. Bohn's Novelists' Library. 1895.

### C. *Separate Novels*

The Adventures of Roderick Random. 2 vols. Printed for J. Osborn, 1748. Many other edns.: 1857 (with memoir by Townsend, J. H.).
The Adventures of Peregrine Pickle. In which are included, Memoirs of a Lady of Quality. 4 vols. 1751. Many other edns.
    Translations: French (Histoire et Aventures de Sir Williams Pickle), 1753; German, 1785.
The Adventures of Ferdinand Count Fathom. By the Author of Roderick Random. 2 vols. 1753.
    Translation: French, 1798.
The Adventures of Sir Launcelot Greaves. By the Author of Roderick Random. 2 vols. 1762. Many other edns.: 1890 (with The Adventures of an Atom).
The History and Adventures of an Atom. 2 vols. 1749. (With The Adventures of Sir Launcelot Greaves.) 1890.
The Expedition of Humphrey Clinker. By the Author of Roderick Random. 3 vols. 1671 [1771]. (2nd and 3rd vols. correctly dated.) Many other edns.
    Translation: French, 1882.

### D. *Plays and Poems*

Advice: A Satire. 1746.
Reproof. A Satire. The Sequel to Advice. 1747.
Advice and Reproof: two Satires. First published in the Year 1746 and 1747. Another edn. 1826.
The Regicide: Or, James the First of Scotland. A Tragedy. By the Author of Roderick Random. Printed by subscription for the Benefit of the Author.
The Reprisal: Or, The Tars of Old England. A Comedy of Two Acts. As it is Performed at the Theatre Royal in Drury Lane. 1757. (Suppl. to Bell's British Theatre, vol. II), 1784; (British Stage), 1786.
Ode to Independence. By the late T. Smollett, M.D. With notes and observations. Glasgow, 1773.
Plays and Poems, with Memoir. 1777.
Poetical Works: Anderson's Poets of Great Britain, vol. x, 1794; Park's Works of the British Poets, 1807; Chalmers's Works of the British Poets, 1810; The British Poets, 1822.

### E. *History of England, and Compilations*

A Complete History of England, from the Descent of Julius Caesar, to the Treaty of Aix-la-Chapelle, 1748. Containing the Transactions of One Thousand Eight Hundred and Three Years. By T. Smollett, M.D. 11 vols. 2nd edn. 1758–60.
Continuation of the Complete History of England. 5 vols. 1762–5.

The History of England from the Revolution to the Death of George the Second. (A remodelled version of the Complete History.) New edn. (5 vols.), 1789. Other edns.: 1790 (5 vols.); 1791 (5 vols.).

A Compendium of Authentic and Entertaining Voyages, Digested in a Chronological Series. The whole exhibiting A clear View of the Customs, Manners, Religion, Government, Commerce and Natural History of most Nations in the Known World. Illustrated and adorned with a variety of genuine Charts, Maps, Plans, Heads, etc., commonly engraved. 7 vols. 1766. Another edn. 1768.

The Present State of All Nations. Containing a Geographical, Natural, Commercial and Political History of all the Countries in the Known World. 8 vols. 1768–9. Another edn. 8 vols. 1784.

*See, also*, bibliography to Chap. xii, *post*.

### F.  *Travels through France and Italy*

Travels through France and Italy. Containing Observations on Character, Customs, Religion, Government, Police, Commerce, Arts and Antiquities. With a particular description of the Town, Territory and Climate of Nice. To which is added, A Register of the Weather, kept during a Residence of Eighteen Months in that City. 2 vols. 1766. With introd. by Seccombe, T. 1901.

### G.  *Fugitive Pieces*

A Faithful Narrative of the Base and inhuman Arts that were lately practised upon the Brain of Habbakuk Hilding, Justice, Dealer and Chapman, who now lies at his House in Covent Garden, in a deplorable State of Lunacy; a dreadful Monument of false Friendship and Delusion. By Drawcansir Alexander, Fencing Master and Philomath. 1742.

Wonderful Prophecies. Being a Dissertation on the Existence, Nature and Extent of the Prophetic powers in the Human Mind: with unquestionable examples of several eminent prophecies, of what is now acting and soon to be fulfilled, upon the Great Theatre of Europe. Particularly those worthy of notice, by Richard Brothers, And a memorable Prophecy of Dr. Smollett, just before his death, also others never before made public by Daniel Defoe, etc. 1795.

### H.  *Translations*

The Adventures of Gil Blas of Santillane. A New Translation, from the best French edition. 5 vols. Numerous other edns.: 1816 (with Sir Launcelot Greaves); 1849 (Bohn's Illustrated Library); 1881 (ed. by Saintsbury, G.).

Remarks upon Proposals lately published for a New Translation of Don Quixote. In which will be considered The Design of Cervantes in Writing the Original, and some New Lights given relative to his Life and Adventures. In a Letter from a Gentlewoman in the Country to a Friend in Town. 1755.

The History and Adventures of the Renowned Don Quixote. Translated from the Spanish of Miguel de Cervantes Saavedra. To which is prefixed, Some Account of the Author's Life. Illustrated by Hayman, F. 2 vols. Numerous other edns.: 1782 (with plates by Stothard, T.); 1833 (with plates by Cruikshank, G., and memoir by Roscoe, T.).

The Works of M. de Voltaire. Translated from the French. With Notes, Historical and Critical. 25 vols. 1761. Vol. ii, etc. by T. Smollett, M.D., T. Franklin, and others. Another edn. 38 vols. 1778–81.

The Adventures of Telemachus, the Son of Ulysses. Translated from the French of F. S. de la Mothe-Fénelon, Archbishop of Cambray. 2 vols. Dublin, 1793.

### I. *Periodicals*

The Critical Review: Or, Annals of Literature. By a Society of Gentlemen. 2 vols. 1756.
The Briton. To be continued every Saturday, price 2½d. 29 May, 1762, to 12 February, 1763.
The British Magazine. A Monthly Repository for Gentlemen and Ladies. 8 vols. 1766–7.

### J. *Biography and Criticism*

Besides the introductions mentioned above, the following may be consulted:
Blackwood's Magazine, vol. x. May, 1900.
Chambers, R. Smollett; his life and selections from his writings. 1867.
Ford, D. Admiral Vernon and the Navy. . . . With a critical reply to Smollett and other historians. . . . 1907.
Hannay, D. Life of Tobias George Smollett (with bibliography by Anderson, J. P.). 1887.
Illustrations of Smollett, Fielding and Goldsmith, in a series of forty-one plates, designed and engraved by Cruikshank, G. . . . 1832.
Macmillan's Magazine, vol. XXI, p. 527.
Masson, D. British Novelists and their Styles. 1859.
Quarterly Review, vol. CIII, no. 205, p. 66. Jan., 1858. Vol. CLXIII, no. 325, p. 34. July, 1886.
Raleigh, Sir W. The English Novel. 1894.
Robinson, C. N. The British Tar in Fact and Fiction. 1909.
Seccombe, T. Articles on Smollett in D. of N. B. (with bibliography) and Encyclopaedia Britannica, 11th edn.
Smeaton, O. Tobias Smollett. 1897.
Wershoven, F. J. Smollett et Lesage. Brieg, 1883.

## CHAPTER III

## STERNE, AND THE NOVEL OF HIS TIMES

### I. Laurence Sterne

A useful bibliography of Sterne's writings will be found in the Appendix to Cross's Life, see sec. C, *post*.

### A. *Collected Works*

Works. 7 vols. Dublin, 1779. 10 vols. 1780. 4 vols. 1819. Ed. Browne, J. P. 4 vols. 1873. Ed. Saintsbury, G. 6 vols. 1894. Ed. Cross, W. L. 12 vols. New York, 1904. French trans. by Michel, F., Paris, 1835.

### B. *Particular Works, including Letters*

Charity Sermon . . . 17 April, 1747. York, 1747.
The Abuses of Conscience. Sermon . . . 29 July, 1750. York, 1750.
A Political Romance addressed to —— —— Esq., of York. [The History of a Warm Watch Coat.] York, 1759. Rptd. in 1769 and 1775.

The Life and Opinions of Tristram Shandy. Vols. I and II, York, 1760; vols.
III to VI, 1761–2; vols. VII and VIII, 1765; vol. IX, 1767. Collective edn.
(9 vols.), 1767, 1769, 1779, etc. Transl. into French by Frénais, 4 vols.,
1784, Wailly, 1842, and others. Also transl. into German by Gelbcke,
F. A., 1865.

For a list of the spurious continuations of Tristram Shandy and of Sterne's
other works, and for notes on forgeries published under his name, see Lee,
Sir S., art. Sterne in D. of N. B., vol. LIV, 1898.

Sermons of Mr. Yorick. 7 vols. 1760–9, 1775, 1777, 1787, etc.

A Sentimental Journey through France and Italy by Mr. Yorick. 2 vols. 1768,
1769, 1778, etc. French trans., by Frénais, 1770, and several later versions.
Also transl. into German, Italian, Polish, Russian and Spanish.

Letters from Yorick to Eliza. 1775.

Letters from Eliza to Yorick. 1775.

Letters to his friends on various occasions. To which is added his History of a
Watch Coat. 1775.

Letters to his most intimate friends. To which are prefixed Memoirs of his Life
and Family. Published by his daughter, Mrs. Medalle. 3 vols. 1775.
German trans., Leipzig, 1776.

The Beauties of Sterne. 1783, 1787, 1809.

Original Letters never before published. 1788.

Seven Letters written by Sterne and his friends. Ed. Cooper, W. Durrant. 1844.

Unpublished Letters. Communicated by John Murray. Philobiblon Soc.
Miscellanies, vol. II. 1855–6.

### C. Biography and Criticism

Behmer, C. A. Laurence Sterne und C. M. Wieland. Muncker's Forsch. zur
neueren Literaturgesch. 9. Munich, 1899.

Cross, W. L. The Life and Times of Laurence Sterne. New York and London,
1909.

Czerny, J. Sterne, Hippel, und Jean Paul. Ein Beitrag zur Geschichte des
humoristischen Romans in Deutschland. Muncker's Forsch. zur neueren
Literaturgesch. 27. Berlin, 1904.

Elwin, W. Sterne. Quarterly Review. March, 1854.

Ferriar, J. Illustrations of Sterne. Manchester, 1798. 2nd edn. 2 vols. 1812.

Fitzgerald, P. Life of Sterne. 2 vols. 1864. Revised edn. 2 vols. 1896.
3rd edn. 1906.

Garat, D. J. Mémoires historiques sur la vie de M. Suard, sur ses écrits, et
sur le XVIIIᵉ siècle. 2 vols. Paris, 1820.

Goethe, J. W. von. Sprüche in Prosa. (Werke, hrsg. im Auftrage der Gross-
herzogin Sophie von Sachsen. Vol. XLII, pt. II, pp. 197–205.) Weimar,
1907.

Melville, L. The Life and Letters of Laurence Sterne. 2 vols. 1911.

Sichel, W. Sterne. A Study. To which is added the Journal to Eliza. 1910.

Stapfer, P. Laurence Sterne, sa personne et ses ouvrages. Étude précédée
d'un fragment inédit de Sterne. Paris, 1870.

Stephen, L. Sterne. Hours in a Library, vol. III. 1892.

Thackeray, W. M. Lectures on the English Humourists: Sterne and Goldsmith.
Works. Biogr. edn., vol. VII. 1898.

Thayer, H. W. Laurence Sterne in Germany. (Columbia Univ. Germanic
Studies, vol. II, pt. I.) New York, 1905.

Traill, H. D. Sterne. (English Men of Letters.) 1882.

## II. Other Writers

### Thomas Amory

Memoirs containing Lives of several Ladies of Great Britain. 1755.
Life of John Buncle, Esq. 4 vols. 1756–66. Rptd., ed. Burn, J. H., 3 vols.,
  1825; with introd. by Baker, E. A., 1904. Transl. into German, 1778.

Hazlitt, W. On John Buncle. The Round Table, No. 14. 17 Sept., 1815.
  Works. Edd. Waller, A. R., and Glover, A. Vol. I. 1902.
Notice of Amory and his works in Retrospective Review, vol. VI, 1822.

### Robert Bage (1728–1801)

Mount Henneth. 2 vols. 1781.
Barham Downs. 2 vols. 1784.
The Fair Syrian. 1787.
James Wallace. 1788.
Man as he is. 4 vols. 1792.
Hermsprong, or Man as he is not. 2 vols. 1796.

### William Beckford

Biographical Memoirs of extraordinary Painters. 1780. Another edn. 1824.
Dreams, Waking Thoughts, and Incidents. 1783.
An Arabian Tale [Vathek], from an unpublished manuscript. With Notes
  [probably by Henley, Sam.]. 1786. In French, 1787. Rptd. 1809. 3rd
  edn. 1815. Other edns.: 1834; ed. Garnett, R., 1893.
Modern Novel Writing, or the Elegant Enthusiast; and Interesting Emotions
  of Arabella Bloomville. 2 vols. 1796.
Azemia, a descriptive and sentimental novel. 2 vols. 1797. 2nd edn. 1798.
The Story of Al Raoui. A Tale from the Arabic. 1799.
Italy, with Sketches of Spain and Portugal. 2 vols. 1834. Another edn. 1840.
Recollections of an Excursion to the Monasteries of Alcobaca and Batalha. 1835.

Melville, L. The Life and Letters of William Beckford of Fonthill. [With
  bibliography and list of authorities.] 1910.

### Henry Brooke

Collected Works. Ed. Brooke, C. 4 vols. 1778. Another edn. 1792.

Universal Beauty. 1735.
Gustavus Vasa, the Deliverer of his Country. A Tragedy. 1739.
Fables for the Female Sex. By Moore, E., and Brooke, H. 1744. Many later
  edns.
The Farmer's Letters to the Protestants of Ireland. 1746.
The Spirit of Party. 1753–4.
The Interests o: Ireland considered. Dublin, 1759.
The Case of the Roman Catholics of Ireland. Dublin, 1760.
Tryal of cause of Roman Catholics. Dublin, 1761.
The Earl of Essex. A Tragedy. 1761.
The Fool of Quality, or the History of Henry Earl of Moreland. 5 vols. 1766–70.
  Condensed by Wesley, J. 1781. Ed. Kingsley, Charles. 2 vols. 1859.
  Ed. Baker, E. A. 1906.
Redemption. 1772.

Juliet Grenville. 3 vols. 1774.

Brookiana. Anecdotes of Henry Brooke. 2 vols. 1804.

*See, also,* bibliography to Vol. IX, Chap. XII.

### *Frances Burney, Madame d'Arblay*

Evelina, or a Young Lady's Entrance into the World. 3 vols. 1778. Ed.
Ellis, A. R. 1881. Ed. Dobson, A. 1904.

Cecilia, or Memoirs of an Heiress. 5 vols. 1782. Ed. Ellis, A. R. 1882. 1904.

Camilla, or a Picture of Youth. 5 vols. 1796.

The Wanderer, or Female Difficulties. 5 vols. 1814.

Tragic Dramas. 1818.

Memoirs of Dr. Burney. 3 vols. 1832.

Diary and Letters. 7 vols. 1842–6, 1854. Ed. Barrett, C. 4 vols. 1891.
Ed. Dobson, A. 1904.

Dobson, A. Fanny Burney. 1903.

Hill, Constance. The House in St. Martin's Street, being chronicles of the
Burney family. 1907.

—— Fanny Burney at the Court of Queen Charlotte. 1912.

Macaulay, Lord. Madame d'Arblay. In last edn. Hist. Essays, vol. II. 1854.

Seeley, L. B. Fanny Burney and her friends. 1890.

### *Thomas Day (1748–1789)*

*See* bibliography to Vol. XI (chapter on Children's Books), *post.*

### *Henry Mackenzie*

Works. 8 vols. 1807, 1808.

The Man of Feeling. 1771.

The Man of the World. 1773.

The Prince of Tunis. A tragedy. 1773.

Julia de Roubigné. 1777.

The Shipwreck. A tragedy altered from Lillo. 1784.

The Mirror. Ed. Mackenzie, H. 1779–80.

The Lounger. Ed. Mackenzie, H. 1785–7.

### *Robert Paltock (1697–1767)*

The Life and Adventures of Peter Wilkins, a Cornish Man. 2 vols. 1751.
With illustrations by Stothard. 2 vols. 1816. Ed. Bullen, A. H. 2 vols.
1884.

### *Rudolf Eric Raspe (1737–1794)*

Baron Munchausen's Narrative of his marvellous travels and campaigns in
Russia. 1785. 2nd edn., Oxford, 1786; 7th edn. 1793. Sequel, 1793. Ed.
Seccombe, T. 1895.

### *Clara Reeve*

The Champion of Virtue, a Gothic Story. 1777. Title changed to The Old
English Baron in second (1778) and all later edns. Rptd., with Memoir by
Scott, Sir W., 1823 and 1883.

The Two Mentors, a Modern Story. 2 vols. 1783.
The Progress of Romance through Times, Countries, and Manners. 2 vols. Colchester, 1785.
The Exiles, or Memoirs of Count de Cronstadt. 3 vols. 1788.
The School for Widows, a Novel. 3 vols. 1791.
Plans of Education. 1792.
Memoirs of Sir Roger de Clarendon, a natural son of Edward the Black Prince. 3 vols. 1793.

### Horace Walpole, Fourth Earl of Orford

The Castle of Otranto. A Story. Translated by William Marshall, Gent. From the Original Italian of Onuphrio Muralto, Canon of the Church of St. Nicholas at Otranto. 1765. 2nd edn. 1765; 5th edn. 1786; 6th edn., Parma, 1791. Rptd. with a Memoir by Scott, Sir W., 1823 and 1883. Transl. into French, 1767; into Italian, 1795.

A. T. B.

## CHAPTER IV

## THE DRAMA AND THE STAGE

*The names of the playhouses given in this bibliography thus—(Drury lane)—are those mentioned in the title-pages of the several plays thus—(as acted at the Theatre Royal, Drury lane). The following abbreviations are used: T. tragedy; C. comedy; O. opera; C. O. comic opera; F. farce. Where there is no entry to the contrary, the author's name appears, either on the title-page or at the foot of the dedication.*

### PARTICULAR AUTHORS

### Isaac Bickerstaff

1756. Leucothoe. A Dramatic Poem. (Anon. In 3 acts. Never acted.)
1761. Thomas and Sally: or, The Sailor's Return. A Musical Entertainment. (Covent garden.) (Anon.) Music by Arne, T. A.
1763. Love in a Village. C. O. (Covent garden.) (Anon.)
1765. The Maid of the Mill. C. O. (Covent garden.) By the Author of Love in a Village.
1765. Daphne and Amintor. C. O. in one act. (Drury lane.) (Anon.)
1766. The Plain Dealer. C. (Drury lane.) With Alterations from Wycherly. (Anon.)
1767. Love in the City. C. O. (Covent garden.) By the Author of Love in a Village.
    This piece, altered and abridged, later appeared as:
    1786. The Romp. A Musical Entertainment. In two acts. Altered from Love in the City, by Mr. Bickerstaff. (Theatres Royal, Dublin and York, and Drury lane.)
1768. [Early imprints read, erroneously, MDCCXLVIII.] Lionel and Clarissa. C. O. (Covent garden.) (Anon.)
    This piece, somewhat altered, later appeared as:
    1773. A School for Fathers. C. O. (Drury lane.) (Anon.) New edn.
1768. The Absent Man. F. (Drury lane.) (Anon.)

1768. The Royal Garland; a new Occasional Interlude in Honour of His Danish Majesty. (Anon.) Music by Arnold, S. (Covent garden.)

1768. The Padlock. C. O. (Drury lane.) (Anon.)

1769. The Hypocrite. C. (Drury lane.) Taken from Molière [Tartuffe] and Cibber [The Non-Juror], by the Author of the Alterations of the Plain-Dealer.

1769. The Ephesian Matron. A Comic Serenata, After the Manner of the Italian. (Ranelagh house.) (Anon.) Music by Dibdin, C.

1769. [Early imprints read, erroneously, MDCCXVIX.] Doctor Last in His Chariot. C. (Haymarket.) (Anon.)

1769. The Captive. C. O. (Haymarket.) (Anon.)

[1769.] Judith, a Sacred Drama: As performed in the Church of Stratford upon Avon, on Occasion of the Jubilee held there, September 6, 1769, in Honour of the Memory of Shakespeare. Music by Arne, T. A.

1770. 'Tis Well it's no Worse. C. (Drury lane.) (Anon.)

1770. The Recruiting Serjeant, a Musical Entertainment. (Drury lane.) (Anon.)

1771. He Wou'd if He Cou'd; or, An Old Fool worse than Any: a Burletta. (Drury lane.) (Anon.) Music by Dibdin, C.

1787. [Acted 1775.] The Sultan, or a Peep into the Seraglio. F. in two acts. (Drury lane and Covent garden.)

1792. The Spoil'd Child; in two acts. (Theatre-Royal, Smoke alley.) (Anon.) Dublin, 1792. [Sometimes ascribed to Bickerstaff.]

### *Mrs. Frances Brooke* (1724–1789)

#### A.  Plays

1756. Virginia. T.
1781. The Siege of Sinope. T.
1783. Rosina. C. O. Numerous edns.

#### B.  Other Works

1763. The History of Lady Julia Mandeville. (Anon.)
1777. The Excursion. 2 vols. [Contains an attack on Garrick.]

### *Henry Brooke*
*See* bibliography to Chap. III, and to Vol. IX, Chap. XII, *ante.*

### *John Brown, Vicar of Newcastle-upon-Tyne* (1715–1766)

#### A.  Plays
1755. Barbarossa. T. (Drury lane.) (Anon.)
1756. Athelstan. T. (Drury lane.) (Anon.)

#### B.  Other Works

1751. Essays on the Characteristics [of the Earl of Shaftesbury]. 5th edn. 1764.

1757. An Estimate of the Manners and Principles of the Times. By the Author of Essays on the Characteristics, &c. 7th edn. 1758.

1763. A Dissertation on . . . Poetry and Music. To which is prefixed, The Cure of Saul. A Sacred Ode. [Performed as oratorio at Covent garden.]

*Henry Carey*

A. Plays

**1715.** The Contrivances; or, More Ways than One. (Drury lane.) (Anon.)

**[1722.]** Hanging and Marriage; or, The Dead Man's Wedding. F. (Lincoln's inn fields.) [Preface dated 1722.]

**1732.** Amelia. A New English Opera. (Haymarket), after the Italian Manner. (Anon.) Music by Lampe, John Frederick.

**1732.** Teraminta. O. (Lincoln's inn fields.) Music by Smith, J. C.

**[1734.]** The Tragedy of Chrononhotonthologos: Being the Most Tragical Tragedy, that ever was Tragediz'd by any Company of Tragedians. Written by Benjamin Bounce, Esq.

**1736.** The Honest Yorkshire-Man. A Ballad Farce. Refus'd to be Acted at Drury-Lane Playhouse: but now Perform'd at the New Theatre in Goodman's Fields, with great Applause.

An earlier, (?) pirated, edn. 1736: A Wonder: or, An Honest Yorkshire-Man. A Ballad Opera; As it is Perform'd at the Theatres with Universal Applause. (Anon.)

**1738.** The Dragon of Wantley, a Burlesque Opera. (Anon.) Music by Lampe, J. F. (Covent garden.) Thirteenth edition, with additions.

**[1743?]** The Dragoness, a Burlesque Opera. (Anon.) Music by Lampe, J. F. [Acted 1738, under title, Margery; or, A Worse Plague than the Dragon.] Alterations of Carey's Nancy; or, The Parting Lovers, acted 1739.

**1755.** The Press Gang: or, Love in Low-Life. (Covent garden.) (Anon.)

**1787.** True-Blue. A Musical Entertainment, As performing at the Royalty-Theatre, Wellclose Square. (Anon.)

**1743.** The Dramatick Works of Henry Carey.

B. Other Works

**1713.** Poems on Several Occasions. [3rd edn., much enlarged, 1729.]

**1737-40.** The Musical Century, in one hundred English Ballads . . . The Words and Musick of the Whole, by Henry Carey. 2 vols. [Vol. II contains Sally in our Alley.]

*Mrs. Susanna (Carroll) Centlivre*

A. Plays

**1700.** The Perjur'd Husband: or, The Adventures of Venice. T. (Drury lane.) Written by S. Carroll.

**1702.** The Beau's Duel: or a Soldier for the Ladies. C. (Lincoln's inn fields.) [Dedication signed Susanna Carroll.]

**[1703.]** The Stolen Heiress, or the Salamanca Doctor Outplotted. C. (Lincoln's inn fields.) (Anon.)

**1703.** Love's Contrivance, or Le Médecin malgré Lui. C. (Drury lane.) [Dedication signed R. M., but play written by Mrs. Centlivre.]

**1705.** The Gamester. C. (Lincoln's inn fields.) (Anon.)

**1706.** Love at a Venture. C. As it is Acted by his Grace the Duke of Grafton's Servants, at the New Theatre in Bath. Written by the Author of The Gamester.

**1706.** The Basset-Table. C. (Drury lane.) By the Author of the Gamester.

**1707.** The Platonick Lady. C. (Haymarket.) By the Author of the Gamester, and Love's Contrivance.

[1709.] The Busie Body. C. (Drury lane.)

[1710?] The Man's bewitch'd; or, The Devil to do about Her. C. (Haymarket.)

This piece was later altered, under the title:

1767. The Ghost. A Comedy of two acts. (Smock alley, Dublin.)

[1710?] A Bickerstaff's Burying; or, Work for the Upholders. F. As it was Acted at the Theatre in the Hay-market, by Her Majesty's Sworn Servants.

1711. Mar-Plot; or, The Second Part of The Busie-Body. C. (Drury lane.)

This piece was later altered, as follows:

1760. Marplot, in Lisbon. Or, The Second Part of the Busie-Body. C. (Theatre-Royal, Crow street. Dublin.)

1712. The Perplex'd Lovers. C. (Drury lane.)

1714. The Wonder: A Woman keeps a Secret. C. (Drury lane) . . . Written by the Author of the Gamester.

1715. The Gotham Election. F.

This piece later appeared, under the title:

1737. The Humours of Elections. By the Author of The Gamester. [Running title: The Gotham Election.]

1715. A Wife Well Manag'd. F. [Frontispiece of Mrs. Centlivre.]

This piece was later altered, under the title:

1732. The Disappointment; a New Ballad Opera of one act. Alter'd from a Farce after the Manner of the Beggar's Opera. (Haymarket.)

1717. The Cruel Gift. T. (Drury lane.) [Running title adds sub-title: "or, The Royal Resentment."]

1718. A Bold Stroke for a Wife. C. (Little Lincoln's inn fields.) By the Author of the Busie-Body and the Gamester. [In A Collection of Plays by Eminent Hands, vol. III, 1719.]

1723. The Artifice. C. (Drury lane.)

1760–1. The Works of the celebrated Mrs. Centlivre. In 3 vols. With a New Account of her Life. Vol. I, 1761, vols. II, III, 1760.

1872. The Dramatic Works of the celebrated Mrs. Centlivre, with a New Account of her Life. Complete in 3 vols.

### B. Other Works

1715. A Poem. Humbly Presented to His most Sacred Majesty George, King of Great Britain, France, and Ireland. Upon His Accession to the Throne. By Susanna Centlivre.

1716. Ode to Hygeia. [In Verses upon the Sickness and Recovery of the Right Honourable Robert Walpole, Esq., in State Poems, by the most Eminent Hands.]

Seibt, Robert. Die Komödien der Mrs. Centlivre. In Anglia, vols. XXXII and XXXIII. Halle a. S. 1909–10.

[Summaries of plays and *dramatis personae*.]

### Colley Cibber (1671–1757)

For bibliography *see ante*, Vol. VIII, pp. 482–3.

### George Colman, the elder

#### A. Plays

1760. Polly Honeycombe, a Dramatick Novel of one act. (Drury lane.) (Anon.)

1761.  The Jealous Wife.  C.  (Drury lane.)
1762.  The Musical Lady.  F.  (Drury lane.)  (Anon.)
1763.  The Deuce is in Him.  F. of two acts.  (Drury lane.)  (Anon.)
1766.  [With Garrick.]  The Clandestine Marriage.  C.  (Drury lane.)
1770.  The Oxonian in Town.  C. in two acts.  (Covent garden.)  (Dedication signed "George Colman.")
1770.  Man and Wife; or, The Shakespeare Jubilee.  C. of three acts.  (Covent garden.)  (Dedication signed "George Colman.")
1770.  The Portrait; a Burletta.  (Covent garden.)  (Anon.)  Music by Arnold.
1774.  The Man of Business.  C.  (Covent garden.)
1776.  The Spleen, or, Islington Spa; a comick piece, of two acts.  (Drury lane.)
1776.  An Occasional Prelude, performed at the opening of the Theatre-Royal, Covent-Garden.  On the Twenty-first of September, 1772.
1776.  New Brooms!  An Occasional Prelude, performed at the opening of the Theatre-Royal, in Drury-Lane, September 21, 1776.
[1780.]  The Manager in Distress.  A Prelude on opening the Theatre-Royal in the Hay-Market, May 30, 1780.
1781.  Songs, Duetts, Trios, &c. in The Genius of Nonsense: an Original, Whimsical, Operatical, Pantomimical, Farcical, Electrical, Naval, Military, Temporary, Local Extravaganza.  (Haymarket.)  (Anon.)
1782.  Songs, Airs, &c. in the Entertainment of Harlequin Teague; or, The Giant's Causeway.  (Haymarket.)  (Anon.)
1789.  Ut Pictura Poesis! or, The Enraged Musician.  A Musical Entertainment. Founded on Hogarth.  (Haymarket.)  Composed by Arnold, S.

## B.  Dramatic Adaptations

1763.  Philaster.  T.  Written by Beaumont and Fletcher.  With Alterations [by C.].  (Drury lane.)
1767.  The English Merchant.  C.  (Drury lane.)  [Based on Voltaire's L'Écossaise.]
1768.  The History of King Lear.  (Covent garden.)
1771.  The Fairy Prince: a Masque.  (Covent garden.)  (Anon.)  [Chiefly from Ben Jonson's Oberon.]
1772.  Comus: a Masque.  Altered from Milton [by C.].  (Covent garden.) Musick by Arne, T. A.
1774.  Achilles in Petticoats.  O.  (Covent garden.)  Written by Mr. Gay, with Alterations [by C.].  The Music by Arne, T. A.
1776.  Epicoene; or, The Silent Woman.  C.  Written by Ben Jonson.  (Drury lane.)  With Alterations, by George Colman.
1777.  The Sheep-Shearing.  A Dramatic Pastoral.  In three acts.  Taken from Shakespeare [Winter's Tale].  (Haymarket.)  (Anon.)
1778.  Bonduca.  T.  Written by Beaumont and Fletcher.  With Alterations [by C.].  (Haymarket.)
1778.  [Acted 1767.]  The Tailors; a Tragedy for Warm Weather, in three acts.  (Haymarket.)  (Anon.)  Later "abridged by Mr. Colman, with some additional touches from his pen" (see Biog. Dram. vol. III, p. 315).
1783.  Fatal Curiosity: a true T.  Written by George Lillo, 1736.  With Alterations [by C.], As revived at the Theatre-Royal, Hay-Market, 1782.
1788.  Tit for Tat.  C. in three acts.  (Haymarket, Drury lane, and Covent garden.)  (Anon.)  [Free alteration of The Mutual Deception, 1785, by Joseph Atkinson.]

1777. The Dramatick Works of George Colman. 4 vols.

C. Other Works

1755–6. The Connoisseur. By Mr. Town, Critic, and Censor-General [chiefly by Colman and Bonnell Thornton]. 2 vols. [140 nos. 31 January, 1754, to 30 September, 1756.]

1760. Ode to Obscurity. (Anon. Published in Two Odes.)

1761. Critical Reflection on the Old English Dramatic Writers. Addressed to David Garrick, Esq. (Anon. In vol. 1 of The Dramatic Works of Philip Massinger, compleat, ed. by Coxeter, T., 4 vols., 1761.

1765. The Comedies of Terence, Translated into Familiar Blank Verse. [Various edns.]

1778 The Dramatick Works of Beaumont and Fletcher; Collated with all the former editions. 10 vols. Preface by Colman.

1783. Q. Horatii Flacci Epistola ad Pisones, De Arte Poetica. The Art of Poetry: an Epistle to the Pisos. Translated from Horace. With Notes.

1787. Prose on Several Occasions; accompanied with Some Pieces in Verse. 3 vols.

---

1841. Memoirs of the Colman Family, including their Correspondence with the most distinguished personages of their time. By Richard Brinsley Peake. 2 vols.

Posthumous Letters . . . addressed to Francis Colman, and George Colman, the Elder. 1820.

### Samuel Crisp (d. 1783)

[Often, erroneously, called "Henry" Crisp.]

1754. Virginia. T. (Drury lane.) (Anon.)

### Elijah Fenton

1723. Marianne. T. (Lincoln's inn fields.)

### Henry Fielding

*See* bibliography to Chap. II, *ante.*

### Samuel Foote

A. Plays

1752. Taste. C. of two acts. (Drury lane.)

1753. The Englishman in Paris. C. in two acts. (Covent garden.)

1754. The Knights. C. in two acts. (Drury lane.)

1756. The Englishman return'd from Paris, Being the Sequel to the Englishman in Paris. F. in two acts. (Covent garden.)

1757. The Author. C. of two acts. (Drury lane.)

1760. The Minor. C. (New Theatre, Haymarket.) By Authority from the Lord Chamberlain.

1762. The Orators. (New Theatre, Haymarket.)

1764. The Lyar. C. in three acts. (Haymarket.)

1764. The Mayor of Garret. C. in two acts. (Drury lane.)

1764. The Patron. C. in three acts. (Haymarket.)

1765. The Commissary. C. in three acts. (Haymarket.)
1770. The Lame Lover. C. in three acts. (Haymarket.)
1776. The Bankrupt. C. in three acts.
1778. The Devil upon Two Sticks. C. in three acts. (Haymarket.)
1778. The Maid of Bath. C. in three acts. (Haymarket.)
    Also, an earlier edn., anon., unauthorised, 1778.
1778. The Nabob. C. in three acts. (Haymarket.)
1778. The Cozeners. C. in three acts. (Haymarket.)
    This and the three preceding plays were published by Colman. Of
    The Cozeners there also appeared an earlier edn., anon., unauthorised, 1778.
1778. A Trip to Calais. C. in three acts. As Originally Written, and Intended
    for Representation, by the late Samuel Foote, Esq. To which is annexed,
    The Capuchin. (Haymarket.) Altered from The Trip to Calais, by the
    late Samuel Foote, Esq. and now published by Mr. Colman.

For some previously unprinted pieces by Foote, see Wilkinson, Tate: The
Wandering Patentee; or, A History of the Yorkshire Theatres from 1770 to
the Present Time, 4 vols., York, 1795. Vol. IV contains The Second Act of
Diversions of the Morning (Drury lane), 1758–9. Vol. I contains: As Acted
1763, at the Hay-Market Theatre. Tragedy A-La-Mode, being the Second
Act of Mr. Foote's Diversions of the Morning, and substituted in lieu of the
former second act in his farce called Tea. Acted by Mr. Foote and Mr. Wilkinson,
in Drury-Lane Theatre, 1758–9. See, also, under Cooke, William, sec. C, post.
    For An Occasional Prologue, performed at the opening of the Theatre-Royal
in the Haymarket, 1767, not inserted in the editions of Foote's Works, see The
Monthly Mirror, vol. XVII, 1804.
[1787?] Dramatic Works. [Individual plays assembled from various edns.,
    1770–86.] 4 vols. (Other 4 vol. collections similarly assembled from differ-
    ent edns. of different dates.)
1799. Works. 2 vols.
1809. Dramatic Works; to which is prefixed a Life of the Author. 2 vols.
1830. Works. With remarks on each play, and an Essay on the Life, Genius,
    and Writings of the Author. By Jon Bee, Esq. [pseud. of John Badcock].
    3 vols.

## B. Other Works

1747. The Roman and English Comedy Consider'd and Compar'd. With
    remarks on the Suspicious Husband. And an Examen into the Merit of
    the present Comic Actors.
1762. The Comic Theatre. Being a Free Translation of all the Best French
    Comedies. By Samuel Foote, Esq. and Others. 5 vols. (According to the
    Advertisement: "One Comedy in each Volume of this work was translated
    by Foote.")

## C. Biography and Criticism

[1777?] Memoirs of the Life and Writings of Samuel Foote, Esq.; the English
    Aristophanes: to which are added the Bon Mots, Repartees, and Good Things
    said by that great Wit and Excentrical Genius.
1778. Aristophanes . . . containing the Jests, Gibes, Bon-Mots, Witticisms,
    and most extraordinary Anecdotes of Samuel Foote, Esq.

Cooke, William.  Memoirs of Samuel Foote, Esq.  With a Collection of his genuine Bon-Mots, Anecdotes, Opinions, &c. mostly original.  And three of his Dramatic Pieces not published in his Works.  3 vols.  1805.  Another edn.  2 vols.  1806.

Forster, John.  Samuel Foote.  In Historical and Biographical Essays, vol. II, pp. 293–437.  1858.

Fitzgerald, Percy.  Samuel Foote, a biography.  1910.

## Thomas Francklin (1721–1784)

### A.  Plays

1766.  The Earl of Warwick.  T.  (Drury lane.)  (Anon.)
1775.  Matilda.  T.  (Drury lane.)  By the Author of the Earl of Warwick.
1776.  The Contract.  C. of two acts.  (Haymarket.)  (Anon.)

### B.  Other Works

1761 etc.  The Works of M. de Voltaire.  Translated from the French.  With Notes, Historical and Critical, by T. Smollett, M.D., T. Francklin, M.A and others.

1765.  Sermons on the Relative Duties.  4th edn., Dublin, 1788.

## David Garrick

### A.  Plays

1742.  The Lying Valet; in two acts.  As it is performed Gratis, at the Theatre in Goodman's-Fields.

1745.  Lethe: or, Esop in the Shades.  As Acted at the Theatres in London, with Universal Applause.  Written by Mrs. Garrick [sic].
    [MS. note in British Museum copy: This is the first Sketch of Mr. Garrick's Lethe and seems to have been surreptitiously printed the year he was absent in Ireland.]

1747.  Miss in her Teens: or, The Medley of Lovers.  F. in two acts,  (Covent garden.)  (Anon.)

1749.  Lethe.  A Dramatic Satire.  (Drury lane.)

1757.  Lilliput.  A Dramatic Entertainment.  (Drury lane.)  (Anon.)

1757.  The Male-Coquette: or, Seventeen Hundred Fifty-Seven.  In two acts.  (Drury lane.)  (Anon.)

1759.  The Guardian.  C. of two acts.  (Drury lane.)  (Anon.)

1760.  The Enchanter; or Love and Magic.  A Musical Drama.  (Drury lane.)  (Anon.)  Music by Smith, John Christopher.

1762.  The Farmer's Return from London.  An Interlude.  (Drury lane.)  (Anon.)  2nd edn.

1766 [with George Colman, the elder].  The Clandestine Marriage.  C.  (Drury lane.)

1766.  Neck or Nothing.  F. in two acts.  (Drury lane.)  (Anon.)

1767.  Cymon.  A Dramatic Romance.  (Drury lane.)  (Anon.)
    This piece was later altered, under the title:
        1792.  Cymon.  A Dramatic Romance.  Written originally by David Garrick, Esq. and first performed as an Opera . . . Dec. 31, 1791.

1767.  A Peep Behind the Curtain; or, The New Rehearsal.  (Drury lane.)  (Anon.)

1772.  The Irish Widow.  In two acts.  (Drury lane.)  (Anon.)

1774. A New Dramatic Entertainment, called A Christmas Tale. In five
parts. (Drury lane.) (Anon.)

1775. Bon Ton; or, High Life above Stairs. C. in two acts. (Drury lane.)
(Anon.)

1775. May-day: or, The Little Gipsy. A Musical F. of one act. To which
is added the Theatrical Candidates. A Musical Prelude. Both: (Drury
lane.) (Anon.)

1768. Dramatic Works; now first collected. In three volumes. Carefully
corrected.

1774. [Another edn.] 2 vols.

1798. Dramatic Works. To which is prefixed a Life of the Author. 3 vols.
[Vol. III includes High Life Below Stairs, by Townley, James.]

## B. Dramatic Adaptations

1750. Romeo and Juliet. By Shakespear. With Alterations, and an additional
Scene. (Drury lane.) (Anon.) 1753 edn. reads: "By D. Garrick."

1752. Every Man in his Humour. C. Written by Ben Jonson. With Alterations and Additions. (Drury lane.) (Anon.)

1755. The Fairies. O. Taken from A Midsummer Night's Dream, Written
by Shakespear. (Drury lane.) (Anon.) The Songs from Shakespeare, by
Milton, Waller, Dryden, Lansdown, Hammond, &c. Music by Smith,
John Christopher.

1756. The Tempest. O. Taken from Shakespear. (Drury lane.) (Anon.)
The Songs from Shakespear, Dryden, &c. Music by Smith, John Christopher.

1756. Catherine and Petruchio. C. in three acts. (Drury lane.) (Alter'd
from Shakespear's Taming of the Shrew. (Anon.)

1757. Isabella: or, The Fatal Marriage. A Play. Alter'd from Southern.
(Drury lane.) (Anon.)

1758. Florizel and Perdita. A Dramatic Pastoral, in three acts. Alter'd
from The Winter's Tale of Shakespear. (Drury lane.)

1758. Antony and Cleopatra; an historical Play, written by William Shakespeare: fitted for the Stage by abridging only; and now acted. (Drury
lane.) [Adapted by Edward Capell and Garrick.]

1758. The Gamesters. C. Alter'd from Shirley. (Drury lane.) (Anon.)

1763. A Midsummer Night's Dream. Written by Shakespeare: With Alterations and Additions, and Several New Songs. (Drury lane.) (Anon.)

1765. Mahomet the Imposter. T. [Originally, 1744, by James Miller and
(?) John Hoadly.] (Drury lane.) (Anon.)
    [1766. 4th edn. With new Improvements.]

1766. The Country Girl. C. (Altered from Wycherley.) (Drury lane.)
(Anon.)

1770. King Arthur: or, The British Worthy. A Masque. By Mr. Dryden.
(Drury lane.) (Anon.) Music by Purcell and Arne. . . . [According
to Advertisement, there were in this "some slight Alterations made, for the
greater Convenience of Representation."]

1771. The Songs, Choruses, and Serious Dialogue of the Masque called The
Institution of the Garter, or, Arthur's Round Table restored. (Anon.)
[Altered from Gilbert West's unacted piece, The Institution of the Order
of the Garter, 1742.]

1773. The Chances. C. [By Beaumont and Fletcher.] With Alterations.
(Anon.)

**1773.** Albumazar. C. As it is now revived at the Theatre-Royal in Drury-Lane. With Alterations [from Thomas Tomkis, by D. G.].

**1773.** Alfred: a Masque. [By Thomson and Mallet.] As it is now revived at the Theatre-Royal, in Drury-Lane, by His Majesty's Servants. (Anon.) ["With some few alterations, and with some New Music."]

**1784.** Cymbeline. T. Altered from Shakespeare, by David Garrick. Marked with the Variations in the Manager's Book at the Theatre-Royal in Drury-Lane. [Biog. Dram. cites an edn. of 1761.]

### C. Other Works

**1769.** An Ode upon Dedicating a Building, and Erecting a Statue, to Shakespeare, at Stratford upon Avon. By D. G.

**1785.** The Poetical Works of David Garrick, Esq. Now first collected into two volumes. With explanatory notes.

**1831–2.** The Private Correspondence of David Garrick with the most celebrated persons of his time . . . illustrated with notes. And a new biographical memoir of Garrick. 2 vols.

**1907.** Some Unpublished Correspondence of David Garrick, edited by George Pierce Baker. Boston, U. S. A.

### D. Biography and Criticism

Davies, Thomas. Memoirs of the Life of David Garrick, Esq. 2 vols. 1780.

Fitzgerald, Percy. The Life of David Garrick. 2 vols. 1868. Revised edn. 1899.

Gaehde, Christian. David Garrick als Shakespeare-Darsteller und seine Bedeutung für die heutige Schauspielkunst. Berlin, 1904.

Hedgcock, F. A. David Garrick et ses Amis Français. Paris, 1911.

    Hedgcock, F. A. A Cosmopolitan Actor. David Garrick and his French Friends. [A very free rendering and adaptation of the above, with bibliography, pp. 430–6.] [1912.]

Knight, Joseph. David Garrick. 1894.

Murphy, Arthur. The Life of David Garrick, Esq. 2 vols. 1801.

Parsons, Mrs. Clement. Garrick and His Circle. (With bibliography, pp. xvii–xx.) New York and London, 1906.

*John Gay*

See bibliography to Vol. **IX**, Chap. **vi**, *ante*.

*Richard Glover*

### A. Plays

**1753.** Boadicia [later edns., "Boadicea"]. T. (Drury lane.)

**1761.** Medea. T.

### B. Other Works

**1737.** Leonidas, a poem. [Numerous edns. 1737–1810.]

**1813.** Memoirs of a celebrated Literary and Political Character [viz. Richard Glover] from . . . 1742 to . . . 1757 etc. New edn. 1814.

See also bibliography to Chap. **vii**, *post*.

*Hall Hartson* (d. 1773)

**1767.** The Countess of Salisbury. T. (Haymarket.) 2nd edn.

## Aaron Hill

### A. Plays

[1710.] Elfrid: or, The Fair Inconstant. T. (Drury lane.) To which is Added the Walking Statue: or, The Devil in the Wine-Cellar. F.

1711. Rinaldo. O. (Haymarket.)

1716. The Fatal Vision: or, The Fall of Siam. T. (Lincoln's inn fields.)

[1721?] The Fatal Extravagance. T. (Lincoln's inn fields.) Written by Mr. Joseph Mitchell [or, rather, (?) by Aaron Hill, in whose Dramatic Works, edn. 1760, it is included]. 4th edn., improv'd into five acts. . . . By Joseph Mitchell, 1726.

1723. King Henry the Fifth: or, The Conquest of France, by the English. T. (Drury lane.)

1731. Athelwold. T. (Drury lane.) [A revision of Hill's Elfrid.]

1753. The Roman Revenge. T.

1758. The Insolvent: or, Filial Piety. T. (Haymarket.) . . . Written by the Late Aaron Hill, Esq.

For Hill's adaptations of Voltaire, viz. 1736, Zara; 1736, Alzira; 1749, Merope, see under English Adaptations of Voltaire, *post.*

1760. The Dramatic Works of Aaron Hill, Esq. 2 vols. [This includes some brief unacted pieces.]

*See also* bibliography to Vol. IX, Chap. VI, *ante.*

### B. Other Works

1731. Advice to the Poets. A Poem.

1743. The Fanciad. An Heroic Poem. In six cantos. (Anon.)

1753. Works; in 4 vols. Consisting of Letters on Various Subjects, and of Original Poems, Moral and Facetious. With an Essay on the Art of Acting.

## Benjamin Hoadly (1706–1757)

1747. The Suspicious Husband. C. (Covent garden.)

## John Home

1757. Douglas. T. (Covent garden.) (Anon.)

1758. Agis. T. (Drury lane.) (Anon.)

1760. The Siege of Aquileia. T. (Drury lane.) (Anon.)

1769. The Fatal Discovery. T. (Drury lane.) (Anon.)

1773. Alonzo. T. In five acts. (Drury lane.) (Anon.)

1778. Alfred. T. (Covent garden.) (Anon.)

1760. Dramatic Works. [Contains only Douglas, Agis, The Siege of Aquileia.]

1798. Dramatic Works. 2 vols. Edinburgh.

1822. Works, now first collected (with Henry Mackenzie's Account of the Life and Writings of John Home). 3 vols. Edinburgh. The Account was also separately printed, Edinburgh, 1822.

## John Hoole (1727–1803)

### A. Plays

1768. Cyrus. T. (Covent garden.)

1770. Timanthes. T. (Covent garden.)

1775. Cleonice, Princess of Bithynia. T. (Covent garden.)

## B.  Other Works

1763.  Tasso's Jerusalem Delivered [translated].  2 vols.  [Numerous edns.]
1783.  Orlando Furioso: translated from the Italian of Lodovico Ariosto; with notes: by John Hoole.  5 vols.  [Numerous edns.]

### *John Hughes*

For bibliography *see ante*, Vol. VIII, p. 493.

### *Charles Johnson* (1649–1748)

1723.  Love in a Forest.  C. [from As You Like It].  (Drury lane.)
1729.  The Village Opera.  As it is Acted at the Theatre-Royal.
1731.  The Tragedy of Medæa.  (Drury lane.)
1733.  Caelia: or, The Perjur'd Lover.  A Play.  (Drury lane.)  (Anon.)
Numerous other plays, 1702–32.

### *Henry Jones* (1721–1770)

1753.  The Earl of Essex.  T.  (Covent garden.)

### *Hugh Kelly*

1768.  False Delicacy.  C.  (Drury lane.)
1770.  A Word to the Wise.  C.  (Drury lane.)
1771.  Clementina.  T.  As it is Perform'd with universal Applause at the Theatre-Royal in Covent garden.  (Anon.)
1774.  The School for Wives.  C.  (Drury lane.)  (Anon.)
1774.  The Romance of an Hour.  C. of two acts.  (Covent garden.)

(1760.  L'Amour A-la-Mode: or, Love A-La-Mode.  F. in three acts.  [Translation from the French, often ascribed to Kelly.]])
1778.  Works.  To which is prefixed the Life of the Author.

### *George Lillo*

1731.  Silvia; or, The Country Burial.  O.  (Lincoln's inn fields.)  With the Musick prefix'd to each Song.  (Anon.)
1731.  The London Merchant: or, The History of George Barnwell.  (Drury lane.)
1735.  The Christian Hero.  T.  (Drury lane.)
1737.  Fatal Curiosity: a True Tragedy of three acts.  (New Theatre, Haymarket.)
This play was later altered, under the title:
1783.  Fatal Curiosity: a true Tragedy.  Written by George Lillo, 1736.  With Alterations [by Colman, G., the elder], As revived at the Theatre Royal, Hay-Market, 1782.
1784.  The Shipwreck: or, Fatal Curiosity.  T.  Altered from Lillo [by Mackenzie, H.].  (Covent garden.)
1738.  Marina: a Play of three acts.  (Covent garden.)  Taken from Pericles, Prince of Tyre.
1740.  Elmerick: or, Justice Triumphant.  T.  (Drury lane.)
1740.  Britannia and Batavia: a Masque.  Written on the Marriage of the Princess Royal with his Highness the Prince of Orange.  By the late Mr Lillo.

1762. Arden of Feversham. An Historical Tragedy: taken from Holingshead's Chronicle, in the Reign of King Edward VI. (Drury lane.) By the late Mr. Lillo.

1740. The Works of the late Mr. George Lillo. [Individual plays with separate titles and different dates. Includes Life of Scanderbeg.]

1775. The Works of Mr. George Lillo; with Some Account of his Life. [By Davies, T.] 2 vols. [2nd edn., improved. 2 vols. 1810.]

1906. The London Merchant or The History of George Barnwell and Fatal Curiosity. . . . Edited, with Introduction by Ward, A. W. (Belles-Lettres Series) Boston, U. S. A., and London. [Contains bibliographies of these two plays and of works biographical and critical concerning Lillo.]

1817. Memoirs of George Barnwell; the unhappy subject of Lillo's Celebrated Tragedy. . . . By a Descendant of the Barnwell Family.

Rapp, Moriz. Studien über das englische Theater. Tübingen, 1862. [Pp. 270–6 on Lillo.]

Hoffman, L. George Lillo (1693–1739). Inaugural Dissertation. Marburg, 1888.

### David Mallet [originally Malloch] (1705?–1765)

1731. Eurydice. T. (Drury lane.) (Anon.)

1739. Mustapha. T. (Drury lane.)

1740. [With Thomson.] Alfred: a Masque. Represented before Their Royal Highnesses the Prince and Princess of Wales, at Cliffden, on the First of August, 1740. (Anon.)

(1751. Alfred: a Masque. (Drury lane.) [See Advertisement as to Mallet's alterations.])

1755. Britannia: a Masque. (Drury lane.) (Anon.)

1763. Elvira. T. (Drury lane.)

1759. Works; in 3 vols. A new edition, corrected.

### Edward Moore

#### A. Plays

1748. The Foundling. C. (Drury lane.) By Mr. Moore, Author of Fables for the Female Sex.

1751. Gil Blas. C. (Drury lane.)

1753. The Gamester. T. (Drury lane.)
The Gamester, a True Story; on which the Tragedy of that Name . . . is Founded. Translated from the Italian. 1753.

Beyer, H. Edward Moore. Sein Leben und seine dramatischen Werke. In-augural Dissertation. Leipzig, 1889.

#### B. Other Works

1744. [Assisted . . . by the author of Gustavus Vasa, i. e. Henry Brooke.] Fables for the Female Sex.

1756. Poems, Fables, and Plays.

*Arthur Murphy*

### A. Plays

1756. The Apprentice. F. in two acts. (Drury lane.)

1756. The Spouter: or, The Triple Revenge. A Comic F., in two acts. As it was intended to be perform'd. With the Original Prologue. Written by the Author; and intended to be spoke by Mr. Garrick, dress'd in Black. (Anon.) [Not included in Murphy's Works.]

1758. The Upholsterer, or What News? F. in two acts. (Drury lane.) By the Author of the Apprentice. Glasgow. 2nd edn. With Alterations and Additions. 1765.

1759. The Orphan of China. T. (Drury lane.)

1760. The Desert Island, a Dramatic Poem, in three acts. (Drury lane.) (Anon.)

1760. The Way to Keep Him. C. in three acts. (Drury lane.) [1761. Ditto. In five acts. 4th edn.]

1761. All in the Wrong. C. (Drury lane.)

1761. The Old Maid. C. in two acts. (Drury lane.)

1763. The Citizen. F. (Covent garden.)

1764. No One's Enemy but His Own. C. in three acts. (Covent garden.) (Anon.)

1764. What we must All come to. C. in two acts, As it was intended to be Acted at the Theatre-Royal in Covent garden. (Anon.)

1767. The School for Guardians. C. (Covent-garden.) (Anon.)

1768. Zenobia. T. (Drury lane.) By the Author of the Orphan of China.

1772. The Grecian Daughter. T. (Drury lane.) (Anon.)

1773. Alzuma. T. (Covent garden.)

1776. Three Weeks after Marriage. C. in two acts. (Covent garden.) [Altered from What we must All come to, 1764.]

1778. Know your own Mind. C. (Covent garden.) (Anon.)

1793. The Rival Sisters. T. Adapted for Theatrical Representation. (Drury lane.)

1798. Arminius. T.

1786. Works [dramatic]. 7 vols. [Vol. IV contains The Choice, acted 1764, and News from Parnassus, acted 1776, apparently not previously printed.]

### B. Other Works

1762. An Essay on the Life and Genius of Henry Fielding. [In vol. I of Works of Henry Fielding, 4 vols.]

1793. An Essay on the Life and Genius of Samuel Johnson, LL.D. [In vol. I of Works of Samuel Johnson, 6 vols., Dublin.]

1801. The Life of David Garrick, Esq. 2 vols.

1811. The Life of Arthur Murphy, Esq. By Jessé Foot, Esq. his executor.

*Mrs. Frances Sheridan* (1724–1766)
[Mother of Richard Brinsley Sheridan]

### A. Plays

1763. The Discovery. C. (Drury lane.) Written by the Editor of Miss Sidney Bidulph.

1764. The Dupe. C. (Drury lane.) . . . By the Author of The Discovery.

## B. Other Works

1761. Memoirs of Miss Sidney Bidulph. [A novel.] 2 vols. Dublin.
1767. The History of Nourjahad. By the Editor of Sidney Bidulph.

Lefanu, Alicia. Memoirs of the Life and Writings of Mrs. Frances Sheridan . . . by her grand-daughter. 1824.

### James Thomson (1700–1748)
See bibliography to Chap. v, *post*

### Richard Tickell (1751–1793)

1778. The Camp. A musical entertainment.
1781. The Carnival of Venice.

### James Townley (1714–1778)

1759. High Life Below Stairs. F. of two acts. (Drury lane.) (Anon.)

### William Whitehead (1715–1785)

1750. The Roman Father. T. (Drury lane.)
1754. Creusa, Queen of Athens. T. (Drury lane.)
1762. The School for Lovers. C. (Drury lane.) By William Whitehead, Esq; Poet Laureat.
1770. A Trip to Scotland. (Drury lane.) (Anon.)
1774. Plays and Poems. 2 vols.

### Edward Young
See bibliography to Chap. VII, *post*.

## II. ENGLISH ADAPTATIONS OF VOLTAIRE

### Performed on the English Stage, 1734–1776

1735 [acted 1734]. Junius Brutus. T. (Drury lane.) [Brutus, adapted by William Duncombe.]
1736. The Tragedy of Zara. (Drury lane.) [Zaire, adapted by Aaron Hill.]
1736. Alzira. T. (Lincoln's inn fields.) [Alzire, adapted by Aaron Hill.]
1744. Mahomet the Imposter. T. (Drury lane.) [Le Fanatisme, ou Mahomet le Prophète, adapted by James Miller and (?) John Hoadly, to whom is ascribed the fifth act.]
1749. Meropé [*sic*]. T. (Drury lane.) [Mérope, adapted by Aaron Hill.]
1759. The Orphan of China. T. (Drury lane.) [Orphelin de la Chine, adapted by Arthur Murphy.]
1760. The English Merchant. C. (Drury lane.) [L'Écossaise, adapted by George Colman, the elder.]
1764. No One's Enemy but His Own. C. in three acts. (Covent garden.) [L'Indiscret, altered by Arthur Murphy.]
1765. Mahomet the Impostor. T. (Drury lane.) [James Miller's 1744 version, altered by (?) Garrick.]
(1769 acted. Orestes. [Oreste, adapted by Thomas Francklin, and acted at Covent garden, but not printed separately. Included in his translation of Voltaire's Works.])
1771. Almida. T. (Drury lane.) By a Lady. [Tancrède, adapted by Dorothea (Mallet) Celesia.]

1771. Zobeide. T. (Covent garden.) [Les Scythes, adapted by Joseph Cradock.]

1776. Semiramis. T. (Drury lane.) [Sémiramis, adapted by George Edward Ayscough.]

In addition to translations and adaptations of Voltaire quoted above, other English dramas show his influence, notably, *e. g.*, John Hoole's Cyrus (1768), Arthur Murphy's Alzuma (1773). For a full discussion of Voltaire's relation to English drama see Lounsbury, T. R., Shakespeare and Voltaire, New York and London, 1902. See also Ballantyne, A., Voltaire's Visit to England, 1726–9, 1893, and Collins, J. Churton, Voltaire, Montesquieu and Rousseau in England, 1908. (Revised from Bolingbroke, a Historical Study, and Voltaire in England, 1886.) For a full bibliography of Voltaire, see that by Anderson, J. P., in Espinasse, F., Life of Voltaire (Great Writers Series), 1892.

### III. Minor Dramatic Pieces Illustrative of the Period

Clive, Mrs. Catherine. The Rehearsal: or, Bays in Petticoats. C. in two acts. (Drury lane.) 1753.

Coffey, Charles. The Devil to Pay; or, The Wives Metamorphos'd. O. (Drury lane.) 1731.

Dodsley, Robert. The Toy Shop. A Dramatick Satire. By Robert Dodsley, Author of The Art of Charming. 1735.

> For full bibliography, *see* Robert Dodsley, Poet, Publisher and Playwright, by Straus, R., London and New York, 1910.

Johnson, Samuel [of Cheshire]. Hurlothrumbo: or, The Super-Natural. (New Theatre, Haymarket.) 1729.

—— The Blazing Comet: The Mad Lovers; or, The Beauties of the Poets. A Play. (New Theatre, Haymarket.) 1732.

Miller, James. The Humours of Oxford. C. As it is Acted at the Theatre-Royal. . . . By a Gentleman of Wadham-College. 1730.

> For Miller's Mahomet the Imposter *see* sec. ii, *ante* (English Adaptations of Voltaire).

Reed, Joseph. The Register Office. F. of two acts. 1761.

### *Pantomimes*, etc.

A Dramatic Entertainment, call'd The Necromancer: or, Harlequin, Doctor Faustus. (Lincoln's inn fields.) 6th edn. 1724.

Argentina Strega per Amore: or Harlequin Multiply'd by Argentina's Witchcraft, for Love. With their wonderful Flights and Apparitions; and the Magick Transformation of Silvio, Cittio, and Brighella. C. (Haymarket.) By the Company of Italian Comedians. 1726.

Perseus and Andromeda. With The Rape of Colombine: or, The Flying Lovers. In five interludes; three Serious, and two Comic. The Serious compos'd by Mons. Roger, and the Comic by Mr. John Weaver, Dancing-Masters. 1728.

Merlin, or The Devil of Stone-henge. An Entertainment. 1734. [Introduces Harlequin.]

A New Dramatic Entertainment called The Royal Chace; or, Merlin's Cave. With several new Comic Scenes of Action introduced into the Grotesque Pantomime of Jupiter and Europa. 1736.

Orpheus and Eurydice. O. (Covent garden.) Music by Lampe, J. F. 1739. [Comic characters include Harlequin, Pantaloon, Colombine, etc.]

Harlequin Student: or The Fall of Pantomime, with the Restoration of the Drama; an Entertainment, As it is now performing . . . at the late Theatre in Goodman's Fields. With the Scenes of Action and Tricks. . . . Also, A Description of the Scenes and Machines . . . And the Words of the Songs and Chorus's. 1741.

Harlequin Sorcerer: with the Loves of Pluto and Proserpine. (Covent garden.) 1752.

[Acted originally at Lincoln's inn fields, 1725. Words by Lewis Theobald.]

O'Hara, Kane. Midas; an English Burletta. (Covent garden.) 1764.

—— The Golden Pippin: an English Burletta, in three acts. (Covent garden.) 1773.

Reed, Joseph. Tom Jones. C. O. (Covent garden.) 1769. [Founded on Fielding's novel.]

### IV. CONTEMPORARY AND EARLY COLLECTIONS OF PLAYS

(In chronological order)

*This list excludes contemporary collections (e. g. Dodsley's) which are confined to earlier English dramas.*

A Select Collection of English Plays. 6 vols. Edinburgh. 1755.

A Select Collection of Farces, As Acted at London and Edinburgh. Edinburgh, 1762.

The English Theatre. . . . Containing the most valuable Plays which have been acted on the London Stage. 8 vols. 1765.

The Theatre: or, Select Works of the British Dramatic Poets. . . . To which are prefixed, the Lives of these celebrated Writers, and Strictures on Most of the Plays. 12 vols. Edinburgh, 1768.

A Collection of New Plays by Several Hands. 4 vols. Altenburg, 1774–8.

The New English Theatre . . . containing the Most Valuable Plays which have been Acted on the London Stage. 12 vols. 1776–7. [Separate plays variously dated, 1775–88.]

Bell's British Theatre, Consisting of the most esteemed English Plays. 24 vols. 1776, etc. 34 vols. 1791, etc.

A Collection of the most esteemed Farces and Entertainments performed on the British Stage. A new edition. 6 vols. Edinburgh, 1786–8.

[Parsons's] The Minor Theatre: being a Collection of the most approved Farces, Operas, and Comedies, in one, two, and three acts. With some account of the respective authors. 7 vols. 1794.

Jones's British Theatre. 10 vols. Dublin, 1795. [Individual plays with separate title-pages and pagination.]

The British Drama; comprehending the best plays in the English language [edited by Sir Walter Scott]. 3 vols. in 5 [vol. I, Tragedies, in two parts; vol. II, Comedies, in two parts; vol. III, Operas and Farces]. 1804.

Sharpe's British Theatre. 18 vols. 1804.

The British Theatre; or, A Collection of Plays . . . with biographical and critical remarks, by Mrs. Inchbald. 25 vols. 1808.

A Collection of Farces and other Afterpieces . . . selected by Mrs. Inchbald. 7 vols. 1809. [Another edn. 7 vols. 1815.]

English Comedy: a Collection of the Most Celebrated Dramas, since the Commencement of the Reformation of the Stage by Sir Richard Steele and Colley Cibber. 6 vols. 1810.

The Modern British Drama. 5 vols. 1811.
The British Drama, a Collection of the most Esteemed Dramatic Productions, with Biography of the Respective Authors; and Critique on each Play, by Richard Cumberland, Esq. 14 vols. 1817.
Oxberry's New English Drama. 20 vols. 1818–25.
The British Drama, a Collection of the most esteemed [engraved title-page reads "approved"] Tragedies, Comedies, Operas, and Farces, in the English Language. 2 vols., 1824–6; 2 vols., Philadelphia, 1837–8; and other later edns.
Dolby's British Theatre. [Individual plays variously dated, 1823–5; frontispiece, "published, Feb. 1825."] [Bound in 7 vols., unnumbered.] 1825.
Cumberland's British Theatre, with Remarks, Biographical and Critical. 43 vols. 1826, etc.
British Theatre, comprising Tragedies, Comedies, Operas, and Farces, from the most classic writers; with Biography, Critical Account and Explanatory Notes by an Englishman [(?) Owen Williams]. Leipzig, 1828.
The London Stage; a Collection of the most reputed Tragedies, Comedies, Operas, Melo-Dramas, Farces, and Interludes. Accurately printed from acting copies, as performed at the Theatres Royal, and carefully collated and revised. [Bound in 4 vols.] [1830.]

### V. COLLECTIONS OF PROLOGUES AND EPILOGUES

#### (In chronological order)

The Court of Thespis; being a Collection of the most admired Prologues and Epilogues. . . . Written by some of the most Approved Wits of the Age, viz. Garrick, Colman, Foote, Murphy, Lloyd, &c. 1769.
A Collection and Selection of English Prologues and Epilogues. Commencing with Shakespeare and concluding with Garrick. 4 vols. 1771.
The Theatrical Bouquet: containing an alphabetical arrangement of the Prologues and Epilogues, which have been published by Distinguished Wits, from the time that Colley Cibber first came on the Stage, to the present Year. 1780.

### VI. THEATRICAL HISTORIES, DICTIONARIES AND GENERAL RECORDS

#### (In chronological order)

*This list excludes (1) general works not largely concerned with mid-eighteenth century English drama, (2) specific works concerning individual dramatists unless, like Cibber's Apology, they deal broadly with general dramatic history and (3) minor publications such as critical, satirical, and controversial tracts, treatises and pamphlets. Some of the more important items under (1) and (2) are entered in the next section of this bibliography. For the multitudinous items under (3) see especially Lowe, R. W., A Bibliographical Account of English Theatrical Literature, 1888, and the catalogues of leading libraries, especially under individual author headings— e. g. the Colman tracts and Garrick items of the British Museum, the Bodleian controversial pamphlets concerning Home's Douglas, etc.*

Cibber, Colley. An Apology for the Life of Mr. Colley Cibber, Comedian . . . With an Historical View of the Stage during his Own Time. Written by Himself. 1740. [2nd edn. 1740. Edited, with Notes and Supplement, by Lowe, R. W. 2 vols. 1889.]

The History of the English Stage, from the Restauration to the Present Time. . . .
By Mr. Thomas Betterton. [Probably not by T. B.] 1741.

An Historical and Critical Account of the Theatres in Europe. . . . By the
famous Lewis Riccoboni of the Italian Theatre at Paris . . . 1741.

Chetwood, W. R. A General History of the Stage, from its Origin in Greece
down to the present Time. . . . Collected and Digested by W. R. Chetwood. 1749.

The British Theatre. Containing the Lives of the English Dramatic Poets with
an Account of all their Plays. . . . To which is prefixed, A Short View
of the Rise and Progress of the English Stage. Dublin, 1750. [Another edn.
London, 1752.]

A General History of the Stage, from its Origin. . . . Translated from the
Eminent Lewis Riccoboni. . . . The Second Edition. To which is
Prefixed, An Introductory Discourse concerning the Present State of the
English Stage and Players. 1754.

Theatrical Records: or, An Account of English Dramatic Authors, and their
Works. Printed for R. and J. Dodsley. 1756.

The Theatrical Review: for the Year 1757, and Beginning of 1758. 1758.

A General View of the Stage. By Mr. Wilkes [pseud. of Samuel Derrick].
1759.

An Essay upon the Present State of the Theatre in France, England and Italy.
1760.

Victor [Benjamin]. The History of the Theatres of London and Dublin, from
the Year 1730, to the present Time. To which is added, An Annual Register
of all the Plays, &c. performed at the Theatres-Royal in London, from the
Year 1712. With Occasional Notes and Anecdotes. 2 vols. 1761.

The Theatrical Review: or, Annals of the Drama. 1763.

[Baker, David Erskine]. The Companion to the Play-House: or, An Historical
Account of all the Dramatic Writers (and their Works) that have appeared
in Great Britain and Ireland, from the Commencement of our Theatrical
Exhibitions, down to the Present Year 1764. 2 vols. 1764. A new edition:
Carefully corrected; greatly enlarged; and continued [by Reed, Isaac]
from 1764 to 1782. 2 vols. 1782. New edn., with the first title Biographia
Dramatica, brought down to the end of November, 1811. By Jones, Stephen.
3 vols in 4. 1812.

Brounsmith, J. (prompter to the Theatre-Royal in the Haymarket). The
Dramatic Time-Piece: or Perpetual Monitor. Being a Calculation of the
Length of Time every act takes . . . at the Theatres-Royal. 1767.

[Gentleman, Francis]. The Dramatic Censor; or, Critical Companion. 2 vols.
1770.

Victor [Benjamin]. The History of the Theatres of London, from the Year
1760 to the Present Time. Being a Continuation of the Annual Register
[see above, under date, 1761]. 1771.

The Theatrical Review, or New Companion to the Play-House: containing A
Critical and Historical Account of every Tragedy, Comedy, Opera, Farce,
&c. exhibited at the Theatres during the last Season. . . . By a Society
of Gentlemen, Independent of Managerial Influence. 2 vols. 1772.

Theatrical Biography: or, Memoirs of the Principal Performers of the Three
Theatres Royal. 2 vols. 1772.

The Playhouse Pocket Companion, or Theatrical Vade-Mecum. . . . To
which is prefixed, A Critical History of the English Stage from its Origin to
the present Time. 1779.

Hitchcock, Robert (prompter of the Theatre-Royal, Dublin). An Historical View of the Irish Stage; from the earliest period down to the close of the season 1788 . . . [or, rather, to 1774. See Preface to vol. ii, (1794)]. 2. vols. Dublin, 1788–94.

A New Theatrical Dictionary. Containing an Account of all the Dramatic Pieces that have appeared from the Commencement of Theatrical Exhibitions to the Present Time. . . . And also a Short Sketch of the Rise and Progress of The English Stage. 1792.

Jackson, John (ten years manager of the Theatre Royal of Edinburgh). The History of the Scottish Stage, from its First Establishment to the Present Time. Edinburgh, 1793.

Oulton, Walley Chamberlain. The History of the Theatres of London . . . from the year 1771 to 1795. 2 vols. 1796.

Dibdin, Charles. A Complete History of the English Stage. 5 vols. [1800.]

The Thespian Dictionary; or Dramatic Biography of the Eighteenth Century . . . forming a concise History of the English Stage. 1802. 2nd edn. 1805.

Holcroft, Thomas. The Theatrical Recorder. 2 vols. 1805–6.

Gilliland, Thomas. The Dramatic Mirror: containing the History of the Stage, from the earliest period to the present time. 2 vols. 1808.

The Drama Recorded; or, Barker's List of Plays . . . from the earliest period, to 1814; to which are added, Notitia Dramatica, or a Chronological Account of Events relative to the English Stage. 1814.

Dibdin, Charles, Jr. History and Illustrations of the London Theatres. 1826.

[Genest, John.] Some Account of the English Stage, from the Restoration in 1660 to 1830. 10 vols. Bath, 1832.

The Dramatic Souvenir: being literary and graphical illustrations of Shakespeare and other celebrated English dramatists. [Especially pp. 94–171.]1833.

[Logan, William Henry.] Fragmenta Scoto-Dramatica. 1715–1758. Edinburgh, 1835.

Tomlins, F. G. A Brief View of the English Drama, from the Earliest Period to the Present Time. 1840.

"Their Majesties Servants." Annals of the English Stage, from Thomas Betterton to Edmund Kean. 2 vols. 1864. [2nd edn., revised. 1 vol. 1865. Edited and revised by Lowe, Robert W. 3 vols. 1888.]

Fitzgerald, Percy. A New History of the English Stage from the Restoration to the Liberty of the Theatres, in connection with the Patent Houses. 2 vols. 1882.

Lowe, Robert W. A Bibliographical Account of English Theatrical Literature. 1888.

Dibdin, James C. The Annals of the Edinburgh Stage with an account of the Rise and Progress of Dramatic Writing in Scotland. Edinburgh, 1888.

Baker, H. Barton. The London Stage: Its History and Traditions from 1576 to 1888. 2 vols. 1889.

Revised as: History of the London Stage and its Famous Players (1576–1903). London and New York, 1904.

Bates, Katherine Lee, and Godfrey, Lydia B. English Drama. A Working Basis. Wellesley College, U. S. A. 1896.

The Haymarket Theatre: some Records & Reminiscences. By Maude, Cyril, edited by Maude, Ralph. 1903.

Adams, W. Davenport. A Dictionary of the Drama. Vol. i, A—G. 1904.

Nicholson, Watson. The Struggle for a Free Stage in London. Boston and New York, 1906. [Also, London edn.]

Wyndham, H. S.  The Annals of Covent Garden Theatre from 1732 to 1897.
2 vols. 1906.

Marks, Jeannette.  English Pastoral Drama . . . (1660–1798).  [With bibliography of English Pastoral Plays.]  [1908.]

The Stage Censor: an historical sketch: 1544–1907: by G. M. G.  1908.

Thorndike, Ashley H.  Tragedy.  Boston and New York, 1908.  [Chap. IX,
with Note on Bibliography.]

Clarence, R.  "The Stage" Cyclopaedia: A Bibliography of Plays.  1909.

Ward, A. W.  Art.  Drama (with bibliography) in Encyclopaedia Britannica,
11th edn., vol. VIII.  Cambridge, 1910.

Materials for the Study of the English Drama (excluding Shakespeare).  A
selected list of books in the Newberry Library.  Chicago, 1912.

VII.  ADDITIONAL WORKS, CHIEFLY BIOGRAPHICAL AND CRITICAL

*This list is limited to a selection from the more considerable works bearing* (1) *on
general phases of the drama, or* (2) *on individual dramatists, discussed in Chap.*
IV.  *Briefer treatises, special dissertqtions* (e. g. *on the sources of separate plays*),
*encylopaedias, general histories of literature or biography, and similar works are
with a few exceptions, omitted.*

Baker, H. B.  Our Old Actors.  2 vols.  1878.

Beers, H. A.  A History of English Romanticism in the Eighteenth Century.
New York, 1899.

Beljame, A.  Le Public et les Hommes de Lettres en Angleterre au dix-huitième
siècle.  Paris, 1881.  With index, Paris, 1897.

Betz, L. P.  La Littérature comparée, essai bibliographique.  Strassburg, 1900.

Boulton, W. B.  The Amusements of Old London.  2 vols.  1901.  [Vol. I,
chap. VI.]

Canfield, D. F.  Corneille and Racine in England.  New York and London,
1904.

Cibber, Theophilus.  The Lives and Characters of the most Eminent Actors
and Actresses of Great Britain and Ireland.  Part I.  Life of Barton Booth.
1753.

—— Dissertations on Theatrical Subjects.  1756.

—— Theophilus Cibber, to David Garrick, Esq; with Dissertations on Theatrical
Subjects.  1759.  [Section V contains attack on Garrick's Shakespearean
perversions.]

Cook, Dutton.  A Book of the Play.  2 vols.  1876.

—— Hours with the Players.  2 vols.  1881.

Cooke, William.  Memoirs of Charles Macklin . . . forming an History of the
Stage during almost the Whole of the last Century.  2nd edn.  1806.

Courthope, W. J.  A History of English Poetry.  London and New York, 1895–
1905.  [Vol. V, chap. XIII.]

Davies, Thomas.  Dramatic Miscellanies.  3 vols.  1783–4.

Dennis, John.  The Age of Pope (1700–1744).  (Handbooks of English Literature.)
1894.

Dobson, Austin.  Introduction to The Good Natur'd Man and She Stoops to
Conquer.  (Belles-Lettres Series.)  Boston and London [1903].

Eloesser, A.  Das bürgerliche Drama.  Seine Geschichte im 18. und 19. Jahrhundert.  Berlin, 1898.

Galt, John.  The Lives of the Players.  2 vols.  1831.

Gosse, Edmund. A History of Eighteenth Century Literature (1660–1780). 1889.

Hastings, Charles. The Theatre: its Development in France and England. 1901.

Hettner, Hermann. Geschichte der englischen Literatur . . . 1660–1770 (Part I: Literaturgeschichte des achtzehnten Jahrhunderts). 1856. [Brunswick, 1894.]

[? Hill, John.] The Actor: a Treatise on the Art of Playing. 1750.

—— The Actor: or, A Treatise on the Art of Playing. A New Work, written by the Author of the former, and adapted to the Present State of the Theatres. 1755.

Kilbourne, Frederick W. Alterations and Adaptations of Shakespeare. Boston, U. S. A., 1906.

Lewes, Charles Lee. Memoirs of Charles Lee Lewes. . . . Written by himself. 4 vols. 1805.

Lounsbury, T. R. Shakespeare as a Dramatic Artist: with an account of his reputation at various periods. New York and London, 1902.

—— The Text of Shakespeare. New York, 1906.

Mantzius, K. A History of Theatrical Art. Translation by Louise von Cossel. 1904, etc. [Vol. v (1909), The Great Actors of the Eighteenth Century.]

Matthews, Brander. The Development of the Drama. New York, 1904.

Millar, J. H. The Mid-Eighteenth Century. Edinburgh and London, 1902. [Chap. vi.]

Molloy, J. F. The Romance of the Irish Stage. 2 vols. 1897.

Morley, Henry. English Plays. (Cassell's Library of English Literature.) [1878.] [Chap. ix.]

Perry, T. S. English Literature in the Eighteenth Century. New York, 1883. [Chap. viii.]

Seccombe, T. The Age of Johnson (1748–1798). (Handbooks of English Literature.) 1899. [Chap. ix.]

Stephen, Sir Leslie. English Literature and Society in the Eighteenth Century. 1904.

Straus, R. Robert Dodsley: Poet, Publisher & Playwright [with full bibliography]. London and New York, 1910.

Ward, A. W. A History of English Dramatic Literature to the Death of Queen Anne. New and revised edn. 3 vols. London and New York, 1899.

Waterhouse, O. The development of English Sentimental Comedy in the 18th century. In Anglia, vol. xxx. Halle a. S., 1907.

Wilkinson, Tate. Memoirs of His Own Life. 4 vols. York, 1790.

—— The Wandering Patentee, or a history of the Yorkshire Theatre from 1770 to the present time. 4 vols. York, 1795.

Wright, C. H. Conrad. A History of French Literature. New York and London, 1912.

## CHAPTER V

## THOMSON AND NATURAL DESCRIPTION IN POETRY

### A. James Thomson

#### (1) *Separate Poems*

Winter. A Poem. 1726. 2nd, 3rd and 4th edns. 1726.

Summer. A Poem. 1727. 2nd edn. 1728; 3rd edn., with additions, 1730.

A Poem sacred to the Memory of Sir Isaac Newton. 1727. 3rd edn. 1727.

Spring. A Poem. 1728. 2nd edn. 1729.

Britannia. A poem written in the year 1729. 2nd and 3rd edns. 1730.

A Poem to the Memory of Mr. Congreve. 1729.

Winter, a Hymn on the Seasons, a Poem to the Memory of Sir Isaac Newton, and Britannia. 1730.

The Seasons, a Hymn, a Poem sacred to the Memory of Sir Isaac Newton, and Britannia. 1730. (Containing Autumn, of which a 2nd edn. appeared in the same year.) Five parts, paged separately. 2nd edn. 1730; 3rd edn. 1734; 4th edn. 1735. A copy in the British Museum (The Four Seasons and other Poems, 1735) is made up in four parts from these later edns. Edns. of the Seasons alone bear dates 1744, 1746, 1752, 1758, 1766, 1768, 1774 (with life of Thomson by Murdoch, P.), 1787 (with Murdoch's life), 1788, 1792 (with essay by Aikin, J.), 1793 (with life and critical essay by Heron, R.), 1793 (with index, glossary and notes by Stockdale, P., another edn. 1794), 1794, 1799 (with Murdoch's life and Aikin's essay), 1802 (with illustrative remarks by Evans, J.), etc. An edn. with notes, etc., by Wright, G., is undated (probably 1770). Illustrated edns. 1792, 1797, 1805, etc. Dublin, 1758, 1761, 1793 (with Johnson's life). Glasgow, 1769. Paris, 1780. Hamburg, 1791 (ed. Timaeus, J. J. C., with Aikin's essay). Parma, 1794.

Antient and Modern Italy compared, being the First part of Liberty, a Poem. 1735.

Greece (Liberty, part II). 1735.

Rome (Liberty, part III). 1735.

Britain (Liberty, part IV). 1736.

The Prospect (Liberty, part V). 1736.

Liberty, a Poem. 1736. (Five parts, made up of copies of the above sections of the poem.) An edn. was published at Glasgow, 1776.

A Poem to the Memory of the Rt. Hon. the Lord Talbot, late Chancellor of Great Britain. 1737.

The Castle of Indolence: an allegorical Poem written in imitation of Spenser. 1748. 2nd edn. 1748.

### (2)  *Pamphlet*

Areopagitica [by John Milton]. With a Preface by another hand. 1738.

### (3)  *Plays*

The Tragedy of Sophonisba. 1730.

Agamemnon, a Tragedy. 1738.

Alfred, a Masque. 1740. Another edn. 1751.

Edward and Eleonora, a Tragedy. As it was to have been acted at the Theatre-Royal in Covent-Garden. 1739. Another edn. 1739. Altered and adapted to the Stage by Hull, T. 1775.

Tancred and Sigismunda, a Tragedy in verse. 1745. Other edns. 1752, 1766, etc.

Coriolanus, a Tragedy, 1749.

Alfred the Great, a Drama for Music. Formerly composed by command of His Late Royal Highness the Prince of Wales, and performed at Cliefdon (*sic*), on the Birthday of her Royal Highness the Princess Augusta. The musical Part of this performance being then too short for an Evening's Entertainment of itself, the Drama is new written, greatly improved from Mallet [D.]'s Play; and the Music (excepting two or three things, which being particularly

Favourites at Cliefdon, are retained by Desire) new-Composed by Arne, T. A. 1753.

### (4) Collected and Modern Editions

Works, vol. II (containing Liberty and Sophonisba, vol. I being the collected ed. of the Seasons, as above, 1730 etc.). 1736.

—— 2 vols. 1738. The British Museum copy is of vol. I alone, containing Thomson's MS. corrections with those attributed to Pope. ♥

—— 2 vols. 1744.

—— 3 vols. 1749.

The Works of James Thomson. In Four Volumes Complete. With his last Corrections, Additions, and Improvements. Vols. II, III, IV. 1750. Vol. I. 1752. Other edns.: 2 vols. (with Murdoch's life), 1762; 2 vols. 1763; 1 vol. (with Murdoch's life), 1768; 4 vols. (with Collins' ode), 1773; 3 vols. 1788; 2 vols. 1788; Edinburgh, 4 vols. 1772.

Poetical Works, collected in British Poets, vols. XXXVIII, XXXIX, 1773; Works of English Poets, ed. Johnson, S., vols. XLVIII, XLIX, 1779; vols. LIV, LV, 1790; Anderson, Complete edn. of Poets of Great Britain, vol. IX, 1793; Chalmers, English Poets, vol. XII, 1810. Also in several other collections.

Poetical Works, ed. Nicolas, Sir Harris. (Aldine edn.) 2 vols. 1830. Also 1862, 1866.

The Seasons and the Castle of Indolence, ed. Cunningham, A. 1841.

The [Seasons, ed. Thomson, A. T. (with notes philosophical, classical, etc.). 1847.

Poetical Works, ed. Gilfillan, G. (with life, etc.). Edinburgh, 1853.

—— ed. Clarke, C. Cowden. Edinburgh, 1868.

—— ed. Rossetti, W. M. 1873, etc.

The Seasons and the Castle of Indolence, ed. Robertson, J. L. Oxford, 1891.

Poetical Works, ed. Tovey, D. C. (Aldine edn.) 2 vols. 1897.

Thomson's Seasons, ed. Zippel, O. Berlin, 1908. Containing the original text with all the various readings of the later edns., historically arranged.

### (5) Translations and Adaptations

Bonducci, Andrea. Le lodi d'Isacco Neuton (with other translations). Naples, 1760.

Brock, B. H. Herrn B. H. Brockes . . . aus dem Englischen übersetzte Jahres-Zeiten des Herrn Thomson zum Anhange des irdischen Vergnügens in Gott. (With English text.) Hamburg, 1745.

Brownell, R. C. Tempora Thomsoni in Latino versu reddita. 1795 (?).

Brugière de Barante. Tancrède et Sigismunde. (Translated in Chefs d'œuvre des Théâtres étrangers, vol. x.)

Castelfranco, A. La libertà . . . Parte iii. Rome. Libera versione poetica. Trieste, 1867.

Châtillon Bontems, Marie-Jeanne de. Les Saisons. (Prose translation.) Paris, 1759. London, 1779.

Daucha, F. Thomsonowy Počasy. V Prasze, 1852.

Foersom, P. Foraaret. Copenhagen, 1807.

—— Vinteren. Copenhagen, 1812.

Harries. Die Jahres-Zeiten. (In iambics.) Altona, 1796.

Mathias, T. J. Il Castello dell' Ozio. Naples, 1826.

Mountfort, D. Palemon and Lavinia. Enlarged from a story in Thomson's Seasons. 1783.

Palthen, J. F. von. Die Jahres-Zeiten. (In prose.) Rostock, 1756.

Petrides, P. Romaic version of part of Summer in Πετρίδου εἰδοποίησισκαὶ πρότασις πρὸς τοὺς νέους τοὺς Ἴωνας. 1817.

Poulm, J. Les Saisons (with English text). Paris, 1802.

Pyra, J. E., and Lange. Thirsis und Damons Freundschaftliche Lieder, ed. Bodmer, J. J. 2nd edn. 1749. Containing translations (Lavinia, Damon, Celadon und Amalia) of three episodes from The Seasons.

Rosenzweig, C. F. von. Die Jahres-Zeiten. (In hexameters.) Hamburg, 1825.

Saint Lambert, C.-F., marquis de. Les Saisons, Poème. 1785. [An adaptation.]

Saurin, B.-J. Blanche et Guiscard, Tragédie. 1763. [Adapted from Tancred and Sigismunda.] New edn. 1772.

Schizzati, F. Le Stagioni. Parma, 1818.

Schlegel, J. H. Eduard und Eleonora: Tankred und Sigismunda. In Trauerspiele. 1764.

Anonymous. La Estate. Modena, 1817.

—— La Primavera. Bologna, 1820.

—— Die Jaargeeijden naar Thomson. Amsterdam, 1803. Adapted for music by Haydn.

## B.  RICHARD JAGO

Edge-Hill; or, the Rural Prospect delineated and moralized. A poem, in four books, 1767.

Labour and Genius. 1768.

Poems, moral and descriptive. . . . To which is added, some account of the life and writings of Mr. Jago. 1784.

Poetical Works, collected in Anderson, Poets of Great Britain, vol. XI, 1793; Chalmers, English Poets, vol. XVII, 1810. Also in other collections.

## C.  LORD LYTTELTON

Blenheim. 1728.

An Epistle to Mr. Pope from a young gentleman at Rome. 1730.

The Progress of Love, in four eclogues. 1732.

Advice to a Lady. 1733.

Letters from a Persian in England, to his Friend at Ispahan. 2 vols. 1735. 2nd, 3rd and 4th edns. 1735; 5th edn. 1744.

Observations on the Conversion and Apostleship of St. Paul in a Letter to Gilbert West. 1747. 9th edn. 1799. Frequently rptd. and transl. into French.

To the Memory of a Lady, a Monody. 1747 [1748].

A Modest Apology for my own Conduct. 1748.

Dialogues of the Dead. 1760.

An additional Dialogue of the Dead, between Pericles and Aristides, being a sequel to the Dialogue between Pericles and Cosmo. 1760.

Four new Dialogues of the Dead. 1765.

The history of the life of Henry II and of the age in which he lived. 3 vols. 1767.

Works . . . now first collected together: with some other pieces never before printed. 1 vol. 1774. 2nd edn. 1775; 3rd edn. (3 vols.) 1776.

A Gentleman's Tour through Monmouthshire, etc. 1781.

Poetical Works, collected in Anderson, Poets of Great Britain, vol. X, 1793; Chalmers, English Poets, vol. XIV (with Johnson's life), 1810; and in other collections.

D. WILLIAM SOMERVILE or SOMERVILLE
As to the spelling of the name, see text, p. 308, note 2.

The Two Springs. A Fable. 1725.

Occasional Poems, Translations, Fables, Tales. 1727.

The Chace, a Poem. 1735. 2nd and 3rd edns. 1735; 4th edn. 1757; 5th edn. 1767; 6th edn. 1773; modern illustrated edn. 1896.

Hobbinol, or the Rural Games. 1740. 2nd and 3rd edns. 1740; 4th edn. 1757; 5th edn. 1758; 6th edn. 1773.

Field Sports. 1742.

The Chase, a Poem: to which is added Hobbinol, or the Rural Games. Birmingham, 1767.

The Wicker Chair, a Burlesque Poem. First ptd. in Waldron's Collection of Miscellaneous Poetry. 1802.

Poetical Works, 2 vols. Glasgow, 1766. See also Anderson, Poets of Great Britain, vol. VIII, 1793; Chalmers, English Poets, vol. XI (with Johnson's life), 1810; and other collections.

E. GENERAL SOURCES OF INFORMATION

Aikin, J. An Essay on the plan and character of Thomson's Seasons. 1778.

B., T. A Criticism by T. B. on the New Sophonisba, a tragedy. 1730.

Bayne, W. James Thomson. (Famous Scots Series.) Edinburgh, 1898.

Beljame, A. Le Public et les Hommes de Lettres en Angleterre au dix-huitième Siècle. Paris, 1881.

Buchan, David Steuart [Erskine], 11th earl of. Essays on the lives and writings of Fletcher of Saltoun and the poet Thomson, with some pieces of Thomson's never before published. 1792.

Courthope, W. J. A History of English Poetry. Vol. v. 1905. [Chaps. x, XII.]

Cunningham, P. (ed.). Unpublished Letters from Thomson to Mallet. (Philobiblon Soc. Biog. and Hist. Miscellanies, vol. IV.)

Gjerset, Knut. Der Einfluss von James Thomsons Jahreszeiten auf die deutsche Literatur des achtzehnten Jahrhunderts, etc. Heidelberg, 1898.

Gosse, Edmund. A History of Eighteenth Century Literature. 1889.

Ibershoff, C. H. A German Translation of Passages in Thomson's Seasons. (Mod. Lang. Notes, XXVI, pp. 107–109. April, 1911.)

Johnson, Samuel. Lives of the English Poets. 1779–81.

Macaulay, G. C. Thomson. (English Men of Letters.) 1908.

More, Jacob. Strictures, Critical and Sentimental, on Thomson's Seasons. 1777.

Morel, Léon. James Thomson, sa vie et ses œuvres. Paris, 1895.

Musidorus: a Poem sacred to the memory of Mr. James Thomson. [1748.]

Phillimore, Sir R. J. Memoirs and Correspondence of George, Lord Lyttelton. 1845.

Schmeding, G. A. Jacob Thomson, ein vergessener Dichter des achtzehnten Jahrhunderts. Braunschweig, 1889.

Shairp, J. C. On Poetic Interpretation of Nature. Edinburgh, 1877.

*See, also*, bibliography to Chap. VII, *post.*

CHAPTER VI

GRAY

For an account of the extant manuscripts of Gray, see notes at end of Gray's Poems, ed. Bradshaw, J. (Aldine edn.), 1891.

## A. EDITIONS PRINTED IN GRAY'S LIFETIME

Ode on a Distant Prospect of Eton College. Dodsley. 1747. (Published anonymously.)
> Dodsley's collection (vol. II, 1748) contains the Eton Ode (anon.), the Ode on the Spring, and the Ode on the death of a favourite Cat, the last two for the first time.

An Elegy Wrote in a Country Church Yard. Dodsley. 1751. 2nd edn. 1751; 4th edn. 1751. (With an Advertisement by Horace Walpole.)
> Printed also in The Magazine of Magazines, Feb. 28, 1751; in The London Magazine, Feb. 28; in The Scots Magazine, Mar. 31; in The Grand Magazine of Magazines, April 30. 8th edn. 1753; 9th edn. 1754. Facsimile of the original manuscript of the Elegy in Pembroke College, Cambridge. 1897.

Designs by Mr. R. Bentley for Six Poems by Mr. T. Gray. 1753, 1765. (The Ode on the Spring; On the death of a favourite cat; On a Distant Prospect of Eton; Hymn to Adversity; Long Story; Elegy.)

Odes by Mr. Gray. Strawberry Hill, 1757.

Poems by Mr. Gray. 1768. Glasgow, 1768. New edn. 1770.

Ode performed in the Senate-House at Cambridge, July 1, 1769, at the Installation of His Grace Augustus Henry Fitzroy, Duke of Grafton, Chancellor of the University. Cambridge, 1769.

## B. LATER EDITIONS, INCLUDING CORRESPONDENCE

Gray's Poems are contained in the principal collections of British Poets (Bell, Johnson, Anderson, Chalmers, etc.).

The Poems of Mr. Gray. To which are prefixed Memoirs of his Life and Writings. By Mason, W. York, 1775. Another edn. 4 vols. 1778.

Poems. 1776, 1778, 1786, 1799 (ed. Jones, S.).

Matthisson, F. von. Letters written from . . . the Continent. . . . With an Appendix in which are included three Letters of Gray's. 1799.

Gray's Works. Ed. Mason, W., with extracts from Gray's MSS. by Mathias, T. J. 2 vols. 1814.
> Mason, W. Poems. 1764. 5th edn. York, 1779. New edn. 3 vols. York, 1796–7.

Poems, with Life, Notes, and an Essay on his Poetry by Mitford, J. 1814.

Works, with a Life of the Author and an Essay on his Poetry, by Mitford, J. 2 vols. 1816.

Poetical Works, with Life etc. by Mitford, J. (Aldine Poets.) 1830.

Works, etc. Ed. Mitford, J. 4 vols. 1836. Vol. v, containing Gray's correspondence with Nicholls, etc. 1843.

Poetical Works. Ed. Moultrie, J. Eton, 1845.

—— with a new life by Mitford, J. 1847.

—— with the new life, and a Lecture on the writings of Gray by the Earl of Carlisle. 4th edn. Eton, 1852. 5th edn. 1854. Other edns. 1863, 1866.

The Correspondence of Gray and Mason, etc. Ed. Mitford, J. 1853. 2nd edn. 1855.

Poems of Gray, Parnell, Collins, Green, and Warton. 1853. Ed. Willmott, R. A. [The account of Gray is brief, but excellent.]

Works. Ed. Gosse, E. 4 vols. 1884.

Gray and his friends. Letters and relics. Ed. Tovey, D. C. Cambridge, 1890.

Poetical Works. New Aldine Edition, with Life, Notes, and Bibliography by Bradshaw, J. 1891.
English Poems of Gray. Ed. Tovey, D. C. Cambridge, 1898.
Gray's Letters. Ed. Tovey, D. C. 3 vols. 1900–12.
[Gives evidence of Sir Walter Scott's interest in Norse literature.]

For translations and parodies *see* Bradshaw's bibliography, *supra*.

### C. Biography and Criticism
*See, also,* sec. B.

Arnold, M. Introduction to the selection from Gray's Poems, printed in T. H. Ward's English Poets, vol. III. 1880.
Gosse, E. Gray. (English Men of Letters.) 1882. New edn. 1889.
Johnson, Samuel. Gray. Lives of the Poets. Ed. Hill, G. B. Vol. III. Oxford, 1905. [For criticisms of the above *see* Bradshaw, *u. s.* p. 317.]
Kittredge, G. L. Gray's Knowledge of Old Norse. In Appendix to Introduction to Phelps's Selections from the Poetry and Prose of T. Gray. Boston, 1894.
Mackenzie, Henry. Introduction to Gray's Fatal Sisters (1768). In Works. vol. VIII. Edinburgh, 1808.
Mathias, T. J. Observations on the writings and on the character of Mr. Gray, 1815.
Stephen, Sir L. Thomas Gray. D. of N. B., vol. XXIII. 1890.

### CHAPTER VII
### YOUNG, COLLINS, AND LESSER POETS OF THE AGE OF JOHNSON

#### I. General
##### A. *Collections*

*The principal works of the writers treated in this chapter will be found in the following Collections of British Poets:*

The Poets of Great Britain from Chaucer to Churchill. (Bell's edn.) 109 vols. Edinburgh, 1777–92.
The Works of the English Poets: with prefaces biographical and critical by Johnson, S. 68 vols. 1779–81.
The Works of the British Poets. Ed. Anderson, R. 14 vols. Edinburgh, 1793–1807.
The Works of the British Poets. Ed. Park, T. 48 vols. 1805–9.
The Works of the English Poets from Chaucer to Cowper including the series ed., with prefaces critical and biographical, by Dr. Samuel Johnson, and the most approved translations. With additional lives by Chalmers, A. 21 vols. 1810.

##### B. *Biography and Criticism*
*See, also,* Vol. IX, bibliography to Chap. VI, sec. I, B.

Millar, J. H. The mid-eighteenth century. (Periods of European literature.) Edinburgh, 1902.
Seccombe, T. The Age of Johnson (1748–98). 1900.

#### II. Particular Writers
##### *Mark Akenside*
Poems. Ed. Dyson, J. 1772.
Poetical Works. Ed. Dyce, A., with a Life. (Aldine Poets.) 1835 and 1857.

Poetical Works of Mark Akenside and John Dyer.  Ed. Willmott, R. A.  1855.

A British Philippic.  1738.
The Pleasures of Imagination.  A poem in three parts.  1744.  4th edn.  1744.
   Ed. Mrs. Barbauld.  1795.
      Transl. into French prose by Holbach, P. H. D. von, Amsterdam, 1759,
   and also into German and Italian.
An Epistle to Curio [i. e. William Pulteney, earl of Bath].  1744.
Odes on several subjects.  1745.  2nd edn.  1760.
An Ode to the Rt. Hon. the Earl of Huntingdon.  1748.
The Remonstrance of Shakespeare.  1749.
An Ode to the Country Gentlemen of England.  1758.
Ode to the late Thomas Edwards, Esq. written in the year 1751.  1766.

Bucke, C.  On the life, writings, and genius of Akenside; with some account
   of his friends.  1832.
Cooper, J. G.  The Call of Aristippus.  1758.  [A panegyric of Akenside.]

### John Armstrong

The Œconomy of Love.  A poetical essay.  1736.  New edn., revised, 1768.  1781.
The Art of preserving Health.  A poem.  1744.  2nd edn.  1745.  Ed. Aikin,
   J.  1795.  1803.
      Transl. into Italian verse by Mathias, T. J., Naples, 1824.
Benevolence.  An epistle.  1751.
Taste.  An Epistle to a young critic.  1753.
Sketches or essays on various subjects, in two parts.  By Launcelot Temple
   [i. e. John Armstrong].  1758.
A Day.  An epistle to John Wilkes, of Aylesbury, Esq.  1761.
Miscellanies.  2 vols.  1770.

### Henry Baker (1698–1774)

Original Poems.  1725.
The Universe.  A Poem intended to restrain the Pride of Man.  [1727.]  With
   a Life.  1805.

### John Codrington Bampfylde (1754–1796)

Sixteen Sonnets.  1778.

### James Beattie

#### (1)  Collected Editions

Poetical Works.  Ed., with a Life, by Dyce, A.  (Aldine Poets.)  1831 and 1866.
Poetical Works of Beattie, Blair, and Falconer.  With Lives, etc., by Gilfillan, G.
   Edinburgh, 1854.
The Poetical Works of James Beattie and William Collins.  With memoirs of
   their lives and writings by Miller, T.  Illustrated.  1846.

#### (2)  Particular Works

Original poems and translations.  1761.  2nd edn.  1766.
The Judgment of Paris.  A poem.  1765.
An Essay on Truth.  1770.  4th edn. 1773; 7th edn. 1807.
      Transl. into French, German, Italian and Dutch.
The Minstrel, or the Progress of Genius.  A poem.  2 parts.  1771–4.  New
   edn., with a few other poems.  1777.  1807.  1819.  Rptd. and illustrated
   by Foster, B.  1858.

Essays. On poetry and music. On laughter. On the utility of classical learning. Edinburgh. 1776.
Dissertations moral and critical. 1783. 2 vols. 1786.
Evidences of the Christian religion. Edinburgh, 1786.
Elements of moral science. 2 vols. 1790–3. 2 vols. Edinburgh, 1807. 2 vols. 1817.

### (3) Biography and Criticism

Bower, A. An Account of the Life of James Beattie. 1804.
Forbes, M. Beattie and his friends. 1904.
Forbes, Sir W. An Account of the Life and Writings of James Beattie, including many of his original Letters. 2 vols. Edinburgh, 1806. 3 vols. 1807. 2 vols. 1824.

#### Robert Blair

*See, also,* Beattie, J., *ante*

The Grave. A poem. 1743.
—— Illustrated by twelve etchings executed by Schiavonetti, L., from the original inventions of William Blake. 1808. 1813.
—— Ed. Farrar, F. W. Illustrated. 1858.

#### Susanna Blamire (1747–1794)

Poetical Works, now for the first time collected by Lonsdale, H. With a preface, memoir, and notes by Maxwell, P. Edinburgh, 1842.

#### Samuel Boyce (d. 1775)

Poems. 1757.

#### John Collier ["Tim Bobbin"] (1708–1786)

View of the Lancashire dialect (by way of Dialogue between Tummus and Meary, etc.). 1746. Frequently rptd., sometimes in edns. including Collier's miscellaneous poems under the title of Works of Tim Bobbin.

#### William Collins

Poetical Works. With Memoirs of the author, and observations on his genius and writings by Langhorne, J. 1765. 1771. 1781. With Johnson's Life added. 1804. 1811.
Poetical Works. Ed. Mrs. Barbauld. 1797.
Poetical Works. To which is prefixed a Life of the Author by Johnson. 1798, 1800. With Johnson's Life, corrected and enlarged by Crowe, W. Bath, 1828.
Poetical Works. With the Life of the Author by Johnson; observations on his writings by Langhorne; and biographical and critical notes by Dyce, A. 1827.
Poetical Works, with a Memoir of the author and an essay on his genius and poems by Brydges, Sir E. (Aldine Poets.) 1830. 1853.
Poems, with Memoir by Thomas, Moy. 1858. 1866. 1894.
Poems. Ed. Stone, C. 1907.
Persian eclogues and odes. 1742. Rptd. 1757 as Oriental eclogues.
Verses to Sir Thomas Hanmer on his edition of Shakespeare's Works. 1743.
Odes on several descriptive and allegoric subjects. 1747.

An Ode occasioned by the death of Mr. Thomson. 1749.
An Ode on the popular superstitions of the Highlands of Scotland considered
as the subject of poetry. 1788. [Published posthumously. The work also
appeared in the Trans. of the Royal Soc. of Edinburgh.]

## Sneyd Davies (1709–1769)

Davies's Poems were never collected. They are to be found in Dodsley's
Collection (1775), vols. V and VI; and in Nichols's Collection (1780), vols. VI
and VII.

## John Dyer

Poems. 1761. 1765.
Grongar Hill. First published in the Miscellaneous Poems and Translations by
several hands of Savage, R. 1726. Rptd. separately, 1727.
The Ruins of Rome. A poem. 1740.
The Fleece. A poem in four books. 1757.

## William Falconer

Poetical Works. Ed. Mitford, J. (Aldine Poets.) 1836 and 1866.

The Shipwreck. A poem in three cantos, by a Sailor. 1762. 2nd edn. 1764;
3rd edn. 1769; 11th edn. 1802.
—— Ed. with a Life by Clarke, J. S. 1804.
—— With Life by Carruthers, R., and illustrations by Foster, B. 1858.
    Friedrich, J. The Shipwreck. A poem by a Sailor. 1762. (Schipper's
    Wiener Beiträge.) Vienna and Leipzig, 1901.

The Demagogue. 1764.
An universal Dictionary of the Marine. 1769, and several later edns., ed. Burney,
W.

## Francis Fawkes (1720–1777)

The Works of Anacreon, Sappho, Bion, Moschus, and Musaeus, translated into
English by a Gentleman of Cambridge. 1760.
Original Poems and Translations. 1761.

## Philip Francis (1708?–1773)

The Odes, Epodes, and Carmen Seculare of Horace in Latin and English. 2 vols.
1743.
The Satires, Epistles, and Art of Poetry of Horace in Latin and English. 2 vols.
1746.
Eugenia. A tragedy. 1752.
Constantine. A tragedy. 1754.

## Richard Glover

Leonidas. A poem. 1737. 5th edn. 1770. Transl. into French and German.
London, or the Progress of Commerce. A poem. 1739.
Admiral Hosier's Ghost. 1740.
Boadicea. A tragedy as it is acted at the Theatre-Royal in Drury Lane. 1753.
Medea. A tragedy. 1761.
The Athenaid. A poem. 1787. [Published posthumously.]
    As to this, see Retrospective Review, vol. II, 1820.

Jason. A tragedy. 1799.
Memoirs by a celebrated literary and political character, from the resignation
of Sir Robert Walpole in 1742 to the establishment of Lord Chatham's
second administration. Written by himself. 1813. [Published by Duppa,
R.]

 An Inquiry concerning the author of the Letters of Junius, with reference
to the Memoirs of a celebrated literary and political character. [By
Duppa, R.] 1814. [Suggesting Glover as the author of the Letters
of Junius.]

### James Grainger (1721?-1766)

The Sugar-Cane. A Poem in four books. 1764.
Poetical Works, with his life. 2 vols. Edinburgh, 1836.

### Matthew Green

The Spleen. An Epistle inscribed to his particular friend, Mr. C. J. (Ed.
Glover, R.) 1737. [Published posthumously.] 2nd edn. 1737; 3rd edn.,
corrected, to which is added some other pieces by the same hand, 1738. Ed.
Aikin, J. 1796.

### Henry Headley (1765-1788)

Poems and other pieces. 1786.
Select Beauties of Ancient English Poetry. With Remarks. 2 vols. 1787.

### John Langhorne (1735-1779)

Poetical Works. 2 vols. 1766. Ed. Langhorne, J. T. 2 vols. 1804.
Plutarch's Lives translated, with notes, by Langhorne, W. and J. 6 vols. 1770.

### Robert Lloyd (1733-1764)

The Actor. A poetical epistle to Bonnell Thornton, Esq. 1760.
Poems. 1762.
Poetical Works. Ed. Kenrick, W. 2 vols. 1774.

### Edward Lovibond (1724-1775)

Poems on several occasions. 1785.

### John Lowe (1750-1798)

Mary's Dream. Printed in Robert Hartley Cromek's Remains of Nithsdale and
Galloway Song. 1810.

### James Merrick (1720-1769)

Poems on sacred subjects. Oxford, 1763.
The Psalms translated or paraphrased in English verse. Reading, 1765.

 Many of his original poems, including The Chameleon, will be found in
Dodsley's Collection.

### William Julius Mickle (1735-1788)

The Lusiad . . . translated from the original Portuguese of Luis de Camões.
1776. 2nd edn. 1778.
Poems, and a Tragedy. 1794.
Poetical Works, with life by Sim, J. 1806.

## Anna, Lady Miller (1741–1781)

Poetical amusements at a villa near Bath. 4 vols. 1775–81.
Letters from Italy. 3 vols. 1776.

## Robert, Earl Nugent (1702–1788)

An Ode on Mr. Pulteney. 1739.
Odes and Epistles. 1739.

## Thomas Russell (1762–1788)

Sonnets and Miscellaneous Poems. Oxford, 1789.

## William Shenstone

Poems on various occasions, written for the entertainment of the author, and printed for the amusement of a few friends prejudiced in his favour. Privately ptd. Oxford, 1737.
The Judgment of Hercules. A poem, inscribed to George Lyttleton, Esq. 1741.
The Schoolmistress. 1742.
Contributions to Dodsley's Collection of Poems, vols. I, III, IV and V. 1748–58.
Works in verse and prose, most of which were never before printed. In two volumes, with decorations. 1764. Vol. III, containing Letters to particular friends, from the year 1739 to 1763. 1769.
(Ed. by Dodsley, R., who added an account of the Leasowes and a character of Shenstone.) 2nd edn., 3 vols., 1765; 5th edn., 3 vols., 1777; 6th edn., 3 vols., 1791.
Essays on Men and Manners. 1802. [First published in vol. II of the Works, 1764.]
Poetical Works. 1812.
—— With Life, critical dissertation, and explanatory notes by Gilfillan, G. Edinburgh, 1854.
Wells, J. E. The Dating of Shenstone's Letters. Anglia, vol. XXXV. Halle, 1912.
*See, also,* bibliography to Chap. XI, sec. II, *post.*

## Christopher Smart

Poems, consisting of his Prize Poems, Odes, Sonnets, and Fables, Latin and English translations; together with many original compositions not included in the quarto edition. To which is prefixed an account of his life and writings. 2 vols. Reading, 1791.
[This edition by no means includes all Smart's poetical works. *See* the bibliography by Gray, G. J., *post.* A Song to David is among the poems omitted from it.]
Carmen cl. Alexandri Pope in S. Caeciliam Latine redditum a Christophero Smart. Cambridge, 1743.
—— Ed. altera. To which is added Ode for Musick on Saint Cecilia's day by C. Smart. Cambridge, 1746.
The Horatian Canons of Friendship. Being the Third Satire of the First Book of Horace imitated. By Ebenezer Pentweazle [*i. e.* C. Smart]. 1750.
On the Eternity of the Supreme Being. (Seatonian Prize Poem for 1750.) Cambridge, 1750. 2nd edn., Cambridge, 1752; 3rd edn., Cambridge, 1756.
On the Immensity of the Supreme Being. (Seatonian Prize Poem for 1751.) Cambridge, 1751. 2nd edn., Cambridge, 1753; 3rd edn., London, 1756.

Poems on several occasions. 1752.
On the Omniscience of the Supreme Being. (Seatonian Prize Poem for 1752.)
Cambridge, 1752. 2nd edn. Cambridge, 1756.
The Hilliad. An epic poem. 1753.
On the Power of the Supreme Being. (Seatonian Prize Poem for 1753.) Cambridge, 1754. 2nd edn. Cambridge, 1758.
On the Goodness of the Supreme Being. (Seatonian Prize Poem for 1755.)
Cambridge, 1756. 2nd edn. Cambridge, 1756.
Hymn to the Supreme Being on recovery from a dangerous fit of illness. 1756.
The Works of Horace translated literally into English prose. 2 vols. 1756.
2nd edn. 1762; 3rd edn. 1770; 6th edn. 1790.
A Song to David. 1763.
Rptd. 1819, 1895; 1898, ed. Tutin, J. R.; 1901, ed. Streatfeild, R. A.
Poems. [Reason and Imagination, etc.] [1763.]
Poems on several occasions. [Munificence and Modesty, etc.] [Probably 1763.]
Ode to the Rt. Hon. the Earl of Northumberland on his being appointed Lord Lieutenant of Ireland. With some other pieces. 1764.
Hannah. An oratorio. [1764.]
A Translation of the Psalms of David. 1765.
A poetical translation of the Fables of Phaedrus, with the Appendix of Gudius. 1765.
The Works of Horace translated into verse. With a prose interpretation for the help of students. 1767.
The Parables of Our Lord and Saviour Jesus Christ done into familiar verse, with occasional applications. 1768.
Abimelech. An oratorio. [1768.]

Browning, R. Parleyings with certain People of Importance in their Day. With Christopher Smart. Poetical Works, vol. II. 1902.
Gosse, E. Smart's Poems. In Gossip in a Library. 1892.
Gray, G. J. Bibliography of the writings of Christopher Smart, with biographical references. (Rptd. from the Bibliographical Society's transactions.) 1903.

### Anna Williams (1706–1783)
Miscellanies in Prose and Verse. 1766.

### Edward Young
#### (1) Collected Editions
Works. 6 vols. 1757–78.
New edn. 1774–8. Revised with a Life by Doran, J. 2 vols. 1854.
Poetical Works. With Life by Mitford, J. (Aldine Poets.) 2 vols. 1834 and 1858.
#### (2) Particular Works
An Epistle to the Right Honourable the Lord Lansdown. 1713.
A Poem on the Last Day. Oxford, 1713. 2nd edn. 1713.
The Force of Religion, or Vanquish'd Love. Illustrated in the story of the Lady Jane Gray. 1714. 2nd edn. 1715; 3rd edn. 1715.
On the late Queen's death and his Majesty's Accession to the Throne. 1714.
A Paraphrase on part of the Book of Job. 1719. 2nd edn. 1719.
Busiris, King of Egypt. A tragedy. 1719.

A Le⁺ter to Mr. Tickell. Occasion'd by the death of the Rt. Hon. Joseph Addison. 1719. 2nd edn. 1719.
The Revenge. A tragedy, as it is acted at the Theatre Royal in Drury Lane. 1721. Ed. Kemble, J. P. 1814.
The Universal Passion. 6 parts. 1725–8. 3rd edn. 1730; 4th edn. 1741.
The Instalment. 1726.
Ocean. An Ode, occasion'd by His Majesty's late royal encouragement of the sea-service. To which is prefix'd an Ode to the King, and a discourse on Ode. 1728.
A Vindication of Providence, or a true estimate of human life. 1728.
Imperium Pelagi. A naval lyrick, written in imitation of Pindar's spirit, occasioned by His Majesty's return, September, 1729, and the succeeding Peace. 1730.
Two Epistles to Mr. Pope concerning the authors of the age. 1730.
The Foreign Address . . . in the character of a Sailor. 1734.
The Complaint, or Night Thoughts on Life, Death, and Immortality. 9 parts. 1742–5. 8th edn. 1749. Transl. into French, 1769. The Complaint and The Consolation. Illustrated by William Blake. 1797.
The Brothers. A Tragedy. Acted at the Theatre Royal in Drury Lane. 1753.
The Centaur not fabulous. 1754. 4th edn. 1786.
Conjectures on original composition in a letter to the Author of Sir Charles Grandison. 1759.
Resignation, in two parts and a postscript to Mrs.******. 1762

(3) Biography and Criticism

Eliot, G. Worldliness and Otherworldliness: the poet Young. Essays. 2nd edn. 1884.
Kind, J. L. Edward Young in Germany. New York, 1906.
Texte, J. Jean Jacques Rousseau and the cosmopolitan spirit in literature. Transl. by Matthews, J. W. 1899. [Young's influence in France.]
Thomas, W. Le poète Edward Young (1683–1765). Paris, 1901.

A. T. B.

## CHAPTER VIII
## JOHNSON AND BOSWELL
### I. Johnson

A bibliography of Samuel Johnson by Cou:tney, W. P., revised by Smith, D. Nichol, was published at Oxford in 1915.

### A. *Collections*
(In chronological order)

The Works of Samuel Johnson, LL.D. Together with his Life, and Notes on his Lives of the Poets. By Hawkins, Sir John. 11 vols. 1787. Vols. xii and xiii (Debates [ed. Chalmers, George], printed for John Stockdale; *see* sec. B, *post*). 1787. Vol. xiv (Miscellaneous Pieces, printed for Stockdale.) 1788. Vol. xv (Miscellaneous Pieces, ed. Gleig, George). 1789.
—— A new edition in twelve volumes. With an Essay on his Life and Genius. By Murphy, Arthur. 1792, 1796, 1801, etc.
—— [edited by Chalmers, A.] 12 vols. 1806, etc.
—— Works, 9 vols.; Debates, 2 vols. (Oxford English Classics.) Oxford, 1825·

—— ed. Lynam, R. 6 vols. 1825.
—— 2 vols. 1850.
—— 16 vols. New York, 1903.
Miscellaneous and Fugitive Pieces. 3 vols. Ed. Davies, T. Vols. I and II
n. d. [1774; ascribed by Boswell to 1773]. Vol. III. 1774.
    The first volume consists wholly of pieces by Johnson. In the second
by far the greater number are his. A few others are in the third.
The Poetical Works of Samuel Johnson, LL.D. Now first collected in one volume
[ed. Kearsley, George]. 1785. New edn., considerably enlarged. 1789.
—— Complete in one volume. A new edition. London and Gainsbrough.
1785.
—— Dublin, 1785.
—— with life by Blagdon, F. W. 1808.
—— ed. Gilfillan, G. Edinburgh, 1855.
—— ed. Ward, T. Methuen. [1905.]
—— ed. Smith, D. Nichol. Oxford. (*In preparation.*)
    Also in The Works of the English Poets, vol. LXXII, 1790; Anderson's
Poets of Great Britain, vol. XI, Edinburgh, 1793; Park's Works of the British
Poets, vol. XXXVII, 1805, and Suppl., vol. VI, 1809; Chalmers's Works of the
English Poets, vol. XVI, 1810.

The Beauties of Johnson: Consisting of Maxims and Observations, Moral,
Critical, and Miscellaneous, accurately extracted from the Works of Dr.
Samuel Johnson, and arranged in alphabetical order, etc. 2 vols. 1782.
7th edn., with biographical anecdotes. One vol. 1787. 8th edn. (with
biographical "augmentations" from Boswell). 1792.
Wit and Wisdom of Samuel Johnson. Selected and arranged by Hill, G. B.
Oxford, 1888.

## B. *Separate Works*

### (In chronological order)

A Voyage to Abyssinia. By Father Jerome Lobo, A Portuguese Jesuit. . . .
With a Continuation of the History of Abyssinia down to the Beginning of
the Eighteenth Century, and Fifteen Dissertations. . . . By Mr. Legrand.
From the French. 1735.
—— To which are added, various other Tracts by the same Author, etc. 1789.
    Also in A General Collection of Voyages and Travels, by Pinkerton,
J., vol. XV, 1814; Cassell's National Library, ed. Morley, H., 1887.
[The History of the Council of Trent, translated from the Italian of Father
Paul Sarpi; with the author's life, and notes etc. from the French.—Pro-
posals issued October, 1738. "Some sheets were printed off, but the design
was dropt." *See* Boswell, ed. Hill, G. B., vol. I, p. 135.]
London: A Poem, In Imitation of the Third Satire of Juvenal. R. Dodsley.
1738. 4th edn. 1739. Also in Dodsley's Collection of Poems, 1748, and
later issues; Two Satires. By Samuel Johnson, A.M., Oxford, 1759; Mis-
cellaneous and Fugitive Pieces, vol. II, 1774.
A Compleat Vindication of the Licensers of the Stage, from the Malicious and
Scandalous Aspersions of Mr. Brooke, Author of Gustavus Vasa. With A
Proposal for making the Office of Licenser more Extensive and Effectual.
By an Impartial Hand. 1739.

Marmor Noftolciense: or an Essay on an Ancient Prophetical Inscription, In Monkish Rhyme, Lately Discover'd near Lynn in Norfolk. By Probus Britanicus. 1739. New edn., with notes and a dedication to Samuel Johnson, LL. D. By Tribunus. 1775. Reprint of edn. of 1739, n. d. [1819 or 1820].

An Account of the Life of Mr. Richard Savage, Son of the Earl Rivers. 1744. 4th edn. 1769.
> Histoires de Richard Savage et de J. Thompson (*i. e.* James Thomson]. Traduites de l'Anglois par M. Le Tourneur. Paris, 1771.
> The Works of Richard Savage, Esq. . . . with an Account of . . . the Author, by Samuel Johnson, LL.D. Vol. 1. 1775. Another edn. 1777. Rptd. in Works of the English Poets, 1781.

An Account of the Life of John Philip Barretier, who was Master of five Languages at the Age of nine Years. 1744. Rptd. from The Gentleman's Magazine.

Miscellaneous Observations on the Tragedy of Macbeth: With Remarks on Sir T. H[anmer]'s Edition of Shakespear. To which is affix'd, Proposals for a New Edition of Shakespear, with a Specimen. 1745.
> [See footnote, *ante*, p. 188, and Courtney and Nichol Smith's Bibliography, p. 18. A copy containing the *Proposals* is in the library of Worcester college, Oxford. The sheet is folded into four, and inserted among advertisements at the conclusion. The bottom half gives two specimen pages, in the small type selected for the edition.]

The Plan of a Dictionary of the English Language; Addressed to the Right Honourable Philip Dormer, Earl of Chesterfield; One of his Majesty's Principal Secretaries of State. 1747.

Prologue and Epilogue, spoken at the opening of the Theatre in Drury-Lane, 1747.
> [The Epilogue was by Garrick.]

The Vanity of Human Wishes. The Tenth Satire of Juvenal, Imitated By Samuel Johnson. 1749. Also in Two Satires, Oxford, 1759; in Dodsley's Collection, and in Miscellaneous and Fugitive Pieces, vol. II, 1774.

Irene: a Tragedy. As it is Acted at the Theatre Royal in Drury-Lane. Dodsley. 1749. Other edns.: (Dublin) 1749, 1754, 1781.

The Rambler. Numb. 1. Price 2d. To be continued on Tuesdays and Saturdays. Tuesday, 20 March, 1749/50.–No. 208. Saturday, 17 [error for 14] March, 1752. [Each number six pages folio.] Collected in 2 (or 4) vols. and issued with the title-page: The Rambler. *Nullius addictus jurare in verba magistri, Quo me cunque rapit tempestas deferor hospes.* Hor. 1751 (some copies 1752, others 1753). Vol. I(-VIII) [superintended by Elphinstone, James]. Edinburgh, 1750–2. 6 vols. [revised by Johnson]. 1752. 11th edn. 1790. Also in Harrison's British Classicks, vol. I, 1796; The British Essayists, ed. Chalmers, A., vols. XIX–XXII, 1802; and other collections.
> *See* Nathan Drake's Essays Illustrative of the Rambler, vol. I, p. 204.
> Thornton, Bonnell. "A Rambler. Number 99999." In the Drury-Lane Journal, No. III, pp. 67–71, 30 January, 1752.

A new Prologue spoken by Mr. Garrick, Thursday, 5 April, 1750. At the Representation of Comus, for the benefit of Mrs. Elizabeth Foster, Milton's granddaughter, and only surviving descendant. 1750.

A Dictionary of the English Language: in which The Words are deduced from their Originals, and Illustrated in their different Significations By Examples from the best Writers. To which are prefixed, A History of the Language, and An English Grammar. By Samuel Johnson, A.M. 2 vols. 1755. 4th edn. (last revised by Johnson), 1773. With numerous corrections and additions . . . by Todd, H. J. 4 vols. 1818. Re-edited by Latham, R. G. 2 vols. 1866–70. And many other edns.

A Dictionary of the English Language . . . abstracted from the Folio Edition. 2 vols. 1756. 5th edn. 1773.

The Prince of Abissinia. A Tale. In Two Volumes. Dodsley. 1759. 6th edn. 1783. The History of Rasselas, Prince of Abissinia. A Tale. 1787. Ed. Hill, G. B. Oxford, 1887.

    Rasselas, Prince of Abyssinia. By Samuel Johnson, LL.D. Being a Facsimile Reproduction of the First Edition published in 1759. In two volumes. With an introduction by Macaulay, James; and a bibliographical list of editions of Rasselas. 1884.

    Rasselas was translated into French (by Baretti, and by others), Italian, German, Dutch, Spanish, Hungarian, Polish, Modern Greek and Bengali.

    Dinarbas: a Tale: being a continuation of Rasselas. [By Cornelia Knight.] 1790.

The Review of A Free Enquiry into the Nature and Origin of Evil. [By Soame Jenyns.] 1759.

The Idler. 2 vols. Newbery. 1761. Published originally in The Universal Chronicle or Weekly Gazette (*v. infra*) from 15 April, 1758, to 5 April, 1760—104 numbers. [In the collected edition Johnson omitted No. 22 and disclaimed in a prefatory note the authorship of Nos. 9, 15, 33, 42, 54, 67, 76, 79, 82, 93, 96, 98.] 3rd edn.; with Additional Essays. 2 vols. 1767. (The additional essays are An Essay on Epitaphs, rptd. from The Gentleman's Magazine; A Dissertation on the Epitaphs written by Pope, from the Universal Visiter; and The Bravery of the English Common Soldiers.) In Harrison's British Classicks, vol. VIII, 1796; The British Essayists, vols. XXXIII–XXXIV, 1802; and other collections.

Three Letters to The Idler. [1761.]

    [Reynolds's three papers, Nos. 76, 79 and 82. This little volume of 20 pages is an offprint from the edition of 1761 and, as is stated in a note in Malone's writing, was specially " taken off " for Johnson for private presentation to Reynolds.]

The Plays of William Shakespeare, 8 vols., with the Corrections and Illustrations of Various Commentators; To which are added Notes by Sam. Johnson. Tonson, etc. 1765. Reissued, 1768. 10 vols., with the Corrections and Illustrations of Various Commentators; To which are added Notes by Samuel Johnson and George Steevens. With an Appendix. 1773. 2nd edn., revised and augmented, 1778; with Supplement, ed. Malone, E., 2 vols., 1780; 3rd edn., revised and augmented by the Editor of Dodsley's Collection of Old Plays, 1785; 4th edn. 1793.

    [Johnson's edition is the basis of the Variorum editions.]

    *See, also,* bibliography to Vol. V, p. 474, *ante.*

Mr. Johnson's Preface To his Edition of Shakespear's Plays. Tonson, etc. 1765.

    [The preface to the edition issued separately, with a special title-page.]

Variorum editions of Shakespeare. (*See* bibliography to Vol. V, pp. 473–475, *ante.*)

    Eighteenth Century Essays on Shakespeare. Ed. Smith, D. Nichol. 1903.

    Johnson on Shakespeare. Essays and Notes with an introduction by Walter Raleigh. 1908.

The False Alarm. 1770. 2nd edn. 1770.

Thoughts on the Late Transactions respecting Falkland's Islands. 1771. 2nd
edn. 1771.
  [Two issues of the 1st edn., with different readings on p. 68: *see* Boswell,
  ed. Hill, G. B., vol. II, p. 135.]
The Patriot. Addressed to the Electors of Great Britain. 1774.
Taxation no Tyranny; An Answer to the Resolutions and Address of the American
Congress. 1775. 4th edn. 1775.
  Political Tracts. Containing: The False Alarm. Falkland's Islands.
  The Patriot; and, Taxation no Tyranny. 1776.
  [All Johnson's political pamphlets were anonymous.]
A Journey to the Western Islands of Scotland. 1775. Many other edns.: 1785,
  1791, etc. French transl. in Nouveau Recueil de Voyages au nord de l'Europe,
  etc. Geneva, 1785.
The Works of the English Poets. With Prefaces, Biographical and Critical.
  By Samuel Johnson. 68 vols. 1779–81. Enlarged edn. 75 vols. 1790.
  Ed. Chalmers, A. 21 vols. 1810
    Johnson's Prefaces are in 10 vols. 1779 (I–IV)–1781 (V–X). [Each
  Preface is paged separately.] Revised and reissued, in different order, as—
The Lives of the most eminent English Poets; with Critical Observations on their
  Works. By Samuel Johnson. 4 vols. 1781. New edn., corrected, 1783;
  with notes, by Cunningham, Peter, 3 vols., 1854; with notes, by Napier, Mrs.
  A., and an introduction by Hales, J. W., 3 vols., 1890; with an introduction
  by Millar, John Hepburn, 3 vols., 1896; with notes and introduction by
  Waugh, A., 6 vols., 1896; edd. Hill, George Birkbeck, and Scott, H. S., 3
  vols., 1905.
    The Six Chief Lives, with Macaulay's Life of Johnson. Ed., with a
    preface, by Arnold, Matthew. 1878.
    Life of Milton. Ed. Firth, C. H. 1888.
    And many other annotated editions of separate lives.
The Principal Additions and Corrections in the third edition of Dr. Johnson's
  Lives of the Poets; collected to complete the second edition. 1783.
Prayers and Meditations, composed by Samuel Johnson, LL.D. and published
  from his manuscripts, by Strahan, George. 1785. 5th edn. 1817; new
  edn., with notes and an introduction by Higgins, Hinchcliffe, and a preface
  by Birrell, Augustine, n. d. [1904].
    Johnsonian Miscellanies. Ed. Hill, G. B. 2 vols. Oxford, 1897. [Vol. I.]
    [Original manuscripts in the library of Pembroke college, Oxford.]
Memoirs of Charles Frederick, King of Prussia . . . with notes and a continuation by Mr. Harrison. . . . 1786. First printed in The Literary Magazine;
  then in Davies's Miscellaneous and Fugitive Pieces, 1774.
Debates in Parliament. [19 Nov., 1740, to 24 Feb., 1743.] By Samuel Johnson,
  LL.D. 2 vols. 1787. Rptd. from The Gentleman's Magazine. [Ed. by
  Chalmers, George: *see* Boswell, ed. Hill, G. B., vol. I, p. 152; commonly said
  to be edited by Stockdale, who was the publisher, and is sometimes confused
  with Percival Stockdale: *see* Boswell, ed. Hill, vol. I, pp. 191, 335, and vol.
  VI, p. 253.] Also 1811, 1825.
A Sermon [on *St. John* xi, 25, 26] written by the late Samuel Johnson for the
  funeral of his wife. Published by Hayes, Samuel. 1788.
Sermons on Different Subjects, left for publication by John Taylor, LL.D.
  Published by Hayes, Samuel. 2 vols. 1788–9. [The second volume has on
  the title: To which is added a Sermon written by Samuel Johnson, LL.D.,
  for the Funeral of his Wife. *See* Boswell, ed. Hill, G. B., vol. III, p. 181.]

The Celebrated Letter from Samuel Johnson, LL.D. to Philip Dormer Stanhope, Earl of Chesterfield; Now first published, With Notes. By James Boswell, Esq. 1790.

A Conversation between His Most Sacred Majesty George III and Samuel Johnson, LL.D. Illustrated with Observations. By James Boswell, Esq. 1790.

An Account of the Life of Dr. Samuel Johnson, from his birth to his eleventh year, written by himself. To which are added, Original Letters to Dr. Samuel Johnson, by Miss Hill Boothby: From the MSS. preserved by the Doctor; and now in Possession of Richard Wright [the editor]. 1805.

Parliamentary Logick: . . . By the Right Hon. William Gerard Hamilton. With an appendix, containing Considerations on the Corn Laws, by Samuel Johnson, LL.D. never before printed. [Ed. Malone, E.] 1808.

A Diary of a Journey into North Wales, in the year 1774; by Samuel Johnson, LL.D. Ed., with illustrative notes, by Duppa, R. 1816.

Letters to and from the late Samuel Johnson, LL.D. To which are added some Poems never before printed. Published from the Original Manuscripts in her possession, by Piozzi, Hester Lynch. 2 vols. 1788.

Original Letters, from . . . Dr. Samuel Johnson, . . . edited by Warner, Rebecca. Bath and London, 1817.

Original Letters of Dr. Samuel Johnson [thirteen in number], communicated by Simeon, Sir John, in Miscellanies of the Philobiblon Society, vol. VI. 1860–1.

Letters of Samuel Johnson, LL.D. Collected and edited by Hill, G. B. 2 vols. Oxford, 1892.

—— Additional Letters. In Johnsonian Miscellanies, ed. Hill, G. B. 1897. [Vol. II.]

### *Wrongly attributed to Johnson*

[There were other writers of the name S. Johnson publishing at the same time— the author of Hurlothrumbo; the president of King's College, New York; and the author of An Essay on Education, a Poem, 1771, An Essay on Woman, a, Poem, 1772, Sensibility, a Poem, 1773, and The Temple of Fashion, a Poem, 1781.]

A Compleat Introduction to the Art of Writing Letters, Universally adapted To all Classes and Conditions of Life. . . . To which is prefixed, A Short but Useful Grammar of the English Language, etc. By S. Johnson. 1758.
[Some of the sentences in the Grammar are taken from the prefatory matter to the Dictionary.]

A History and Defence of Magna Charta. . . . With an introductory discourse, containing a short account of the rise and progress of national freedom. 1769.
[By Samuel Johnson, rector of Corringham.]

The Right of the British Legislature to tax the American Colonies vindicated; and the means of asserting that right proposed. 1774.
[Attributed to Johnson in British Museum catalogue.]

Hypocrisy Unmasked; or, a short inquiry into the religious complaints of our American Colonies. To which is added, a Word on the Laws against Popery in Great Britain and Ireland. 1776.
[Attributed to Johnson in British Museum catalogue.]

The Sixteenth Ode of the Third Book of Horace imitated. With a dedication to the Right Honourable the Lord N[ort]h. 1777.
[Dedication signed S . . . . l J . . . . n.]

The Patriot, A Tragedy. From a Manuscript of the Late Dr. Samuel Johnson, Corrected by Himself. 1785.
[By Joseph Simpson: *see* Boswell, ed. Hill, G. B., vol. III, p. 28.]

## C. *Contributions to Periodicals*

The Gentleman's Magazine.

*Most of the contributions marked as doubtful are ascribed to Johnson by Boswell*

Latin verses Ad Urbanum. (March, 1738.)
Latin verses Ad Richardum Savage. (April.)
Greek and Latin verses to Eliza (Elizabeth Carter). (April.)
Latin verses "to a Lady who spoke in defence of liberty." (April.)
(?) Introduction to "Debates in The Senate of Magna Lilliputia." (June.)
(?) English translation of verses "to Eliza" signed Urbanus. (August.)
To Lady F[irebra]ce at Bury Assizes. (September.)
The Life of Father Paul Sarpi. (November.)
Greek verses "to Birch." (December.)
"To the Reader" prefixed to the collected numbers for 1738.
Introductory letter to Mr. Urban. (January, 1739.)
The Life of Boerhaave. (Jan., Feb., March, April.)
An Appeal to the Publick. (March.)
To the Reader. (May.)
The Life of Admiral Blake. (June, 1740.)
The Life of Sir Francis Drake (Aug., Sept., Oct., Dec., Jan., 1741.)
Epitaph upon Claudy Philips, Musician. (Sept.)
An Essay on Epitaphs. (Dec.)
Some Account of the Life of Barretier. (Dec., and Feb., 1741.)
Preface to collected numbers for 1740.
(?) A Debate upon the Petition of Parliament to Cromwell to assume the Title of King. (February, March, 1741.)
Translation of the Abbé de Guyon's Dissertation on the Amazons. (April.)
Translation of Fontenelle's Panegyric on Dr. Morin, with two notes. (July.)
(?) Translation of the Jests of Hierocles, with introductory note. (September.)
Debates on The Senate of Lilliput. (July–December, and Supplement.)
Preface to collected numbers for 1741.
Essay on the Account of the Conduct of the Duchess of Marlborough. (March, April, May, June, 1742.)
An Account of the Life of Peter Burman. (April.)
(?) Additional Account of the Life of Barretier. (May.)
(?) Essay on the Description of China by Père du Halde. (June.)
(The continuation in July, is clearly not by Johnson.)
The Life of Dr. Sydenham. (December.)
Proposals for printing Bibliotheca Harleiana, with an account of the Harleian Library. (December.)
(?) Abridgment of "Foreign History." (December.)
Debates in The Senate of Lilliput. (January—December, and Supplement.)
Preface to collected numbers for 1742.
Considerations on Crousaz and Warburton. (March, November, 1743.)
Friendship; an Ode. (July.)
The Young Author. (July.)
Ad Lauram parituram Epigramma. (July.)

Letter on the forthcoming Life of Savage. (August.)
Latin translation of Pope's verses on his grotto. (October.)
(?) Advertisement of Bibliotheca Harleiana. (October.)
Proposals for the Harleian Miscellany. (Supplement, end.)
Debates in The Senate of Lilliput. (January–December, and Supplement.)
Preface to collected numbers for 1743.
Debates in the Senate of Lilliput. (Jan.–March, 1744.)
(?) Preface to collected numbers for 1744.
(?) Latin epitaph on Sir Thomas Hanmer, and translation. (May, 1747.)
(?) To Miss —— on her giving the Author a Gold and Silver Net-Work Purse. (May.)
(?) Stella in mourning. (May.)
(?) The Winter's Walk. (May.)
(?) An Ode, beginning "Stern winter now, by spring repress'd." (May.)
(?) To Lyce, an elderly Lady. (May.)

> [The preceding six pieces, each signed * * *, have been included among Johnson's poetical works since 1785. Boswell says "it is supposed" they were by Johnson; Malone suggests Hawkesworth. Some are certainly not by Johnson, and there is no proof of his authorship of any. The Winter's Walk is said to be "by Samuel Johnson, LL.D." in the Scots Magazine for December, 1767. Other pieces from the Magazine about this time are included among his collected poems, but without reason. Twelve pieces, including four of the above, had been definitely ascribed "to S—— J——, LL.D." in Pearch's Collection of Poems, vol. III, 1770.]

Prologue spoken at the opening of Drury Lane Theatre. (October, 1747.)
Life of Roscommon. (May, 1748.)
(?) Foreign History. (November.)
Prologue at the representation of Comus. (April, 1750.)
Life of Edward Cave. (February, 1754.)
Review of Tytler's Vindication of Mary Queen of Scots. (October, 1760.)
Account of the detection of the Imposture in Cock-Lane. (February, 1762.)
Prologue to the Good-Natur'd Man. (February, 1768.)
Prologue to the Word to the Wise. (June, 1777.)
On the Death of Dr. Robert Levet. (August, 1783.)
Letter, with memorandum on the authors of the Ancient Universal History, dated 6 December, 1784 ("the last scrap he ever dictated for the press"). (December, 1784.)
Speech on the subject of an address to the Throne after the expedition to Rochfort in September, 1757, dictated to a friend who delivered it at a certain respectable talking society. (October, 1785.)
Considerations on the case of Dr. Trapp's Sermons abridged by Mr. Cave (written 1739). (July, 1787.)

The General Advertiser.

Letter announcing the representation of Comus for the benefit of Milton's granddaughter. (4 April, 1750.)

The Student, or, The Oxford and Cambridge Monthly Miscellany. Vol. II. 1751.

The Life of Dr. Francis Cheynel (Nos. VII–IX,? April–June, 1751).
   [Signed S. J——N.]

The Adventurer.

Nos. 34, 39, 41, 45, 50, 53, 58, 62, 67, 69, 74, 81, 85, 92, 95, 99, 102, 107, 108, 111, 115, 119, 120, 126, 128, 131, 137, 138. (From 3 March, 1753, to 2 March, 1754.)
  [Signed T. Johnson's sole authorship of Nos. 34, 41, 53, 62—which are letters signed Misagryus or Misargyrus—is doubtful: *see* Boswell, ed. Hill, G. B., vol. I, p. 254. According to Hawkins, Johnson "did not himself write" No. 81 (on "Admirable Crichton"), but "dictated" it to Hawkesworth: *see* Life, 1787, pp. 294, 309.]

The Universal Visiter, and Memorialist.  For the Year 1756.

Further thoughts on Agriculture.  (March.)
Latin verses beginning: Nequicquam Danaen includit ahenea turris.  (March.)
Reflections on the present State of Literature.  (April.)
A Dissertation on the Epitaphs written by Pope.  (May.)
  [All signed **(*i. e.* S. J.); other contributions signed ** are clearly not his.]

The Literary Magazine: or, Universal Review.

  Articles:
Preliminary Address.  (May, 1756.)
An Introduction to the Political State of Great Britain.  (May.)
Observations added to "An authentic Account of the present State of Lisbon."
  (May.)
Observations on the Militia Bill.  (June.)
Observations on his Britannick Majesty's Treaties with her Imperial Majesty
  of all the Russias and the Landgrave of Hesse-Cassel.  (July.)
Observations on the present State of Affairs.  (August.)
Memoirs of the King of Prussia.  (November, December, January, 1757.)
  Reviews:
Birch's History of the Royal Society.  (May, 1756.)
Murphy's Gray's Inn Journal.  (May.)
Warton's Essay on the Writings and Genius of Pope.  (May.)
Hampton's Polybius.  (May.)
Blackwell's Memoirs of the Court of Augustus.  (May.)
Russell's Natural History of Aleppo.  (June.)
Newton's Letters to Bentley containing arguments in proof of a Deity.  (June.)
Borlase's Observations on the Islands of Scilly.  (June.)
Home's Experiments on Bleaching.  (July.)
Browne's Christian Morals.  (July.)
Hales "on distilling sea-water, the great benefit of ventilators, and curing an
  ill-taste in milk."  (July.)
Lucas's Essay on Waters.  (August, September.)
Keith's Catalogue of the Bishops of Scotland.  (August.)
Browne's History of Jamaica.  (August.)
Parkin's Account of the Invasion under William Duke of Normandy.  (August.)
Philosophical Transactions, vol. XLIX.  (August.)
Mrs. Lennox's translation of Sully's Memoirs.  (October.)
Miscellanies by Elizabeth Harrison.  (October.)
Evans's Map and Account of the Middle Colonies in America.  (October.)
Letter on the case of Admiral Byng.  (October.)
Appeal to the people concerning Admiral Byng.  (October.)
Hanway's Eight Days Journey . . . to which is added an essay on Tea.  (November, May, 1757.)
The Cadet.  A military treatise.  (November.)

Further Particulars relating to the case of Admiral Byng. (November.)
The Conduct of the ministry impartially examined. (November.)
A Free Inquiry into the Nature and Origin of Evil. (May, 1757, June, July.)
A Reply to a Paper in the Gazetteer of May 26, 1757 [by Hanway]. (June, 1757.)
The London Chronicle.

Introduction. (1 January, 1757.)
Character of the Rev. Mr. Zachariah Mudge. (2 May, 1769.)
The Universal Chronicle, or Weekly Gazette.

The Idler, from 15 April, 1758, to 5 April, 1760.
Advertisement against reprinting the Idler without leave. (5 January, 1759.)
The Gazetteer.

Three letters on the plans for Black-Friars bridge. (1, 8, 15 December, 1759.)
The Critical Review.

Review of Graham's Telemachus, a Mask. (April, 1763.)
Review of Grainger's Sugar-Cane. (October, 1764.)
Review of Goldsmith's Traveller. (December.)
The London Magazine.

Elegy on the Death of Mr. Levet. (September, 1783.)
["Incorrect copies of this effusion of the most friendly regard have been distributed; that which you will now receive, is genuine," p. 229.]

The Morning Chronicle.

Communication showing that a passage in The Rambler, No. 85, did not favour suicide. (May 29, 1782.)
(*See* Gentleman's Magazine, February, 1786, pp. 93-5.)

D. *Contributions to Books: Assistance to other Writers*
A Miscellany of Poems By several Hands. Publish'd by J. Husbands, A.M., Fellow of Pembroke-College, Oxon. Oxford, 1731.
Messia (pp. 111-117).
["The Translation of Mr. Pope's Messiah was deliver'd to his Tutor as a College Exercise, by Mr. Johnson, a Commoner of Pembroke-College in Oxford, and 'tis hoped will be no Discredit to the excellent Original." Preface.]
The Works of Dr. Thomas Sydenham, newly made English from the original Latin. By John Swan, M.D. 1742.
The prefatory Life of Sydenham, printed also in The Gentleman's Magazine.
A Medicinal Dictionary. By Robert James, M.D. 3 vols. 1743-5.
Dedication to Dr. Mead.
["I helped in writing the proposals for his Dictionary, and also a little in the Dictionary itself." *See* Boswell, ed. Hill, G. B., vol. III, p. 22.]
Catalogus Bibliothecæ Harleianæ. 1743-4.
An Account of the Harleian Library, vol. I, already printed in Proposals for Printing Bibliotheca Harleiana.
Preface to vol. III.
Proposals for printing the Harleian Miscellany, prefixed to vol. III.
The Harleian Miscellany. Vol. I. 1744.
Introduction, afterwards entitled An Essay on the Origin and Importance of small Tracts and Fugitive Pieces.

Boulter's Monument. A Panegyrical Poem, sacred to the Memory of that great and excellent Prelate and Patriot, Dr. Hugh Boulter, late Lord-Archbishop of Ardmagh. [By Madden, Samuel.] Dublin, 1745.

> "Castigated" by Johnson at the author's request: see Boswell, ed. Hill, G. B., vol. I, p. 318.

The Preceptor: containing A General Course of Education. Dodsley. 1748.

> Vol. I. Preface.
> Vol. II. The Vision of Theodore, the Hermit of Teneriffe. The Picture of Human Life: from the Greek of Cebes (see Monthly Review, March, 1790, p. 282).

An Essay on Milton's Use and Imitation of the Moderns, in his Paradise Lost. [By Lauder, William.] 1750.

> Preface and Postscript.

A Letter to the Reverend Mr. Douglas, occasioned by his Vindication of Milton. By William Lauder. 1751.

> Beginning dictated by Johnson.

The Female Quixote: or, the Adventures of Arabella. By Charlotte Lennox 1752.

> Dedication to the Earl of Middlesex.

Shakespear Illustrated. By the Author of the Female Quixote. 1753.

> Dedication to the Earl of Orrery.

Familiar Letters and Poems on several occasions. By Mary Masters. 1755.

> ["Mrs. Masters, the poetess, whose volumes he revised, and, it is said, illuminated here and there with a ray of his own genius." Boswell, ed. Hill, G. B., vol. IV, p. 246.]

An Account of an Attempt to ascertain the Longitude at Sea, by an Exact Theory of the Variation of the Magnetical Needle. . . . By Zachariah Williams 1755.

> [Written for Williams by Johnson; with an Italian translation, printed on the right-hand pages, by Baretti. In the Bodleian copy, which was presented by Johnson, there are three notes in Johnson's handwriting, and an unidentified newspaper cutting about Williams, evidently written by Johnson.]

Christian Morals: by Sir Thomas Browne, of Norwich, M.D. With a Life of the Author, by Samuel Johnson; and explanatory notes. 1756.

An Introduction to the Game of Draughts. By William Payne. 1756.

> Dedication to the Earl of Rochford; and Preface.

A New Dictionary of Trade and Commerce. By Richard Rolt. 1756.

> Preface.

Designs of Chinese Buildings, Furniture, Dresses, Machines, Utensils, etc. By William Chambers. 1757.

> "The first two Paragraphs." See Boswell, ed. Hill, G. B., vol. I, p. 21; cf. vol. IV, p. 188.

The Evangelical History of our Lord Jesus Christ, harmonized, explained, and illustrated, etc. By a Society of Gentlemen. [1757.]

> Dedication to The Lords Spiritual and Temporal and Commons.
> [Johnson's authorship of this Dedication was denied by Boswell, ed. Hill, G. B., vol. IV, p. 383. But see Anderson's Life of Johnson, 1815, pp. 257–8.]

New Tables of Interest. By John Payne. 1758.

> Preface.

Stenography; or, Short-hand Improved. . . . By John Angell. n.d. [?1758].

(?) Dedication to the Duke of Richmond.

(?) Preface.

["I remember one, Angel, who came to me to write for him a Preface or Dedication to a book upon short-hand." Boswell, ed. Hill, G. B., vol. II, p. 224. Whether it was the Dedication or the Preface that Johnson supplied, it cannot have been printed as he wrote it, or dictated it.]

The Greek Theatre of Father Brumoy, translated by Mrs. C. Lennox. 3 vols. 1759.

> Translation of A Dissertation on the Greek Comedy, and The General Conclusion of the Book.

The World displayed; or, a Curious Collection of Voyages and Travels, selected from the Writers of all Nations. 20 vols. 1759–61.

> Introduction, vol. I.

A Dictionary of the English and Italian Languages. By Giuseppe Baretti. 2 vols. 1760.

> Dedication.

> > Baretti, G. An Account of the Manners and Customs of Italy. 1766.
> > —— A Journey from London to Genoa. 2 vols. 1770.
> > —— Discours sur Shakespeare et sur Monsieur de Voltaire. 1777.
> > Collison-Morley, L. Giuseppe Baretti; with an account of his literary friendships and feuds. 1909. (Bibliography.)

An Address of the Painters to George III on his Accession to the Throne of these Kingdoms. 1760.

> Written by Johnson: see Boswell, ed. Hill, G. B., vol. I, p. 352.

Proceedings of the Committee appointed to manage the contributions begun at London, December 18, 1759, for cloathing French Soldiers, Prisoners of War. 1760.

> Introduction.

The English Works of Roger Ascham. With notes and observations, and the author's life. By James Bennet. [1761.]

> Dedication to the Earl of Shaftesbury; and the Life of Ascham.

Thoughts on the Coronation of his present Majesty King George the Third. By John Gwynn. 1761.

> "Corrections and Improvements." See Boswell, ed. Hill, G. B., vol. I, pp. 21, 361.

A complete System of Astronomical Chronology. . . . By John Kennedy. 1762.

> Dedication; and concluding paragraph.

Catalogue of the Artists' Exhibition. 1762.

> Preface. See Boswell, ed. Hill, G. B., vol. I, p. 367.

Jerusalem Delivered, an heroic poem; translated . . . by John Hoole. 1763.

> Dedication to the Queen.

The Poetical Calendar. Containing a Collection of scarce and valuable Pieces of Poetry: with Variety of Originals and Translations, by the most eminent hands. Written and Selected by Francis Fawkes, M.A., and William Woty. In Twelve Volumes. 1763.

> Some Account of the Life and Writings of Mr. William Collins. (Vol. XII. For December.)

The Traveller; or, a Prospect of Society. 1764.

> Ll. 420, 429–434, 437–8. See Boswell, ed. Hill, G. B., vol. II, p. 6.

Reliques of Ancient English Poetry. [Edited by Percy.] 3 vols. 1765.

> Dedication to the Countess of Northumberland [partly by Johnson:

*see* Anderson's Life of Johnson, 1815, p. 309, and G. B. Hill's paper on Boswell's Proof-sheets in Johnson Club Papers, 1899, p. 69.]

Miscellanies in Prose and Verse. By Anna Williams. 1766.

    Advertisement.

    Several Poems, including The Ant.

    The Fountains: A Fairy Tale. [Prose.]

    ["Most of the pieces in this volume have evidently received additions from his superiour pen." Boswell, ed. Hill, G. B., vol. II, p. 26.]

London and Westminster Improved, Illustrated by Plans. . . . By John Gwynn. 1766.

    Dedication to the King.

A Treatise describing and explaining the construction and use of new celestial and terrestrial globes. By George Adams. 1766.

    Dedication to the King.

The Good-Natur'd Man; a Comedy. 1768.

    Prologue.

The Deserted Village. 1770.

    The last four lines. *See* Boswell, ed. Hill, G. B., vol. II, p. 7.

A Dictionary of Ancient Geography. . . . By Alexander Macbean. 1773.

    Preface.

Easy Phraseology, for the use of Young Ladies, who intend to learn the colloquial part of the Italian Language. By Joseph Baretti. 1775.

    Preface.

The Lusiad. Translated by William Julius Mickle. 1775.

    Sentence in introduction. *See* Boswell, ed. Hill, G. B., vol. IV, p. 251.

Occasional Papers by the late William Dodd, LL.D.

    Suppressed, but rptd., from one of the few undestroyed copies, in The Life of Samuel Johnson (attributed to Cooke), published by Kearsley in 1785, pp. 130–140. The pamphlet contained, besides editorial matter, Dr. Dodd's Account of Himself; a Declaration inclosed by Dodd in a letter to a friend; his Letter to the Lord Chancellor; his Letter to the Earl of Mansfield; his petition to the King; Mrs. Dodd's petition to the Queen; and Observations on the propriety of pardoning Dodd, sent by Johnson to the public papers. All were written by Johnson, except Dodd's Account of Himself, which he revised.

    Johnson wrote also Dodd's Speech to the Recorder of London; a petition from the City of London, which "they mended"; and Dodd's last solemn Declaration. *See* Boswell, ed. Hill, G. B., vol. III, pp. 141, etc.

The Convict's Address to his Unhappy Brethren; Being a Sermon preached by the Rev. Dr. Dodd, Friday, June 6, 1777, in the Chapel of Newgate.

    [Johnson marked for Boswell "such passages as were added by Dr. Dodd." *See* Boswell, ed. Hill, G. B., vol. III, p. 142. Several issues, from London and provincial presses, *e. g.* Salisbury and Newcastle-upon-Tyne, with varying titles.]

A Commentary, with Notes, on the Four Evangelists and the Acts of the Apostles, etc. By Zachary Pearce. 1777.

    Dedication to the King; and Additions to Pearce's autobiography.

Seven Discourses delivered in the Royal Academy by the President [Sir Joshua Reynolds]. 1778.

    Dedication to the King.

Memoirs of Garrick. By Thomas Davies. 1780.

    The first two sentences.

An Enquiry into the Authenticity of the Poems ascribed to Ossian. With a Reply to Mr. Clark's Answer. By W. Shaw. 1782.
> Appendix, containing A Reply to Mr. Clark.

The Village. 1783.
> Lines 15–18 and 20; and general revision. *See* Boswell, ed. Hill, G. B.,' vol. IV, p. 175.

E. *Biography and Personalia*<br>(In chronological order)

The Race. By Mercurius Spur, Esq. 1764. 2nd edn. 1766.
> [By Cuthbert Shaw: see Boswell, ed. Hill, G. B., vol. II, p. 31, and Monthly Review, April, 1766, p. 321.]

Johnsoniana: or, a Collection of Bon Mots, etc. By Dr. Johnson, and Others. Together with the Choice Sentences of Publius Syrus. 1776.

—— A new edition, Considerably enlarged and improved; being the only Jest Book extant, proper to be read in families, in which no obscenity, or profane oath is to be found. 1777.

Ode, by Dr. Samuel Johnson, to Mrs. Thrale, upon their supposed approaching nuptials. 1784.

A Biographical Sketch of Dr. Samuel Johnson. In The Gentleman's Magazine for December, 1784. Signed T. T. (*i. e.* Thomas Tyers).

—— Published separately. 1785.

An authentic copy of Dr. Johnson's Will, and the Ceremonial of Dr. Johnson's Funeral—communicated by Sir John Hawkins. In The Gentleman's Magazine for December, 1784.

An Account of the Writings of Dr. Samuel Johnson, including some Incidents of his Life. In The European Magazine, December, 1784, and January–April, 1785.

Johnsoniana [by George Steevens]. In The European Magazine for January, 1785.

The Life of Samuel Johnson, LL.D. With Occasional Remarks on his Writings, an Authentic Copy of his Will, and a Catalogue of his Works. To which are added Some Papers written by Dr. Johnson, in behalf of a late unfortunate Character, never before published. Kearsley. 1785.

—— Dublin, 1785.
> [The Preface is dated Dec. 28, 1784. The authorship is attributed to William Cooke, a member of the Essex Head Club. *See* Nichols, Illustrations of Lit. Hist., vol. VII, p. 467.]

—— The second edition, with considerable additions and corrections. To which is added, Johnsoniana; or, a selection of Dr. Johnson's Bon-Mots, Observations, &c., most of which were never before published. 1785.

A Catalogue of the valuable Library of Books, Of the late learned Samuel Johnson, Esq; LL.D. deceased; Which will be Sold by Auction, (By Order of the Executors) By Mr. Christie, At his Great Room in Pall Mall, On Wednesday, February 16, 1785, and three following days.

—— Fac-Simile of the Sale Catalogue. . . . Reprinted for the Meeting of the Johnson Club at Oxford, June 11, 1892.

Memoirs of the Life and Writings of the late Dr. Samuel Johnson; containing Many valuable Original Letters, and several Interesting Anecdotes both of his Literary and Social Connections. The whole authenticated by living evidence. 1785.
> [Apparently by William Shaw, whose share in the Ossian controversy, in which he had Johnson's assistance, is described fully.]

The Journal of a Tour to the Hebrides, with Samuel Johnson, LL.D. 1785.
*See* Boswell.

Dr. Johnson's Table Talk: or, Conversations of the late Samuel Johnson, L.L.D.
on a variety of useful and entertaining subjects. (Arranged in Alphabetical
Order, after the manner of Selden's Table Talk.) 1785.
["Compiled by Mr. [Stephen] Jones." Anderson, Life of Johnson, 1815,
p. 625.]

An Ode on the Much lamented Death of Dr. Samuel Johnson. Written the 18th
December, 1784. n. d. [1785].

Elegy to the memory of Doctor Samuel Johnson; By Thomas Hobhouse, Esq.
1785.

Verses on the Death of Dr. Samuel Johnson. 1785.
[By Thomas Percy, nephew of the bishop.]

Johnson's Laurel: or, contest of the poets; a poem. 1785.

Anecdotes of the late Samuel Johnson, LL.D. during the last Twenty Years of
his Life. By Hesther Lynch Piozzi. 1786. 4th edn. 1786.

An Essay on the Life, Character, and Writings, of Dr. Samuel Johnson. By
Joseph Towers, L.L.D. 1786.
[Also an issue without the author's name on the title-page.]

A Poetical Review of the Literary and Moral Character of the late Samuel Johnson, L.L.D., with Notes. By John Courtenay, Esq. 1786. 3rd edn. 1786.

A Monody on the much lamented Death of Samuel Johnson, LL.D. 1786.

A Poetical Epistle from the Ghost of Dr. Johnson, to his four friends: the Rev.
Mr. Strahan, James Boswell, Esq., Mrs. Piozzi, J. Courtenay, Esq., M. P.
From the original Copy in the Possession of the Editor. 1786.

Anecdotes of the Learned Pig. With Notes, critical and explanatory; and
Illustrations, from Bozzy, Piozzi, &c. 1786.

The Life of Samuel Johnson, LL.D. By Sir John Hawkins, Knt. 1787. 2nd
edn. revised and corrected. 1787.

The Olla Podrida [a periodical, conducted by Thomas Monro, Magdalen college,
Oxford]. No. 13 (9 June, 1787) on Johnson, written by George Horne,
President of Magdalen, afterwards bishop of Norwich.

More last words of Dr. Johnson. Consisting of important Anecdotes, and a curious Letter from a Medical Gentleman. . . . By Francis Barber. 1787.
[By "a Mr. *Francis*, who had been barber to the Doctor."]

The Witticisms, Anecdotes, Jests, and Sayings, of Dr. Samuel Johnson . . .
collected from Boswell . . . and other Gentlemen. . . . And a full
Account of Dr. Johnson's Conversation with the King. To which is added
a great Number of Jests, in which the most distinguished wits of the present
Century bore a Part. By J. Merry, Esq., of Pembroke College. 1791.
Also 1793 and 1797.

A Dialogue between Dr. Johnson and Mrs. Knowles. In The Gentleman's
Magazine. June, 1791. Rptd. separately 1799.

The Life of Samuel Johnson, LL.D. By James Boswell, Esq. 1791.
*See* Boswell.

The Character of Doctor Johnson. With illustrations from Mrs. Piozzi, Sir
John Hawkins, and Mr. Boswell. 1792.
["Written soon after the Publication of his Lives of the Poets."]

An Essay on the Life and Genius of Samuel Johnson, LL.D. By Arthur Murphy,
Esq. 1792. (Preface to edition; published separately.)

An unfinished Discourse by Reynolds, dealing with Johnson's influence, printed
in The Works of Reynolds, ed. Malone, Preface, vol. I. 1797.

Two Dialogues by Reynolds in imitation of Johnson's style of conversation. Privately printed [for Lady Thomond]. 1816.
    A paper by Reynolds on Johnson's character, printed in Leslie and Taylor's Life of Reynolds, vol. II, 1865.
The Life of Samuel Johnson, LL.D., with Critical Observations on his Works. By Robert Anderson, M.D. 1795. 3rd edn., enlarged. 1815.
Dr. Johnson's Table-Talk: containing Aphorisms on Literature, Life, and Manners; with Anecdotes of Distinguished Persons. 1798. 2 vols. 1807.
    The Table Talk of Samuel Johnson, LL.D., comprising his most interesting remarks and observations. Collected by James Boswell, Esq., F. R. S. 2 vols. 1818.
Narrative of what passed in the visits paid by J. Hoole to Dr. Johnson, in his last illness. By John Hoole. In The European Magazine, September, 1799.
An Account of the Life of Dr. Samuel Johnson, from his birth to his eleventh year, written by himself. 1805.
    See sec. B, ante.
    Anecdotes, references, etc., by contemporaries in Nichols's Literary Anecdotes, vol. II, p. 550; vol. V, p. 15; vol. IX, p. 778, etc. (cf. Gentleman's Magazine, Dec., 1784), and Illustrations, vols. IV–VIII, passim; European Magazine, Oct. 1799 (by Lady Knight), etc.; Seward's Anecdotes of Distinguished Persons, 1795, and Biographiana, 1799; Mant's Memoirs of Thomas Warton, 1802; Wooll's Memoirs of Joseph Warton, 1806; Cumberland's Memoirs, 1807; Pennington's Memoirs of Mrs. Carter, 1808; Percival Stockdale's Memoirs, 1809; Northcote's Memoirs of Reynolds, 1813; Beloe's Sexagenarian, 1817; Lætitia Hawkins's Memoirs, 1824; Joseph Cradock's Literary Memoirs, 1828; J. T. Smith's Nollekens and his Times, 1828 (ed. Gosse, E., 1895); Roberts's Memoirs of Hannah More, 1834; Madame D'Arblay's Memoirs of Dr. Burney, 1832, and Diary and Letters, 1842; Prior's Life of Malone, 1860; Autobiography of Mrs. Piozzi, ed. Hayward, A., 1861; Diary of William Windham, 1866; Croker's Correspondence, 1884; Letters of Horace Walpole, Cowper, etc.
Johnsoniana; or, Supplement to Boswell. Edited by Croker, J. W. 1836.
A Diary of a Visit to England in 1775. By an Irishman [Dr. Thomas Campbell]. With Notes by Samuel Raymond, M.A., Prothonotary of the Supreme Court of New South Wales. Sydney, 1854.
    On the authenticity of this Diary, see The Edinburgh Review, October 1859, and Boswell, ed. Hill, G. B., vol. II, p. 338.
    [Campbell, Thomas.] A Philosophical Survey of the South of Ireland, in a series of Letters to John Watkinson, M.D. 1777.
Unpublished Episodes in the Life of Dr. Johnson. By Jewitt, Llewellynn. The Gentleman's Magazine. December, 1878.
Johnsoniana. Newly collected and edited by Napier, Robina. 1884.
Johnsonian Miscellanies. Arranged and edited by Hill, George Birkbeck. 2 vols. 1897.
The Reades of Blackwood Hill and Dr. Johnson's Ancestry. By Reade, A. L. 1906.
Johnsonian Gleanings. By Reade, A. L. Part I, 1909. Part II, 1912.
Bi-Centenary of the Birth of Dr. Samuel Johnson. Commemoration Festival at Lichfield, September 15th to 19th, 1909. Reports . . . edited by Raby, J. T. 1909.
    [Contains hitherto unpublished material.]
Doctor Johnson and Mrs. Thrale: including Mrs. Thrale's unpublished journal of the Welsh tour made in 1774 and much hitherto unpublished correspond-

ence of the Streatham coterie.   By Broadley, A. M.   With an introductory
essay by Seccombe, T.   1910.

### F.   *Contemporary Criticism*
### (In chronological order)

*In addition to the books or pamphlets noted below, there are the notices and reviews
in the periodicals, such as The Gentleman's Magazine, The London Magazine,
The Monthly Review, The Edinburgh Review, 1755–6, The Annual Register,
and The Critical Review.*

An Essay on Tragedy, with a Critical Examen of Mahomet and Irene.   1749.

A Letter from a friend in England to Mr. [John] Maxwell . . . with a character
of Mr. Johnson's English Dictionary lately published, and Mr. Maxwell's
Justification of himself. . . .   Dublin, 1755.

A Poetical Epistle to Mr. Samuel Johnson, A. M.   By Mr. Murphy.   1760.

A Review of Dr. Johnson's New Edition of Shakespeare: In which the Ignorance,
or Inattention, of that Editor is exposed, and the Poet defended from the
Persecution of his Commentators.   By W. Kenrick.   1765.

An Examination of Mr. Kenrick's Review.   [By James Barclay.]   1766.

A Defence of Mr. Kenrick's Review. . . .   By a Friend.   [R. R.—? W. Kenrick.]   1766.

The Sale of Authors, A Dialogue, In Imitation of Lucian's Sale of Philosophers.
1767.
    [By Archibald Campbell.]

Lexiphanes, A Dialogue.   Imitated from Lucian, and suited to the present Times.
    . . .   Being An attempt to restore the English Tongue to its ancient Purity,
And to correct, as well as expose, the affected Style, hard Words, and absurd
Phraseology of many late Writers, and particularly of Our English Lexiphanes,
the Rambler.   1767.   [By Archibald Campbell.]   3rd edn.   1783.

Prose on Several Occasions.   By George Colman.   Vol. II.   1787.
    [Contains Letter from Lexiphanes, dated 4 December, 1770; and A
Sketch of Dr. Johnson, signed Chiaro Oscuro.   London Packet, 22 December,
1775.]

A Letter to Samuel Johnson, LL.D.   1770.   [By Wilkes.]

The Crisis.   In answer to The False Alarm.   1770.

The Constitution Defended, and Pensioner Exposed; in remarks on The False
Alarm.   1770.
    [By John Scott, of Amwell.]

A Refutation of a Pamphlet called Thoughts on the late Transactions respecting
Falkland's Islands.   In a Letter addressed to the Author, and dedicated to
Dr. Samuel Johnson.   1771.

Remarks on the Patriot &c.   [By John Scott, of Amwell.]   1775.

An Answer to a Pamphlet, entitled Taxation no Tyranny.   Addressed to the
Author, and to Persons in Power.   1775.

Tyranny Unmasked.   An Answer to a Late Pamphlet, entitled Taxation no
Tyranny.   1775.

Taxation, Tyranny.   Addressed to Samuel Johnson, L.L.D.   1775.

The Pamphlet, entitled, Taxation no Tyranny, candidly considered, and it's
arguments, and pernicious doctrines, exposed and refuted.   n.d. [?1775].

Resistance no Rebellion: in answer to Doctor Johnsons Taxation no Tyranny.
1775.

A Defence of the Resolutions and Address of the American Congress, in reply
to Taxation no Tyranny.   By the Author of Regulus.   n.d. [?1775].

A Letter to Dr. Samuel Johnson; occasioned by his late political publications. . . . 1775.

    [By J. Towers.]

Remarks on a Voyage to the Hebrides, in a Letter to Samuel Johnson, LL.D. 1775.

A Letter to Dr. Samuel Johnson, on His Journey to the Western Isles. By Andrew Henderson. n.d.[1775].

A Second Letter to Dr. Samuel Johnson, in which his wicked and opprobrious invectives are shewn &c. n.d. [1775].

A Journey to the Highlands of Scotland. With Occasional Remarks on Dr. Johnson's Tour: By a Lady [Mary Ann Hanway]. n.d. [?1776].

An Essay upon the King's Friends, with an account of some discoveries made in Italy, and found in a Virgil, concerning the Tories. To Dr. S——l J——n. 1776.

Remarks on Dr. Samuel Johnson's Journey to the Hebrides. . . . By Donald M'Nicol, Minister of Lismore in Argyleshire. 1779. Rptd. 1817.

Remarks on Johnson's Life of Milton. To which are added Milton's Tractate on Education and Areopagitica. 1780.

    [By Archdeacon Francis Blackburne.]

A Cursory Examination of Dr. Johnson's Strictures on the Lyric Performances of Gray. 1781.

Deformities of Dr. Samuel Johnson. Selected from his Works. 1782.

    [By John Callander, of Craigforth.]

Remarks on Dr. Johnson's Life, and Critical Observations on the Works of Mr. Gray. 1782.

    [By "William Tindal"—British Museum Catalogue.]

Remarks on Doctor Johnson's Lives of the most eminent English Poets. By a Yorkshire Freeholder. 1782.

Observations on Dr. Johnson's Life of Hammond. 1782.

    [By William Beville. *See* Anderson's Life, 1815, p. 401, and Gentleman's Magazine, 1822, Part 2, pp. 188 and 278.]

A Critical Review of the Works of Dr. Samuel Johnson, containing A particular Vindication of several eminent Characters. 1783.

    [By John Callander.]

A Criticism on the Elegy written in a Country Church-Yard. Being a continuation of Dr. J——n's Criticism on the Poems of Gray. 1783. 2nd edn. 1810.

    [By John Young, professor of Greek in the university of Glasgow.]

An Inquiry into some Passages in Dr. Johnson's Lives of the Poets: Particularly his Observations on Lyric Poetry, and the Odes of Gray. By R. Potter. 1783.

A Dialogue between Dr. Johnson and Dr. Goldsmith, in the Shades, relative to the former's Strictures on the English Poets, particularly Pope, Milton, and Gray. 1785.

Devotional Poetry Vindicated, in some Occasional Remarks on the late Dr. Samuel Johnson's animadversions upon that subject in his Life of Waller. . . . By Daniel Turner. Oxford [1785].

The Life of Isaac Watts. By Samuel Johnson, LL.D. With notes, containing animadversions and additions [by Samuel Palmer]. 1785.

Essay on the Style of Dr. Samuel Johnson. By Robert Burrowes. In Transactions of the Royal Irish Academy, vol. 1. 1787.

Two Dialogues; containing a comparative view of the Lives, Characters, and Writings, of Philip, the late Earl of Chesterfield, and Dr. Samuel Johnson. 1787.

    [By William Hayley.]

An Unfinished Letter to the Right Honourable William Pitt, concerning the New Dictionary of the English Language. By Herbert Croft. 1788.

The Art of Criticism; as exemplified in Dr. Johnson's Lives of the Most Eminent English Poets. 1789.

    [By Robert Potter.]

A Critical Enquiry into the Moral Writings of Dr. Samuel Johnson. . . . To which is added an Appendix containing A Dialogue between Boswell and Johnson in the Shades. By Attalus. 1802.

    [By William Mudford, whose name is given in the edition of 1803.]

### G. *Later Criticism, Biography, etc.*

Bailey, John. Dr. Johnson and his Circle. 1913.

Carlyle, Thomas. Essay on Boswell's Life of Johnson. Fraser's Magazine, May, 1832.

—— On Heroes, etc. (The Hero as Man of Letters.) May, 1840.

Chalmers, Alexander. Essays on the Rambler and Idler. The British Essayists, vols. XIX, XXXIII. 1802.

De Quincey, Thomas. On Johnson's Life of Milton. Works, ed. Masson, D., vol. IV. 1859.

Dobson, Austin. Johnson's Library. Eighteenth-Century Vignettes. Second series. 1894.

—— Dr. Johnson's Haunts and Habitations. Introduction to Boswell, ed. Glover, A., 1901. Rptd. in Side-Walk Studies, 1902.

Drake, Nathan. Essays illustrative of The Rambler, Adventurer, and Idler. 2 vols. 1809.

Grant, Lieut.-Col. F. Life of Samuel Johnson. With a bibliography by Anderson, J. P. (Great Writers.) 1887.

Hill, George Birkbeck. Dr. Johnson: His Friends and His Critics. 1878.

—— Footsteps of Dr. Johnson (Scotland). 1890.

    *See, also*, Rasselas, Lives of the Poets, Letters of Johnson, Johnsonian Miscellanies, Johnson Club Papers, and Boswell.

Hutton, W. H. The Religion of Dr. Johnson. Burford Papers. 1905.

Johnson Club Papers by Various Hands. 1899.

Macaulay, Lord. Essay on Boswell's Life of Johnson, edited by Croker, J. W. The Edinburgh Review. 1831.

—— Samuel Johnson. Encyclopædia Britannica. 1856.

Murray, Sir James A. H. The Evolution of English Lexicography. (Romanes lecture.) 1900.

Nichols, John. The Rise and Progress of the Gentleman's Magazine . . . being a prefatory introduction to the general index of that work from 1787 to 1818. 1821.

Raleigh, Sir Walter. Samuel Johnson. (Leslie Stephen lecture.) 1907.

—— Johnson on Shakespeare. 1908.

—— Six Essays on Johnson. 1910.

Scott, Sir Walter. Life of Johnson. (Novelist's Library.) 1821.

Stephen, Sir Leslie. Samuel Johnson. (English Men of Letters.) 1878.

—— Art. on Johnson in D. of N. B., vol. XXX. 1892.

Timmins, S. Dr. Johnson in Birmingham. (Transactions of the Birmingham and Midland Institute, Archaeological Section, 1876.) 1880.

Welsh, C. A Bookseller of the Last Century. Being some Account of the Life of John Newbery, etc. 1885.

Wheatley, H. B. Dr. Johnson as a Bibliographer. (Transactions of the Bibliographical Society, vol. VIII.) 1907.
White, T. Holt. A Review of Johnson's Criticism on the Style of Milton's English Prose. 1818.

## II. Boswell

### A. *Works separately published*

An Elegy on the Death of an Amiable Young Lady. With an Epistle from Menalcas to Lycidas. To which are prefixed three critical recommendatory letters. Edinburgh, 1761.
An Ode to Tragedy. By a Gentleman of Scotland. Edinburgh, MDCLXI (error for 1761).
The Cub at Newmarket: a tale. 1762.
A Collection of Original Poems, by the Rev. Mr. Blacklock, and other Scotch Gentlemen. Vol. II. Edinburgh, 1762.
    [Boswell had a share in editing this volume, to which he contributed.]
Critical Strictures on the new Tragedy of Elvira, written by David Malloch. Flexney, 1763.
    [By Boswell, Andrew Erskine, and George Dempster.]
Letters between The Honourable Andrew Erskine, and James Boswell, Esq. Flexney, 1763. Ed. Hill, G. B. 1879. Selection, in Letters of Boswell to Temple. 1857 and 1908.
Dorando, A Spanish Tale. London and Edinburgh, 1767.
The Essence of the Douglas Cause. To which is subjoined, Some Observations on a Pamphlet lately published, intitled, Considerations on the Douglas Cause. 1767.
    Long extracts are given in the Scots Magazine, Nov., Dec., 1767, and Nov., 1768.
—— Observations on the Douglas Cause in General; . . . In a Letter to a Noble Lord, From a Gentleman in ****. With The Essence of the Douglas Cause. 1769.
    For the letter by Francis Douglas, *see* Notes and Queries, Sept., 1861, p. 222.

*The following, except where otherwise noted, were published
with Boswell's name:*

An Account of Corsica, The Journal of a Tour to that Island; and Memoirs of Pascal Paoli. Glasgow, 1768. 3rd edn., corrected. 1769.
British Essays in favour of the Brave Corsicans: by several hands. Collected and published by James Boswell, Esq. 1769. [Preface dated 15 October, 1768.]
The Decision of the Court of Session upon the question of Literary Property; in the cause John Hinton of London, Bookseller, Pursuer, against Alexander Donaldson, &c. Edinburgh, 1774.
A Letter to the People of Scotland, On the Present State of the Nation. Edinburgh, 1783.
A Letter to the People of Scotland, on the Alarming Attempt to infringe the Articles of the Union, and introduce a Most Pernicious Innovation by diminishing the number of the Lords of Session. 1785.
The Journal of a Tour to the Hebrides, with Samuel Johnson, LL.D. 1785. 3rd edn. 1786. Ed. Croker, J. W., 1831, etc.; ed. Carruthers, R., 1851; ed. Fitz-

gerald, Percy, 1874; ed. Napier, A., 1884; ed. Hill, G. B., 1887. *See, also,* The Life of Johnson, *post.*
A Conversation between His Most Sacred Majesty George III and Samuel Johnson, LL.D. Illustrated with Observations. 1790.
The Celebrated Letter from Samuel Johnson, LL.D., to Philip Dormer Stanhope, Earl of Chesterfield; Now first published, With Notes. 1790.
The Life of Samuel Johnson, LL.D. Comprehending an account of his studies and numerous works, in chronological order; a series of his epistolary correspondence and conversations with many eminent persons; and various original pieces of his composition, never before published. The whole exhibiting a view of literature and literary men in Great-Britain, for near half a century, during which he flourished. 2 vols. Dilly. 1791. 2nd edn., revised and augmented. 3 vols. 1793. 3rd, revised and augmented [edited by Malone, Edmond]. 4 vols. 1799. Ed. Chalmers, Alex. 4 vols. 1822. [Ed. Walesby, F. P., of Wadham College.] 4 vols. Oxford, 1826. Ed. Croker, J. W. 5 vols. 1831; 2nd edn., ed. by Wright, J. 10 vols. 1850. Ed. Carruthers, R. 4 vols. 1851–2. Ed. Fitzgerald, P. 3 vols. 1874. Reissued with a bibliography of Boswell's Life by Tedder, H. R. 1888. Ed. Napier, A. 5 vols. 1884; also 6 vols. 1884. Ed. Morley, Henry. 5 vols. 1885. Ed. Hill, G. B. 6 vols. 1887. Ed. Morris, M. 1 vol. (Globe edn.) 1893. Ed. Birrell, A. 6 vols. 1896. Ed. Glover, A., with introduction by Dobson, Austin. 3 vols. 1901. Ed. Ingpen, R. (with many illustrations). 1907.
[The later editions include the Journal of a Tour to the Hebrides. For further details *see* the bibliography by Tedder, H. R., in P. Fitzgerald's edition, 1888.]
The Principal Corrections and Additions to the First Edition of Mr. Boswell's Life of Dr. Johnson. 1793.
No Abolition of Slavery; or the Universal Empire of Love: a Poem. 1791. [Anon.]
Songs in the Justiciary Opera, Composed fifty years ago, By C—— M—— and B——. I.C.C. Auchinleck, 1816.
["Those that are here preserved are given from memory." Advertisement.]
Privately printed for Sir Alexander Boswell; included in Maidment's Court of Session Garland, 1839 etc.
Letters of James Boswell, addressed to the Rev. W. J. Temple. Now first published from the original MSS. With an introduction and notes [by Francis, Philip]. 1857.
—— with an introduction by Seccombe, T. 1908.
Boswelliana. The Commonplace Book of James Boswell. With a memoir and annotations by the Rev. Charles Rogers . . . and introductory remarks by . . . Lord Houghton. Printed for the Grampian Club. 1874.
[A selection limited to "anecdotes personal to the writer" had been contributed by Milnes, R. M., afterwards Lord Houghton, to the Miscellanies of the Philobiblon Society, vol. II, 1855–6.]

*Wrongly attributed to Boswell*

The Speeches, Arguments, and Determinations of The Lords of Council and Session in Scotland, upon [the Douglas Cause]. With an Introductory Preface. By a Barrister at Law. Almon. 1767.
[Attributed to Boswell in Halkett and Laing.]

A Letter to Robert Macqueen Lord Braxfield, on his promotion to be one of the
Judges of the High Court of Justiciary. Edinburgh, 1780.
[Attributed to Boswell in the Bodleian Catalogue.]

### B.  *Contributions to Periodicals*
The Scots Magazine.

Verses on the equestrian statue of King Charles II in the Parliament close, being
painted white. September, 1767.
Prologue at the opening of the Theatre-Royal in Edinburgh. November, 1767.
Memorial in behalf of the Corsicans. December, 1768.
[The numbers for June, July, August, 1768, contain correspondence be-
tween the Hon. Miss Primerose and the author of the Essence of the Douglas
Cause reprinted from the Edinburgh Courant.]

The London Magazine.

Memorial in Behalf of the Corsicans. December, 1768.
A Letter from James Boswell, Esq., on Shakespeare's Jubilee at Stratford-upon-
Avon: An Account of the Armed Corsican Chief at the Masquerade, followed
by Boswell's poem. September, 1769. Pp. 451–6.
On the Profession of a Player. August, September, October, 1770.
Letter, with an unpublished song by Goldsmith, intended to have been sung in
She Stoops to Conquer. June, 1774.
The Hypochondriack. Seventy numbers, from October, 1777, to August, 1783.
(?) The Story of Mr. Levet. Signed S. Y. September, 1783.
(?) Memoirs of Mrs. Anne Williams. Signed B. December, 1783.

The Gentleman's Magazine.

Two Letters in reply to criticisms on the Journal. April, 1786.
Ode to Mr. Charles Dilly. April, 1791 (cf. June, p. 564).
Letters in reply to Miss Anna Seward. November, 1793, January, 1794.
[He was preparing a reply to Samuel Parr shortly before his death.
June, 1795, p. 525.]

The European Magazine.

Memoirs of James Boswell, Esq. May, June, 1791.

The Edinburgh Courant.

Correspondence on the Douglas Cause, reprinted in the Scots Magazine for
June, July, August, 1768.

The Public Advertiser.

Letter, with "a genuine copy" of the Theatre-Royal Prologue. 12 January, 1768.
[In this letter Boswell is an "old correspondent."]

The St. James's Chronicle.

Letter on Hackman, the murderer. 17 April, 1779. [*See* Notes and Queries,
September, 1863, p. 232.]

### C.  *Contemporary Criticism (apart from Reviews in Periodicals)*
An Epistle to James Boswell, Esq., occasioned by his having transmitted the moral
writings of Dr. Samuel Johnson to Pascal Paoli. By W. K[enrick]. 1768.
A Poetical and Congratulatory Epistle to James Boswell, Esq., on his Journal of
a Tour to the Hebrides. By Peter Pindar. 1786.
Picturesque Beauties of Boswell—twenty caricatures in illustration of Boswell's
Journal. [By Collings and Rowlandson.] 1786.

Remarks on the Journal of a Tour to the Hebrides. In a Letter to James Boswell, Esq. [Signed Verax.] [? 1786.]

A Defence of Mr. Boswell's Journal, in a Letter to the Author of the Remarks. 1786.

The Remarker Remarked; or, a Parody on the Letter to Mr. Boswell, on his Tour, etc. 1786.

An Epistle to James Boswell, Esq.; occasioned by his long-expected, and now speedily to be published Life of Dr. Johnson. 1790.

A Letter to James Boswell, Esq. With some Remarks on Johnson's Dictionary, and on Language, etc. 1792.

### D. *Later Biography and Criticism*

[*See, also, ante,* JOHNSON, secs. E, F, G.]

Biographicus [Temple, J. W.?]. Letter. The Gentleman's Magazine, August, 1795.

C. [Courtenay, J.?] Letter. The Gentleman's Magazine. June, 1795.

Carlyle, Thomas. Essay on Boswell's Life of Johnson in Fraser's Magazine. May, 1832.

Fitzgerald, Percy. Life of James Boswell. 2 vols. 1891.

Forbes, Sir William. Life of Beattie. 1806.

Green, M. Letter. The Gentleman's Magazine. June, 1795.

Henley, W. E. Views and Reviews. 1902.

Hill, G. Birkbeck. Boswell's Proof Sheets, in Johnson Club Papers. 1899.

Holcroft, Thomas. Memoirs. 3 vols. 1816.

Johnson, Lionel. Post Liminium: Essays and Critical Papers. 1911.

Leask, W. Keith. James Boswell. (Famous Scots Series.) 1897.

Macaulay, Lord. Essay on Boswell's Life of Johnson. The Edinburgh Review. September, 1831.

Mallory, George. Boswell the Biographer. 1912.

Malone, Edmond. Letter. The Gentleman's Magazine. June, 1795.

Nichols, John. Literary Anecdotes. 9 vols. 1812–15.

—— Illustrations of the Literary History of the Eighteenth Century. 8 vols. 1817–58.

R., J. B. Memoirs of Boswell. The Gentleman's Magazine. June, 1795.

Raleigh, Sir Walter. Six Essays on Johnson. 1910.

Rogers, Charles. Memoir, prefixed to Boswelliana. 1874.

Stephen, Sir Leslie. Art. on Boswell in D. of N. B., vol. II. 1886.

Taylor, John. Records of my Life. 2 vols. 1832.

Whyte, E. A. Remarks on Boswell's Life of Johnson. Dublin, 1797. (Included in A Miscellany by Whyte, S., and E. A., 1799; reissued as Miscellanea Nova, 1800 and 1801.)

## CHAPTER IX

## OLIVER GOLDSMITH

### I. COLLECTED WORKS

The Miscellaneous Works of Oliver Goldsmith, M.B. Compiled for Bishop Percy, and edited by Rose, Samuel. 4 vols. 1801. (Includes the so-called Percy memoir, and unpublished prologues to She Stoops to Conquer.) In the 4th edn., 1820, was first printed the oratorio The Captivity, afterwards issued separately in 1837.

The Miscellaneous Works of Oliver Goldsmith. Ed. Prior, James. 4 vols. 1837. (Contains "a variety of pieces now first collected.")

The Works of Oliver Goldsmith. (Murray's British Classics.) Ed. Cunningham, Peter. 4 vols. 1854. (First printed translation of Vida's Game of Chess.)

The Works of Oliver Goldsmith. With memoir by Spalding, William. 1858. (Contains facsimile of important letter to Mrs. Lawder (Jane Contarine).)

The Works of Oliver Goldsmith. With life, etc., by Waller, J. F. 1864–5.

The Miscellaneous Works of Oliver Goldsmith. Globe edn. Biographical introduction by Masson, David. 1869.

The Works of Oliver Goldsmith. (Bohn's Standard Library.) With notes and life by Gibbs, J. W. M. 5 vols. 1885–6. (Contains some "hitherto uncollected" pieces.)

## II. Part Collections

Poems and Plays, 1777; Poetical and Dramatic Works, 2 vols. 1780; Poetical Works, Aldine edn., ed. Mitford, John, 1831; new edn., 1895; Poetical Works, ed. Corney, Bolton, 1846; Goldsmith's Select Poems, ed. Lobban, J. H., 1900; Complete Poetical Works, ed. Dobson, A., Oxford edn., 1906; Plays of Goldsmith, Belles Lettres Series, edd. Dobson, A., and Baker, George P., 1903; and Plays and Vicar of Wakefield, by Doble, C. E., and Ostler, G., Oxford edn., 1909. (This last contains a valuable glossarial index.)

## III. Separate Works

The Memoirs of a Protestant, condemned to the Galleys of France, for his Religion. Written by Himself. . . . Translated from the Original, just published at the Hague, by Willington, James. 2 vols. 1758. Reprint published in 1895, with introduction by Dobson, A., and facsimile of Goldsmith's receipt to Edward Dilly.

An Enquiry into the present state of Polite Learning in Europe. 1759. 2nd edn., "revised and corrected," 1774. (In this edn. much is omitted, including the verses from Macrobius (Prologue of Laberius).)

The Bee. 6 October to 24 November, 1759. Issued in a volume, December, 1759. Annotated edn., by Dobson, A. (Temple Classics.) 1903.

Memoirs of M. de Voltaire. The Lady's Magazine. 1761.

The Mystery Revealed. (Pamphlet on the Cock-lane Ghost.) 1742 [1762].

The History of Mecklenburgh. 1762.

The Art of Poetry. 2 vols. 1762. (Said to have been revised by Goldsmith for Newbery.)

The Citizen of the World; or, Letters from a Chinese Philosopher, residing in London, to his Friend in the East. Appeared in The Public Ledger as Chinese Letters from 24 January, 1760, to 14 August, 1761; published in two volumes, May, 1762. Separate annotated edns. by Knight, Charles, 1840; and Dobson, A. (Temple Library), 2 vols., 1891; and Temple Classics, 2 vols., 1900.

Plutarch's Lives, abridged from the Greek. By Goldsmith and Joseph Collyer. 7 vols. 1762.

The Life of Richard Nash, of Bath, Esquire, 1762. 2nd edn., revised. Same year.

An History of England in a Series of Letters from a Nobleman to his Son. 2 vols. 1764.

The Traveller; or, a Prospect of Society. Published 19 December, 1764 (dated 1765). Three edns. quickly followed, and a 9th was issued in 1774, the year of the author's death. (Numerous alterations were made between the 1st and the 6th edn., of 1770.)

Essays. By Mr. Goldsmith. 1765. 2nd edn., corrected, 1766.

Edwin and Angelina (The Hermit). Printed privately for the amusement of the Countess of Northumberland. [1765.] (Afterwards included in The Vicar of Wakefield.)

The Vicar of Wakefield. 2 vols. 1766. Pub. 27 March. 2nd edn., 31 May; 3rd edn., 29 August; 4th edn., 1770; 5th edn., April, 1774 (dated 1773). (Johnson's "exact narration" in Boswell (ed. Hill, G. B., 1887, vol. I, p. 416, and vol. III, p. 321), of which most other accounts are variations, was that, some time before the publication of The Traveller in 1764, having been applied to by Goldsmith in distress and durance, he [Johnson] sold the MS. to a bookseller for £60 (or guineas). In Charles Welsh's life of Newbery, 1885, pp. 58–9, that writer pointed out that he had found in some old account-books an entry showing that Goldsmith had sold a third share of the book to Benjamin Collins, printer, of Salisbury (who afterwards printed it), 28 October, 1762, for £21. That The Vicar was being written in 1761–2, is plain from internal evidence (references to the musical glasses, the Auditor, etc.); but no conclusive solution of the apparent conflict between the two stories has yet been propounded, although it may be a very simple one.)

A detailed bibliography of The Vicar, coming down to 1885, is prefixed to Stock's facsimile reprint of that date. There is also a bibliography in the Great Writers series. Separate annotated editions were issued in The Parchment Library, 1883, rev. 1908; by Macmillan, Michael, 1897; and Doble, C. E., Oxford edn., 1909.

A Concise History of Philosophy and Philosophers. Translated by Goldsmith from the French of Formey, J. H. S. 1766.

A Short English Grammar, 1766.

Poems for Young Ladies. Collected, with Preface by Goldsmith. 1767.

Beauties of English Poesy. 2 vols. 1767.

The Good Natur'd Man, a Comedy. 1768 (5 February). Produced at Covent garden, 29 January. 5th edn. 1768.

The Roman History. 2 vols. 1769. Abridged by the author for the use of schools, 1772.

The Deserted Village. Published 26 May, 1770. Four more edns. in the same year.

The Life of Thomas Parnell. 1770. Also prefixed to Parnell's Works, same year.

The Life of Henry St. John, Lord Viscount Bolingbroke. 1770. (Originally prefixed to Bolingbroke's Dissertation on Parties.)

The History of England. 4 vols. 1771.

Threnodia Augustalis. Monody on the Death of the Princess Dowager of Wales. 1772. Performed, on 22 February, the day of publication, at Mrs. Cornely's rooms in Soho square.

She Stoops to Conquer, a Comedy. 1773 (26 March). Produced at Covent garden, 15 March.

[For a Song by Dr. Goldsmith, originally intended to be sung by Miss Hardcastle in this comedy, see a letter by James Boswell in The London Magazine for June, 1774.]

Retaliation, a Poem, 1774 (19 April). 2nd edn., with "explanatory notes," same year. Fifth edn., 1774, with supplementary epitaph on Caleb Whitefoord. To an 8th edn., 1777, other poems were added, together with a life varied from Glover's Anecdotes, Annual Register, 1774, pp. 29–34.

An History of the Earth and Animated Nature. 8 vols. 1774.

The Haunch of Venison, a poetical epistle to Lord Clare. 1776. (Contains H. W. Bunbury's portrait.)

A Survey of Experimental Philosophy. 2 vols. 1776.
The Comic Romance of Monsieur Scarron. 2 vols. [1780.] Translation attributed to Goldsmith.

IV. Biography and Criticism

Black, W. Goldsmith. English Men of Letters. 1878.
Boswell, James. Life of Samuel Johnson, etc. 2 vols. 1791.
Cooke, W. European Magazine. 1793. Pp. 91–5, 170–4, 258–63.
Courthope, W. J. History of English Poetry. 1905. (Vol. v, pp. 209–19.)
Cox, M. F. The Country and Kindred of Oliver Goldsmith. Journal of the National Literary Society of Ireland, 1900. (Vol. i, pt. ii, pp. 81–111.)
Cumberland, Richard. Memoirs . . . written by Himself. 2 vols. 1807. (Vol. i, pp. 350–74.)
Davies, T. Memoirs of David Garrick. 2 vols. 1780. (Vol. ii, pp. 142–64.)
De Quincey, Thomas. Works, 1853–60. (Vol. vi, pp. 194–233.)
Dobson, Austin. Life of Goldsmith. Great Writers, 1888. Contains three hitherto unpublished letters; and a Bibliography by Anderson, John P. Rev. edn., without Bibliography, New York, 1899.
Ford, E. Names and Characters in the Vicar of Wakefield. National Review, May, 1883.
Forster, J. Life and Adventures of Oliver Goldsmith, A Biography. 1848. 2nd edn. 2 vols. 1854. Final edn. 1877.
    Article on this in Quarterly Review, vol. xcv (pp. 394–448).
Forsyth, W. Novels and Novelists of the Eighteenth Century, etc. 1871. (Chap. x.)
Glover, William. Anecdotes of the late Dr. Goldsmith. Annual Register, 1774. (Pp. 29–34.)
Hawes, W. An Account of the late Dr. Goldsmith's Illness, etc. 1774. 4th edn. 1780.
Hawkins, Sir John. Life of Samuel Johnson. 1787. Pp. 416–21.
Howitt, W. Homes and Haunts of the most eminent British Poets. 1857. Pp. 195–228.
Hunt, Leigh. Classic Tales, etc. 1806. Vol. i, pp. 41–80. (Contains an essay on Goldsmith.)
Irving, Washington. Life of Oliver Goldsmith. 1844. 2 vols. Revised from Forster, 1849.
King, R. Ashe. Oliver Goldsmith. 1910.
Leslie, C. R., and Taylor, Tom. Life and Times of Sir Joshua Reynolds. 1865. 2 vols.
Lytton, Lord. Article on Forster's Life. Edinburgh Review, vol. lxxxviii, pp. 193–225.
Macaulay, Lord. Article on Goldsmith in Encyclopaedia Britannica, 1856. Vol. x. Rptd. in Miscellaneous Writings. 1880.
Mangin, E. An Essay on Light Reading. 1808. (Contains, at pp. 136–50, the letter from Strean referred to, p. 220, ante.)
—— The Parlour Window. References to Goldsmith, pp. 2, 4, 26.
Mason, W. S. A Statistical Account . . . of Ireland. 1814–49. 3 vols. (Vol. iii, pp. 356–66.) (Contains particulars of the Goldsmith family.)
Minto, W. Manual of English Prose Literature. 1886. (Goldsmith: pp. 461–73.)
Monthly Review. 1757. (Nos. from April to September contain Goldsmith's review work for Ralph Griffiths.)

Moore, F. Frankfort. Goldsmith. 1910.
Nichols, J. Literary Anecdotes, 1812–15, and Illustrations, etc. 1817–58.
Northcote, J. Memoirs of Reynolds, 1813. (Many references to Goldsmith.)
Prior, Sir James. Life of Oliver Goldsmith. 1837. 2 vols.
Taine, H. A. Histoire de la Littérature Anglaise. 1863–4. 4 vols. (Vol. III, pp. 330–6.)
Thackeray, W. M. English Humourists, 1853. Pp. 269–322. Rptd. in Centenary Biographical Edn., 1912, vol. XI.
Thrale, H. L. Anecdotes of the late Samuel Johnson, 1786; and Autobiography, edited by Hayward, A. 2nd edn. 1861. 2 vols.
Welsh, C. A Bookseller of the Last Century (John Newbery). 1885. Pp. 54–62.

CHAPTER X

THE LITERARY INFLUENCE OF THE MIDDLE AGES

I. GENERAL WORKS

Addison, J. On Chevy Chase, Spectator, 70 (21 May, 1711) and 74 (25 May, 1711).
Beers, H. A. History of English Romanticism in the 18th century. [Adds items to Phelps's treatment of Norse influences.] 1899.
[Drummond, W.] Polemo-Middinia inter Vitarvam et Nebernam. Acc. Jacobi id nominis quinti, Regis Scotorum, cantilena rustica vulgo inscripta Christs Kirk on the Green. Recensuit notisque illustravit E. G[ibson]. Oxford, 1691.
Dryden, John. Miscellany Poems. Part VI. 2nd edn. 1716.
    Contains Hervor at Angantyr's Grave, rptd. from Hickes's Thesaurus.
Farley, F. E. Scandinavian Influences on the English Romantic Movement. Harvard Studies in Philology, no. 9. Cambridge, Mass., 1903.
    [Extremely valuable for the bibliography of translations from the Scandinavian and of original poetic treatment of Scandinavian subjects to the end of the 18th century.]
Herzfeld, G. Bemerkungen über die nordischen Stoffe in der englischen Poesie des vorigen Jahrhunderts. Appendix to William Taylor von Norwich. Eine Studie. Halle, 1897.
Hickes, G. Institutiones grammaticae Anglo-Saxonicae Mœso-Gothicae, etc. Oxford, 1689.
—— Linguarum vett. septentrionalium thesaurus grammatico-criticus et archaeologicus. 2 vols. Oxford, 1703–5.
Hurd, R. Letters on Chivalry and Romance, 1762. Ed. Morley, E. J. 1911.
Metcalfe, F. The Englishman and the Scandinavian. 1880.
Nordby, C. H. The influence of old Norse literature upon English literature. Columbia, 1901. [Briefly reviews some of the authors discussed in Farley's dissertation, but is for the most part concerned with a later period.]
Phelps, W. L. The beginnings of the English Romantic movement. Boston, 1893.
Temple, Sir William. On the Death-Song of Ragnar Lodbrok, etc. Essays Upon·Heroick Virtue; Upon Poetry. Miscellanea. Pt. II. 1690.

II. PARTICULAR WRITERS

*Michael Bruce* (1746–1767)

Poems on several occasions. [Including two Danish Odes.] 1770. Rptd. in Works. Ed. Grosart, A. B. Edinburgh, 1865.

## Thomas Chatterton

### (1) Collected Editions

Miscellanies in prose and verse. (Ed. Broughton, J.) With supplement. 1778–84.

Walpole, H. Letter to the editor of the Miscellanies of Thomas Chatterton. Strawberry Hill. 1779.

Works. Edd. Southey, R., and Cottle, J. With Life by Gregory, G. 3 vols. 1803.

Poetical Works. Ed. Willcox, C. B. 2 vols. Cambridge, 1842.

Poetical Works, with an essay on the Rowley poems by Skeat, W. W., and a memoir by Bell, E. 2 vols. 1871. 2 vols. 1875 (Aldine Poets).

Complete Poetical Works. Ed. with a biographical introduction, notes, glossary, and bibliography by Roberts, H. D. 2 vols. 1906.

Poetical Works. With an introduction by Lee, Sir S. 2 vols. 1906–9.

Chatterton's writings were translated into French by Pagnon, J., with a memoir by Callet, A. 2 vols. 1839.

### (2) Separate Works

An elegy on the much lamented death of William Beckford, Esq. 1770.

The Execution of Sir Charles Bawdin. (Ed. by Eagles, T.) 1772.

The Revenge: a burletta. With additional songs. 1795.

### (3) The Rowley Poems, including the controversial literature as to their authorship

Poems supposed to have been written at Bristol by Thomas Rowley and others in the 15th century. Ed. Tyrwhitt, T. 1777; 2nd edn. 1777; 3rd edn. 1778 (with Appendix). Ed. Milles, J. 1782. Ed. Sharpe, L. Cambridge, 1794. Ed. Steele, R. 1898. Ed. Hare, M. E. Oxford, 1911. (A reprint of Tyrwhitt's third edn. with a useful bibliography.)

[?Dampier, H.] Remarks upon the eighth section of the second volume of Mr. Warton's History of English Poetry. [1779.]

[Warton had included an account of the Rowley Poems in his History; but he viewed them with suspicion.]

Bryant, J. Observations upon the Poems of T. Rowley, in which the authenticity of those poems is ascertained. 1781.

An Examination of the Poems attributed to Thomas Rowley and William Canynge, with a defence of the opinion of Mr. Warton. Sherborne. [1782.]

Greene, E. B. Strictures upon a pamphlet [by Malone, E.] entitled Cursory observations, etc. With a postscript on Mr. Thomas Warton's Inquiry into the same subject. 1782.

Hickford, R. Observations on the Poems attributed to Rowley, tending to prove that they were really written by him and other ancient authors. With Remarks on the Appendix of the editor [Tyrwhitt, T.] of Rowley's Poems. [1782.]

Malone, E. Cursory observations on the Poems attributed to Thomas Rowley. 1782.

Tyrwhitt, T. A Vindication of the appendix to the Poems called Rowley's, in reply to the answers of the Dean of Exeter [Milles], Jacob Bryant and a third anonymous writer. 1782.

Warton, T.   An Inquiry into the authenticity of the Poems attributed to Thomas Rowley.   In which the arguments of the Dean of Exeter [Milles] and Mr. Bryant are examined.   1782.

Mathias, T. J.   An essay on the evidence, external and internal, relating to the poems attributed to T. Rowley.   1783.

Sherwen, J.   The introduction to an examination of some part of the internal evidence respecting the authenticity of certain publications said to have been found in manuscripts at Bristol.   Bath, 1809.

For various satires in prose and verse dealing with the Rowley controversy, *see* Lowndes's Bibliographer's Manual, ed. Bohn, H. G., part VIII, 1864, and the Catalogue of Printed Books in the British Museum.

## (4)   Biography and Criticism

Britton, J.   The Life, Character, and Writings of Chatterton.   In his Historical and architectural essay relating to Redcliffe Church, Bristol.   1813.

Croft, Sir H.   Love and Madness.   A story too true, in a series of letters between parties whose names would perhaps be mentioned, were they less known or less lamented.   1780.   4th edn.   1780.

—— Love and Madness: in a series of letters, one of which contains the original account of Chatterton.   New edn.   1786.

—— Love Letters of Mr. Hackman and Miss Reay, 1775–1779.   Ed. by Burgess, G.   1895.   [A re-issue of Love and Madness.]

   Chatterton and Love and Madness: a letter from Sir Herbert Croft to Mr. Nichols.   1800.

Davis, J.   The Life and Letters of Thomas Chatterton.   1806.

Gregory, G.   The life of Thomas Chatterton, with criticisms on his genius and writings.   1789.   Republished in Southey and Cottle's edn. of Chatterton's Works.   1803.

Ingram, J. H.   The True Chatterton.   A new study from original documents.   1910.

Lacy, Ernest.   Chatterton.   (Tragedy.)   In Plays and Sonnets.   Philadelphia, 1900.

Maitland, S. R.   Chatterton.   An essay.   1857.

Masson, D.   Chatterton.   A story of 1770.   In Essays biographical and critical.   1856.   Reissued 1874.   New edn.   1899.

Pryce, G.   Memorials of the Canynges' family and their times.   To which is added inedited memoranda (42 pp.) relating to Chatterton.   Bristol, 1854.

Puettmann, H.   Chatterton.   Leben des Dichters und Dichtungen.   2 vols.   Barmen, 1840.

Richter, H.   Thomas Chatterton.   Schipper's Wiener Beiträge.   Vienna, 1900.

Ross, J. [formerly J. Dix].   The life of Thomas Chatterton; including his unpublished poems and correspondence.   1837.   1851.

Russell, C. E.   Thomas Chatterton, the marvellous boy.   The story of a strange life, 1752–1770.   1909.

Vigny, A. de.   Chatterton.   Drame.   1835.

Watts-Dunton, T.   Thomas Chatterton.   Prefixed to the selection from his poems in T. H. Ward's English Poets.   Vol. III.   1880.

Wilson, D.   Thomas Chatterton.   A biographical study.   1869.

### Amos Simon Cottle (1768?–1800)

Icelandic Poetry, or the Edda of Sæmund translated into English verse.   Bristol, 1797.

*George Ellis* (1753–1815)

Specimens of the early English poets. 1790. New edn. 1801.

Vol. I of the 1801 edn. contains John Hookham Frere's translation of *Brunanburh*, with the following note by the editor: "This was written several years ago during the controversy occasioned by the poems attributed to Rowley, and was intended as an imitation of the style and language of the fourteenth century. The reader will probably hear with some surprise that this singular instance of critical ingenuity was the composition of an Eton school-boy."

Specimens of early English Metrical Romances chiefly written during the early part of the fourteenth century; to which is prefixed an historical introduction. 1805.

*Evan Evans* (1731–1789)

Some Specimens of the poetry of the antient Welsh Bards. 1764.

*Thomas Gray*

*See* bibliography to Chap. VI, *ante*.

*David Herd* (1732–1810)

*See* Vol. IX, Chap. XIV, bibliography.

*Richard Hole* (1746–1803)

Arthur, or the Northern Enchantment. A poetical romance in seven books. 1789.

*Edward Jerningham* (1727–1812)

The Rise and Progress of the Scandinavian Poetry. 1784.

*James Macpherson*

(1) Poetical Works

The Poems of Ossian, containing the poetical works of James Macpherson in prose and rhyme. Ed. by Laing, M. 2 vols. Edinburgh, 1805.

A. *Ossianic Poetry.*

A good bibliography of Macpherson's Ossian, and of the literature of the Ossianic controversy, will be found in Lowndes's Bibliographer's Manual, ed. Bohn, H. G., part VI. 1861.

Fragments of Ancient Poetry collected in the Highlands of Scotland, and translated from the Galic or Erse language. Edinburgh, 1760.

Fingal. An ancient epic poem. In six books. With several other poems translated from the Galic language by James Macpherson. 1762.

Temora. An ancient epic poem. In eight books. With several other poems translated from the Galic language by James Macpherson. 1763.

The works of Ossian, translated by James Macpherson. 3rd edn. with a critical dissertation on the Poems of Ossian by Blair, Hugh. 2 vols., 1765; 2 vols., 1773; I and II, 1773; III and IV, Frankfort and Leipzig, printed for J. G. Fleischer, 1777 [edited by Goethe and Merck; Goethe engraved the title-vignette]; 2 vols., 1784; 2 vols., 1796; new edn., with Blair's critical dissertation, 2 vols., 1806; ed. Campbell, H. 2 vols., 1822; ed. Sharp, W. Edinburgh. 1896.

As to the numerous renderings of portions of the Ossianic poems into verse, *see* the bibliography in Lowndes mentioned above.

The Ossianic poems have been translated into Greek, Latin, French, German, Italian, Spanish, Dutch. Swedish, and Danish. As to these translations *see* the bibliography in Lowndes and the B. M. Catalogue *s. v.* Ossian.

The following selection of editions of Ossianic texts will be useful for purposes of comparison. For a fuller bibliography, *see* Nutt, A., Ossian and the Ossianic Literature. Popular Studies in Mythology, Romance, and Folk-Lore, 3. 1899.

The Poems of Ossian in the original Gaelic, with a literal translation into Latin by Macfarlan, R., together with a dissertation on the authenticity of the poems by Sinclair, Sir J., a translation from Cesarotti's dissertation, and notes by McArthur, J. 3 vols. 1807.

Ahlwardt, Christian Wilhelm. Die Gedichte Ossian's aus dem Gaelischen im Sylbenmasse des Originals. 3 vols. Leipzig, 1811.

The Genuine Remains of Ossian literally translated, with a preliminary dissertation by Macgregor, P. 1841.

Transactions of the Ossianic Society for the years 1853–8. 6 vols. Dublin, 1854–61.

Simpson, J. H. Poems of Oisin, Bard of Erin. 1857.

Campbell, J. F. Popular Tales of the West Islands. 4 vols. Edinburgh, 1860–2. New edn. Paisley, 1890–3.

Lismore. The Dean of Lismore's Book. Ed. by McLauchlan, T. Edinburgh 1861. [A new edn., by Quiggin, E. C., is in preparation.]

The Poems of Ossian. In the original Gaelic. With a literal translation into English and a dissertation on the authenticity of the poems, by Clerk, A. Together with the translation by Macpherson. 2 vols. Edinburgh, 1870.

Revue Celtique. For a note as to the Ossianic contributions to this periodical, 1870, etc., *see* Nutt, A., Ossian and the Ossianic Literature.

Campbell, J. F. Heroic Gaelic Ballads collected in Scotland from 1512 to 1871. Arranged by Campbell, J. F. 1872.

Meyer, K. Cath Finntrága, or the Battle of Ventry. Ed. by Meyer, K. Oxford, 1885.

MacInnes, D. Folk and Hero Tales. Collected, edited in Gaelic, and translated by MacInnes, D. With a study on the development of the Ossianic saga and notes by Nutt, A. 1890.

Campbell, J. G. The Fians, or Stories, Poems, and Traditions of Fionn and his Warrior Band. Collected from oral sources by Campbell, J. G. 1891.

MacDougall, J. Folk and Hero Tales. Collected, edited, and translated by MacDougall, J. With introduction by Nutt, A. 1891.

Campbell, J. G. Clan Traditions and Popular Tales of the Western Highlands and Islands. 1895.

B. *Other Poetical Works.*

The Highlander. An heroic poem in six cantos. 1758.
The Iliad of Homer translated into prose. 1773.

(2) Historical Works

An Introduction to the history of Great Britain and Ireland. 1771.

The History of Great Britain from the Restoration to the Accession of the House of Hanover. 2 vols. 1775.

Original papers, containing the secret history of Great Britain from the Restoration to the Accession of the House of Hanover. To which are prefixed extracts from the life of James II as written by himself. 2 vols. 1775.

The rights of Great Britain asserted against the claims of America. 1776.

A short history of the Opposition during the last session of Parliament. 1779.

### (3) Biography and Criticism

Heuer, O. Eine unbekannte Ossianübersetzung Goethes. In Jahrbuch des Freien Deutschen Hochstifts. 1908.

Macbain, A. Macpherson's Ossian. Celtic Magazine. Feb.–April, 1887.

Report of the Committee of the Highland Society of Scotland appointed to enquire into the nature and authenticity of the Poems of Ossian. 3 vols. Edinburgh, 1805.

Saunders, T. B. The Life and Letters of James Macpherson. 1894.

Scott, Sir W. Review of Laing's edition of Ossian in Edinburgh Review. July, 1805.

Shaw, W. An Enquiry into the authenticity of the Poems ascribed to Ossian. 1781.

Smart, J. S. James Macpherson. An episode in literature. 1905.

[A very clear account of the whole business.]

Stern, L. Chr. Die ossianischen Heldenlieder. Zeitschrift für vergleichende Litteraturgeschichte. Vol. VIII. Weimar, 1895.

### Paul Henri Mallet (1730–1807)

L'Introduction à l'Histoire de Dannemarc. 2 vols. Copenhagen, 1755–6.

Gibbon, E. An Examination of Mallet's Introduction. Miscellaneous Works. Vol. III. 1814.

Goldsmith, O. Volume II of Mallet's Introduction reviewed in Monthly Review, April, 1757. Rptd. in Works. Vol. IV. 1885.

### Thomas James Mathias (1754?–1835)

Runic Odes imitated from the Norse tongue in the manner of Mr. Gray. 1781.

### Thomas Percy

Hau Kiou Choaan, or the Pleasing History. A translation from the Chinese. To which are added (1) the Argument or story of a Chinese play; (2) a collection of Chinese proverbs; and (3) fragments of Chinese poetry; with notes. 4 vols. 1761.

Miscellaneous pieces relating to the Chinese. 2 vols. 1762.

Five pieces of Runic poetry translated from the Islandic language. 1763.

The Song of Solomon newly translated from the original Hebrew; with a commentary and annotations. 1764.

Reliques of Ancient English Poetry. 3 vols. 1765. 2nd edn. 1767; 3rd edn. 1775; 4th edn., by his nephew, Percy, T., 1794; 5th edn. 1812; ed. Willmott, R. A., 1857; ed. Gilfillan, G., 1858; ed. Prichard, J. V., 2 vols., 1876 (Bohn's Standard Library); ed. Wheatley, H. B., 3 vols., 1876–7. Reissued 1891.

The Household Book of the Earl of Northumberland in 1512, at his castles of Wressle and Leconfield in Yorkshire. Ed. Percy, T. 1768. 1770. 1827.

A Key to the New Testament. 1769. 3rd edn. 1799. New ed. Cambridge, 1823.

Northern Antiquities, or a description of the manners, customs, religion, and laws of the ancient Danes . . . . With a translation of the Edda and other pieces from the ancient Islandic tongue. Transl. from Mallet's Introduction à l'Histoire de Dannemarc, etc. With additional notes by the English translator and Goranson's Latin version of the Edda. 2 vols. 1770. 2 vols. Edinburgh, 1809.

The Hermit of Warkworth. A Northumberland Ballad. In three fits or cantos. 1772. 3rd edn. 1772. Frequently reprinted.
Letters from Thomas Percy, John Callander, David Herd, and others to George Paton. Edinburgh, 1830.
Gaussen, A. C. C. Percy, Prelate and Poet. With a preface by Douglas, Sir G. 1908.
Bishop Percy's Folio Manuscript. Edd. Hales, J. W., and Furnivall, F. J. 3 vols. 1868.

Percy had a copious correspondence with literary men of his time. Practically the whole of the 856 pages of vol. II (1848) and 436 pages of vol. VIII (1858) of Nichols's Illustrations of the Literary History of the 18th Century are occupied by letters to and from Percy, his correspondents including George Steevens, Dr. Grainger, James Boswell, Michael Lort, Dr. Thomas Birch, Archdeacon Nares, Dr. Thomas Campbell, the Moira family, John Nichols and John Pinkerton.

### John Pinkerton (1758–1826)

Vitae antiquae Sanctorum qui habitaverunt in ea parte Britanniae nunc vocata Scotia, et in ejus insulis. 1789.

### Richard Polwhele (1760–1838)

Poems chiefly by Gentlemen of Devon and Cornwall. Ed. by Polwhele, R. 2 vols. Bath, 1792. [Including The Incantation of Herva, and other poems on Scandinavian subjects.]

### Joseph Ritson

A select collection of English Songs. 3 vols. 1783. 2nd edn., by Park, T. 3 vols. 1813.
Remarks critical and illustrative on the text and notes of the last edition of Shakespeare. 1783. The Quip Modest. Supplement to Remarks. 1788. (A virulent attack on Steevens's edition.)
Ancient Songs from the time of King Henry III to the Revolution. 1790. 2nd edn., enlarged. 2 vols. 1829. 3rd edn. by Hazlitt, W. C. 1877.
Pieces of ancient popular poetry. 1791. 2nd edn. 1833.
Cursory criticisms on the edition of Shakespeare published by Malone, E. 1792.
Scotish Songs. 2 vols. 1794. Rptd. 1866. 2 vols. Glasgow, 1869.
The English Anthology. Ed. by Ritson, J. 3 vols. 1793–4.
Robin Hood. A Collection of all the ancient poems, songs, and ballads, now extant, relative to that celebrated English outlaw. 2 vols. 1795. 2nd edn. 1832. Rptd. 1885.
Poems on interesting events in the reign of King Edward III. written in 1352 by Laurence Minot. Ed. Ritson, J. 1795. Rptd. 1825.
Ancient Engleish metrical romanceës. 3 vols. 1802.

Reviewed, together with Ellis, by Scott, Sir W., in The Edinburgh Review, 1806. The following is an extract from this article: "Much coarse and insolent invective is poured on Bishop Percy, who seems to have incurred the editor's resentment in a double capacity—as a dignitary of the Church, and a successful publisher of ancient poetry. We do not think Mr. Ritson imbibed this spirit from the works which he studied. Surely neither the gallant Sir Lancelot nor the courteous Sir Gavain, would have given the reverend Bishop the lie direct on account of a disputed reading in the old song of Maggie Lauder!"

Bibliographia poetica. A Catalogue of English poets of the 12th, 13th, 14th, 15th, and 16th Centuries, with an account of their works. 1802.

Northern Garlands. 1810. Rptd. Edinburgh, 1887–8.
   (The four Garlands here republished were originally printed between 1784 and 1793.)

The Caledonian Muse. A chronological selection of Scotish poetry from the earliest times. 1821.
   (Printed in 1785, but not published.)

The Life of King Arthur from ancient historians and authentic documents. 1825.

Memoirs of the Celts or Gauls. 1827.

Annals of the Caledonians, Picts, and Scots. 2 vols. 1828.

Fairy Tales. Now first collected. To which are prefixed two dissertations. I. On Pigmies. II. On Fairies. 1831. Rptd. 1875.

The Letters of Joseph Ritson. To which is prefixed a memoir of the author by Nicolas, Sir H. (Ed. Frank, J.) 2 vols. 1833.

Haslewood, J. Some account of the life and publications of Ritson, J. 1824.

MacCunn, F. A. Sir Walter Scott's Friends. [Ritson, Ellis, etc.] Edinburgh, 1909.

### Anna Seward (1747–1809)

Llangollen Vale and other Poems. 1796. [Including Herva at the Tomb of Argantyr.]

—— Harold's Complaint. Poetical Works. Ed. Scott, Sir W. Vol. III. 1810.

### Joseph Sterling

Poems. 1789. [Including Odes from the Icelandic.]

### William Bagshaw Stevens (1756–1800)

Poems, consisting of Indian Odes and miscellaneous pieces. Oxford, 1775. [Including Herva and Argantyr. An Ode, imitated from an antient scald, etc.]

### Thomas Tyrwhitt

An Epistle to Florio at Oxford. 1749.

Translations in verse. 1752.

Proceedings and debates of the House of Commons 1620–1 from an original manuscript at Queen's College, Oxford. 2 vols. 1766.

Observations and conjectures upon some passages of Shakespeare. 1766.

The Manner of holding Parliaments in England. By Henry Elsynge. Corrected and enlarged by Tyrwhitt, T. 1768.

The Canterbury Tales of Chaucer. To which are added an essay on his language and versification and an introductory discourse, together with notes and a glossary. By Tyrwhitt, T. 5 vols. 1775–8. 2nd edn. Oxford, 1798.
   Tyrwhitt's text was frequently reprinted. Cp. Chaucer: a bibliographical manual, by Hammond, E. P., p. 206, New York, 1908.

See, also, under Chatterton, sec. 3, ante. As to Tyrwhitt's editions of the classics see the list in the Dict. of Nat. Biog.

### Thomas Warton the elder

Poems on several occasions. (Ed. by his son Warton, J.) 1748.

### Thomas Warton the younger

The Pleasures of Melancholy. 1747.

The Triumph of Isis. A Poem. Occasioned by Isis, an Elegy [by Mason, W.]. [1749.]

A description of the City, College, and Cathedral of Winchester. . . .[1750].

Newmarket. A Satire. 1751.

Ode for Music as performed at the Theatre, in Oxford on the second of July 1751. Oxford [1751].

The Union, or select Scots and English poems. Edinburgh, 1753. 3rd edn. 1766.

Observations on the Faerie Queene of Spenser. 1754. 2nd edn. 2 vols. 1762. New edn. 2 vols. 1807.

    (Further remarks by Warton on Spenser will be found in the edition of Spenser's Works published in 1805.)

    [Huggins, W.] The Observer observ'd. [Attack on Warton's Observations.] 1756.

A Companion to the Guide, and a Guide to the Companion; being a Complete Supplement to all the accounts of Oxford hitherto published. 1760. 1806.

The life and literary remains of Ralph Bathurst, M.D., President of Trinity College, Oxford. 1761.

The Oxford Sausage, or select poetical pieces written by the most celebrated wits of the University of Oxford. 1764. 1772. 1814. 1815.

Theocriti quae supersunt. Accedunt variorum notae. Ed. T. Warton. 2 vols. Oxford, 1770.

The Life of Sir Thomas Pope, Founder of Trinity College, Oxford. 1772. 2nd edn. 1780.

The History of English Poetry from the close of the eleventh to the commencement of the eighteenth century. To which are prefixed [three] dissertations. 3 vols. 1774–81.

    Ed. Price, R., with numerous notes. 4 vols. 1824; 3 vols. 1840. Ed. Hazlitt, W. C. 4 vols. 1871. First edn. rptd. 1875.

    A fragment of vol. IV of Warton's work was printed.

    Observations on the three first volumes of the History of English poetry. [By J. Ritson.] 1782.

    Index to the History of English Poetry. [By T. Fillingham.] 1806.

Poems. 1777. 3rd edn. 1779; 4th edn. 1789; 1791. Ed. Mant, R., with a memoir. 2 vols. Oxford, 1802.

Specimen of a history of Oxfordshire. (History of Kiddington.) 1781. 2nd edn. 1783; 3rd edn. 1815.

An Inquiry into the authenticity of the Poems attributed to Thomas Rowley. 1782.

    *See, also,* under Chatterton, sec. 3, *ante.*

Poems upon several occasions by John Milton. Ed. Warton, T., with notes, critical and explanatory. 1785. 2nd edn. 1791.

    [This volume contains Milton's early poems.]

Austin, W. S., and Ralph, J. Lives of the Laureates. 1853.

Blakiston, H. E. D. Thomas Warton and Machyn's Diary. Engl. Hist. Rev. Vol. XI. 1896.

Dennis, J. The Wartons. Studies in English literature. London, 1876.

Drake, N. On Thomas Warton. Essays. Vol. II. Pt. III. Essay III. 1810.

*Joseph Warton*

Ode on reading West's Pindar. 1744.

Odes on various subjects. 1746. 2nd edn. 1747.

Essay on the genius and writings of Pope. 2 vols. 1756–82. 5th edn. 2 vols. 1806.

The Works of Virgil in English verse by Christopher Pitt and Joseph Warton. (Ed. by Warton, J.) 4 vols. 1753 (with the text); 1763.

The Works of Alexander Pope. With notes and illustrations by Warton, J., and others. 9 vols. 1797.

Wooll, J. Biographical memoirs of the Rev. Joseph Warton; to which are added a selection from his works, and a literary correspondence. . . .Vol. I. (No more published.) 1806.

Mant, R. Verses to the memory of Joseph Warton. Oxford, 1800.

Pattison, M. Pope and his editors. Essays. Ed. Nettleship, H. Vol. II. Oxford, 1889.

*See, also,* under Thomas Warton, *ante.*

A. T. B.

## CHAPTER XI

### LETTER-WRITERS

### I

#### FANNY BURNEY (MME. D'ARBLAY)

Diary and Letters of Madame D'Arblay, 1778–1840. Edited by her niece Charlotte Barrett, 1842–6. 7 vols. Frequently rptd. Rptd. "with Preface and Notes by Austin Dobson." 1904–5. 6 vols.

Early Diary of Frances Burney, 1768–1778, with a Selection from her correspondence and from the Journals of Susan and Charlotte Burney. Ed. by Ellis, A. R. 1889. 2 vols. Rptd. in Bohn's Standard Library.

Seeley, L. B. Fanny Burney and her Friends. Select passages from her Diary and other writings. 2nd edn. 1890.

*See, also,* bibliography to Chap. III, *ante.*

#### MARGARET CALDERWOOD (1715–1774)

Letters and Journals of Mrs. Calderwood of Polton. Ed. Fergusson, A. Edinburgh, 1884. (Earlier edn. in Coltness Collections, Maitland Club Publ., 1842.)

#### DAVID GARRICK

The Private Correspondence of David Garrick with the most celebrated persons of his Time. 1831–2. 2 vols. 4°.

Some Unpublished Correspondence of David Garrick. Ed. by Baker, George Pierce. Boston, Mass., 1907. 8°.

*See, also,* bibliography to Chap. IV, *ante.*

#### MRS. ELIZABETH MONTAGU

The Letters of Mrs. Elizabeth Montagu, with some of the Letters of her Correspondents. Part the first. Letters from an early age to the age of 23. Published by Matthew Montagu, M.P. 1809. 2 vols. 8°. Part the Second. Letters from the age of 23 to 40. Vols. III, IV. 1813.

A Lady of the last Century (Mrs. Elizabeth Montagu) illustrated in her Unpublished Letters. Collected and arranged by Dr. Doran. 1873.

*See, also,* bibliography to Vol. XI, chapter on The Blue Stockings.

## HANNAH MORE

Memoirs of the Life and Correspondence of Mrs. Hannah More, by Roberts, W.
1834. 4 vols. Rptd. and also abridged.
Hannah More. By Harland, Marion. (Literary Hearthstones.) G. P. Putnam's Sons, New York and London, 1900.
Hannah More, a Biographical Study. By Meakin, Annette M. B. 1911.
See, also, bibliography to Vol. XI, chapter on The Blue Stockings.

## SIR JOSHUA REYNOLDS

The several Discourses of Sir Joshua Reynolds were first published separately as they were delivered.
Seven Discourses delivered in the Royal Academy by the President. 1778.
The complete series of fifteen Discourses was published by Malone, E., in the first volume of his edition of Reynolds's Works, 2 vols., 1797. The Discourses have been frequently reprinted and edited; among others, by Burnet, J., 1842; Gosse, E., 1884; Fry, Roger, 1905; Dobson, Austin, 1907.

## PHILIP DORMER STANHOPE, FOURTH EARL OF CHESTERFIELD

Miscellaneous Works of the late Philip Dormer Stanhope Earl of Chesterfield with Memoirs of his Life by Maty, M. [Ed. by Justamond, J. O.] 2 vols. 1777.
Letters of Philip Earl of Chesterfield. Ed. with Notes [and Memoirs] by Mahon, Lord. 5 vols. 1845. (Vols. I, II, Letters on Education and Characters; vols. III, IV, Letters Political and Miscellaneous; vol. v, 1853, Miscellanies.)
Letters to his son Philip Stanhope. Published by Mrs. Eugenia Stanhope. 2 vols. 1774. Ed. Strachey, C., with Notes by Calthrop, A. 2 vols. 1901.
Letters to A. C. Stanhope Esq. relative to the Education of his Lordship's godson Philip the late Earl. 1817.
Letters to his Godson and Successor. Now first edited from the originals with a Memoir of Lord Chesterfield by the Earl of Carnarvon. Oxford, 1890. Appendix. Letters to A. C. Stanhope. 1890.

Ernst, W. Memoirs of the life of the fourth Earl of Chesterfield; with numerous letters now first published. 1893.
Hayward, Abraham. Lord Chesterfield and George Selwyn. 1854.
Tovey, D. C. Chesterfield's Letters. In Reviews and Essays in English Literature. 1897.

## HORACE WALPOLE, FOURTH EARL OF ORFORD

### A. *Collected Works*

The Works of Horatio Walpole, Earl of Orford. 5 vols. 1798. [Ed. Berry, Mary.]
Vol. I, Miscellaneous, and Catalogue of Royal and Noble Authors; vol. II, The Castle of Otranto, Richard III, Ædes Walpolianæ etc.; vol. III, Anecdotes of Painting; vol. IV, Catalogue of Engravers, Miscellaneous; vol. v, Miscellaneous Letters.
Subsequently were added:
Vol. VI, 1818, Letters to George Montagu, 1736–76, to the Rev. William Cole and others 1745 to 1782; vol. VII, 1822, Memoirs of the last ten years of the reign of George II, vol. I; vol. VIII, Memoirs, vol. II; vol. IX, 1825, Letters to the Earl of Hertford and to the Rev. Henry Zouch.

Memoirs of the last ten years of the reign of George II. 2 vols. 1822.
Memoirs of the reign of King George II. Ed. Holland, Lord. 3 vols. 1846.
Memoirs of the reign of King George III. Ed. Le Marchant, Sir D. 2 vols.
1845. New edn., by Barker, G. F. R. 4 vols. 1894.
Journal of the reign of George III from 1771–1783. Ed. Doran, J. 2 vols.
1859. New edn. by Steuart, A. F. 2 vols. 1910.

### B.  *Collected Editions of Correspondence*

1820.  Private Correspondence of Horace Walpole now first collected. 1820.
4 vols. 8°.

> First collected edition, arranged chronologically. It "includes the whole
> of [Walpole's] letters hitherto published," and comprises a period of above
> sixty years, 1735–1797. Rptd. twice in 1837.

1840.  Letters [ed. by Wright, John]. 6 vols. 1840. Rptd. several times.
1857–9.  Letters; ed. by Cunningham, Peter. 9 vols. Rptd.
1903.  Letters, ed. by Toynbee, Mrs. Paget. Oxford. 16 vols.

### C.  *Separate Collections of Letters*

1798.  Letters to Conway, etc. *See* Works, vol. v.
1818.  Letters to Montagu and Cole. *See* Works, vol. vi.
1825.  Letters to the Earl of Hertford and the Rev. Henry Zouch. *See* Works,
vol. ix.

1833.  Letters to Sir Horace Mann, 1741–60. Ed. by Dover, Lord. 1833. 3 vols.
1840.  Letters to the Berrys, first published in Collected edition of Walpole's
Letters. 1840. (*See above.*)
1843–4.  Letters to Mann 1760–85. Concluding series. 1843–4. 4 vols.

> Dr. Doran edited a selection from Mann's Letters to Walpole under the
> title of Mann and Manners at the Court of Florence, 1740–1786. 1786.
> 2 vols.

1848.  Letters to the Countess of Ossory, 1769–97. Ed. by Smith, R. Vernon.
2 vols.
1851.  Correspondence of Horace Walpole and the Rev. W. Mason. Ed. by
Mitford, J. 2 vols.
1902.  Some unpublished Letters of Horace Walpole. Ed. by Walpole, Sir
Spencer. 1902.

> Mostly written to the Hon. Thomas Walpole, second son of the first
> Lord Walpole of Wolterton.

Walpole's Letters to Mme. Du Deffand were destroyed by the writer's desire.
For her letters to him *see* Letters of the Marquise Du Deffand to the Hon.
Horace Walpole. . . . Published [by Miss Mary Berry] from the Originals
at Strawberry Hill. 4 vols. 1810. [Containing 353 letters and fragments.]
These letters were rptd. in Paris in 1811, 1812 and 1824.

> Lettres de la Marquise Du Deffand à Horace Walpole, 1766–1780.
> Ed. by Toynbee, Mrs. Paget. 3 vols. 1912. This collection, published
> from the Walpole Papers belonging to Jervis, W. R. Parker, consists of
> 838 letters, more than double the number in Miss Berry's edition.

### D.  *Biography and Criticism*

Berry, Miss. Extracts of the Journals and Correspondence of. Ed. Lewis, Lady
T. 3 vols. 1865.
Dobson, Austin. Horace Walpole, a Memoir. New York, 1890. 2nd edn.,
London, 1893; new edn., London, 1910.

Dobson, Austin. Eighteenth Century Vignettes. Series 1. A Day at Straw-
    berry Hill. 1892. Series 3. The Officina Arbuteana. 1896.
Greenwood, Alice D.  Horace Walpole's World.  1913.
Havens, M. A.  Horace Walpole and the Strawberry Hill Press.  Canton, Penn.,
    1901.
Hayward, A.  Strawberry Hill.  Quarterly Review, October, 1876.  Rptd.
Macaulay, Lord.  Edinburgh Review, October, 1833.  Rptd.
Seeley, L. B.  Horace Walpole and his World.  1883.
Walpoliana.  [By Pinkerton, John.]  2 vols.  1799.
Warburton, Eliot.  Memoirs of Horace Walpole and his Contemporaries, in-
    cluding numerous Original letters chiefly from Strawberry Hill.  2 vols.
    1851.
Wheatley, H. B.  The Strawberry Hill Press.  Bibliographica. May, 1896.
    *See, also,* bibliography to Chap. III, *ante.*

## GILBERT WHITE

Natural History and Antiquities of Selborne.  1789.  4°.
    Repeatedly rptd., and successively edited by distinguished naturalists,
including Buckland, F., 1875; Bell, T., 2 vols., 1877; Miall, L. C., and Fow-
ler, W. W., 1901; Allen, Grant, 1902; Kearton, R., 1911.

## II

### THE WARWICKSHIRE COTERIE

Many MSS of these writers still exist, the letters of Dodsley to Shenstone
in the British Museum, and much of the private correspondence of Shenstone,
Lady Luxborough, Somerville, and others, is preserved in private collections,
a great deal still unpublished.

### A.  *Collections of Letters and Verses*

Letters written by the late Right Honourable Lady Luxborough to William
    Shenstone, Esq.  1775.
Select Letters between the late Duchess of Somerset, Lady Luxborough, Miss
    Dolman, Mr. Whistler, Mr. R. Dodsley, William Shenstone, Esq., and
    others; including a sketch of the manners, laws, etc. of the republic of Venice,
    and some poetical pieces.  The whole now first published from original
    copies by Mr. Hull.  2 vols.  1778.
Correspondence between Frances, Countess of Hertford (afterwards Duchess
    of Somerset), and Henrietta Louisa, Countess of Pomfret, between the years
    1738 and 1741.  3 vols.  1805.
Hecht, H.  Thomas Percy and William Shenstone.  1909.  [A Collection of
    original letters between them.]

### B.  *Particular Authors*

Robert Dodsley

*See* bibliography to Vol. IX, Chap. VI.

Richard Graves

The Festoon, a collection of Epigrams.  1766.
The Spiritual Quixote, or the Summer's Ramble of Mr. Geoffry Wildgoose.
    A comic romance.  3 vols.  1772.  2nd edition, 1774; 1792, 1808.  Rptd.
    in the British Novelists.  2 vols.  1820.

Euphrosyne, or Amusements on the Road of Life.　1776.　2 vols.　1780.
Columella, or the Distressed Anchoret.　A colloquial tale.　2 vols.　1779.
Eugenius, or Anecdotes of the Golden Vale.　2 vols.　1785.
Lucubrations.　1786.
Recollections of some particulars of the life of William Shenstone, Esq.　1788.
The Rout, or a sketch of modern life.　1789.
Plexippus, cr the Aspiring Plebeian.　2 vols.　1790.
The Reveries of Solitude.　Consisting of essays in prose, a new translation of the Muscipula, and original pieces in verse.　1793.
Senilities, or solitary amusements in prose and verse.　1801.
The Invalid, with the obvious means of enjoying health and long life.　1804.
The Triflers, consisting of trifling essays, trifling anecdotes, and a few poetical trifles.　1805, 1806.
　　And other works.

Richard Jago

See bibliography to Chap. v, ante.

William Shenstone

See bibliography to Chap. vii, ante.

William Somerville (or Somervile)

See bibliography to Chap. v, ante.

A few letters of Somerville, in the possession of the last descendant of his cousin and correspondent Lord Somerville, were published in The Monthly Packet, November, 1898.

C.　Modern Books

Courtney, W. P.　Dodsley's Collection of Poetry, its contents and contributors. A chapter in the history of English literature in the eighteenth century. (Privately printed.)　1910.
Hutton, W. H.　Burford Papers.　1905.　[Accounts of the Warwickshire coterie and of Richard Graves.]
Kilvert, F.　Remains in prose and verse.　1866.
　　[Includes an account of Richard Graves.]
Sichel, W.　Bolingbroke and his times.　2 vols.　1901 and 1902.　[Memoirs of Lady Luxborough, printing Bolingbroke's correspondence with her.]
Straus, R.　Robert Dodsley, poet, publisher, and playwright.　1910.
　　An eighteenth century correspondence, ed. Dickins, L., and Stanton, M., 1910.

CHAPTER XII

HISTORIANS I

HUME AND MODERN HISTORIANS

James Anderson (1662–1728)

An historical essay showing that the crown and kingdom of Scotland is imperial and independent.　1705.　[A reply to The Superiority and Direct Dominion of the Imperial Crown and Kingdom of England over the Crown and King- dom of Scotland, 1704, by Atwood, William, sometime chief justice of New York.　Anderson criticised and condemned as forgeries the documents relating to the homage of the Scottish kings which John Hardyng supplied to the English treasury in 1457.　Atwood replied with The Scotch patriot unmasked. Anderson's book caused great excitement in Scotland; and the Scottish parliament voted him £4800 Scots and ordered Atwood's books to be burnt.]

Collections relating to the History of Mary, Queen of Scots, etc. 4 vols. 4to. 1727–8. [Of great value.]

Selectus diplomatum et numismatum Scotiae thesaurus, etc. 1739. [A magnificent compilation finished shortly before Anderson's death, and published by Ruddiman, Thomas, with an introduction, translated and published independently, 1773.]

### Thomas Birch

As to his edition of the Thurloe Papers, *see* bibliography to Vol. VII, Chaps. VIII and IX, p. 491, *ante*.

Lives and characters in Houbraken's Heads of illustrious persons of Great Britain. 1743. With additions. 2 vols. 1747–51.

Life of the Hon. Robert Boyle, prefixed to Boyle's Works. 1744.

An Inquiry into the share which King Charles I had in the Transactions of the earl of Glamorgan for bringing over a body of Irish rebels to assist that King in which Mr. Carte's imperfect account is impartially considered. (Anonymous.) 1747. 2nd edn., with appendix containing letters of the king to the earl of Glamorgan. 1756.

> The case of the Royal Martyr considered with candour in Answer to some libels, &c., by John Boswell, vicar of Taunton. 1758. [Reply to Inquiry.]

An historical view of the negotiations between the courts of England, France, and Brussels, 1592–1617, extracted chiefly from the State papers of Sir T. Edmonds, and of A. Bacon. 1749.

Life of Dr. John Tillotson, archbishop of Canterbury, compiled chiefly from his original papers. 1752.

> Remarks on the Life, etc. 1753. 3rd edn., with additions. 1755. [Reply by Smith, George, editor of Bede, a nonjuring bishop.]

Memoirs of the reign of Queen Elizabeth from 1581 to her death, from the original papers of A. Bacon, and other manuscripts [at Lambeth]. 2 vols. 1754.

The Life of Henry, Prince of Wales, eldest son of James I, chiefly from his own papers. 1760.

Letters between Colonel R. Hammond and the Committee of Lords and Commons at Derby House relating to Charles I while confined in Carisbrooke castle. 1764.

The Court and Times of James the First, illustrated by authentic and confidential Letters, etc. 2 vols. 1848.

The Court and Times of Charles the First, illustrated, etc., including memoir of the mission in England of the Capuchin friars in the service of Queen Henrietta Maria, etc. 2 vols. 1848.

> Both these were transcribed by Birch, and ed. by the author of Memoirs of Sophia Dorothea. [Williams, R. F.]

### Sir William Blackstone (1723–1780)

An Analysis of the Laws of England. 1754. 3rd edn. Oxford, 1758.

Commentaries on the Laws of England. 4 vols. 1765–9. For a list of the subsequent edns. and adaptations *see* bibliography appended to notice of Blackstone in D. of N. B., vol. v. The work was translated into French, German and Italian.

Tracts chiefly relating to the antiquities and laws of England. 2 vols. 1762. 3rd ed. Oxford, 1771.

Reports of cases determined in the several courts of Westminster Hall, from 1746 to 1779. 2 vols. 1781. (With a life by Clitherow, J.)

### Archibald Bower

The History of the Popes from the foundation of the see of Rome to the present time. 7 vols. 1748–66. [Vol. v, 1761, contains A summary view in 186 pp., of the controversy between the papists and the author.] An edn. with continuation by Cox, S. H. Philadelphia, 1844.

The more noteworthy pamphlets on Bower and his History are: A dialogue between Archibald and Timothy, Douay, 1748; Remarks on the first two volumes of the late Lives, etc., Douay, 1754; Six Letters from A——d B——r to Father Sheldon, 1756; Mr. Bower's answer to a scurrilous pamphlet, etc., 1757; Bower and Tillemont compared, 1757 (Douglas); Mr. Bower's answer to Bower and Tillemont compared, 1757; A full confutation of Bower's three defences, 1757 (Douglas); A complete and final detection, 1758 (Douglas). [A collection of the Bower pamphlets, including most of above, with portrait of Bower, is in the Brit. Mus. Library.]

### Thomas Carte

The Irish Massacre set in a clear light. Wherein Mr. Baxter's account of it in the history of his own life and the Abridgment thereof by Dr. Calamy is fully considered. Together with two replies from Mr. Chaundler, etc. [1714.] 2nd edn., with additions [1715], and in Somers Tracts, vol. III, 1809.

The Life of James, Duke of Ormond, to which is added a very valuable collection of letters, etc. 3 vols. Vol. III containing the letters, 1735; vols. I and II the life, 1736. Revised edn. 6 vols. Oxford, 1851.

A general account of the necessary materials for a History of England, etc. [1738.]

Collection of original letters and papers concerning the affairs of England 1640–1661, etc. 1739.

The History of the Revolution in Portugal from the foundation of that kingdom to 1667, with letters of Sir R. Southwell to the Duke of Ormond. 1740.

Collection of several papers published by Mr. T. C., etc. 1744.

A general History of England by Thomas Carte, an Englishman. 4 vols. 1747–55. See under Birch, Thomas, ante.

### Arthur Collins (1690?–1760)

The Life of William Cecil, Lord Burghley, from the original manuscript wrote soon after his lordship's death, etc., with other matters relating to the Cecil family, 1732.

Letters and Memorials of State in the reigns of Queen Mary, Queen Elizabeth, King James, Charles I, part of the Reign of Charles II, and Oliver's usurpation from the originals at Penshurst Place and the Office of Papers and Records of State. With genealogical and historical illustrations by the editor. 2 vols. 1746. [Generally known as The Sydney Papers. (See Vol. VIII, p. 304, note 1, ante.)]

Collins was the compiler of a Peerage and of various family histories.

*George Crawfurd* (d. 1748)

A genealogical history of the Stewarts from 1034 to 1710, to which is prefixed a description of the shire of Renfrew. 2 pts. 1710. The Shire of Renfrew continued by Semple, W. 1782. 2nd edn., continued. 1818.

Lives and characters of the officers of the Crown and State of Scotland from David I to the Union. Vol. I. 1726. (All published.)

Memoir of Henry Guthrie prefixed to reissue of The Memoirs of Henry Guthry, late bishop of Dunkeld. 1748.

[Though Crawfurd's works are now superseded, he was a learned and laborious man. He was author of The Peerage of Scotland, 1716.]

*Sir David Dalrymple*
*See* Lord Hailes.

*Sir John Dalrymple*

Essay towards a general history of feudal property in Great Britain. 1757. 4th edn., enlarged and corrected. 1759.

Criticised in A discourse on the bookland and folkland of the Saxons, wherein the nature of those kinds of estates is explained and the notion of them advanced by Sir John Dalrymple confuted, Cambridge, 1775.

Memoirs of Great Britain and Ireland from the dissolution of the last parliament of Charles II until the sea battle of La Hogue. 2 pts. 1771. 2nd edn., with continuation, Until the capture of the French and Spanish fleets at Vigo. 3 vols. 1790. New edn., with appendixes. 1796.

French tr. of the earlier part, 1776. Criticised by O'Halloran, S., in Observations on the Memoirs, etc., 4to, 1772; in the Letters of Lady Rachel Russell, with an introduction vindicating the character of Lord Russell against Sir John Dalrymple, 1773, 7th edn., 1809; and in Lord [John] Russell's Life of William Lord Russell, 1819, 4th edn., 1853.

*Jean Louis Delolme*

La Constitution de l'Angleterre. Amsterdam, 1771.

A parallel between the English constitution and the former government of Sweden containing some observations on the late revolution in that kingdom, etc. 1772. [Probably a tr. of Delolme's work by another hand.]

The Constitution of England or an account of the English government in which it is compared with the republican form of government. 8vo. 1775. 4th edn., enlarged. 1784. New edn., corrected. 1789. With supplementary notes and a preface biographical and critical, by Coote, C. 1807. New edn., with life and notes by Macgregor, John, Bohn's Standard Library, 1838. French edns., Geneva, 1788, 1790; German, 1776, ed. Dahlmann, F. C., 1819; Spanish, Oviedo, 1812.

The History of the Flagellants or the advantages of discipline, a paraphrase and commentary on the Historia Flagellantium of the Abbé Boileau by somebody who is not a doctor of the Sorbonne. 1777. Under title Memorials of human superstition, etc. 1784.

The British Empire in Europe, pt. I, containing an account of the connection between England and Ireland previous to the year 1780, etc. 1787.

*Adam Ferguson*

The History of the Progress and termination of the Roman Republic. Illustrated with Maps. 3 vols. 1733.

An Essay on the History of Civil Society. 1767. 3rd edn., corrected. 8vo.
    1768. New edn. Bâle, 1789. German trans., 1768; French trans., 1783.
Principles of Moral and Political Science. 2 vols. Edinburgh, 1792.

### Oliver Goldsmith

A History of England in a series of Letters from a Nobleman to his son. 2 vols.
    1764. [A school-book published anonymously and attributed to Lyttelton
    and others.] Various edns. and continuations; French tr., 1777.
The History of England from the earliest times to the death of George II. 4 vols.
    8vo. 1771. 11th edn., revised and continued to 1815 by Coote, C. 1819.
    French trans., 1837; Spanish, 1853.
An Abridgment of foregoing. [Posthumous.] 1774.

### Walter Goodall (or Goodal)

An examination of the letters said to be written by Mary, queen of Scotland, to
    James, earl of Bothwell. 2 vols. 1754.
    [Goodall edited the Scotchironicon, 1759.]

### William Guthrie

A general History of England from the invasion of Julius Caesar to the revolution
    of 1688. 4 vols. 1744-51.
A general History of Scotland from the earliest accounts to the present time. 10
    vols. 1767.

### Sir David Dalrymple, Lord Hailes

Memorials and letters relating to the History of Britain in the reign of James I.
    1762. 2nd edn., corrected. 1766.
Memorials and letters, etc., in the reign of Charles I. 1766.
The secret correspondence between Sir Robert Cecil and James VI. 1766.
Remarks on the history of Scotland. 1773.
Annals of Scotland from Malcolm Canmore to Robert I. 1776. Continued to
    the accession of the house of Stuart. 1779. New edn., to which are added
    several texts relative to the history. 3 vols. 1797.

### Philip Yorke, second Earl of Hardwicke

Letters to and from Sir Dudley Carleton, Knt. [Viscount Dorchester], during his
    embassy in Holland, 1616-1620, with historical preface. 1757. 3rd edn.
    1780.
Miscellaneous State Papers from 1501 to 1726 (the Hardwicke Papers). 2 vols.
    1778. (Anonymous.)

### Robert Henry

The History of Great Britain from the first invasion by the Romans, written on a
    new plan. 5 vols. 1771-85. Vol. VI, posthumous, ed. Laing. 1793.
    12 vols., with life of author. 1805. French tr. by Boulard, A. M. H. Paris,
    1789-96. [Hume wrote a laudatory review of the first volume for The
    Edinburgh Magazine and Review, which Gilbert Stuart (see post), the editor,
    suppressed, substituting a violent attack of his own.]

### David Hume

History of Great Britain [containing the reigns of James I and Charles I]. Vol. I.
    4to. Edinburgh, 1754. Vol. II, reigns of Charles II and James II. 1756.

History of England under the House of Tudor. 2 vols. 1759. From the invasion of Julius Caesar to the accession of Henry VII. 2 vols. 1761. From the invasion, etc., to the revolution in 1688. With the author's last corrections and an account of his life written by himself. 8 vols. 1778. With portraits, 8 vols., and Smollett, 5 vols. Oxford, 1826. [Best edition.] With Smollett and continuation by Hughes, T. S. 21 vols. 1836, 1848. Continuation to 1835. 18 vols. 1854. Histoire de la Maison de Stuart. French tr. by Prévost d'Exilles, A. F. 3 vols. 1760; by Mme. Belot. (Plantagenets and Tudors.) 4 vols. 1763; 6 vols. 1765. With continuations by Smollett, Adolphus and Aikin. By Campenon, V. 13 vols. 1839–40. [This presents Hume's last corrections.]

Compare bibliography to Chap. II, ante.

### Thomas Lediard (1685–1743)

The Naval History of England, in all its branches, from the Norman Conquest . . . to the conclusion of 1734. 2 vols. 1735.
The Life of John, Duke of Marlborough. 3 vols. 1736.
The History of the Reigns of William III and Mary and Anne, in continuation of the History of England by Rapin de Thoyras. 1737.

### Thomas Leland

A History of Ireland from the invasion of Henry II, with a preliminary discourse on the ancient state of that kingdom. 3 vols. 1773. 3rd edn., corrected. 1774.

### George Lyttelton, Baron Lyttelton

The History of the Life of King Henry II and of the Age in which he lived. 2 vols., and one unnumbered of notes. 1767.

### Mrs. Catherine Macaulay (or Macaulay Graham) (1731–1791)

The History of England from the accession of James I to that of the Brunswick Line. 8 vols. 4to. 1763–83. In vol. III and onwards and 2nd edn. of vols. I and II title substituted " to the elevation of the House of Hanover," from vol. V title " to the Revolution," 1688, at which date vol. VIII ends. French trans. [undertaken at the suggestion of Mirabeau], 5 vols., 1791–2.
The History of England from the Revolution to the present time in a series of letters to a Friend. Vol. I. Bath, 1778. [All published.]

[The author was sister of John Sawbridge, the democratic lord mayor, and was herself a violent republican. Her History is strongly coloured by her political opinions: it is badly constructed and ill-written. She wrote a Reply to Burke's Thoughts on the Present Discontents, 1770, in connection with which Lecky describes her as " the ablest writer of the new radical school."]

### Joseph McCormick (1733–1799)

See Carstares, William, in bibliography to Vol. IX, Chaps. VII and VIII.

### James Macpherson

Introduction to the history of Great Britain and Ireland, or an enquiry into the origin, religion, etc. of the Britons, Scots and Irish, and Anglo-Saxons. 1771. Enlarged, 1772.

Criticised by O'Halloran, Sylvester, in Introduction to the study of the History and antiquities of Ireland, 1772; by Whitaker, John, *see post*, and by Pinkerton, John, *see post*.

A History of Great Britain from the Restoration to the accession of the House of Hannover. 2 vols. 1775.

Original papers: containing the secret history of Great Britain from the Restoration to the accession of the house of Hannover. To which are prefixed extracts from the Life of James II as written by himself. 2 vols. 1775.

　　*See* Ranke, L. von, History of England, vol. VI, pp. 35 ff. (Eng. trans. 1875).

### Simon Ockley

The Conquest of Syria, Persia, and Ægypt by the Saracens [The History of the Saracens]. Vol. I, 1708; vol. II, 1718, with new edn. of vol. I and the Sentences of Ali published separately in 1717. 3rd edn., with Life of Mahomet [by Dr. Long]. 2 vols. Cambridge, 1757. 5th edn., with memoir of Ockley. Bohn's Standard Library, 1848. Fr. tr. [by Jault, A. F.]. Paris, 1748.

### Robert Orme

A History of the military transactions of the British nation in Indostan from 1745. 2 vols. Vol. II in two parts. 1763–78. Edn. revised by author. 1803.

Historical Fragments of the Mogul empire, of the Morattoes, and of the English concerns in Indostan from 1659. 1782. With Memoir of author. 1805.

### John Pinkerton (1758–1826)

The History of Scotland from the Accession of the House of Stuart to that of Mary. 2 vols. 1797.

### Humphry Prideaux (1648–1724)

The Life of Mahomet. 1697.

### William Robertson

Works, with account of life by Stewart, D., 8 vols., 1817. Oxford, 8 vols., 1825. French tr., by Suard, J.-B. A., Morellet, A., et Campenon, V., 12 vols., 1829; ed. Buchon, J.-A., 2 vols., 1843.

History of Scotland during the reigns of Queen Mary and of King James VI till his accession to the crown of England. With a review of the Scotch History before that period and an appendix containing original papers. 2 vols., 1759; 11th edn., corrected, 1787; 19th edn., 1812, and others. French tr., 3 vols., 1764. [*See under* Tytler, William, and Stuart, Gilbert, for replies.]

History of the reign of the Emperor Charles V, with a view of the progress of society from the subversion of the Roman empire to the beginning of the sixteenth century, 3 vols., 4to, 1769. Philadelphia, 1770. New edn., with corrections, 1777. 17th edn., with life by Stewart, Dugald, 1806. With an account of the emperor's life after his abdication, by Prescott, W. H., 1857; in vols. XII–XV of Prescott's Works, ed. Munro, W. H., 1905. French tr. by Suard, J.-B. A., 2 vols., Amsterdam, 1771. German, 3 vols., Brunswick, 1770–1. Italian, Palermo, 1835. Spanish, Barcelona, 1846.

History of America, 2 vols., 1777; 3 vols., 1778. With corrections, 1788; 9th edn., with posthumous vol., 4 vols., 1800. French tr. by Suard, J.-B. A. and Morellet, A., 1778; 6th edn., 1845. Geschichte von Amerika übersetzt von Schiller, J. F., 3 vols., Leipzig, 1777. Mod. Greek, 4 vols., Vienna, 1792–3.

An Historical Disquisition concerning the knowledge the Ancients had of India,
1791. With the author's last corrections, etc., 1794. French tr., Paris, 1792.
Italian, ed. Romagnosi, 1832.

## William Russell

A History of America from its discovery by Columbus to the conclusion of the
late war. 2 vols. 1778. [Contains notices of famous buccaneers.]
The History of Modern Europe to the Peace of Paris, 1763, in a series of Letters
from a Nobleman to his son. 5 vols. 1779–86. With continuations by
Coote, C. and others. 1818, 1827, 1850.

## Thomas Rymer

See bibliography to Vol. IX, Chaps. VII and VIII.

## Edmund Sawyer (d. 1759)

Memorials of Affairs of State in the reigns of Queen Elizabeth and King James
collected chiefly from the original papers of the Right Hon. Sir Ralph Winwood, Kt., and some time one of the principal secretaries of state. 3 vols.
1725. [The Winwood Memorials, from 1590–1614, are an important selection
from the official correspondence of Sir Ralph Winwood while ambassador
at the French court and the Hague. The Winwood papers, though some in
Sawyer's collection are missing, are calendared in the Hist. MSS. Com-
missioners' Report on the manuscripts of the duke of Buccleuch and Queens-
berry, vol. I, 1899.]

## Tobias George Smollett

A compleat History of England deduced from the descent of Julius Caesar to
the Treaty of Aix la Chapelle, 1748, containing the transactions of one
thousand eight hundred and three years. 4 vols. 1757–8. 2nd edn. 11
vols. 8vo. 1758–60. [Published in monthly parts at a shilling each.]
Continuation of the Complete History of England. 5 vols. 1763–5.
The History of England from the Revolution to the death of George II. (Designed as a continuation of Mr. Hume's History.) 5 vols. A new edn. 1789.

## Gilbert Stuart (1742–1786)

An historical disquisition concerning the antiquity of the English constitution.
1768. 2nd edn., corrected. 1770.
A view of society in Europe in its progress from rudeness to refinement. 1778.
French tr., by Boulard, A. H. M., 2 vols., Paris, 1789.
History of the establishment of the reformation in Scotland, a collection of the
principal records concerning it. 1780.
The History of Scotland, from the establishment of the reformation to the death
of Queen Mary. 2 vols. 1782. 2nd edn., to which are added Observations
concerning the public law and constitution of Scotland, originally published
in 1779. 1784. [This book, written in a polished style, with well-balanced
sentences, and occasionally high-flown expressions, contains a vindication of
Mary; in an appendix are some letters referring to the treatment of her by
Robertson, against whom Stuart had a personal grudge; cf. Gent. Mag., vol.
LII (1782), p. 167. He was editor of the Edinburgh Magazine and Review,
1773–6, and known as an unprincipled and slashing reviewer; for his conduct
with regard to Robert Henry, see ante.]

### William Tytler

An historical and critical inquiry into the evidence against Mary, queen of Scots, etc. 1760. 1772. With answer to Robertson, Hume, etc., 1772. With additional chapters. 2 vols. 1790. French tr., Paris, 1772. Ed. Prince Lobanov-Rostovsky. Paris, 1860.

### Horace Walpole, Earl of Orford

Historic Doubts on the life and reign of Richard III. 4to. 1768. [The first edn. of 1200 copies " sold so very fast that a new edition was undertaken the next day of 1000 more."] With additions and reply to Dr. Milles, 1770. H. W.'s Works, vol. II, 1798, with replies to criticisms of Hume and others, of Dr. Milles, in Observations on the wardrobe account for 1483, 1770, and in Archaeologia, vol. I, p. 361, and of Masters, Robert, in Archaeologia, vol. II, p. 198.

### Robert Watson

The History of the Reign of Philip II, King of Spain. 3 vols. 4to. 1777. Several 8vo edns., 7th 1812. French tr., by Mirabeau and Durival, J. Amsterdam, 1778.

History of the Reign of Philip III. Ed. and completed by Thomson, W. 2 vols. 1783. 3rd edn., enlarged. 1808. French tr., by Bonnet, L. J. A. Paris, 1809.

### Peter Whalley (1722–1791)

An Essay on the Manner of Writing History. [Anon.] 1746.
An Enquiry into the Learning of Shakespeare. 1748.
The Works of Ben Jonson. Ed. by Whalley, P. 7 vols. 1756.
The History and Antiquities of Northamptonshire. Compiled from the manuscript collections of John Bridges. 2 vols. 1791.

### John Whitaker

See bibliography to Chap. XIII, post.

## CHAPTER XIII

## HISTORIANS II

### I. EDWARD GIBBON

#### A. MSS.

The following MSS. in the British Museum are unprinted, except in part. (See Harrison, F., Proceedings of the Gibbon Commemoration, 1794–1894, p. 32.) Journals of Edward Gibbon, 1762–4. Consisting of:

1. Journal de mon Voyage dans quelques endroits de la Suisse: 21 September–20 October, 1755. (Autograph to 15 October.) [In English; partly printed in Miscellaneous Works, 1796.]

2. Ephemerides, or Journal of my actions, studies and opinions: vol. II, 17 August, 1762–May, 1763. In French.

3. Ephemerides, or Journal de ma vie, de mes études et de mes sentimens; vol. III, August–November, 1763. In French.

4. Journal (without title), including the tour in Italy; December, 1763–June 1764. In French.

5. Journal (without title); written in Italy, June–December, 1764. In French.

[According to Harrison, F., the above fill not less than 720 pp. of quarto and folio in Gibbon's very close handwriting, and small excerpts of them are inserted as notes in the published Memoirs and in a few other parts of the Miscellaneous Works.]

Outlines of the History of the World. Written (in Gibbon's early hand) between 1758 and 1763.

Extraits raisonnés de mes Lectures, beginning with general remarks upon Reading; written at Dover, 17 March, 1761.

Common Place Book, in which I purpose to note what I find most remarkable in my Historical Readings. Begun at Lausanne, March 19, 1755.

Observations on various subjects, written in French, at Lausanne and Buriton, 1756–8.

Note-Book, containing four pages of Materials for corrections and improvements for the 1st vol. of my History, followed by two pages of Materials for the fourth volume of [the same], November 8, 1781.

## B. *The Decline and Fall*

### (1) Editions

Gibbon, Edward. The Decline and Fall of the Roman Empire. Vol. I. 1776. Vols. II and III. 1781. Vols. IV–VI. 1788.

—— The History of the Decline and Fall of the Roman Empire. With notes by Milman, H. H. 12 vols. 1838–9. With notes by Milman, H. H. and Guizot, F. P. G. With additional notes by Smith, William. 8 vols. 1854. New edn., 1872. [Of Milman's Preface a considerable part first appeared in The Quarterly Review, vol. I, January, 1834.]

—— The History of the Decline and Fall of the Roman Empire. Ed. Bury, J. B. 7 vols. 1896–1900. New edn. 7 vols. 1909–13. [Now the standard edition, containing, besides a pregnant introduction, a series of longer notes or excursuses, with select bibliographies of later works, appended to each volume, and forming a supplement to the work, especially in those parts in which it falls short of the results of later research.]

Gibbon, Edward. Histoire de la Décadence, etc. Trans. by Le Clerc de Sept-Chênes (the reader of Louis XVI, who was supposed to have been the actual translator of this portion!), Demeunier, Boulard, Cautwell and Marignie. 18 vols. Paris, 1777–95. New edn., revised by Mme. Guizot, with Lettre sur la vie et le caractère de Gibbon by Suard, J.-B. A., and Notes by Guizot, F. P. G., 13 vols., Paris, 1812; 3rd edn., 1828–9.

—— Geschichte des Verfalls und Untergangs des Römischen Reiches. Übers. und mit einigen Anm. herausg. von Wenck, Friedrich August Wilhelm. 19 vols. 1779. 2nd edn. 1820.

German translation of c. XLIV by Hugo, G. H. under the title: Gibbon's Übersicht des römischen Rechts. Göttingen, 1789.

Istoria della Decadenza e Rovina dell' Imperio Romano. Trans. by Fabbroni and Foggi, vols. I–IX. Pisa, 1779–86. [Vol. X, though printed, was never published.]

### (2) *Adversaria*, etc.

Apthorpe, East. Letters on the Prevalence of Christianity before its Civil Establishment; with Observations on the late History of the Decline of the Roman Empire. 1778.

Burgh, William.  An Enquiry into the Belief of the Christians of the first three centuries respecting the one Godhead.  York, 1778.

(Chelsum, James.)  Remarks on the two last Chapters of Mr. Gibbon's History, etc., in a Letter to a Friend.  1776.  Rptd. in an enlarged form, with the author's name, Oxford, 1778.  [Chelsum was assisted in his task by Thomas Randolph.]

—— A Reply to Mr. Gibbon's Vindication.  Winchester, 1785.

Davis, Henry Edwards.  An Examination of the Fifteenth and Sixteenth Chapters of Mr. Gibbon's History of the Decline and Fall, etc.  In which his view of the Progress of the Christian Religion is shewn to be founded on the Misrepresentation of the authors he cites: and Numerous Instances of his Inaccuracy and Plagiarism are produced.  1778.

Edwards, Thomas.  The Jewish and Heathen Rejection of the Christian Miracles.  Preached before the University of Cambridge.  March 7, 1790.

Hailes, Lord (Sir David Dalrymple.)  An Inquiry into the Secondary Causes which Mr. Gibbon has assigned for the Rapid Growth of Christianity.  1786.

Loftus, Smyth.  A Reply to the Reasonings of Mr. Gibbon, etc.  Dublin, 1778.

Milner, Joseph.  Gibbon's Account of Christianity considered; together with some Strictures on Hume's Dialogues concerning Natural Religion.  1781.

Priestley, Joseph.  An History of the Corruptions of Christianity.  1782.  [The challenge to Gibbon is in Part I of the General Conclusion.]

Randolph, Thomas (President of Corpus Christi College, Oxford).  The Proof of the Christian Religion drawn from its Successful and Speedy Propagation, etc.  In two sermons.  Oxford, 1777.  [Against Gibbon's chap. xv.]

Taylor, Henry.  Thoughts on the Nature of the Grand Apostacy, with Reflections and Observations on the XVth Chapter of Mr. Gibbon's History of the Decline and Fall, etc.  1781.

—— Further Thoughts, etc.  1783.

Travis, George (archdeacon).  Letters to Edward Gibbon, Esq., author of the History of the Decline and Fall, etc.  Chester, 1785.  3rd edn. (enlarged).  1794.

> Porson, Richard.  Letters to Archdeacon Travis in Answer to Defence of the Three Heavenly Witnesses.  The Gentleman's Magazine, 1788–9.  Rptd. 1790, and with an additional letter (or this only?) in Porson's Tracts and Miscellaneous Criticisms.  Ed. Kidd, T.  1815.

Watson, Richard (bishop of Llandaff).  An Apology for Christianity in a Series of Letters to Edward Gibbon, Esq.  1776.

—— Two Apologies, one for Christianity in a series of letters addressed to Edward Gibbon, Esq., 1776, the other for the Bible, in answer to Thomas Paine, etc., 1805.

Whitaker, John.  Gibbon's History of the Decline and Fall of the Roman Empire, in vols. IV, V and VI quarto, reviewed.  1791.  [Originally published in The English Review.]

White, Joseph.  Sermons containing a View of Christianity and Mahometanism, in their history, their evidence and their effects, preached before the University of Oxford.  Bampton Lectures, 1784.  3rd edn.  1789.

---

Gibbon, Edward.  A Vindication of Some Passages in the XVth and XVIth Chapters of the History of the Decline and Fall of the Roman Empire.  By the Author.  1779.  (Rptd. in Misc. Works, vol. IV.)

**C.** *Other Writings (including Memoirs and Letters)*

Miscellaneous Works of Edward Gibbon, with Memoirs of his Life and Writings
Composed by Himself. Ed. John, Lord Sheffield. Vols. I and II, 1796;
vol. III, 1814; new edn., 5 vols., 1814. [Vol. I: Memoirs and Letters; vol. II:
Letters; vol. III: Historical and Critical; vol. IV: Classical and Critical;
vol. V: Miscellaneous.]

## (1) Memoirs and Letters

Autobiographies, the, of Edward Gibbon. Printed verbatim from hitherto
unpublished MSS., with an introduction by the Earl of Sheffield. Ed.
Murray, John. 1896. Contains (though in different order):
    A. The Memoirs of the Life of Edward Gibbon, with various observa-
tions and excursions by himself. Written in 1788-9, but only giving particulars of his family.
    B. My own Life. Written in 1789-90, and ending in April, 1764.
    C. Memoirs of the Life and Writings of Edward Gibbon; written in
1789-90, and brought down to October, 1772.
    D. Memoirs (without title); written in 1790-1, and brought down to
October, 1772.
    E. My Own Life; dated at end "Lausanne, March 2, 1791," and
ending with the death of Deyverdun in July, 1789; with notes added in
1792-3.
    F. Memoirs (without title); written in 1792-3, but only brought down
to the date of Gibbon's leaving Oxford in June, 1753. [Described by
Murray as the latest and most perfect. A fragment of headings from June,
1753 to April, 1758, with two pages on ancestry, containing the famous
passage on Tom Jones and the house of Austria.]
Life, the, of Edward Gibbon, Esq., With Selections from his Correspondence,
and illustrations by Milman, H. H. 1839. [The Memoirs, divided into
chapters, with extracts from the Journals, and selected Letters to Lord
Sheffield and others.]
Private Letters of Edward Gibbon (1753-1794). With an Introduction by the
Earl of Sheffield. Ed. by Prothero, Rowland E. 2 vols. 1896.
Memoirs, the, of the Life of Edward Gibbon, with various Observations and
Excursions by himself. Ed. Hill, George Birkbeck. 1900. [Contains
ample notes, and in the appendix, valuable excursuses.]

## (2) Other Writings

Antiquities of the House of Brunswick. Miscellaneous Works, vol. III. 1814.
Essai sur l'Étude de la Littérature. 1761. Rptd. in Miscellaneous Works,
vol. IV.
Mémoire justificatif pour servir de réponse à l'Exposé, etc., de la Cour de France.
1779. [Published anonymously.] Rptd. in Miscellaneous Works, vol. V,
1814.
Mémoires Littéraires de la Grande-Bretagne. 2 vols. 1767-8. [Ed. by
Gibbon and Deyverdun, George.] Rptd. in Miscellaneous Works, vol. IV,
1814.
Observations on the Design of the VIth Book of the Aeneid. Rptd. in Miscellaneous Works, vol. IV.

### D.  *Biography and Criticism*

(Writings not previously mentioned under B)

Adeane, Jane H.  The Girlhood of Maria Josepha Holroyd (Lady Stanley of
    Alderley), recorded in letters.  Ed. J. H. A.  1896.  [She was the daughter
    of Gibbon's chief friend, the first Lord Sheffield.]
        *See, also,* Adeane, Jane H., The Early Married Life of Maria Josepha,
    Lady Stanley, 1899.
Bagehot, W.  Estimates of some Englishmen and Scotchmen: E. Gibbon.  1858.
Morison, James Cotter.  Gibbon.  (English Men of Letters series.)  1878.
Proceedings of the Gibbon Commemoration, 1794–1894.  Royal Historical
    Society.  1895.  [Contains Introductory Speech of Sir Mountstuart Grant
    Duff, Address by Frederic Harrison, and Catalogue of the Exhibition at
    the British Museum of Autograph Memoirs, Journals and Notebooks,
    Correspondence, Early Impressions, Relics and Portraits.]
Read, General Meredith.  Historic Studies in Vaud, Berne and Savoy, from
    Roman Times to Voltaire, Rousseau and Gibbon.  2 vols.  1897.  [*See* vol.
    II for much about Gibbon and the relics of him at Lausanne and elsewhere.]
Smith, James.  Junius Unveiled.  1909.  [An unconvincing attempt to prove
    that Gibbon was Junius.]

### II.  OTHER WRITERS ON ANCIENT HISTORY

*See* bibliography to Chap. XII, *ante.*

Hooke, Nathaniel (d. 1673).  Roman History, from the Building of Rome to the
    Ruin of the Commonwealth.  4 vols.  1738–71.
        For titles of a series of dissertations by Hooke on the Roman Senate
        see art. Hooke, Nathaniel, in Dictionary of National Biography,
        vol. XXVII.
Middleton, Conyers.  The History of the Life of Marcus Tullius Cicero.  2 vols.
    1741.
Middleton, Conyers.  The Miscellaneous Works.  4 vols.  1752.  2nd edn.
    5 vols.  1755.  [Contains, besides the Life of Cicero:]
——  A Dissertation concerning the Origin of Printing.  1735.
——  The Epistles of M. T. Cicero to M. Brutus, and of Brutus to Cicero.
    With English notes and a prefatory dissertation.  1743.
    A Treatise on the Roman Senate.  1746–7.
    *See, also,* bibliography to Vol. IX, Chap. XII.
Mitford, William.  The History of Greece.  10 vols.  1784–1810.  New edn.
    10 vols.  1819–20.
        Macaulay, Lord.  Review of the above.  In Knight's Quarterly Mag-
        azine for November, 1824.  Rptd. in Miscellaneous Writings, vol. I,
        1860.
        Memoir, by the author's brother, Lord Redesdale.  In History of Greece.
        8 vols.  1829.  Revised by King, W.
Whitaker, John.  The Course of Hannibal over the Alps ascertained.  2 vols.  1784.
        Tytler, Alexander Fraser (Lord Woodhouselee).  A Critical Examination
    of the above.  1794.
——  The History of Manchester.  In Four Books.  Book I (Roman and Roman-
    British Period), 1771; Additional vol. of Principal Corrections, and 2nd edn.
    of vol. I, 2 vols., 1773; Book II (Saxon Period, to foundation of Heptarchy,
    and descent upon it of the Danes), 1775.  [No more published.]

Whitaker, John. The Genuine History of the Britons, a refutation of Macpherson's Introd. to the History of Great Britain and Ireland. 1772.
—— Mary Queen of Scots vindicated. 3 vols. 1787; volume of Additions and 2nd edn., 1790. [An uncompromising defence, now of no importance. His unfinished MS. of the Private Life of Mary Queen of Scots was used by Chambers, G. as a basis for his Life of Mary, 1818.]
—— Life of St. Neot (posthumous).

CHAPTER XIV

PHILOSOPHERS

*General Authorities:* Histories of philosophy and of political economy; Forsyth, T. M., English Philosophy, 1910; McCosh, J., The Scottish Philosophy, 1875; Pringle-Pattison, A. S., Scottish Philosophy, 1885; Seth, J., English Philosophers, 1912; Stephen, Sir L., A History of English Thought in the Eighteenth Century. 2 vols. 1876.

I. DAVID HUME

A. *Works*

(In chronological order)

A Treatise of Human Nature: being an Attempt to introduce the experimental Method of Reasoning into Moral Subjects. Vols. I and II, 1739; vol. III, 1740.
Essays Moral and Political. Edinburgh, 1741. Vol. II, 1742.
Philosophical Essays concerning Human Understanding. 1748.
An Enquiry concerning the Principles of Morals. 1751.
Political Discourses. Edinburgh, 1752.
Essays and Treatises on Several Subjects. In four volumes. 1753–4 (final edition, 1777).
The History of Great Britain. (The History of England.) *See* bibliography to Chap. XII, *ante.*
Four Dissertations. I. The Natural History of Religion. II. Of the Passions. III. Of Tragedy. IV. Of the Standard of Taste. 1757.
The Life of David Hume, Esq. Written by himself. 1777.
Two Essays [on Suicide and on Immortality]. 1777.
Dialogues concerning Natural Religion. 1779.
Editions of A Treatise of Human Nature and Dialogues concerning Natural Religion, by Green, T. H. and Grose, T. H. (with philosophical introductions by Green, T. H.), 2 vols., 1874; of Essays (complete) by the same (with bibliographical introduction by Grose, T. H.), 2 vols., 1875; of the Treatise, Oxford, 1896, and of the two Enquiries, *ib.*, 1894 (with indexes) by Selby-Bigge, L. A.; of the Dialogues, by McEwen, B., 1907; of the Political Discourses, by Robertson, W. B., 1908.

B. *Selected Biography and Criticism*

Bonar, J. Philosophy and Political Economy. 1893.
Burton, J. H. Life and Correspondence of David Hume. 1846.
—— Letters of Eminent Persons addressed to David Hume. 1849.
Gižycki, G. von. Die Ethik Humes. 1878.
Green, T. H. Introductions to Hume's Treatise. Vols. I and II. Works. **Vol.** I. 1885.
Hedvall, C. Humes Erkenntnistheorie. 1906.

Hill, G. Birkbeck.   Letters of David Hume to W. Strahan.   1888.
Huxley, T. H.   Hume.   (English Men of Letters series.)   1879.
Jodl, F.   Leben und Philosophie Humes.   1872.
Klemme, M.   Die volkswirtschaftlichen Anschauungen Humes.   1900.
Lechartier, G.   David Hume, moraliste et sociologue.   1900.
Marcus, E.   Kant's Revolutionsprinzip.   Eine exakte Lösung des Kant-Hume'-
   schen Erkenntnisproblem.   1902.
Meinong, A.   Hume-Studien.   I, 1877; II, 1882.
Pfleiderer, E.   Empirismus und Skepsis in Humes Philosophie.   1874.
Quast, O.   Der Begriff der Belief bei Hume.   1903.
Teisseire, M.   Les Essais économiques de David Hume.   1902.
Thomsen, A.   David Hume.   Sein Leben und seine Philosophie.   1912.

## II.   ADAM SMITH

### A.   *Works*

The Theory of Moral Sentiments; or an essay towards an analysis of the principles
   by which men naturally judge concerning the conduct and character, first
   of their neighbours, and afterwards of themselves; to which is added, a
   Dissertation on the Origin of Languages.   1759.   6th edn.   2 vols.   1790.
An Inquiry into the Nature and Causes of the Wealth of Nations.   2 vols.   1776.
   6th edn.   3 vols.   1791.   Edd. McCulloch, J. R., 1828, etc.; Rogers, J. E. T.,
   1869;   Nicholson, J. S., 1884;   Cannan, E., 1904.

Essays on Philosophical Subjects.   To which is prefixed an account of the life
   and writings of the author.   By Stewart, Dugald.   1795.
Lectures on Justice, Police, Revenue and Arms . . . reported by a student in
   1763.   Ed. by Cannan, E.   Oxford, 1896.

### B.   *Biography and Criticism*

Bagehot, W.   Economic Studies.   1880.
—— Biographical Studies.   1881.
Bonar, J.   Philosophy and Political Economy.   1893.
—— A Catalogue of the Library of Adam Smith.   1894.
Farrer, J. A.   Adam Smith.   (English Philosophers series.)   1881.
Haldane, Viscount.   Adam Smith.   (Great Writers series.)   1887.
Hasbach, W.   Die allgemeinen philosophischen Grundlagen der von Quesnay
   und Smith begründeten politischen Ökonomie.   Leipzig, 1890.
—— Untersuchungen über Adam Smith.   Leipzig, 1891.
Hirst, F. W.   Adam Smith.   (English Men of Letters series.)   1904.
Leslie, T. E. Cliffe.   Essays in Political and Moral Philosophy.   1879.
Nicholson, J. S.   A Project of Empire.   1909.
Oncken, A.   Adam Smith in der Culturgeschichte.   1874.
—— Adam Smith und Immanuel Kant.   1877.
Rae, John.   Life of Adam Smith.   1895.
Stewart, Dugald.   Biographical Memoir of Adam Smith in Trans., R. S. E.   1793.
   (In vol. containing also memoirs of Robertson and Reid, 1811; in Works, vol.
   x, 1858.)

### III.   OTHER PHILOSOPHICAL WRITERS

#### *James Beattie*

An Essay on the Nature and Immutability of Truth in opposition to sophistry
   and scepticism.   Edinburgh, 1770.   With other essays.   Edinburgh, 1776.

Dissertations moral and critical. 1783.
Elements of Moral Science. 1790-3.

Forbes, Sir W. Life and Writings of Beattie. 2 vols. 1806.
Forbes, M. Beattie and his friends. 1904.
*See, also*, bibliography to Chap. VII, *ante*.

### George Campbell (1719-1796)

A Dissertation on Miracles. 1762.
The Philosophy of Rhetoric. 1776.

### William Derham (1657-1735)

Physico-Theology. 1713.
Astro-Theology. 1715.
Christo-Theology. 1730.

### John Douglas (bishop of Salisbury) (1721-1807)

Criterion of Miracles. 1752.

### Adam Ferguson

Essay on the History of Civil Society. 1767.
History of the Progress and Termination of the Roman Republic. 1783.
Principles of Moral and Political Science. Edinburgh, 1792.

Huth, H. Soziale und individualistische Auffassung . . . bei Adam Smith und
Adam Ferguson. 1907.
*See, also*, bibliography to Chap. XII, *ante*.

### James Harris (1709-1780)

Hermes, or a Philosophical Inquiry concerning Universal Grammar. 1751.
Philosophical Arrangements. 1775.
Philological Inquiries in three parts. 2 vols. 1781.

### David Hartley

Conjecturæ quædam de sensu motu et idearum generatione. 1746. In Parr's
Metaphysical Tracts, 1837.
Observations on Man, his frame, his duty, and his expectations. 1749.
(The edition of 1791 is accompanied by a sketch of the author's life, and
by notes and additions translated from the German of Pistorius, H. A.)

Hartley's Theory of the Human Mind, on the principle of the Association of Ideas.
With essays by Priestley, J. 1775.

Bower, G. S. Hartley and James Mill. (English Philosophers Series.) 1881.

### Henry Home, Lord Kames (1696-1782)

Essays on the Principles of Morality and Natural Religion. 1751. (German
trans. 1772.)
Introduction to the Art of Thinking. 1761.
Elements of Criticism. 1762.
Sketches of the History of Man. 1774.

Tytler, A. F., Lord Woodhouselee. Life of Lord Kames. 1807.

## Nathaniel Lardner (1684–1768)

The Credibility of the Gospel History. 1727–55.
Works. 11 vols. 1788. 4 vols. 1817. 10 vols. 1827.

## James Burnett, Lord Monboddo (1714–1799)

Of the Origin and Progress of Language. 3 vols. Edinburgh, 1773–6. 2nd edn.
6 vols. 1774–92.
Antient Metaphysics: or, the Science of Universals. 6 vols. Edinburgh,
1779–99.

Knight, W. Lord Monboddo and some of his contemporaries. 1900.

## James Oswald (1715–1769)

An Appeal to Common Sense in behalf of Religion. Edinburgh, 1766.

## William Paley

The Principles of Moral and Political Philosophy. 1785. Ed. Whateley, R.
1859. Ed. Bain, A. (Moral Philosophy only). n.d.
Horæ Paulinæ, or the Truth of the Scripture History of St. Paul evinced. 1790.
A View of the Evidences of Christianity. 1794.
Natural Theology, or Evidences of the Existence and Attributes of the Deity
collected from the Appearances of Nature. 1802. With notes by Brougham,
Lord, and Bell, Sir C. 1836.
Works. 7 vols. 1825.

## Richard Price

A Review of the Principal Questions and Difficulties in Morals. 1757. 3rd edn.
1787.
Observations on Reversionary Payments. 1771. 4th edn. 1783.
An Appeal to the Public on the subject of the National Debt. 1772.
Observations on the nature of Civil Liberty, the Principles of Government, and the
Justice and Policy of the War with America. 1776.
Additional Observations [on the same subject]. 1777.
The General Introduction and Supplement to the two Tracts on Civil Liberty.
1778.
An Essay on the Population of England. 1780.
A Discourse on the Love of our Country. 1789.

## Joseph Priestley

The History and Present State of Electricity. 1767.
An Essay on the First Principles of Government. 1768. 2nd edn. 1771.
A Free Address to Protestant Dissenters as such. 1769.
Institutes of Natural and Revealed Theology. 3 vols. 1772–4.
Experiments and observations on different kinds of Air. 6 vols. 1774–86.
An Examination of Dr. Reid's Inquiry . . . , Dr. Beattie's Essay . . . , and
Dr. Oswald's Appeal to Common Sense. 1774.
Disquisitions relating to Matter and Spirit. 1777.
The Doctrine of Philosophical Necessity illustrated. 1777.
A Free Discussion on the doctrines of Materialism, &c. 1778.
Observations on the Importance of the American Revolution. 1784.
(And many other works chiefly scientific and theological.)

Theological and Miscellaneous Works, ed. Rutt, J. T. 25 vols. 1817–32.

Thorpe, T. E. Priestley. (English Men of Science Series.) 1906.
*See, also, under* David Hartley, *ante.*

## John Ray

The Wisdom of God manifested in the Works of the Creation. 1691.
(And many other works, chiefly botanical.)

## Thomas Reid

An Essay on Quantity, in Phil. Trans. 1748.
An Inquiry into the Human Mind on the Principles of Common Sense. 1764.
A Brief Account of Aristotle's Logic, in Lord Kames's History of Man. 1774.
Essays on the Intellectual Powers of Man. Edinburgh, 1783.
Essays on the Active Powers of Man. Edinburgh, 1788.

Works, ed. Hamilton, Sir W. 2 vols. 1846–63.
Fraser, A. C. Reid. (Famous Scots Series.) 1898.
Pringle, Pattison A. Seth. Scottish Philosophy. 1885.
Stewart, Dugald, in Works, vol. x, and in Hamilton's Reid, vol. 1.

## Sir James Steuart [Denham]

An Inquiry into the Principles of Political Economy: being an Essay on the Science
of Domestic Policy in Free Nations. 2 vols. 1767.

Hasbach, W. Untersuchungen über Adam Smith. 1891. (Pp. 369–381.)

## Abraham Tucker (1705–1774)

The Light of Nature pursued. 7 vols. 1768–78. [Vols. v–vii published posthumously by his daughter.] *See, also,* Hazlitt's Preface to an abridgment
of Tucker's work, Works, edd. Waller, A. R. and Glover, A., vol. iv, 1902.

## CHAPTER XV

### DIVINES

#### A. General Works

Abbey, C. J. The English Church and its Bishops, 1700–1800. 2 vols. 1887.
Abbey, C. J. and Overton, J. H. The English Church in the 18th century.
2 vols. 1878. New edn. 1887.
Hunt, J. Religious Thought in England to the end of the 18th century. 3 vols.
1870–3.
Hutton, W. H. The English Church from the accession of Charles I to the death
of Queen Anne. [With useful bibliographies.] 1903.
Lathbury, T. History of the Nonjurors. 1845.
Millar, J. H. The mid-eighteenth century. Edinburgh, 1902.
Overton, J. H. Life in the English Church, 1660–1717. 1885.
—— The Nonjurors: their lives, principles, and writings. 1902.
—— The English Church from the accession of George I to the end of the eighteenth century. 1906.
Stephen, Sir L. English Thought in the 18th century. 2 vols. 1876.

## B.  Particular Writers

### Francis Atterbury, Bp. of Rochester

Miscellaneous Works.  With historical notes by J. Nichols.  5 vols.  1789–98.
A Discourse occasion'd by the death of Lady Cutts.  1698.
The Rights and Privileges of an English Convocation stated and vindicated.  1700.
*See, also*, Vol. IX, Chap. xiii, and bibliography.

Beeching, H. C.  Francis Atterbury.  1909.

### Joseph Bingham

Works.  2 vols.  1726.  9 vols.  Ed. Pitman, J. R.  1840.  New edn by
Bingham, R.  10 vols.  Oxford, 1855.
Origines ecclesiasticae, or the antiquities of the Christian church.  10 vols.
1708–22.
Transl. into Latin by Grischow, J. H., 10 vols.  Halle, 1724–9.

### Thomas Brett (1667–1743)

A Sermon on remission of sins according to the Scriptures and the doctrine of
the Church of England.  1711.  2nd edn.  1712; 3rd edn.  1715.
A Sermon of the honour of the Christian priesthood.  1712.
The divine right of episcopacy.  1718.
A general history of the world.  1729.  2nd edn.  1732.

### Joseph Butler

See Vol. IX, Chap. xi, bibliography.

### Richard Cumberland, Bp. of Peterborough

See Vol. IX, Chap. xi, bibliography.

### Thomas Deacon

A Communion Office [for Non jurors].  1718.
A compleat collection of devotions.  1734.
A full, true, comprehensive view of Christianity.  1747.  2nd edn.  1748.
Sutton, C. W.  The writings of T. Deacon and J. Owen.  Manchester, 1879.

Broxap, H.  A biography of Thomas Deacon, the Manchester Non-Juror.
Manchester, 1911.

### Henry Dodwell (d. 1711)

See Vol. VIII, Chap. xii, bibliography, and Vol. IX, Chaps. xi and xiii,
bibliographies.

### John William Fletcher

Works.  8th edn.  7 vols.  1826.
Checks to Antinomianism.  1771, etc.
Zelotus and Honestus reconciled; or an Equal Check given to Pharisaism and
Antinomianism.  1774.

### Thomas Herring, Abp. of Canterbury

Seven Sermons on public occasions.  1763.
Letters to William Duncombe, Esq., deceased, from the year 1728 to the year 1757.
With notes and an appendix.  1777.

## James Hervey

*See* Vol. IX, Chap. xi, bibliography.

## Benjamin Hoadly, Bp. of Winchester

Works. Published by his son John Hoadly. With a life. 3 vols. 1773.
A Plain Account of the Nature and End of the Sacrament of the Lord's Supper.
1735.
    [Answered by Waterland in A Review of the Doctrine of the Eucharist.]
    *See, also,* Vol. IX, Chap. xi, bibliography.

## Humphrey Hody (1659–1707)

The Resurrection of the (same) Body asserted. 1694.
A History of English Councils and Convocations. 1701.
De Bibliorum textibus originalibus. Oxford, 1705.

## Richard Hurd, Bp. of Worcester (1720–1808)

Moral and Political Dialogues. 1759.
Letters on Chivalry and Romance. 1762.
An Introduction to the Study of the Prophecies concerning the Christian Church,
    and in particular concerning the Church of Papal Rome. 1772.

## John Johnson (1662–1725)

Theological Works. 2 vols. 1847.
The Clergyman's Vade Mecum. 2 pts. 1708–9.
The Unbloody Sacrifice and Altar unvail'd and supported. 2 pts. 1714–17.

## Samuel Johnson (d. 1703)

*See* Vol. IX, Chap. xi, bibliography.

## White Kennett, Bp. of Peterborough

Parochial antiquities attempted in the history of Ambrosden, etc. 1695.
Ecclesiastical Synods and Parliamentary Convocations . . . historically stated
    and vindicated from the misrepresentations of Mr. Atterbury. 1701.

Life, by Newton, W. 1730.
    *See, also,* Vol. IX, Chaps. vii and viii, bibliography.

## Thomas Secker, Abp. of Canterbury

Works. Ed. Porteus, B. 6 vols. 1825.
Sermons on several subjects. Ed. Porteus, B. and Stinton, G. To which is
    added a review of his life and character. 7 vols. 1770–1.
Lectures on the Catechism of the Church of England. 1769.

## Thomas Sherlock, Bp. of London

Remarks on the Bp. of Bangor's [Hoadly's] treatment of the Clergy and Con-
    vocation. 1717.
A Letter to the Clergy and People of London and Westminster on occasion of the
    late Earthquakes. 1750.
    *See, also,* Vol. IX, Chap. xi, bibliography.

### George Smalridge, Bp. of Bristol

Sixty sermons preach'd on several occasions.  1726.  2nd edn.  1727.  New edn
2 vols.  Oxford, 1852.

### Augustus Montague Toplady

Works.  New edn. with a memoir of the author.  6 vols.  1825.  6 vols.  1828.
The Historic Proof of the Doctrinal Calvinism of the Church of England.  1774.
Psalms and Hymns for public and private worship.  1776.

Wright, T.  A. M. Toplady.  1911.

### Thomas Wagstaffe, the elder (1645–1712)

A Vindication of King Charles the Martyr proving that His Majesty was the
author of Εἰκὼν βασιλική.  1693; 1697.
A Defence of the Vindication.  1699.

### William Wake, Abp. of Canterbury

See Vol. IX, Chap. XI, bibliography.

### Daniel Waterland

A Review of the doctrine of the Eucharist.  Cambridge, 1737.  Rptd., Oxford,
1896.
See, also, Vol. IX, Chap. XI, bibliography.

### John Wesley

Works.  32 vols.  Bristol, 1771–4.  11th edn.  15 vols.  1856–62.
A Collection of Psalms and Hymns.  Charlestown, 1737.
        For later Collections of Hymns issued by John and Charles Wesley,
    see Julian, J., Dictionary of Hymnology, 2nd edn., 1907.
Journal.  21 pts.  [1739]–91.  4 vols.  1827.  Abridged, 1902.  Ed. Curnock,
    N.  (Standard edn.)  1909–  (in course of publication).

Coke, T. and Moore, H.  Life of John Wesley.  1792.  New edn.  2 vols.  1824–5.
Green, R.  Bibliography of the works of John and Charles Wesley.  1896.
Southey, R.  Life of Wesley.  2 vols.  1820.
Tyerman, L.  The life and times of Wesley.  3 vols.  1870–1.
Whitehead, J.  Life of John Wesley.  2 vols.  1791–3.

### Charles Wesley

Journal.  Ed. Jackson, T.  2 vols.  1849.
Jackson, T.  Life and Correspondence of Charles Wesley.  2 vols.  1841.
Telford, J.  Life of Charles Wesley.  1887.  New edn.  1900.
    See, also, John Wesley.

### George Whitefield

Works.  Ed. Gillies, J.  6 vols.  1771–2.
Journals.  1738–41.
A Short Account of God's dealings with G. Whitefield.  1740.
A Full Account.  1747.
A Further Account.  1747.

Journals; to which is prefixed his Short Account and **Further Account. Ed.**
Wale, W. 1905.

Tyerman, L. Life of G. Whitefield. 2 vols. 1876.

### *Thomas Wilson, Bp. of Sodor and Man*

Collected Works. 2 vols. 1781. 6 vols. Oxford, 1847–63.
Principles and Duties of Christianity. In English and Manks. 1707.
A short and plain Instruction for the better understanding of the Lord's Supper.
1736. 32nd edn. 1807.
The knowledge and practice of Christianity made easy. 3rd edn. **1742.**
Sacra privata. Bath, 1786.
Parochialia. 1791.

Keble, John. The Life of Th. Wilson. 2 vols. Oxford, 1863.

**A. T. B.**

## CHAPTER XVI

### THE LITERATURE OF DISSENT, 1660–1760

The general literature of the history of dissent is in an unsatisfactory condition.
Since Daniel Neal's History of the Puritans (extending only to 1688; best edition
5 vols. 1793–7) no great synoptic work has been attempted, for Bogue and Bennett's History of Dissenters 1688–1804 (4 vols. 1808–12) and Joshua Toulmin's
Historical view of . . . Protestant Dissenters and of the progress of free inquiry
and religious liberty, 1814, are not comparable to Neal's work as to breadth of
treatment and documentary thoroughness, and the same may be said of Stough-
ton's Religion in England, 1702–1800, 2 vols. 1878. To these works succeeded
a lesser series of merely denominational histories, and to these, again, the modern
race of mere church monograph writers. (Burrage, C., The Early English Dissenters in the light of recent research, 2 vols. Cambridge, 1912, purports to reach
only to 1641.) Apart from the literary activity of the Society of Friends [see
Vol. VIII] the foundation of the Congregational Historical society and the Baptist
Historical society promises some day to remove this reproach from dissent. The
latter society in particular, under the guidance of Whitley, Dr. W. T., is supplying
exactly what is required. But much of this preliminary work still remains to
be done before a broad synopsis on the lines of Neal's work can be attempted.

The biographical literature of dissent is, comparatively, abundant, especially
in Calamy, Edmund, Abridgement of Baxter's life, 1702: 2nd edn., 2 vols. 1713
and continuation 1727, 2 vols.; inefficiently re-edited as The Nonconformist's
Memorial, 3 vols. 1802–3; *see, also,* Wilson, Dissenting Churches in London,
4 vols. 1808–14. But the early portion of it (in Calamy especially) stands greatly
in need of a general searching revision such as Nightingale, B., has furnished for
Cumberland and Westmorland.

### I. DENOMINATIONAL HISTORIES

#### A. *Congregational*

Dale, Robert William. History of English Congregationalism. Completed and
ed. by Dale, A. W. W. 1907.
Fletcher, Joseph. A History of the revival . . . of Independency in England.
4 vols. 1847.

Hanbury, Benjamin. Historical Memorials relating to the Independents from their rise to the Restoration. 1839–44.
Waddington, J. Congregational History. 5 vols. 1869–80.

### B. *Presbyterian*

Drysdale, A. H. History of the Presbyterians in England. 1889.
History, opinions and legal position, The, of the English Presbyterians. 1834.
McCree, Thomas. Annals of English Presbyterianism. 1872.
Murch, J. History of the Presbyterian and General Baptist Churches in the West of England. 1835.
Wilson, J. Historical enquiry concerning the principles . . . of the English Presbyterians. 1835.

### C. *Baptist*

Armitage, T. History of the Baptists. 1887.
Benedict, D. General History of the Baptist Denomination. 2 vols. 1813.
Crosby, T. History of the English Baptists. 4 vols. 1738–40.
Douglas, D. History of the Baptist Churches in the North of England. (1846.)
Fuller, J. G. Brief History of the Western Association. 1843.
Ivimey, J. History of the English Baptists. 4 vols. 1811–30.
Taylor, T. History of the English General Baptists. 2 vols. 1818.
Thomas, J. History of the Baptist Association in Wales. 1795.
Whitley, W. T. History of the Baptists in Cumberland, Lancashire and Cheshire. [In preparation.]

### D. *Unitarian*

Brief History of the Unitarians called also Socinians. 1687.
Hebard, J. Historical sketch of Unitarianism. 1834.
Herford, B. Story of religion in England. 1883.
Lindsey, Theophilus. Historical view of the state of Unitarian doctrine and worship. 1783.
Lloyd, W. Story of Protestant Dissent and English Unitarians. 1899.
New, H. Unitarian and Free Christian Churches in England. 1883.

---

Woolman, John (1720–1772). Works. Philadelphia, 1774.
—— Journal. 1775. With an introduction by Smellie, A., and an appreciation by Whittier, J. G. 1898.

## II. Toleration and Removal of Disabilities

The general history of the legislation on the subject of dissenters' disabilites is fairly well covered in Skeats, Herbert S., History of the Free Churches of England, 1868 (continued by Miall, E.); but the literary side of the subject has not received the special and complete treatment which it deserves. Schaff, P., The Progress of Religious Freedom, and Ruffini, F., Religious Liberty, English translation, 1912, are too broad in their sweep to be able to particularise the purely dissenting phase of the literary side of this controversy; while the ordinary dissenting authorities such as Bogue and Bennett, Waddington, Toulmin and Brook, B. (Sketch of the History and proceedings of the Deputies appointed to protect the civil rights of Protestant Dissenters, 1813) treat it too much as an isolated and sectarian phenomenon.

The following may be cited among earlier writers or writings, Dissenting or secular, on the subject of toleration:

An Humble Supplication to the King's Majesty. 1620. (Anonymous.)
Busher, Leonard. Religion's Peace. 1614. To which are appended Certain
  Reasons against Persecution. Reissued by the Hanserd Knollys Soc. 1846.
Goodwin, John.
Persecution for Religion judged and condemned. 1615. (Anonymous.)
Richardson, Samuel. The Necessity of Toleration in Matters of Religion. 1647.
Robinson, Henry.
Sturgion, John. A Plea for Toleration. 1661.
—— Sion's Groans for her Distressed. 1661.
The Ancient Bounds: or Liberty of Conscience. 1645. (Anonymous.)
The Humble Petition of the Anabaptists. 1660.

See, also, bibliographies to Vol. VII, Chaps. v (Milton), and vii (Bunyan),
ante; Vol. IX, Chap. 1 (Defoe), ante; Vol. VIII, Chap. xiv (Locke), ante.

### III. THE ANTI-TRINITARIAN AND DEISTIC CONTROVERSIES

The bibliography of the several successive phases of the anti-Trinitarian controversy are covered by several general authorities. Wallace, R., Anti-Trinitarian Biography, 3 vols. 1850 (vol. 1, Introduction); Hunt, J., Religious Thought
in England, 3 vols. 1870–3 (vol. 11, pp. 273–8); Bogue, D. and Bennett, J., A
History of Dissenters, 1688–1808, 4 vols. 1808–12 (vol. 111); Curteis, G. H.,
Dissent in relation to the Church (Bampton Lecture), 1871. But none of these
is complete. Several of the dissenting colleges possess large collections of the
pamphlet literature of this subject; but, probably, the most comprehensive of
these collections is in Dr. Williams's Library, Gordon Square, where a special
catalogue of this subject, containing several hundred items, has lately been compiled. The whole subject is at present being specially studied by Colligan, J. H.,
of Liverpool.
  The literature of the deistic controversy is fully surveyed in Dr. John Leland's
View of the Principal Deistical Writers, 3 vols. 1755; Stephen, Sir Leslie, History
of English Thought in the Eighteenth Century, vol. 1, 1876; Lechler, G. V.,
Geschichte des englischen Deismus, 2 vols. 1841; Farrar, S., A Critical History
of Free Thought (Bampton Lecture), 1862; and also in general authorities such
as Abbey and Overton, The English Church in the Eighteenth Century, 2 vols.
1878. As the dissenting contribution to this controversy constitutes the chief
claim of dissent to purely literary notice, a list is appended here of the chief
works by nonconformist writers:

Bennet, Benjamin. On the truth, inspiration and usefulness of the sacred scrip-
  tures. 1730.
Benson, George. The Reasonableness of the Christian Religion. 1743.
Browne, Simon. A fit rebuke. 1732.
—— Defence of the religion of nature. 1732.
Calamy, Edmund. Sermons on the inspiration of the holy writings. 1710.
Chandler, Samuel. Reflections on the conduct of the modern Deists. 1727.
—— A Vindication of the Christian Religion. 1728.
—— A Vindication of . . . Daniel's prophecies. 1728.
—— Plain reasons for being a Christian. 1730.
—— The witnesses of the Resurrection. 1744.
Doddridge, Philip. The Redeemer and the Sanctifier. 1736.
—— Of the Evidences of Christianity. In answer to [Dodwell's] Christianity
  not founded in Argument. 1742–3.

Duchal, James.  On the presumptive arguments for the truth of the Christian religion.  1753.
Fleming, Caleb.  Various Answers etc. to Thomas Chubb.  1738, etc.
Foster, James.  A Letter to a Deist.  1729.
—— The Usefulness, Truth and Excellence of the Christian Religion.  1731.
Hallett, Joseph.  A Free and Impartial Study of the Holy Scriptures recommended.  3 vols.  1729–36.
—— The Immorality of the Moral Philosopher.  1737.
—— The Consistent Christian.  1738.
Harris, William.  Two Sermons against Woolaston.  1738.
Jones, Jeremiah.  A new and full method of settling the canonical authority of the New Testament.  1726.
Lardner, Nathaniel.  The Credibility of Gospel History.  1727.
Leland, John.  The advantage and necessity of the Christian Revelation.  1764.
—— The divine authority of the Old and New Testament.  1738.
—— Remarks on a pamphlet.  1744.
—— Reflections on the late Lord Bolingbroke's letters.  1753.
—— An Answer to Tindal's Christianity as old as the Creation.  1733.
—— A View of the principal Deistical writers.  1754–6.
Lowman, Moses.  Dissertation on the civil government of the Hebrews.  1740.
—— The argument from prophecy.  1733.
Morgan, Thomas.  The Moral Philosopher.  1737.
Watts, Isaac.  Three Sermons on the Inward Witness of Christianity, or An Evidence of the Truth of the Gospel from its Divine Effects.  1730.

## IV.  Writers of Hymns and Religious Verse

### A.  *Congregationalists*

Doddridge, Philip.  Hymns.  (Posthumous; ed. Orton, J.)  Salop, 1755.  Reissued, with additional hymns, as Scriptural Hymns, ed. Humphreys, J. D. 1839.
Newton, John.  Olney Hymns.  1779.  (With his friend Cowper.)
Watts, Isaac.  (Of his six hundred hymns, many are still sung, and formed part of his Horae Lyricae (1706), Hymns (1707), Divine Songs (1715), and Psalms of David (1719).)

### B.  *Presbyterians*

Brown, Simon.  Hymns and Spiritual Songs.  3 books.  1720.
Slater, Samuel (died 1704).  Poems.  1679.

### C.  *Baptists*

Keach, Benjamin (1640–1704).  Spiritual Melodies . . . Psalms and Hymns from the Old and New Testament.  1691.
—— A Feast of Fat Things . . . Spiritual Songs.  1692.
Robinson, Robert (1735–90).  Hymns for the Fast-Day.  (Issued by Whitefield, 1757.  See, as to these and others of like merit, D. of N. B. vol. XLIX.)
Ryland, John Collett (1723–92).  Life and Actions of Jesus Christ, by Way of Question and Answer, in Verse.  1767.
Steele, Anne (1717–78).  Poems on Subjects chiefly Devotional (1760).
Stennett, Joseph (1663–1713).  Hymns in vol. IV of his Works, 4 vols.  1732.  (Originally publ. 1697–1712; version of Solomon's Song, 1700.)

CHAPTER XVII

POLITICAL LITERATURE, 1755–75

I. POLITICAL CONTROVERSY, 1754–75

A. *Periodicals*

The Auditor. June, 1762–Feb., 1763. (Ed. Murphy, A.)

The Briton. May, 1762–Feb., 1763. (Ed. Smollett, T.)

The Con-Test, Nos. 1–38. 23 Nov., 1756–6 Aug., 1757. (Ed.? Ruffhead, O., or? Francis, P.)

The Monitor, or British Freeholder, Nos. 1–403. 9 Aug., 1755–6 Oct., 1763. (Ed.? Entick, John.)

The North Briton. 1762–3. (By John Wilkes and Charles Churchill.) 2nd edn., with notes. 3 vols. 1763. Continued 1768–9.

The Test, Nos. 1–35. 6 Nov., 1756–9 July, 1757. (Ed. Murphy, A.)

Wilkes, J. C. The Political Controversy, or weekly magazine of ministerial and anti-ministerial essays. 5 vols. 1762–3. (This includes reprints of the issues for 1762–3 of The Monitor, The Auditor, The Briton, The North Briton, and other papers.)

B. *Separate Works*

The most important tracts of this period (1763–1770) are reprinted in: Almon, J. A collection of scarce and interesting tracts. 4 vols. 1787–8.

Bath, W. Pulteney, Earl of. Seasonable hints from an honest man on the new reign and the new parliament. 1761.

Burke, Edmund. Short account of a late short administration. 1766.

—— Observations on a late State of the nation. 1769.

—— Thoughts on the cause of the present discontents. 1770.

Candor. A Letter to the Public Advertiser. 1764.

—— A Letter concerning libels, warrants, etc. 6th edn. 1766.

For a list and account of other pamphlets, some signed Phileleutherus Anglicanus, which have been attributed to Candor, see W. J. Smith's essay in Grenville Papers, vol. III, pp. CLXXVI ff.

Francis, P. A Letter from the Cocoa Tree to the Country Gentleman. 1762.

Grenville, G. The present state of the nation. 1768.

—— Speech on the motion for expelling Mr. Wilkes, 3 February, 1769.

Guthrie, W. An Address to the Public on the late dismission of a General Officer [Conway]. 1764.

Jenyns, Soame. Poems. 1752.

—— A Free Enquiry into the Nature and Origin of Evil. 1757.

—— View of the Internal Evidence of the Christian Religion. 1776.

—— Disquisitions on Several Subjects. 1782.

—— Thoughts on Parliamentary Reform. 1784.

—— Works. Ed. Cole, C. N. 4 vols. 1790.

Johnson, Samuel. The False Alarm. 1770. [On the Middlesex Election.]

—— Thoughts on the late transactions respecting Falkland's Islands. 1771.

—— The Patriot. Addressed to the Electors of Great Britain. 1774.

Lloyd, Charles. A Vindication of the conduct of the ministry in the case of Mr. Wilkes. 1763.

—— The anatomy of a late negotiation. 1763.

—— A defence of the Majority in the House of Commons on the question of general warrants. 1764.

Lloyd, Charles. A critical review of the new administration. 1765.
—— The conduct of the late administration examined. 1765.
—— An honest man's reasons for declining to take part in the new administration. 1765.
—— An examination of the principles of a late Rt. Hon. Gentleman [Pitt]. 1766.
—— A true history of a short administration. 1766.
Massie, Joseph. An Essay on the governing causes of the natural rate of Interest. 1750.
—— A Representation concerning the Knowledge of Commerce as a National Concern. 1760.
Shebbeare, J. Letters to the people of England. 8 parts. 1756–70.
—— Letters on the English nation. 2nd edn. 2 vols. 1756.
—— The history of the excellence and decline of the constitution . . . of the Sumatrans. 2 vols. [1763.]
Townshend, C. A Defence of the Minority in the House of Commons on the question relating to general warrants. 1764.
—— The State of the Nation in 1766 and 1767.
Walpole, Horace. The opposition to the late Minister [Bute] vindicated. 1763.
—— A Counter Address to the Public on the late dismission of a General Officer [General Conway]. 1764.
Whately, T. Remarks on The Budget. 1765.
—— Considerations on the trade and finances of the kingdom. 1766.
Wilkes, John. A Letter to Earl Temple. 1763.
—— A Letter to the Duke of Grafton. 1767.
—— A Letter to Mr. Grenville in answer to his Speech. 1769.

### C.   Biography and Criticism

Almon, J. Biographical, literary, and political Anecdotes of several of the most eminent persons of the present age. 3 vols. 1797.
Andrews, A. History of British Journalism to 1855. 2 vols. 1859.
Bourne, H. R. F. English Newspapers. Chapters in the history of Journalism. 2 vols. 1887.
Escott, T. H. S. Masters of English Journalism. 1911. (Chap. IV.)
Fitzgerald, P. Life and Times of John Wilkes. 2 vols. 1888.
Johnstone, C. Chrysal, or the Adventures of a Guinea. 4 vols. 1760–5. New edn. by Baker, E. A. 1908. [Contains an account of Medmenham.]
Stephens, A. Memoirs of John Horne Tooke, interspersed with original documents. 2 vols. 1813.
Wilkes, J. Correspondence . . . With memoirs of his life by Almon, J. 5 vols. 1805.
Wright, T. England under the House of Hanover; its history during the reigns of the three Georges, illustrated from caricatures and satires. 2 vols. 1848. Another edn. 1868.

### II.   CHARLES CHURCHILL

#### A.   Collected Editions

Poems. 1763–5, 1766; 7th edn., 1772; 1774, 1776.
Poetical Works, with an authentic account of his life [by Tooke, W.]. 2 vols. 1804.
Poetical Works. With notes and a life of the author by Tooke, W. (Aldine Poets.) 3 vols. 1844. (Tooke's edition of 1804 reprinted and enlarged.)
Poetical Works, with memoir, etc., by Gilfillan, G. Edinburgh, 1855.

Poetical Works, with a memoir by Hannay, J. L., and copious notes by Tooke, W. 2 vols. 1866. Revised edn. 1892.

## B. *Separate Works*

The Rosciad. By the Author. 1761. 9th edn. 1765.
Reviewed in Critical Review, March, 1761.
The Apology. Addressed to the Critical Reviewers. 1761.
These three reprinted and annotated by Lowe, R. W., 1891.
Night. An Epistle to Robert Lloyd. 1762.
The Ghost. 4 books. 1762–3.
The North Briton. (By Churchill and Wilkes.) 1762–3.
The Prophecy of Famine; a Scots pastoral inscribed to John Wilkes, Esq. 1763.
An Epistle to William Hogarth. 1763. 2nd edn. 1763.
The Conference. 1763.
The Duellist. In three books. 1763.
The Author. 1763.
Gotham. In three books. 1764.
The Candidate. 1764.
The Farewell. 1764.
The Times. 1764.
Independence. 1764.
Sermons, with a satirical dedication in verse to Warburton. (Published posthumously.) 1765.

## C. *Biography and Criticism*

(In addition to the memoirs cited above under sec. II, A.)

Courthope, W. J. History of English Poetry. 1905. (On Churchill: vol. v, pp. 224–37.)
Forster, J. Charles Churchill, 1731–1764. The Edinburgh Review for January, 1845. Rptd. 1855 and in Historical and Biographical Essays, vol. II, 1858.
Fitzgerald, P. The Life and Times of John Wilkes. 2 vols. 1888.
Genuine memoirs of Mr. Charles Churchill. 1765.
Putschi, F. Charles Churchill, sein Leben und seine Werke. [Wiener Beiträge zur engl. Philologie.] Vienna and Leipzig, 1909.
Scott, R. F. Admissions to the College of St. John the Evangelist. Cambridge, 1903. [Notice of Churchill, pt. III, p. 580.]
Stephen, Sir L. Charles Churchill. D. of N. B. vol. x. 1887.

## III. OTHER SATIRISTS IN VERSE

Chatterton, T. The Consuliad. Poetical works. Ed. Roberts, H. D. 1906.
Falconer, W. The Demagogue. Poetical works. Aldine edn. 1836.
Mason, W. [Malcolm MacGreggor.] Ode to Mr. Pinchbeck upon his newly invented patent candle-snuffers. 1776.
—— An Epistle to Dr. Shebbeare; to which is added an Ode to Sir Fletcher Norton. 1777.
—— The Dean and the Squire. A political eclogue, humbly dedicated to Soame Jenyns, Esq. 1782.
Whitehead, Paul (1710–1774). Poems and miscellaneous compositions. Ed. with a life by Thompson, E. 1777.
—— Manners. A Satire. 1739.
—— Honour. A Satire. 1747.
—— Satires. 1748.

## IV.  OTHER PUBLIC LETTER-WRITERS, 1758–75.

These will be found in the following:

The Public Advertiser (ed. Woodfall, H. S.); The Gazetteer and Almon's Political Register. The following were the principal signatures to letters contributed to The Public Advertiser: Anti-Sejanus (1766); Cato Redivivus (1766); A. B. (1766–7); Onustus (1767); One of the People (1767), etc.

A full general account will be found in Parkes-Merivale, under sec. v, B, *post*.

Scott, James. A collection of interesting letters. 1767. (These first appeared in The Public Advertiser under the pseudonym of Anti-Sejanus.)

—— Fugitive Political Essays which have appeared in The Public Advertiser during the last winter, 1769–70. 1770.

## V.  JUNIUS

The Letters of Junius originally appeared in The Public Advertiser.

A full annotated bibliography (12 columns) of the Letters of Junius, and of the controversial literature relating to them, is given in Lowndes's Bibliographer's Manual, new edn. by Bohn, H. G., part 5, 1860. In the preface will be found some account of a secret letter addressed to Grafton and signed Lucius. This letter cannot now be found.

An elaborate bibliography of 49 editions of the Letters and of 289 works and articles about Junius, compiled by Edmunds, J., appeared in vol. II of the Bulletin of the Mercantile Library of Philadelphia, 1890–2.

An annotated list, by Wheatley, H. B., of the 46 persons to whom the authorship of the Letters has been assigned is included in Halkett and Laing's Dictionary of Anonymous and Pseudonymous Literature (1882–8).

### A.  *Collected Editions*

The Political Contest; containing a series of letters between Junius and Sir W. Draper; also the whole of Junius's letters to the D[uke] of G[rafton]. 2 pts. 1769. 3rd edn. 1769.

Almon, J. A Collection of the Letters of Atticus, Lucius, Junius, and others. 1769.

The Letters of Junius. 2 vols. 1772. (The first authorised edition; as to the previous unauthorised editions by Wheble and others, *see* Bohn's bibliography mentioned above.) Other edns.: 1783, 1788, 1789, 1797, 1802 (with notes by Heron, R.), 1806 (ed. Almon, J.), etc.

Junius, including letters by the same writer under other signatures (now first collected). To which are added his confidential correspondence with Mr. Wilkes, and his private letters to H. S. Woodfall; with a preliminary essay [by Good, J. M.]. 3 vols. 1812. 2nd edn. 1814.

The Letters of Junius, with preliminary dissertations and copious notes by Atticus Secundus [M'Diarmid, J.]. 2 vols. Edinburgh, 1822.

Junius. New edn., enlarged, with new evidence as to the authorship. 2 vols. London, 1850. Reprinted.

[In vol. II. is an important essay of 80 pages, in which the editor, Wade, John, assumes Sir Philip Francis to be the author of the Junius Letters. In addition to the letters collected by Junius himself, this edn. contains miscellaneous letters written by or attributed to him.]

## B. *Critical and Controversial Works*

Barker, E. H.   I. The claims of Sir Philip Francis to the authorship of Junius's Letters disproved.   II. Some enquiry into the claims of the late Charles Lloyd, Esq. to the composition of them.   1831.   [Opposes the claims of Francis and Sackville, and advocates those of Charles Lloyd.]

Brockhaus, F.   Die Briefe des Junius.   Leipzig, 1876.

Chabot, C.   The handwriting of Junius professionally investigated.   With preface and collateral evidence by Twisleton, Edward.   1871.

Chatham, William Pitt, earl of.   Correspondence.   Edd. by Taylor, W. S. and Pringle, J. H.   4 vols.   1840.   [Contains two secret letters of Junius to Lord Chatham in 1768 and 1772.]

Cockburn, Sir G.   Inquiry as to who was the author of Junius.   Dublin, 1845.   [Argues strongly for Charles Lloyd.]

Coleridge, S. T.   Notes on Junius.   Literary Remains.   Ed. Coleridge, H. N.   Vol. I.   1836.

Dilke, C. W.   Junius.   In Papers of a Critic, vol. II.   1875.

Francis, H. R.   Junius revealed, by his surviving grandson, Francis, H. R.   1894.

Francis, Sir P.   Memoirs, with correspondence and journals.   Commenced by Parkes, J.   Completed and edited by Merivale, H.   2 vols.   1867.   [Contains a cogent statement of the Franciscan case, especially with regard to dates and to the identity of Francis's and Junius's political opinions.   It also has a full account of the principal letter-writers in The Public Advertiser unfortunately identifying them all with Francis and Junius.]

Francis, Sir P. and others.   The Francis Letters.   By Sir Philip Francis and other members of the family.   Ed. by Francis, B. and Keary, E.   2 vols.   1901.   [With a note on the Junius controversy by Keary, C. F.]

Grafton, A. H. F., 3rd duke of.   Autobiography and political correspondence.   Ed. Anson, Sir W. R.   1898.   [Gives the inner history of many political events Commented upon by Junius.   Sir William Anson suggests that "whatever part Francis may have played in the composition of the Letters, Temple directed their policy, supplied much of their information, and may conceivably have polished their invective."]

Grenville Papers.   Correspondence of R. Grenville, Earl Temple, and Rt. Hon. G. Grenville, their friends and contemporaries.   4 vols.   1852–3.   [Contains three secret letters written by Junius to George Grenville in 1768.   The editor, Smith, W. J., argues that Lord Temple was Junius and gives much information on the political pamphleteering of the time in a valuable preface to vol. III.]

Hayward, A.   More about Junius.   The Franciscan theory unsound.   Rptd. from Fraser's Magazine.   1868.   [Against Parkes and Merivale.]

—— The handwriting of Junius.   1874.

—— Junius.   Encyclopaedia Britannica.   Edn. 9, vol. XIII.   1881.

Jaques, J.   The history of Junius and his works.   1843.

Lecky, W. E. H.   History of England in the eighteenth century.   3rd edn.   Vol. III.   1887.   [Account and critique of Junius.]

Macaulay, Lord.   Essay on Warren Hastings.   Works, vol. IX.   1898.

Merivale, H.   Junius, Francis, and Lord Mansfield in December, 1770.   Fortnightly Review.   1 March, 1868.   [Replying to Hayward.]

Newhall, I.   Letters on Junius . . . showing that the author of that celebrated work was Earl Temple.   Boston, 1831.

Rae, W. Fraser. Facts about Junius and Francis, with other notes on the Junius controversy. Contributed to the Athenaeum in 1888 and following years.

Smith, James. Junius unveiled. 1909. [Argues that Gibbon was Junius.]

Stephen, Sir L. Sir Philip Francis. D. of N. B. vol. xx. 1889.

—— Chatham, Francis, and Junius. Eng. Hist. Rev. April, 1888.

Taylor, J. A discovery of the author of the Letters of Junius. 1813. [In favour of Dr. Philip Francis and Sir Philip Francis.]

—— The identity of Junius with a distinguished living character [Sir P. Francis] established. 1816. 2nd. edn. 1818.

—— Supplement to Junius identified. 1817. 2nd. edn. 1818.

A. T. B.

# TABLE OF PRINCIPAL DATES

1641 Henry Dodwell born (d. 1711).
1657 William Wake born (d. 1737).
1663 Francis Atterbury born (d. 1732).
1663 Thomas Wilson, bp. of Sodor and Man born (d. 1755).
1667? Susannah Centlivre born (d. 1723).
1674 Isaac Watts born (d. 1748).
1675 William Somerville born (d. 1742).
1676 Benjamin Hoadly born (d. 1761).
1678 Simon Ockley born (d. 1720).
1678 Thomas Sherlock born (d. 1761).
1683 Conyers Middleton born (d. 1750).
1683 Daniel Waterland born (d. 1740).
1683 Edward Young born (d. 1765).
1685 Aaron Hill born (d. 1750).
1686 Thomas Carte born (d. 1754).
1688? Thomas Warton the elder born (d. 1745).
1689 Samuel Richardson born (d. 1761).
1692 Joseph Butler born (d. 1752).
1693 George Lillo born (d. 1739).
1696 Matthew Green born (d. 1737).
1699 Robert Blair born (d. 1746).
1700 Death of Dryden.
1700 James Thomson born (d. 1748).
1700? John Dyer born (d. 1758).
1702 Philip Doddridge born (d. 1751).
1703 John Wesley born (d. 1791).
1703? Henry Brooke born (d. 1783).
1705 Abraham Tucker born (d. 1774).
1707 Henry Fielding born (d. 1754).
1707 Charles Wesley born (d. 1788).
1708 Ockley's *History of the Saracens* begins to appear (completed 1757).

1709 John Armstrong born (d. 1779).
1709 Samuel Johnson born (d. 1784).
1709 George, Lord Lyttelton born (d. 1773).
1709 Mrs. Centlivre's *The Busy Body*.
1709 First Copyright Act passed.
1710 Thomas Reid born (d. 1796).
1711 David Hume born (d. 1776).
1712 Richard Glover born (d. 1785).
1712 Edward Moore born (d. 1757).
1713 Laurence Sterne born (d. 1768).
1714 James Hervey born (d. 1758).
1714 William Shenstone born (d. 1763).
1714 George Whitefield born (d. 1770).
1714-27 George I.
1715 Richard Graves born (d. 1804).
1715 Richard Jago born (d. 1781).
1715 William Whitehead born (d. 1785).
1716 Thomas Gray born (d. 1771).
1717 David Garrick born (d. 1779).
1717 Horace Walpole born (d. 1797).
1717-20 The Bangorian Controversy.
1719 Death of Addison.
1719 Edward Young's *Busiris*.
1720 Samuel Foote born (d. 1777).
1720 Mrs. Elizabeth Montagu born (d. 1800).
1720 Gilbert White born (d. 1793).
1721 Mark Akenside born (d. 1770).
1721 William Collins born (d. 1759).
1721 William Robertson born (d. 1793).
1721 Tobias Smollett born (d. 1771)
1722 John Home born (d. 1808).
1722 Thomas Leland born (d. 1785).
1722 Christopher Smart born (d. 1771).
1722 Joseph Warton born (d. 1800)

1723  Richard Price born (d. 1791).

1723  Sir Joshua Reynolds born (d. 1792).

1723  Adam Smith born (d. 1790).

1726  Law's *Absolute Unlawfulness of the Stage Entertainment fully demonstrated*.

1726  Thomson's *Winter*.

1727  Arthur Murphy born (d. 1805).

1727  John Wilkes born (d. 1797).

1727  Death of Newton.

1727  Dyer's *Grongar Hill*.

1727  Thomson's *Summer*.

1727–60  George II.

1728  Oliver Goldsmith born (d. 1774).

1728  Thomas Warton the Younger born (d. 1790).

1728  Fielding's *Love in Several Masques*.

1728  Gay's *Beggar's Opera*.

1728  Thomson's *Spring*.

1729  John William Fletcher (of Madeley) born (d. 1785).

1729  Thomas Percy born (d. 1811).

1729  Clara Reeve born (d. 1807).

1729  Thomson's *Sophonisba*.

1730  Fielding's *Tom Thumb*.

1730  Thomson's *Seasons* (including *Autumn*).

1731  Charles Churchill born (d. 1764).

1731  Death of Defoe.

1731  *The Gentleman's Magazine* first appears.

1731  Lillo's *London Merchant*.

1732  George Colman born (d. 1794).

1732  William Falconer born (d. 1769).

1732  David Hartley born (d. 1813).

1733  Joseph Priestley born (d. 1804).

1734  Henry Carey's *Chrononhotonthologos*.

1735  James Beattie born (d. 1803).

1735  Somervile's *The Chace*.

1736  James Macpherson born (d. 1796).

1736  Butler's *Analogy*.

1736  Fielding's *Pasquin*.

1736  Aaron Hill's *Zara*.

1736  Lillo's *Fatal Curiosity*.

1737  Death of Queen Caroline.

1737  Edward Gibbon born (d. 1794.)

1737  Fielding's *The Historical Register for 1736*.

1737  Green's *The Spleen*.

1738  Johnson's *London*.

1739  Hugh Kelly born (d. 1777).

1739  War declared against Spain.

1739–40  Hume's *Treatise of Human Nature*.

1740  James Boswell born (d. 1795).

1740  Sir Philip Francis born (d. 1818).

1740–1  Richardson's *Pamela*.

1741  Middleton's *Life of Cicero*.

1741  Resignation of Walpole.

1742  Battle of Dettingen.

1742  Fielding's *Joseph Andrews*.

1742–5  Young's *Night Thoughts*.

1743  William Paley born (d. 1805).

1743  Blair's *The Grave*.

1743  Fielding's *Miscellanies*.

1744  William Mitford born (d. 1827).

1744  Pope died.

1744  Akenside's *Pleasures of the Imagination*.

1744  Armstrong's *Art of preserving health*.

1744  Sarah Fielding's *David Simple*.

1744  Johnson's *Life of Savage*.

1745  Henry Mackenzie born (d. 1831).

1745  Hannah More born (d. 1833).

1745  Death of Swift.

1745–6  Jacobite Rebellion.

1746–7  Hervey's *Meditations*.

1747  Collins's *Odes*.

1747  Gray's *Ode on a distant prospect of Eton College*.

1747  John Hoadly's *Suspicious Husband*.

1747  Lyttelton's *Monody*.

1747–8  Richardson's *Clarissa Harlowe*.

1747–55  Carte's *History of England*.

1748  Hume's *Philosophical Essays concerning Human Understanding*.

1748  Smollett's *Roderick Random*.

1748  Thomson's *Castle of Indolence*.

1749  Fielding's *Tom Jones*.

1749  David Hartley's *Observations on Man*.

1749 Johnson's *Vanity of Human Wishes* and *Irene*.

1750 First number of *The Rambler*, 20 March. (Last, 14 March, 1752).

1750 Fielding's *Enquiry into the Causes of the late Increase of Robbers*.

1750 Whitehead's *The Roman Father*.

1751 Sheridan born (d. 1816).

1751 Fielding's *Amelia*.

1751 Gray's *Elegy*.

1751 Hume's *Enquiry concerning the Principles of Morals*.

1751 Smollett's *Peregrine Pickle*.

1752 Frances Burney (Mme. d'Arblay) born (d. 1840).

1752 Thomas Chatterton born (d. 1770).

1752 Joseph Ritson born (d. 1803).

1752 Smollett's *Adventures of Ferdinand Count Fathom*.

1753 Edward Moore's *The Gamester*.

1753–4 Richardson's *Sir Charles Grandison*.

1754–61 Hume's *History of Great Britain*.

1755 Fielding's *Voyage to Lisbon*.

1755 Johnson's *Dictionary*.

1755 Shebbeare's *Letters to the People of England* begin.

1755 *The Monitor* established.

1756 Home's *Douglas*.

1757–60 The great years of Pitt.

1757 Battle of Plassey.

1757 The Strawberry Hill Press opened.

1757 Gray's *Odes*.

1757 Price's *Review of the principal questions in Morals*.

1757–8 Smollett's *History of England*.

1758 H. S. Woodfall assumes control of *The Public Advertiser*.

1758–60 Johnson's *Idler*.

1759 Battle of Minden. Capture of Quebec.

1759 Johnson's *Rasselas*.

1759 Robertson's *History of Scotland*.

1759 Adam Smith's *Theory of Moral Sentiments*.

1760 Lyttelton's *Dialogues of the Dead*.

1760 Macpherson's *Fragments of Ancient Poetry*.

1760 Rousseau's *Nouvelle Héloïse*.

1760–7 Sterne's *Tristram Shandy*.

1760–1820 George III.

1761 Churchill's *The Rosciad* and *The Apology*.

1761 Colman's *The Jealous Wife*.

1761 Diderot's *Éloge de Richardson*.

1761 Resignation of Pitt. Bute at the head of affairs.

1762 Isaac Bickerstaff's *Love in a Village*.

1762 Falconer's *The Shipwreck*.

1762 Goldsmith's *Citizen of the World*.

1762 Macpherson's *Fingal*.

1762 Smollett's *Sir Launcelot Greaves*.

1762 Walpole's *Anecdotes of Painting in England*.

1763 No. 45 of *The North Briton* appears.

1763–5 Continuation of Smollett's *History of England*.

1763 Macpherson's *Temora*.

1763 Percy's *Five Pieces of Runic Poetry*.

1763 Resignation of Bute.

1763 Smart's *Song to David*.

1764 Goldsmith's *The Traveller*.

1764 Reid's *Inquiry into the Human Mind*.

1764 Shenstone's *Works in Prose and Verse*.

1764 Horace Walpole's *Castle of Otranto*.

1764 The Candor pamphlets.

1765 The Stamp Act.

1765 Johnson's edition of Shakespeare.

1765 Percy's *Reliques*.

1765 Tucker's *Light of Nature pursued*, Vols. I-IV. (Completed 1778).

1766 Colman's *Clandestine Marriage*.

1766 Goldsmith's *Vicar of Wakefield*.

1766 Repeal of the Stamp Act. The Chatham Ministry.

1766 Smollett's *Travels through France and Italy*.

1766–70 Henry Brooke's *The Fool of Quality*.

1768 Goldsmith's *The Good-Natur'd Man.*

1768 Gray's *Poems.*

1768 Kelly's *False Delicacy.*

1768 Priestley's *Essay on the first principles of Government.*

1768 Resignation of Chatham.

1768 Sterne's *Sentimental Journey.*

1768 Horace Walpole's *H i s t o r i c Doubts.*

1769 The Letters of Junius begin to appear in *The Public Advertiser.*

1769 Reynolds's first *Discourse.*

1769 Robertson's *History of Charles V.*

1769 Smollett's *History and Adventures of an Atom.*

1769 Wilkes expelled from the House.

1770 Goldsmith's *Deserted Village.*

1771 Goldsmith's *History of England.*

1771 Mackenzie's *Man of Feeling.*

1771 Smollett's *Humphrey Clinker.*

1771 *Encyclopaedia Britannica.* Edn. I.

1771–4 Beattie's *The Minstrel.*

1772 Graves's *Spiritual Quixote.*

1772 The Letters of Junius collected.

1773 Goldsmith's *She stoops to conquer.*

1773 Leland's *History of Ireland.*

1773 Mackenzie's *Man of the World.*

1773 The Boston Tea Riots.

1774 Chesterfield's *Letters to his Son.*

1774–81 Warton's *History of English Poetry.*

1775 Charles Lamb born (d. 1834).

1775 Johnson's *Journey to the Western Islands of Scotland.*

1775–8 Tyrwhitt's edition of Chaucer published.

1776 American Declaration of Independence.

1776 Gibbon's *Decline and Fall of the Roman Empire,* Vol. I. (Vols. II, III, 1781; Vols. IV–VI, 1788.)

1776 Adam Smith's *Wealth of Nations.*

1777 Chatterton's *Rowley Poems* published.

1777 Mackenzie's *Julia de Roubigné.*

1777 Clara Reeve's *Old E n g l i s h Baron.*

1778 Death of Voltaire.

1778 Death of Rousseau.

1778 Fanny Burney's *Evelina.*

1778 Walpole's *Miscellaneous Letters* appear as Vol. v of his *Collected Works.*

1781 Johnson's *Lives of the Poets.*

1782 Fanny Burney's *Cecilia.*

1783 Peace of Versailles.

1784 Death of Johnson.

1784 Death of Diderot.

1784 Mitford's *History of Greece,* Vol. I (completed 1810).

1786 Boswell's *Tour to the Hebrides.*

1788–95 Trial of Warren Hastings.

1789 White's *Natural History of Selborne.*

1791 Boswell's *Life of Johnson.*

1794 Death of Gibbon.

1794 Paley's *Evidences.*

1796 Fanny Burney's *Camilla.*

1796 Gibbon's *Memoirs of my Life and Writings* published with his *Miscellaneous Works.*

1842–6 Fanny Burney's *Diary and Letters* published.

1857 Horace Walpole's *Letters,* ed. P. Cunningham.

1903 Horace Walpole's *Letters,* ed. Mrs. Paget Toynbee.

# CORRIGENDA AND ADDENDA

## THE CAMBRIDGE HISTORY OF ENGLISH LITERATURE

### VOLUME X. THE AGE OF JOHNSON

The following footnote should be added on p. 179 to ' book,' l. 2.
A book bound by Johnson was in Boswell's sale catalogue.
p. 231, l. 25 *for* invented *read* adopted.
The following should be added to the bibliographies:
Chapter I. Richardson.
The discussion concerning Richardson's supposed indebtedness to Marivaux
has recently been revived, and new evidence brought forward. See Mod. Lang.
Rev. vol. VIII, pp. 464 ff. Oct., 1913, and Modern Philology, vol. XVI, No. 9, January, 1919.

Chapter II. Fielding and Smollett.
*Under Fielding:*
Cross, W. L. The History of Henry Fielding. 3 vols. Yale and Oxford, 1919.
Fielding, H. Selected Essays. Ed. Gerould, G. H. Boston, 1905.
Dobson, A., Fielding and Andrew Millar. The Library. July, 1916.
Wells, J. E. Fielding's *Champion* and Captain Hercules Vinegar. Mod. Lang.
Rev. April, 1913.
—— Some New Facts concerning Fielding's Tumble-Down Dick and Pasquin.
Mod. Lang. Notes (Baltimore). May, 1913.
Wells, J. E. Fielding's Political Purpose in *Jonathan Wild*. Pub. Mod. Lang.
Ass. America. March, 1913.
*Under Smollett:*
Works. 6 vols. 1904.
Henderson, Andrew. A Second Letter to Dr. Samuel Johnson . . . with an
impartial character of Doctor Smollet. n.d. [1775].

Chapter III. Sterne, and the Novel of his Times.
*Under Sterne:*
Melville, Lewis. Sterne's Eliza. In Some Eccentrics and a Woman. 1911.
Paul, H. Sterne, In Man and Letters. 1901.
*Under William Beckford:*
The History of the Caliph Vathek. Ed. Ross, E. Denison. 1901.
The Episodes of Vathek. Translated by Sir Frank T. Marzials. With an
Introduction by Lewis Melville. 1912.
Melville, Lewis. William Beckford of Fonthill Abbey. In Some Eccentrics and
a Woman. 1911.
*Under Frances Burney:*
Saintsbury, G. In Essays on English Literature 1780–1860. 2nd Series. 1895.

*Under Henry Mackenzie:*

Kluge, J. Henry Mackenzie. Sein Leben und seine Werke. Anglia, xxxiv. Halle, 1911.

Chapter vi. Gray.

Essays and Criticisms. Ed. Northup, C. S. Boston and London, n.d. [1909].

Phelps, W. L. (ed.). Gray's Poetry and Prose (selections). Boston, 1894.

Thomas Gray. Poems. Ed. Poole, Austin Lane. Oxford, 1917.

Cook, Albert S. (ed.). A Concordance to the English Poems of Thomas Gray. Boston and New York, 1908.

Elwin, W. Some Eighteenth Century Men of Letters. Vol. ii. 1902.

Farley's Scandinavian Influences. 1903.

Lowell, J. R. Latest Literary Essays. 1891.

Northup, C. S. In Notes and Queries. 1911.

Warren, Sir T. H. Gray and Dante in Essays of Poets and Poetry, Ancient and Modern. 1909.

Shelley, H. C. Edward Young, Life and Letters of. 1914.

Chapter vii. Young, Collins and Lesser Poets of the Age of Johnson.

William Collins. Poems. Ed. Stone, Christopher, and Poole, Austin Lane. Oxford, 1917.

Chapter viii. Johnson and Boswell.

*Under Johnson:*

Dobson, Austin. A Garret in Gough Square. Eighteenth Century Vignettes, 1st series. 1892.

Rosebery, Lord. Address at Lichfield. 1909 (printed in the bicentenary report).

Saintsbury, G. The Peace of the Augustans. A survey of 18th century literature as a place of rest and refreshment. 1916.

[Swift, Pope, Johnson, Goldsmith and others.]

Stephen, Leslie. Johnsoniana, in Studies of a Biographer. Vol. i. 1898.

Chapter x. The Literary Influence of the Middle Ages.

*Under Thomas Chatterton:*

Clarke, Sir Ernest. New Lights on Chatterton. Bibliographical Society (read, 21, xii. 1914; published, 1916).

*Under Thomas Percy:*

Dobson, A. Percy and Goldsmith. In Old Kensington Palace. 1910.

Percy had a copious correspondence with literary men of his time. Practically the whole of the 856 pages of vol. ii (1848) and 436 pages of vol. viii (1858) of Nichols's Illustrations of the Literary History of the 18th century are occupied by letters to and from Percy, his correspondents including George Steevens, Dr. Grainger, James Boswell, Michael Lort, Dr. Thomas Birch, Archdeacon Nares, Dr. Thomas Campbell, the Moira family, John Nichols and John Pinkerton.

*Under Anna Seward:*

Lucas, E. V. A Swan and her Friends. 1907.

Chapter xi. Letter-writers.

*Under Sir Joshua Reynolds:*

Phillips, Claude. Sir Joshua Reynolds. n.d. [1893].

*Under Philip Dormer Stanhope, fourth Earl of Chesterfield:*

Collins, J. C. In Essays and Studies. 1895.

*Under Horace Walpole, fourth earl of Orford:*

Two Supplementary Volumes of Letters were added to the Paget Toynbee edn. Oxford, 1919.

Goad, Caroline. Horace in the English Literature of the Eighteenth Century. Yale and Oxford, 1918.

[Contains a valuable appendix of instances of indebtedness to Horace in 18th century English writings—Rowe, Addison, Steele, Prior, Gay, Pope, Swift, Fielding, Richardson, Sterne, Smollett, Johnson, Chesterfield, Walpole.]

Stephen, Sir Leslie. In Hours in a Library. Vol. I. 1874.

*Under Gilbert White:*

Jardine, Sir W. and Jesse, E. (ed.). 1841.

Chapter XIII. Historians II.

*Under Edward Gibbon:*

Stephen, Sir L. Gibbon's Autobiography in Studies of a Biographer. Vol. I. 1898.

Chapter XV. Divines.

### Alban Butler (1711–1773)

The Lives of the Fathers, Martyrs, and other principal Saints; compiled from original monuments and other authentick records; illustrated with the remarks of judicious modern criticks and historians. 4 vols. 1756–9. 12 vols. Dublin, 1779–80; 12 vols. Edinburgh, 1798–1800; etc.

### Richard Challoner (1691–1781)

The Garden of the Soul. c. 1740 and numerous edns.

Memoirs of Missionary Priests, as well secular as regular, and of other catholics of both sexes that have suffered death in England, on religious accounts, from the year of our Lord 1577 to 1684. 2 vols. 1741–2 and later edns.

The Rheims New Testament and the Douay Bible, with annotations. 5 vols. 1749–50 and several later edns.

Chapter XVI. The Literature of Dissent, 1660–1760.

Parker, J. Dissenting Academies in England. Cambridge, 1915.

Chapter XVII. Political Literature (1755–75).

Bleackley, Horace. Life of John Wilkes. 1917.

# INDEX

[The letters ff. after an entry imply that references to the same subject occur on at least two succeeding pages. Birth and death dates are not, as a rule, given in the case of writers whose work is treated in other volumes.]